THE NEAR EAST SINCE THE FIRST WORLD WAR

A History of the Near East
General Editor: Professor P.M. Holt

*The Prophet and the Age of the Caliphates: the Islamic Near East from the sixth to the eleventh century
Hugh Kennedy

*The Age of the Crusades: the Near East from the eleventh century to 1517
P.M. Holt

The Rise of the Ottoman Empire 1300–1574
Colin Imber

The Decline of the Ottoman Empire 1574–1792
R.C. Repp

*The Making of the Modern Near East 1792–1923
M.E. Yapp

*The Near East since the First World War
M.E. Yapp

*Medieval Persia 1040–1797
D.O. Morgan

**Already published*

The Near East since the First World War

M.E. Yapp

Longman
London and New York

Longman Group UK Limited
Longman House, Burnt Mill, Harlow,
Essex CM20 2JE, England
and Associated Companies throughout the world

Published in the United States of America
by Longman Inc., New York

First published 1991

British Library Cataloguing in Publication Data
Yapp, Malcolm 1931–
The Near East since the First World War.–(A history of the Near East)
1. Middle East, history
I. Title II. Series
956

ISBN 0–582–49500–8 CSD
ISBN 0–582–49499–0 PPR

Library of Congress Cataloging in Publication Data
Yapp, Malcolm.
The Near East since the First World War / M.E. Yapp.
p. cm. — (A History of the Near East)
Includes index.
Includes bibliographical references.
ISBN 0–582–49500–8 (cased). — ISBN 0–582–49499–0 (pbk.)
1. Middle East—History—20th century. I. Title. II. Series.
DS62.4.Y36 1991
956.04—dc20 90-36319
CIP

Produced by Longman Singapore Publishers (Pte) Ltd.
Printed in Singapore

Contents

List of Maps

List of Abbreviations

AIOC	Anglo–Iranian Oil Company
ANM	Arab Nationalist Movement
ARAMCO	Arabian–American Oil Company
ASU	Arab Socialist Union (Egypt)
CENTO	Central Treaty Organisation
CFTU	Council of Federated Trade Unions (Iran)
CGS	Chief of the General Staff
DP	Democrat Party (Turkey)
FLOSY	Front for the Liberation of South Yemen
GCC	Gulf Co-operation Council
GDP	Gross Domestic Product
GNA	Grand National Assembly
GNP	Gross National Product
HQ	Headquarters
ICO	Islamic Conference Organisation
ICP	Iraq Communist Party
IDF	Israel Defence Forces
ILO	International Labour Organisation
IMF	International Monetary Fund
IPC	Iraq Petroleum Company
IRP	Islamic Republican Party (Iran)
JP	Justice Party (Turkey)
KDP	Kurdish Democratic Party
LF	Lebanese Forces
LNM	Lebanese National Movement
MB	Muslim Brotherhood
mbd	million barrels a day
MESC	Middle East Supply Centre
MMNE	*The Making of the Modern Near East*

MP	Motherland Party (Turkey)
NAP	National Action Party (Turkey)
NATO	North Atlantic Treaty Organisation
NCRC	National Council of the Revolutionary Command (Iraq)
NDP	National Democratic Party (Egypt)
NLF	National Liberation Front (South Yemen)
NRC	National Revolutionary Council (Iraq)
NSP	National Salvation Party (Turkey)
NUC	National Unity Committee (Turkey)
OPEC	Organisation of Petroleum Exporting Countries
PDFLP	Popular Democratic Front for the Liberation of Palestine
PDRY	People's Democratic Republic of Yemen
PFLOAG	Popular Front for the Liberation of the Occupied Arab Gulf
PFLP	Popular Front for the Liberation of Palestine
PLO	Palestinian Liberation Organisation
PUK	Patriotic Union of Kurdistan
RAF	Royal Air Force
RCC	Regional Command Council (Baᶜth)
RCC	Revolutionary Command Council (Egypt)
RCD	Regional Co-operation for Development
RPP	Republican People's Party (Turkey)
SEATO	South-East Asia Treaty Organisation
SSNP	Syrian Social Nationalist Party (Known in French as the Parti Populaire Syrien and hence commonly referred to as PPS.)
TPP	True Path Party (Turkey)
TWP	Turkish Workers' Party
UAR	United Arab Republic
UN	United Nations (Organisation)
UNEF	United Nations Emergency Force
UNIFIL	United Nations Interim Force in Lebanon
UNSCOP	United Nations Special Committee on Palestine
UNRWA	United Nations Relief and Works Agency
USA	United States of America
USSR	Union of Soviet Socialist Republics

Note: Names, Titles and Dates

NAMES AND TITLES

Near Eastern Muslim names usually consisted of five elements: the personal name, the formal name, the patronymic, the group name and the honorific.

1. The personal name (*ism* or ᶜ*alam*), for example, Muḥammad, Aḥmad, ᶜAlī or Ḥusayn, the last two being especially popular among Shīᶜīs. Sometimes individuals are known by two personal names in combination, for example Ṣaddām Ḥusayn or Muḥammad Riżā. A common form of the personal name is the compound usually formed by the combination of ᶜAbd (slave) with one of the 99 names or attributes of God. Examples include ᶜAbd al-Hādī (slave of the Guide), the name of a well-known Nablus notable family, and ᶜAbd al-Karīm (slave of the Generous One). Although it is not included among the 99 names, al-Nāṣir (the giver of victory) is also understood to designate an attribute of God. It will be noted that the definite article *al-* is always attached to the possessor and not the thing possessed; the form "Abdul" is a solecism.
2. The formal name (*kunya*), usually denoting the relationship of the name bearer to another person, for example Abū (Father of) accompanied by the name of the other person. The *kunya* may also describe a metaphorical relationship or a relationship to a familiar object or activity, amounting in this last usage to a nickname. Names of this type have been popular among Palestinian guerrilla leaders; thus Khalīl al-Wazīr, the head of the PLO military department, adopted the name of Abū Jihād (the father of war) and his wife, who called herself Intiṣār al-Wazīr (the victory of Wazīr), also became known as Umm Jihād (mother of war). Such nicknames

were often terms of opprobrium; thus the Muslim opponents of Ḥāfiẓ al-Asad called him Abū Righāl, after a legendary traitor said to have guided the Christian Yemeni forces against Mecca in AD 572. The famous Egyptian singer, Umm Kulthūm (literally, mother of the elephant), derived her *kunya* from Muḥammad's daughter, Fāṭima.

3. The patronymic (*nasab*) indicating the genealogy of the name bearer by listing the names of his or her ancestors, each name being preceded by the word *ibn* (son of) or *bint* (daughter of). Thus Fahd ibn ᶜAbd al-ᶜAzīz signifies Fahd, the son of ᶜAbd al-ᶜAzīz. In Persian the suffix -zāda (son of) was often added to a name to fulfil the same purpose and a similar office is performed in Turkish by the suffix -oğlu, for example Karaosmanoğlu.
4. The group name (*nisba*) often denoting the place of origin or residence, for example al-Miṣrī (the Egyptian), and al-Takrītī (from Takrīt in Iraq) or the occupation, for example al-Ṣayrafī (the banker or moneychanger). The *nisba* often signified the tribe (*qabīla*), for example al-Dosarī from the important south Nejdi tribal confederation, or family or clan (*ahl*). The *nisba* is an adjective and appears in a name with the ending *-ī* or *-iyya* and is almost always preceded by the definite article *al-*. One should distinguish this use of *al-* plus adjective from the use of *Āl* with a noun, as in Āl Bū Saᶜīd and Āl Saᶜūd, to signify the *ahl* in the sense of dynasty. It should be noted that the *nisba*, by betraying the regional or tribal origin of an individual, could expose the undue predominance of a particular group or encourage tribal or regional identities to flourish and for these reasons the use of certain forms of the *nisba* has been discouraged or made illegal in some Near Eastern states.
5. The honorific (*laqab*) may be either a nickname or a title. An example of a nickname may be found in the name of the Syrian Druze family, al-Aṭrash (the deaf). Titles were bestowed upon rulers, princes, soldiers and officers of State and were often compounds with terms signifying the state (*dawla* or *mulk*), the ruler (*sulṭān* or *malik*) or religion (*islām* or *dīn*). In Qajar Iran bureaucrats were frequently known by titles, for example Qavām al-Salṭana. One should also note the use of religious titles, for example *ḥājj* (one who has made the pilgrimage), *sharīf* and *sayyid* (descendants of the Prophet), *āyatallāh* and *ḥujjat al-islām*, all of which may become annexed to the name by which an individual is known.

An individual might be known by names chosen from any of the above groups or by combinations of them. In Arabia and in some other parts of the Arab world traditional practice continued throughout the period with which this book is concerned. But in Turkey, following the adoption of a new civil code, the law of 28 June 1934 (which also abolished non-military titles) made it compulsory for Turkish citizens to adopt surnames, hitherto rare, from 1 January 1935. Surnames were chosen in various ways: families, places, associations and qualities. ᶜIsmet Pasha became known as Inönü, after the famous battle in which he was triumphant; and Muṣṭafā Kemāl selected that of Atatürk (father of the Turks). In 1925 official and religious titles were abolished in Iran and this act also accelerated a change in the style of personal names. Family or place names or other styles came to be used as surnames: thus Qavām al-Salṭana became Aḥmad Qavām and his cousin, Muṣaddiq al-Salṭana, Muḥammad Muṣaddiq. In many Arab countries it also became common to employ surnames, notably in Lebanon. It has usually been the *nasab*, the *nisba* and the *laqab* which have formed the surname, occasionally undergoing some evolution, for example the dropping of the definite article in the *nisba*. The practice of adopting surnames, however, was more common among some social groups than others: Christian more than Muslim, non-Arab rather than Arab, secular more than religious, richer rather than poorer, urban more than rural. One is still in danger of committing solecisms in treating as surnames names which do not yet quite have that status; in search of simplicity I fear I have done so in this book.

Finally, we may note the evolution of names in Israel. Most immigrants from Europe arrived with names in a Europeanized form but the practice developed and increased after the establishment of the state of converting these names into Hebraized forms, thus Moses Shertok became Moshe Sharrett.

DATES

In this book only Christian dates (Gregorian calendar) have been provided. To find the Muslim (*hijrī*) date it is necessary to use a conversion table, for example W. Haig, *Comparative tables of Muhammadan and Christian dates* (London 1932), or G.S.P. Freeman-Grenville, *The Muslim and Christian calendars* (London 1963). Turkey adopted the Gregorian calendar in 1925 in place of the solar calendar based on the Muslim era in use until that time. In the same year Iran adopted a solar calendar based on the Muslim era in place of the *hijrī* calendar which continued to be used for religious purposes. In 1976 Iran changed the era to one based on the year of the alleged establishment of the Iranian monarchy but the new calendar was abandoned in 1978. In Arabia the *hijrī* calendar is in regular use; in other Arab countries Muslim and Gregorian calendars are used.

Preface

This book is a sequel to *The Making of the Modern Near East* which was published in the same series in 1987. The latter work took the story of the Near East down to to the peace settlement which followed the First World War and which created a new state structure in the region. The present book takes up the story where its predecessor left off and has as a central theme the fortunes of the new system of states. As with the previous book, however, the emphasis is not on international relations but on internal change, political, economic and social. It is an obvious advantage to read the new book with its predecessor and with other volumes in the series but the work is intended to be complete in itself and to furnish the reader with a general history of the modern and contemporary Near and Middle East.

It must be emphasised that it is a work of history which is the study of the past based primarily on written records. Much writing on the contemporary Near East is the work of social and political scientists; I have drawn heavily and gratefully on their work and I hope many of them will profit from this book. But neither the materials, nor the methods nor the purposes of social and political scientists are identical with those of historians; each discipline has its peculiar characteristics and its particular insights. It is illuminating to combine disciplinary approaches but dangerous to mix them. Man has invented several ingenious devices for extracting corks from bottles, each of which works well in its own way and according to its own principles, but an instrument which possessed the features of all of them would be fairly useless. To put one aspect of the matter more plainly: either directly by extrapolation from existing trends or indirectly by the creation of models most social and political scientists are concerned with prediction, or with advising policy makers how to avoid or palliate the consequences of the contemplated course of events. History is unconcerned with prediction; it has only one basic question: how did this get to be what it is? I have sought to explain (starting from the end of the First World War) how the Near East got to be how it was in 1989 and not to predict how it will look in 2000 or even 1990. The selection of material has been governed by the consideration of what was important in the historical process, not by what is significant to the understanding of the present situation or the prospects for tomorrow. In borrowing freely from the writings of social and political scientists I have sought to disentangle their material from the frameworks in which they commonly presented it. The task of so doing seems to me to be one of those problems (and pleasures) of the historian of contemporary events which distinguish his work from that of his colleagues who write about more remote periods of the past.

Neither of the two other problems of writing contemporary history which are commonly mentioned – those of sources and perspective – seem to me to present especial difficulties. Sources, as shown in the Bibliographical Guide, are in abundance and although perspectives change it is not demonstrable that new and later perspectives are any better (in the eye of eternity) than older, contemporary ones. The problem is not that of discerning the process which is at work but of not knowing the end of it; and the consequence of that ignorance is ultimately a longer book because one must also signpost the history that will never be.

Because of its subject matter this book may be read by many who are not academic specialists on the Middle East; that is certainly the hope and intention. Commonly, books designed for such a readership do not have a scholarly apparatus of transliteration; usually they include a remark to the effect that for the general reader it is discouraging to have names in such forms and for the specialist unnecessary and that the authors have therefore adopted a simple system by which they mean no system at all. This book, like other books in the series, does have a consistent system of transliteration (based on that employed in the *Cambridge History of Islam*). It should be said that for the specialist it is necessary and for the general reader helpful to have such a system. The non-specialist reader may at least learn something of the structure of Muslim names and of their pronunciation and avoid the comical errors perpetrated by, for example, football commentators at the World Cup.

It is with pleasure and gratitude that I once again acknowledge the help and advice of my editor, Professor P.M. Holt, who read the manuscript and the proofs and whose sharp eye, knowledge and judgement enabled me to make several improvements to the text, and of my publishers, Messrs Longman. Several years ago I contracted with Longmans to produce one medium sized book. They have waited patiently for more than twice the time agreed and accepted two long books. Moreover they responded to every nervous request for further delay and more words not with frowns and monitory remarks but with encouragement, support and even enthusiasm. It helped a lot.

Introduction: Social, Economic and Political Change in the Near East

GENERAL

The Near East is a term which serves the historian well until the end of the First World War. Coined in the late nineteenth century it was employed as a convenient shorthand for the Ottoman Empire and its successor states. The Near East was therefore the region west of the Iranian frontier and could be distinguished from the Far East, composed of China and Japan, and the Middle East, comprising the area which intervened between the Near and the Far Easts. After the First World War the Near East became gradually engulfed in the Middle East as the latter term began to be used to include the Arab states which emerged from the Ottoman Empire. During the Second World War the triumphant Middle East marched yet further westwards into North Africa and subsequently began to send feelers into Pakistan. More recently the term has been used especially to describe Israel and its Arab neighbours. The name "Near East" survived principally as an expression used to delineate the region of western Asia in the period before the arrival of Islam; one speaks of the ancient Near East but not usually of the ancient Middle East. "Near East" is not now applied to the states of south-eastern Europe, for which the term had been especially coined; and Turkey itself has been left to inhabit a sort of geographical limbo, uneasily poised between Europe and the Middle East and commonly neglected by specialists dealing with each of them.

To an historian who wishes to write about Turkey, Iran, Egypt, Israel and the Arab world of Asia in the twentieth century this terminological mess is distressing for he can find no completely satisfactory term to describe an area which warrants being treated as a region in the sense that the cultural and historical links across the region, the common experiences of its states and peoples and their interconnections provide a basis for a unified treatment. "Near East" remains as good a term as any but those who are looking for the Middle East will probably find it in this book.

During the period covered by this book the Near East changed more than it had done during any comparable period in its history. The change may be encompassed in the term "modernization". It is a term used frequently in this book and it is necessary to define what is meant by modernization at the outset because the term is used by various writers with different meanings or emphases. In this book it is used to signify the transition from a traditional to a modern society. The terms "traditional" and "modern" are themselves the subject of dispute; here they are used to denote ideal types of societies characterized by certain attributes. Briefly, a traditional society is one which socially has a compartmentalized system in which groups are not arranged in any systematic hierarchy and in which most people are illiterate; economically it is largely engaged in subsistence agriculture or pastoralism; and politically it is characterized by minimal government, that is the state has few functions and those mainly concerned with defence. A modern society is divided into horizontally-banded classes and is mainly literate; economically, production is for the market, industry and services predominate and most people live in towns; and politically it is distinguished by a powerful state with a wide range of social and economic functions. The argument of this book is that during the period under consideration the Near East moved decisively from a structure which still approximated more closely to the traditional model to one which imitated more nearly the concept of a modern society.

The direction of change is unmistakable but modernization did not take place evenly in time, place or sector. In time the greatest changes took place after 1950, Turkey and Egypt experienced the earliest transformations and Arabia lagged behind, and political changes were greater than economic or social changes. It is these variations and especially the leading role of the state which have dictated the form of this book. I had supposed that the work might have been cast in the form of thematic chapters which would have facilitated a constant comparison of developments in different parts of the region. But it eventually became apparent that to adopt such a structure would obliterate the most distinctive feature of Near Eastern development – the creation and development of a novel state system. This feature could only be described through an examination of the history of individual states. This examination is conducted in Sections II and III, the engine room of the book; only in this introductory chapter is a broad comparative approach adopted.

In this book, as in its predecessor in this series, a major problem has been to balance internal and external factors in change. It is easy to write that both were important and that one should not attempt to arrange them according to degree of importance but in fact a decision about their relative importance and a decision about the structure of the historical account are inextricably linked. To introduce a substantial discussion of the international concerns of states into an account of their internal history would have the effect of giving too great a weight to the international factor in their development. In theory this emphasis is not inevitable but in practice it has been the outcome in books which have adopted this form. As a consequence the history of the modern Near East has often been written as though the states were driftwood in the sea of international affairs, their destinies shaped by the decisions of others. This I believe to be a false picture, popular as it has been among Near Easterners and outsiders alike. As will become apparent, in my view the main motor of change has been internal and for that reason, at the cost of introducing a different (although, I think, a lesser) distortion, international affairs have been largely confined to Section III.

Three outside influences may be distinguished: the Ottoman, the European and the superpower. Of these the first is indeed an internal influence but it has been externalized by writers who have labelled the period of Ottoman rule the time of alien Turkish oppression in much of the Near East and gone on to suggest that Ottoman influence was minimal. The universal denigration of Ottoman rule by Arab and Turkish nationalists and by Europeans has obscured the importance of the Ottoman legacy to the Near East from 1923 until about 1950. In those years politics were dominated by men educated in Ottoman schools and colleges many of whom had served the Empire as soldiers and bureaucrats. They affected Ottoman styles of dress and behaviour and many spoke Ottoman Turkish for preference; Ṣubḥī Barakāt, the first president of the Syrian federal council spoke little Arabic and to accommodate him and those who shared his background Turkish was made an official language of the Aleppo council. The Ottoman administrative system remained the foundation of government in much of the area and the Ottoman codes of law, notably the Mecelle, persisted in parts of the region. The passing of the last Ottoman generation in mid-century was one of the events contributing to the transfiguration of Near Eastern politics around that time.

The second outside influence is the European, primarily conveyed through Britain and France. In the nineteenth century France had been the European model for imitation by the Near East and French institutions, moderated by their passage through Ottoman hands, remained of central importance in most of the region. French law, educational structures and administrative styles prevailed in the former Ottoman territories and extended into Iran. The French language remained the first choice of European language for those who lived outside the region of direct British domination. Even in Egypt French was the preferred language and in 1946 Lord Stansgate was chosen to lead the British negotiators under Ernest Bevin not because of his skills as a negotiator but because he had a command of French which few of his Labour colleagues possessed. European influence, exerted through ideas and through models of institutions, dress and behaviour, exercised a profound influence over the Near East particularly during that period when a small élite dominated access to European thought. What Albert Hourani has called the liberal age was essentially the age of European influence and it endured from the late nineteenth century until the middle of the twentieth century. Its decline was partly the result of the decline of European influence and of Europe itself but more the consequence of the enlargement of the Near Eastern élite. The men who came to power from the mid-twentieth century onwards were not untouched by European influence but were much more responsive to indigenous sentiment. By comparison with the ideological influence the direct impact of Europe in economics and politics was smaller. The structure of European economic domination withered quickly after the 1920s and in the same period Europe sought to reduce her direct involvement in the internal politics of the Near Eastern states. Turkey and Iran went their own way; from the time of Egyptian independence in 1922 Britain was a declining influence in the internal affairs of that state: much the same evolution took place in Iraq; and most of Arabia was left to its own devices. Only in Greater Syria was the direct experience of European government and administration prolonged until the end of the Second World War. Contemplating the style of European political intervention in the Near East one is struck by how cautious and conservative it was by comparison both with the late Ottoman rule which preceded it and with the indigenous regimes which succeeded it. Europe was not much interested in the Near East, was unwilling to invest large resources in the region or to commit numerous forces and sought a quiet life by working with traditional leaders. Palestine, where Britain nurtured the revolutionary philosophy of Zionism, is the only major exception.

The third and least important of the outside interventions in the

Near East is that of the superpowers, the United States and the Soviet Union. They did not replace Britain and France after 1956 because they never possessed the influence which the two European states had enjoyed before 1945. European influence was replaced primarily by Near Eastern independence; only a residual element was inherited by the superpowers. The principal role of the USA and the USSR was that of providers of economic and military aid and this office supplied them with little influence. More often they found themselves manipulated by their alleged clients. The interventions of the superpowers may be compared to the part played by thunder and lightning in the hands of primitive magicians – spectacular, unpredictable and very shortlived.

SOCIETY

Ortega y Gasset once remarked that Spain consisted of a series of watertight compartments. His observation would fit most traditional societies and is especially applicable to the Near East in 1923. The family, the tribe, the religious community, the village and the urban quarter were still the institutions around which the lives of most people in the Near East revolved and transactions between inhabitants of different compartments were limited. The political and economic changes which had taken place during the previous century had made little alteration in this social particularism; the compartments stood in a different relationship to the state and the economy from what their situation had been in 1800 but the containers themselves had proved most durable. (See *The Making of the Modern Near East* (*MMNE*), 9–10.) During the period with which this book is concerned, however, substantial changes in social organization did take place and an account of the Near East may appropriately begin with a description of social institutions and a glance at the character of the changes they underwent.

The basic social unit in the Near East in 1989, as in 1923, was the family. Unfortunately we know very little of its evolution over the intervening period. It seems probable, however, that at the beginning of the period the extended family, consisting of two or more nuclear families living together in a single household, was the most common arrangement. This hypothesis rests on some very limited observations by contemporary observers, on the assumption that the extended family pattern was usual in rural areas, and on the knowledge that more than four out of every five people in the Near East lived in rural areas. What evidence we have from censuses and extrapolations from surveys suggests that in 1989 much less than a quarter of the population lived in extended families. The change may be partly attributed to a decline in extended families in rural areas but chiefly to urbanization. Statistics for Turkey in 1965 show that while 27 per cent of village households fell into the extended family category only 15 per cent of those in small towns did so and only 10 per cent of those in cities.

The decline of the extended family was matched by the decline of other kinship groupings from the clan to the tribal federation. The decline of pastoral nomadism was a factor in this change but the epithet "tribal" had never been synonymous with nomads in the Near East; the majority of tribal people had for long been cultivators. Tribalism in the traditional Near East was a matter of customary law, marriage patterns, obedience to a collective leadership of elders under a shaykh, and a sense of identity (*ʿaṣabiyya*) based on genealogy, historical memory and arrangements for defence against outside enemies. The interposition of the state deprived the tribe of many of its legal, educational, political and economic functions; and the operation of economic change, in particular the factor of migration, reinforced the impact of the state.

This is not to say that kinship links did not continue to be important. Tribal links remained of fundamental importance in Arabia throughout the period and in Iraq, Syria and Jordan a substantial portion of the population was classified as tribal. In eastern Turkey the Kurdish population preserved strong tribal links and tribal affiliations were also important among the Kurds, Lurs and other groups in Iran. In some ways political change reinforced kinship links; in autocratic states where political power was contested by factions within numerically small élites it was natural to turn first to kinsmen as the most reliable allies and to reward them with powerful appointments. The regimes of Ḥāfiẓ al-Asad in Syria and Ṣaddām Ḥusayn in Iraq were distinguished by the prominence of the families of the rulers. More democratic statesmen, such as Turgut Özal in Turkey, also looked to the support of their kin. The centrality of family was implicit in the political structure of the monarchical states of Arabia and of Jordan and they saw no reason to hide the fact; on the other hand republics were ashamed of kin and other tribal links and often attempted to disguise their significance by, for example, banning the use of tribal names. It is a not unusual experience that the decline of a social institution is accompanied by its politicization and its invasion of the state system; kinship ties provide one example of the phenomenon as religious ties provide another. Economic development also provided opportunities for kinship ties to flourish.

In 1923 the Near East was overwhelmingly Muslim. About three or four per cent of the population was Christian, concentrated mainly in Egypt, Syria, Lebanon and Palestine, and about one per cent Jewish, scattered all over the region. Leaving aside insignificant numbers of Hindus in the Gulf and members of tiny sects such as the Yazīdīs of Syria and Iraq the remainder were Muslim, about four-fifths Sunnīs and the rest Shīʿīs. The Shīʿīs belonged to various sects but by far the largest was that of the Imāmī or Twelver Shīʿīs who made up 90 per cent of the population of Iran and about half that of Iraq. In 1989 the breakdown of the population was similar; the proportion of Christians had fallen slightly and the Jews were redistributed so as to be concentrated almost exclusively in Israel.

The religious community was an important social organization. Although the state had made inroads into the functions of the religious community before 1923 the latter still retained responsibilities in personal law and education as well as a role in defining social boundaries which were observed especially in marriage; also the community maintained religious buildings and institutions. The religious community continued to be important throughout the period but its significance varied according to region and community. Broadly speaking the more Muslim a state the less the religious community mattered, and the more divided its religious composition the more significant was the religious community. A second factor was that of European intervention. The European states had established before 1923 a tradition of protecting the interests of non-Muslim minorities in the Near East and this tradition was expressed in the mandates acquired in 1920 by Britain and France which enjoined them to have especial regard to the rights of religious communities. It was in Lebanon and in Palestine where each factor reinforced the effect of the other that religious communities had the largest social role and eventually became political communities in response to the same imperatives which had affected kinship links. The most important of these imperatives was the growth of the state and its invasion of other social compartments.

Confronted by the greater demands of the state non-Muslim minority communities had a choice of strategies. They could keep their political heads down and live obscure lives hoping to be left to carry on their economic and social avocations. Such was the choice of the Armenians and the Bahā'īs of Iran and the Armenians and Greeks who remained in Istanbul after 1923. The Bahā'īs often concealed their identity completely. As it happened these quietist groups were sometimes not left undisturbed. During the Second World War the non-Muslim minorities of Turkey were subjected to a capital levy imposed with great severity and the Greeks suffered again when anti-Greek feeling flourished during the Cyprus problems of the 1960s and 1970s. The Bahā'īs, perched uneasily on the fringes of Shīʿī Islam, were still more unlucky; in 1955 they were a target for persecution in Iran and were again the particular victims of Muslim rage in 1979. This strategy of obscurity was especially that chosen by Jewish communities outside Palestine but just as the Greeks were affected by animosities caused by the activities of their co-religionists elsewhere so the position of the Jewish communities was undermined by Zionist actions in Palestine. From 1936 onwards Jewish communities in the Near East came under increasing pressure and in June 1941 in Baghdad popular hostility was vented in a massacre of Jews. As in Iran in 1955 the government found it convenient to allow the persecution to proceed for a time in order to defuse opposition over other matters. Nevertheless, the Jewish strategy was generally successful and in most states of the Near East the Jews prospered until their position was almost completely destroyed by the Palestine war of 1948. Most then left to go to Israel although a few remained in other Near Eastern states; in Iran Jews flourished under the Pahlavīs; in Damascus Jewish doctors retained the traditional respect they had enjoyed; and in Egypt a poor and tiny community remained in the Jewish quarter of Cairo.

A second strategy was what may be called the chameleon strategy, that is to attempt to downgrade the importance of identification by religious community and to assert instead some other banner of identity under which the non-Muslim minority would escape from its disadvantage and become equal with Muslims. The favourite banners were those of nationalism and communism. Communist parties in the Near East during the 1920s and 1930s had a disproportionate number of members drawn from minorities and foreigners; the Alexandria branch of the Egyptian communist party was led by a foreign Jew, Joseph Rosenthal, and Jews were especially prominent during the 1930s. Several members of the Greek Orthodox community in Syria chose Syrian nationalism; one of them, Anṭūn Saʿāda, founded the Syrian Social Nationalist Party (SSNP) which was primarily a Greek Orthodox party. The ideology of Saʿāda's party fitted the situation of the Greek Orthodox, spread as they were throughout greater Syria and lacking a foreign protector. The favourite choice, however, was Arab nationalism; one of the founders of the Baʿth Party was a Greek Orthodox, Michel ʿAflaq; and it was through the Baʿth that the heterodox Muslim communities of the Ismāʿīlīs, the Druzes and especially the ʿAlawīs (Nuṣayrīs) sought to escape their disabilities. It is interesting to note that when the young Ḥāfiẓ al-Asad considered a political career he saw the choice as being between the SSNP and the Baʿth. Of course the corollary of the choice of the strategy of the secular ideological banner was that the member of the minority community gave up much of what had made his community distinctive, often separate schools, courts and language. It was a choice for an individual rather than a community. The strategy had another disadvantage, namely that the secular character of the state institutions might after all not be preserved but that they might become infused with Islam.

Some Christians eventually despaired of all secular assimilation strategies and concluded that greater concessions must be made to Islam. ʿAflaq tried to find a way out of the dilemma by his formula that Christians must revere Islam because of its peculiar place in the history and culture of the Arabs but eventually began to think that only conversion would answer. Khalīl Sakākīnī, a Palestinian Greek Orthodox writer and civil servant, came to a similar view. "As long as I am not a Moslem," he wrote to his son in 1932, "I am naught. If you desire to amount to anything then be a Moslem and that will be peace." [1] Sakākīnī spent his life in a ceaseless hunt for some panacea which would enable him to escape from the inherent inferiority which was the fate of the Christians in a Muslim state; any ism or none would do – "I am a member of humanity," he asserted hopefully but unavailingly.

A third strategy was to try to create some territorial political framework which would enable the community to retain its social organization and yet enjoy unrestricted access to economic and political benefits. For hopes of success this strategy required that the minority should be fairly numerous and concentrated in a compact territorial area and that it should have some powerful protector. Several communities had some experience of this strategy but most, including the heterodox Muslim communities of Syria, abandoned it. Some, like the Assyrian Christians of Iraq, who relied too heavily on a foreign protector, suffered for their dependence when the protection was withdrawn. The two non-Muslim communities which adopted this strategy with some success were the Zionists in Palestine under British protection and the Maronites in Lebanon under French protection. Under the umbrella of the British mandate the Zionists built up a community, defined by religion but possessing its own language and a full range of institutions, which in 1948 converted itself into a sovereign state in which the former minority became a majority. Nevertheless, Israel could still not do without a powerful protector. The Maronites persuaded France to create Greater Lebanon as a vehicle for their ambitions, a sovereign state with a small Christian majority and the Maronites as the largest single community. Within the state each community ran its own affairs with its own laws, courts and schools. Even the political system came to be partitioned on communal lines. Such a system, however, depended for its success on very limited powers being given to the state, on the acceptance by the communities of their place in the system and on the willingness of outsiders to support it. In fact these conditions were not met and the system broke down progressively from 1958.

The largest non-Muslim community of the Near East is the Coptic Christian community in Egypt. Its experience is an instructive one. Despite their numbers the Copts were nowhere a majority; even in the region of their greatest concentration around Asyūṭ they were still a minority. They could not hope for a territorial solution therefore and variously looked to foreign protection, political assimilation through Egyptian nationalism, striking a deal with a Muslim group which would allow them to retain their institutions and also reserve jobs in the public services for the Copts as a community, and obscurity. None was wholly successful and as the strategies were often pursued simultaneously they tended to cancel each other out. Foreign (British) protection was incompatible with nationalism (and in any case Britain was not interested in acting as protector of the Copts); and trying to turn a cultural community into a political community so as to bargain for jobs could not easily be combined with obscurity. Finally, during the 1970s the rise of Muslim assertiveness was matched by a new Coptic assertiveness under a new Coptic pope and clashes between the two communities were the result. The Copts had found no satisfactory way of combining their cultural identity with the political changes which had taken place.

One may conclude that with few exceptions the non-Muslim social compartments in the Near East lost ground during the period. They lost many of the educational and legal functions which they had formerly possessed; they found that they were at a disadvantage in competition for jobs in the enlarged state sector; and their former economic eminence, developed especially during the nineteenth century, became more difficult to sustain in the face of nationalization. In the end the preferred solution was often emigration, to Israel for the Jews, or to Europe or the Americas for the Christians.

Something has already been said of Muslim religious compartments in relation to the heterodox Muslim communities of the Near East. Muslim religious compartments were of two sorts: the orthodox compartments dominated by the ulema and the popular compartments represented by the Ṣūfī orders. Both supplied religious services but the first concentrated on legal and educational activities and the second on social functions.

Faced with the seemingly inexorable advance of the powers of the state the Muslim compartments had five main strategies open to them. First they could adopt the strategy of the secular states which dominated the Near East from 1923 until 1978, that is to say they could accept the loss of their traditional legal and educational functions and offer only facilities for the expression of personal belief, in other words give up their claims to be social organizations and become purveyors of worship. This was the reaction of most of the orthodox Sunnī ulema of the Near East who endeavoured to hold on to control of a few institutions but otherwise agreed to endorse the policies of the secular state in return for permission to continue their religious activities with state support. Thus the leading shaykhs of the Azhar endorsed Jamāl ᶜAbd al-Nāṣir's socialist measures in the 1960s and Sādāt's Camp David policy in 1978–9. In essence this was the traditional orthodox strategy carried forward from the age of minimal government into the era of state intervention. A second strategy was that of obscurity; hide from the state and carry on some traditional functions in secrecy. This was the policy of several Ṣūfī orders, notably those of the North Caucasus under Soviet rule but including many others in the Near East. This policy had the by-product of making it more difficult for outsiders to obtain information about the Ṣūfī orders and their work. As long as the functions did not obtrude unduly into the political arena the state was usually willing to allow the Ṣūfī orders to carry on in this fashion. A third strategy was that of violent resistance to the state. This strategy was also adopted by some Ṣūfī orders, notably the Qādirī and Naqshbandī orders among the Kurds of Iraq and Turkey during the 1920s and 1930s and among the former for many years thereafter. In Pakistan and the Sudan one can observe another Ṣūfī strategy. In those states the Ṣūfī orders, reinforced by tribal links, espoused secular nationalism, formed political parties and took power. That I have been unable to discover evidence of this phenomenon in the Near East proper may well be my failure rather than the absence of the strategy there.

A fourth strategy was to attempt some compromise between the religious community and the state, based upon traditional Muslim scholarly methods. This was the strategy of the Islamic modernists.

Islamic modernism began in the nineteenth century and its techniques were featured in the work of Sayyid Aḥmad Khān in India, Nāmik Kemāl in the Ottoman Empire and Muḥammad ᶜAbduh in Egypt. The problem was that the Sharīᶜa, the code of rules which governed the behaviour of Muslims, included many rules which forbade certain new social and economic practices. The Sharīᶜa was constructed from the Qur'ān and the Sunna or Traditions of the Prophet, that is the record of the sayings and actions attributed to Muḥammad, together with the product of scholarly reasoning applied to the Qur'ān and Traditions in accordance with accepted techniques. The object of the modernists was to create room for manoeuvre and compromise within the Sharīᶜa while staying within the conventional bounds of argument. The modernists accomplished this end through various devices which may be grouped under three headings, namely the exercise of personal judgement or *ijtihād* to choose between conflicting rules, the reduction of the number of rules by questioning the authenticity of some of the Traditions, and by the development of principles derived from the revised Sharīᶜa and their application to modern problems. This last device was especially important because it changed the whole character of the Sharīᶜa which, like the English common law, had always been a large body of precise rules and precedents and not a reservoir of principles. Rules are difficult to escape from but principles are keys to many doors.

The Islamic modernist movement continued through most of our period and considerably developed its critique of traditional Islam. The questioning of the authenticity of the Traditions was carried to great lengths in Egypt and very many long established Traditions were struck out of the canon on the grounds that the chain of transmission was unreliable; in particular a quarter or more of the Traditions are cited on the authority of Abū Hurayra, one of the companions of the Prophet, and by the simple device of questioning Abū Hurayra's veracity many sources of awkward rules were removed. Muᶜammar Qadhdhāfī in Libya went further and declared that none of the Traditions was binding and all that mattered was the Qur'ān itself, which contains surprisingly few rules for the guidance of society as opposed to the individual. To dispute the validity of the Qur'ān, of course, was impossible but it was another matter with rules derived from it. Thus the Qur'ān permits a man to have four wives but insists that he treats all fairly. The modernists argued that while such a feat was possible for the Prophet it was not feasible for lesser men and used this as an argument to restrict polygamy. More and more recourse was had to principles which opened up almost unlimited possibilities of reinterpretation. A particularly important principle was that of *istiṣlāḥ* (public interest or expediency) by which it was argued that whatever was necessary to protect the religion, the life, intellect, generation and property of the people was legitimate. Astonishingly, in the hands of some Muslim teachers such as Muṣṭafā al-Sibāʿī in Egypt and Syria and Dr ʿAlī Sharīʿatī in Iran, Islam was turned into a religion of social protest. "I...am expecting," wrote Sharīʿatī, "a sudden world revolution in favour of truth and justice and of the oppressed masses." [2] Through such devices Islamic law was substantially modified and the life of the Muslim community changed. The modernist movement was of particular importance because it gave intellectual respectability to change in the eyes of conservative Muslims.

The fifth strategy pursued by Muslims in the face of modernity was that known as fundamentalism or revivalism, although neither term accurately conveys the essence of the movement which became so prominent during the latter part of the twentieth century. The fundamentalists' strategy was to take over the state, that is to insist that the business of the state was conducted in strict accordance with the Sharīʿa. In making this demand they did not oppose the main elements of modernization, namely a powerful state, a programme of rapid economic development and social investment, especially in education and health. On the contrary they welcomed these developments. But they insisted that modernization should not be accompanied by Western social fashions, notably drink, drugs and dancing and by a relaxation of personal morality. And in certain economic matters, for example the charging of interest, they demanded that Sharīʿa rules should be strictly observed and that there should be no compromises such as those advocated by the modernists.

The fundamentalist movement began during the 1920s in Egypt and Syria in the form of several Muslim social organizations concerned with educational and similar social activities. To some extent their appearance was a response to the activities of Christian missionary organizations: the Young Men's Muslim Association (1927) was clearly a Muslim reply to its Christian equivalent. The best known of these societies was the Muslim Brotherhood which appeared in Egypt in 1928. Like its predecessors the Brotherhood was primarily an educational and welfare organization and only gradually developed a fuller programme and did not become closely concerned with politics until the 1940s. Its aim, at least until the late 1940s, was always to influence politicians and not to seek power for itself. The Muslim Brotherhood spread into other Arab countries and similar organizations sprang up elsewhere and organized themselves in more overtly political ways, for example the National Salvation Party in Turkey.

The fundamentalist movement was new in two ways. First its doctrine of modernization under Sharīʿa rules was fresh: other movements had either opposed modernization completely or accepted modernization but ignored or compromised the Sharīʿa. Second, it attracted a novel following from among new immigrants to cities, those who by coming to the city had chosen modernization but who resented the circumstance that most of the benefits appeared to flow to a Westernized urban élite. For these new urban dwellers fundamentalist doctrines with their unique combination of familiar Islamic resonances and modernizing promises provided a means to challenge the establishment. And the fundamentalists were quick to recruit them; the contrast in Cairo between the involvement of the Brotherhood and the indifference of the established ulema worked greatly to the advantage of the Brothers.

In Shīʿī Islam movements took place which were comparable to all of those described above, although the nature of Shiʿism and the peculiar authority of the *mujtahids* (whose title embodied the acceptance of the notion of *ijtihād*) meant that it was easier for them (if they so wished) to convert the Sharīʿa into a body of changing doctrine than it was for the reformers within Sunnī Islam. In Iran a mixture of modernism, fundamentalism and orthodoxy produced the most remarkable reversal of fortune among any Muslim community. One can write of a Shīʿī system which existed in Iran and was dominated by religious functionaries who supplied educational, legal, social and religious services in return for contributions from members of the community. From 1923 until 1978 this Shīʿī system remained important but steadily declined in stature against the state which took over several of its functions and asserted increasing control over its finances. In 1979 this process was reversed: the Islamic revolution involved the takeover of the state by the religious community under its traditional leadership, the only example of such a development in the modern Near East.

Muslim fundamentalism became, in the last two decades of our period, the principal challenge to the secular governments which had dominated the Near East since 1923. Its rise owed something to events such as the defeat sustained by radical Arab nationalism in 1967, to the wealth of Saudi Arabia given in support of Islamic causes and the publicity given to matters such as the fate of Jerusalem. But its main strength came from the progress of modernization itself.

One may summarize the changes in Muslim society in terms of the roles of Islam. Islam performs political, legal and educational functions, sets values for the society and defines the framework of personal belief, that is sets out what it is to be a Muslim through the five pillars of prayers, fasting, charitable payments, pilgrimage and above all the declaration of the unity of God. Down to 1970 Islam seemed to be on the retreat in each of these areas: its political, legal and formal educational functions were usurped by the state, its values were challenged by secular values and unbelief and non-observance increased. From about 1970 Islam advanced in each of these areas: constitutions gave greater prominence to Islam, laws were given a more distinctively Muslim element, state educational systems allocated additional time to Islamic matters, and the personal behaviour of Muslims became more conspicuously Islamic – fasts were observed, pilgrimages performed, and beards and veils (or at least headscarves) acquired a new popularity. One may regard this change either as a real change in the behaviour of Muslims or as the consequence of the new salience of a group which was always Muslim but hitherto obscured.

Ethnic compartments became more important in the Near East during the period with which we are concerned. In 1923 ethnic identities, based on language, were just beginning to come to the fore, notably in the demands of Arab and Turkish nationalism. Still these identities were less important than religious identities and often acted as a cover for them; the Turkish national movement was essentially a Muslim protest against Christian assertion. It was only as the role of the state increased, literacy spread and language became an essential qualification for jobs in the expanding government services of the new states that ethnic identities became more significant. Some consequences of this development are considered below.

One may also consider social organization in terms of rural and urban societies, the former dominated by the village and the latter by the urban quarter. Both of these traditional organizations were substantially modified during the period covered by this book. The village was changed by land reform, the removal of the landlord and his agent, and the substitution for him of the influence of the state, usually exercised through a new socio-economic organization, the co-operative. In fact, in many areas the co-operatives were unsuccessful in achieving their expressed purposes and served to obscure the changes which were taking place in villages. About these changes there is considerable controversy, especially concerning the role of the rural notable. According to one theory the removal of the big absentee landlord did not produce a new, more egalitarian rural society but paved the way for the rise of a class of medium proprietors who controlled the new rural institutions, assumed the role of intermediaries between peasant and state and sometimes moved into prominent positions in state institutions.

Probably bigger influences on the traditional village, however, were the rise in population which led to emigration to the cities, the developments in communications which broke down rural isolation and the arrival of the state in the form of a variety of agencies and demands. In a study of rural change in Iran and the effects of the invasion of the countryside by the Shah's corps, Eric Hoogland captures the effect of this last change in the statement of a peasant: "before we were ignorant but now we know that pills and shots can help us .... Before the elders said that if a child dies it was the will of God, but now, I think that it is the will of government." [3] But one should beware of attributing too much effect to state provision. In a similar study of Egypt James Mayfield relates the story of the young idealistic doctor from Alexandria who was sent to a remote village where the dirt so horrified him that he dared to eat nothing and after three days returned to the city.

Damascus may serve as an example of the evolution of a Near Eastern city. Within its walls the old city had ten quarters each of which could be cut off from the others. The inhabitants, who tended to be divided on ethnic and religious lines, included tradesmen, merchants, religious functionaries and other notables and their families. Quarters were ruled by headmen and councils which included the religious and lay notables. At lower levels kinship groups, religious associations, sporting clubs or other types of gangs possessed power on the streets. The leaders of these gangs were powerful men. An example was Abū ᶜAlī al-Kilāwī, a prominent gang leader of the 1920s, the list of whose attributes tell us something of what was required of a quarter leader. He was strong, a good wrestler, swordsman and horseman, he won fights and he collected followers. It was the alliances between such men and the religious and lay notables which were significant in the politics of traditional Damascus as in other cities. One could find similar men in every quarter of every city, for example, Shaᶜbān the Brainless who led the demonstrations in the Tehran bazaar against Muṣaddiq in August 1953.

Long before 1923 Damascus had expanded beyond its walls, particularly to the south in the direction of the Ḥawrān towards which ran a long suburb called the Maydān. Under French rule the city suffered heavily under bombardment in 1925/6 but it was increasing prosperity which led to a movement outwards into new suburbs, in particular into the government and European region to the north west of the city. New quarters grew up all around the city and by the 1930s not more than a quarter of the people lived in the old city which had been deserted by many of the non-religious notables. One of the effects of this movement was to weaken the traditional structure and the alliance between lay notables and gang leaders. The power of the traditional gang leaders also slipped away; in Iran it is noticeable that the influence of the gang leaders, so powerful in the 1940s and 1950s declined after 1963. Merchants also moved out; unlike other Near Eastern towns where the old bazaar was bulldozed to drive roads through or to construct a new business centre on the site, the Damascus bazaar was left intact and a new business centre established outside the old city. The traditional structure was further impaired by the influx of immigrants from the countryside. It is noticeable that the new immigrant suburbs or shanty towns did not develop the same corporate spirit and institutions which the older quarters possessed; the Maydān was never dominated by quarter leaders. In the last stage the old bazaaris began to move out to better accommodation, the bazaars were partly deserted and the old quarters were themselves often taken over by new immigrants. In the process the corporate identity of the city crumbled and the dominant influence throughout became the government. The process took a long time, however, and the influence of the old bazaar and its traditional leaders long persisted in some cities. In Iran, where modernization was especially compressed into the period after 1960, the survival of the old organization in many cities was an important factor in the success of the 1979 Islamic revolution.

One may also consider Near Eastern social organization in terms of classes. Many writers would deny that Near Eastern society, traditional or modern, can ever be arranged into classes; the old networks of kin and religion and the old divisions of ruler and ruled, they argue, were and are too powerful for broad economic interest groups to have much weight. Certainly, hostility to the notion of class was expressed from every side of the Near Eastern political spectrum. The Turkish constitution banned political parties based on class (and religion) and in 1944 Muḥammad Riżā Shāh banned the mention of the term in newspapers. The radical socialist regimes of the 1950s and 1960s never contemplated a class-divided society; ᶜAbd al-Nāṣir spoke of melting the differences between society's various forces. The Muslim radicals also meant by socialism only a movement for social justice; Muṣṭafā al-Sibāᶜī, the author of a book on Islamic socialism, condemned Marxism and the class war. Deeply rooted in Near Eastern thought was an ancient concept of a harmonious, organic society in which the various parts co-operated to their mutual advantage. The object of social and political policy was to restore this harmony when it was unnaturally disturbed by an oppressive regime or group which exploited others. Outside a small group of Marxist intellectuals, mainly in Turkey and Egypt, there was little notion of antagonisms decreed by the impersonal forces of production.

It would be difficult to argue that either in 1923 or in 1989 there existed substantial classes based on their relationship to the means of production in the Near East. Nevertheless, group interests based on economic circumstance did exist and changed throughout the period. From 1923 until the 1950s and 1960s the dominant group was that of the large landowners, the leading element in the group referred to in this book as notables. They had been prominent components of the Ottoman system and after 1923 dominated the political systems of most Near Eastern countries. Although one could write the political history of the period in terms of squabbles among notables it is also clear that they recognized a group interest; they formed landowner associations and used their political power, for example in Egypt during the interwar depression, to safeguard their economic interests. The story of their rise and fall is one of the leading themes in the history of the Near East during the period covered by this book.

The place of the landowning notables was taken from the 1950s onwards (earlier in Turkey) by another distinct interest group; namely an urban middle class. It must be made clear that this class was not one dominated by manufacturers, but was a professional class including lawyers, engineers, doctors, teachers and students and was dominated by bureaucrats and military officers. Directly or indirectly the whole class was dependent upon the state. Many writers may respond that this situation represents no change in the Near East; the leading social group had always been that of state functionaries. Such a view seems to under-rate the significance of the switch from a minimal state to one in which the state dominated employment; in earlier periods there had been plenty of room for other social groups to enjoy high status but the expansion of state power made the new effendi class wholly dominant from about 1960 onwards.

Other groups may be mentioned briefly. The religious notables declined in relative importance throughout the period or at least until 1979 in Iran. The traditional bazaaris remained a significant urban phenomenon through most of the period and many adapted successfully to the economic changes which took place. Industrial workers never became a distinct social class. There were industrial workers, concentrated in transport, textiles, food processing and oil, and there were trade unions and strikes, but there was little which could be seen as part of a consistent recognition of a group interest; rather worker associations were manipulated by other groups for their own interests. New immigrants to cities were a phenomenon but not a class. The controversy about the development of a class of middling rural notables has been mentioned; much of its force has come from the circumstance that many Near Eastern army officers had precisely such an origin. But army officers were essentially part of the state interest, not representatives of a rural interest they had left behind although they often found it useful to employ old regional and kin links in their search for advancement. As for peasants they lived up to Marx's despairing comment that they were not a class and resembled nothing so much as a sack of potatoes; with the minor exception of the Socialist Party of Akram al-Ḥawrānī in Syria in the 1950s there was nothing which could be described as a peasants' party.

Lastly, mention should be made of the rise of new social organizations. Some were outside the state, for example, many political parties, youth organizations such as the Boy Scouts, student associations, professional associations, employers' associations and worker associations. An increasing number from 1950 onwards were essentially outgrowths of the state or rather of the regime which controlled the state and included the mass political parties, such as the Arab Socialist Union in Egypt and the short-lived Resurgence Party in Iran, and the characteristic transmission belts, those social organizations intended to mobilize people in support of the policies of the regime. They included organizations of women, peasants, youth etc. None, it may be said, achieved the importance of older social organizations.

One of the most dramatic social changes in the Near East during the period 1923 to 1989 took place in education. In 1923 a little over 1 million children were in school, representing about 2 per cent of the total population: by 1980 there were 32 million in school representing about 15 per cent of the population. Down to 1950 the main concentration was on provision for primary education. The period from 1950 to 1960 saw a considerable enlargement of secondary education and the last 20 years was the age of mass higher education. By the end of our period primary education was virtually universal for boys and well over three-quarters of girls also experienced some primary education. Between a half and three-quarters of all boys enjoyed some secondary education, including middle school and vocational, and between one-third and a half of girls. As for higher education, by 1989 the region had about 100 universities, together with a number of other institutions of higher education, and about 16 per cent of children went on to some form of higher education, a figure similar to that of the United Kingdom. Literacy, about 10 per cent in 1923, rose to around 65 per cent at the end.

With the exception of some parts of Arabia, notably North Yemen, the record is very similar over the whole region although the timing differs; Turkey, Egypt and the Levant states led and Iran and Arabia lagged behind at first but moved forward more rapidly at the end; the oil states of Arabia were fortunate in that they did not require first to build up a supply of trained teachers but could hire them from other Arabic-speaking countries, in particular from Egypt. In 1980 over 90 per cent of teachers in the United Arab Emirates were not citizens of that state and two-thirds were from Egypt. Another pattern of uniformity is in state spending on education; over the period from 1950 to 1989 most states spent around 12 per cent of their budgets on education, which usually ranked second only to defence.

Educational development in the Near East was dominated by the state. At the beginning of the period most education was provided from non-governmental sources, including the religious communities, missionary organizations and private educational enterprises both local and foreign. In the mandated territories this situation persisted down to independence but in the independent states of Turkey, Iran and Egypt and in the former mandated territories after they gained independence (with the exception of Lebanon) the emphasis was entirely on the state. Provision by religious communities continued but was overtaken by state provision and the state also exercised control over teaching in religious schools. In Israel the religious parties were able to make a favourable arrangement with the state concerning their schools. Independent governments evinced increasing hostility to the activities of foreign schools and in most countries such schools were nationalized or brought under close state control. State control was a reality: the selection of teachers, books and curricula was supervised by the ministries of education.

Despite its domination of education the state was not able to dictate every line of development but increasingly found itself responding to a demand for education. The nineteenth century state concept of education in the Near East had been to produce men trained to fill certain slots in government services and had been focused on higher education. In the twentieth century this concept was overtaken by educational philosophies which stressed education as the key to progress by overcoming ignorance. During the period with which we are concerned the main driving force became not social progress but individual advancement; education was seen as the key to government jobs and in Egypt in particular the state found itself obliged to promise jobs to all graduates. In expanding the educational system so rapidly in the years after 1950 the state was often bowing to the weight of popular opinion. The rate of expansion far outran resources available and there was a substantial deterioriation in the quality of education.

Another educational development during our period was the ending of the two track system which had come into being in the early part of the twentieth century. It had soon become apparent to nineteenth century reformers that there were problems in lifting students out of the traditional system and putting them into a college with a modern curriculum. During the nineteenth century modern secondary schools had been developed and eventually elementary schools as well. There emerged in most Near Eastern countries a two track educational system: the state system which led towards government jobs and the religious system which led to religious jobs. There began a major debate about how to pull the two tracks together, a debate which was partially resolved by the victory of the state system and its establishment of a substantial monopoly over the provision of education. But the debate did not stop there, because from the 1930s in Egypt and increasingly elsewhere there was a dispute about the Islamic content of education in state schools. On this matter also the state made concessions from the 1950s onwards although without substantially altering the basically secular curriculum.

The other pillar of the social system is law. Well before 1923 the state had invaded the legal system and by that date Egypt and the former Ottoman territories possessed state courts and European-style codes of commercial, penal and civil law. Personal law, governing marriage, divorce and inheritance, was still the province of the religious communities whether administered in state courts or in their own community courts, including Sharīʿa courts. The general tendency of developments after 1923 was for the extension of the power of the state over the legal system in two ways: first by trying to ensure that all cases were heard in the state courts by judges whose training was approved by the state and, second, by trying to modify personal law.

The degree of success varied from one country to another. In Arabia generally, apart from South Yemen, Sharīʿa law and Sharīʿa courts survived. At the other end of the spectrum the whole of the law of Turkey and its courts were secularized and brought under state control. Other countries were arrayed between; Sharīʿa courts survived in many states but not in Egypt, and Sharīʿa personal law was modified in new codes of law which claimed to be based on Islamic principles but which incorporated elements of non-Sharīʿa law or the products of the work of the Islamic modernists. A good example is the Tunisian law of personal status of 1956 which claimed to be an adaptation of traditional Islamic law but which changed Sharīʿa law out of all recognition and banned polygamy. Most other legal reformers contented themselves with restricting polygamy but hesitated to go so far as to ban what was permitted in the Qur'ān. In Iran under the Pahlavīs state control over law went far but the Islamic republic after 1979 set itself to reverse the process and reinstate the Sharīʿa law and religiously-trained judges. But the Iranian reformers did not seek to push back the bounds of the state, rather to make the state courts and law Islamic.

The period of radical secular revolution from 1950 to 1970 was the heyday of the extension of state power and the attack on Sharīʿa law. The state by no means had everything its own way, however; in 1960 the ingenious President Bourguiba (Abū Ruqayba) in Tunisia tried to abolish the Ramaḍān fast, arguing that the Sharīʿa permitted those engaged in *jihād* to be relieved of the requirement to fast and since all developing countries were engaged in a variety of *jihād* the relaxation should apply to them. Bourguiba failed to convince anyone with this piece of modernism and was obliged to give way. During the period after 1970 the question of the role of Sharīʿa law in Muslim countries (and of Jewish law in Israel) became a bitterly contested issue and modifications were made in some legal codes and constitutions to give a more prominent place to Islamic principles and the Sharīʿa. It would be wrong, however, to say that the system constructed before 1970 was substantially challenged except in Iran.

One of the effects of legal reform was to improve the legal position of women. The extent of the improvement varied from state to state; only in Turkey with the adoption of the Swiss civil code in 1926 were women given something like legal equality. In most countries the legal changes had the effect of restricting polygamy, raising the age of marriage and improving the position of women in divorce and inheritance. Constitutional changes also extended the rights of women. Again the process began in Turkey when women were given the vote in 1930 and allowed to sit in parliament from 1932 but the franchise and the right to sit in parliament were granted (mainly during the 1950s) in every state which had a parliament except Kuwayt. The improvement in educational provision for women has already been noted: of the 32 million in school in 1980 about 12 million were girls. In employment, however, the picture was very different: in the Near East in 1975 female employment in towns represented only 5 per cent of women against an average for developing countries of 25 per cent. Given that opportunities for female employment were greater in rural areas it is the case that the effect of modernization in the Near East was to reduce the proportion of women in work. There was a substantial contrast between the success of middle and upper class women in finding jobs and the performance of poorer women. Finally, a feature of the Near East has been the development of women's organizations. In 1923 the Egyptian feminist, Hudā Shaᶜrāwī, founded the first feminist union in Egypt, the same year that she shocked public opinion by removing her veil at Cairo railway station. She was one of the first of many Near Eastern women to take that step, sometimes with the support of the state, often reluctantly at the behest of the state.

ECONOMY

The outstanding fact about the economic performance of the Near East during the period 1923 to 1989 is the increase of population. In 1923 the population of the region was about 52 million (Turkey 13 million, Egypt 13, Iran 12, Iraq 3, Greater Syria 4, made up of Syria 2.2, Palestine 0.8, Lebanon 0.7 and Transjordan 0.3, and Arabia 7). By the late 1980s the population had increased almost exactly four times to 210 million (Turkey, Iran and Egypt all being in the region of 50 million, Iraq 16, Syria 10, Israel 4, Lebanon 3, Jordan 3 and Arabia 24). The rate of increase accelerated throughout the period: between 1920 and 1940 it was in the region of 1.5 per cent a year; between 1940 and 1960 over 2 per cent; and between 1960 and 1980 nearly 3 per cent. No useful estimates can be made for the 1980s but while the rate of increase may have slowed in Turkey, Israel and Lebanon to around 2 per cent a year it appears to have been over 3 per cent throughout most of the region.

The cause of this increase in population was primarily a reduction in the death rate, more particularly the fall in the death rate among young children. The longest run of reasonably reliable statistics exists for Egypt and there the death rate fell from about 40 per thousand in the early twentieth century to about 16 per thousand in the mid-1960s. In the same period the birth rate also fell from about 50 per thousand to 44 per thousand. The fall in the birth rate was far from equalling the fall in the death rate and the differential accounts for the increase in population growth from 1 per cent a year to nearly 3 per cent during the period. No-one can be sure why the death rate should have fallen so rapidly but the favourite theories include a general improvement in the standard of living, an improvement in education, and medical advances especially in the control of epidemic and debilitating diseases.

Migration was a much less important factor in population change although over the period as a whole the Near East was probably a net gainer of population. The period begins with the major population exchanges between Greece and Turkey when Turkey was a net loser but subsequently Turkey received many Turkish immigrants from Balkan states especially Bulgaria. An unknown number arrived during the early 1920s, about 150,000 in 1950-51 and 300,000 in 1989. Counterbalancing this flow was the emigration of Turkish workers to Europe, especially West Germany, from the 1960s. Technically they were guest workers but many, perhaps 500,000, settled permanently in Germany. Syria, and especially Lebanon, showed a net emigration over the period: about 4,000 Lebanese a year went to the New World and Africa during the interwar period and the flow continued thereafter. Throughout the period there was constant immigration of Jews into Palestine and later Israel, in all perhaps 1.5 million from outside the region although many Israelis, possibly 500,000 by 1989, went outside the state, mainly to Europe and America to live. From the 1960s the Arabian peninsula received many foreign workers notably from India and Pakistan. The numbers of these cannot be estimated. Finally, one should note the movements caused by political turmoil in the 1980s. These movements particularly affected Iran which received about 2 million refugees from Afghanistan and hundreds of thousands from Iraq. Iran also exported refugees; perhaps 1 million went outside the region, mainly to Europe and North America after 1978.

Migration also affected the internal distribution of population. Until 1960 a striking characteristic of the people of the Near East, except for the Lebanese, was their reluctance to move (one should not forget the involuntary movement of some 700,000 Palestinians in 1948) but since that time a growing number has gone to other parts of the region to work and often to settle. The main cause of this flow has been the oil wealth of Arabia and the demand for unskilled workers for construction and services and for highly trained specialists. The principal exporting countries have been Egypt and the two Yemens together with the Palestinians (often appearing as Jordanians), and the principal importers of labour have been Iraq, Saudi Arabia and the smaller Gulf states. Once again it is difficult to estimate the numbers of those who have moved but the figure may be of the order of 5 millions and represents a substantial, if possibly temporary shift in the balance of the population in the Near East. Finally, political change and turbulence also affected movements between Near Eastern states: the transfer of Hatay to Turkey led to the emigration of many non-Turks to Syria in 1939; after 1975 Kurds fled from Iraq to Iran; and after 1979 Iranians departed for Turkey.

The principal factor in the redistribution of population was urbanization. In 1923 about one-fifth of the people of the Near East lived in towns. The proportion changed little before 1945: the growth of the urban population was in line with the general growth of population. After 1945 the urban proportion began to rise and by 1968 about one-third of the population was urban and by 1989 about one-half. In 1923 the Near East had no city with as many as a million people; by 1989 it had at least 12, led by Greater Cairo with 13 million. The rate of growth of large cities during the period was such that at any time from 1960 onwards between one-third and one-half of their populations was composed of new immigrants. Housing construction could not keep up with the flow and around each major city grew large squatter settlements.

There has been much discussion of the urbanization phenomenon and it has focused on two issues: why did the new immigrants come to the city and what sort of life did they enjoy when they got there? We now have enough information from studies of individual cities and immigrant groups to answer these questions with some accuracy. First, the immigrants came overwhelmingly because they wished to better themselves and believed they could have an improved life in the city. The picture of peasants driven to the city by lack of any alternative seems to have little merit as a general explanation. On the whole the new immigrants tended to be the younger, better educated and more enterprising members of the rural or small town community. A survey in Turkey in the 1970s showed that 84 per cent of peasants would have liked to live in the city. Second, when they arrived in the city the immigrants tended to join people from the same village, region, ethnic group or religious association and be supported by them in the early months. They frequently revisited their villages and the early years of urban life had a transitional nature; there was rarely a clean break and the theory that new immigrants fell victim to Durkheimian anomie seems not to be substantiated. The new immigrants went into unskilled employment in construction or services; jobs in the modern sector went almost exclusively to second generation city dwellers. Finally, one should beware of assuming that all squatter settlements were flimsy, unpleasant structures: many were solidly built and inhabited by prosperous people with steady jobs. Successful people moved up the housing ladder and often the settlement itself was rebuilt by government, shanties being replaced by high-rise apartments as in Revolutionary City outside Baghdad.

The principal economic problems of the Near East during the 70 years following the First World War were to feed, house, clothe, educate and provide jobs for this increased population and in addition to provide it with a constantly rising standard of living. These tasks the Near East accomplished with considerable success.

From 1923 until 1945 the Near East stood still economically, that is to say that the increase in GNP equalled the increase in population and the standard of living remained about the same. Of course there was some variation throughout the region in place and time. Turkey advanced rapidly during the 1920s and 1930s partly because of the very low baseline from which she started as a result of the damaging wars she had fought from 1911 until 1923. Egypt also did well on the strength of high cotton prices during the same period. Palestine prospered because of the influx of immigrants and capital from abroad. Iran made considerable advances by virtue of oil revenues and, during the 1930s, invested a high proportion of national income although this was not reflected in an increase in the standard of living. From 1930, however, economic growth slowed through most of the region. The two great events were the interwar depression and the Second World War.

It is difficult to estimate the effect of the depression on the economies of the Near East. Until recently the conventional view was that primary producers were hit harder than industrialized states during the depression and that the Near East suffered badly, and there is some evidence to support this view. Prices of cereals and cotton fell considerably. In Turkey cereal prices fell by 70 per cent between 1928 and 1933 whereas the prices of textiles and sugar fell by only 25 per cent. In Egypt cotton prices had fallen by August 1931 to one-third of what they had been in 1929. And prices were slow to recover; even in 1939 cotton fetched only half what it had done in the halcyon days of the early 1920s. Government help cushioned the impact on producers in both countries and agricultural production continued to rise during the 1930s but at a slower rate than it had done in the 1920s. But it could be argued that the conditions of the 1920s were exceptionally favourable in both countries and some slowdown in agriculture was inevitable. A new revisionist view propounded in relation to other Asian countries questions this picture of unrelieved gloom, however, and points to new opportunities which opened up for the region. One could also construct for the Near East a list of counterbalancing advantages, notably the impetus given by the depression to government efforts to promote industrial development. These efforts were most conspicuous in Turkey where a system of state- directed industrialized planning was inaugurated with some success but there is also evidence of new industrial development in Egypt helped by tariff protection and in Iran there was some stimulus to the development of communications. On balance there seems no doubt that the depression contributed to a reduction of economic growth – in Egypt GDP fell by 2.5 per cent a year between 1929 and 1935 – but it also assisted the process of making the Near East more independent of Europe.

The effect of the Second World War was also mixed. Initially the war led to shortages, particularly of shipping which caused severe problems in some parts of the region until the problems were alleviated by the work of the Middle East Supply Centre. Generally speaking the situation was worst in the northern part of the region; the closure of the Mediterranean hurt all countries dependent upon its use and the inadequacy of land communications meant that it was difficult to find substitutes. The southern part of the region, on the other hand, could draw on supplies from Africa and Asia and reach markets there. Inflation and shortages were more acute in the north than in the south. The war also created opportunities for local industrialists, now insulated from European competition, in supplying the wants of the local market and of Allied troops in the region. In this way the war gave a boost to local industry in Egypt and Syria. German demands helped Turkish industry and mining. On the other hand the war had the effect of deferring planned oil production in Arabia, although its longer term effect was to promote more rapid development of Middle Eastern oil. The war also had the consequence that the Near East was forced into involuntary saving through inflation and the inability of Britain to pay for goods. The effect was to restrict consumption and to enable the Near East to repatriate foreign debt and build up a reserve in the form of frozen sterling balances which became available to finance investment after the war. One could regard the Second World War as having built a somewhat uncomfortable platform from which the Near East could move forward in the post-war period.

After a slow post-war recovery the Near East took off economically from 1950. Between 1950 and 1970 the economies of the Near East grew at an average rate of about 5 per cent a year or more. Allowing for population increase this still represented an increase of per capita income of well over 2 per cent a year. Once again there were variations in place and time; the Korean War was a boon for the Near East and the early 1950s were blessed by good weather and large harvests.

The period after 1965 was generally less prosperous than the preceding years had been. But the picture is remarkably even.

Why did the Near East do so well in this period ? Oil is certainly one factor and rapidly increasing oil revenues may account for much of the growth which took place in Iran, Iraq and Arabia. But countries which did not have oil did even better; the two leading performers in this period were Jordan and Israel with economic growth in the region of 8–10 per cent a year. Both of these states may be regarded as special cases since they benefited more than other countries from outside aid and Jordan was one of the first countries to profit considerably from remittances from Jordanian Palestinians employed in Arabia. But Turkey had no oil and yet averaged between 5 and 6 per cent growth per year over the same period. At the time credit was claimed by the new radical regimes which appeared in several parts of the Arab world but a comparison of the performance of the state-planned radical economies with the so-called conservative states shows no significant difference in their economic performance; if anything the conservatives did slightly better. The stimulus provided by the demands of an increasing and restless population was one factor and another was the sustained world economic boom.

In the decade 1970 to 1980 the Near East did even better and in this period the main impetus certainly came from oil. The oil price rises, which began in 1970 and subsequently increased in two great leaps in 1973 and 1979, made available very large sums for investment by the oil-rich states and most countries of the region now benefited directly from that oil wealth through employment and remittances, through selling goods or through offering services of various kinds to the oil-rich states. For other states there was plenty of foreign credit. Only Lebanon, which had done so well before 1970 by providing tourist facilities and financial services to oil-rich states, missed out on this new round as the civil war ruined her attractiveness and her economy. The oil boom ran on into the early 1980s but by the middle 1980s the Near East was running into harder times; the world recession, the fall in demand for oil, the Iran–Iraq war and a growing burden of foreign debt all combined to force the Near East to restrict economic growth. In some cases, notably in Iran, there was a sharp reversal and the standard of living was considerably reduced.

By 1980 the average Near Eastern citizen was twice as well off as he or she had been in 1950. But since there is no such animal as the average Near Eastern citizen who or what benefited? One answer is the state: between 1950 and 1970 the state share of consumption increased by an average of 50 per cent. The only exceptions were

Turkey and Syria, and during the 1970s Syria made up for its slow start. A substantial share of the extra income therefore was taken by the state and returned in the form of services, especially education, health and defence. Not all was returned, however; a large part went in paying the greatly increased number of state functionaries. Those who did best out of the Near Eastern boom were army officers, bureaucrats, teachers and those working for the state in other capacities as managers, workers and contractors. To this group we may add officials of the government-sponsored political parties. The second major group to profit was urban dwellers of all types. Most state services in education, health and housing were provided for their benefit. They also enjoyed food and other subsidies which grew rapidly during the 1970s. Those who did least well out of the boom were those in agriculture.

During the whole period from 1923 to 1989 the economy of the Near East was transformed. In 1923 the economy of the whole region had been dominated, as it had been in the past, by agriculture, which employed about 75 per cent of the work force. By 1985 no more than one-third worked in agriculture and this figure exaggerates the relative significance of agriculture because it includes a large number of women. The change did not take place evenly; down to 1945 agriculture more or less held its own; indeed the 1920s saw considerable extensions of cultivation in several countries, notably in Turkey and Syria. Throughout this period the economy of the Near East was dominated by cereal cultivation, mainly for domestic consumption. Only cotton (Egypt, Turkey, Iran, Iraq and Syria), dates from Iraq, and citrus fruit from the Levant were major exports, although Turkey did begin exports of grain from 1930. The balance began to shift from 1950. Several countries enjoyed agricultural booms during the 1950s and there were big extensions of the area available for cultivation in Syria, Iraq and especially Iran, where the irrigated area increased from 1.6 million hectares in 1950 to 5.25 million in 1971. Agricultural production, assisted by mechanization increased throughout the region. Nevertheless, by 1970 the percentage of the Near Eastern workforce in agriculture had fallen to between 40 and 50 per cent and agriculture's share of GDP was down from about 35 per cent in 1950 to below 20 per cent. From 1970 the move out of agriculture quickened in pace. Total numbers employed in agriculture did not reduce but most of the increase in population went into other economic activities.

From the 1950s the shape of Near Eastern agriculture was changed by land reform although the effect of land reform on the decline of agriculture was minimal. There is a danger of exaggerating the economic effect of land reform. Even before land reform small holders predominated in the Near East. There were very large landholders in every country and especially in Iraq, Iran, Syria and Egypt. But with the exception of southern Iraq it was only a small part of the cultivated land which was in very large estates; in Egypt in 1952 only 20 per cent of the land was in holdings of 84 hectares or more and half of these holdings were exactly 84 hectares. In Iran two-thirds of cultivated land was held by proprietors whose holdings were in the range of 5 to 50 hectares and only 3 per cent of holdings were over 500 hectares. The small number of great landlords who could turn their concentrations of landed wealth into political power was a very important political phenomenon in the Near East but the great landlords were few – no more than a few hundred at most in any state – and their economic influence was inevitably slight. Economically, land reform had the effect of confirming the predominance of the small and medium proprietor throughout the Near East. The big landlords disappeared and, eventually, the landless declined for there was not enough land to accommodate them. There appears to be very little connection between land reform and economic performance: in Iran production increased, in Iraq it fell and in Syria and Egypt it is difficult to discern any change which can be attributed to land reform. Land reform, so great an episode in the history of the Near East from 1952 to 1968, was a political, not an economic event.

It was only to a very limited extent that manufacturing industry filled the place of agriculture in the Near East. The share of manufacturing industry in GNP increased throughout the period but by 1985 was still only in the region of 15 per cent. Textiles and food processing predominated thoughout and especially during the period before 1970. Before that date only Turkey (in 1939) and Egypt (in 1958) had established the beginnings of heavy industry by the construction of iron and steel plants and most of the development in this sector in the Near East occurred during the years after 1970. It was after 1970 that refining and petrochemicals also began to develop. Before 1950 refineries had often been located in producer countries. By that date there were 12 refineries in the Near East, most of them small and serving local purposes but including four large refineries at Ābādān (1912), Baḥrayn (1937), Ra's al-Tanūra in Saudi Arabia (1945) and Mīnā' al-Aḥmadī in Kuwayt (1949). Between 1950 and 1970 although many more refineries were built in the region, including the substantial Aden refinery (1954), the preferred locations were in the consumer countries. After 1970 this practice was reversed and the largest development of refining and associated petrochemical industries took place during the 1970s and 1980s as the oil-rich states sought to diversify their economies. Construction was also always important but its importance is disguised in statistics because of the extent to which the work is carried on inconspicuously by casual labour which does not appear in statistics. It is very clear, however, that the building of cities, ports, communications systems, etc., involved a great deal of capital and many men, and that in the period after 1970 construction was one of the major economic activities of the Near East, as, indeed, it probably always had been.

Oil is the industry most closely associated with the Near East and it is also one of the most awkward for the historian who is trying to present a broad picture. The reason is that just as fluctuations in agricultural production and prices due to variations of weather and the vagaries of the market had a dramatic effect on production and therefore on the relative contribution of all sectors to GNP in the first half of our period so fluctuations in oil prices had the same type of effect in the years after 1970. It will be sensible to begin, therefore, with a brief account of the development of the oil industry in the region.

If we exclude the earlier development of Baku, the oil industry in the Near East began with the discovery of oil in commercial quantities at Masjid-i Sulaymān in south-west Iran in 1908 and the formation of the Anglo–Persian Oil Company to exploit the deposits. Production began in 1912 and the Ābādān refinery was opened in the same year. The next substantial development took place in Iraq when the Kirkuk field was opened in 1927. Oil was taken out by pipeline to Haifa and Tripoli. During the 1930s the most interesting developments took place in Arabia and oil was discovered in Baḥrayn, Qaṭar, Saudi Arabia and Kuwayt, although with the exception of Baḥrayn production did not get going until the end of the Second World War. Subsequently there were further discoveries on the Arabian shore of the Gulf and during the 1960s Abū Dhabī became a major producer. Oil production extended to other Near Eastern countries, in particular to Libya and Egypt in the 1960s.

Near Eastern oil was slow to make a major impact on the world. At the beginning of our period it represented only about 2 per cent of world production which was dominated by the United States. The Near East's share rose to 5 per cent in 1935, 17 per cent in 1950 and 25 per cent in 1960, and to a peak of nearly 40 per cent in 1973 (and was still 35 per cent in 1980) before declining in the 1980s.

The Near Eastern oil industry was developed through concessions given to European and American oil interests. The concessionaires formed producer companies and eventually the oil industry came to be dominated by a small number of large multi-national companies which controlled all aspects of oil exploration, production, processing, distribution and marketing. From an early period there were disputes between Near Eastern governments and the oil companies about the way in which shares in the profits of oil should be divided. In 1950 a system of equal shares was established, although it failed to avert the oil nationalization crisis in Iran. After 1970 the whole system was challenged by the governments and between 1972 and 1976 all the major producing companies were taken over by the states in which they operated, in Iraq by nationalization and in other states by the government taking a controlling shareholding in the companies.

Until 1970 the price of oil (outside the Communist world) was effectively controlled by US production and attempts by Iran in the 1950s and Iraq in the 1960s to impose their will on the system had failed. By 1970, however, it became clear that US oil production could not be sustained, that more oil was being used than was being discovered and that in the future the Near East would become the dominant producer of oil for sale, the more so because its reserves of commercial oil amounted to 60 per cent of world stocks. Further, the USA, which as late as 1967 had imported only 3 per cent of its oil from the Near East began to increase its demands which amounted to 14 per cent of its requirements in 1973. The Near Eastern states took advantage of this circumstance to force up the price of oil, their efforts being co-ordinated by the Organisation of Petroleum Exporting Countries (OPEC) which was originally formed in 1960 to fight a cut in oil prices. During the 1970s, and especially in the years 1973 and 1979, the price of oil was increased from under 2 dollars a barrel in 1970 to nearly 40 dollars by the end of 1980. The resulting increase in the incomes of the governments of oil-producing states was dramatic and the revenues financed the great economic boom of the 1970s and early 1980s in the Near East. But the oil producers had overplayed their hand: demand fell, other oil and energy sources were tapped and the price of oil fell through most of the 1980s to between one-quarter and one-half of its peak. The Near Eastern boom lost much of its power.

The great importance of the oil industry to the Near East was as a source of funds to finance government expenditures and investments. It was not itself a substantial employer of labour; directly it employed less than 100,000 people in the Near East in the 1960s. Furthermore, the circumstance that oil deposits were mainly sited in remote regions meant that the oil industry was partly insulated from the rest of the economy and had little direct spin off in established urban activities. Nor did the indirect spin off have the impact which it might have done in creating employment in the Near East because many of the largest oil deposits were located in the less developed states of the Near East. As a consequence the governments concerned chose to spend much of the money they received on goods from the USA, Europe and Japan, and spending in the Near East on goods and services, although considerable, was less influential than it might have been under a different dispensation.

Of other economic activities one should note the development of communications. Between the two world wars railway construction was the major investment as much of the Near East sought to catch up with other regions of the world; between 1914 and 1957 there was a fourfold increase in the length of track and Iran and Turkey spent especially heavily. But emphasis soon shifted to roads which came to dominate the transport system. Ports were also developed. Older patterns of communications were disrupted by the political division of the Near East in 1920–3, established ports were cut off from their natural hinterlands and new ports were required by new states. Thus Alexandretta, cut off from Iraq and eventually from Aleppo, declined and its place was taken partly by Latakia. The British mandates in Palestine and Iraq made Haifa into the main regional port but the result of the 1948 war cut Haifa off from the Arab world and it sank to being an Israeli local port. Iraq developed Basra and later Umm Qaṣr, and Jordan built ᶜAqaba. But generally the Near East never quite came to terms with the economic consequences of political frontiers: port capacity in the Near East and its supporting transport systems lagged behind the development of trade and when the great economic boom arrived in the 1970s the system was found inadequate.

In terms of its contribution to GNP and employment the major economic activity of the Near East, replacing agriculture during our period, was services, and especially government services. Except for Turkey among major states and Lebanon and North Yemen among the smaller states, the state became the dominant economic factor in the economy of the Near East and we must soon turn to consider its evolution. But before we look at the politics of the independent states in the Near East it will be useful to glance at the economic contribution of the outside world.

At the beginning of our period European states were an important factor in the economy of the Near East. Most Near Eastern trade was conducted with Europe, a high proportion of the debt was held by foreigners, the banking and credit system was dominated by foreign banks and insurance companies, and much of industry was owned by foreigners. In addition Britain and France ruled directly in the mandated territories whose currencies were tied to sterling and the franc.

Between 1923 and 1956 this structure of European economic eminence was dismantled. The Ottoman public debt was divided among the successor states in 1923 and Turkey, which assumed responsibility for the greatest part found the burden of repayments very troublesome in the 1920s so much so that she sought and was granted a rescheduling of the debt. Thereafter interest reductions and the liquidation of parts of the debt reduced the problem, the Debt Administration was closed in 1940 having ceased to function for some years and the debt was finally extinguished in 1948. Turkey had done well out of the bargaining and the other successor states hastened to take advantage of the concessions offered to her and they also escaped much of the burden. The transformation of the Egyptian debt into an internal debt had already begun during the First World War when half the debt had been Egyptianized and the process continued until in 1943 it became wholly an internal Egyptian matter. The Caisse de la Dette was suppressed in 1940. European central banking control also disappeared. The note issue role of European banks was assumed by Turkey in 1930, Iran in 1932, Egypt in 1951, Syria in 1956 and Lebanon in 1964. Insurance companies in Egypt and Syria were nationalized in the 1950s. Foreign domination of industry was ended in Turkey and Iran during the 1930s and the greatest industrial enterprise of all, the Anglo–Iranian Oil Company, was nationalized in 1951. In Egypt the proportion of shares in Egyptian companies held abroad fell from 70 per cent in 1914 to 50 per cent in 1934 and 13 per cent in 1940. Most of Egyptian industry was then owned by foreigners resident in Egypt; in 1948 still only 40 per cent of nominal capital was owned by Egyptians. But in 1947 a law was introduced to promote Egyptianization and eventually between 1956 and 1961 Egyptian industry was nationalized, including the Suez Canal Company. French-owned companies in Syria were nationalized in the 1950s and those in Lebanon were Lebanized in the same period. Finally, Europeans lost their domination of Near Eastern trade.

Foreign economic influence in the Near East continued to be important after 1956 but never regained the significance it had had in the early years. The states of the Near East continued to conduct most of their trade with Europe, the United States and Japan and some states became heavily dependent on foreign aid, notably Israel, Jordan, Turkey and Egypt. But all retained ownership and control of their own economies.

POLITICS

The outstanding political development, indeed the greatest phenomenon of any sort in the Near East since 1923, has been the growth and consolidation of the state and the state system established in 1923. In 1923 the Near East was divided between a number of weak states which possessed very few institutions and which felt themselves vulnerable both to international powers and to social forces within their borders. By 1989, with few exceptions, the same states were firmly established on the international map and dominant over society and the economy within their frontiers. It is this pre-eminence of the state which has determined the shape of this book. The arena of the state provided the contours of all other activities and an arrangement which was not based upon the individual states would obscure the central feature of Near Eastern development since 1923. It is also plain, however, that there have been many uniformities in the progress of the different states and in the following section these will be briefly explored together with some of the ideas which have underpinned the state system. An examination of alternatives to the state system which have been offered will also be provided.

One problem which has agitated writers on the politics of the Near East has been that of legitimacy, that is the notion derived from Weber that in order to succeed political systems must be acceptable to the people who live in them and acceptance depends upon the establishment of some plausible title to authority derived from tradition, rationality or charisma. There has been much confusion in the discussion of this issue, the consequence of the habit of writers of mixing up states, regimes, governments and individual leaders and not making clear whether they are talking of the legitimacy of one or the other. The result has been that the debate has often been at cross purposes. For example Michael Hudson wrote an influential book in which he argued that the central problem of Arab politics was the failure of *regimes* to establish their legitimacy and Gabriel Ben-Dor attacked his argument with a book about the authority of *states*. Two comments may be made on the legitimacy debate: first that states, regimes, governments and individual leaders have all been attacked on the grounds that they had no title to authority and all have attempted to establish some such title. Second, that on the whole the debate has not mattered much: it has been the power of the institutions of the state, at the disposal of regimes, government and individual leaders, which has given them authority; legitimacy, like the Chinese mandate of heaven, has gone to those who controlled the power of the state and the states survived because their very power drew support to themselves.

The collapse of the Ottoman Empire during and after the First World War led to the establishment of a new state system throughout most of the Near East. The new states were obliged to equip themselves with constitutions. Although many of the provisions of the constitutions were flouted the constitutions were important because they defined the nature of the states and the arena within which political activity could legitimately take place and therefore helped to shape the nature of that activity and the direction in which the states developed. Turkey's decision to opt for a republic and the sovereignty of the people exercised through a single chamber parliament was a momentous change of direction which contrasts sharply with the decision of Riżā Shāh to stay within the 1906 Iranian monarchical constitution. The political development of Egypt and Iraq was shaped by the uneasy balance within their constitutions between the king and the politicians. And the decision not to include a timetable for the introduction of an organic law in the Palestine mandate, the effect of which was that mandatory Palestine had no constitution other than the mandate itself, was a crucial one for the future of the state. It helped to ensure, indeed, that Palestine had no future and, alone among the states of the 1923 settlement outside Arabia, did not survive.

The most important institutions established by the new states were their armies. The central function of government and its only ultimate title to authority is the maintenance of security for life and property. During and after the First World War security had broken down in much of the region and the first task of governments was to equip themselves with adequate security forces. In this respect there is a clear distinction between the development of the three main states of the region. Turkey inherited the traditions and some of the personnel of the old Ottoman army and the circumstances of the war of 1919–22 ensured that the army predated the new state. The problem was not to build up an army but to make the army fit the new state in terms of its demands on resources and to ensure that the army accepted the new state. These ends were accomplished with such success that the army became the guardian of the institutions and ideals of the new republic. In Iran the army was the creation not of the state but of the Pahlavī regime. Its success in holding the state together and defeating its internal enemies was considerable but its loyalties were always to the Pahlavī regime rather than to the secular state created by the Pahlavīs and the army collapsed in 1979 when the Pahlavīs deserted it. Egypt, on the other hand, had nothing which could be called an army of its own until after 1936; the ultimate guarantor of the state was Britain. When the Egyptian army was created it was very much the product of the state. In this respect Egypt resembled Syria and Lebanon, but not Iraq or Transjordan where the army and the state grew up together. In Palestine there was no state army, only those of Britain and of the two main communities.

After 1923 the states of the Near East established, on the foundations of the systems set up before that date, central governments in which duties were divided between functional ministries and provincial governments on the French (and Ottoman) model, that is a centralized structure of provinces and smaller units dependent upon them. In Arabia these governmental structures developed much more slowly than elsewhere; governments remained basically of the old household style until the 1960s and when the forms of modern governments were adopted the result resembled the old households writ large and functionally divided. The heart of the matter was, however, the identification of functions and the construction of a logical system for managing those functions. The functional character of the new governments cut across older social institutions which performed functions but were not conceived in terms of functions. The advance of the state involved the stripping of functions from these older institutions, notably defence, education, law and some economic functions. The process was a long one because the state was unable to find the resources in men and money to discharge the functions to which it aspired and the social institutions resisted the change. But the process was inexorable and by the end of our period the state had, except in a few pockets of the Arabian peninsula and in Lebanon, established a virtual monopoly of these functions. The question had become only that of who should manage the state.

The Near Eastern political élite in 1923 may be divided into three categories. In Turkey the élite was largely composed of the old Ottoman civil and military bureaucracy supported by a class of rural notables in western Anatolia and Kurdish tribal chiefs in the east. In Arabia and Transjordan the élite was tribal, owing its position to birth and in some cases to British endorsement, and it was supported by a class whose influence derived from its religious status. Throughout the rest of the area, that is to say in Egypt, the Fertile Crescent and Iran, the core of the élite was composed of big absentee landowners who lived in towns and dominated the politics of them. Under the Ottoman system these notables had served as the interface between the Ottoman government and people, acting as brokers between government agencies and rural notables and urban interest groups. The notables had competed for jobs within the Ottoman and Islamic systems and the central question of politics was what they would do now the Ottoman system had gone.

Albert Hourani, who more than anyone has been responsible for identifying the central political role of the notables, argued that what they would really have liked would have been to recreate the Ottoman system and that much of their behaviour is best understood on the basis that they were acting as they had done under the Ottomans. Their demand for supreme power, therefore, was not serious; it was a bargaining counter designed to secure their position as brokers and help them against their rivals. Their problem was that they could not find a political authority prepared to behave like the Ottomans or, for that matter, the Qājārs either. Notable politics depended upon restraint by the state and governments run by notables were small governments. The state had to leave the notables room but instead, by expanding its functions, it threatened their role. The heyday of the notables was from 1923 until 1950; in that period they and their lawyer allies and instruments dominated the politics of the states mentioned either alone or with other groups: the European mandated governments, the Egyptian monarchy, the soldiers who supported Rižā Shāh in Iran and the Hashimites. During the 1950s and 1960s the notables were swept away.

The principal turning point in the history of the Near East since 1923 is neither the end of European domination nor the rise of the oil industry but the replacement of the notables by new groups composed of what one might call a state middle class of bureaucrats and army officers during the great secular revolutions of the 1950s and 1960s. It is true that these three events apparently coincided in time but they did not have the same impact. Long before the Suez fiasco of 1956 European domination was no more than a convenient fiction which served to satisfy the *amour propre* of Britain and France on the one hand and, on the other, the need for a convenient peg on which some Near Easterners could hang their complaints against others. And the presence or absence of oil wealth in any state was evidently irrelevant to the question of whether there was a secular revolution or not as any consideration of the revolutions would show.

During the 1950s and 1960s there was a debate about the nature of the contemporary revolutionary movement in the Near East. The participants in the debate may be divided into two groups: those who argued that the revolutionaries were trying to achieve their proclaimed goals and were effecting a real change in the nature of the Near

East; and those who claimed that the revolutions were purely rhetorical, that the revolutionaries were not serious in their proclamations and did not carry them out and that no real change had taken place other than that one group had replaced another in control of the states concerned. Both sides in the debate were right and both were wrong. The revolutionaries did not achieve many of their proclaimed goals and may well have had no intention of doing so but there was, nevertheless, a real change. Moreover, this change was not confined to the states which proclaimed themselves to be revolutionary but very similar changes took place in the so-called traditional or reactionary states.

Initially, the revolutionaries enunciated their goals in terms of the things they were against rather than what they wanted. Thus the earliest theme is hostility to corruption; that was the only justification for the revolutionaries' intervention cited in the announcement of the Egyptian revolution on 23 July 1952. Secondly, they were against injustice, perhaps the oldest and most traditional of all Islamic calls to revolution. Later, the revolutionaries declared themselves to be against imperialism. At first they opposed only specific features of foreign political and economic influence; thus on 16 January 1953 the Egyptian revolutionaries announced, in contradiction of their July 1952 proclamation, that the principal object of the revolution was to evict the foreigners. It was only in the 1960s that the revolutionaries fastened on to the notion of imperialism as a broad and vague concept embracing features of political, economic and social domination; thus the Syrian revolution of March 1963 was stated as being "to liberate your Arab land from imperialism ".[4] Anti-imperialism became the stock in trade of the radical revolutions of the 1960s. Anti-capitalism joined it; initially there was no criticism of capitalism but hostility to the system was voiced in the Egyptian constitution of January 1956 and this hostility became general among the later revolutionaries.

Opposition to so-called feudalism appeared in the Egyptian constitution of 16 January 1956 when the intention to abolish "feudalism" was stated. The meaning is vague but was plainly linked to the reduction of the power of the big absentee landlords which had already taken place through land reform. In the charter of the South Yemen National Liberation Front of 1965 anti-feudalism was more specifically directed against the power of the sultans and chiefs of the Aden protectorate states. A peculiar feature of the radical revolutionary movements of Arabia was opposition to "tribalism" by which was meant the projection of tribal links into politics rather than pastoral nomadism.

The list of things the revolutionaries wanted began with nationalism. "We are Arab nationalists before anything else," stated Ḥusnī al-Zaʿīm, Syria's first revolutionary dictator in April 1949.[5] But nationalism was an ambiguous concept; Zaʿīm also propounded a narrower Syrian version: on 30 March 1949 he claimed that the "Syrian nation will seize glory and climb the ladder of greatness to eternity."[6] The tension between Arab nationalism and the nationalisms of the various Arab states runs through the history of Arab radical nationalism. And there were intermediate varieties of nationalism – Greater Syrian, Yemeni, Nile, etc.

The revolutionaries also claimed to be for the people. From an early period there were frequent references to the mandate of the people as a principal source by which the revolution was legitimized. "The people alone are the source of power; they must be consulted at every juncture," stated Adīb al-Shishaklī in June 1953.[7] ʿAbd al-Karīm Qāsim announced his revolution in Iraq with a proclamation to the effect that authority must be entrusted to a government which stems from the people and is inspired by their wishes. Freedom was also a prominent goal of the revolutionaries but after the early days this goal was expressed not in terms of individual freedoms but of collective freedom. Thus the March 1963 revolutionaries in Iraq defined freedom as "the collective expression of popular responsibility" and added that there was no freedom without socialism.[8] The revolutionaries never favoured parliamentary democracy except within strict limits but preferred that freedom should be exercised through direct democracy (like the committees which abounded in Libya) and popular choice expressed through a single party or dedicated group (such as the army) acting in the name of the people, nation or history. The revolutionaries were always élitist.

The revolutionaries were for progress and, especially from 1959, for socialism. The period 1959–61 in Egypt was a major turning point in the history of the secular revolutions because it was then that Egypt turned to socialism. From then on socialism became one of the main planks of the revolutionaries until it began to go out of fashion in the 1970s and 1980s. In fact, as remarked above, Near Eastern socialism was unlike European socialism because of the predominance of an organic view of society and the state. Class parties did not succeed. Essentially, socialism in the secular revolutions meant a dominant role for the state in the economy and society.

When one cuts through the vague rhetoric of the revolutionaries and asks what did they actually do one sees that they greatly enlarged the role of the state, broke the power of the landowner notables through land reform, transferred resources from the rural sector to the urban sector, brought into being a new state-based urban élite, and transferred power from the old to the young. The rest was mainly froth. If one compares these achievements with what happened in states which were said to be reactionary one sees that exactly the same things happened during the same period. The White Revolution in Iran was similar in its concept and its results to the radical revolution in Egypt, Syria and Iraq. The secular revolutions all transferred power from the private sector to the state, from the rural sector to the urban and from the old to the young.

The secular states desired ideologies to fit their existence and such ideologies evolved on similar lines in most states during the period after 1923, often drawing on themes enunciated during the nineteenth century and taken ultimately from European sources. All sought the origin of the state in a pre-Islamic period. Turkish nationalism stressed a Turkish identity which went back in one direction to the Turkish peoples of Central Asia and in another to earlier peoples inhabiting the region; thus the two great banks of Atatürk's creation were named the Sumerian and Hittite banks. In Iran the history of the pre-Islamic Achaemenid and Sassanid dynasties was stressed and Persepolis was chosen as the site for the celebration of the alleged 2500th anniversary of Persian kingship. In Egypt during the 1920s the continuity of Egypt from the Pharaonic period was emphasized by many writers and among the Catholic Christians of Lebanon the Phoenician origins of the state were discussed. Iraq's rich history of Babylonian and Assyrian relics became a cult and was powerfully featured by the regime of Ṣaddām Ḥusayn during and after the Iran–Iraq war. History was reinforced by language; in Turkey and Persia a movement took place to assert the purity of the languages and to remove from them the evidence of foreign intrusions.

Like the secular states themselves the ideologies which supported them were the product of the work of a small élite. The new ideologies made little appeal to the mass of the people although one should not underestimate the effect of the exposure of young people to such ideologies; the size of the élite which subscribed to them increased rapidly although not so rapidly as the number of those who were drawn into the orbit of the state. But the secular state did not triumph by virtue of the appeal of its ideology but because of the power it wielded and the benefits it offered to those who embraced it. The alternatives, despite the rhetorical importance given to them and despite the circumstance that they often had a broader emotional appeal, failed to replace the states. The alternatives were the movements of Pan-Arabism, Pan-Turkism and Pan-Islamism and the ethnic separatist movements within states.

Pan-Arabism appeared in various forms throughout the period. In its earliest manifestation it was the programme of the Hashimite rulers who had adopted it during the First World War and who continued in their separate states to cherish the hope that the promise of an Arab union under Hashimite leadership might be revived. Thus Fayṣal I in Iraq and ᶜAbdallāh of Transjordan each sought to widen the scope of his authority by joining with Syria and Lebanon. In Iraq the Fayṣal tradition was inherited by his political followers, notably by Nūrī al-Saᶜīd, who produced several schemes for Fertile Crescent union. For the Sunnī Arabs of Iraq Arab nationalism in this form was an attractive option because it promised to strengthen their vulnerable position in Iraq itself where they were a minority political élite contending against the possibility of a Shīᶜī or Kurdish challenge. To neither of these latter groups did such schemes appeal either then or later. ᶜAbdallāh also had political clients, particularly the group associated with the Syrian, ᶜAbd al-Raḥmān Shahbandar. The Hashimites and their followers continued to hope until 1958 that with British support they might accomplish some measure of Arab union. Britain, however, was never very interested.

Pan-Arabism also appeared in an ideological form during the inter-war period, notably in the writings of the former Ottoman official, Sāṭiᶜ al-Ḥuṣrī, who asserted that the essence of Arabism was language and that was the ultimate basis of Arab unity. Similar ideas provided the impetus for several political parties which sprang up in Arab countries during the 1930s, including the League of National Action in Syria, the Istiqlāl party in Palestine and the Syrian Social Nationalist Party and it was in this milieu that the Baᶜth Party had its origins. In Jerusalem in 1931 the ideals were set out in the Pan-Arab National Covenant which declared the Arab countries to be indivisible.

Between 1936 and 1945 the Pan-Arab cause advanced as a popular and political interest and achieved some institutional recognition in the Arab League. The Palestine question gave an impetus to Pan-Arabism as popular sympathies with the Palestinian Arabs were expressed in several Arab countries especially in 1936. The involvement of Arab states in discussions on Palestine between 1936 and 1939 increased the sense that there were Arab issues which transcended the bounds of the established states. In particular it was at this time that Egypt, hitherto regarded as standing outside the mainstream of Pan-Arab thought which was concentrated in the Fertile Crescent, became a prominent actor on the Arab scene. In the Second World War the question of the future of Syria and Lebanon as they approached independence was also treated as an Arab question. At that time the ambitions of the Hashimites, the enthusiasms of the radicals, the calculations of other Arab rulers, and the political interests of Britain came together in the formation of the Arab League in 1945. The Arab League, however, reflected the Egyptian view that what was required was an association of Arab states and involved a rejection of the proposals for Arab union espoused by the radical Pan-Arabs and by Nūrī al-Saᶜīd.

Pan-Arabism reached its peak during the 1950s and 1960s when it became the creed of the radical Arab parties which achieved power in Egypt, Syria and Iraq. There were numerous projects of union of which one, that between Egypt and Syria in the United Arab Republic from 1958 to 1961, appeared to be the prototype for a general union of Arab countries. The UAR failed when Syrians rejected it and a renewed effort to establish a union in 1963 broke down because President ᶜAbd al-Nāṣir of Egypt was too doubtful of the intentions of Syria and Iraq. The Pan-Arab movement failed partly through tactical errors but principally because it gave insufficient weight to differences between the political and cultural traditions of the Arab states, because the economic basis for a union did not exist, because many Arabs did not want a Sunnī Arab or Egyptian dominated union and non-Arab minorities such as the Kurds of Iraq rejected Pan-Arabism, and especially because the interests vested in the continuation of the existing states were too strong. Political unity remained an ideal but the emphasis turned to various forms of association between Arab states.

Pan-Turkism was a much less significant movement. It remained throughout our period an intellectual movement, promoted especially by Turks outside Turkey but also by many groups within. The movement stressed the cultural links which bound Turks together and envisaged a political entity composed of the Turks of Turkey, the USSR, China and possibly Iran and Afghanistan. Unlike the Pan-Arab programme, which could be accomplished by the joining of existing states, Pan-Turk plans could not be realized without the breakup of major non-Turkish states and therefore was too dangerous a policy to be espoused by the politicians who ruled Turkey. From 1921 onwards Atatürk set his face against Pan-Turkism and only during the Second World War did its programme briefly appear to be feasible when, in 1941–2, it seemed possible that the USSR might break up under the German onslaught. But even then, although Pan-Turks were given a free rein, the Turkish government never espoused their projects and when it became clear that the USSR would emerge on the victorious side Inönü hastily shut down the activities of the Pan-Turks in 1944. Pan-Turkism continued as an intellectual movement and in the 1960s it was given a new political significance in relation to the Turks of Cyprus. The National Action Party of Alparslan Türkeş became a vehicle for Pan-Turk ideas although it never adopted the Pan-Turk programme. Pan-Turkism was an aspiration but never a serious challenge to the state system.

Another movement to challenge the dominance of the secular state was Pan-Islamism. The notion that Muslim states and peoples should come together in some association, federation or unity under a supreme Muslim ruler was one that was given prominence in the nineteenth century in the writings of Jamāl al-Dīn al-Afghānī; and during the same period the view that among Muslim rulers the Ottoman Sultan and Caliph had some pre-eminence was also widely held. (See *MMNE*, 181–2.) To Muslims living under non-Muslim rule, particularly those in India, Pan-Islamism had attractive possibilities. The abolition of the Caliphate by the Turkish Republic in 1924 led to claims to the office being lodged by King Ḥusayn of the Ḥijāz and Fu'ād I of Egypt. Muslim intellectuals who dreamed of the creation of a Muslim state also saw the opportunity to create some permanent Muslim organization which might become the seed of a closer association. Popular Muslim feeling was also aroused by the problems of the pilgrimage after the occupation of the Ḥijāz by the Wahhābī ruler, ᶜAbd al-ᶜAzīz Āl Saᶜūd, and by the apparent threat to Jerusalem posed by Zionist activities which led to the Wailing Wall riots of 1929. These different political, intellectual and popular elements came together in a number of Islamic congresses held between the world wars. The congresses, however, failed to create any permanent organization principally because the interests of those concerned were so widely divergent; in particular the ambitions of Muslim states and rulers conflicted and ᶜAbd al-ᶜAzīz was unwilling to allow the pilgrimage to become the occasion for a political gathering.

For some time Pan-Islamism slipped into the background as a political programme although it remained an ideal of the popular Muslim movements of which the most notable was the Muslim Brotherhood of Egypt. For the Brothers the existence of separate Muslim states was an aberration; for them Islam was a universal movement and they spread their activities into other states. But from 1950 to 1967 the Muslim movements were driven out of politics by the dominance of the secular states. Only after the Arab defeat in 1967 did the idea of a Muslim association return.

In 1971 the Islamic Conference Organisation (ICO) was established. The ICO was an organization of Muslim states which arranged periodic meetings of Muslim heads of states and of foreign ministers with a view to co-ordinating policies. It owed its foundation first to the leading role assumed by Saudi Arabia after 1967 and, second, to the attempted burning of the Aqṣā mosque in Jerusalem in 1969. The ICO, however, remained an association of existing states and there was no attempt to move beyond this to threaten the sovereignty of the states themselves. Nor did the Islamic revolution in Iran, although it gave so great an impetus to the political claims of Islam, express any direct challenge to the existence of states. It challenged states to become more Muslim but not to sacrifice their identity as states. Pan-Islamism remained a movement which attracted widespread popular sympathy but little serious political attention and it made no challenge to the existing state structure.

The third type of challenge to the state system came from inside the states themselves in the form of ethnic separatist movements. These were challenges to the existing state system but not to the idea of the state because what the ethnic movements proposed was either a new type of federal or confederal state or the redrawing of state boundaries and the creation of new states. By ethnic movement we mean essentially a movement based on language. In a situation of minimal government language has little political significance; if government has only a modest presence then it makes small difference to the ordinary citizen if it uses a different language. The matter is otherwise when the role of government is enhanced and the citizen is brought into contact with its schools, courts, army and administrative apparatus. Those who speak a language which is not the official language of the state are then at a disadvantage compared with native speakers of the state's language and find it difficult to compete for state employment. Those ethnic minorities which are small in number or live in scattered areas have little choice; they can emigrate, resign themselves to poor and obscure lives or learn the state language and make the best of the business. But those ethnic minorities which are substantial in number and inhabit a compact area have the option of striving for autonomy or separation. If they inhabit a frontier region adjacent to another group of their ethnic community their chances of success are strengthened.

There were many such minorities in the Near East during the nineteenth century but after 1923 their number was much fewer: the Dhufāris (Ẓufāris) in Oman were the only such group in the Arabian peninsula and their uprising was crushed in the 1970s. Egypt had none. Syria had a classic example of such a minority in the form of the Turks of Alexandretta, whose proximity to Turkey facilitated an escape from the Syrian state in 1939. Israel acquired a minority of this character in 1948 in the form of the Arabs whose greatest concentration is in Galilee adjacent to the Lebanese border. Iran had several, including the Balūchīs, the Turkomans, the Azerīs and the Arabs of Khūzistān, all of whom produced movements aiming at autonomy or separation; and the speakers of various Persian dialects for whom it was a question whether they would assimilate their dialect to the Persian of the state or whether they would regard their language as a distinctive emblem which warranted regarding themselves as a separate community. But the most threatening of all the ethnic movements was that of the Kurds.

The Kurds inhabit a fairly compact area which includes areas of eastern Turkey, north eastern Syria, northern Iraq and western Iran. In each of these states Kurdish movements with demands ranging from requests for cultural recognition to armed assertions of the right to outright separation took place after the First World War. The Kurdish movement in its origins was primarily a tribal affair, at other times it took on a religious colour through the participation of Ṣūfī orders, but increasingly from the 1960s it adopted the aspect of a classic ethnic movement, finding supporters among literate urban Kurds. Except in Iraq, where the Kurds secured an autonomy agreement, the Kurds failed to win any outstanding success and their attempts to exploit the possibilities opened up by the Iran–Iraq war led to a determined effort to suppress their demands when the war was concluded. The Kurdish challenge to the established state system of the Near East was the greatest of the ethnic challenges but it failed to upset the system because the states involved limited the aid they were prepared to give to Kurds in other states, and other outside powers declined to aid a movement which threatened the state system.

The international system of states supported the state system of the Near East through the League of Nations, the United Nations and through the activities of individual states which, except in very limited circumstances, notably in Lebanon but also in relation to the Palestine Liberation Organisation and the Kurds, dealt with established states and were reluctant to take or support any action which would destroy them. The international system, therefore, assisted the maintenance of the state system and through economic and military aid promoted the growth of state power in individual states. But the principal factor in the growth of state power and the stability of the states was the behaviour of the states themselves and the interests of the steadily enlarging élites which directed or operated them.

NOTES

1. Quoted Elie Kedourie, *The Chatham House Version*, 1970, 340.
2. Ali Shariati, "Intizar, the Religion of Protest", in John L. Donahue and John L. Esposito (eds), *Islam in Transition*, 1982, 303.
3. Quoted Eric Hoogland, *Land and Revolution in Iran, 1960–1980*, Austin 1982, 137.
4. Ministerial Statement by the Government of Syria, 14 March 1963, in *Arab Political Documents 1963*, Beirut, n.d., 48.
5. Speech by Ḥusnī al-Za^{c}īm 3 April 1949, in Muhammad Khalil (ed.), *The Arab States and the Arab League*, 2 vols, Beirut 1962, i, 527.
6. Statement by the Syrian General Command of the Army and the Armed Forces, 30 March 1949, Khalil, *op.cit.*, i, 521.
7. Statement by Brigadier A. ash-Shishakly, Khalil, *op.cit.*, i, 560.
8. Transitional Programme of the National Revolutionary Command of Iraq broadcast by Major General Aḥmad Ḥasan al-Bakr, 15 March 1963, in *Arab Political Documents 1963*, 55.

SECTION I

THE YEARS OF THE NOTABLES

CHAPTER ONE

Egypt to 1952

Geographically Egypt consists of a broad area of desert which occupies over 95 per cent of the country and a long valley formed by the Nile river. In the north the valley broadens into the Delta of Lower Egypt. All but 1 per cent of the population live in the Nile valley. In 1920 nearly 90 per cent of the population of 13 million was rural, living in villages; there was also a small nomadic bedouin population principally in the western desert although many of the bedouin were settled or semi-settled. One quarter of the population lived in towns, notably in Cairo which had a population of 900,000 and Alexandria (500,000). In the towns there was also a resident foreign European population of about 200,000, half of whom were of Greek origin and the remainder mainly Italian, British and French. Other significant foreign minorities were the Syrians and the Armenians. Over 90 per cent of the population was Muslim, nearly all Sunnī. Egypt also possessed the largest indigenous Christian group in the Near East in the form of the Coptic community, resident mainly in the towns and in Upper Egypt, and a small Jewish community.

About 70 per cent of the working population was engaged in agriculture. Many of these were employed in growing foodstuffs but the most distinctive feature of Egyptian agriculture was the growth of cotton for the international market. In 1921 cotton landlords established the Egyptian General Agricultural Syndicate to improve their negotiating position with the cotton purchasers. Of the remainder of the population 20 per cent was employed in construction, services or transport and 8 per cent in manufacturing industry, which in 1920 was still dominated by foreign enterprises especially in textiles and continued to be so throughout the following years The industrial labour force in 1920 was put at 250,000.

Until 1914 Egypt had been an autonomous province of the Ottoman empire ruled by a hereditary ruler entitled khedive. In 1882 Egypt had been occupied by Britain and in 1914 Britain had ended Ottoman authority and declared Egypt a protectorate. The last khedive was deposed and his uncle put in his place with the title of sultan. In 1922 Britain issued a unilateral declaration of Egyptian independence having failed to negotiate an agreement with an Egyptian government. At the same time she reserved four points pending a treaty with Egypt. These reserved points concerned the Suez Canal, Egyptian defence and foreign policy, the Sudan and the capitulations (see *MMNE*, 344-5). Accordingly, the condition of Egypt was what may be termed neo-independence and a situation was created in which three groups shared or contended for power within Egypt. These were the Crown, the politicians and the British. The history of Egypt between 1922 and 1952 was dominated by their conflicts and co-operation.

The political framework was provided by the Egyptian constitution of 1923. This constitution was, like many Near Eastern constitutions, modelled on the Belgian constitution of 1831 and therefore ultimately on the unwritten English constitution. It was drafted not by a constituent assembly but by a commission appointed by the sultan who had not wanted a constitution but had been obliged to give way to British insistence. Even so he was determined that he should retain substantial powers and although the drafters strove to produce a liberal document the outcome was a compromise. Egypt was to be a monarchy; in fact the ruler, Aḥmad Fu'ād, had already assumed the title of king in March 1922. The constitution and the accompanying electoral law provided for a two chamber parliament, the lower house indirectly elected by universal manhood suffrage, the upper chamber partly appointed and partly elected on a very narrow franchise. The king retained the power to appoint the prime minister, dismiss the government, dissolve or prorogue parliament, and all bills required his assent. He also retained powers over a range of appointments, especially religious, and over *waqfs* which embraced nearly one tenth of land under cultivation in Egypt.

The king also developed other instruments of power. He had his own palace staff, known from 1936 as the royal cabinet, to which he recruited influential politicians such as ᶜAlī Māhir. Fu'ād's son and successor, Fārūq, made considerable use of his own personal staff, including his ambitious former tutor, Aḥmad Ḥasanayn, and even his cooks, butlers and his Italian pimp, Pulli. Another important source of royal influence was the ulema. Fu'ād presented himself as the protector of al-Azhar and of the claims of the ulema in general against the secular minded politicians. His religious influence was both a useful source of propaganda through the mosque and a way into the streets where he could mobilize support.

The effect of the constitution was that the king could keep out of power any government which he did not like but he could not keep his own chosen government in power unless he won an election or governed without parliament. As every election under the 1923 constitution was won by his opponents this meant that Egypt was commonly ruled without a parliament. One way out of the dilemma was to replace the constitution and the electoral law by instruments more favourable to the crown and this was done in 1930 with the help of one of the most able of Egyptian politicians, Ismāʿīl Ṣidqī. Ministers were made responsible to the king, the electorate was greatly restricted by introducing financial and educational voting qualifications and professional men were disqualified from standing in rural areas. These changes were sufficient to induce the king's opponents to boycott the elections, which Ṣidqī's newly created People's Party won. Ṣidqī ruled for three years. In 1935, however, Fu'ād was obliged to restore the 1923 constitution. Even so it was found possible in 1938 to rig the election so as to return a government of the monarch's choice.

The death of Fu'ād in 1936 and the circumstance that his son and designated successor, Fārūq, was a minor, meant that for over a year the crown was effectively removed from politics. But from the end of 1937 the young Fārūq reasserted his influence and installed once more a succession of congenial governments which ruled until the power of the king was successfully challenged by the British in 1942. In 1944 Fārūq regained his freedom of action and from then until 1952 the crown was once more a central factor in Egyptian political life.

The second element in the Egyptian political scene was the politicians. The core of the Egyptian political class consisted of a number of wealthy absentee landowners. Egypt was a country of great landed estates. In 1939 less than 13,000 landowners owned more than 40 per cent of the cultivated area of Egypt. Wealthiest of all was the royal family which alone owned nearly one-tenth. The landowner politicians were well educated, often abroad and usually in France and commonly in law. Most were Muslims although there were some Christians but they were secular in outlook. Their ideology was that of Egyptian nationalism in the fashion articulated by the journalists and intellectuals, Aḥmad Luṭfī al-Sayyid and Muḥammad Ḥusayn Haykal. The older distinction between notables of Turko-Circassian origin and those native Arabic-speaking Egyptians had largely disappeared although the Turkish language and Turkish styles of dress and behaviour were still common. ᶜAdlī Yegen was clearly identifiable as a member of the old Turkish group and Fu'ād himself was a poor speaker of Arabic. But the breaking of the Ottoman connection in 1914 and subsequent changes in Turkey itself did much to eliminate the old Ottoman tradition in Egypt. Many notables had substantial interests in cotton cultivation but some had invested in industry. It is interesting that Egyptian industry was owned not by a new business class but by foreigners and notables. Although the notables were resident in Cairo they retained their power bases in their provinces and when they changed their political allegiances they took their provincial base with them. So, when Muḥammad Maḥmūd left the Wafd Party his province of Buḥayra went with him to the new Liberal Constitutionalist party.

Landowners constituted the core of the political class but around them was a penumbra of professional administrators and politicians who had risen either through the bureaucracy or the professions, especially law and journalism, and whose evident abilities had recommended them as suitable recruits for the landowner-controlled political parties. Such men would often marry into the landowning notable class as did the two successive leaders of the Wafd Party, Saᶜd Zaghlūl, who married a daughter of Muṣṭafā Fahmī, a long serving prime minister during the period of British control, and Muṣṭafā al-Naḥḥās, who married into the great al-Wakīl family. And there was also a small number of traditional figures such as ᶜAlī Shaᶜrāwī, a wealthy landowner from Minya province who spoke only Arabic. Most of the notables were comfortable in French.

Notables engaged in politics principally because they required access to government patronage. They wanted to persuade government to protect their interests as landowners or industrialists with cheap credit or protective tariffs and during the great depression they secured such assistance. They also liked the prestige of government office and many were genuinely concerned to play a part in the development of their country. Some were concerned to enrich themselves. But the heart of the matter was patronage; notables wished to be able to reward their supporters by contracts, licences and jobs. At every turn of the political wheel in Egypt there was a change in the personnel of the administration as each party advanced its own supporters and their relatives in the central and provincial bureaucracy. Ties of kinship and region linked notables to their followers; political parties were alliances of the networks thus formed. It follows that notables did not welcome long periods of exclusion from government unless they controlled patronage networks outside the realm of government and as government expanded outside networks became fewer and smaller. The object of politics was to establish a position from which the notable could bargain his way into power. Political positions in Egypt were adopted not from principle or conviction but from expediency. The best model for the student of Egyptian politics between 1922 and 1952 remains the account of the relations between George III and his politicians by Sir Lewis Namier.

An analysis of Egyptian governments from 1922 to 1952 discloses the same characteristics which distinguished those of Iraq and Lebanon during the same period, that is the appearance of political instability and the reality of ministerial continuity. The average life of the 32 cabinets during that period was just under one year but the ministers who held office were drawn from a few individuals who merely took turns to occupy the various posts. Sixty per cent were landholders.

Of the several parliamentary political parties which existed in Egypt one, the Wafd Party, was in a class of its own. The Wafd had begun not as a party but, as the name indicates, as a delegation of Egyptian politicians who had endeavoured to open negotiations with Britain in 1919. In the words of its leader, Zaghlūl, it was "a delegation empowered by the nation and expressing its will about a matter which it has assigned to us. This matter is complete independence and we strive to this end alone."[1] The Wafd found it difficult to live down these high sentiments and become an ordinary political party after 1922. The Wafd found it repugnant to recognize the legitimacy of other political parties and declined to accept that they had any right to negotiate with Britain. Nor, with rare exceptions, would it form coalitions with other parties. Furthermore, the Wafd continued after 1922 to concentrate on the issue of independence almost to the exclusion of other issues. It is true that the Wafd put forward a detailed programme of social and economic reform in 1925 which gave the party a radical appearance but in practice this programme had a low priority. Partly this attitude of the Wafd was due to the towering influence of Zaghlūl who was a leader regarded by his followers with almost religious awe as someone under the direct protection of God. Zaghlūl found it easier to live with principles than compromise and his inability to work with Fu'ād ensured the exclusion of the Wafd from power despite its regular successes at elections. His successor, Naḥḥās, was of a more amenable disposition but there was something of Zaghlūl in him also and his relations with his colleagues were a history of disputes.

Like other parties the Wafd was dominated by landowners but among its leaders it also had several administrators, industrialists and financiers. For most of the Wafd's history landowners composed 40 per cent of its leadership although the proportion fell well below this at times, notably in the mid 1930s. The party had a large following in urban areas among bureaucrats, the intelligentsia and workers, and considerable strength in rural areas through the support of provincial administrators, rural notables and village headmen. Unlike other parties the Wafd possessed a strong organization. In 1919 a central organization and provincial branches had been created to control the agitation against Britain. The provincial branches became the basis of a constituency organization but the central organization remained dominant and was controlled by a small group around Zaghlūl and Naḥḥās. Within the central organization was the mysterious and sinister secret apparatus which was supposed to plan assassinations and other nefarious activities. The early history of the Wafd and its later exclusion from power for long periods inclined the Wafd to promote extra-parliamentary agitation and violence and its rural and urban organization enabled it to arrange riots and other disturbances in village, street and college. In the 1930s it organized its young followers in a paramilitary group known as the Blue Shirts.

Other parliamentary political parties in Egypt originated in breakaway movements from the Wafd. Most prominent among these during the 1920s was the Liberal Constitutionalist Party which was founded in 1922 although it had its beginnings in the split between Zaghlūl and ^{c}Adlī Yegen in 1921. Even more than the Wafd it was a party of big landowners but it was also the party richest in intellectual talent numbering among its members Luṭfī al-Sayyid and Ḥusayn Haykal. The Union Party (1925) of Ḥasan Nash'at was composed of large landowners willing to work closely with the palace. Another palace party which attracted large landowners and some of the urban middle class was the People's Party of Ismā^{c}īl Ṣidqī (1930), a former Wafdist. The 1937 Sa^{c}dist party was formed by a splinter group from the Wafd led by Maḥmūd Fahmī al-Nuqrāshī and Aḥmad Māhir. It included a number of industrialists and gave prominence in its programme to their needs. Another Wafd splinter was the Independent Wafd of Makram ^{c}Ubayd, the Coptic former general secretary of the party who had been dropped by Naḥḥās after ^{c}Ubayd criticized the corrupt practices of Naḥḥās's wife's family. Founded in 1942 the Independent Wafd espoused a radical programme. These other parties had no substantial party organization, especially at constituency level. If they were in power they used the government apparatus at election times; otherwise they were coalitions of factions and individuals.

The third element in the Egyptian political scene was the British. After 1922 British influence was maintained through the high commissioner (British ambassador from 1936) and his staff in Cairo, through advisers with the Egyptian government in the departments of justice and finance, through command of the Egyptian army, through the British garrison in Egypt and through the British presence in the Sudan. If necessary British power could be supported by a naval demonstration in the Mediterranean. Of the four British high commissioners three were strong uncompromising men. Lord Allenby (1922–5) interfered in the making of the making of the constitution and the formation of governments and was personally responsible, anticipating the approval of London, for the ultimatum delivered to the Egyptian government in 1924 after the murder of the British commander in chief of the Egyptian Army, Sir Lee Stack. Allenby demanded an apology, the prosecution of the assailants and an indemnity and coupled with these items further demands for the withdrawal of Egyptian troops from the Sudan, a large extension of the irrigated area in the Sudan (using Nile water), and an end to opposition to British upholding of the capitulatory privileges of foreigners. His successor, Lord Lloyd, 1925–9, also interfered in the formation of governments, declining to accept Zaghlūl as prime minister in 1926 unless he would accept the 1922 declaration and be respectful to the king. After Zaghlūl refused and ᶜAdlī Yegen formed a government Lloyd insisted on excluding radical Wafdists from the coalition. Lloyd also defeated Egyptian attempts to interfere in the command of the Egyptian army. Lloyd's successor, Sir Percy Loraine, 1929–34, was more conciliatory, but he was replaced by Sir Miles Lampson (later Lord Killearn), 1934–46, who won a reputation for great severity during the Second World War although in his early years this reputation was undeserved.

The prominence of Britain in Egyptian public life was to some extent a self-inflicted wound for Egypt for it was Egyptian politicians who made the question of an Anglo–Egyptian treaty the principal item on the Egyptian political agenda and also made it almost impossible to reach a decision on the matter. As remarked above the Wafd refused to allow others to negotiate a treaty or to join in a concerted approach to Britain but was itself unwilling to offer sufficient concessions to secure a treaty. Although Zaghlūl showed himself more ready to compromise in government than outside he was neither prepared nor willing to offer enough to reach an agreement which would have substantially reduced British interference in Egypt. Zaghūl tried and failed in 1924 and the Wafd blocked the attempt by ᶜAbd al-Khāliq Tharwat in 1927. In 1929 Muḥammad Maḥmūd reached agreement on a treaty more favourable to Egypt but Naḥḥās would not accept what he himself had not negotiated and in 1930 could do no better when he had his own opportunity. By now the British were reluctant to try for an agreement without the Wafd and accordingly discouraged Ṣidqī from serious negotiations. Only in 1936, with the crown out of the way and a Wafd government in power which was willing to allow other parties into a joint negotiating team, was an agreement at last negotiated.

Egyptian politics went through a minor revolution in 1935–6. In 1930 Fu'ād and Ṣidqī, under the pressure of the need for government action to combat the effects of the depression on Egyptian society and economic life and in despair at the political stalemate, had tried to force Egyptian politics into a new, more authoritarian mould. They had failed. Ṣidqī had resigned in 1933, ostensibly through ill health but in reality because he had lost Fu'ād's confidence. His successors lacked his abilities and had no support except that provided by the palace. Nor did they even have a constitutional basis; Fu'ād abolished Ṣidqī's 1930 constitution without restoring that of 1923 and so achieved his 1922 goal of dispensing with any legal restrictions on his power. Parliament was dissolved. In 1935 the government of Muḥammad Tawfīq Nasīm was confronted by a Wafd-led coalition of almost all the politicians excluded from power and demands for a return to the 1923 constitution. Throughout 1935 there was unrest culminating in strikes and demonstrations in December. On 12 December Fu'ād at last fulfilled his April promise and reinstated the 1923 constitution. Nasīm resigned and a coalition government under ᶜAlī Māhir was formed in January 1936 to arrange for new elections. These elections, held in May 1936, were won by the Wafd and Naḥḥās became prime minister. The success of the Egyptian agitation was an important factor in setting off the wave of political protest in the Arab world which was a feature of 1936.

The Anglo–Egyptian treaty of 1936 was partly a consequence of the changes which had taken place inside Egypt. In addition to the factor of the restoration of the constitution the death of Fu'ād on 28 April 1936 meant that the crown could not interfere with negotiations. The treaty was also a consequence of changes in the international scene, in particular the threat of Italian ambitions in the Near East demonstrated by the Italian invasion of Ethiopia in October 1935. Mussolini, who since 1934 had been developing roads and railways in Libya up to the Egyptian border, apparently had ambitions in Egypt and Italy was perceived by both Britons and Egyptian politicians to menace their interests. The matter of treaty negotiation with Britain had been linked with the agitation for the restoration of the constitution and one of the acts of the coalition government of ᶜAlī Māhir was to appoint a joint all-party delegation to negotiate with Britain. This delegation continued its work under the Wafd government and the treaty was signed on 26 August 1936.

The 1936 treaty dealt with the four reserved points of 1922. The questions of foreign and defence policy were dealt with by forming a 20-year offensive/defensive military alliance between Britain and Egypt. The two states were to co-operate in foreign affairs. A British garrison would remain in the Canal Zone for 20 years and in the event of war Britain would have the right to use all Egyptian facilities. After 20 years it was supposed that the Egyptian army would be ready to take over the duties of defence. The Egyptian army would continue to use British equipment and advisers but the British inspector general would be withdrawn. The British judicial and financial advisers would also go. It was agreed that the capitulations should be abolished and this was accomplished in 1937 at Montreux. Egypt was to be admitted to the League of Nations. The outstanding point concerned the Sudan on which all negotiations since 1924 had broken down. The two sides agreed to shelve the issue although Egypt gained some concessions on irrigation. Egypt could have had the same deal in 1930 and probably earlier; the delay had its penalties for Egypt and its political system. It is difficult to avoid the view that the question of relations with Britain was employed by all Egyptian politicians as a useful diversion from the difficult internal problems of Egypt.

The Wafd government fell from power in December 1937. It had some minor social and economic reforms to its credit, including the introduction of industrial injury compensation, and it made a start on the army expansion which was necessary if Egypt was to be finally rid of the British presence. But it was racked by internal disputes which culminated in the departure of Nuqrāshī and Aḥmad Māhir to establish their own Saᶜdist party. And it was confronted by growing unrest on the streets from Muslim and workers' organizations. The major factor in the fall of the Wafd, however, was the return of the palace to politics. King Fārūq was determined to be his own master and he could not get on with Naḥḥās. Muḥammad Maḥmūd became prime minister once more and in 1939 was replaced by Fārūq's favourite, ᶜAlī Māhir, the chief of his royal cabinet.

The Second World War deeply affected Egypt. For Britain Egypt was of great strategic importance and, after the entry of Italy into the war, Egypt, the headquarters of Middle East Command, became both part of the front line and the main base for British operations in the area. Under the 1936 treaty Britain had the right to use Egyptian facilities and she wanted to be assured that that right would not be impaired by a hostile or even unenthusiastic Egyptian government. It was tolerable that Egypt should remain neutral but not that she should deal with the Axis powers. Accordingly ᶜAlī Māhir had to go in June 1940 and in February 1942, with Rommel advancing on Egypt, Britain decided that only a Wafdist government would answer. Fārūq resisted the demand and in a dramatic move, Lampson surrounded the Abdin palace with tanks and on 4 February went to demand Fārūq's abdication. Fārūq avoided abdication by proposing a Wafdist government under Naḥḥās. Lampson, deprived of his victim, reluctantly agreed. The incident provided a powerful memory of humiliation not only for Fārūq but also for many Egyptian nationalists and redounded to the eventual detriment of its immediate beneficiary, the Wafd.

The Wafd government endured until 1944 when Fārūq was permitted to rid himself of it. By that time, with North Africa secured, Britain had no more interest in the fate of the Wafd. The fall of the Wafd was little regretted by others. It was denounced for subservience to Britain and the Wafd's radical image was much damaged by the publication in 1943 of the so-called Black Book of its discarded general secretary, Makram ᶜUbayd, containing embarrassing revelations of Wafd corruption. The main concern of Egyptian politicians was now to prepare for yet another negotiation with Britain as soon as the war ended. To ensure that Egypt acquired a place at the post-war settlement Egypt at last declared war on Germany on 26 February 1945. To the Nuqrāshī government of 1945 a successful agreement with Britain seemed the only way to save itself from the domestic problems which threatened to overwhelm it. In the event the task of conducting the negotiations fell to a new Egyptian government under Ismāᶜīl Ṣidqī.

Ṣidqī was the most talented Egyptian politician of his generation. Highly intelligent, adept in government and politics, unscrupulous and corrupt, Ṣidqī triumphed in the 1946 negotiations with Britain. In matters which concerned Egypt he won every point and had the draft treaty been ratified he would have taken Britain out of Egypt and out of Egyptian politics by 1949. The stumbling block was the Sudan. Ṣidqī and the British foreign secretary, Ernest Bevin, evolved a delicate form of words the import of which was that each side could claim that its position was intact while the situation of the Sudan remained unchanged. Partly through Ṣidqī's own carelessness and partly through the hostility of his political rivals the Sudan formula was exploded, the agreement failed and Ṣidqī resigned.

The years 1945 to 1952 saw the breakdown of the Egyptian government and the Egyptian revolution. To understand the causes of those events it is necessary to examine economic, social and political change in Egypt over a much longer period.

During the period 1922 to 1952 Egypt lost ground economically. The nineteenth century had seen an unprecedented surge of prosperity in Egypt based on specialization in cotton production for the international market. By 1900 Egypt not only supported a much larger population but almost everyone was better off. At some time in the early twentieth century various economic indicators began to suggest that, although there was still much benefit to be derived from the further development of cotton production, returns to investment were beginning to fall and it was time to begin to diversify. The prosperity of cotton during the First World War postponed the need for decision but after 1918 some action was required. One possibility was to expand the cultivated area by investment in irrigation and to promote agricultural diversification but little was done on this front. Between 1920 and 1952 the cropped area increased only by 30 per cent, a rate far below that achieved in earlier years.

An obvious alternative or supplement to further agricultural development was industrialization. Some government help to industry was given through tariffs which were raised to an average of 20 per cent in 1930. In general government assistance was small and down to 1952 the state share of industry was negligible. There was some growth of an Egyptian entrepreneurial class. In 1920 Muḥammad Ṭalᶜat Ḥarb and others founded the Bank Misr to provide investment for economic development (rather than practising the type of lending to finance trade common among foreign banks). The Bank Misr group had much success and invested in cotton textiles, communications, films and other industrial or commercial undertakings. But this indigenous development did not compensate for the growing hostility to foreign and minority influence in the economy which discouraged investment in long term projects. Nevertheless, private investment in industry did increase rapidly especially as a consequence of the incentives provided by the demands of the Second World War. By 1952 industry was taking a quarter of total investment and between 1938 and 1951 production rose by more than 10 per cent a year. Even so in 1952 industrial production still constituted no more than 15 per cent of the gross national product and most of this was in non-manufacturing industry. Egyptian industry also had many unsolved problems including poor management, low labour productivity, high transport costs and a lack of raw materials. Wealthy Egyptian consumers preferred to buy foreign goods.

Egypt was already experiencing the human costs of industrialization especially in Cairo and Alexandria where about half the larger firms were located. In 1932 an International Labour Organisation (ILO) report disclosed that a 15-hour day was common, that factories employed children under ten years old, and that weekly holidays were unknown. Unions were weak but strikes were frequent. The number of industrial workers increased rapidly, however, and by 1952, although still representing only one-tenth of the total labour force, amounted to nearly 2 million people. Cuts in production after the war enhanced the dissatisfactions of workers and contributed to unrest which was manipulated by politicians. A feature of Egyptian industrialization was that partly because of fears for the future foreign industrialists preferred to finance expansion out of retained profits. It would seem likely that this system also implied an element of retained wages. Egyptians spent over 60 per cent of their income on food alone.

Statistically Egypt stood still in the 40 years before 1950. The average rate of economic growth over the whole of this period was about 1.5 per cent per annum. This figure almost exactly matched the rate of population increase over the same period. The average Egyptian should have been just about as well off in 1950 as he was in 1910, In fact most were worse off because of the deterioration in Egypt's terms of trade over the period as a whole, the greater share taken by the state, and the more unequal distribution of incomes, partly as a result of inflation. At the same time people in towns had higher expectations.

Another significant development in independent Egypt was the expansion of education. Under British control investment in education had been given a very low priority and much provision had been left to private schools. In 1914 38 per cent of all students attended foreign schools. The contribution of foreign schools remained important throughout the period 1922 to 1952 although increasing efforts were made to exercise some control over them and what they taught. But the state sector developed rapidly. Spending on education rose from 4 per cent of government expenditure in 1920 to 13 per cent of a much larger budget in 1951. The commitment to education was real although it was often overambitious. In 1923 elementary education was declared to be free and compulsory although it was not possible to implement this declaration; by 1950 only 30 per cent of Egyptian children received elementary education. In 1951 Egypt did at last unify the two streams of elementary education; the traditional system which led nowhere except to the madrasa and the modern system which prepared children for secondary education. Secondary pupils also increased from about 5,000 in 1920 to 120,000 in 1951. In 1950 another optimistic pledge declared secondary education to be free leading to a flood of applicants which overwhelmed the school system. By 1952 there were nearly 2 million children in schools at all levels, four times the figure at the beginning of the period. Higher education also expanded. The Egyptian university founded in 1908 was a private institution teaching arts subjects. Some specialized colleges of law, medicine, etc. also existed. In 1925 these institutions were brought together in the Egyptian state university in Cairo. By 1952 there were three modern universities: Cairo, Alexandria (1942) and ᶜAyn Shams on the outskirts of Cairo (1950). In addition there was the Azhar which, with royal help, had more or less successfully resisted all attempts to reform it. The number of university students increased from 3,000 in 1925 to 32,000 in 1950.

One can measure statistically a marked growth in the relative weight of the state in Egypt between 1913 and 1952 although the growth in no way compares with the expansion of the state after 1952. Nevertheless, government expenditure as a proportion of national income rose from 10 per cent to 20 per cent in those years. In fact it reached the figure of 20 per cent by 1938 but fell back during the Second World War and only regained its former peak some five years later. Partly this rise represents a real increase in spending on state services, notably education and defence, but partly it indicates an expansion of the bureaucracy in order to provide jobs.

Another important change in Egypt during the period after 1930 was the revival of Islam. During the 1920s the tone of Egyptian intellectual life had been set by the small secular élite which dominated politics and the press. This élite had played down the Islamic element in the Egyptian past, denied that Islam had a role in politics and even questioned the nature of the Qur'ān. Islam had been excluded from developments in education and legal reform had also reduced its scope. Instead the élite had stressed the geographical, historical and cultural identity of Egyptians and Egypt's continuity from ancient times when it was the standard bearer of world civilization. There grew up a romantic image of the Egyptian peasant who was held to exemplify the true immemorial Egyptian virtues of endurance, pragmatism, realism and humour. Egyptians also looked more and more to Europe for ideas; the writer, Ḥusayn Fawzī, regarded France as his true home and Western civilization as the ideal. Socialism, social Darwinism and positivism were only some of the ideas which fascinated Egyptian writers of the period.

In the 1930s secularism gave way increasingly to a Muslim revival.

In 1931, the blind philosopher, Ṭāhā Ḥusayn, who had opposed traditional interpretations of the Qur'ān in his book on pre-Islamic poetry, was dismissed from his post in the Egyptian state university. The incident demonstrates the change in the intellectual climate of Egypt. Within a short time several writers who had sturdily proclaimed their secular gospel in the 1920s were writing Muslim apologetics. Muḥammad Ḥusayn Haykal produced a number of books about the early history of Islam intended to demonstrate the fundamental rationality of the religion. The effort to reform Sharīʿa law was abandoned and after 1930 an agitation to reform the 1883 Egyptian civil code so as to bring it more in line with the Sharīʿa began. A new, more Islamic civil code was finally introduced in 1949 but was promptly attacked for being insufficiently Muslim. The most distinctive evidence of the Muslim revival, however, was the growth of the Muslim Brotherhood.

The Muslim Brotherhood was one of the most remarkable political phenomena in the Near East during the first half of the twentieth century. It was founded in 1928 by an Egyptian schoolteacher, Ḥasan al-Bannā, who had been deeply influenced by the ideas of earlier Muslim reformers, notably Jamāl al-Dīn al-Afghānī and Muḥammad ʿAbduh, and by the religious element in the Egyptian National Party. Al-Bannā's aim resembled in some ways that of the Ṣūfīs; namely, to build around himself a group of carefully educated and trained followers who would become the agency of the purification of Islam. Education and other aspects of social work including health care always remained the central concerns of the Brotherhood and the dedicated Brothers were regarded with admiration. But al-Bannā's aims eventually went further into economics and politics. The Brothers developed their own industrial establishments and put forward their own ideas for the reorganization of economic and political life. The core of their doctrine was that Egypt should proceed with modernization but this modernization should be conducted according to the Sharīʿa . These ideas constituted a challenge both to the traditional ulema and to the secular élite but the real challenge came less from the ideas than the large following which the Brotherhood attracted and their dedicated pursuit of their aims through direct action.

The Brotherhood was tightly organized, control being vested in the general guidance council dominated by Ḥasan al-Bannā, the Supreme Guide. The Brotherhood had a branch organization and from an early period paramilitary groups. After the Second World War it also developed a secret apparatus to conduct assassinations. The Brotherhood was essentially an urban party; it was founded in Ismailiya and was strongest in the Canal Zone, Cairo and Alexandria. Its leaders came from the *effendi* class of state functionaries, most of its members from the middling urban class and its mass following was recruited especially from new immigrants to towns. How large its following was it is impossible to say for the Brotherhood was a secretive organization. It has been estimated, however, that at the peak of its popularity in 1949 it may have had half a million members and as many more supporters. For a party which was not an official government party this would be an astonishing performance and marks the Brotherhood out as the largest grass roots movement in the Near East, a development at once indigenous and new.

The Brotherhood was the most powerful of a number of extra-parliamentary ideological parties which opened their challenge to the political system in the 1930s. The Communist Party, founded in 1922, was never a prominent element on the streets as its appeal was chiefly to the minorities. Much more important was the Young Egypt Party of Aḥmad Ḥusayn which was first formed in 1933 and was launched as a political party in 1936. Aḥmad Ḥusayn was the son of a government official from a small landowning family and his appeal was directed to the same middling urban group as the Brotherhood as well as to workers and students. In 1936 more than half of Young Egypt's members lived in Cairo and its suburbs. The Young Egypt Party put forward a strong Egyptian nationalist policy with state sponsored economic development and an emphasis on military training and a powerful army. In the late 1930s in the face of the Islamic revival Aḥmad Ḥusayn emphasized Islam, renamed his party the Nationalist Islamic Party in 1940 and substituted for the slogan "God, Fatherland and King" a new slogan "God is Great and Glory belongs to Islam."[2] After the war, when Soviet successes made the left more popular, his party became the Egyptian Socialist Party (1949). Behind these chameleon changes the composition of the party remained the same with its tight organization under an all-powerful leader and its para-military units, the Green Shirts.

Already in the 1930s the new parties were making extensive inroads into the Wafd's urban following and by the end of the Second World War it was they who controlled the streets, organized strikes, demonstrations, riots and assassinations. Violence was not new in Egyptian politics but had continued after the disturbances of 1919. The Wafd, doomed to almost permanent opposition, had taken to the streets and villages in the 1920s. Urban political unrest had increased in the 1930s with the development of the paramilitary forces of both parliamentary and extra parliamentary forces. It was after 1945, however, that violence truly became part of the political structure and the standard resort of opposition. The Cairo disturbances of February and March 1946 were a potent factor in the British decision to change their stance in the negotiations and after the failure of those negotiations attacks on British personnel and property became common. The Muslim Brotherhood was at the centre of these disturbances and the Nuqrāshī government made an effort to crush the organization in 1948. In May martial law was proclaimed in connection with the Palestine war – another disastrous blow to the prestige of the parliamentary system – and in October the government dissolved the Brotherhood. In January 1949 the Brothers responded by murdering Nuqrāshī and the following month al-Bannā was killed, it is assumed on government orders.

The crown and the parliamentary parties failed to find any adequate response to this challenge to their system. In July a coalition government was formed but the politicians could not agree among themselves, the government collapsed and in January 1950 the Wafd won a last, unconvincing victory in the ensuing election. The Wafd tried once more for agreement with Britain and discussions proceeded throughout 1950 and most of 1951. They broke down over military arrangements in Egypt and, as usual, the question of the Sudan. In October 1951 Naḥḥās made a leap into the lawless dark when he unilaterally abrogated the 1936 treaty. Britain refused to recognize the abrogation and British forces stayed but now the Egyptian government was obliged to regard them as illegal occupiers. An economic boycott was begun and attacks on the British forces by the Brothers, the Socialists and other groups which the government could scarcely restrain. A clash was inevitable and came when British forces overcame and killed Egyptian police in the Canal zone. This event was followed by unprecedented riots in Cairo on Black Saturday (26 January 1952) which left 30 dead and parts of Cairo in ruins. It was the end for the Wafd and indeed for the political notables as an effective force; a few short-lived governments of independents followed and, as the last element of the old order, the crown was left to defend the system with the aid of the army.

It was the army which eventually put an end to Egypt's constitutional government. From 1882 until 1922 and substantially until 1936, the Egyptian army had been under British control. Britain considered a large Egyptian army to be both unnecessary and dangerous and had maintained only a small force for internal security in Egypt. For long much of the Egyptian army was retained in the Sudan and recruited from the Sudanese. The 1936 treaty, the international situation and the need to develop the Egyptian army to take over from Britain had led to a rapid expansion. Within a short period the army had grown from 11,000 to 22,000 and in 1939 a territorial army was established. More officer trainees were required and these were recruited not as had been the case since 1882 from well-to-do sons of notables, often from Turko-Circassian military families, but mainly from the sons of middling landowners and minor government officials. Among the 1938 graduates from the first intake at the military academy were second lieutenants Jamāl ᶜAbd al-Nāṣir (Nasser) and Anwar al-Sādāt. By 1952 the officers of this generation held the ranks of major and lieutenant-colonel. Their careers had been frustrating ones, however. During the Second World War they had been treated with justified suspicion by the British and seen Egypt's independence disregarded. In 1948 they had been pitched into the Palestine War without preparation and indeed in the expectation that they would not have to undertake any serious fighting. Instead of which they had been defeated by Israel. In 1952 they were called upon to take the place of the police and deal with street violence, defending a government and a system in which they had no confidence and of which they were contemptuous.

It was almost inevitable that an army called upon to support the ordinary processes of civil government would claim a share in the policies of that government. In fact an organization engaged in planning a takeover was already in being within the army. The Free Officers Movement Committee was formed in 1949 and in January 1950 ᶜAbd al-Nāṣir became its chairman. The movement demonstrated its strength in December 1951 when it secured the election of its own candidate, General Muḥammad Najīb (Neguib), as President of the Officers Club. The government perceived the danger and endeavoured to conciliate the officers with pay rises, etc. Fārūq, however, rejected a proposal to make Najīb minister of defence and by July 1952 the only question was whether the crown or the army struck first against the other. In the event it was the army which made its move on 23 July 1952. The coup was a model of military planning and execution, the most efficient thing done in Egypt for many years.

The military coup of July 1952 was the opening shot of the Egyptian revolution and the event which marks the beginning of the end of the old political order not only in Egypt but in the Near East. Within three years all the elements of the old Egyptian system had disappeared. Fārūq abdicated on 26 July leaving his infant son, Aḥmad Fu'ād, and a regency. But a year later the crown itself went and Egypt became a republic. Soon the notables were also out of power, their places taken by army officers and other professionals. In 1954 the army contrived the agreement with Britain which had so long eluded the politicans. By 1955 British troops had also gone from Egypt and the country was at last truly independent.

NOTES

1. Quoted Albert Hourani, *Arabic Thought in the Liberal Age, 1798–1939*, 1962, 221.
2. Quotations from P.J. Vatikiotis, *The Modern History of Egypt*, 1969, 328-9.

CHAPTER TWO

Iraq to 1958

Physically Iraq is dominated by the valleys of the rivers Tigris and Euphrates, the waters of which support its agriculture. To the east Iraq is separated from Iran by the Zagros range; to the west and south there is no clear physical separation from the plateaux and deserts of Syria and Arabia. In the north the Mosul region is carved from the contorted mass of mountains of eastern Asia Minor. In these areas the political boundaries of the state are not reinforced by nature. Nor are they endorsed by cultural distinctiveness: the Iraqi state which emerged in 1921 had a majority of Arabic speakers (80 per cent), the remainder being Kurds (15 per cent, principally in the north), Turkomans (especially in the Kirkūk region) and Persian speakers. More than 90 per cent of Iraq's population of 3 million was Muslim but the Muslims were divided between Shīʿis and Sunnīs in a ratio of 7:5. There was also a small but important Jewish population of 100,000 mainly resident in Baghdad. About 80 per cent of the population lived in the countryside; most of the cultivators accepted a tribal social structure but only about 10 per cent of the total population consisted of pure nomads. The remaining 20 per cent of the population lived in towns. The largest town was Baghdad with a population of about 200,000. Mosul and Basra were the only other towns of any size, the former with rather more than 50,000 inhabitants, the latter with rather less than that figure. About 5 per cent of the population was literate.

Very few citizens of the new state thought of themselves as Iraqis. Most thought of themselves as members of tribes and religious communities, a few as members of other cultural or political groupings. Among the older élite nostalgia for the Ottoman Empire was strong; among younger men there was a new-found enthusiasm for Arabism. Iraq's first ruler, Fayṣal I, defined the problem graphically in 1933:

> In Iraq there is still . . . no Iraqi people, but unimaginable masses of human beings, devoid of any patriotic ideal, imbued with religious traditions and absurdities, connected by no common tie, giving ear to evil, prone to anarchy, and perpetually ready to rise against any government whatsoever.[1]

Under a mandate from the League of Nations the administration of Iraq was entrusted to Britain but in 1921 Britain adopted a policy of devolving responsibilities to an Iraqi government. This arrangement was formalized by the Anglo–Iraqi treaty of 1922 modified by a supplementary military agreement in 1924. Britain controlled Iraq's foreign and defence policies and was able to exercise influence over Iraq's internal affairs through advisers and through ultimate financial control. In practice Britain quickly reduced her interference in internal affairs; the number of advisers was cut from nearly 3000 in 1920 to 100 in 1932 when the advisers became employees of the Iraqi government. Britain thus paved the way for a new treaty in 1930 which further restricted British powers and led to the independence of Iraq and her admission to the League of Nations in 1932. The remarkable pace at which Britain quitted her mandate responsibilities was due to a desire to reduce her financial commitments (down to less than £500,000 per annum in 1930) and a wish to avoid becoming involved in any possible internal disturbances comparable to the 1920 uprising (see *MMNE*, 335–6). Britain safeguarded her strategic interests in communications and oil by the 1930 treaty of alliance which gave her sovereign rights in two bases (at Habbāniyya, 50 miles from Baghdad, and Shaʿība near Basra) and the right to use all Iraqi facilities in case of war. The consequence of Britain's decision to terminate her mandate responsibilities so quickly was that the Iraqi state had to create hastily the institutions required to sustain itself.

Iraq was successful in creating a political system which held the state together and attracted a small élite committed to working that system. The 1924 constitution was democratic in form but not in practice. It provided for a monarch, a government, a judiciary and a two-chamber parliament. The judiciary and the parliament were under government control; the upper chamber was appointed and dismissed by the monarch and the lower chamber elected under strict government supervision. On paper the chamber of deputies had large powers but its members lacked either the will or the political skills to use them. The real tension was between monarch and cabinet: the monarch appointed the cabinet but could not dismiss it until the constitution was amended in 1943. The result was that Iraqi monarchs habitually resorted to political intrigue to get rid of governments they did not like and so contributed to the backstairs atmosphere of Iraqi politics. Another characteristic of Iraqi politics was the propensity to resort to violence and it may be accounted one of the successes of the monarchical period that this feature was restrained.

Iraq was a monarchy ruled by members of the Hashimite family of Mecca which traced its descent from Hāshim, the great-grandfather of the Prophet Muḥammad. The monarchy was reluctantly accepted and its first ruler was slow to find a place among the affections of his people. Three years after he came to the throne the king was still named after the Ottoman Sultan and Caliph in the *khuṭba*. Fayṣal I (1921–33) was, however, a skilful and determined politician who played a major part in the state building of the first decade. Fayṣal was able but unpopular; his son, Ghāzī I (1933–39), was popular but not able. Ghāzī's death in a car accident left his four-year-old son, Fayṣal II (1939–58) as heir to the throne and a regency was created with Ghāzī's cousin, ᶜAbd al-Ilāh as regent. The regent, a mild man who looked to Britain for support, was commonly regarded as neither able nor popular.

The principal supporters of the monarchy and of the Iraqi state were the small group of men, composed largely of ex-Ottoman army officers of Iraqi origin, who had linked their fortunes to those of Fayṣal I either during the Arab Revolt or in Damascus in 1918–20 and who returned with him to Iraq in 1921. Most were by origin middle or lower class Arabs from Baghdad and the north of Iraq. They lacked landed wealth and looked to government service for advancement. Most had chosen a military career in the Ottoman service and had been educated at the military colleges at Baghdad and Istanbul. Even before 1914 some had begun to doubt the wisdom of linking their fortunes to the survival of the Ottoman empire and had joined the society of Arab officers known as The Covenant. Among this last group were some of the best known politicians of Hashimite Iraq including Nūrī al-Saᶜīd, Jamīl al-Midfaᶜī and the brothers Ṭāhā and Yāsīn al-Hāshimī. The ex-Ottoman officers were of much the same age – in 1921 they were in their thirties; Nūrī, Ṭāhā and ᶜAlī Jawdat had been at military preparatory school together. During the pre-independence period the ex-Ottoman officers held more than half of all cabinet posts in Iraqi governments and although their influence declined under Ghāzī they remained very prominent.

The older notables were slower to recognize that the Ottoman system had gone for ever and to accept Fayṣal and they were jealous of the influence of those who had come with him. Nevertheless, they were by inclination government men and gradually came to terms with the new establishment. The old notables came from different backgrounds, although the great majority had been educated in Ottoman schools and colleges, many at the Istanbul law college or the Mülkiye, and had served as Ottoman bureaucrats. Traditionally, the leading figures came from the Sunnī *sayyid* families (that is those claiming descent from the Prophet) which had migrated to Iraq from Arabia, Syria and Iran during the Ottoman period and whose prestige derived from their status and education reinforced by wealth from land, *waqfs* and administrative posts. Typical of these was the Gaylānī family, which provided the *naqībs* of Baghdad. The influence of the *sayyid* families had tended to decline during the late Ottoman period when professional skills came to count for more than religious status in the hunt for office and they had felt especially threatened under the Young Turk regime. For them the Fayṣal regime offered an opportunity to regain their position; during the pre-independence period they held nearly one third of cabinet posts and provided 9 of the 13 prime ministers.

A second group of notables comprised the bureaucratic families, some with a regional base and several of Caucasian origin who had entered Iraq during the Mamlūk ascendancy. The largest section of the bureaucratic group was the Turks, who had enjoyed an advantageous position in the search for office under the Ottomans and suffered a set-back with the advent of the Hashimites. Gradually many reconciled themselves to the new regime and took office under it. The extent of the rehabilitation of the bureaucrats may be gauged from the success of the Bābān family of Sulaimaniyya. Between 1930 and 1958 four members of the Bābān family served in a total of 31 cabinet posts (39 including multiple posts) and there was a Bābān in every other cabinet during the period. Most of the posts they held were minor ones but they included the last prime minister of the monarchy. Yet another group of old notables was composed of the merchant families. The leading merchant family in Iraq was the Jewish Sāsūns who were prominent in international trade. Their expertise in finance was invaluable to early Iraqi governments but during the 1930s the Jews came under a political cloud and were much less conspicuous in administrative posts. The Muslim merchant families tended to be confined to local trade and were generally poorer than the Jewish and Christian merchants. Several of the Muslim merchant families had originated outside Iraq, for example the Pachāchīs from Syria. The merchants had only a minor part in government during the 1920s and tended to support opposition groups. From the mid-1930s, however, they played an increasing role in Iraqi governments.

A third group of men who played a part in the political arena of the new Iraq was the tribal shaykhs. Although the late Ottoman period had seen the integration of some tribal shaykhs into the state they had still been regarded with suspicion as a group and their position had been a lowly one. None ever sat in the Ottoman parliament. The British occupation presented the shaykhs with an opportunity. The British perceived them as dangerous enemies to be conciliated, potential allies against the Ottomans and useful aids in preserving peace in tribal areas. What began as an expedient continued as a policy and the power of shaykhs was steadily increased. "Many of them were small men of no account until we made them powerful and rich" complained one British political agent.[2] The policy of winning over the shaykhs was continued under the Hashimite monarchy. An effort was made to associate them with administration; the Tribal Disputes Regulation of 1924 confirmed tribal law and extended the jurisdictional rights given to the shaykhs by the British. Above all they were given land and government projects for their regions. Politically, tribal shaykhs constituted the largest group in the Iraqi chamber of deputies but were poorly represented in governments. Between 1920 and 1936 only 8 of 59 cabinet postholders were tribal shaykhs. The shaykhs enjoyed their benefits at the provincial level where they formed a major prop of the new state.

The political élite of Hashimite Iraq was strongly Sunnī. Between 1921 and 1936 71 per cent of cabinet posts were held by Sunnīs and only 24 per cent by Shīʿīs, who held mainly minor posts, for example the education portfolio. Their role in cabinets, however, was often to act as intermediaries with the Shīʿī tribes rather than to provide professional expertise. Shīʿīs were also under-represented in the chamber: in 1928 of 88 deputies elected only 26 were Shīʿīs. The small representation of the Shīʿīs reflected both the traditional Sunnī predominance and the suspicion with which the Shīʿīs were regarded. The Shīʿī *mujtahids* of Karbalā and Najaf had opposed the state in its early years and in 1923 they staged a demonstration intended to bring the government down. The demonstration failed to achieve its effect and some of its leaders were exiled. Thereafter the power of the Shīʿī religious leaders was diminished but they retained considerable influence among the Shīʿī tribes and were believed to foment tribal risings. The Shīʿīs only gradually reconciled themselves to the state. During the second half of the life of the monarchy Shīʿīs came to play a larger part in politics and between 1947 and 1958 there were four Shīʿī prime ministers. They were talented individuals like Ṣāliḥ Jābir rather than Shīʿī leaders, however, and they never challenged the Sunnī ascendancy. If one takes the five major posts (prime minister, finance, interior, defence and foreign affairs) then between 1921 and 1958 80 per cent were held by Sunnīs and only 20 per cent by Shīʿīs. At the provincial level Shīʿīs were even more poorly represented; in 1933 only 1 out of 14 provincial governors was a Shīʿī and only 4 of 47 heads of districts.

The short life of Iraqi governments – between 1921 and 1958 there were 59 cabinets with an average life of about eight months – gives the impression of political instability. Closer inspection reveals that most of the cabinet changes were simply reshuffles around different prime ministers. Only 166 individuals were involved and some of these held many posts. Easily the most enduring Iraqi politician of the monarchy was Nūrī al-Saʿīd, who held no less than 47 cabinet posts, but other names also appear again and again, for example those of ʿUmar Nadharī (21), Tawfīq al-Suwaydī (19), ʿAlī Mumtāz al-Daftārī (18) and Jamīl al-Midfāʿī (14). In addition there was considerable ministerial continuity. The same individual might hold the same ministry under successive governments: thus Jaʿfar Pasha al-ʿAskarī, Ṭāhā al-Hāshimī and Nūrī al-Saʿīd all held the defence portfolio for long periods. The frequent elections did not signify instability either. In monarchical Iraq all elections were controlled by the government and each election was a ritual by which a new government, formed as a result of negotiation in Baghdad, confirmed its ascendancy by bringing its supporters into the chamber of deputies.

Political parties were little more than the labels of the factions and alliances which were the stuff of Iraqi politics. Thus the Progress Party of 1925 was the vehicle of the ambitions of the Saʿdūns, the National Party that of the ambitious Shīʿī politician Jaʿfar Abū al-Timmān, the Iraqi Covenant of Nūrī al-Saʿīd and the People's Party of Yāsīn al-Hāshimī. Politics were about personalities not policies although divisions were often presented in the latter form. Before 1932 the nominal dispute was commonly between those who were willing to work with Britain and those who demanded greater independence. After 1932 relations with Britain continued to be a prominent bone of contention but other issues also appeared. But these were superficial features. Men sought office because of the rewards it brought in wealth and patronage and they formed alliances, often cemented by marriages like those which linked the Hāshimī, Daftārī and Chādirchī families, to facilitate these purposes. Alliances were made not only between politicians but between politicians and judges and central and local officials. Alliances with local officials were especially useful for electoral purposes and some important politicians such as Ṣāliḥ Jābir in Basra and ʿUmar Nadharī in Kirkuk began their careers as district officials. The rewards of a political career were considerable. Politicians made money from gifts, bribes, licences, sale of jobs, partnerships with merchants (in the 1950s the Gaylānīs held the Pepsi Cola agency for Iraq) and speculation in land. The receipts were used to pay followers, support relatives and to maintain the style of gracious living and hospitality which was regarded as an essential attribute of the notable. Wealth was usually converted into land.

Hashimite Iraq was a country of great landowners. In 1930 it was estimated that 20 per cent of Iraq was cultivable, less than 10 per cent cultivated and only 3 per cent in any given year. During the Hashimite period the last figure was more than doubled. Under the old Ottoman system most land was state land (*mīrī*). Under the 1858 land law it had become possible to register in the name of the holder state land which had been cultivated for a number of years. By 1918 almost one-fifth of the land of Iraq was held under this so-called *tapu* system. Nearly 80 per cent of land was still state land but during the Hashimite period much of this land was converted to a new category of *lazma* (land cultivated by the claimant for 15 years). Under the 1930 land law land (other than the 4 per cent held as *milk* and *waqf*) was divided into three classes: *tapu*, *lazma* and *ṣirf* (land with no established tenancy). It is difficult to estimate the proportions of land in these classes because there was no complete survey and much depends on what land is counted. One estimate is that by 1933 50 per cent of Iraqi land was *tapu* or *lazma* and mainly in the hands of big landowners and that by 1958 the proportion had risen to 60 per cent. According to another estimate only one-third of land in 1950 consisted of *tapu* and *lazma*. On their newly acquired land the landlords introduced pump irrigation and the cropped area rose from under 1 million acres in 1913 to over 4 million in 1943. It is interesting to note that pump irrigation was congenial to private landlordism whereas the large scale irrigation schemes which became a feature of the planning of the 1950s shifted the emphasis back towards state control; the ministry of agriculture, abolished in 1931, was reinstated in 1952.

The landlords' gain was achieved partly at the expense of the peasants. Peasants lost traditional rights and in 1932 a new law bound indebted peasants to the land although this law was virtually unenforceable. Many peasants became sharecroppers and by 1958 one and a half million had no land at all. Many also went to the cities and it is noticeable that the largest number of new migrants to Baghdad came from the provinces of Kūt and ᶜAmāra which also had most land in large estates. Southern Iraq was especially the region of landlordism; by contrast small holdings were much more common in northern

Iraq. The landlords' gain was achieved also at the expense of the state; land tax, which had produced over 40 per cent of national revenue in the late Ottoman period had fallen to under 2 per cent in 1958 although this relative decline was partly accounted for by the increase in other sources of revenue, notably oil which provided 60 per cent of state revenues in the 1950s. Whatever may be said of the distribution of rewards, however, it is evident that landlordism contributed considerably to the prosperity of Iraq under the monarchy.

The ex-Ottoman officers returned to Iraq poor men but they quickly acquired great wealth, especially in land. Ja^cfar Pasha secured large areas of former public land near Baghdad. And other groups also gained land, especially the tribal shaykhs including the leaders of the great Shīʿī tribes. By 1958 six of the seven largest landowners in Iraq were Shīʿīs. Ṣāliḥ Jābir, the son of a carpenter, acquired great landed wealth and married into a prominent shaykhly family. The historian, Hanna Batatu, has calculated that by 1958 49 families owned 17 per cent of all privately held agricultural land. The Hashimite regime was one in which power and wealth were concentrated in a very small élite.

A second important element in the consolidation of the state was the development of the educational system. In 1920 Iraq had only 8,000 students in state primary schools and 200 in secondary schools. By 1930 these figures had risen to 34,000 and 2,000 and by 1958 there were 74,000 in secondary education alone as well as 3,500 in higher education. Education was still available to only a small section of the Iraqi population, mainly urban and mainly male, and 85 per cent of Iraqis were illiterate in 1958. But those who did go through the state educational system were exposed to steady indoctrination in state values. During the 1920s the director of education was Sāṭiʿ al-Ḥuṣrī, the former Ottoman official who became the principal intellectual exponent of Arab nationalism, emphasizing especially the factor of language. Under al-Ḥuṣrī Iraqi education adopted the French academic style and stressed Arabic language and history. His successor during the 1930s, Muḥammad Faḍl al-Jamālī, gave greater weight to American educational philosophy and emphasized practical skills but he also put much weight on the inculcation of Iraqi patriotism through history teaching. There were 40 official Iraqi heroes ranging from those of pre-Islamic times to Ghāzī I. In the late 1930s education came under the control of Sāmī Shawkat who was considerably influenced by German National Socialist ideas and who recommended the prominence of military training in schools. Iraq was represented as the

Piedmont or Prussia of the Arab world, destined to be the architect of its future unity.

The most important of all new Iraqi institutions was the army. Before 1914 the Ottomans had kept a force of 16,000 in Iraq of which the rank and file were recruited locally. By the end of the war this force had disappeared and military forces in Iraq consisted of British and Indian forces together with the Iraq Levies, a force recruited largely from Kurdish and Assyrian volunteers with British officers. With the British decision to withdraw ground forces from Iraq the need for an Iraqi army to take over internal security duties became urgent. From the beginning there were other motives behind the development of the army. In the first place there was the practical need to find employment for the 640 ex-Ottoman officers in Iraq. Secondly, there was the predisposition in favour of the army by those former Ottoman officers who were the main supporters of Fayṣal. Army expansion was also supported by nationalists who saw an army as an integrating force. These Iraqis favoured a large army recruited by conscription. Jaᶜfar Pasha al-ᶜAskarī was put in charge of the army programme and recruiting began in June 1921. By March 1922 a force of 3,500 men was in existence. By 1932 the size of the army had reached 11,500, still short of the target of 15,000, but the introduction of conscription in 1934 led to further expansion and by 1941, when it was easily defeated by British forces, the army had a strength of 44,000. Thereafter, the size of the army was reduced to 30,000.

In the early years nearly all officers were former Ottoman officers who, as late as 1932, still numbered 50 per cent of the officer corps. New Iraqi officer recruits entered from the Baghdad military college. At first officer cadets came mainly from well-to-do urban families with some sons of tribal shaykhs, but after the introduction of conscription many officer recruits came from poorer families and from outside Baghdad. After the Second World War these new officers were to play a significant political role but down to 1941 the higher ranks were dominated by the ex-Ottoman officers. In 1936, when the first Iraqi army coup took place, 50 of the 61 Iraqi officers of the rank of commander and above were ex-Ottoman officers educated in Istanbul. Three-quarters were born in Baghdad and 58 of the 61 were Sunnīs. In the early years the rank and file were mainly tribesmen but this situation changed after the introduction of conscription.

Throughout the 1920s proposals to introduce conscription were opposed by the Shīᶜīs, the Kurds and the tribal shaykhs as well as by the British who said that Iraq could neither afford nor enforce conscription. During this period the army was generally unpopular but attitudes towards the army changed when Iraq began its move towards independence and after the army won its first major success against the hated Assyrians in 1933. The Assyrian (Nestorian Christian) community in Iraq was largely composed of First World War immigrants from Turkish territory who had never assimilated and who were extensively employed in the Iraq Levies. The Assyrians were unhappy at the prospect of Iraqi independence and had sought autonomy. The League of Nations had, however, contented itself with securing a guarantee of protection, after independence negotiations between the Assyrians and the Iraqi government broke down and there were disturbances leading to the army intervention. After their bloody defeat one-third of the Assyrians sought refuge in Syria and most of the remainder were integrated in Iraq. During the mid-1930s the army again demonstrated its abilities when it suppressed the serious tribal uprisings of that period (which were caused by the Tigris floods of 1934–5, conscription, local disputes and religious propaganda combined with political intrigue) and effectively broke the military power of the tribes. This was an historic achievement in Iraq; the power of the tribes had been formidable to all governments and as late as 1933 the tribes were estimated to have 100,000 rifles against 15,000 in the possession of the Iraqi army. In regard to the tribes the Hashimites continued and completed the policy of the Ottomans of combining military coercion with settlement and employment. Supported by the Iraqi Police, a force of 10,500 by 1939 (19,000 by 1945, 23,000 by 1958 including an 8,000 strong mobile force which formed the chief repressive force in the hands of the monarchy) the Iraqi army showed itself capable of ensuring the internal security of the state and controlling the sporadic violence which jeopardized the peace of the country. Only in Kurdistan was the army unable to establish full control.

Kurds composed the majority of the population of the former Mosul vilayet. After the First World War they had enjoyed the brief prospect of a Kurdish state embracing all the Ottoman Kurdish territories except those reserved for an Armenian state but this vision had foundered as a result of the victory of the Turkish nationalists and the absence of any strong sentiment among the Kurds in favour of a separate state. Theirs remained an essentially tribal society although some Kurdish leaders who had lived in Istanbul or in Europe continued to cherish dreams of a Kurdish national state and to oppose the claims of the Iraqi state. In 1919 the leading intellectual centre in Kurdistan was Sulaimāniyya, site of the Ottoman military college, the doorway through which many Kurds had passed into Ottoman military service. Shaykh Maḥmūd, a Ṣūfī leader of the Qādirī order from the Barzinjī family of Sulaimāniyya, became the first leader of Kurdish risings initially against the British and then against the Iraqi state. The contradictory character of the appeal of Shaykh Maḥmūd well sums up the nature of Kurdish resistance at this period. His principal following came through the use of traditional tribal networks but he added appeals to Islam and to the principle of self-determination and assumed the title of king of Kurdistan in 1922. After his capture he recited to Arnold Wilson, the British Deputy Commissioner, the twelfth of Woodrow Wilson's Fourteen Points together with the Anglo–French Declaration of 8 November 1918. He carried strapped to his arm a Kurdish translation of these documents written on the fly leaf of a Qur'ān. It may be taken as evidence of change in Iraq that his son was a member of the first cabinet formed by General Qāsim in 1958.

From about 1930 onwards the leadership of Kurdish opposition passed from the Sulaimāniyya Qādirī Barzinjīs to the Bārzān family of Mosul represented first by Shaykh Aḥmad Bārzānī and subsequently by his better known brother, Mullā Muṣṭafā Bārzānī. The Bārzāns were a leading family of the rival Naqshbandī order. Disturbances continued reaching a new climax at the end of the Second World War when the independent Kurdish Republic of Mahābād was established in Iranian Kurdistan by Mullā Muṣṭafā with Soviet support. The collapse of the Republic in 1946 led to a temporary diminution of Kurdish unrest. Maḥmūd, Aḥmad and Muṣṭafā were all leaders who combined tribal and religious appeals, drawing on the extensive Kurdish support for the reformed militant Ṣūfī orders of the Naqshbandiyya and Qādiriyya. A second line of Kurdish political development took place during the period after 1932 when demands of a secular character were formulated by Kurdish intellectuals. This initiative found expression in the establishment of the Kurdish Democratic Party in 1946. The secular Kurds had no tribal following, however, and constituted no threat to the Iraqi state before 1958. But the Iraqi state had found no solution to the Kurdish problem: neither coercion nor conciliation through the employment of Kurdish officials and the Kurdish language had either broken or won over the dissidents. Kurdistan remained the major military commitment of the Iraqi army until the end of the monarchy.

That the Iraqi state should depend upon its army for its existence was inevitable, but it seems also inevitable that states which come to depend upon their armies for the conduct of the ordinary processes of civil government will be eventually obliged to admit them to a share in the making of the policies which the armies are called upon to administer. In 1936 the Iraqi army made its first political intervention when General Bakr Ṣidqī, victor over the Assyrians and the tribes, forced the resignation of the government of Yāsīn al-Hāshimī. It may be said that Yāsīn had reaped where he had sown because he had helped to provoke the tribal risings of 1935 in a successful attempt to get rid of the government of Jamīl al-Midfāʿī and had persuaded the army to hold back from military action against the tribes until his purpose was accomplished. It was poetic justice that one of his allies in the tribal provocation, Ḥikmat Sulaymān, now joined forces with Bakr Ṣidqī to overthrow Yāsīn himself.

The Ṣidqī/Sulaymān government lasted only a year before it was itself overthrown by military action. Ṣidqī was disliked for allegedly favouring Kurds and for failing to fulfil his promises of improved supplies to the army; Ḥikmat was generally thought to have overstepped the boundary of acceptable behaviour in notable politics and was driven permanently from political life. A new government under Jamīl al-Midfāʿī was formed but it proved unable to keep the army out of politics. The army officers who had taken part in the coups began to fear for their own safety in the event of retribution and therefore sought to protect themselves by forming political links with other willing notables. Jamīl was replaced by Nūrī who also sought to put the army back in the bottle with equal lack of success. By 1940 the dominant group in the army and the final arbiter of politics was a combination of four colonels known as the Golden Square. The leading figure in this combination was Colonel Ṣalāḥ al-Dīn al-Ṣabbāgh, a former Ottoman army officer like his companions (although none of them was one of the favoured followers of Fayṣal), and a man also strongly influenced by ideas of Arab nationalism and a keen supporter of the cause of the Palestinian Arabs. Pan-Arabism, Iraqi nationalism and Islamic sentiment were all powerful influences among Iraqi army officers. It should not, however, be supposed that there was unity of ideas or action among army officers; the army was as riddled with factionalism as was Iraqi society and politics.

The new military mould of Iraqi politics was destroyed as a result of the Second World War. For Iraq the war presented a problem: whether to co-operate fully with Britain as Nūrī urged or to maintain good relations with the Axis powers. After the fall of France in 1940 neutralist and pro-Axis sentiments strengthened and the policies of the government of Rashīd ʿĀlī al-Gaylānī accorded with these views. Rashīd ʿĀlī was removed from power in February 1940 but restored in April by an army coup. The regent and the pro-British politicians fled from Baghdad and Rashīd ᶜAlī began negotiations with the Axis. In May there followed a British military intervention which overthrew Rashīd ᶜĀlī and the Golden Square and restored the authority of the regent. The army was driven from politics until after the war.

Even during the period of army domination Iraqi politics had followed the established pattern with the same men pursuing similar domestic politics. After 1941 Iraq continued in the same manner without the army. From 1943 the power of the monarchy was strengthened although it was still difficult for the regent to dismiss a cabinet he did not want and he tended to use the chamber of deputies to control the cabinet. Within government the old alliances and factional struggles continued; disputes continued to be about personalities and power rather than about policies even when presented as differences about policies. During the 1950s the principal conflict within government was that between Ṣāliḥ Jābir and Nūrī al-Saᶜīd.

Outside government a change did come over the Iraqi political landscape with the rise of new ideological parties and the politicization of the streets. This change may in part be attributed to the working through of developments during the monarchy, particularly in education. In 1920 the size of the bureaucracy was 3,000 but less than 100 college students graduated each year to staff it. The number of civil servants increased to 8,000 in 1935 and 18,000 in 1947 of whom 7,000 were in the educational service. By 1958 the bureaucracy had grown to 20,000 but 8,500 secondary graduates a year sought jobs. One should think of the bureaucracy in this period as a necessary device for distributing rewards rather than for supplying services. About two-thirds of government expenditure before 1950 went on salaries. Competition for the spoils was keen, graduate unemployment and student unrest were features of the post-war scene and it was natural that the students should turn to those parties which advocated a major expansion of state activities. One cannot over-emphasize the small scale of Iraqi government before 1950 and its puny impact on society.

A second factor was the growth of towns and especially of Baghdad. By 1947 the population of Greater Baghdad had reached 500,000 and in 1957 it attained 800,000. A 1957 survey showed that many of the new immigrants failed to find manufacturing employment and drifted into poorly paid service employment; 75 per cent were in construction or services. Even so most believed their condition had considerably improved as compared with their rural situation. Nevertheless, they were now exposed to political influences from which they had formerly been insulated. The ending of the wartime boom added to their grievances.

Ideological parties had first made their appearance in the 1930s. The Ahālī Party, founded in 1931, was composed of young well-to-do notables, especially from merchant families, and advocated a programme of social reform and liberal democracy with tinges of socialism. In 1936 members of the Ahālī Party had filled half the seats in Ḥikmat Sulaymān's cabinet but they had quickly resigned and the party had declined to be revived after the war as the National Democrat Party. The Muthannā Club, founded in 1935 with a programme of Pan-Arabism, was not a political party but rather a grouping of professionals, intellectuals and army officers. After 1945 most Pan-Arabists joined the Istiqlāl Party (1946) although some Pan-Arabists regrouped under the Baᶜth party (1952) which, however, remained a tiny force before 1958. The Iraq Communist Party had been insignificant before 1939 but it expanded rapidly after 1941 when Soviet prestige increased and socialism became respectable. The Communist Party played a prominent role in organizing the first major street disturbances in January 1948. These disturbances were directed against the Anglo–Iraqi Treaty of Portsmouth and toppled the government of Ṣāliḥ Jābir. Subsequently, the party was crushed but quickly revived. Its main support came from students but it also had a following among workers.

The Portsmouth agitation provided a model for subsequent political street demonstrations. In 1952 further riots in support of the Egyptian revolution convulsed Baghdad and in 1954 another street protest brought about the fall of the government of Muṣṭafā al-ᶜUmarī. The new ideological groupings also made some progress in elections to the chamber of deputies; in 1946 they succeeded in getting 14 of their number elected although government control of the chamber ensured that their progress within the system was always very limited. It is interesting to observe that the élite politicians were much more circumspect in their dealings with the new forces than they had been in their dealings with the army and the tribes in the 1930s. The government was also reluctant to call in the army to quell urban disturbances preferring to rely upon the enlarged police force. It was, however, unable to adhere entirely to this policy.

Government policy for dealing with Iraq's problems was geared to long-term agricultural development based on new, large scale irrigation projects. Oil revenues, which increased from 10 per cent of GNP and 34 per cent of foreign exchange earnings in 1948 to 28 per cent of GNP and 59 per cent of foreign exchange earnings in 1958, were earmarked primarily for this purpose rather than being handed out in shorter term rewards. At the time Hashimite policy was regarded as wise and provident: post-revolutionary wisdom asserted that more should have been spent on bread and circuses.

The end of the Hashimite monarchy of Iraq came in 1958. Of all the revolutions in the Near East that which took place in Iraq in 1958 is one of the least easy to explain because it was an army coup and we know too little about developments in the army after 1941. The memory of the 1941 humiliation was strong among Iraqi army officers; the careers of many were ruined by their association with the Golden Square, including the uncle of Ṣaddām Ḥusayn (the future president of Iraq), who was brought up to regard al-Ṣabbāgh (who had been extradited to Iraq and hanged), as a hero and martyr. Another memory of humiliation was Palestine in 1948 when the Iraqi forces had been wholly inadequate to achieve their uncertain goals. The example of the success of the Egyptian officers in 1952 was a powerful one and it was from that date that a Free Officer movement began among Iraqi officers but the movement was never strong; by 1958 it included only 200 officers, less than 5 per cent of the Iraqi officer corps. It is noticeable that the Iraqi Free Officers came from the new generation recruited in the 1930s and not from the old ex-Ottoman officers who had completed their military careers by 1958. All 15 members of the Supreme Committee of Free Officers were born between 1914 and 1921. In a vague way one can point to the influence of the ideological parties and to inflation but no precise links can be established with these phenomena. Similarly, one can note the great political movements of the period, the successes of radical ideas represented by Egypt and the decline of the influence and prestige of Britain, the patron of the Hashimite monarchy. But when all this is said it was and is surprising that a regime which appeared to have weathered its earlier difficulties and in the 1950s entered a period of stability and increasing prosperity supported by buoyant oil revenues should have collapsed so quickly and completely.

The leader of the revolution was Brigadier ᶜAbd al-Karīm Qāsim, (1914–63) the son of a small farmer from south of Baghdad. Qāsim had passed through the Baghdad Military College in the early 1930s and served in Palestine in 1948. He joined the Free Officers in 1957 and the same year became chairman and commenced planning the coup. Qāsim was a secretive, withdrawn man and a passionate Iraqi nationalist. When he was later accused of betraying the principles of the revolution he made a revealing remark. How could he be accused of betraying the principles, he asked, when only he knew what they were?

An opportunity was presented by troop movements in July 1958.

Only 3,000 troops were involved and two-thirds of these were unarmed. A decisive factor may have been the massive street demonstrations which accompanied the coup in Baghdad. The revolution was a bloody one: the royal family, Nūrī and the principal supporters of the Hashimite regime were killed. And perhaps this event may suggest both the principal reason for the revolution and for its success. The Hashimite élite was so small that it could be eliminated at a stroke; its monopoly of power and its unwillingness to admit sufficient new members sealed its doom. Notable politics were by definition restricted and incapable of rapid enlargement.

NOTES

1. Hanna Batatu, *The Old Social Classes and the Revolutionary Movements of Iraq*, Princeton 1978, 28.
2. Quoted Marion Farouk-Sluglett and Peter Sluglett, "The Transformation of Land Tenure and Rural Social Structure in Central and South Iraq, c.1870–1958 ", in *International Journal of Middle Eastern Studies, 15* (1983), 496.

CHAPTER THREE

Syria and Lebanon to 1958

SYRIA

The main geographical divisions of Syria run from north to south. Enumerated from east to west they consist first of a narrow coastal strip along the shore of the Mediterranean, second, a mountain ridge (the Jabal Anṣāriyya), third, the valley of the Orontes, fourth, a second range of mountains, known as the Anti-Lebanon range, in the south, and fifth, a plateau of steppe and desert extending to the Euphrates in the east. These natural features do not lend themselves to political frontier making and, in fact, the frontiers of the Syrian Republic are entirely the result of political arrangements, primarily those made after the First World War by agreement between Britain, France and Turkey. Syria did not exist as an entity before 1920; under Ottoman rule the region was divided among a number of provinces and special districts.

The population of Syria in 1920 was about 2.2 million of whom about half a million lived in towns and the remainder in the countryside. Syria had two major towns: Aleppo with 200,000 people and Damascus with 175,000. The market towns of Homs and Hama had around 50,000 each and other towns were insignificant. The rural population consisted mainly of cultivators; between 10 and 15 per cent were bedouin who carried on pastoral activities in the east. The population was largely Arabic speaking although there were numbers of Turkish speakers in the north. Eighty-five per cent of the population was Muslim, four-fifths Sunnīs, the remainder Shīʿīs, consisting of Druzes, Ismāʿīlīs and ʿAlawīs or Nuṣayrīs, the last named group being much the largest Shīʿī sect comprising nearly 12 per cent of the total population. The remaining 15 per cent of the population was

Christian, including various Catholic and Orthodox sects, the largest being the Greek Orthodox.

The legal basis of French rule in Syria was a mandate from the League of Nations, approved in 1922. The mandate defined the objects of French rule as "to facilitate the progressive development of Syria and the Lebanon as independent states". No time limit was set but it was indicated that an organic law or embryonic constitution should be introduced within three years. France was also enjoined to organize an efficient administration and a suitable legal system to replace the capitulations. The mandate also emphasized the avoidance of actions which would infringe upon the activities of the various religious communities. Thus, from the outset it was decided that Syria should be separated from Lebanon and that the Ottoman *millet* system (which involved the delegation by the state of certain functions to religious communities) would survive in some form.

France had sought the mandate for Syria for a number of reasons. These included hopes of economic advantage from French investments in ports, railways and roads and from trade, hopes of strategic advantage from the extension of France's Mediterranean interests into the eastern part of the region, and a belief in a civilizing mission associated with the protection of Catholic Christians and the extension of educational and missionary activities. These prospective advantages were emphasized by clerical and business groups and especially by the so-called Colonial Party in France but it is doubtful whether they ever commanded the support of a majority in France and none was realized. Without Cilician cotton the economic attractions of Syria diminished. The returns from investments were small and France's hopes of discovering oil were disappointed. Syrian trade was also slight and by 1933 France controlled only 14 per cent of it. The strategic gains were also viewed sceptically as an unnecessary diversion from France's true interests on the Rhine and in the Western Mediterranean. And support for the civilizing mission was sharply reduced by the discovery that Syria was a financial loss. In any case it was Lebanon which was the main centre of Catholic work. It is probably true to say that France took the mandate for prestige and kept it for the same reason.

France did not choose the approach to mandate which was adopted by Britain in Iraq, that is to devolve authority as quickly as possible to a single Arab government and seek to safeguard her own interests by treaty. Instead France embarked upon a policy of creating an elaborate structure of French power and on a detailed administrative reorganization of Syria. The French model was taken from Morocco under Lyautey and its principles were those of indirect rule, collaboration with local élites and respect for local customs and institutions. The early French administrators of Syria themselves had experience of Morocco.

The French administrative structure consisted of a high commissioner, responsible for both Syria and Lebanon, his secretary general and staff together with officials in charge of central activities. These were located in the central headquarters in Beirut. Second were the delegates, that is the representatives of the high commissioner in the capitals of the various states into which Syria was divided. The delegates had large staffs, for example the delegate to the government of Damascus had more than 20 French officials in key posts in departments of the Damascus government. Third, there were joint delegates placed in the districts into which the states were divided for purposes of local government and in some cases in sub-districts as well. Fourth, there were a number of indirect agents, that is French officials placed in states nominally at the request of the governors. Last, there were French officials in autonomous organizations supported by the states as a common interest, for example the customs service. During the 1920s there were in total about 350 French officials in Syria and Lebanon. Many were army officers on secondment: others were officials transferred from departments of government in Paris. In addition to the officials there were also some 1,000 French officers serving with the Armée du Levant and about 3,000 unofficial French residents in Syria and Lebanon, mainly in Beirut and principally engaged in educational or business activities. Unlike the situation in North Africa there was no French settler group in Syria.

French administrative control was extended to all appointments, laws and regulations, finance and important administrative decisions. Through the Common Interests France exercised control over the largest source of revenue, customs, as well as over a number of key services. French financial control was further reinforced by French domination of banking and by the linking of Syria's currency to the French franc. French judges inspected Syrian courts and interfered even in personal law and *waqf* administration. Behind the administrative control was military control.

French military control of Syria rested ultimately on the Armée du Levant which was composed of some French and Foreign Legion forces but principally of French colonial troops from Africa and Madagascar. In 1921, at the height of the initial struggle to pacify the region, the Levant Army numbered 70,000 but by 1924 this strength was reduced to 15,000. The Levant Army was supported by the Troupes Spéciales du Levant, a locally recruited force with French and local officers. The Troupes Spéciales were steadily expanded; in 1924 they numbered 6,500 and by 1935 14,000 although they were subsequently reduced to 10,000. Recruits were principally Christians and Shīʿīs: officers were former Ottoman officers supplemented by Syrians trained in the military academy of Damascus until 1932 and then in the academy at Homs. A third element of coercion was the Syrian Gendarmerie, another locally recruited force with a strong minority element, which was used for constabulary duties in rural areas.

The administrative structure devised for Syria and Lebanon involved the division of the region into a number of small states. This structure may be interpreted as a device for ensuring French domination by dividing the nationalist opposition and forcing the small states to depend upon the Common Interests under French control. Such indeed was the apparent effect of the arrangement but the reason for the division appears to have been the French view of the region as one comprising a number of distinct areas and communities each of which required different administrative arrangements adapted to its peculiar conditions. Historically, the region had never been treated as a single political unit and there seemed no reason why it should be so treated in the future; nationalist agitation could be dismissed as unrepresentative and unrealistic rhetoric. The French view found favour among the minorities who were given their own regions.

About the character of the division French officials disagreed. The able secretary general, Robert de Caix, favoured the complete exclusion of Lebanon and the division of Syria into some eight or nine federated administrative cantons on a Swiss model. The high commissioner, General Henri Gouraud, preferred a confederation which would include Lebanon and consist of a smaller number of larger political rather than administrative units. Gouraud's views prevailed in the original dispositions of 1 September 1920 when four large autonomous units were created consisting of Greater Lebanon, a Damascus state (including Homs and Hama), an Aleppo state and an ʿAlawī territory (in effect an enlargement of the Ottoman district of Latakia in which the ʿAlawīs had a small majority). Within the Aleppo state Alexandretta was made an autonomous district and Dayr al-Zūr in the north east became partly autonomous. The bedouin areas of the east were placed under a special military regime, the Contrôle Bédouin. A fifth autonomous region, that of the Jebel Druze with its capital at Suwayda, was created in 1921. However, Gouraud's plan was modified in an important manner in 1922 when Greater Lebanon was excluded from the confederation.

The French administrative structure quickly broke down. In 1924

Aleppo and Damascus, the two largest states were united and remained so. France still endeavoured to exclude the ᶜAlawī and Druze regions from the Syrian state but in 1936 agreed to their incorporation into a unitary Syrian state under special guarantees, although this decision was subsequently briefly reversed from 1939 to 1942. Only Greater Lebanon and Alexandretta were eventually excluded from the Syrian state. The crucial decision was that to unite Aleppo and Damascus in 1924 and this decision was taken partly because of nationalist pressure, evinced by the vote for union by the Syrian federal council in January 1924, and partly because the separate administrations were too expensive. The eventual shape of the Syrian state owed something to France, therefore, but rather more to local pressure. The exclusion of Greater Lebanon was as much the result of Lebanese demands as of French desires and the exclusion of Alexandretta and its eventual incorporation into Turkey was the consequence of local demands reinforced by a reluctant French recognition of the necessity of conciliating Turkey in the period immediately preceding the outbreak of the Second World War.

The French system depended upon finding local collaborators. In Lebanon the Maronite community provided such assistance but in Syria the matter was more difficult. In the minority areas grateful local notables could be found but in Aleppo and Damascus (and also in Homs and Hama) the French had to deal with the great Sunnī urban notables who had dominated the provincial councils of Syria under the Ottomans and the General Syrian Congress of Fayṣal in 1919–20. These notables were absentee landowners who lived in the cities and traditionally competed for religious or bureaucratic offices and the rewards and prestige which accompanied them. They belonged to a small number of powerful families. These families included in Damascus the Mardams, Quwwatlīs and ᶜAẓms; in Aleppo the Qudsīs, Jābirīs and Kīkhyās; in Hama the Kaylānīs, Barāzīs and ᶜAẓms: and in Homs the Ātāsīs and Jundīs. There were also notable families in the Druze region including the Aṭrash and ᶜAsalīs and among the Christian groups. A further account of the notables is given below. Here it may only be remarked that they were the most important single factor in Syrian politics down to 1963.

The French could find collaborators among the Syrian notables but they were obliged to choose from those who did not espouse nationalist sentiments. Those chosen tended to be men with a strong Ottoman background and often from religious families; the more "modern" notables, who were often the most suitable for administrative posts, tended to be nationalists. Of the 38 men who held ministerial or equivalent posts in Syria between 1920 and 1936 only five were nationalists. A good example of the type of Damascus notable who collaborated was Shaykh Tāj al-Dīn al-Ḥasanī (d. 1943), who served as prime minister from 1928–32 and from 1934–36. He was a man of moderate nationalist sympathies from a religious family and enjoyed the support of the Damascus ulema. In a society in which the Ottoman fez was almost *de rigeur* he wore a turban. Another was Muḥammad ʿAlī al-ʿĀbid, the first president of the Syrian Republic who came from an old Ottoman service family in Damascus and was the son of Aḥmad ʿIzzat Pasha, a close advisor of Sulṭān ʿAbd ül-Ḥamīd. He was also reputed to be the wealthiest man in Damascus. Some members of the ʿAẓm family were also willing to accept office under the French. In Aleppo it was easier to find collaborators because of the presence of many ex-Ottoman bureaucrats with little interest in Arab nationalism: indeed the problem was often to find enough jobs to satisfy them. One such was Ṣubḥī Barakāt who served as president of the short lived federation of Aleppo and Damascus in 1922. Typical of his class Ṣubḥī spoke little Arabic. In Aleppo the French could also appeal to resentment of Damascene claims to leadership.

Down to 1925 France could be reasonably satisfied with the development of her policy in Syria. The first task of pacification had been accomplished. Between 1919 and 1921 France had faced major challenges to her rule from the Turkish nationalists in the north and from Fayṣal and his followers in Damascus as well as several other uprisings, Kurdish and bedouin raids and sporadic banditry. Fayṣal's regime was defeated in July 1920 and the Turkish nationalists bought off in 1921 by the heavy sacrifice of Cilicia. Armed revolts in the Aleppo–Hama region and in the ʿAlawī districts had been suppressed after Turkish assistance was withdrawn from them. Bedouin and Kurdish raids were gradually curtailed. The military garrison and the costs of ruling Syria had been substantially reduced. The new administrative structure was in place and although parts of it had had to be modified it was functioning adequately. A beginning had been made in an attempt to create a political structure in the form of elected representative councils. Under Gouraud's successor, General Maxime Weygand (1923–24), a start had been made on economic development.

A change in French policy took place under Weygand's successor, General Maurice Sarrail. Sarrail was an oddity among French generals who tended to be conservative and Catholic. An atheist and radical, Sarrail was the darling of the French left which had triumphed in the 1924 elections. Sarrail had little sympathy for the sensitivities of the religious communities of Syria whether Christian or Muslim and appears to have aimed at creating a secular state in Syria. Authoritarianism and liberalism were curiously blended in Sarrail and he both encouraged nationalism, urging a delegation of notables to create a political party, and trampled on opposition. In the end he alienated almost everyone. The end of his government of Syria came, however, as a result of a major uprising which broke out in the summer of 1925 and was not finally suppressed until 1927.

The Syrian rebellion of 1925–7 began as a tribal disturbance in the Druze region and spread to many areas of the country. The story of its origins is interesting because it affords an insight into both the nature of French rule at the lower levels and Druze politics. The Jebel Druze is a mountainous region south east of Damascus with a 1920 population of about 50,000, consisting of Druze cultivators and herdsmen many of whom were the descendants of nineteenth century immigrants from Mount Lebanon. It was a fierce tribal society which had been a constant source of irritation to the Ottoman authorities. By an agreement in 1921 an autonomous government, headed by a Druze governor assisted by a council of notables, had been established in the Jebel Druze. The governor, Salīm al-Aṭrash, worked contentedly with the French until his death in 1923 but in the factional Druze society was opposed by his rivals, one of whom, Sulṭān al-Aṭrash, led an unsuccessful rising in 1922. Other Druze notable families also took sides for and against French rule according to their factional disputes. These disputes made it difficult to choose a successor to Salīm and the French political agent, Captain Carbillet, became acting governor and then, in 1924, permanent governor of the Druze region. Carbillet was a zealous reformer anxious to modernize Druze society and politics and he saw the notables as an obstacle to his schemes which were designed to benefit the cultivators. He succeeded in alienating the notables who took the opportunity presented by Carbillet's absence on leave to bring their complaints to Sarrail. It seems likely that they were encouraged to do so by Carbillet's deputy who hoped to be put in that officer's place. Sarrail supported Carbillet and arrested the complaining notables. There followed a Druze uprising led by Sulṭān al-Aṭrash who may well have planned it in advance. His demands were essentially particularist Druze demands. They were for a Druze governor, no French garrison and no disarmament of the Druzes.

At this point the uprising acquired a new, nationalist dimension when the Druze rebels were joined by a group of nationalist notables from Damascus led by ʿAbd al-Raḥmān Shāhbandar, a former member of Fayṣal's government who had recently returned to Syria from exile and founded the People's Party. It is worth noting as further evidence of the persistence of Ottoman patterns of thought that in his inaugural speech Shāhbandar compared his new party to the Committee of Union and Progress. There followed a fresh declaration by the rebels. This was a curious mixture of holy war, demand for independence for Syria, and appeals to the principles of the French Revolution and the rights of man.

During the latter part of 1925 and in 1926 the rising spread. Its most menacing feature from the French viewpoint was the attempt by Sulṭān al-Aṭrash to extend the Druze revolt to embrace the Druzes of Mount Hermon, the Wādī al-Taym and the Shūf but the Druze advance was defeated in November 1925 and thereafter the disturbances were confined to Syria. Within Syria there were disturbances in the bedouin areas, in Hama and in Damascus and its environs. The Damascus disturbances began with the penetration of the southern suburbs by Druze rebels and were supported by the lower classes in the city. The French countered with heavy bombardments of the offending areas. Outside Damascus disturbances took place in the orchard area of the Ghūṭa which was the scene of much fighting. Gradually French military control was reasserted, the Jebel was reconquered in April 1926 and the embers of the revolt finally extinguished in the early part of 1927.

The Syrian uprising of 1925–7 has been presented as a nationalist movement and certainly it had a nationalist element represented by Shāhbandar and his associates. But only a small minority of notables took part. Indeed very few people did take part in it, probably no more than 10,000 all told of whom more than half were Druzes. The north of the country was quiet, Christians opposed the revolt and despite the drought of 1925 the peasantry did not join in, except in the special circumstances of the Ghūṭa. The disturbances were largely tribal (Druzes and bedouin) with some participation by the working class of the towns of Damascus and Hama. The uprising was at heart a traditional movement fuelled by religion, factional rivalries and ambitions, and hopes of plunder. There was some support for the revolt from Muslim merchants, jealous of Christian competition and unsettled by economic depression and inflation, and from notables who had close links with the Druzes. The revolt often spread through traditional networks as may be illustrated from the role of Naṣīb Bey al-Bakrī, a member of a prominent Damascus family of religious notables who was made head of the provisional government set up by the rebels in August 1925. Al-Bakrī had strong links with the Druzes: his Ghūṭa village was inhabited by Druzes and he had contacts in the southern, partly Druze areas of Damascus. He provided an essential link between Shāhbandar and the Druzes.

The principal effect of the uprising was that it led to a complete change in French policy. Sarrail was recalled on 30 October 1925 and replaced by a civilian high commissioner, the journalist and politician Henri de Jouvenal. De Jouvenal's new policy was modelled on British policy in Iraq, that is to isolate the extremists, conciliate the moderate nationalists and work towards an independent Syrian federation linked by treaty to France. Talks began with the nationalist notables who demanded the unity of Greater Syria, a constitution, a treaty with France and the gradual removal of French troops. De Jouvenal negotiated on this basis while at the same time he sought to draw the nationalists into the existing state governments. The price demanded by the nationalists was too high for the new government of Poincaré in Paris, however, and in July 1926 de Jouvenal resigned. He was succeeded by Henri Ponsot (1926–33), a career diplomat who proceeded more cautiously than his predecessor. Ponsot offered a greater share of power to the nationalists but dropped discussion of independence and a treaty. In 1928 a constituent assembly was elected to draw up a constitution for Syria.

The new political initiative failed. Although the constituent assembly was composed mainly of moderate rural notables well inclined towards the French it was dominated by the great urban notables among whom the leading group was the National Bloc, at this time still an informal organization. Only the urban politicians had the skills to operate the assembly and the National Bloc inevitably dominated the constitutional drafting committee. It would be fair to say that only the urban grandees understood what a western type constitution was. Compromise was still low in the list of their skills, however, and the constitution produced was wholly unacceptable to France. In style it was a democratic, secular document. It declared Syria (including Lebanon, Palestine and Transjordan) to be one and indivisible and transferred all power to that non-existent polity. France, the mandatory authority, was left with no power at all. Ponsot was willing to try for a compromise but Paris refused. The assembly was prorogued in February 1929 and France introduced her own constitution for Syria by decree in August 1930. In the French instrument over-riding powers were retained by France.

Between 1930 and 1936 France sought to make the new constitution work, bring to power a strong government and make an Iraqi-style treaty with it. She failed. The Syrian Republic was inaugurated, elections were held and the first president elected in 1932. But the

National Bloc held one quarter of the seats in the new parliament and was strong enough to block any attempts to make a treaty. Ponsot was replaced by another diplomat, Charles Damien de Martel, in 1933 and Martel did conclude a treaty in November of the same year but it was a dead letter.

In 1936 the Syrian political landscape was transformed by two events: the general strike in January and the coming to power of a left wing government in France in June. The general strike grew out of local clashes but was also inspired by the example of the successful Egyptian strike and demonstrations in December 1935. It was organized by students, quarter leaders and a new political party, the League of National Action. The urban notables of the National Bloc did not take the initiative and were alarmed by the violence and demonstrations. To try to check its development they were obliged to assume the lead and it was to the National Bloc leaders that the French turned in an effort to find a solution to the problems of Syria. A Syrian delegation, dominated by the National Bloc, was invited to France to negotiate a treaty. Success in the negotiation was facilitated by the advent of the Léon Blum Popular Front government and a treaty was signed in September 1936.

The Franco–Syrian treaty of 1936 (like the Franco–Lebanese treaty of the same year) was modelled on the Anglo–Iraqi treaty three years earlier. Syria gained its independence and the Druze and ᶜAlawī territories were incorporated into the state with limited autonomy similar to that given to Alexandretta. The nationalists accepted the exclusion of Lebanon and through the 25-year treaty of alliance conceded some French control over foreign and defence policy including French base rights. France also retained powers in the Common Interests.

The 1936 settlement was a real achievement but one must ask why it was accomplished in 1936 and not ten years earlier. Partly the answer lies in a change in the regional and international climate. Events in Egypt, Palestine and Lebanon, as well as the example of the progress of Iraq, all combined to make the nationalists more anxious for a settlement. In the international field the tensions produced by the activities of Italy and Germany made France more ready to disentangle herself from Syria. Partly the answer is weariness on both sides. And partly it was the general strike with its threat of a new type of urban violence and a new surge of unrest which led both France and the urban notables to fear for their own interests. But there is also a personal factor. From the nationalist ranks there arose a politician of great skill in the person of Jamīl Mardam who since the early 1930s had been the architect of a new policy of compromise. It was Mardam who took the lead in the treaty negotiations and it was he who became prime minister in the nationalist government formed after the landslide victory of the National Bloc in the Syrian elections of November 1936.

The story of the years 1936–9 is of the gradual breakdown of the 1936 settlement. One reason for the failure was the shift back towards the right in Paris, opposition to the settlement from the colonial party and French concerns about Arab nationalism and Muslim resurgence and their effects upon North Africa. There were also fears for the security of French strategic and economic interests. In November 1938 France refused to ratify the 1936 treaty. Another reason was the divisions among the nationalists themselves and their failures in government, particularly in their relations with the minority groups within Syria.

The divisions among the nationalists had their origin in the characteristic factional disputes of notables although they were expressed in terms of differences about policies. Within the National Bloc the principal clash was that between Jamīl Mardam and Shukrī al-Quwwatlī; within the broader nationalist movement it was between Shāhbandar and Mardam. The clashes were expressed in terms of criticism of Mardam for offering too many concessions in his unsuccessful attempt to persuade France to ratify the treaty but the heart of them was the conflict of personal ambition. Mardam was eventually forced to resign and in February 1939 the National Bloc broke up.

The troubles with the minorities arose partly from the nationalists' ideological predisposition towards an integrated Syria and partly from the desire of Damascus politicians to enjoy the spoils of office at the expense of the minority groups. In the ʿAlawī, Druze and Jazīra regions and in Alexandretta nationalist policies produced strong reactions from local groups whose insulated political life was disturbed. In the ʿAlawī territories the great majority of ʿAlawīs opposed union which appeared to mean the political reinforcement of the economic power of the absentee Sunnī landowners who dominated the region. The Druzes were more evenly divided in their attitudes but a majority still favoured autonomy. In the Jazīra the Christians (who dominated the towns) and the Kurds (who comprised about 50 per cent of the population) were both opposed to integration and their hostility was vented in an uprising in 1937 which obliged France to restore order by force. The outcome was that in July 1939 each of the three areas was given back its autonomy, the Jazīra being placed under direct French rule.

The most serious nationalist failure was in Alexandretta in the north west. In 1936 the population of Alexandretta was about 200,000 of whom some 40 per cent were Turks, 30 per cent ᶜAlawīs, 20 per cent Christians (half of whom were Armenians) and 10 per cent Arab Sunnī Muslims. Between 1921 and 1936 Alexandretta had enjoyed a limited uneasy autonomy (under the provisions of the 1921 Franco–Turkish agreement) during which time the Syrian nationalists pressed for integration and Turkey supported the existing system. In 1936 the prospect of integration caused Turkey to press for independence for Alexandretta and many Turks within the district to demand integration with Turkey. In 1938, for reasons of international politics, France wished to conciliate Turkey and a Franco–Turkish treaty was followed in September 1938 by the establishment of the independent state of Hatay, its integration into Turkey in February 1939 and its annexation in June. Fifty thousand Armenians, ᶜAlawīs and Sunnī Arabs left the district. The loss of the region was felt as a grievous blow by Syrian nationalists and the loss of its established port of Alexandretta injured Aleppo which had already been hurt by political separation from its natural economic hinterland in Turkey and Iraq.

In July 1939 political life in Syria came to a temporary halt. The new high commissioner, Gabriel Puaux, another diplomatist, in addition to restoring autonomy to the minority areas, suspended the constitution, dissolved parliament and administered the country through a directorate. Martial law was established. Still, politicians could be found who were willing to co-operate with France, notably Shāhbandar, who had always looked for support outside Syria to the Hashimites and beyond them to Britain. In the past this attitude had made Shāhbandar unacceptable to France even without his radical nationalist record but in the circumstances of the war Anglo–French differences were healed and Shāhbandar rose to prominence. In June 1940 he was assassinated and in the same month the fall of France and the installation of a Vichy high commissioner, General Henri Dentz, in Syria completely changed the political situation.

It was Britain who was ultimately responsible for ending French rule in Syria. The British aid for which the Syrian nationalists had looked in vain in 1919 was at last provided between 1941 and 1945. In June 1941, fearing that Syria might become a base for Axis operations in the Middle East, British and Free French forces invaded Syria and Lebanon and replaced the Vichy government with a Free French one. On 8 June 1941 the Free French commander, General Catroux, issued a proclamation in which he stated that "I come to put an end to the mandatory regime and to proclaim you free and independent".[1] But although the Syrian constitution was restored and the Druze and ᶜAlawī areas put back under Damascus control Syria was not given its independence. The Free French hoped to link the grant of independence to a treaty which would safeguard French interests: the nationalists demanded independence immediately and before the negotiation of any treaty. After the nationalist victory at the elections in July 1943 a clash was inevitable. A united front in opposition to France was formed by Syrian and Lebanese nationalists.

In the situation which developed in 1943 it was difficult for Britain to stand aloof. Her principal concern was that Syria and Lebanon should remain peaceful but when in November 1943 the French authorities arrested the Lebanese ministers it seemed impossible that peace could be maintained. Accordingly, Britain demanded that the French should release the ministers and French compliance spelled the beginning of the end of French authority. So long as France retained control of the Troupes Spéciales, however, she still had some power and the denouement did not take place until May 1945 when clashes took place between the French and the Syrian nationalists and Britain delivered a second ultimatum obliging France to give way. By August 1946 all British and French troops were withdrawn and the independence of Syria and Lebanon was secured.

The Syrian hero of eventual independence was Mardam's great rival, Shukrī al-Quwwatli. Quwwatlī's star had risen after the death of Shāhbandar and the flight of Mardam and others to Baghdad. In 1940–1 Quwwatlī's pro-Axis policy had found favour with the Vichy authorities. After the British occupation he had fled but he swiftly switched his allegiance and persuaded the British authorities that he was the man with whom they could deal. In 1943 he played a leading role in the reform of the National Bloc and its conversion into the National Party and it was his coalition which won the 1943 election, and he then became president. The relationship which he had formed with the British authorities was an important factor in persuading them to back him against the French in 1943–5 as the man who could best deliver a trouble free Syria. Mardam, the man of compromise with France, was eclipsed.

Syrian independence was a victory for the Sunnī notables and it was they who inherited power. Their pre-eminence was the consequence of their education, their experience, their ability to manipulate networks involving merchants and artisans, and their wealth, derived from landholding. Their landed position was already well established during the Ottoman period and they had continued to extend their holdings during the mandatory period by purchases of state land. Many were adept at utilizing the opportunities for commercial exploitation. A few, but not many, had industrial or financial interests as well. They formed a tiny group: according to one calculation no more than 50 families controlled the political system in 1946. They were much fewer in number than the rural and tribal notables who formed a majority in every parliament between 1919 and 1949 but despite the French support given to this latter group the urban notables were always dominant. This was hardly because of their better organization; at elections most notables stood as independents and in parliament their parties were factional alliances. The National Bloc (founded in 1931) was a grand coalition of factions and exemplified the character of notable politics. It was a party of Sunnī urban notables, two-thirds of its members being absentee landlords and a quarter merchants. More than 90 per cent of its leaders was Sunnī, half of them from Damascus and a third from Aleppo. They were well educated, mainly in Ottoman state colleges, especially the Harbiye and the Mülkiye, and many had served in the Ottoman bureaucracy. They were secular in style and they adopted a secular nationalist ideology. They had no economic programme and they had no support outside the towns either from the peasantry or the minorities. Their moderate notable rivals were identical other than that they were more likely to come from religious families and to hold a government job.

In many ways the conflict of nationalists and moderates during the French mandate resembles the conflict of Arab nationalists and pro-Ottomans during the period before 1914. Only the rhetoric is modified. Even conflicts within the nationalist ranks seem determined by attitudes developed during the Ottoman period. During the 1920s the divisions between nationalists in exile betrayed the same pattern. On the one side was the group associated with Shakīb Arslān, which was composed of old Ottoman loyalists who in the new circumstances looked to Turkey, Germany, Islam and Saudi Arabia for help. On the other side were those around Shāhbandar whose attitudes resembled those of the earlier Arab nationalists: pro-Hashimite, pro-British and secular. It is difficult to over-estimate the extent to which Syrian politics during the mandate period were shaped by the Ottoman experience whether in ideas, styles, expectations or cleavages. What the notables wanted was a substitute for the Sublime Porte, an institution which would behave in the same way. It was their misfortune that the Third Republic had a different political culture.

Independence achieved, the coalition which had secured it quickly broke up and by 1948 two successor groups had emerged: the National Party, dominated by Damascus politicians, and the People's Party which represented the notables of Aleppo. In government the notables were strangely inept. The post-war situation was admittedly difficult. Economically, Syria had enjoyed a boom during the war as a result of the cessation of imports and the demands of Allied troops in the region. Syrian industry, especially textiles, had expanded rapidly and there had been a large increase in agricultural production especially in the Jazīra. The post-war slump in demand caused discontent among several groups. The progress of urbanization also raised problems of housing and employment, and the expansion of education, the area in which the government concentrated its principal efforts, produced a group of people for whom jobs did not exist. The discontented turned to new political parties, which promised an expansion of state activities, and showed their unhappiness in strikes and demonstrations. Nor was the international situation more comforting: the great issue which confronted Syria was the Palestine war of 1948, which inspired considerable popular enthusiasm but Syria lacked the forces to influence the result.

It was the army which first challenged the domination of politics by the notables. The Syrian army was essentially the old Troupes Spéciales of the mandate. It was composed largely of minority groups and especially of ᶜAlawīs who predominated among the NCOs and rank and file. By independence several infantry battalions were composed entirely of ᶜAlawīs. Sunnī notables had avoided the army; only during the 1930s had some young Sunnīs and those not from the leading families entered the officer academy. In the light of its record under the French, when it had been used against the notables, and the predominance of the minorities within the force it is unsurprising that the Sunnī notables regarded the Troupes Spéciales with suspicion. Between 1946 and 1948 the Syrian government reduced the size of the army from 7,000 to 2,500 seeing it as an unnecessarily large and expensive burden on the state. When the army failed in Palestine the government blamed the army and the army blamed the government. In these circumstances it was unfortunate that the government called upon the army to restore order when, paralysed by its own divisions, it could find no answer to the internal problems. That was in December 1948. After four more months without a government the army did not wait to be invited but in March 1949 intervened on its own account.

Syria experienced three military coups in 1949. The first in March was led by the commander in chief, Ḥusnī al-Zaᶜīm, a former Ottoman officer of Kurdish origin who had served in the Arab revolt and subsequently joined the Troupes Spéciales. In July he made himself president of Syria, but in August was overthrown in a second coup led coup led by another ex-Ottoman officer whose career had followed a similar pattern, Colonel Muḥammad Sāmī al-Ḥinnāwī. Zaʿim, however, had in his short reign effected a transmutation in the position of the army, the size of which he increased from 5,000 to 27,000. The army and its demands would henceforth be a major factor in Syrian politics. But his career had also shown that the army could not do without the politicians who were needed to run the government. Ḥinnāwī, during his equally short eminence, did endeavour to pull the army back from involvement in politics and restore the old notables to power, but he failed. Ḥinnāwī, from Aleppo, found himself supporting the old Aleppine dream of unity with Iraq, an aim to which all Syrian politicians subscribed in theory but to which Damascenes always objected in practice. Ḥinnāwī made too many enemies among both new and old politicians as well as within the army and in December he was overthrown in the third coup which was led by Colonel Adīb al-Shishaklī, a veteran of the first two coups. Shishaklī was a much younger man than his predecessors, however, and had not served in the Ottoman army but was entirely a product of the French Troupes Spéciales.

Shishaklī's domination of Syria from 1949–54 marks an important stage in the evolution of the army's role in politics. During the first two years he tried to carry out the aim of Ḥinnāwī by withdrawing the army from politics and restoring power to the notables. He found it impossible to work out a satisfactory compromise with the notables, however, and in November 1951 staged a second coup by which he dispensed altogether with the notables and established a highly centralized dictatorship with a programme of radical reform. At first he sought the co-operation of some of the new ideological political parties but eventually broke with them as well.

Shishaklī's government was the most efficient Syria had known for several years. It was under Shishaklī in 1953 that the last vestiges of the system of communal representation established by the French and reduced by the independent government of 1947–9 were abolished. ʿAlawī and Druze personal laws were abolished and all citizens were brought under Syrian law. Shishaklī was helped by a great agricultural boom based especially on the exploitation of the Jazīra. Syria had come to fear the possible loss of the Jazīra if it remained a minority-dominated province and since independence it had promoted settlement in the region which thus acquired an Arab Muslim majority. At the same time the Christian merchants of Aleppo had seen the Jazīra as a new outlet for their capital and energies. The combination of labour and capital had produced an enormous expansion of cultivation from

20,000 hectares in 1942 to over 400,000 in the 1950s. The boom had the incidental effect of greatly enriching the ᶜAẓm family whose main lands were in the Jazīra.

The circumstances of Shishaklī's fall from power were unusual. It is a characteristic of coups in general and those in the Near East in particular that they take place in the capital city. The centralization of power in the second half of the twentieth century is such that so long as a regime controls the capital it may retain power and those who wish to overthrow it must concentrate their efforts on asserting their mastery in the capital. The Syrian coup of 1954 was quite different and the nature of the difference is instructive to those who endeavour to understand the evolution of Syrian politics in that period. Shishaklī's domination over Damascus was never broken, indeed there was no group in the capital which could challenge his power. The challenge came first with a revolt in the Jebel Druze in 1953 followed by strikes, demonstrations and eventually an army coup in Aleppo which spread to Homs, Hama and Latakia. Shishaklī eventually bowed to a provincial movement rather than endure a civil war. His situation was a consequence of the bipolar structure of Syrian society in which Aleppo was a true rival of Damascus.

The fall of Shishaklī allowed the return of the old notables to power in Syria. The army broke into factions and withdrew from politics; elections were held and a large majority of those elected were urban notables or their representatives. But the 1954 elections exposed a new challenge to the power of the old élite. This challenge came from the ideological parties who for the first time secured a sizeable representation in the assembly.

Ideological parties were not a new feature in Syria. Shāhbandar's 1932 Popular Front had had a strong ideological element. The 1933 League of National Action founded by young Pan-Arabs for a few years had attempted to rally support on a nationalist programme before it had succumbed to the lures of the politics of notables. During and after the Second World War ideological parties grew quickly. The Syrian Social Nationalist Party, founded by a Greek Orthodox, Anṭūn Saᶜāda, with a Greater Syrian programme, appealed to intellectuals, workers and to the minorities. The Syrian Communist Party shed some of its minority origins under the leadership of Khālid Bakdāsh, an Arabized Kurd from Damascus, where his power base was in the Kurdish quarter. Bakdāsh, who had spent the years 1933-5 in Moscow, was elected to parliament in 1954. In 1944 the Syrian Muslim Brotherhood was formed out of one of the many Muslim benevolent societies which had been established in the 1920s and 1930s. The

Muslim Brotherhood drew its support from the bazaar and from new immigrants from the countryside and its leadership from religious and professional figures. It concentrated on social issues and in 1944 it clashed with government over the wearing of the veil.

Most important of the new ideological parties was the Baᶜth (Renaissance) Party which was formally constituted in 1946, although it had existed as a movement since the late 1930s when it was founded by two Paris-educated school teachers, a Sunnī Muslim, Ṣalāḥ al-Dīn al-Bīṭār, and Michel ᶜAflaq, son of a Greek Orthodox merchant from the southern Maydān quarter of Damascus, home of the new immigrants from the Jebel Druze and the Ḥawrān. More significantly, in the 1950s the Baᶜth extended its appeal to Latakia where it replaced the SSNP as the most popular party among the ᶜAlawīs. . The Baᶜth appealed to romantic nationalism. In the words of the Baᶜthist poet, Kamāl Nāṣir:

> And the years shall pass,
> And the Baᶜth will remain
> Beyond the years
> A beautiful dream.[2]

The Baᶜth's organization reflected its aspirations: its national command was all-Arab and its regional command the state in which it operated, in this case Syria. In 1952 the Baᶜth merged with the Arab Socialist Party of Akram al-Ḥawrānī, son of a minor rural notable of Hama. The merged party professed Arab unity, freedom and socialism. In the 1954 elections the Baᶜth made substantial advances.

The advance of the ideological parties was associated with the entry into the political arena of new groups. This phenomenon was the result of the expansion of the ambit of state activity notably under Shishaklī, the process of urbanization and the educational expansion which took place after independence. Although the state educational system had expanded under French rule the main emphasis had been given to private schools run by missions, by charitable groups and especially by the religious communities. As late as 1939–40 there were only seven state secondary schools, together with ten others which provided elements of secondary education. In all about 4,000 pupils were receiving state secondary education. There were also some 450 elementary schools with rather more than 50,000 pupils. Three times this number were in private schools. Opportunities for higher education were largely confined to the Damascus law and medical schools. After independence governments gave priority to state education: expenditure was increased several times and by 1955–6 there were 258 state secondary schools with over 60,000 pupils. Higher education also greatly expanded: Damascus University was founded in 1946 and there was a rush for admission. Graduates found their path to advancement barred by the dominance of the urban notables and turned to those who challenged the old political system. To the minorities, no longer insulated from national politics by the French arrangements ideological parties had a special appeal for they offered a way out of the restrictions imposed by religious differentiation. If class or language became the qualification for membership of the political community Christians, ᶜAlawīs, Druzes and others might hope to escape from their disabilities. To new immigrants to the towns ideological parties offered a platform from which they could challenge the established élite.

After 1954 the notable politicians had to contend not only with the internal problems of Syria but also with the regional and international problems which derived from the polarization of the Arab world between Egypt and Iraq and the involvement of the Near East in the Cold War. In these circumstances some strange configurations were produced. In 1955 Syria, led by its foreign minister, Khālid al-ᶜAẓm, a wealthy member of one of the most prominent of all the notable families of Syria and a politician who had recently been ejected from power for pursuing a policy too favourable to the West, linked herself to the Soviet bloc and to Egypt with whom she concluded a defence pact. Inevitably, the opposition in Syria looked to the West and to Iraq. In 1956 the ground was cut from under the opposition by the Suez War, which marked the eclipse of British and French influence and by an abortive Iraqi plot to procure a coup in Syria. Egyptian influence rose in Syria as a consequence.

By the end of 1957 the notables were in disarray, their system penetrated by ideological groupings with which they were in alliance. The strongest forces were those of Nāṣirism, Baᶜthism and Communism while in the wings lurked the army. To save themselves from the left and the army and convinced that Egypt held the key to Arab unity the Baᶜth asked President ᶜAbd al-Nāṣir for a federal union. ᶜAbd al-Nāṣir insisted on a full union and control of the Syrian army and this was eventually agreed. In February 1958 Syria and Egypt formed the United Arab Republic.

The temporary disappearance of Syria as a political entity in 1958 in many ways seemed a logical consequence of a political philosophy which had always denied the existence of Syria. Before 1936 the notables had insisted on Greater Syria while the ideological parties all identified with something other than the Syrian Republic whether it was Greater Syria, the Arab nation, Islam or the international working class. The minorities in many cases still looked to their own communities. Regional rivalries also played their part, in particular the different outlooks of Aleppo and Damascus. Syria presented a curious spectacle in 1958: in social life orderly and traditional, economically prosperous, in politics almost anarchic. As the Syrian president, the experienced, long enduring Shukrī al-Quwwatlī, is reported to have remarked to ᶜAbd al-Nāṣir at the time of the union: "You have acquired a nation of politicians: fifty per cent believe themselves to be national leaders, twenty five per cent to be prophets, and at least ten per cent to be gods."[3]

LEBANON

Greater Lebanon was created by France in 1920. Under Ottoman rule there had existed only the autonomous district of Lebanon, consisting of Mount Lebanon alone with a 1914 population of about 400,000, four-fifths Christian and one-fifth Muslim. Among the Christians easily the largest group was the Maronite community which comprised nearly 60 per cent of the entire community. During the First World War Lebanon lost its autonomous status and, as a result of famine, disease and emigration, the total population fell substantially, according to some estimates by as much as one third, and the losses among the Maronites may have been disproportionately large. The discontent of many Maronites with the status and size of the district was increased. In 1919 their apprehension about the future was made stronger by the strident claims of the Syrians who surrounded Fayṣal in Damascus. The Maronites demanded a state which should include, in addition to Mount Lebanon, Tripoli and ᶜAkkār in the north, the Biqāᶜ valley in the east, Ḥāṣbayyā, Rāshayyā and Jabal ᶜĀmil in the south, and the coastal strip including Tyre, Sidon and, above all, Beirut in the west. The Maronites based their demands on appeals to history, geography and economics. In Paris, after the war their claims were pressed by the Central Syrian Committee of Shukrī Ghānim and by delegations sent by the Maronite Patriarch, Ilyās al-Ḥuwayyik.

The French decision to establish Greater Lebanon was made in consequence of Maronite pressure and for want of a reliable alternative. Many Frenchmen favoured a united Syria with a small autonomous Lebanon on the Ottoman model and it was hoped that agreement could be reached with Fayṣal on this basis. Doubts about Fayṣal's willingness or ability to make and keep an agreement caused France to turn to the Maronites as being the only community in the region which could be trusted to promote French interests. On 10 November 1919, in a letter to Ḥuwayyik, Clemenceau committed France to support an independent Lebanese state. The size of that state was still undecided, however, and in January 1920 it seems that France contemplated a state much smaller than that which was eventually called into existence. Robert de Caix would have excluded Tripoli and the northern region, an idea to which Jouvenal returned briefly in 1926. It was General Henri Gouraud who made the decision to adopt the full Maronite territorial demands.

The choice of the larger, independent state was a fateful one. The Maronites wanted two things: they wanted a state which would be large enough to stand on its own and one in which Christians could control their own destinies. Yet in the territories newly added to the former district Christians numbered little more than one-third of the population and while Christians still formed a majority of the population of the whole of Greater Lebanon they comprised only 55 per cent of the population and the Maronites, while still the largest single community, were now only one-third of the whole. The second largest community at one-fifth of the whole was the Sunnī Muslims who bitterly resented their separation from Syria, the loss of their former supremacy and their subjection to Maronite rule. Moreover, the demographic balance was moving against the Christians. Because of a lower rate of emigration and a higher natural increase the Muslims, and especially the Shīʿīs (17 per cent in 1921), were eroding the Christian numerical superiority. By 1932 the balance was 51 per cent against 49 per cent. After that date Lebanon stopped official counts of its population. It was evident that Lebanon could not be both Greater and Christian except by subterfuge. To find a solution to this dilemma became the central problem of Lebanese politics.

Between 1920 and 1925 Lebanon was ruled by French governors assisted by advisory councils, which were replaced in 1922 by representative councils. The existence of a Maronite community willing and anxious to co-operate with France made the task of finding collaborators easier than in Syria but Caix held back from transferring power quickly to the advisory council and the representative council in Lebanon was introduced at the same time as those in Syria. The representative council was fashioned in a manner which was significant for the future of Lebanon because deputies were elected on a confessional basis, that is they were divided proportionately among religious communities. The Sunnī Muslims, however, boycotted the 1922 election.

In 1926 the Lebanese Republic was established under the constitution of 23 May 1926. The transition from representative assembly to chamber of deputies was not accomplished as smoothly as this presentation of events suggests, however, and, in fact, in 1925–6 the Lebanese polity passed through a major crisis. In 1925 the representative council was abolished by Sarrail who disliked the whole confessional system and proposed for Lebanon a quite different mode of development, namely that Lebanon should become a secular state. Sarrail wanted to end the system of representation of religious communities, to replace the administrative organization of Lebanon with new arrangements which obliterated the old confessional divisions, and to break the hold of the religious communities on education which should henceforth become the responsibility of the secular state. Sarrail's proposals encountered widespread opposition not only from the Maronites but from other religious communities in Lebanon and they were aborted partly for this reason and partly because of the Druze revolt. Even so Lebanon was not out of the wood for Sarrail's successsor, Jouvenal, proposed new concessions at the expense of Lebanon in his effort to win over the Syrian nationalists. These schemes came to nothing but another of Jouvenal's initiatives bore fruit in the Lebanese constitution.

The Lebanese constitution of 1926 preserved the confessional system established four years earlier and in its origins dating back to the middle of the nineteenth century. There was an elected chamber of deputies, a senate nominated by the French high commissioner on a confessional basis, a president and a cabinet. The first president was Charles Dabbās, a Greek Orthodox chosen by Jouvenal. Although French control was still secured through the influence of the high commissioner, the control of military forces and the Common Interests, the Lebanese Republic provided an arena in which the political life of Lebanon could develop. For the time being, however, that development was impaired by the continued refusal of about half of the population of Lebanon to work the system. The Sunnīs were wholly opposed to the state; the Shīʿīs were suspicious, although Shīʿī notables were more willing to co-operate; and many Greek Orthodox, although concerned about the prospect of Muslim rule, continued to resent Catholic pre-eminence. The Druzes were divided: they disliked Maronite domination but were in favour of an independent Lebanon; some notables, like the Jānbulāṭs (Jumblatts) were willing to co-operate with France and some, like the Arslāns, refused.

Between 1926 and 1943 Lebanese politics became a rather artificial power struggle between Maronite factions. To a considerable extent these struggles were about personal rivalries but they also contained an element related to differing views of the future of Lebanon. Some Maronites believed the whole venture of Greater Lebanon had been a mistake and that a small autonomous Christian Mount Lebanon on the Ottoman model was preferable, a view shared by many Sunnī Muslims. Something like this scheme was at one time favoured by one of the most prominent of Lebanese politicians, Emile Eddé (Iddī), who in 1919 had been one of the foremost advocates of a Greater Lebanon. Faced with the difficulty of securing Muslim co-operation he suggested abandoning the northern and southern regions and leaving only the Mountain, the Biqā^{c} and Beirut under unassailable Christian domination. Other Maronites believed that the future lay with Greater Lebanon but that it must always expect Muslim hostility and therefore lean wholly on French support. For much of his career Eddé took this view as did his great rival, Bishāra al-Khūrī, in the early years of the state. Non-Maronites like Charles Dabbās and Fu'ād Arslān also thought French protection essential. A third view, which was very much a minority view before 1943, was that in the long run a Greater Lebanon could work only if the Muslims were persuaded to accept it. For long no prominent Maronite politican adopted this view but eventually it was taken up by Bishāra al-Khūrī. It is probable that the concept could not have succeeded earlier; it was necessary that first a generation of Sunnī politicians with memories of Ottoman domination should pass away and be replaced by a new group whose attitudes were not shaped by the past.

Although of so much interest and future importance the arguments about the political direction of Lebanon were of less immediate consequence for the political history of that state than the squabbles of factions which made Lebanese politics a turbulent business and obliged the French to suspend the constitution in 1932. More will be said of these factions and of the dynamics of Lebanese politics below but for the moment it is sufficient to note that the French act had the effect of uniting against France many groups which were suddenly deprived of the spoils of politics they had come to enjoy. Lebanese politicans now sought greater independence and for this purpose followed the example of the Syrian nationalists in seeking to substitute for the mandate arrangements an independent Lebanon in treaty relations with France. The unratified Franco–Lebanese Treaty of 1936 was a move in this direction.

The main provisions of the Franco–Lebanese Treaty were similar to those of the contemporary treaty with Syria. An annex provided for the continuation of the confessional system as the basis of the division of power in Lebanon. The treaty was well received by Christians and bitterly opposed by the bulk of the Muslim community still unwilling to accept an independent Greater Lebanon. Its main effect was to provide a basis for the full restoration of the constitution, a situation which lasted until September 1939 when, following the outbreak of war in Europe, the French high commissioner suspended the constitution once more. In June 1941 Lebanon was occupied by British and Free French forces, its independence being promised in the announcements of General Catroux. As in Syria, however, the Free French wished to prolong their hold in order to secure a treaty guaranteeing French interests. And, as in Syria, a number of politicians, of whom the most prominent was Bishāra al-Khūrī, turned to Britain for assistance. These politicians found some Muslims willing to co-operate in a bid for immediate independence. Obliged to make concessions, in March 1943 France announced the restoration of the constitution. Elections held in the summer of 1943 gave a large majority to those who sought immediate independence and in September Khūrī was elected president. The stage was set for a full scale confrontation which took place the following November. The Lebanese chamber amended the constitution without reference to France; the French delegate general, Jean Helleu, suspended the constitution and arrested Khūrī and the offending ministers; there was widespread resistance and British pressure; and France backed down. In 1945 France made a last attempt to salvage some of her interests in Lebanon but once more was obliged to give way to Britain. Lebanese independence was finally secured.

A key factor in the achievement of Lebanese independence had been the co-operation of Christian and Muslim politicians. This co-operation was founded on an unwritten understanding about power-sharing known as the National Pact. Many earlier proposals for securing Christian–Muslim co-operation in Greater Lebanon had been based on the Sarrail model of individual equality in a secular state. The National Pact adopted the opposite approach and endeavoured to secure co-operation in a pluralist polity in which power was shared on a confessional basis. It incorporated both the ideas of men like Michel Shīḥā, a Greek Catholic banker and one of the architects of the 1926 constitution, and the experience gained in working the system since 1926. In many ways the National Pact merely endorsed the practice of Lebanese politics.

To understand the power sharing system it is first necessary to enumerate the religious communities of Lebanon in more detail. The largest single community was the Maronite, 29 per cent of the population in 1932, located in the northern and central parts of Mount Lebanon and in east Beirut. The second was the Sunnī Muslims, 23 per cent, mainly urban and in the coastal towns of Tripoli, Sidon and Beirut. The Shīʿīs, still a predominantly rural community in 1943, had 20 per cent and were located in the south and in the northern Biqāʿ. The Greek Orthodox (10 per cent) were, like the Sunnīs, mainly urban but were also found in the Kūra in north Lebanon. Next came the Druzes (7 per cent) in the southern part of Mount Lebanon, notably in the Shūf. The Greek Catholics (6 per cent) were a prosperous urban community strong in Beirut and in the town of Zaḥla. The remaining 5 per cent of the population consisted mainly of Christian sects living in Beirut of which the most important was the Armenians, essentially an exile community whose politics were still formed around earlier struggles for Armenia and a contest for control of the Armenian church organization. The percentages given for these groups are all from the 1932 census although they no longer truly reflected the situation in 1943. In particular they overestimated the Christian proportion and underestimated the weight of the Shīʿī population. Nevertheless, they formed the basis of the division of power agreed primarily by Maronites and Sunnīs.

The division of power was as follows. The president was to be a Maronite (as he had been since 1934), the prime minister a Sunnī Muslim (since 1937), and the president of the chamber of deputies a Shīʿī. Representatives in the chamber of deputies were to be apportioned on the basis of six Christians to five Muslims, an arrangement introduced in the summer of 1943. Thereafter the number of deputies was a multiple of 11. Confessional representation was also extended to the cabinet. Cabinets consisted of eight or ten members including two (or three) Maronites, two (or three Sunnīs) and one each from the Greek Orthodox, the Greek Catholics, the Shīʿīs and the Druzes.

A second feature of Lebanese politics was the regional factor. The religious communities had geographical situations which coloured their outlook. For example, the situation of the Maronites of the north, in the vicinity of Tripoli, was such as to incline them more than the Maronites of the south towards co-operation with Syria. The southern Maronites were obliged to work with the Druzes. A second example of the regional factor was the rivalry between Beirut and Tripoli. So small a country could scarcely afford two major ports and Beirut won the race. Had Syria and Lebanon been united it is difficult to believe that this would have been the result because Tripoli was much better placed to serve the larger unit. The resentment of Tripoli at its eclipse by Beirut was a factor in Lebanese political alignments. The growth of Beirut itself was an important element in the political situation. In 1921 the population of Beirut was 94,000 of whom a slight majority was Muslim. By 1943 the population had risen to 170,000 with a small Christian majority, primarily the consequence of the settlement and naturalization of 40,000 Armenians after 1920. So large a city cast an increasing shadow over the rest of the country. The total population of Lebanon in 1943 was 1.5 million.

The leading feature of the Lebanese political system was the predominance of notables. The Sunnī notables resembled those of Syria with their Ottoman education and experience although their wealth often derived more from their urban activities than from their landholding. The cousins, Sāmī al-Ṣulḥ and Riyāḍ al-Ṣulḥ came from an old Ottoman bureaucratic family from Sidon, now settled in Beirut, although they had adopted Arab nationalist views before 1918. ʿAbd al-Ḥamīd al-Karāmī and his son Rashīd al-Karāmī came from a religious family in Tripoli which had held the office of *muftī*. Ṣā'ib Salām was the son of a deputy in the Ottoman parliament from a Beirut merchant family. An interesting personality was Shaykh Muḥammad al-Jisr, from a religious family in Tripoli with a record of Ottoman service. He was one of the earliest of the Sunnī notables to co-operate with France and served as president of the senate and later of the chamber of deputies from 1926 to 1932. Another member of an old Tripoli family was Khayr al-Dīn al-Aḥdab who moved to Beirut and established a newspaper which became the vehicle for his Pan-Arab views. Later, he modified his views and in 1937 he became the first Muslim prime minister of Lebanon. The Shīʿī notables, on the other hand, were usually large landlords. Prominent among them were the Asʿads of the south and the Ḥamādas of the Biqāʿ. The Druze leaders, like the Shīʿīs, tended to favour traditional status. In terms of status the leading family was that of the Arslāns but in terms of landholding the most wealthy was the Jānbulāṭs. The rivalry between these two families was an important factor in Druze and Lebanese politics for it determined with whom they would work.

The Christian notables had a rather different background for most of them had studied in non-Ottoman schools and colleges, notably at the Jesuit college of St Joseph, and learned their political craft in the autonomous district of Mount Lebanon. Many were landowners but many also had moved into urban occupations. The Greek Catholic notables, Michel Shīḥā and Salīm Taqlā, were bankers. The Greek Orthodox were often from long established merchant families like that of the lawyer and millionaire, Petro Ṭrād. Among the Maronites there were many landowners but professional men were the leaders in politics. Emile Eddé was a Paris-educated lawyer, more at home in French than in Arabic. Bishāra al-Khūrī, son of a civil servant who had served in the old autonomous district, was also trained as a lawyer. An interesting example of the composite nature of the Christian notable was Kamīl Shamʿūn (Camille Chamoun) who came from a landowning family in the Shūf but acquired a legal education and entered politics: in the Shūf he was a traditional notable; in Beirut a modern political leader. A similar appearance was made by Sulaymān Faranjiyya from the north: in his stronghold of Zāghurtā he was a traditional figure while in Beirut he played the modern game of politics. In the career of the Lebanese notable the two elements balanced and supported each other: his political base was his region; to reward his followers he was obliged to seek office. To stand aloof from politics altogether was a luxury which few notables could afford; the new political arena reshaped their traditional life.

By independence the ingredients of success in politics were established. They were a landowning base with local followers, urban wealth, modern skills and good alliances. Landowners were the leading group in Lebanese chambers down to independence and beyond falling from nearly 60 per cent in the 1920s to 40 per cent in 1957 and only 10 per cent in 1968. In Lebanon, however, those with modern skills came more quickly to the fore than in other countries of the region. By 1929 lawyers already numbered a quarter of the chamber and by 1943 they were nearly 40 per cent. In this shift Christians took the lead and Muslims followed. Lawyers also predominated in governments. Between 1926 and 1972 8 out of 12 presidents and 7 prime ministers were lawyers. The proportion of lawyers in cabinets between 1943 and 1972 was between one third and two thirds. By contrast businessmen did not go into government in large numbers: only 6 per cent of members of Lebanese cabinets were in this category. In the rise of the professional politician one can begin to see the seeds of major change in Lebanon, namely the passing of many of the traditional notable families who could not well adapt to the requirements of the new political arena. In 1936 38 per cent of chamber seats were held by notable families which dated back to the nineteenth century; by 1972 such families held only 7 per cent of seats.

The changing character of Lebanese politics was disguised by the pre-eminence of a few families at the highest levels. This phenomenon was especially pronounced among the Sunnīs. Of 35 cabinets formed between 1943 and 1964 no less than 31 were headed by members of four families, the Ṣulḥs, the Karāmīs, the Yāfis and the Salāms. These Sunnī prime ministers formed alliances with Maronite presidents. Such alliances were those of Emile Eddé and Khayr al-Dīn al-Aḥdab, of Bishāra al-Khūrī and Riyāḍ al-Ṣulḥ, of Kamīl Shamᶜūn and Sāmī al-Ṣulḥ and of Fu'ād Shihāb and Rashīd al-Karāmī. Similar alliances were formed with notables from other communities. The electoral system also promoted the formation of alliances across confessional frontiers. From 1922 to 1952 Lebanon was divided for electoral purposes into five vast multi-member constituencies, electing as many as 15 deputies. After 1952 these were broken up into 26 multi-member constituencies electing between two and eight deputies each. As deputies were often elected by the votes of members of other religious communities politicians were obliged to form alliances to secure the votes. Local political bosses were a vital element in the system.

The large number of cabinets and their short life (between 1926 and 1964 there were 46 cabinets with an average life of less than eight months) gave Lebanon the appearance of great political instability. Just as in Iraq, however, this phenomenon disguised ministerial stability. Only 134 individuals held ministerial office in that period and many had long periods in office. Defence was usually reserved for the Druze member and Majīd al-Arslān held the defence portfolio in many governments.

In a political system dominated by confessional, regional, family and individual influence there was little room for conventional political parties. Such parliamentary parties that existed were factional groupings or coalitions like the National Bloc, a Maronite grouping created by Emile Eddé in the 1920s, which his son, Raymond, endeavoured to convert into a mass party in the 1950s. A similar grouping was the Constitutional Bloc of Bishāra al-Khūrī, which was formally constituted in 1934. In 1943 it became the vehicle of his victorious alliance with Riyāḍ al-Ṣulḥ. In the 1950s the Constitutional Bloc sought to become a mass party as the Constitutional Union (1955). The National Liberal Party of Kamīl Shamᶜūn, which was formed at the end of the 1950s, was little more than a vehicle for Shamᶜūn's political ambitions. Even more amorphous and more short-lived were the coalitions of opposition factions such as the so-called Socialist Front which overthrew Khūrī in 1952 and the National Front which confronted Shamᶜūn in 1958.

The ideological parties which came into being outside parliament (although some managed to secure representation within the chamber) also had many of the characteristics of the parliamentary factions despite their names and programmes. One of the earliest of these parties was the Syrian Social Nationalist Party, already mentioned in connection with Syria but more influential in Lebanon. It was founded in 1932 and it was especially a party of the Greek Orthodox, to whom the doctrine of a united, secular Syria was especially congenial. In the mid 1930s the party grew rapidly and took part in the demonstrations of 1936. Suppressed, it revived after 1944 and attempted to launch an armed uprising in 1949. As a result the party was again suppressed and its leader, Anṭūn Saʿāda, executed. Whether as an underground or a legal party it continued to be active in Syria and Lebanon after that date. In 1961 it made another unsuccessful attempt to mount a coup in Lebanon. Like many parties of the 1930s the SSNP adopted the styles of Fascism: Saʿāda was known as *al-zaʿīm* (the Führer) and the party anthem was "Syria, Syria, über alles" sung to the same tune as the German national anthem. Another Fascist style organization was the Katā'ib (Phalanges Libanaises) a Maronite party created by Pierre Jumayyil in 1936 under the influence of the Berlin Olympics. The Phalanges was not a party of notables; like many of the ideological parties it appealed to the middle class and small business men. It preached democratic Lebanese nationalism. Its Sunnī counterpart was al-Najjāda (the Helpers) founded in 1937 and emphasising Islam and Arabism. The latter's members came mainly from Beirut and the Biqāʿ and were workers, peasants and students.

The ideological parties which grew up in the post-war climate espoused leftist ideologies. These included the Progressive Socialist Party founded in 1949 by the young, ambitious and well-educated Druze leader, Kamāl Jānbulāṭ. Despite its secular programme and a number of Christians on its council it was essentially a Druze party. The Arab National Movement, at first a loose grouping but from 1960 more tightly organised, was largely a Sunnī Muslim party stressing Pan-Arabism under Egyptian leadership and especially hostile to Israel. The Baʿth party had few followers in Lebanon and the Lebanese Communist Party appealed principally to the smaller minorities and to the Palestinian refugees.

From 1943 until 1958 the Lebanese political system was successful in providing a basis for considerable freedom and prosperity in Lebanon and with some modifications after that year it continued to do so until 1975. That it could do so depended upon it being asked to do very little. Whereas in every other part of the Near East one witnesses the often spectacular expansion of government activity, during the same period in Lebanon the government remained modest and unambitious. One may take as an example the provision of education. Most Lebanese went to private schools, usually maintained by the religious communities. In 1924 only 12 per cent were in public schools and as late as 1959 only 40 per cent. Higher education was provided mainly by two private foreign institutions, the American University of Beirut and St Joseph; the unfashionable Lebanese University was founded only in 1958. The largest institution in terms of numbers was another private venture, the Arab University, founded in 1960. Relative to the size of the population the bureaucracy and the army were much smaller than in other countries of the region, although the pressure of patronage demands tended always to expand the number of civil servants. It is arguable that the division of power on a confessional basis is only tolerable so long as there is not much power to divide; if the stakes become too great then those who feel that they have too small a share of the spoils will challenge the division or even the basis of the system.

The Lebanese economy ran with the minimum of government control and with much success. Lebanon is a small, densely populated mountainous country. Only one-quarter of the land is cultivable with the consequence that urbanization proceeded more rapidly in Lebanon than elsewhere. By the late 1960s about 50 per cent of the population of Lebanon lived in towns. Most, however, did not work in manufacturing industry but in construction or services. Of the gross national product 18 per cent came from agriculture, 12 per cent from industry and 70 per cent from services. An economy based upon private service industries is peculiarly well adapted to flourish without government controls. In 1948 Lebanon had adopted a policy of free trade and free currency exchange. Trade expanded and Beirut became the leading banking centre of the Near East. The economic and the political systems of Lebanon were in harmony. On the other hand the benefits accrued especially to those groups, mainly Christian but also including Sunnī Muslims, who controlled the service industries. Agricultural and industrial workers were much less content. For them increased state intervention in the economy could bring increased prosperity.

By 1958 the pressures from those who were discontented with the allocation of economic and political benefits in Lebanon had become strong, especially in Beirut whither had come migrants from hitherto quiescent rural communities, notably the Shīʿīs. The discontented were mobilized by two political leaders, Kamāl Jānbulāṭ and Ṣā'ib Salām in a challenge to the Maronite ascendancy personified by Kamīl Shamʿūn, who had succeeded Khūrī as President in 1952. The opportunity for their challenge was provided by the decision of Shamʿūn to seek a further term of office. Shamʿūn had made many enemies beginning with Kamāl Jānbulāṭ who had received no reward for helping Sham^{c}ūn to overthrow Khūrī and including many Maronites, notably the Patriarch himself. The international situation also favoured a challenge. Sham^{c}ūn and his foreign minister, Charles Mālik, were especially identified with a pro-Western policy and in 1957 had accepted the Eisenhower doctrine (see p.414). Inevitably this action placed Lebanon in opposition to Egypt, whose leader, ^{c}Abd al-Nāṣir, had become a hero for Lebanese Sunnī Muslims and all those who believed that Lebanon should pursue a Pan-Arab policy.

The disparate coalition of the National Front which confronted Sham^{c}ūn received a setback in the parliamentary elections of 1958 when many of its leaders were defeated. The National Front then turned to street demonstrations, strikes and violence. The Lebanese army refused to suppress the disturbances and the government sought help from the United States which landed a force of marines in July 1958. In fact a political solution was found when the commander of the Lebanese army, General Fu'ād Shihāb, was elected to succeed Sham^{c}ūn as president. Shihāb chose a member of the National Front, Rashīd al-Karāmī, as prime minister and, reluctantly, Karāmī gave places in his cabinet to followers of Sham^{c}ūn.

In many ways the events of 1958 were no more than another struggle between Lebanese notable factions and the solution was cast in a familiar form. The new features were first the international dimension and the way groups in Lebanon sought to enlist outsiders by representing their struggle as part of the Cold War or the fight for Arab nationalism: and second the involvement of the urban poor. In the longer term these two new elements would threaten the Lebanese political system as it had existed hitherto.

NOTES

1. Quoted Albert Hourani, *Syria and Lebanon*, 1946, 241.
2. Quoted Kamel S. Abu Jaber, *The Arab Ba'th Socialist Party*, New York 1966, xvii.
3. Quoted Abu Jaber, *op.cit.* 48.

CHAPTER FOUR

Palestine and Transjordan to 1950

PALESTINE

Palestine was another creation of the post First World War settlement. Under Ottoman rule there had been no Palestine; the region had been divided among three districts, each with its Ottoman officials and a representative council of local notables. One of these districts, the Sanjak of Jerusalem, covering southern Palestine, had had a special status and was directly responsible to the government in Istanbul. The other districts were parts of *vilayets* which included areas of Syria and Lebanon. To the Muslim population Palestine was only a geographical expression; to the Christians it was an historical memory with religious significance; and to the Jews it was roughly conterminous with the land of Israel. There was no agreement on what were the boundaries of Palestine, however, and the boundaries fixed were the result of political decisions and bargaining between Britain and France.

Geographically, Palestine was a southerly extension of Syria and possessed the same features, namely a coastal plain and a hilly interior dipping in the east to the deep valley of the Jordan. Beyond the Jordan the Jordanian hills were a prolongation of the anti-Lebanon range. The economy was mainly agricultural with some pastoral activity and handicrafts in a few modest towns of which the most important were Jerusalem in the interior and the coastal cities of Haifa, Jaffa and the new Jewish town of Tel Aviv.

The settled population of Palestine at the end of the First World War was of the order of 700,000; there were a further 50,000 or so nomads. Divided according to religion nearly four-fifths were Muslim, rather more than 10 per cent Christian and rather less than 10 per cent Jewish. The Muslims were mainly Sunnī but there were some Shīʿis and Druzes. The Muslim population was almost entirely Arabic-speaking and predominantly rural. The Christians included virtually all the sects common to the Near East although the largest number were Greek Orthodox and Catholics with the former having a slight preponderance. The Christians were also almost entirely Arabic speakers but proportionately more lived in towns, especially Jerusalem and other Christian holy centres. The Jewish population of about 65,000 was composed of several distinct groups: a few were descended from Jews who had never left Palestine, some (especially in Ṣafad in eastern Galilee) were descended from sixteenth-century Sephardic settlers from Spain, and about half were the product of the various Zionist settlements of the nineteenth and early twentieth centuries. Zionists in the narrower sense of adherents of the Zionist Congress probably composed about one quarter of the total Jewish population. The Jewish population included a number in agricultural settlements and some engaged in market gardening but the majority of Jews lived in towns, especially in Jerusalem and Tel Aviv. The Jewish population spoke several languages but Zionist policy was to promote the use of modern Hebrew.

The central feature of the history of Palestine under the British mandate is the change in the size and structure of the population. By 1947 the total population had increased to nearly two million. Of this total over two thirds were Arabs (including bedouin), both Christian and Muslim, and a little under one third Jewish. The Arab element had grown largely by natural increase assisted by some immigration from Syria, Lebanon and Transjordan. The Jewish element had grown principally by immigration. Of the population of 404,000 Jews in 1936 some 280,000 were immigrants. Jewish immigration was the principal political issue of the mandate period: to the Zionists it was the key to the construction of the Jewish state and to the Arabs it was a threat to their enjoyment of their country.

Jewish immigration into Palestine did not take place gradually but in waves. Zionist hopes of a sudden influx of Jewish immigrants into Palestine at the end of the war were disappointed. They blamed the attitude of the British military administration but there seems to have been no great enthusiasm by Jews to come to Palestine. Between 1920 and 1923 immigration averaged only 8,000 a year. Between 1923 and 1926 it rose substantially due in part to the ill-treatment of Jews by the nationalist Polish government and the severe restrictions placed in 1924 on immigration to the United States, the favoured destination of Jewish emigrants from eastern Europe. In the late 1920s, however, Jewish immigration into Palestine declined again and between 1927 and 1929 more Jews left Palestine than entered that country. Immigration did not pick up strongly again until 1933 but between 1933 and 1936 it reached its peak. In those years 166,000 immigrants entered Palestine. Jewish emigration to Palestine in this period is often associated with the coming to power of the Nazi party in Germany but although the number of German Jews among the immigrants increased considerably the majority came as before from eastern Europe and especially from Poland where the largest number of European Jews lived.

Three points may be noted about the Zionist immigration. First, the origin of the immigrants had a profound effect upon the character of the Jewish community in Palestine. They were east European and strongly Zionist. The leadership, which was drawn from those who had entered before 1914, was socialist. In background and outlook they had little in common with the Arabs, the older Jewish immigrants or the British administrators. Second, there was no clear relationship between immigration and Arab hostility. During the period before 1923 when immigration was small there was considerable expressed hostility. From 1923 until 1926, a period when many Jews entered Palestine, the country was quiet. In 1929, at a time when Jewish immigration was at an all time low, the most serious riots until that time occurred. Only in 1936 did the peak of immigration and widespread disturbances coincide. This apparent lack of connection between immigration and disturbances led some observers to conclude that hostility to Jewish immigration was not the major factor which Arab politicians declared it to be. Third, the size of the Jewish population was of crucial importance in shaping its political attitudes. Put simply, before 1936 the Jewish community was too small to stand alone and it needed the protection of the British umbrella. After 1936, at 400,000 and 30 per cent of the population, it could contemplate forming a state and if necessary dispense with British supervision.

The Jewish community in Palestine, the Yishuv, constituted under the British mandate a *millet* par excellence. It had what almost amounted to its own government in the form of the Jewish Agency. Article 4 of the mandate provided for the establishment of a Jewish Agency to advise and co-operate with the administration on matters affecting the establishment of the Jewish national home and the interests of the Jewish population in Palestine. The Zionist Organisation was selected to constitute the Agency but in the late 1920s this was dominated by the Yishuv representatives. The Yishuv also had its own national council, recognized by the administration in 1927. Through these and other bodies the Yishuv was able to exercise many of the functions of government. It ran its own schools, which taught in Hebrew; it had its own system of local government; and it had its own enclosed economy. The Jewish Federation of Labour (Histadrut, founded 1920) insisted that Jewish employers should employ only Jewish labour, a policy explicitly accepted by the administration in 1931. The Yishuv also had what amounted to its own army in the form of the Hagana, founded in 1920 in place of the system of settlement guards which had existed hitherto. By 1937 Hagana was over 10,000 strong with some 40,000 reservists.

The Yishuv had its own political structure composed of numerous political parties representing the many different shades of view in the Yishuv. The dominant group was the Labour party, which also was the controlling force in Histadrut and the Hagana. Its leader was David Ben Gurion who in the Yishuv was the counterpart of Chaim Weizmann in the Zionist Organisation. Weizmann dominated the international work of the Zionists especially among the Diaspora and Ben Gurion shaped the policy of the Yishuv. Of the other groups it is only necessary to note two. One was the bi-nationalists who advocated the creation of a bi-national state in Palestine with equal power for Jews and Arabs. The best known personality among the bi-nationalists was Judah Magnes. The other was the Revisionists whose leader was Vladimir Jabotinsky. The Revisionists opposed the British decision to separate Transjordan from the rest of the mandated area and generally declined any compromise which would endanger the goal of establishing a Jewish state in the whole of Palestine. It would be wrong to suppose that the Yishuv was preoccupied with its relations with the British and the Arabs. Rather it was concerned with the development of the Jewish community alone and endeavoured to shut itself off from outsiders.

Under its own management the Yishuv developed into a well-educated, relatively prosperous, mainly urban, European community. Education was given great prominence by the Yishuv. Article 15 of the mandate guaranteed communities the right to education in their own language and the Yishuv chose Hebrew. In 1925 the religious communities ordinance gave communities the right to tax their own members for education and the Yishuv took full advantage of this so that the budget for Jewish schools came to exceed that for government schools. The Yishuv also received financial support from the Diaspora through the Zionist Organisation. Because of the publicity given to the Zionist agricultural settlements it is sometimes supposed that the Yishuv was predominantly rural. This is a misapprehension: the great majority lived in towns and by 1935 more Jews lived in towns than

Arabs despite the fact that the Jewish population was less than a third of the size of the Arab. Of the Jewish agricultural population the majority were engaged in capitalist farming, market gardening around the towns or the production of citrus fruit for export. Others went into a variety of settlements, co-operative and communal. It was the communal settlements (kibbutzim) which attracted attention and admiration as examples of pioneering socialism and these came to be regarded as archetypes of Jewish settlement in Palestine. In fact only about 12 per cent of the Yishuv lived in kibbutzim although men from the kibbutzim came to exercise a powerful influence over the political life of the Yishuv and in the Hagana.

A final feature of the activities of the Jewish community to be considered was the programme of land purchase. It was the object of the Zionists to buy land on which to found settlements. In the early years of the mandate such purchases were mainly of sparsely inhabited uncultivated land purchased in large blocks from absentee landlords, for example the land of the Sursuq family in the Jezreel valley. From 1929 land purchases became a major issue in Palestine politics and it became difficult to find large tracts of suitable land for sale; purchases tended to be in smaller packets from private landlords and the Jewish National Fund played a larger part in the purchasing. In the 1930s and especially from 1936 onwards land purchases assumed a different character. With the prospect of partition purchases were directed towards securing possession of strategic tracts of land intended to consolidate Jewish settlements and ensure control of coastal and valley areas. In 1940 regulations were introduced to control Jewish purchases but these regulations had little effect. By May 1948 Jews had acquired by purchase some 2 million dunums (200,000 hectares) out of 26 million (2.6 million hs.) in Palestine, mainly in the coastal plain, the Jordan and Jezreel valleys, and in Galilee and Gaza. It is difficult to estimate how many Arabs were evicted but probably it was no more than a few thousands. The true importance of land purchases, however, lay in establishing a pattern of Jewish settlement which helped to shape the partition plan of 1947.

The majority of the Arab population of Palestine lived in villages working as cultivators, often as sharecroppers on the land of absentee landowners; in 1936 of an Arab population of 968,000 670,000 were cultivators living in 850 villages. The villages also contained a wealthier class of rural notables. Rather less than one third of the Arab population lived in towns where they were employed in construction, service industries, traditional handicrafts, a few modern industries and as professional teachers, bureaucrats, etc. There were also a number of merchants engaged in local, regional or international trade and many of the latter and the professionals were Christian.

The towns were also the homes of the Sunnī Muslim urban notables, a group very similar in style and composition to the urban notables of Syria and Iraq but with a drabber, provincial flavour. Palestine had no cities comparable to Aleppo, Baghdad and Damascus, all of which had been capitals of Ottoman provinces and its notables had competed for smaller prizes or departed to try to make their marks on a broader canvas. Nevertheless, Jerusalem possessed great religious prestige and its leading offices had been sought with passion. The urban notables had increased their power considerably during the late nineteenth and early twentieth centuries at the expense of the tribal shaykhs whose power the Ottomans had sought to limit. The 1858 Ottoman land law, which had promoted individual landownership, helped the urban notables to increase their landholding and their domination of local administrative posts and of the district councils gave them a substantial role in provincial government.

Nearly 50 urban notable families have been identified. In Nablus in central Palestine two notable families maintained a rivalry which had endured throughout the nineteenth century. These were the ᶜAbd al-Hādī family which, with the Nimrs, led the Yamanī faction, and the Tawqān family, leader of the Qaysī faction. (The epithets Yamanī and Qaysī once described Arabian tribal groups but in the course of time they had become mere labels for rival political factions.) In Acre in the north west were the Khalīfa and Shuqayrī families. Haifa was especially the centre of the Greek Catholics who continued to look longingly across the border towards their co-religionists in Lebanon. Jaffa had notables but was also a town of merchants. The principal centre of the notables was Jerusalem. One of the oldest families was the Khālidīs who claimed descent from Khālid ibn al-Walīd, the companion of the Prophet and the conqueror of Palestine. The Ḥusaynī family, which possessed extensive lands in southern Palestine, had risen to eminence in the nineteenth century. The principal rivals of the Ḥusaynīs during the mandate were the Nashāshībīs who had achieved distinction during the early twentieth century when they had acquired considerable lands. An indication of the standing of the Jerusalem families may be gained from noting that before 1914 all the representatives of Jerusalem in the Ottoman parliament came from four families: the ᶜAlamīs (another old Jerusalem family), the Ḥusaynīs, the Khālidīs and the Nashāshībīs.

The rivalry of the Ḥusaynīs and the Nashāshībīs was a crucial factor in shaping the politics of the Palestinian Arab community during the early years of the mandate. The leader of the Ḥusaynī faction, Kamāl al-Ḥusaynī, who co-operated with the British, died in 1921 and was succeeded as *muftī* of Jerusalem by al-Ḥājj Muḥammad Amīn al-Ḥusaynī. The office of *muftī* of Jerusalem, which combined the roles of giver of legal opinions with some administrative functions, had not been especially important in the past but it had increased in significance during the late Ottoman period and under the British it became an office of power. The choice of Ḥājj Amīn was contrived by Britain and was controversial because of Amīn's youth and lack of religious knowledge. His position was greatly enhanced in January 1922 when he was chosen to head the new Supreme Muslim Council, an institution created by Britain to look after the affairs of the Muslim community, including the Sharīᶜa courts and the *waqfs*. At once Ḥājj Amīn was given control of considerable financial resources (*waqf* income was £50,000 p.a. and rising), patronage and networks. He was not the undisputed leader of the Ḥusaynī faction, however. A feature of notable politics was not only the rivalries between families but the rivalries within them; until his death in 1934 the most respected member of the Ḥusaynī family was the venerable Mūsā al-Kāẓim al-Ḥusaynī. Another office of power and prestige was that of mayor of Jerusalem and this was held by the leader of the Nashāshībī faction, Rāghib Bey, a former deputy in the Ottoman parliament.

Down to 1936 Palestine Arab politics were the politics of notables. All political parties were based on families or clans and on traditional alliances. Notables controlled the early local Muslim–Christian associations and the national organization, the Arab Executive. During the 1930s parties with a more modern style and ideological programmes made their appearance but they were essentially notable parties. The Palestine Arab Party (1935) was the party of the Ḥusaynīs and the National Defence Party (1934) of the Nashāshībīs: the Reform Party (1935) was a party of lesser notables under Khālidī leadership, and the Istiqlāl Party (1932) was dominated by the ᶜAbd al-Hādīs. These parties, and especially the Istiqlāl Party, did include a number of young professionals, but they remained essentially vehicles of the ambitions of their leaders. All had basically the same objective: an independent Arab Palestine; their differences were about tactics and allies. The Ḥusaynīs and the ᶜAbd al-Hādīs favoured a Pan-Arab stance; the Nashāshībīs and Khālidīs looked to Amir ᶜAbdallāh in Transjordan. The notables also dominated the Arab Higher Committee, the party leaders' coalition formed in 1936, but they lost some control over events during the Arab rebellion of 1937–9 when power slipped to new groups. But the notables returned to dominate Palestinian Arab politics again in the 1940s. The 1944 Ḥusaynī Palestinian Arab Party was better organized with local branches, more efficient and embraced even peasants, but it remained a notable party.

To what extent did Palestinian Arabs think of themselves as a political community? Before 1918 there was very little idea of Palestine among them although they were conscious of a certain common interest in opposing Zionist settlement. Nor was Arabism so prominent in Palestine as it was in Syria. In 1918 Palestinian Arabs faced the same dilemma as other Ottoman Arabs: what political identity and goals should replace their lost Ottoman personality. Those in Nablus looked to Fayṣal in Damascus and accepted the view of Palestine as southern Syria; those in Jerusalem were less anxious to acknowledge Fayṣal's rule. Most Palestinians organized themselves as local communities through the Muslim–Christian associations. In July 1920 the southern Syrian option was excluded by the fall of Fayṣal and Palestinians were obliged to choose again. Under the leadership of the Ḥusaynīs they emphasized a Palestinian identity which permitted Muslim–Christian co-operation, was acceptable to Britain and fitted the political arena in which they operated. The Palestinian Arab identity was very much an élite choice, however, and it had little appeal to the masses. When peasants and the lower classes in towns became drawn into the political struggle during the 1930s the most powerful bond proved to be Islam. Also during the 1930s, with the rise of other Arab states, the appeal of Pan-Arabism strengthened again. Even in 1948 Palestinian Arabs still thought of themselves primarily as members of families or of local, religious or ethnic communities rather than as Palestinians. Nevertheless, during the mandate Palestinians had acquired Palestinian institutions and the habit of working in and with these institutions had promoted in some measure the growth of a Palestinian identity. For, during the mandate government institutions were Palestinian Arab institutions, the Yishuv having opted out.

The British administration of Palestine began in 1917 as a military administration in the occupied territories and it continued as a military administration until 1 July 1920 when a civil administration assumed control of Palestine. Under the civil administration power passed to civilians, to a high commissioner in Jerusalem and the central departments of government, six district governors (later commissioners) and a structure of district officers who included a number of Arabs (26 in 1925). In London control passed in 1921 from the Foreign Office to the Colonial Office. Within the Colonial Office there was established a Middle East department the officials of which were given immediate charge of Palestine affairs. The dominant influences on policy down to 1936 were the high commissioner and the colonial secretary and their permanent officials. Except in 1929–31 the cabinet made no significant intervention. From 1936 the matter was different; then the Foreign Office, through the cabinet, began to assert a leading role in policy in Palestine.

The British programme for Palestine was contained in the mandate, the drafting of which was carried out during the latter part of 1919 and early 1920, although the mandate was not published until 1922 and formal ratification of the award by the Council of the League of Nations took place in 1923. The Palestine mandate differed from other class A mandates in certain important respects. In Syria, Lebanon and Iraq it was required that the mandatory should work towards the independence of the country concerned and while setting out no detailed timetable stated that a start should be made within three years. In Palestine there was no such stipulation. Instead the Palestine mandate incorporated the Zionist programme. In the preamble the Balfour Declaration of 1917 was repeated and some articles related to aspects of progress to be made in establishing the Jewish national home. Article 2 stated that the mandatory should establish "such political, administrative and economic conditions as will secure the establishment of the Jewish national home".[1] Article 6 obliged the mandatory to facilitate Jewish immigration and encourage close settlement by Jews on the land. Both of these articles also contained provisions that the rights of other sections of the population should not be prejudiced but the thrust of the mandate was plainly towards the fulfilment of the Zionist programme. This circumstance was unsurprising as the original draft had been prepared by the Zionist Organisation which had been closely involved throughout the discussions.

The British commitment to Zionism was criticized from the beginning. The military administration had urged the British government to slow down implementation, the Foreign Office had expressed grave reservations about the wisdom of the policy and the appropriateness of the mandate and even some earlier supporters of Zionism such as Ronald Graham became disillusioned. "Weizmann", Graham remarked to Ronald Storrs, "has sold us a pup."[2] Lloyd George and Balfour remained solid in their support of the policy, however, the commitment was confirmed, some of the doubters removed and in 1920 the military administration itself was replaced against its own advice. The downfall of the military administration was precipitated by the Jerusalem disturbances of Easter 1920. Criticism of the Zionists by Palestinian Arabs had been gathering strength for a year and there were demonstrations in Jerusalem in February, March and April 1920. The last of these erupted into riots, the military administration was blamed and it was decided that the civil administration should take over in the summer. Herbert Samuel was appointed high commissioner.

From 1920 until 1923 Britain began implementation of the Zionist programme and tried to win acceptance of the mandate from Palestinian Arabs and establish some representative institutions. Samuel, a former Liberal cabinet minister and a Jew, had been a strong supporter of Zionism since 1914 but he was also conscious of the strength of Palestinian opposition to Zionism. Samuel was confirmed in his fears by the Jaffa riots of May 1921. These disturbances, which began as a conflict between rival Jewish groups, transposed into Arab–Jewish clashes and spread to include attacks on neighbouring Jewish settlements, were the most serious of the early years of the mandate. They had a powerful effect upon Samuel who temporarily suspended Jewish immigration, endeavoured to allay Arab fears about the Zionist programme and increased his constitutional offers to the Arabs.

Samuel made three attempts to draw in the Arabs: through an advisory council, a legislative council and an Arab agency. The advisory council was established before the Jaffa riots in October 1920. It had 21 members of whom 11 were officials and 10 non-officials, The latter number included 4 Muslims, 3 Christians and 3 Jews, all nominated by the high commissioner. Although it had no power the advisory council functioned satisfactorily in that useful exchanges of views took place on routine matters of government. After the riots Samuel opened constitutional negotiations. These negotiations were conducted partly in London with an Arab delegation which was chosen by the fourth Palestinian Arab Congress at the end of May 1921. The leader of the Arab delegation was Mūsā al-Kāẓim al-Ḥusaynī, who had been chosen to head the Arab Executive Committee set up by the third Palestinian Congress in December 1920.

Negotiations of one sort and another were carried on in London, with frequent references to Palestine, for more than a year. The Arabs demanded a national government, the abandonment of the Zionist programme and unity with other Arab states. They made it plain, however, that they would accept a representative council so long as it had power to control Jewish immigration. This was the sticking point because the British government would not concede what amounted to abandonment of the Zionist programme. To do so, the cabinet minuted, " would seriously reduce the prestige of this country in the eyes of Jews throughout the world".[3] Instead Britain tried to promulgate her own constitution. The scheme, published in August 1922, provided for a representative assembly consisting of 22 elected members, including at least 2 Christians and at least 2 Jews. The assembly could discuss any matter it chose but it could make no law which was inconsistent with the mandate. Samuel called elections but they were boycotted by the Arabs and he was obliged to abandon the scheme. Instead he tried to reconstitute the advisory council but the Arabs had now come to see that institution as a stalking horse for the unwanted legislative council and refused to co-operate.

Samuel's last attempt to draw in the Arabs was the scheme for an Arab agency. The scheme was Samuel's but it was produced by a cabinet sub-committee on Palestine appointed in July 1923. The sub-committee included opponents of the Zionist programme among whom was the foreign secretary, Lord Curzon, himself. Curzon, inevitably, was the dominant figure. It was hoped by the Arabs that Britain would now pull back from Zionism. The Arabs were disappointed. The sub-committee reported that there could be no retreat from commitment to the Zionist programme without giving up the mandate, the consequence of which would be that Palestine would be occupied by France, Italy or even Turkey. Moreover, the abandonment of the Balfour promise would involve too great a sacrifice of British honour. All that was offered was the Arab agency, a body to represent Arab interests as the Jewish agency represented Jewish. Its members were to be nominated by the high commissioner. The agency was a good deal inferior to the legislative council which had already been spurned and the Arabs again rejected the offer. There were no further offers of constitutional progress at the centre for some years.

There is little doubt that the Palestinian Arabs missed a great opportunity during the years 1921–3. A legislative council would have given them a platform, the elections would have spurred on their political organization and they would have been better placed to form an effective alliance with sympathizers in the administration and the Colonial Office. They rejected the chance because they were unable to see past the limited powers of the council to its potential as a pressure point, because they hoped for better offers from a new government in London and because of their own factional differences which made it difficult for any of them to compromise for fear of being outbid by rivals.

The negotiations took place against a background of events elsewhere which inevitably influenced the position of those involved.

One factor was the circumstance that the mandate had yet to be finally approved by the League. Another was the struggle in Turkey which resulted in the defeat of the Greeks in September 1922 and the long delicate negotiations leading up to the Treaty of Lausanne in July 1923. A government which had been obliged to abandon one of the main pillars of the Near Eastern settlement was unlikely to wish to be seen to relinquish another. The example of developments in Iraq and Egypt also encouraged the Palestinian Arabs to hope for better offers. And in London the period was one of dramatic political change with the fall of the coalition government of Lloyd George. The impact of these events is uncertain but students of Palestine would be unwise to ignore them.

One initiative which came out of these years was the White Paper of June 1922. This was a redefinition of the meaning of the mandate which emphasized Britain's commitment to support of Zionism but played down the implications of Zionism for Palestine. On immigration the White Paper established the principle of regulation according to "the economic capacity of the country at the time to absorb new arrivals".[4] It was also the vehicle of constitutional promises. The White Paper represented no change of policy, however. The general remarks about British policy involved no commitment, regulation according to economic absorptive capacity was impossible to operate and the constitutional plans bore no fruit.

Samuel's successor, Lord Plumer (1925–8), turned away from constitutional development towards the encouragement of local institutions of self government and the enlargement of Samuel's policy of the increased employment of Arabs in the administration. He introduced elected municipal councils, employed more Arab district officers and tried to increase the powers of the village headmen (*mukhtārs*). Plumer was able to put off further consideration of constitutional developments because of the general economic prosperity of the period and the quietness of the political scene. Arab demands did not cease but they did not seem importunate. It began to seem as though anti-Zionism had run its course and the original hopes that Palestinian opposition would pass would be realized.

It was the so-called Wailing Wall riots of August 1929 which challenged these optimistic speculations and ushered in the next crisis in Palestinian affairs. The riots began in Jerusalem in a dispute over Jewish access to the western wall of the temple mound for prayer and spread to other parts of the country. The riots had three main effects. Within the Arab community they enhanced the position of Ḥājj Amīn al-Ḥusaynī who could depict himself as the defender of Muslim rights. Within the Jewish community they inspired fear and distrust of the Arabs. And to the British they indicated the need to think again about the mandate policy.

Proposals which would have drastically modified the Zionist programme were brought forward by the high commissioner, Sir John Chancellor (1928–31). Chancellor interpreted the riots as indicating widespread Arab opposition to Zionism and argued that the only way to carry out the mandate was by force. The alternative was to ask for a revision of the mandate to eliminate the clauses which gave Jews a privileged position in Palestine. He proposed the revival of the legislative council scheme and the introduction of controls on Jewish immigration and land purchases. Many of Chancellor's arguments were supported by a commission of inquiry into the causes of the riots and by a separate inquiry into the land problem. His proposals resulted in a new White Paper issued by the colonial secretary, Lord Passfield, in October 1930.

The Passfield White Paper rejected the idea of a revision of the mandate and reaffirmed the interpretation of the mandate given in the Churchill White Paper of 1922. But it also stated that new proposals for a legislative council would be brought forward and gave clear indications that restrictions on Jewish immigration and land purchases would be introduced. The new White Paper produced strong criticism from the Zionists, from members of the Conservative opposition and from others inside and outside Britain. In February 1931 the cabinet decided to draw back, a decision announced in a public letter from the prime minister, Ramsay Macdonald to Weizmann. The White Paper was not repudiated but it was made clear that there would be no additional restrictions on immigration and no restrictions on land transfers pending a further inquiry. The legislative council remained on the agenda but talks on this broke down because of Zionist demands for parity.

The failure of the 1930 attempt to change direction in Palestine was partly due to pro-Zionist sentiment in the governing Labour Party, partly to the circumstance that the Macdonald government was a minority government dependent upon Liberal votes when the Liberals were supportive of Zionism and partly because of Foreign Office opposition on the grounds that a change in policy would have a bad effect on Britain's international interests. Passfield informed Chancellor that political and international reasons were paramount in present circumstances. Reading the discussions of the period it is plain that what weighed chiefly with Britain was, once again, prestige. In 1929 the Foreign Office had refused to contemplate going to the League to ask for the revision of the mandate which Chancellor had requested and the strongest argument levelled against the White Paper was that it constituted a breach of the mandate for which Britain could legally be called to account.

The period from 1931 to 1935 saw significant changes in Palestine. The politicization of the Arab community gained pace. Among the notables the events of 1929 to 1931 had strengthened the position of the Ḥusaynīs and of Ḥājj Amīn in particular. He now appeared as both a radical and Muslim leader. Islam grew as a force in the Palestinian politics: at one level Ḥājj Amīn promoted a World Islamic Congress and at another there was a growth of lower class Muslim organizations. The most spectacular example of the new salience of Islam was the career of Shaykh ᶜIzz al-Dīn al-Qassām, who collected a following of peasant immigrants to Haifa and began attacking Jewish settlements in the Jezreel valley in the early 1930s. He was eventually killed in November 1935 and became a martyred hero to those who followed. A second challenge to notable leadership came from young urban nationalists with a professional background who were organized into several youth societies. By 1935 Palestinian Arabs were more self-conscious, more organized, more radical, more Muslim and more ready for violence. At the same time the Yishuv was far stronger as a result of the development of its own institutions and the great inflow of immigrants from 1933. The stage was set for a major confrontation which took place in 1936.

By 1936 the path of constitutional advance seemed closed. In the autumn of 1935 the high commissioner had put forward a new proposal for a partly elected, legislative council of 28 members (14 Arabs, 7 Jews, 2 commercial representatives and 5 British officials) with powers limited by the high commissioner's veto, together with suggestions for restrictions on Jewish immigration and land purchase. The Arab political parties were divided in their reaction to the scheme; the Zionists were strongly hostile. It was opposed in Parliament and the government abandoned the scheme.

In April 1936 disturbances commenced in Palestine, influenced by the successful riots, demonstrations and strikes in Egypt and Syria. The disturbances began on 15 April, and on 20 April the Nablus nationalist committee called for a national strike. The notables, taken unawares, struggled to gain control of events and on 25 April formed a coalition of party leaders, the Arab Higher Committee to organize the strike. The strike spread in urban areas, accompanied by violence which from May extended to rural areas. Armed bands with Muslim slogans were formed. Volunteers entered Palestine from Iraq, Syria and Transjordan.

The strike and its accompanying violence continued until 10 October when the Arab Higher Committee called it off in response to appeals from Arab governments. The involvement of the Arab states was one of the most important results of the events of 1936. Hitherto Britain had resisted any attempts by outsiders to become involved but from April 1936 onwards there were approaches from Arab governments and in June Britain changed her policy and invited assistance in settling the disturbances. Much controversy attends both the reasons for the involvement of other Arabs and the wisdom of the British decision to admit them to discussions on the future of Palestine.

The Arab states became involved partly because they were impelled by popular pressure and partly to advance their interests or enhance their own importance. There was popular Arab interest in affairs in Palestine in 1936 and earlier. Arab intellectuals, students and many of the poorer inhabitants of Damascus, Cairo and Baghdad took part in demonstrations, fund raising or served as volunteers. There was genuine popular pressure on Egyptian governments to intervene in a matter about which they cared little. The position of the National Bloc in Syria was similar. There was also a Muslim interest, strengthened as a result of the events of 1929–30, and this interest was especially marked in Saudi Arabia. Arab governments could represent themselves as responding to popular enthusiasm in making representations about Palestine. It is also true that some Arab governments, notably that of ᶜAbdallāh in Transjordan, had ambitions in Palestine and others were unwilling to allow Transjordan, or any other state, to claim an influence when they were excluded. The British decision to allow intervention was shaped partly by a belief that the Arab states could help to end the strike but also by a notion that for international reasons it was as well to conciliate Arab states in the region. Britain made no concession to the Arab states other than that they might give evidence to a new inquiry into the affairs of Palestine.

The British commission of inquiry, the Peel Commission, was a watershed in the affairs of Palestine. The causes of the disturbances, it reported on 7 August 1937, were the Arab desire for independence and Arab hatred of Zionism. Its verdict was that the mandate was unworkable because the Jewish and Arab communities were irreconcilable. and it recommended partition as the best solution.

Britain accepted the recommendation, the Zionists agreed with reservations about the size of the Jewish state, and the Arabs rejected partition. Some moderate Arabs might have accepted the proposal had the proposed Jewish state been smaller and if there had been immediate restrictions on immigration and land purchase but as it was there were no takers and at the Bludan conference of 8 September 1937 the Palestinian Arabs were supported by Arabs from other countries. Arab rejection was followed by the great Arab rebellion of 1937–9, an event comparable in magnitude to the 1919 uprising in Egypt, the 1920 rising in Iraq and the Syrian rebellion of 1925–7.

The Arab rebellion was primarily a rural movement. There were disturbances in towns but these were kept under control. In rural areas, however, the violence of 1936 had never entirely subsided and in October 1937 turned into widespread revolt. There were three main areas of disturbance: in Galilee in the north, in the region south and west of Jerusalem and the most serious disturbances in the central region of Tulkarm, Jenin, Nablus and Ramallah. The revolt had no general leadership: in October 1937 the British arrested some members of the Arab Higher Committee and others, including the Muftī, Ḥājj Amīn, fled. From Damascus the Muftī endeavoured to direct events but control was in the hands of local commanders. About 10,000 villagers were involved in all with a hard core of 3,000 full time guerrillas. They directed their attacks primarily against government property: roads, bridges, telegraph wires, police stations and officials although their principal targets were often Arabs suspected of collaborating with government. The revolt had many aspects apart from the struggle against government, including factional disputes within villages, peasants against landlords, Muslim against Jew, Christian and Druze, and political rivalries – several moderates were killed by partisans of the Ḥusaynīs. There was also an element of traditional banditry. Economic misery does not seem to have been a major factor: Palestine had never been more prosperous and the regions worst affected were not the areas where Jewish land purchases had taken place and peasants been evicted. The rebels received help from outside: money, especially from Iraq, volunteers from Syria and sympathy from several Arab states.

Although the high commissioner and the colonial secretary argued in favour of an attempt to end the revolt by conciliation of the Arabs the cabinet decided on military repression. Reasons of strategy and prestige demanded that Britain should not give way to violence. But the British found it no easy task to suppress so widespread a movement and for the first year the revolt continued to grow reaching a peak in October 1938. Thereafter, with the resolution of the Munich crisis Britain was able to send reinforcements, and patrols, village searches and collective punishments eventually reduced the disturbances to no more than sporadic troubles by March 1939.

The revolt had four main results. First, it caused a widespread breakdown of economic and social institutions. Under dual pressure from the rebels and the British, village structures crumbled. Second, it led to a temporary breakdown of government and a permanent blow to the administrative structures Britain had created. Pressure on Arab government servants – district officers, *mukhtārs* and schoolteachers – was often unbearable and the pattern of collaboration built up since the 1920s was destroyed. Third, the revolt strengthened the Yishuv's military position through the experience of the revolt and the training received, increased support for the Revisionists who launched their own campaign of killing, and greatly weakened the position of the bi-nationalists. Fourth, the revolt helped to persuade Britain to abandon partition.

Between 1937 and 1939 Britain completely changed her plans for the future of Palestine. This was partly for practical reasons concerned with the difficulties revealed when the question of partition was studied in detail. It was partly because of Zionist lack of enthusiasm and Arab hostility. The main reason was international. The support of other Arab states for the Palestinian Arabs suggested that if Britain persisted with the partition scheme she would risk alienating those states. With the prospect of war with Germany and Italy in Europe and the danger that these powers might establish their influence in the Arab Near East across Britain's imperial communications this risk was unacceptable, the Foreign Office argued. The cabinet agreed. Partition was finally abandoned in September 1938, the month of Munich.

The new policy was announced in a White Paper in May 1939. It was preceded by an attempt to procure agreement between the Arabs (including representatives of Egypt, Iraq, Transjordan, Saudi Arabia and Yemen) and the Zionists at a conference in London. When this conference failed to produce agreement Britain produced her own solution. Britain announced that Palestine would become independent in ten years. In the interim self-governing institutions would be established and Jewish immigration would be limited to 75,000 over the next five years. Further, immigration thereafter would be subject to an Arab veto. There would also be strict control over land sales. The plan was rejected by Zionists and Palestinian Arabs. The rejection by the former was unsurprising because the scheme ended all hope of a Jewish state in Palestine and put a question mark against the future of the Jewish community in Palestine, condemned as it was to become a permanent and diminishing minority in the population. The Arab rejection, apparently because of a provision for a constitutional review after five years, was another sign of the curious, uncompromising appearance of the politics of notables; compromise was always sought but could not be sought visibly.

The war prevented the full implementation of the 1939 scheme and changed the nature of the Palestine question. First, the circumstance that the Near East was a centre of military operations until 1943 ensured that Britain had neither the time nor the inclination for a major constitutional experiment in Palestine. Land sale regulations were introduced in 1940 and immigration was controlled, but, despite pressure from Arab states, no serious action was taken on other proposals. In 1943 the possibility of partition was reopened by a Cabinet sub-committee but the initiative was abandoned after the murder of Lord Moyne, the Minister Resident in the Middle East, by Jewish terrorists on 6 November 1944. In any case Britain could not easily find Palestinian Arabs with whom to deal. Ḥājj Amīn threw in his lot first with Britain's opponents in Iraq and subsequently with Germany and there were no obvious alternative leaders.

Second, the attitude of the United States became a factor in the Palestine situation. The Nazi onslaught on the Jews of Europe led to strong pressure from several sources, notably from Zionists in the United States, to open Palestine to unrestricted Jewish immigration. Disasters to two ships carrying Jewish refugees, the *Patria* (blown up by Zionists in Haifa harbour on 25 November 1940) and the *Struma* (sunk in the Black Sea on 25 February 1942), publicized the plight of Jews seeking to escape to Palestine. Nazi persecution of the Jews persuaded Jews everywhere to support the Zionist demand for a Jewish state in Palestine. In 1939 Zionism had been a minority movement among American Jews: by the end of the war an estimated 80 per cent were supporters. Efforts to mobilize American Jews against the 1939 White Paper had not been very successful but news of the Final Solution which spread in the latter part of 1942 changed attitudes dramatically. The May 1942 American Zionist Biltmore declaration for a Jewish Commonwealth in Palestine became the policy of American Jews in general in 1943. Skilful organization notably by Stephen Wise of the American Jewish Committee and his rival, Abba Silver, ensured that their views became dominant in the United States Congress.

A third change was in the position of the Yishuv. The war had placed the Yishuv in a difficult position; it was totally opposed to British policy in Palestine but supported Britain against Nazi Germany. Some Revisionists (the Stern Gang) maintained their armed struggle against Britain but the leadership of the community sought on the one hand to acquire military experience and weapons by fighting alongside Britain and on the other to circumvent the White Paper. Illegal immigration continued and the land sale regulations were evaded. Hagana increased its strength and by 1944 numbered 37,000 although only 6,000 were well trained troops. By 1945 the Yishuv was much better placed to resist by force the imposition of uncongenial policies. In October 1945 it launched a general campaign against Britain in Palestine. The Hagana concentrated on illegal immigration and attacks on British communications and the Revisionist organizations attacked British personnel. Their single greatest success was the blowing up of the British headquarters in the King David Hotel in Jerusalem on 22 July 1946 but between 1945 and 1947 they contrived to disrupt British government in Palestine.

Britain returned to serious consideration of the future of Palestine in 1945. The central figure in the making of British policy was Ernest Bevin, foreign secretary in the newly elected Labour government. The Labour Party had historically been sympathetic to the claims of Zionism but Bevin considered the question from the point of view of British interests in the Middle East as a whole. The options were to continue with the 1939 White Paper policy of a unitary Arab-dominated state, partition, a Palestine solution within an Arab federation, cantonization or some other scheme of provincial autonomy within Palestine, or a reference to the United Nations. There was no longer any serious idea of continuing with the original mandate policy. Bevin held no strong views about what the solution should be but was convinced that it must be acceptable to the Arab states of the region and that the United States must be persuaded to support that solution. To Bevin Palestine was less important for its own sake than for the effect of British policy there on the Middle East as a whole.

In addition to the question of the long term future government of Palestine there was a short term problem of the Jewish refugees in Europe. Largely through the efforts of Zionists the notion became current that there were 100,000 Jewish refugees in Europe who wanted to start a new life in Palestine. It was demanded that these should be admitted at once and in the circumstances of the revelations of the dreadful fate which had befallen the Jews of Nazi-controlled Europe there was widespread support for this demand. To admit them would breach the 1939 White Paper policy which until December 1945 remained official British policy and Bevin was reluctant to do this until he had another policy to put in its place. He saw the opportunity to enlist the aid of the United States in solving the problem of the refugees and proposed an Anglo–American committee of inquiry into the matter. At United States' insistence the scope of the inquiry was widened to take in the situation in Palestine and the committee's inquiry inevitably turned into one which was in part about the future of Palestine.

Bevin failed to obtain United States help in Palestine. The Anglo–American Committee reported on 1 May 1946 in favour of the immediate admission of the 100,000 refugees and the establishment of a bi-national state in Palestine under United Nations' trusteeship. It was a solution which no-one wanted. It was opposed by Arabs and Zionists; the British government eventually concluded it was impractical although Bevin was willing to try if the United States agreed; and whilst President Truman endorsed the recommendation for the admission of the refugees he did nothing effective about the bi-national proposal. An Anglo–American group set up to study the recommendation came up with a different proposal for a provincial autonomy scheme but Truman refused to endorse this scheme either. In August Truman indicated his own preference for partition, a view he made public in a speech on 4 October 1946.

The American refusal to be drawn into an Anglo–American scheme for the solution of the Palestine question was a heavy blow to Britain. It was unlikely that the Zionists could have been brought to agree to the provincial autonomy scheme or, indeed, that the Arabs would have accepted it either. The scheme was drafted with such skill that the Arabs claimed it was a step towards partition and the Zionists a move towards an Arab-dominated unitary state. It was recognized by Britons that either could be the result. However, any chance of agreement at the London conference summoned by Britain to discuss the question in September–October 1946 evaporated in the light of Truman's attitude. In August 1946 the Zionists had come to realize that a Jewish state in the whole of Palestine was not a practicable goal under the circumstances and had opted for partition in preference to provincial autonomy. Truman's support confirmed them in the wisdom of their choice. In December the moderate Zionist leaders, Weizmann and Wise, who still favoured continued negotiation with Britain, were overthrown by the radicals, Ben Gurion and Silver. When the London conference reassembled in January–February 1947 to reconsider the provincial autonomy scheme there was no agreement. It was also clear that no scheme of partition would be agreed.

In February 1947 Britain referred the Palestine question to the United Nations. It is important to understand that this was not a surrender of the mandate but a decision to seek advice and it is pertinent to ask what Britain expected would be the result. No doubt some Britons supposed that it was the prelude to getting out of Palestine; after all, at almost the same time Britain had taken the much larger decision to set a time limit to leave India. But it is doubtful if those most closely involved in Palestine affairs saw the matter in this light. It was generally believed that the United Nations would fail to find a solution if for no other reason than that the USSR would prevent agreement on one. In that case the UN was likely to come back to Britain whose position in enforcing a solution would be immeasurably strengthened and who would now be supported in her efforts by the United States for want of any alternative to Britain.

The United Nations solution to the Palestine question was partition. The United Nations Special Committee on Palestine (UNSCOP), appointed 13 May, delivered two reports on 31 August 1947. The majority recommended the partition of Palestine into three elements: an Arab state, a Jewish state and an international zone embracing Jerusalem. The minority recommended an independent, federal state. With modifications the majority scheme was adopted by the United Nations on 29 November by a vote of 33:13 with 10 abstentions. The British mandate was to terminate on 1 May 1948. The result was assured first by the support of the USSR for partition and second by the efforts of the United States to mobilize votes in favour of the recommendation.

The United States played a decisive role in the resolution of the Palestine question in 1946–7. US policy was determined almost wholly by the White House. Neither the State Department nor Defence was happy with US policy, believing that US interests would be better served by a more even-handed policy which might safeguard US interests in the Arab world. As late as February–March 1948 the State Department tried to change US policy, postpone the application of the UN decision and substitute a scheme of trusteeship for Palestine. Truman, however, stood firm for partition. Truman's policy was guided by several considerations. Simple humanitarianism played a significant role in his attitude to the refugees. Another factor was a desire to avoid entering into financial or military commitments in Palestine: trusteeship it was calculated would have required more than 100,000 troops. Yet another was to uphold US and UN prestige once the UN decision was taken. But very high in Truman's mind were political considerations, namely the importance of the Jewish vote.

Britain had already taken her decision to withdraw from Palestine in September 1947. Partly this decision was the result of the UNSCOP recommendation but partly it was the burden of Palestine. Palestine locked up 80,000 British troops supported by 20,000 police and cost nearly £40 million a year. In the difficult economic position of post-war Britain this drain on resources was difficult to tolerate. Moreover, the effort had failed to achieve the end of establishing security in Palestine where civil and military authority were breaking down. The murder of two British sergeants by Revisionists on 20 July 1947 caused widespread revulsion in Britain against the Palestine connection. Palestine was also very damaging to Britain's international reputation. The episode of the *Exodus*, a ship loaded with refugees which in the summer of 1947 sailed from Marseilles to Palestine in the full glare of publicity, was turned away and eventually arrived in Germany, was extremely embarrassing.

Britain had also decided that she would not implement the United Nations solution. The UNSCOP recommendations had been based on the assumption that Britain would administer their solutions for two or three years but Britain decided that to associate herself with partition would inevitably damage her relations with the Arab states which opposed that solution. Britain's decision was confirmed by the cabinet in November when it was decided that British troops would be withdrawn by 1 August 1948, and on 11 December it was announced that Britain would surrender the mandate on 15 May. The last British troops left Haifa on 30 June 1948. During the period before May 1948 Britain refused to take any action which might aid either side and refused also to permit the entry into Palestine of other forces, whether Arab or United Nations observers. The result was that Arabs and Jews were left to fight for Palestine.

From November 1947 until May 1948 a civil war took place in Palestine between Jews and Arabs. In numbers of fighters the two sides were roughly equal although the Jews had a superiority in men in the military age group which gradually had its effect. More to the point Jewish operations were better co-ordinated. From November until March the Jews were on the defensive, partly because their strategy of holding settlements tied down numbers of troops in small packets, but they succeeded in holding the territories allocated to them. In April and May they shifted to the offensive, gained control of the towns of mixed population, including Haifa and Jaffa, and extended their control in areas allocated to Arab Palestine. The Arabs were disorganized. The nominal leader was Ḥājj Amīn but different groups fought without co-ordination and sometimes, as in Lydda, fought each other. The Palestinian Arabs received only limited help from outside, mainly consisting of some 3,000 volunteers of the Arab Liberation Army.

On the Arab side power had shifted from the Palestinian Arabs to the Arab states, now grouped in the Arab League. In Palestine the position of the old notables had declined owing to economic changes, which had led to the greater prominence of the new commercial towns of Haifa and Jaffa, and the political blows suffered by the Palestinian notables after 1936. But the new forces had not produced new political organizations and leaders and the strongest political force in Palestine after 1945 was the reconstituted Palestinian Arab Party of the Ḥusaynīs. The British preferred to deal with the Arab states and it was the Arab League which took the lead in the recreation of the Arab Higher Committee in June 1946. The Arab states rejected entirely the UN decision on Palestine and prepared for war in May 1948. During the winter of 1947–8 the Arab states (Iraq, Lebanon, Syria, Transjordan and the Palestinian Arabs) set up a military committee and tried to co-ordinate military and political action. They found it impossible to agree what that action should be or to allocate adequate forces to Palestine. One problem was the attitude of ᶜAbdallāh of Transjordan who foresaw that the Palestinian Arab state would be unable to stand alone and hoped, with the aid of his Arab Legion and with British and Jewish consent, to take over Arab Palestine. He would not commit his forces to co-operation with other Arab forces for indeterminate operations in Palestine aimed at eliminating the Jewish state. The consequence was that when the Arab states intervened with their own forces in May 1947 they did so with no agreed goals or plan of action and each fought as a separate army.

From May 1948 until January 1949 the war was an international war between the newly established state of Israel (proclaimed 14 May 1948) and the Arab states of Egypt, Iraq, Lebanon, Syria and Transjordan. It was punctuated by a number of truces during which the UN tried in vain to mediate a settlement. The truces divide the war into stages. Before the first truce on 11 June 1948 the two sides had reached a military stalemate. In the second stage of the war (8–18 July) the Israelis, rearmed and equipped, launched an offensive which gave them control of the whole of Galilee, including western Galilee which had been allocated to the Arab state. In the third stage of the war in October 1948 the Israelis fought Egypt successfully for control of the Negev and in the fourth round from 22 December to 8 January 1949 they accomplished the final defeat of the Egyptians. In the meantime ᶜAbdallāh had secured control of much of Arab Palestine and old Jerusalem, new Jerusalem having been held by Israel. UN efforts to end the war by inducing Israel to surrender either Galilee or the Negev were made abortive by the Israeli successes.

The war was terminated not by a peace treaty but by a number of armistice agreements signed between February and July 1949. Those with Lebanon and Syria confirmed their pre-war frontiers with Palestine; around Lake Tiberias demilitarized zones were established. The treaty with Egypt also confirmed the old frontier but left Egypt in control of Gaza. The frontier with Jordan was the ceasefire line.

As a result of the war the original UN settlement had been drastically modified. The UN plan had proposed a Jewish state in which the numbers of Jews and Arabs would have been roughly equal, an Arab state almost entirely Arab in population, and an international zone. In consequence of the fighting the last two elements had disappeared: the Arab state and the international zone had been divided between Israel and Jordan; only Gaza, under Egypt, was outside. There had also been a major shift of population. Through apprehension, through fear of Jewish actions such as the massacre of Dayr Yāsīn (9 April 1948), and in some cases through expulsion by Jewish forces, some 700,000 Arabs had fled from their homes in territories under Jewish control and at the end of the war were not allowed to return.

The Palestine mandate had been based on the supposition that there was a natural harmony between the strategic interests of Britain, the Zionist desire for a national home and the well-being of the indigenous Muslim and Christian inhabitants of Palestine. The assumption was wrong: the Zionists would accept nothing less than a state; the Palestinian Arabs, rather than Muslims and Christians, were determined that this should not happen; and the circumstance that Palestine under the mandate was probably the most prosperous area in the Near East with GDP rising at 13.7 per cent a year and per capita income at 5 per cent did not count in the balance. The strategic arguments over Palestine changed . Although the chiefs of staff continued to argue that Palestine was a valuable British possession which should be retained it was clear to many politicians by 1947 that Palestine was a strategic liability, from which Britain should try to withdraw with the least damage to her interests. At this point even prestige, to preserve which had been for many years the main British purpose in Palestine, was discarded. Of Britain's career in Palestine it may be said that nothing became her less than the leaving of it.

TRANSJORDAN

The area east of the river Jordan which came to form the Amirate of

Transjordan in 1921 was, under Ottoman rule, no more than a southerly extension of the province of Syria, chiefly notable for commanding the pilgrim route from Damascus to the Ḥijāz and therefore the scene of the construction of a section of the Ḥijāz railway. In 1921 its total population was between two and three hundred thousand (excluding Maᶜān and ᶜAqaba which at that time did not form part of the Amirate). Of this number about half were nomadic and half settled. The nomadic population consisted of bedouin tribes, of which the most important were the Ḥuwayṭāt (the only Jordanian tribe to take part in the Arab revolt), the Banū Ṣakhr and the ᶜAdwān. The settled population, partly urban but mainly cultivating, inhabited some 12 small towns and 200 villages. Like the nomads the settled population was mainly Arab and tribally organized but it also included some 20,000 Circassians settled in the region since 1878. The towns, of which the largest were Salṭ, Irbid and Karak, were basically villages built up to function as fortresses or staging posts to support the pilgrim route. Amman, which was chosen as the capital of the state, was a Circassian settlement. In the early years of the state it was used only as a summer residence; the first ruler, ᶜAbdallāh spent the winter months in the Jordan valley. The population was 90 per cent Muslim; the remainder being nearly all Christian, principally of the Greek Orthodox rite. By 1938 the population of the slightly enlarged Amirate was 300,000 and by 1948 about 400,000. At that time the state was further enlarged by the addition of part of Palestine and the population was considerably inflated by an influx of refugees. By 1949 the population of what had become the Hashimite Kingdom of Jordan was 1,350,000.

Of all the new states of the Arab east none had a less promising birth than did Transjordan. The creation of the separate administration of Transjordan in 1921 had provided an answer to two pressing problems which confronted Britain: what to do with the territory east of the Jordan and what to do with ᶜAbdallāh ibn Ḥusayn. Before 1921 it had been supposed that Fayṣal's administration would take care of Transjordan but the overthrow of his government in Damascus in 1920 had left Britain with the expensive responsibility. ᶜAbdallāh was not, as once contemplated, to get Iraq which was to go to his brother Fayṣal and Britain certainly did not wish ᶜAbdallāh to try his fortunes in Syria against the French. The solution was not expected to endure. ᶜAbdallāh still yearned for some greater prize than Transjordan – "I have had enough of this wilderness of Trans-Jordania"[5] he told his British adviser – and looked to Syria or even Palestine. On the other hand Britain did not think that ᶜAbdallāh had either the ability or the local support to form a lasting government in Transjordan. In Jerusalem it was expected that Transjordan would pass under the control of the Palestine administration.

To most people's surprise ᶜAbdallāh survived. He was helped initially by favourable reports by T.E. Lawrence and H. St John Philby and by the Saudi occupation of Jauf in 1922 which made ᶜAbdallāh seem a valuable buffer against Wahhābī raids and an insertion of Saudi power into the area between Palestine and Iraq. There was still concern, however, about his ambitions and his ability to administer efficiently. In October 1922 ᶜAbdallāh asked for independence and a treaty on the Iraqi model but the British government was unenthusiastic and offered only autonomy within the Palestine mandate. Nevertheless, in May 1923 ᶜAbdallāh was given an assurance that Britain would recognize an independent government in Transjordan under his rule provided that government was properly constituted, efficient and constitutional and subject to a satisfactory agreement with Britain. Dissatisfaction with ᶜAbdallāh's administration persisted, however, and in August 1924 Britain demanded that ᶜAbdallāh accept much greater British control over his government, in particular over financial and military affairs. ᶜAbdallāh accepted what was an ultimatum and from 1924 to 1939 British control was exercised through the British representative in Amman, Colonel Henry Cox.

After the resolution of the crisis in 1924 Transjordan began to prosper and to develop the basic institutions of a state. Under British supervision the central administration was rebuilt. Many of the Syrian officials who had entered the region after 1920 and who were widely believed to be using Transjordan as a base for their activities in Syria were dismissed in 1923 and a new staff largely recruited from young Palestinians was built up. After a survey the tax system was made more efficient. A land registration programme was introduced aimed at giving greater security to the cultivators although this was only partly completed and a feature of Transjordanian development was the emergence of a group of large landowners, recruited mainly from the tribal shaykhs (especially those of the Banū Ṣakhr) who became one of the principal props of ᶜAbdallāh's government. The position of the tribal shaykhs was strengthened by the grant of legal privileges via the 1924 Tribal Courts Law and the 1929 Bedouin Control Board. ᶜAbdallāh himself was given a large estate at British instigation. There was also some educational development and by 1941 there were 73 government schools and 92 private schools of which 6 were secondary schools (4 public and 2 private). For higher education Transjordanians were still obliged to go outside the state, mainly to Palestine, Lebanon or Syria.

The principal achievement of the early years of the state was the establishment of security in the region. This was the result of the development of adequate military forces. The task of constructing a military force had begun before the arrival of ᶜAbdallāh by the creation of what was known as the Reserve Force. This force was the nucleus of the Arab Legion established in 1923 when all forces in Transjordan were amalgamated under the command of a British officer, Frederick Peake. The Legion was at first recruited from peasants and was intended to be used against unruly tribes; the officers, inevitably, were ex-Ottoman officers and continued to be until 1940. Tribesmen were not recruited in numbers until the 1930s and officers of tribal origin became common only in the 1940s as they were promoted from the ranks. In 1926 the task of external defence, which had also fallen on the Legion, was taken away from it and given to the Transjordan Frontier Force, a Palestinian force with only British officers under the command of the General Officer Commanding in Palestine. At that time the strength of the Legion was reduced from 1,600 to 900 in keeping with the reduction of its function to purely police duties. In 1930, however, the Transjordan Frontier Force was returned to Palestine and a new force known as the Desert Mobile Force was organized as part of the Arab Legion by a British officer, John Glubb. It was the Desert Mobile Force which set out from the beginning to recruit bedouin and thereby give the nomads a new, powerful interest in the success of the state of Transjordan. By 1939 the strength of the Legion was still only 1,600 but during the Second World War it expanded to 8,000, including recruits under training. The Desert Mobile Force was converted into an armoured brigade of 3,000.

A further achievement was the settlement of the frontiers of Transjordan. The boundaries with Iraq and Palestine were defined fairly easily as these states were also under British control. The mid-desert frontier with Iraq, however, was not drawn in detail until 1932 and although the line of the Jordan river provided a clear demarcation of the northern section of the western frontier with Palestine there remained problems in the southern Negev. The northern frontier with Syria was based upon the original 1918 division into enemy territory administrations as modified by the Anglo–French boundary agreement in 1921 but was not defined in detail until 1931–2. The most difficult problem, however, concerned the southern frontier. Before 1925 this frontier had been left vague because of some ambiguity about the position of ᶜAbdallāh in relation to his father in the Ḥijāz. Ḥusayn regarded ᶜAbdallāh rather as his lieutenant in Transjordan than as an independent ruler. Wahhābī inroads after 1921 into territory claimed by Transjordan caused unease and the problem of the southern frontier became imperative after the Saᶜudi conquest of the Ḥijāz in 1926. In particular there was the matter of the possession of Maᶜān and ᶜAqaba which had been left under Ḥijāzī control but which it was thought inadvisable to leave to the Saᶜūdīs. Accordingly, to the disgust of ᶜAbd al-ᶜAzīz Āl Saᶜūd, Maᶜān and ᶜAqaba were attached to Transjordan. The ownership of these areas remained a bone of contention although agreement was reached on the eastern part of the southern frontier by the treaty of Hadda (2 November 1925). At Hadda the future Saudi state was given the Wādī al-Sirḥān which earlier had been thought to be essential to the protection of the British territories.

Political development was slow before the Second World War. In 1928 an agreement with Britain provided for only a small constitutional advance. Transjordan was given an organic law, liberal in appearance but weak in practice, establishing an elected legislative council (chosen partly on a confessional basis with over-representation of minorities) and an executive council. Wide powers were retained by the amir. ᶜAbdallāh was disappointed that Britain retained close control over finance and defence, but in truth his government could not have survived without a British subsidy which between 1925 and 1930 covered more than a third of government expenditure, leaving aside other defence costs which were covered by Britain. ᶜAbdallāh's government was essentially a personal one; ministers were glorified clerks rather than politicians although some were able enough. As in other Arab countries the Ottoman influence was strong; most of ᶜAbdallāh's senior advisers were graduates of Ottoman civil and military colleges and some of them had studied in Istanbul during the time when he himself had lived there. Among this number were three early chief ministers of Syrian or Lebanese origin, Rashīd Ṭalīᶜa, Maẓhar al-Raslān and ᶜAlī Riḍā Pasha al-Rikābī, who had at one time led the government of Fayṣal in Syria. Other chief ministers were of Palestinian origin, notably the long serving, Tawfiq Abu'l Hudā.

Opposition to ᶜAbdallāh's rule came from various elements. The most serious challenge in the early years came from the ᶜAdwān tribe which resented the favour shown to their rivals, the Banū Ṣakhr and marched on Amman in September 1923. The ᶜAdwān were defeated by the Arab Legion. Another source of opposition was the townsmen of the Jordan valley who resented their own subordinate position and whose own local rivalries were exploited by ᶜAbdallāh. An example may be taken from Karak where two local notable families vied for influence, the Majālīs and the Ṭarawnas. When the Majālīs seemed to find favour with ʿAbdallāh the Ṭarawnas swung to the opposition. The establishment of the legislative council in 1928 gave these minor urban notables an opportunity to demonstrate their hostility to ʿAbdallāh's government although it seems likely that ʿAbdallāh himself encouraged their criticisms in order to obtain an extra lever to resist British demands. Another opportunity for criticism was provided by ʿAbdallāh's dealings with the Zionists in Palestine during the 1930s. Opposition to ʿAbdallāh tended to be voiced in Pan-Arab terms, despite ʿAbdallāh's own claims to represent Arab nationalist sentiments. Challenges also came from within ʿAbdallāh's own family. His eldest son, Ṭalāl, supported the opposition to his father and in 1941 paid the price for this when he was temporarily excluded from the succession, although a contributory factor was his unstable personality. But in Transjordan political opposition like political forms in general was elementary and presented no dangers beyond the capacity of ʿAbdallāh and his British allies to deal with.

A problem which persisted in Anglo–Transjordanian relations and which caused the British to look upon ʿAbdallāh with suspicion was the ambitions of the amir, himself. ʿAbdallāh was never satisfied with his Transjordanian state and hoped always to become a larger figure in the Arab world. Until 1933 he looked to the reconquest of the Ḥijāz from Ibn Saʿūd and he always hoped to gain a throne in Damascus. For this purpose he cultivated Syrian nationalists, notably ʿAbd al-Raḥmān Shāhbandar, and constantly jeopardized good Anglo–French relations by his activities, although at one point the French high commissioner, Henri Ponsot, apparently toyed with the idea of making ʿAbdallāh king of Syria. ʿAbdallāh also believed he had a role to play in Palestine and this notion grew after the publication of the report of the Peel Commission in 1937. ʿAbdallāh conceived that he might become the ruler of Arab Palestine in the event of a partition and built up close contacts with Palestinian notables, especially the Nashāshībīs. Not only did these activities of ʿAbdallāh cause concern to Britain but they also were the cause of his poor relations with other Arab states which viewed his ambitions with distaste and often with contempt.

In 1947 ʿAbdallāh's Palestinian ambitions appeared in a different light. The prospect of the imminent partition of Palestine raised the question of the future of Arab Palestine. Few thought that it could stand alone and a link with Transjordan seemed appropriate to Britons. Most Palestinians and the Arab states did not share this view, however, and with Britain unwilling to admit any other power in Palestine before the termination of her mandate ᶜAbdallāh was obliged to wait impatiently during 1947 and the first months of 1948. When he was permitted to intervene he was instructed by Britain not to violate the territory assigned to the Jewish state. In the fighting of 1948–9 the Arab Legion was the most successful of the Arab armies but its lack of reserves and adequate supply system meant that it was fully stretched in the operations which it undertook. Nevertheless, when the fighting was terminated ᶜAbdallāh was in possession of the West Bank and the old city of Jerusalem. He was not permitted to annex these territories directly in breach of the United Nations plan but over the following two years he accomplished the same end by stealth. He introduced his supporters into key positions in the administration of the territories and in 1950 was able to muster enough supporters in the West Bank to unite the two banks of the Jordan. In the 1950 Jordanian parliament half the seats were allocated to the West Bank and half to the East. Parliament voted to unite the two portions and the enlarged state was established. A year later ᶜAbdallāh was assassinated in Jerusalem.

Transjordan had achieved its independence before the resolution of the Palestinian dispute. During the Second World War Transjordan had proved a reliable pillar of British influence in the region and the greatly enlarged Arab Legion had been a useful adjunct of British military power, notably in the Iraqi operation of 1941. Transjordan also enjoyed an economic boom. ᶜAbdallāh's reward came in 1946 when the United Nations agreed to a British request to terminate the mandate and give independence to Transjordan. The mandate was replaced by a treaty of alliance (22 March 1946). Britain kept ultimate military control and Transjordan continued to receive British financial support, although new oil pipeline revenues considerably enlarged the income of the Jordanian government. The British Resident, Sir Alec Kirkbride, still retained considerable influence in Transjordan. The substantial degree of British control visible in the 1946 treaty was much reduced by a further treaty (15 March 1948). On 25 May 1946 the Hashimite Kingdom of Jordan was proclaimed although the state continued to be known as Transjordan for a further three years.

NOTES

1. A copy of the mandate is in J.C. Hurewitz (ed.), *The Middle East and North Africa in World Politics*, 2nd edn, vol. 2, New Haven 1979, 305–9.
2. Graham to Storrs, 27 May 1920, quoted Bernard Wasserstein, *The British in Palestine*, 1978, 55.
3. Cabinet Minute on Palestine, 18 August 1921, quoted Wasserstein, *op.cit.*, 113.
4. Hurewitz, *op cit.*, 302–5.
5. Quoted Mary C. Wilson, *King Abdullah, Britain and the Making of Jordan*, Cambridge 1987, 47.

CHAPTER FIVE

Turkey to 1950

The Turkey which emerged from the long bruising wars of 1912 to 1922 was an accident. The territories which it comprised were those which the nationalist leaders of 1919 to 1922 were able to claw back from their opponents. Subsequently, nationalist doctrines rationalized the result of pragmatic military and political decisions and endowed the shape of Turkey with some element of design but this intellectualization was only an attempt to make sense of history. One writes 'only' but in truth much of the early history of the Turkish Republic was a grand and largely successful attempt to render reality acceptable by making it myth.

Geographically Turkey consisted of six areas. One was the small area of the once-extensive Ottoman European territories left to the state in eastern Thrace. This included the city of Istanbul. The other five areas were in Anatolia and comprised the so-called central plateau, a high, dry upland area riven by hills and mountains, the steep and fertile coastlands of the Black Sea, the rich regions bordering on the shores of the Aegean and the Mediterranean, the flat, low lying region south of the Taurus mountains and the high, mountainous region of eastern Anatolia.

The population of the Turkish territories had changed considerably between 1912 and 1923 as a result of war, famine and population exchange. It had fallen by about 30 per cent to no more than 13 million: the first census in 1927 showed a population of 13.6 million. The substantial Greek and Armenian populations had been reduced by about 2.5 million and the places of a fifth of them were taken by Muslim immigrants mainly from the former European territories. The population was now more than 98 per cent Muslim. The majority of these were Sunnīs; the proportion of Shīʿis has been a matter of controversy, estimates ranging from 5 per cent to 40 per cent. The discrepancy may be the consequence of profound ignorance of basic Muslim doctrines by a large part of the population allowing inquirers to draw whatever conclusions pleased them. Linguistic divisions of the population depend on how one classifies dialects and how one numbers the Kurds. A reasonable estimate is that 85 per cent spoke Turkish as their mother tongue, 10 per cent Kurdish and the remainder Caucasian languages, Greek and Armenian.

The population was largely rural: three-quarters lived in villages and over 80 per cent was dependent on agriculture. The majority of these were small peasant proprietors; a partial survey in the late 1930s indicated that 86 per cent of the land was held by people with a holding of less than 50 hectares. There were large estates in eastern Anatolia, on the Aegean and in the south but there was no dominant class of large landowners as in other parts of the Near East. There were attempts at land reform but little was accomplished before 1950; in any case inequalities of land holding were a local problem. The greatest problems were those of what to do with the vacated lands of the Christians who had gone, how to settle the new immigrants, how to find more people to cultivate the land, and how to increase production. The area of cultivated land in Anatolia had fallen dramatically from 5.5 million hectares in 1912. Even after four years of recovery it was still under 4 million hectares in 1927. The loss of livestock had been especially heavy. The region which had suffered most was eastern Anatolia. The main crop was grain: in 1927 about 90 per cent of the sown land was under wheat. The most important commercial crops were cotton, tobacco and figs. About half the exploited land was pasture and wool was an important item of production.

About one-quarter of the population was urban but the bulk of the urban labour force was engaged in service industries, including government. The great majority of industrial workers were in handicrafts: a census of 1922 disclosed 75,000 workers in 33,000 establishments, a very clear indication of their character. A survey of 1915 had found less than 300 industrial enterprises employing more than five people and only 15,000 workers in these. Before the war sections of industry had been dominated by the Ottoman minorities and by foreigners – many of the larger manufacturing enterprises, a lot of the mining, most of the public utilities and all but 13 per cent of the railways. Filling the places of the Christians who had gone was a considerable problem for the new state. It was a problem especially of the two largest cities of Istanbul and Izmir which between them had over half of Turkey's industrial enterprises. Both cities had suffered severely as a result of the war of 1919–22 and the population exchange. The population of Istanbul, over one million in 1914, had shrunk by a third and three-quarters of Izmir had been destroyed at the time of the nationalist occupation in September 1922. The population of Izmir was between 100,000 and 150,000. Two other Turkish cities – Adana and Bursa – had around 50,000 people each and the rest, including the new capital, Ankara, were under this figure. Ankara, when it became the nationalist headquarters in 1919, had no more than 20,000 people.

By 1950 the population of Turkey had risen to 21 million but the basic characteristics of its population distribution had not changed greatly. Urbanization and industrialization had proceeded slowly. Turkey was still agricultural: 68 per cent of the population was rural and 71 per cent dependent on agriculture. Towns grew slowly: at one million Istanbul in 1950 was nearly back to where it had been in 1914 and Izmir had 230,000 people. The largest growth was, of course, in Ankara which, with nearly 300,000 people, now surpassed Izmir. But of other towns only Adana exceeded 100,000 people. Much of this urban growth took place in the latter part of the period; during the 1920s the urban population grew more slowly than the rural. Less than 10 per cent of the population was dependent upon industry. When one looks for the dynamics of change in Turkey before 1950 one should not look at the economy or at society but at politics. Change still came from above.

Turkey formally became a republic on 29 October 1923 when it revised its constitution, although the die had been effectively cast when the sultanate had been abolished a year earlier. The origins of the constitution were revolutionary. It had been necessary for the nationalists to find some way of legitimizing their authority after their breach with the Allied-controlled government of the Sultan in 1920 and an organic law had been adopted in January 1921 declaring that sovereignty belonged to the nation, which was represented by the nationalist parliament, the Grand National Assembly, which in turn possessed all power, legislative and executive. The problem of the sultan had been set on one side at that time on the grounds that he was not a free agent. The fate of the sultanate had been sealed when his government was invited by the Allies to negotiate on behalf of Turkey. In 1923 the task was not only to tidy up the matter of sultanate and republic but also to curb the powers of the assembly. Accordingly, the amended constitution provided for a president, elected by the assembly. The president chose the prime minister, who in turn chose his ministers. The assembly approved the choice but it no longer had the power to choose ministers itself and it never exercised its power to dismiss a government. Even so the powers of the single chamber

Turkish parliament elected for four years far exceeded those of any other such institution in the Near East. The assembly had supreme legislative power, could not be dissolved but by itself and commanded its own armed forces. It had to be managed, not ignored, because the state could not function without it.

A major institution of the republic was the army. War had always been the principal function of Ottoman government and the improvement of the Ottoman army had been the main object of the nineteenth century reformers. Under the Young Turks the army had dominated politics through the activities of army officers and through the share of the budget appropriated to its maintenance. For the Republic it was essential to bring the army under control, reduce its demands on the budget and take it out of politics. These ends were accomplished in considerable measure before the Second World War. Serving officers were excluded from the assembly, although the proportion of former military officers among its members remained high, reducing slightly from one-sixth in 1920 to one-eighth in 1943. The army share of the budget fell from 40 per cent in 1926 to 28 per cent in the early 1930s. A drastic change took place only with the Democrat victory in 1950 when former military officers numbered only one-twentieth of the assembly. The size of the army was held at about 80,000 for most of the period, taking a diminishing share of the budget and leaving resources available for civil development. During the late 1930s, however, the deteriorating international situation led to a big expansion of the army and a large increase of its share of the budget which reached a peak of 56 per cent between 1940 and 1945. Despite one isolated military conspiracy there was no interference in politics after the resentment of some senior military commanders had been expressed through the Progressive Party in 1925–6. Under its chief of staff, Fevzi Çakmak, the army remained loyal and docile. Through training in basic skills and its inculcation of nationalist values among recruits the army contributed to the strengthening of the republic.

The Turkish political élite was quite different in character from the élites of other Near Eastern states. A study of the membership of the Grand National Assembly reveals that it was dominated by men whose background was that of civil and military officials; between 40 and 50 per cent of deputies between 1920 and 1950 were in this category. The next largest category comprised those in professional occupations: these rose from just under 18 per cent in 1920 to 35 per cent in 1946. Businessmen amounted to an average of 15 per cent, rising sharply to 24 per cent in 1946. Men of religion on the other hand fell from 17 per cent in 1920 to only 7 per cent in 1923 and dwindled to

1 per cent by 1943. Landowners, the dominant group in other Near Eastern assemblies, were under 5 per cent. Another feature which distinguished the Turkish élite was its local character. Whereas other assemblies were dominated by absentee landlords nearly 60 per cent of GNA members represented their own localities; only 16 per cent came from Istanbul. The war of independence had been won by an alliance of which the core was formed by officials and local notables. Between 1920 and 1925 the alliance was put under strain by the increasing demands of the state but it was re-established in the republican era; local notables retained a considerable influence in the provinces, where the old Ottoman structure of local government continued with modifications. Elected provincial councils to advise governors remained and these were dominated by local notables. Thirdly, the élite was well-educated; a considerable majority had some form of higher education. Lastly, the members were not only young – in their early 40s – but they stayed young. This phenomenon was the consequence of the steady turnover of members; apart from the second assembly which had only one-third of those who had served in the first, about 50 per cent of the membership changed at each four-year election; on balance older people went and younger members entered keeping the age of the élite about the same. Although at the very top some leaders went on and on, as a whole the élite had an unusual capacity for renewing itself.

The differences between the political élite of republican Turkey and the élites of other Near Eastern countries in the same period are only partly accountable by reference to the revolutionary circumstances in which the regime came to power. One reason for the differences is simply that Turkey had no great class of landed proprietors. Another factor was that Turkey, much more than other states, was the inheritor of the Ottoman tradition of rule by a civil and military bureaucracy; 93 per cent of staff officers and 85 per cent of civil servants retained their places under the republic. The Ottoman élite had been transfigured during the Young Turk revolution of 1908 to 1918 when the old Porte bureaucracy had lost power to a younger group of men from humbler, provincial backgrounds. The Turkish nationalists of 1922 were the inheritors of the Young Turk revolution; indeed although the policies of the leaders of the Committee of Union and Progress (CUP) were denounced for having ruined the Ottoman Empire many of the nationalists were by origin themselves Unionists and the Defence of Rights groups which had been the precursors of the GNA were commonly built on the base of branch organizations of the CUP. It is a nice irony that the nationalists, in denouncing the

Ottoman and Unionist legacies, were condemning two major components of their own pre-eminence.

The new republic had a very stable political structure. Before 1950 only once (in 1946) were elections held before the completion of the four-year term of the assembly. This stability was partly due to the dominance of the assembly by one political party, the People's Party (from 1937 the Republican People's Party (RPP)), founded in September 1923 but effectively in existence as a political grouping under the name of the Defence of Rights Group for Anatolia and Rumelia from May 1921. The RPP was quite different from any other Near Eastern political party before 1950. It was the source of policy, which was executed by ministers, and through its branch organization it controlled the work of local government officers. All appointments were made through the party. In some ways it resembled European totalitarian parties of the same period but there was one significant difference; the RPP was never a mass party and never sought to organize the masses; it was a party of the élite which gave or transmitted orders.

The overwhelming majority of members of the Assembly were members of the RPP. In the first assembly there was opposition from a substantial cohort known as the Second Group (the progenitor of the RPP being the First). The Second Group was eliminated at the elections for the second assembly and a new opposition party, the Progressive Party, appeared on 17 November 1924, offering a programme similar to that of the RPP but more liberal. The Progressives lasted only until June 1925 when they were abolished. In August 1930 the regime itself tried to create a parliamentary opposition (the Liberal Party) but this experiment lasted only until December. Thereafter, until 1945, opposition came only from groups within the RPP and from a few independents who were allowed to win seats where the RPP deliberately refrained from putting up candidates. After 1945 there was an efflorescence of political parties but the RPP held firmly to its control of the assembly and political power until its defeat at the elections of 1950. It need hardly be said that the reason for the domination of the RPP was not its inordinate popularity but the close interlocking of party and government at the centre and in the provinces, a system which was able to procure whatever electoral result was desired and ensure that only tolerated opposition existed.

Extra-parliamentary opposition was not substantial and was kept under control without excessive difficulty. The most serious challenge proceeded from tribal and religious elements in 1925. This was the revolt of Şeyh Sait, a Naqshbandī Kurdish leader in eastern Anatolia. The Kurdish population of the region may be divided into two sections: the tribal Kurds of the hills who were mainly peasant proprietors, and the largely detribalized Kurds of the plains who were mainly sharecroppers. The tribal Kurds may be further subdivided into two subsections: large and small tribes. It was among the small tribes that Ṣūfī religious men had especially assumed the role of leaders and it was here, in the Zaza tribe, that Şeyh Sait had his particular following and the revolt primarily involved the Zaza tribe. The revolt was indeed planned as part of a much broader movement in which the lead had been taken by Kurdish nationalists. But they were so few that they found it necessary to call on the help of the religious men who had the influence they lacked. In the event it was the religious men who took over the revolt bringing their own tribal following and giving the movement a mainly religious character as a *jihād* for a Kurdish state in which Islam would be respected. The secular nationalists played little part, as did the large Kurdish tribes or the sharecroppers. Nor indeed did the rebels link with other internal opposition to the republic or with outsiders. The revolt, which broke out in February 1925, covered an extensive area west of Lake Van before it was suppressed in November. However, the rebels failed to take any major town and once troops had been brought in from outside the region the principal obstacle to the restoration of control was the difficulty of the country. The leaders, including Şeyh Sait, were captured and hanged. There were continued disturbances in the Kurdish regions throughout the history of the republic as indeed there had been under the Ottoman regime but none represented more than a troublesome irritation. Another violent religious protest in western Anatolia was suppressed in 1930.

The Şeyh Sait rising provided the occasion for the nearest approach of the Turkish revolution to a reign of terror. The regime took advantage of the atmosphere of fear and suspicion caused by the revolt and the discovery of a separate plot against the life of the president to deal with other elements of opposition. Revolutionary courts which had existed during the period 1919–22 were reconstituted in 1925 as Independence Tribunals and held sway for two years during which period they staged several trials and at one time threatened to become, like a committee of public safety, the dominant power in the state. Many alleged enemies of the regime were executed, driven from public life or otherwise silenced by the tribunals. They included former leaders of the Committee of Union and Progress such as Cavid Paşa and Dr Nazım, who were hanged, and Kara Kemal, who shot himself; so-called communists; and, most important of all, several of the most prominent of the nationalist leaders during the struggle for independence, including Rauf Orbay, Kâzim Karabekir, Ali Fuat Cebesoy and Refet Bele. The latter men had been the leaders of the Progressive Party and although they were acquitted they were excluded from political life either permanently or for some years. In 1927 the tribunals were disbanded, however, and the republic abandoned the path of revolutionary legality.

Students of the Turkish Republic will be bewildered that an account of its early history could proceed so far without mentioning the name of its manager, Gazi Mustafa Kemal Paşa, better known by the surname he adopted in 1934 as Atatürk. At the cost of being anachronistic I shall refer to him by his surname. It is indeed because accounts of the republic are rightly dominated by the figure of Atatürk that it seemed worthwhile to analyse first other features of the political landscape before they were dwarfed by the personality of the creator of the republic and of most of its institutions and its first president. Atatürk was born in Salonika, probably in 1881, the son of a minor government official turned failed timber dealer who died early in Atatürk's life. Like many Turks in similar circumstances Atatürk took up a military career, went to military school, was a cadet at Monastir, attended the war college in Istanbul and graduated from the staff college in 1905. He was a supporter of the Young Turks but failed to prosper in politics and made his name as a military commander at Gallipoli and in Syria during the First World War. In 1919 he assumed the leadership of the nationalist struggle in Anatolia and it was in no small measure due to his will and determination that the struggle was brought to a successful conclusion with the defeat of the Greeks in 1922 and the conclusion of peace with Europe at Lausanne in 1923. During those years of struggle he also created the nationalist political institutions which were carried on into the republic and he beat off challenges from Ottomanists, Unionists, leftists and religious elements (see *MMNE*, 307–22).

Atatürk ruled Turkey from 1923 until his death in 1938. He brought to this work great qualities: intellectual ability to contemplate any situation dispassionately and rationally and to think through the logical consequences of a course of action; marvellous ability to calculate the chances and a highly developed sense of the possible; clear-sighted concentration on the essential objective and inflexible will in driving towards his goal. As a man he was unattractive: ruthless, ambitious, ungenerous, intolerant of any criticism and given to impulsive rages. His pleasures were drink, cards and women. His health from 1919 was poor: he suffered from kidney disease and died of cirrhosis of the liver. Constant pain and debility may partially account for his erratic behaviour and his autocratic style. He was a dictator but not one in the mould of contemporary European dictators: rather he was a modern paşa working with modern instruments towards modern goals.

Atatürk's principal goals after 1923 were to secure the independence, peace and modernization of the Turkish Republic. His policy was expressed in terms of six principles, adopted by the RPP in 1931 and inserted into the Turkish constitution in 1937. It should not be assumed, however, that Atatürk's policy was ideological in inspiration: the principles were rationalizations of the programmes which circumstances had obliged him to adopt and in some cases rather woolly rationalizations at that. Nevertheless, the principles provide convenient, if inelegant pegs on which to hang an account of the main features of Turkish development in this period. The principles are republicanism, nationalism, secularism, statism, populism and revolutionism.

The basic principle was republicanism which could not even be discussed, let alone challenged; an attempt by the Nation Party to raise the matter in 1949–50 was firmly silenced. It may be that Atatürk had always had a republic in mind but it is very doubtful if the idea appealed to more than a small minority of his followers. The prestige of the Ottoman dynasty was high; it was difficult for men to imagine any other form of government and its presence also seemed to guarantee the position of Islam. In 1922 events played into Atatürk's hands enabling him not only to drive out the sultan but to end the sultanate. Opposition in the assembly was over-ridden with threats from Atatürk. It was theoretically possible either that Turkey might have become a caliphal state or that the Ottomans might have been replaced by another dynasty but the operation was difficult to contemplate in practice. So a republic, hard as the word was for Muslims to accept because of its connotations of irreligion, was inevitable. But in Atatürk's vision the republic became more than a political convenience; it also grew into a symbol of the rejection of the past and the regeneration of the Turkish nation.

The concept of the Turkish nation was one which was unfamiliar to many Turks and it was necessary to promote it under the principle of nationalism. Of course, Turks had long been aware of a cultural identity as Turks but the attempt to change that cultural identity into a political identity had begun only at the end of the nineteenth century and, despite some progress under the Young Turks through the operations of the Turkish Hearth Society and the writings of men like Ziya Gökalp, Turkish nationalism remained a minority movement until the end of the empire. Like their predecessors the Young Turks nearly all supposed that their political identity was that of Ottomans, strongly reinforced by their religious identity as Muslims. The majority of those who followed Atatürk between 1919 and 1922 thought that they were indeed fighting for the freedom of Ottomans and Muslims. Atatürk's realism in adopting the 1918 armistice boundaries as the basis of his claims and in stopping the war when Anatolia and Thrace were liberated created a state which could not be rationalized in either Ottoman or Muslim terms but which made sense in terms of ethnic Turkish nationalism. The move of the capital to Ankara, although partly for security reasons, dramatized the change in the character of the state; cosmopolitan and Ottoman Istanbul, like the former St Petersburg for the young Soviet state, had too many echoes of an imperial past.

History was therefore rewritten to persuade men that they had indeed been fighting for a Turkish national state and had accomplished that goal. The rewriting of history went further and an attempt was made to demonstrate the continuity and excellence of Turkish civilization from the time of the Hittites. In the so-called "sun language" theory which flourished for some time the Turkish language was claimed to be the original language from which Semitic and Indo–European languages were descended. Proof of Turkish antiquity was found in the circumstance that the Turkish word for man "adam" was also the name of the first man who, it followed, must have been a Turk. Other linguistic absurdities served further to enhance Turkish self esteem. In addition the Turkish language was reformed. Words of Arabic and Persian origin were eliminated where possible and replaced by words coined from Turkish roots or borrowed from European languages and sometimes given a spurious Turkish ancestry. As 80 or 90 per cent of the vocabulary of Ottoman Turkish came from the languages in disfavour the consequences for the Turkish language were dramatic. For some years readers and writers floundered in a cloud of incomprehension whilst new words flowed like a meteor storm through the pages of newspapers and periodicals. On top of it all Turkey adopted a Latin alphabet in 1928 in place of the Arabic script in which Ottoman Turkish was written. The decision was defensible on phonetic grounds for Turkish, with its strong vowels, is unsuited to the Arabic script. But the motive was again to break with the past and assert the separate identity of the nation.

Turkish nationalism had also its problems. One concerned those citizens of Turkey who were not Turks. The largest group of non-Turks was the Kurds and the problem was dealt with by declaring them to be a particular variety of Turk, namely 'mountain Turks'. For some time there was no mention of Kurds and the Kurdish language was banned from print. A second problem concerned the position of Turks outside the bounds of the Republic, whether in the former Ottoman territories or in those of the Soviet Union, China, Iran and Afghanistan. If Turkey was for the Turkish nation should not these groups also be included? Such was the contention of the Pan-Turks. In fact the Pan-Turks were kept under strict control by Atatürk and his successors. Pan-Turk irridentism was a threat to Turkey's good relations with her neighbours and these ranked much higher in Atatürk's calculations. Mosul was grumblingly left to Iraq in 1926 in the interests of peace with Britain and the only success was in the recovery of Hatay in 1939, the outcome of a carefully calculated manoeuvre initiated by Atatürk before his death and based on his accurate assessment of France's priorities at the time. Turkish nationalism was for the consolidation of the Turkish state and not the dissipation of its energies and resources in foreign adventure.

One of the most important principles was secularism. Secularism had two aspects: one concerned the political or public claims of Islam and the other its social influence. Islam's political claims were dismissed: the Caliphate, which had been exploited by Ottoman sultans since the eighteenth century in an attempt to magnify their authority, was abolished in 1924 and the role of Islam in law and education terminated. The post of Shaykh al-Islām was eliminated and the ministry of the sharīʿa and waqfs closed. The superintendence of *waqfs* was placed in a special office under the control of the prime minister and control of religious education was transferred to the ministry of education. The Sharīʿa courts were abolished and in 1926 Sharīʿa personal law covering marriage, divorce and inheritance was replaced by a version of the Swiss civil code of law. In 1925 also the Ṣūfī orders were banned and their religious houses closed. In 1928 a constitutional amendment removed the article which named Islam as the state religion. Turkey was henceforth a purely secular state. In all these changes Atatürk had been following the lines of early Turkish reformers; what was striking was the speed and comprehensiveness of the changes which he introduced. Islam had been reduced to something it had never been, a system of personal belief. Worship was tolerated within limits: the number of mosques was reduced in 1931–2, government preachers were obliged to include practical information in their Friday services and it was forbidden to wear religious dress outside places of worship. But education and law were secular, incorporating concepts such as the equality of men and women which were abhorrent to the orthodox.

Atatürk claimed that his policy of secularization was designed only to terminate the political role of Islam and that one effect would be to purify and revive Islam. But, as is plain from the account of the reforms given in the preceding paragraph, taking Islam out of politics meant taking it out of much of social life as well. In fact the majority of Turks, especially those in the countryside, refused to accept this situation, quietly ignored and avoided the institutions of the secular state and continued to patronize religious institutions. The great increase in illegitimate births which occurred in Turkey was the consequence not of a sudden access of immorality but of the introduction of a civil law which was ignored. Traditional Muslim medicine continued to be practised and visits to shrines did not cease because the state disapproved. In the short term secularism was an affair of the élite and the cities; only in the longer term did the changes in education and law work deeper into the fabric of society.

Atatürk attacked other social practices related to Islam directly. In 1925 he abolished Maḥmud II's judicious sartorial compromise, the fez, and insisted on the wearing of hats or other headgear distinguished by the detested brim which obstructed the devotions of the believer. The same year he adopted the Christian Gregorian calendar and ten years later declared Sunday, not Friday to be the day of rest. The introduction of the Latin script, the attack on Arabic and the adoption of surnames (1934) also had implications for Islamic social practices. There was one practice he did not dare to ban although he was tempted to do so: he would not abolish the veil although he encouraged women to discard it.

Secularism went farther in Turkey than in any other part of the Near East. Only in the Muslim republics of the Soviet Union were there changes of similar magnitude. Whether there is any significance in the circumstance that secularization made the greatest progress among Sunnī Turkish populations is a matter for speculation; it may be that to Arabs Islam was a stronger element of identity. The absence of sustained violent resistance was a factor in the progress of secularization. But another was the view of Atatürk and much of the Turkish élite that there was only one civilization and that was western civilization based on science; the rest was superstition. Turkish secularism may be seen partly as a pragmatic response to the challenges to the republic but it must also be seen as a Turkish expression of the ideas of the European enlightenment, transmitted via Auguste Comte and H.G. Wells, two of the writers most admired by Atatürk.

There was a public revival of Islam during and after the Second World War. This was witnessed by increased interest in pilgrimage, fasting, prayer, religious publications and in demands for religious education and for religious discussion. Appeals to religious sentiments were forbidden to political parties but support for the National Party of Fevzi Çakmak owed something to the accurate supposition that the party was sympathetic to the claims of Islam. In the more relaxed political atmosphere of the times the government made some concessions to this interest; religious education in primary schools was allowed in 1949 and some religious schools reopened. Some attempt was made to remedy the problem of the shortage of religious teachers by introducing training for such teachers in the Ankara Theological Faculty. But these were minor changes which did not breach the secular principle on which the state was built.

Statism was a late addition to the principles of the Turkish Republic and was especially a recognition of the new role of the state in the Turkish economy after 1929. A common view is that Turkey had a liberal economy until 1929–32 and a state-directed economy thereafter, the change from the one to the other being associated with ideology and the great depression. This formulation has some merit but it overstates the contrast between the two periods. In the first period liberalism was not complete; during the 1920s the state assumed responsibility for much of the railway network and its development and operated a number of state monopolies, for example in tobacco. Although the state did not run the monopolized industries itself it exercised some control through licensing. Nor was liberalism a matter of conviction. It has been suggested that the adoption of a liberal economic policy was a conscious decision at the Izmir Economic congress in 1923 but a study of the inconclusive discussions at that meeting indicates that no clear decision emerged. The truth was that the regime had neither the ability nor the wish to interfere in the economy much beyond what was necessary to raise revenue. There was no tradition of state planning: Atatürk was not interested; his prime minister, İsmet İnönü was not especially competent in the economic field; and Turkey's freedom to intervene in the economy was severely limited by the capitulations which prevented her raising tariffs until 1929 although the monopoly system enabled Turkey to circumvent some of the restrictions of the capitulations.

The recovery of tariff freedom made protection possible: the new Turkish tariff of 1929 replaced average duties of 13 per cent with duties of around 46 per cent. A second practical consideration was that after many delays Turkey was obliged to commence repaying her share of the Ottoman debt in 1929. This was a heavy drain on foreign exchange and required action to reverse the adverse balance of trade;

Turkey's monetary crisis began some months before the Wall Street crash. The depression itself was, however, a significant factor in the decision to move to state control. Agriculture had enjoyed a boom in the 1920s under the effects of buoyant demand after the restoration of peace, rising prices and particularly favourable tax treatment: the abolition of the tithe in 1925 saved proprietors more than the nominal 12.5 per cent because they avoided payments to tax farmers. Between 1923 and 1929 output more than doubled, commercial crops being exceptionally successful. Wheat prices now fell by two-thirds between 1929 and 1931 and remained depressed. Cotton and tobacco did slightly better but the effect was to make it exceedingly difficult for farmers to meet their fixed charges. Industry suffered also though to a lesser degree. Some state action to alleviate the problems was seemingly required. That it was concentrated more on industry than on agriculture may owe something to the circumstance that the government was more responsive to urban discontent than to rural but it owes something also to ideology. Turks did come to believe in the doctrine that states should strive for economic independence and for a powerful industrial base.

The principal element in the new structure was state control of investment through new development banks. In the 1920s banking in Turkey was still dominated by foreign banks. Some private Turkish banks for economic development had been founded during the 1920s including the Business Bank and the Bank for Industry and Mining. In addition the old Agricultural Bank had been reorganized. Now there was a rearrangement. A central bank was founded in 1930 to be followed by the Sumerian Bank, which took over from the Bank for Industry and Mining (1933), and by the Hittite Bank (1935) which eventually assumed responsibility for mining. Later, further elements were added. A number of public utilities were nationalized, the former state monopolies were converted into state-managed enterprises and a five-year plan (1934) completed the edifice.

State control was still of an elementary character. The greater part of the economy, notably agriculture, was outside. Small industry remained in private hands. Primarily, the new policy was a matter of strict control of foreign trade, the promotion of import substitution and of exports to protect the balance of payments, the development of a heavy industrial base and some protection to agriculture through subsidized grain prices. During the Second World War controls were further increased to deal with the serious economic consequences of the war.

Statism was in part a delayed, pragmatic reaction to the problems of the Turkish economy, notably the disappearance of the minorities and the shortage of entrepreneurial and managerial skills and, especially, of domestic or foreign capital for investment. It had also an ideological aspect. In part the ideological impulse derived from the Ottoman tradition of the paternalistic state, Baba Devlet, now greatly extended from the simple notions of the establishment of justice; and in part it was inspired by the example of developments in other parts of the world and the apparent success of state intervention in the economy of the Soviet Union. Soviet advice was sought in drawing up the first five-year plan.

Judged by economic criteria it is difficult to say whether statism was successful or not. Calculations of Turkish national income indicate growth at a rate of over 11 per cent per annum under the comparatively liberal regime of the 1920s, principally due to the rapid agricultural recovery during the years 1923–6. During the 1930s economic growth fell to about 6 per cent a year, industry growing at twice the rate of agriculture. On the other hand conditions were much more difficult during the 1930s and it might well be argued that growth would have been lower without state control. Statism did create a problem for the longer term future in the shape of a large and inefficient state industrial sector and a subsidized agriculture. But by 1939 the results were encouraging; although Turkey was still a poor country the average Turk was 40 per cent better off than he had been in 1930. The severest problems were the result of the war when national income fell by an average of 7 per cent a year and the rise in the standard of living since 1930 was wiped out. Despite the recovery after 1945 Turkey in 1950 was still worse off than she had been in 1939.

Populism is a vague and difficult concept. It contained several notions but especially the belief that the revolution was for all the people; class divisions, it was claimed, did not exist in Turkey and all should unite for the progress of the nation; trade unions were illegal until 1947. The state saw its role to foster this idea of popular unity for progress especially through education. Education was to train personnel, obliterate the unhappy past and implant the goals of the national future. The republic inherited an education system divided between a public sector and a private sector which embraced both the community schools and foreign schools run especially by missionaries. Like other Near Eastern countries Turkey had a two-track educational system: the state system, emphasizing Ottoman Turkish, which led on towards government employment; and the religious system, emphasizing Arabic in the case of Muslim schools, which produced clerics. In 1924 the state assumed control of all education and Turkey acquired a unified educational system using Turkish and emphasizing Turkish history; religious schools were closed and religion excluded from the curriculum. An increased share of resources went into education. The 1924 constitution declared elementary education to be free and compulsory; although this ambition was not attained elementary school attendance rose from less than a quarter of children in 1924 to over half in 1950. During the 1920s attention was focused on secondary education and during the 1930s on vocational, technical and adult education. A particular feature of adult education was the People's Houses and village institutes which were also used to mobilize support for the social and economic policies of the regime. They were unpopular, being seen as instruments of the élite. In higher education the University of Ankara was established in 1925 and there was a crash programme of teacher training. The results were fairly impressive: in 1923 literacy in Turkey was about 10 per cent; by 1950 one third of Turks had some modest degree of literacy. Development was uneven: literacy among townspeople was much greater than in rural areas and among men much more than women. Eastern Anatolia lagged far behind the west.

Vaguest of all the principles of Kemalism was revolutionism. At its heart was the notion that Turkey was in the throes of a continuing and fundamental revolution which involved a complete break with its past. Alternatively, the principle was defined as reformism with connotations of more moderate change. To an extent the difference reflected enduring divisions among Turkish leaders about the pace and exent of change. The progressives and liberals like Ali Fethi Okyar argued for slower movement at a pace which was more acceptable to the mass of the population: the radicals, such as Recep Peker, secretary general of the RPP during the early 1930s, favoured rapid change enforced by the state. Atatürk switched from one to the other as seemed appropriate and İnönü doggedly carried out the policies Atatürk devised. Two general points may be made about the character of the revolution. First, it was in the old tradition of revolution from the top; despite the principle of populism Turkey was to have what its élite thought good for it. Second, it was primarily a political revolution; for all the emphasis on social change and economic development the pace was slow outside the towns. The educational and legal changes were real but their effects took a long time to work through society.

Atatürk died in 1938 and was succeeded as president by his old ally and long-serving prime minister, İsmet İnönü. İnönü was seen as a dull, inferior edition of Atatürk, lacking ideas and imagination, but this view, as time was to show, was unjust. Atatürk could conceive change and force it through; İnönü could manage change. His skills were quickly tested: he had immediately to confront the grave crisis of the Second World War and thereafter to manage the shift to a multi-party system.

Turkish foreign policy under Atatürk had been aimed at securing peace. In pursuit of this end treaties were signed with Turkey's neighbours and these came to form the basis of two regional pacts: the Balkan Pact (1934) with Greece, Yugoslavia, Hungary and Bulgaria which protected Turkey's western frontier, and the Saadabad Pact (1937) with Iraq, Iran and Afghanistan which gave security on the east. These uneasy alliances of minor powers, however, provided no real answer to Turkey's quest for international security and, particularly, security against any threat from the Soviet Union. Quite apart from her vulnerable eastern frontier Turkey had a constant concern deriving from the existence of the Straits. At Montreux in 1936 the regime of the Straits established in 1923 at Lausanne was modified: the Straits Commission disappeared and Turkish troops were allowed to reoccupy the demilitarized zone. Turkey was also allowed to close the Straits in the event of war or the imminent threat of war. The new regime was not satisfactory to the Soviet Union which argued that all Black Sea powers had a right to control the use of the Straits. Turkey confronted the possibility that the Soviet Union might take advantage of any international crisis to present new demands. Accordingly, Turkey looked for help to the west. During the 1930s Turkey drew closer to Germany which came to predominate in Turkey's trade. But when obliged to choose politically between Britain and France on the one hand and Germany and Italy on the other Atatürk chose the former grouping and İnönü continued this policy.

In 1939 Turkey did not make the mistake the Ottoman empire had made in 1914. When war broke out in September Turkey stayed neutral although in October she signed a treaty of alliance with Britain and France. According to that treaty Turkey should have entered the war when Italy did so but in fact in June 1940 Turkey remained neutral. By that time France had fallen and the German–Soviet alliance seemed to be in the ascendant. It seemed that only Germany could protect Turkey from the USSR and in June 1941 Turkey signed a treaty of friendship with Germany with whom she continued to conduct a valuable trade, notably by the export of chrome. Some Turks hoped for a German victory over the USSR, the collapse of that state and the establishment of a federation of Turkey with the Soviet Turkish regions. These Pan-Turk ambitions seem not to have had any considerable weight in the calculations of İnönü and the Turkish leadership, however. Turkey did not join the Axis and the wisdom of her decision was shown when the war turned in favour of the Allies in the autumn of 1942. From that time onwards Turkey came under considerable pressure, especially from Britain, to enter the war but Turkey refused. Turks asked who would protect them from Germany and the Soviet Union and believed that Britain would abandon them to Soviet mercies. Only in 1944 when it became obvious that the Allies would win and that hopes that Germany could survive as a major factor in the European balance were doomed did Turkey change her position. It then became a matter of concern that the victorious allies might leave unhelpful Turkey to the USSR. Turkey declared war on Germany on 23 February 1945 in order to earn a little gratitude and find a place at the United Nations.

Turkey had survived the war and ended up on the winning side. Her anticipations of Soviet threats were to be realized in 1946 when from the Soviet Union came demands for a change in the regime of the Straits and for a revision of frontiers in eastern Turkey. Turkey's reaction and that of the western powers to that threat are dealt with in Chapter 15.

As remarked earlier the effects of the war on the Turkish economy were disastrous. Despite conducting a good trade with the belligerents and amassing a hoard of foreign currency reserves which she could not spend, Turkey's national income fell considerably. The effect upon individuals and groups was uneven partly due to a price rise of nearly 600 per cent between 1938 and 1943. The consequential pressure on state finances persuaded the government to institute a capital levy in 1942. Nominally, the levy was to be paid by all property owners and was allegedly aimed at war profiteers. It was so arranged, however, that it fell very heavily on the minorities who paid ten times as much as Muslims. Those who could not pay were sent to forced labour. The tax was abandoned in 1944.

By the end of the war social and economic discontent in Turkey was very great. Political demands for liberalization also arose encouraged by the circumstance that the democratic countries had triumphed. Looking to the future Turkey's leaders perceived the need to stand better in the eyes of Britain and the United States. And, in some cases, there was a genuine, frustrated impulse towards liberalism; İnönü confessed that he felt personally ashamed that Turkey was a one party state. In these circumstances, for domestic and international reasons, İnönü announced on 19 May 1945 that the time had come to move towards democracy.

Turkey's movement towards democracy was conducted within strict limits. Freedom was not allowed to the left, the extreme right or to religious malcontents. İnönü's notion of an opposition was a party of the moderate right, a new version of the 1930 Freedom Party. Such a party was the Democrat Party (DP) , founded 7 January 1946, by four former prominent members of the RPP. The chairman was Celâl Bayar, the founder of the Business Bank and later minister of the interior and prime minister from 1937 to 1939. The other three were Adnan Menderes, from a rich landowning family in Aydin, Refik Koraltan and Fuat Köprülü. From among the many parties founded in the immediate post-war period the Democrat Party emerged as the principal challenger to the dominance of the RPP, attracting support from commercial farmers in western Anatolia, businessmen tired of controls and unhappy Muslims. So great was the support that the RPP became alarmed and called a quick, partially-controlled election in order to strike before the DP was ready. Nevertheless, at the July 1946 election the DP won 62 seats and at once became the most considerable opposition the government had faced since 1924.

Breaking the mould of autocracy was no easy task. The Democrats had to learn the novel skills of opposition; confronted by government manipulation of the system against them the DP threatened extra-parliamentary opposition. The radical, authoritarian faction within the RPP led by the prime minister, Recep Peker, demanded the termination of the DP challenge and a reversion to the tested one-party system. İnönü, the arbiter, held firm to his chosen course. Peker was replaced by a more moderate RPP prime minister in 1947 and a yet more moderate leader took over in 1949 to superintend the elections of 1950. The Democrats also had their problems. Their success had attracted to them every group opposed to the RPP and the DP was in danger of becoming an incoherent coalition. In July 1948 a dissident group which included a number of men with Muslim sympathies broke away to form the Nation Party. For a time it seemed that the DP challenge might burn itself out among the cross fires.

The Democrats triumphed at the elections of 14 May 1950. Only with difficulty was the RPP brought to agree that the 1950 elections should be wholly free but having taken the decision in December 1949 they stuck to it. In the event it is interesting that the RPP did so well. The RPP retained much of its urban support and its hold on the notables of the east and polled 39 per cent of the votes cast in a poll in which 80 per cent of the electorate voted. For a party which had compelled Turks to do what they did not want to do for 25 years that was a creditable result and suggests that an élite party had found a way of securing a mass following. They won only 69 seats, however, against the 408 obtained by the DP who took 53 per cent of the votes. The RPP stepped down, Bayar replaced İnönü as president and Menderes became prime minister. It was a remarkable and devastating victory but in many ways its most interesting feature is that an authoritarian regime should have permitted it.

CHAPTER SIX

Iran to 1960

Of all the states of the Near East, outside Arabia, Iran, in 1921, had the least experience of modernization. The physical form of Iran had contributed to this circumstance. The vast deserts of central and south eastern Iran pushed human activity into the north and west so that two thirds of the population was strung out along the chains of the Elburz and the Zagros and in the rolling plains of the north western provinces. In so large a country lacking modern technology the decentralization of political authority was a natural consequence; the provinces paid small attention and less taxation to the Qājār monarchy in Tehran. At central and provincial levels power was in the hands of notables whose wealth was based primarily on landholding, sometimes on tribal or religious status, occasionally on wealth derived from trade. Under the constitution of 1906–7 Iran was a monarchy with a two chamber parliament which had extensive powers over legislation and finance and a veto over concessions, loans, railways and roads. It could also force the dismissal of governments. In fact most of the constitution was inoperative; the second chamber had never been created and the assembly (Majlis) had not met since 1915.

The population of nearly 12 million was about 20 per cent urban, 20 per cent nomadic tribesmen and 60 per cent peasant cultivators. Economic production was mainly cereals and livestock for subsistence and local exchange; some cotton and opium were produced for export. Leaving aside oil, industry consisted largely of artisan production in the bazaar and rural handicrafts. Trade was small partly because communications were poor; the journey from Tehran to the Gulf ports took two months in 1920. There were no railways except for a short extension of the Russian system into the north western province of Azerbaijan and roads were suitable only for animal transport. The population was well over 95 per cent Muslim and 80 per cent Imāmī

(Twelver) Shīʿīs. The non-Muslim groups included small communities of Jews, Christians, Zoroastrians and Bahā'īs, members of a universal religion which had broken away from Shīʿī Islam. Ethnically, Iran was more divided: there were Turkish, Kurdish, Arabic and Baluch-speaking minorities and some Persian dialects were so far from the language of Fars as almost to qualify as separate languages. If all were counted as ethnic minorities true Persian speakers numbered little more than half the population. The political élite, however, was overwhelmingly Persian in culture.

In 1921 Iran was still recovering from the effects of the war during which Ottoman and Russian armies had fought over her soil and government had almost broken down. In the aftermath of the war Britain, as the surviving Great Power in Iran, had attempted to establish her own predominance in Iran through the device of an Anglo–Iranian agreement but the agreement was never ratified and was abandoned at the end of 1920. One reason for the failure of the agreement was the refusal of Britain to defend Iran against a Soviet threat represented by the landing of Bolshevik forces in May 1920 in support of a rebellion in the Caspian province of Gilan. In February 1921 the prospects for Iran, threatened by Soviet invasion, provincial separatism and financial collapse, seemed gloomy indeed. At this juncture the government was overthrown by a military coup (see *MMNE*, 345–8).

The coup of 21 February 1921 was carried out by the recently reorganized Persian Cossack Brigade led by Riżā Khān who had planned the move in concert with a number of radical reformers in Tehran led by Sayyid Żiyā al-Dīn Ṭabāṭabā'ī. Subsequently a government was formed by Żiyā. The old politicians had been imprisoned and the new government consisted of old bureaucrats and inexperienced amateurs. In the circumstances in which Iran found itself the government programme was Utopian: to reform the administration, the army, the judiciary and land tenure, to abolish foreign concessions and the capitulations, and to improve communications. Hated by the old politicans and by Aḥmad Shh Qājār, disliked by Russia and spurned by Britain, Żiyā's government lasted only three months before it was replaced by a government of the old politicians, newly released from jail. The immediate cause of its fall was a dispute between Żiyā and Riżā over the role of British military advisers in the army. Its single noteworthy achievement was the signature on 26 February of a treaty with Soviet Russia which normalized relations with that power and paved the way for the withdrawal of Bolshevik forces from Iran.

The years 1921 to 1926 witnessed the rise to power of Riżā Khān who displaced Aḥmad Shāh Qājār and established the Pahlavī dynasty with himself as first Shah in 1926. Riżā Khān was an almost illiterate soldier who had served all his career in the Cossack Brigade, a Russian-officered force employed on internal security duties in northern Iran. After the dismissal of the Russian officers and the reorganization of the force by British officers in the autumn of 1920 he had been given command of the Brigade. In April 1921 he was made minister of war and he retained that post in the succeeding governments. His main task was to construct an army which could re-establish the authority of the central government and maintain internal security in Iran. His control of the army became the principal factor in his bid for supreme power.

The Pahlavī army was the key institution in the centralization of power in Iran. That Iran needed a modern army had been common ground among Iranian reformers since the early nineteenth century. Most recently Britain had brought forward a plan for army reform and the Żiyā government gave first priority to army reform: "an army before and above everything".[1] Riżā was entirely in agreement with this aim: "the object of the movement of February 21," he said four years later, "was to rescue the army – which is the soul of the nation – from the hands of foreigners and to make it independent".[2] But in 1921 Iran did not have an army; instead she had a variety of small coercive forces – police, provincial forces and central forces such as the Cossack Brigade and the Gendermerie. Many had foreign officers. Out of these units Riżā created a unified force: the British-controlled South Persia Rifles was disbanded and the Gendermerie amalgamated with the Cossacks in December 1921. Foreign officers were replaced with Iranian officers, many trained abroad. Until 1925 the army was recruited from volunteers; in that year conscription was introduced. The army steadily grew in size. In 1927 it numbered 40,000 and by 1941 130,000 together with some 20,000 in the reconstituted gendarmerie. Iran was divided into military districts and the regional military commanders, usually former Cossack officers loyal to Riżā, formed a vital source of support to him and a means of influencing civilian government at elections and in other ways.

The army played the principal role in the crushing of provincial and tribal resistance to the Tehran government. Four major regions, Gilan, Khurasan, Azerbaijan and Kurdistan, were restored to central control by the end of 1922. The Jangalī movement in the northern province of Gilan was a Muslim movement directed originally against the pre-1914 Russian occupation, but which after 1917 exhibited a radical, anti-landlord character under the leadership of a religious radical, Kūchik Khān . After the entry of Bolshevik troops in May 1921 a Soviet Republic of Gilan was proclaimed with Kūchik as president (4 June 1921). Shortly afterwards the Jangalīs split between a communist faction drawn mainly from the Caucasus and a local group under Kūchik. Despite efforts to patch up the differences divisions persisted and prevented the rebels from launching their projected attack on Tehran. In autumn 1921 the reformed government forces attacked and defeated the rebels. Kūchik died of exposure and order was quickly restored in the province.

The rebellion in Khurasan was compounded of Kurdish tribal elements, the grievances of Turkish-speaking immigrants from Azerbaijan and the ambitions of the local commander of the Gendarmerie, Muḥammad Taqī Khān, Pisyān. Taqī, like several Gendarmerie officers, was a supporter of the Democrat party, a liberal/radical group which had led the opposition to Anglo–Russian dominance in Iran and which had looked to Germany and the Ottomans during the war. Taqī himself had spent part of the war in Berlin. In April 1921 he arrested the Governor of Khurasan and obtained recognition as military governor of the province. He was brought down not by government troops but by government-fostered divisions among his supporters which grouped against him a number of tribes. His power collapsed and he was killed in October 1921. It was another five years, however, before Riżā's army finally brought the tribes of Khurasan under control.

A movement of autonomy sprang up in Azerbaijan after 1917 following the withdrawal of Russian troops and influenced by the example of the independent state of former Russian Azerbaijan in 1918–20. The leadership of the movement was assumed by Shaykh Muḥammad Khīābānī, a former Democrat Party member of the Majlis. On 7 April 1920 the Azerbaijani Democrat Party seized power in Tabriz and expelled the governor and on 23 June proclaimed the autonomous government of Āzādistān. By July they were in control of the entire province. Their programme called for the autonomy of Azerbaijan within a republican Iran. A plan for extending the use of the Azerī language in schools, courts, etc., was announced but appeals to Azerī nationalism, a divisive element in Azerbaijan because of the presence of non-Turkish groups, were muted. The central government reacted fiercely and promptly; in September 1920, government forces crushed the rebellion. Khīābānī was killed. The Azerbaijani movement had a brief sequel in the rebellion of Major Abu'l Qāsim Lāhūtī, another Gendarmerie officer whose career resembled that of

Taqī Khān. Lāhūtī's seizure of Tabriz on 1 February 1922 and call for a march on Tehran reflects the continuing discontent among radical Gendarmerie officers at their subordination to the Cossack officers whom they despised as being of inferior birth, education and ability. Lāhūtī's rebellion was crushed by the Cossacks after a week. Lāhūtī escaped to Russia and lived to become a noted poet in Tajikistan.

The fourth rebellion was in Kurdistan and was led by one Ismāᶜīl Āqā, better known as Sīmtqū, chief of the Shakkāk tribe of Kurds. Sīmtqū's rebellion was basically a Kurdish tribal revolt but, like other Kurdish movements of the same period in Turkey and Iraq, it also had Ṣūfī and nationalist features. Sīmtqū was in touch with Kurdish nationalists in Paris and was designated minister of war in the projected government of Kurdistan. In 1919 Sīmtqū established himself at the head of 10,000 Kurdish tribesmen in the region around Lake Urmiyah and defied government forces and opposing tribal groups for three years before Riżā's new army defeated him in August 1922. The Kurdish tribal forces disintegrated and Sīmtqū fled to Turkey. He continued to trouble the frontier until his death in 1929 but no longer threatened the integrity of Iran.

By the end of 1922 the movements in northern Iran which had threatened the cohesion of Iran had all been defeated. Because each had contained an element of separatism and because of their location in frontier provinces with the prospect of foreign assistance they had seemed a serious menace to the Iranian state. In retrospect it is clear that the separatist element was not prominent; the object of the rebels was to influence affairs in Tehran and to obtain some degree of autonomy. Separatist demands were used as a lever on Tehran or became a last refuge when all attempts to obtain concessions from Tehran had failed. An important factor in their failure was that they received no foreign help apart from that given to the Gilan rising in 1920–1, notwithstanding all the many accusations of British, Russian and Turkish support. They failed also because they were weak and divided, particularly in their tribal support, and they were ultimately defeated by the determination and skill of the Tehran governments and their army.

During the years which followed the Tehran government extended its authority over southern Iran at the expense of the great tribal confederations and in defiance of Britain. A major step in this process was the reduction of the power of Shaykh Khazᶜal of Muḥammara (modern Khurramshahr) which extended over much of the province of Arabistan (Khuzistan). Taking advantage of the weakness of the central government since 1909 and with British assistance and Arab tribal support Khaz^c^al had established effective autonomy in the region and it seemed possible that Arabistan might go the way of Kuwayt. Britain, however, had always stopped short of giving Khaz^c^al any assurance of protection against the legitimate demands of the Tehran government and despite the advice of many officials who pointed to Britain's interests in the Gulf and her oil investment in Khuzistan and urged that Britain should back Khaz^c^al, Britain declined to do so when Riżā demanded Khaz^c^al's submission. As the ambassador, Sir Percy Loraine, wrote: 'it must be borne in mind that Tehran is the ultimate criterion of our relations with Persia and the cohesion of the Persian Empire as a whole is far more important to British interests generally and in the long run than the local supremacy of any of our particular protégés".[3] In November 1924 Riżā ordered his armies into Khuzistan and Khaz^c^al submitted on 6 December. The Arab chief was subsequently arrested and kept under house arrest in Tehran until his death in 1936. Arabistan was renamed Khuzistan, Persian-speaking officials were brought in and Persian was introduced as the language of instruction in the schools.

The pacification of the tribes of southern Iran was a long process pursued through a variety of means and one which was not completed until 1930. Riżā set tribe against tribe, exploited differences within tribes, set up and deposed chiefs, offered alternative employment to chiefs in the administration and to tribesmen in the army, opened roads into tribal territory such as the road from Dizfūl to Khurramābād which penetrated the wild region of Luristan, blocked annual migration routes and encouraged settlement. His army and gendarmerie fought annual campaigns.

It would be impossible to describe all these campaigns even if the details were available but mention may be made of the reduction of the two principal southern tribes, the Bakhtiyārī and the Qashqā'ī. The power and wealth of the Bakhtiyārī made them a formidable enemy. In 1909 they had been a principal agency of the deposition of the Qājār Shah, Muḥammad ^c^Alī, and they had dominated the government of Tehran and of several provinces for years afterwards. Furthermore, they enjoyed British support and British subsidies by virtue of their control of the oil fields. In 1923 Riżā demanded money and disarmament from the Bakhtiyārīs but accepted a compromise by which they paid over a sum of money but kept their arms. The episode, however, made it clear to all that the Bakhtiyārīs would not have British support in the future. The Qashqā'īs were the dominant tribe in Fars and possessed large stocks of arms; there was, however, no question of their receiving support from Britain with whom relations had been bad for years. Riżā left the Qashqā'īs alone until 1926 when he detained the Qashqā'ī chief in Tehran and carried through a partial disarmament of the tribe. The resentment of the Qashqā'īs and the Bakhtiyārīs was demonstrated in 1929 when they joined with other tribes in a major challenge to Riżā's government, demanding tribal autonomy, the release of their chiefs, an end to disarmament, lower taxes and above all, an end to conscription. For a time government control over large areas of southern Iran was lost. The government's answer was a major military campaign in 1929–30 which broke the back of tribal resistance. Riżā offered some concessions to the rebels but never implemented them and during the next few years suppressed further uprisings. Several chiefs were executed or kept in prison and the tribes, deprived of leadership, eventually subsided into grumbling submission. In a few brutal years Riżā had changed the course of Iranian history by reducing the major source of opposition to central government. Nomadism declined to embrace no more than 10 per cent of the population by 1941.

In the meantime Riżā had established his own control over the central government. From 1921 to 1923 Iran was governed by cabinets of old politicians responsible to parliament, the Majlis. The new parliament (the fourth since the establishment of the constitution in 1906) assembled in June 1921. It was dominated by large landowners and clerics, who comprised 40 per cent of the fourth Majlis as they did of its two successors. The Majlis had no parties but there were a number of factions including a small leftist group (led by a Qājār prince, Sulaymān Mīrzā), a conservative, nationalist and religious faction of which the most prominent spokesman was Sayyid Ḥasan Mudarris, and a secular liberal group within which the best known figure was Sayyid Muḥammad Tadayyun. The great notable politicians usually remained aloof from the factions but sought their help in the search for office. Of these old politicians the most able was the great northern landowner, Qavām al-Salṭana, brother of Vusūq al-Dawla, the main author of the agreement with Britain. Qavām was prime minister twice during the years 1921 and 1922 and was the principal rival to Riżā. He lost the battle for power partly because of Riżā's control of the army but also because he was unable to win sufficient support in the Majlis, especially from the conservative, clerical faction, and because he incurred the dislike of the Soviet Union with which he failed to negotiate a trade treaty. Qavām went into exile in October 1923 the month in which Riżā became prime minister.

In control of the government and of the army and able to interfere in the elections for the fifth Majlis which met in January 1924, Riżā was in a position to bid for supreme power. His first thought was to become president of a republic like Muṣṭafā Kemāl in Turkey. He allowed the notion to be mooted in the spring of 1924 and secured strong backing for the republican concept from Tadayyun and the liberal group. Mudarris and the clerical party, supported by the Shīʿī *mujtahids* outside parliament, opposed the establishment of a republic (which they equated with atheism just as Riżā, Tadayyun and others associated a republic with progress). The religious group raised powerful support on the streets and even caused divisions within the army. Riżā hastily pulled back, dropped his support for a republic, made his peace with the ulema at Qum, reunited his army supporters and persuaded the Majlis to recall him to the office of prime minister from which he had resigned. The episode had demonstrated that Riżā was not yet all-powerful and he adopted a cautious and conciliatory approach and set himself to win more support in the Majlis before trying again. A visit to the Shīʿī shrines in Iraq helped to win clerical approval.

In 1925 Riżā made a second bid for supreme power. In the late summer and autumn of that year he orchestrated a campaign against Aḥmad Shāh Qājār, who had been abroad in Europe since 1923. On 30 October the intimidated Majlis passed a law to abolish Qājār rule and appointed Riżā provisional head of state. On 15 December 1925 Riżā accepted the offer of the crown from a constituent assembly called into being for that purpose and crowned himself in a ceremony on 25 April 1926.

As Shah Riżā developed an autocratic style of rule. During his rise to power he had developed some political skills but political manoeuvre was not congenial to him. He was too inarticulate to argue and too poor a reader to master paperwork. He was accustomed to command and quick to resort to violence to get his way. Riżā also believed that an aloof style of kingship, punctuated with lightning personal interventions, was most consistent with the traditions of Iran and with its immediate needs. He had a very clear idea of the direction in which Iran should move, a vision of the rapid creation of a modern national state. Riżā took over and implemented a concept of Iran as a distinct cultural and political entity moulded by history and language. During his reign there was an emphasis upon the pre-Islamic past of Iran; ancient history was taught at the expense of the study of the Islamic period. The language was reformed to try to eliminate foreign words (although Riżā retained the Arabic script). For Riżā Iran was a teleological as well as an historical concept; the greatness of Iran was in the future as well as the past and it depended upon modernization.

Riżā needed new men to implement his policies. For the time being he made do with many of the old politicians and some of these continued to be prominent into the 1930s, notably Muḥammad ᶜAlī Furūghī, who served as prime minister for several years. Riżā also introduced men of his own choice and these men became dominant from 1933 onwards. From 1926 until 1932 his principal minister was ᶜAbd al-Ḥusayn Khān Taymūrtāsh, a member of a wealthy Khurasani land-owning family who had received a military education, travelled abroad and spoke several languages. Taymūrtāsh had all the skills and graces which Riżā lacked and he came to control Iran's foreign affairs and exercise an important influence over domestic affairs. Taymūrtāsh was an ambitious opportunist who made several serious errors and was eventually dismissed, imprisoned and possibly murdered in 1932. No subsequent minister obtained such power. Another prominent minister was ᶜAlī Akbar Dāvar, successively minister of the interior, justice and finance. In the latter two posts he presided over the major legal reforms of the period and over the programme of economic development. In provincial posts Riżā often employed his generals.

Riżā brought the Majlis under firm control. He used his influence at the 1928 elections to eliminate many of his more vocal critics. During the following years the character of the Majlis changed: clerical representation fell dramatically and the Majlis became dominated by big landlords. Riżā allowed them to retain their lands and local influence; in return they refrained from opposing his policies. There were no political parties.

Riżā's policy of conciliating landlords requires further comment because it goes to the heart of the Pahlavī regime in the period before 1960. Big landlords owning one or more villages and receiving rent from peasant cultivators dominated Iranian agriculture and local life. Landlords improved their position under Riżā Shāh. After 1924 they benefited from sales of state land and they profited also from the abolition of the land tax in 1934. Their ranks were joined by Riżā himself who became the greatest landlord in Iran, owning nearly 1.5 million hectares, mainly in the northern provinces and acquired by methods which do not bear examination. Some of the new men who rose under the Pahlavī regime also turned their influence into land. Riżā's regime was a landlord regime and this circumstance meant that the impact of the changes he introduced could have little effect in the countryside and the bases of power and authority in Iran would remain unchanged.

Riżā avoided a direct conflict with the great leaders of Shīʿī Islam but he contrived increasingly to reduce the role of Islam. It was during the 1920s that the shrine at Qum developed into one of the most important centres of Shīʿī teaching and the base of several notable *mujtahids*. In his early years Riżā cultivated the support of the ulema but from 1926 onwards he showed increasing disregard for their views. The extension of state control over education and the reform of law and law courts reduced their role; government control of *waqfs* left part of their income at Riżā's mercy; and their opinions were flouted over the introduction of western costume. But Riżā also feared the power of the ulema. In 1938 he confided to a United States' diplomat that dark forces of religious fanaticism existed in Iran which were more powerful and more hostile to progress than those which existed in Turkey. Certainly the Iranian religious classes were treated much more warily than were Turkey's ulema: some reforms, such as the adoption of a Latin script, were dropped for fear of religious opposition; and the ulema of Iran remained a large and wealthy group, deeply influential in the social life of Iran.

Riżā introduced profound changes in law and education. Legal reform was required as a necessary preliminary to ridding Iran of the capitulations (accomplished in 1928), to provide a firmer basis for the conduct of economic transactions and to extend the power of the state. Modern codes had been devised in the past but there were neither courts nor trained lawyers to apply them. After the reorganization of the ministry of justice in 1927 European-trained lawyers were substituted for clerics and a steady expansion of state courts took place. A new civil code was introduced progressively from 1928 and issued as a complete code in 1939. The code was modelled on French law but the section dealing with personal law was taken from the Sharīʿa.

France also provided the model for the reform of education. Once again there had been several attempts at reform in the past but all had foundered for want of money and will. The results of Riżā's reforms were impressive. Between 1919 and 1940 state spending on education multiplied 20 times: the number of schools increased from less than 300 to over 8,000, and the number of pupils from 23,000 to half a million. Higher education and teacher training also developed: in 1934 the University of Tehran was founded by amalgamating a number of existing institutions and a major programme of teacher training resulted in the establishment of 36 colleges by 1941. Many students were in religious schools but the expansion of religious schools peaked in 1936 while that of the state schools accelerated. By 1940 most pupils were in the state system and an overwhelming majority at the secondary level. Private schools run by foreign missionaries and non-Muslim religious communities also played an important part but Riżā regarded these with suspicion, closed some of the non-Muslim schools and expelled the missionaries in 1940. In many ways the education provided in Pahlavī Iran was superficial and it remained largely an urban phenomenon. Nevertheless, Riżā's schools and his adult education programme launched in 1936 substantially reduced illiteracy in Iran.

Several other changes were introduced in the social life of Pahlavī Iran. Standards of health were improved, particularly for town dwellers; women were given new rights in property and divorce and polygamy were discouraged: and there were many sumptuary laws. In 1928 Riżā effectively forced the widespread adoption of western dress and in 1935 abolished the veil, an act which had the effect of confining many conservative women to their houses.

Economic development was at the centre of Riżā's programme of reform from 1930. During the early years of his reign he was too concerned with other matters and handicapped by the capitulations. An unfavourable trade agreement forced upon Iran in 1927 by her major trade partner, Russia, the achievement of tariff autonomy in 1928, and the world depression of 1929 were key factors in persuading Riżā to sponsor a programme of state-directed economic development. In this programme agriculture was ignored and the principal features were the development of modern industry based on import substitution (mainly textiles and food processing) and the construction of a nationwide system of communications – roads, ports and, above all, the Trans-Iranian railway, the centre piece of Riżā's programme. The railway, extending 1,800 kilometres from the Gulf to the Caspian, absorbed the largest part of Iran's development budget and has been widely regarded as a wasteful investment. Critics have argued that a cheaper railway system, orientated on an east–west axis, would have been more profitable, or that Iran would have been better to have spent the money on roads. It is certainly true that Iran saw very little immediate benefit from her substantial expenditure. One is left with the impression that for Riżā a railway was less an economic choice than a symbol of modernity and an assertion of independence, an instrument required to free northern Iran from the economic dominance of Russia.

Iran's economic development could have been financed by borrowing; in her oil resources Iran had excellent security for foreign loans. But Riżā shared the common Iranian antipathy to foreign loans and, having squeezed the Anglo–Persian Oil Company for all he thought he could obtain in the renegotiation of the concession in 1933, Riżā relied on internal resources raised through indirect taxes, namely monopolies on tea and sugar. By so doing he ensured that the costs of development would fall most heavily on the poorest section of the population and especially on the countryside. No single decision, except for conscription, contributed more to his unpopularity. And he was unrelenting. After the completion of the railway he might have relaxed but instead he pressed on with ambitious plans for an iron and steel industry and with an extensive programme of military expenditure. In this last period he financed his projects by printing money and between 1936 and 1939 prices rose 50 per cent, representing another burden on the poor.

The Second World War was a blow to Riżā's plans for modernization. Iran's neutrality was inevitable: she could not afford to alienate either Germany, Britain or the USSR and was terrified that the Soviet Union might take the chance to assert her dominance over Iran. But the supplies of civil and military goods on which Iran's development plans depended dried up, her oil revenues fell and foreign currency reserves abroad were frozen. For two years Iran limped along until the German invasion of Russia in June 1941 and the formation of the Anglo–Russian alliance. Iran now had to confront again the situation which had left her impotent between 1907 and 1917; the two Great Powers which she most feared were once more in alliance.

During the summer of 1941 Iran tried to buy time in the hope that the USSR might collapse under the German onslaught. She resisted the Anglo–Soviet demands for the dismissal of the Germans employed in Iran. But Britain and the USSR were in no mood to be patient and began to plan military action as early as July. On 16 August the British and Russian demands were presented to Iran and after their anticipated rejection the two powers invaded Iran on 25 August. On 16 September, the day Tehran was occupied by Allied forces, Riżā Shāh abdicated in favour of his son, Muḥammad Riżā Shāh. Neither the British nor the old politicians wanted him. The ex-Shah died three years later in South Africa.

Iran was under occupation from 1941 until 1946. The occupation was legalized by a tripartite treaty signed on 29 January 1942 according to which the occupation was not an occupation. Britain and the USSR pledged themselves to respect Iran's territorial integrity, sovereignty and political independence and to evacuate Iran not later than six months after the end of the war. Iran agreed to Allied control of Iran's communications for the purpose of sending supplies to the USSR through Iran. By the Tehran Declaration of 1 December 1943 the United States joined Britain and the USSR in a further pledge to respect Iran's independence. In order to execute the treaty Soviet forces were stationed in northern Iran and British forces in the south. From 1942 US forces organized much of the supply system. Inevitably, the foreign powers interfered widely in Iranian government both in the provinces and in Tehran, especially in the area of financial and economic policy. In addition the United States supplied a number of advisers to departments of Iranian government to assist with security forces, the economy and finance. The most important of these advisers was Arthur Millspaugh, who headed the financial mission (as he had led a similar mission during the 1920s) and who used his powers to attempt an extensive redirection of Iranian development.

Iranian independence was considerably abridged by the occupation and the power of government reduced. The demands of the Allied powers also imposed on Iran much economic hardship leading to inflation (300 per cent in the years 1941–3), shortages of food and other commodities and even famine. At the same time the removal of Riżā Shāh led to much greater political freedom and there developed in Iran during the years after 1941 a tripartite struggle for influence between the Shah, the Majlis and the occupying powers.

The new Shah was young (22) and inexperienced. More importantly he could no longer rely on the instruments which had supported his father's regime. The army had collapsed in 1941 and because of the occupation could not be used freely against the Shah's enemies. The Shah could no longer control the Majlis and therefore his power over government was much reduced. The Pahlavī lands were taken by the state. In the circumstances Muḥammad Riżā played for time, seeking to keep control of the army of which he was commander in chief, to defend the military budget and to rebuild the army in the hope that at the end of the war he might use it to restore the power of the monarchy. The strength of the army recovered to 80,000 in 1943, 100,000 in 1946 and 120,000 in 1949.

The Majlis, as previously, was dominated by big landowners. There were still no parties but members grouped themselves into several factions, the number of which fluctuated during the war. The factions were based partly on kinship and regional links, partly on the attitude of individuals to the occupying powers and to the Pahlavīs and partly on ideology. One group, mainly from central and western Iran, was sympathetic to the Pahlavīs. Another group, mainly from the south, looked to Britain. From 1943 the leading figure in this group was Sayyid Żiyā al-Dīn Ṭabāṭabā'ī, Riżā's fellow conspirator in 1921. A third group, from the north west, consisted of a number of former Qājār notables who were hostile to the Pahlavīs and allegedly sought Soviet support. In this group the leading figure was Aḥmad Qavām, the former Qavām al-Salṭana, Riżā's principal rival in 1922-3. These and other factions were essentially coalitions which sought to protect the local interests of their members and to form alliances in order to achieve ministerial office or to extract patronage from ministers. Under the constitution the Majlis possessed the power, which it could now exercise, to choose and dismiss governments. There was, however, a broader sentiment, namely to defend the independence of Iran; the Majlis opposed the granting of an oil concession in the northern provinces to the USSR in 1944 and obstructed the attempts of the US financial adviser to dominate Iranian government in 1943–5.

The consequence of greater political freedom and the balance of power was political instability which persisted in Iran down to 1953. There were 31 cabinets and 148 ministers in the 12 years after 1941 compared with 10 cabinets and 50 ministers in the previous 16 years of Riżā's rule. Cabinets during the second period were commonly coalitions formed by arrangements in which the designated prime minister bought votes in return for portfolios. Cabinets were dominated by old notables; although several of Riżā's new men held office 81 of the 148 ministers came from old notable families. The fall of Riżā had meant the return of the notables and one is confronted once more with the irony that Near Eastern notables prospered most under the European influence which they resisted most fiercely.

The period of the occupation also led to the recovery of some of their lost power by religious leaders and tribal chiefs, who were released from detention. By 1943 there was virtually no government presence in the Bakhtiyārī area and the Qashqā'īs also asserted their independence. Nomadism and semi-nomadism are said to have doubled in the years after 1941. Religious leaders were wooed by government, *waqf* lands and religious schools were returned to their control and they were allowed to vent their animosity towards non-Muslim groups. In Khuzistan, Kurdistan and Azerbaijan ethnic movements developed.

The greater political and press freedom led also to the appearance of new, more ideological urban parties. The most prominent of these parties was the Tūdah Party, founded in September 1941, by a group of Marxists who had been imprisoned in 1937 and were released after Riżā's abdication. Its first leader was the veteran radical, Sulaymān Mīrzā. The party quickly acquired a large following among intellectuals and professional people and began to appeal to organized labour; in 1944 the Tūdah formed the Council of Federated Trade Unions

(CFTU) out of an organization established in 1942 and began arranging strikes. The party spread out from Tehran into the north, where it enjoyed Soviet patronage. and then into the south where it acquired a considerable following among oil workers in Khuzistan. In July 1946 it organized a massive strike in Khuzistan. The party's main strength was outside parliament but in 1944 it succeeded in electing eight of its supporters. Its programme was that of a national democratic revolution; it was strongly opposed to landlord domination. The Tūdah was at the peak of its influence in 1946 with 50,000 members and a claimed industrial following through the CFTU of 350,000. It had three cabinet ministers and controlled the administration in many towns.

A number of nationalist parties made their appearance, including the Iran Party, a moderate party of young liberal intellectuals, some of a secular disposition, others, like the engineer Mahdī Bāzargān, of a more religious inclination who looked to the traditional bazaar for support. The Iran Party was one of the constituents of a loose grouping known as the National Front (NF) which came into existence in 1944.

The conflicts which had developed in Iran during the war came to a head in 1946. At that time it is possible to discern three main groups. The Shah and his supporters wanted to re-establish the power of the monarchy, end the foreign occupation and resist the claims of ethnic groups aiming at autonomy, of radicals intent on social and political revolution and of notables insistent on reducing the power of the monarchy. They looked to the western powers for outside support. Second were the notables who wanted to end the occupation, preserve the integrity of Iran, avoid social revolution but replace the Pahlavīs as the dominant group in Iran. Third were the radicals who favoured a reconstruction of Iranian society and politics possibly with Soviet assistance; some hoped to establish autonomous governments in ethnically distinct regions, notably in Kurdistan and Azerbaijan.

The most urgent problem was the evacuation of Soviet forces from northern Iran. British and American forces were withdrawn within the timetable laid down in 1942 but in March 1946 Soviet forces still remained. On the matter of evacuation the views of the old notables and the Pahlavīs coincided and an uncertain, working alliance was achieved. A government was formed in January 1946 under Qavām, who reached an agreement with the Soviet Union in April 1946 by which the Soviet troops would be withdrawn in mid-May and an oil concession for the northern provinces would be given to the USSR. Qavām pointed out, however, that the agreement required the assent of the Majlis. He had carefully waited until the dissolution of the twelfth Majlis in March 1946 and he argued that a new Majlis could not be elected until Soviet forces had gone. Soviet forces were withdrawn by 9 May but elections were delayed because of the situation which had developed in Azerbaijan and Kurdistan.

In October and November 1945 an armed uprising in Azerbaijan had brought to power the Democratic Party of Azerbaijan, an organization founded in September 1945 which included many of the former supporters of Khīābānī's abortive movement of 1917–20. The leader was Jaᶜfar Pīshāvarī, who had been released from prison in 1941. The Azerbaijan Democrat Party allied with the Tūdah and received Soviet help. In December 1945 Pīshāvarī became prime minister of the newly proclaimed autonomous government of Azerbaijan. The programme of the new government was radical and embraced land reform, support for the rights of workers and women and the use of Azerī in schools and government offices. The Democrats encountered opposition from several quarters – Kurds and other tribes as well as from supporters of the authority of Tehran, they were handicapped by a poor harvest in 1946 and their autocratic rule made them increasingly unpopular.

Government authority had also weakened in Kurdistan during the war. As early as 1942 a Kurdish national organization, the Association for the Renaissance of Kurdistan, had been founded in Mahābād under the leadership of a prominent religious figure, Qāżī Muḥammad. In 1945 this organization merged with a leftist group to form the Democratic Party of Kurdistan, also led by Qāżī Muḥammad. At this time the Kurdish nationalists were reinforced from Iraq with the arrival of Muṣṭafā Bārzānī and his followers, who were avoiding British and Iraqi efforts to subdue them. The Kurdish Democrats' programme had called for Kurdish autonomy but on 22 January 1946 Qāżī Muḥammad went beyond this and proclaimed the foundation of the Kurdish Republic of Mahābād, a direct challenge, apparently with Soviet encouragement, to the integrity of Iran.

Qavām pursued a devious policy during the summer of 1946. On the one hand he offered to recognize limited Azerbaijani autonomy and made overtures to the left. He also launched his own party, the Democrat Party, with a programme of radical reform and in August formed a coalition with the Tūdah and Iran parties. The evidence does not permit us to be sure about his motives and intentions. On the one hand it seems possible that he was preparing to carry out his aim of reducing the power of the monarchy by allying with the radicals; on the other it is possible that he was merely playing for time until Iran was ready to reassert her power in Azerbaijan and Kurdistan and could be sure that the Soviet Union would permit her to do so. In the autumn of 1946 he turned against the left and in December ordered the army to re-enter Azerbaijan and Kurdistan where the nationalist governments were quickly destroyed.

Qavām had preserved the unity of Iran but the real winner was the monarch. Although Qavām's supporters were most numerous in the new Majlis they lacked cohesion and there was a strong body of conservative support for the crown, especially from the newly recovered regions. When Qavām eventually submitted the oil agreement with Russia to the Majlis for approval in October 1947 it was promptly rejected and Qavām immediately resigned. It seems probable that Qavām had always known that the Majlis would reject his bargain – he made no attempt to persuade the assembly – and that he had worked the Soviet Union out of Iran by a confidence trick. Like Curzon in 1919 Molotov had not understood the importance of Majlis ratification of an agreement.

At the end of 1947 it seemed that the Shah was on the verge of rebuilding Pahlavī power. His enemies were divided; he had control of the army, the government and bureaucracy; and he had recovered the Pahlavī estates. He went on to complete the destruction of the left and strengthened his position against the Majlis by constitutional changes which established a second chamber under his control and gave him the right to dissolve parliament. Royal influence in the 1949 elections was strong and the 16th Majlis, which met in 1950 contained a majority of supporters of the monarchy. But the appearance was deceptive: the Shah's opponents were still intent upon limiting his power and an opportunity to do so was presented by the Anglo–Iranian oil dispute.

The Shah needed money to relaunch Iran's modernization programme of which the centre piece was the mighty seven year plan announced in 1946. He had hoped for substantial United States' aid but was disappointed. It was the more important, therefore, to achieve a quick and profitable renegotiation of the Anglo–Iranian concession. An agreement was signed in July 1949 but there was insufficient time for the 15th Majlis to consider it and it was left over for the new parliament.

The 16th Majlis declined to accept the oil agreement and called for the nationalization of the oil industry. There has been a good deal of argument about the terms which were offered but this discussion seems to miss the point that at bottom the complaints of the Majlis were not financial but political. Iranian oil was not a mere commodity, like cotton, but a symbol of Iranian independence. Furthermore, it was feared that oil revenues in the hands of the Shah could corrupt the liberties of Iran and subvert the constitution. As so often in contemplating the relations of Shah and notables in twentieth century Iran one is reminded of the struggles of Crown and Whigs in eighteenth century England; oil, like India, stood at once for prestige and corruption.

The Shah's response was to choose as prime minister a tough soldier, General ᶜAlī Razmārā, to push the oil agreement through the Majlis. Razmārā, however, frightened many of his potential allies among the landowners with a radical programme which in some ways foreshadowed the White Revolution of the 1960s. Opposition to him was widespread by the time he was assassinated on 7 March 1951. The Majlis was then thoroughly alarmed by the demonstrations of popular hostility to the oil agreement. There had been a growth of religious protest, led by Āyatallāh Abu'l Qāsim Kāshānī, against foreign influence in general and the Anglo–Iranian Oil Company (AIOC) in particular; a member of a group of religious terrorists (the Fidā'iyān-i Islām) had been responsible for the murder of Razmārā. Also, the Tūdah party, which had quickly revived, organized street demonstrations.

Thoroughly intimidated the Majlis passed a bill to nationalize the oil industry on 20 March 1951 and in May found a prime minister willing to implement it. This was Muḥammad Muṣaddiq, an elderly politician who had been a prominent opponent of Riżā Shāh in the 1920s, had returned to politics in 1944, and in 1950, as chairman of the Majlis oil committee, had emerged as the most prominent opponent of the agreement. Muṣaddiq was strongly supported by the National Front. He had a high reputation for ability and integrity but he lacked the political judgement of Qavām.

Muṣaddiq dominated the Iranian political scene from 1951 to 1953. He had two objectives: to expel the AIOC and to reduce the power of the Shah. Muṣaddiq was an independent with no clear basis of support. He endeavoured to obtain a sympathetic Majlis by stopping the elections when a bare quorum of 69 members had been elected so as to exclude the conservative landlords from the countryside and magnify the effect of his own urban following. Even so, landlords were still the largest group in the new Majlis and Muṣaddiq could not rely on it for support. The National Front itself was divided and as time went on the religious element abandoned Muṣaddiq. As a consequence Muṣaddiq tended to appeal to the streets where he received support from the Tūdah Party in his struggles against the Shah; thus, in July 1952, when he resigned after a clash with the Shah over control of the army, massive street demonstrations forced the Shah to recall him. But Muṣaddiq's dependence upon the streets tended to alienate not only the conservative landlords but also the religious leaders. By August 1953 Muṣaddiq was driven to seek support through a national referendum which he won by a large majority.

Muṣaddiq failed to reach agreement with the AIOC over the nationalization of oil: the great Abadan refinery was closed down in October 1951 and subsequent efforts to find a compromise also failed. It is still difficult to explain Muṣaddiq's unwillingness to accept the offers made to him. One view is that he thought Iran could do without oil revenues; another view is that he believed Iran could sell her oil independently; a third is that he thought the United States would bail Iran out with aid to save her from communism; and another possibility is that he kept the crisis going in order to prosecute his second aim of reducing the power of the Shah. There is also disagreement about the effects of the cessation of oil revenues. It has recently been argued that Iran managed not too badly but the more common view is that Iran suffered and that the consequent discontent increased opposition to Muṣaddiq.

Muṣaddiq came close to destroying the power of the Pahlavīs but in the end he failed. His first major clash with the Shah occurred in July 1952 when he forced the Shah to allow him to govern without parliament and to make him minister of war. Muṣaddiq used his new position to try to undermine the Shah's control of the army and appointed military commanders favourable to himself. A crisis in the relations of Shah and prime minister occurred in August 1953. On 16 August the Shah dismissed Muṣaddiq and appointed General Fażlallāh Zāhidī to succeed him. Muṣaddiq refused to go, the Tūdah demonstrated in his support, and the Shah fled abroad. Interestingly, Muṣaddiq himself feared that the Tūdah might be the real gainers from the fall of the Shah and he ordered the army to clear the streets. Subsequently, Tūdah leaders claimed that they had indeed planned a coup. It seemed that Muṣaddiq had won but on 19 August Muṣaddiq was overthrown by army action and street demonstrations against himself. One factor in the fall of Muṣaddiq was an Anglo–American plot whereby contact was made with Zāhidī and other opponents of Muṣaddiq and funds supplied to pay for street demonstrations. But this plot could not have succeeded if it had not been that Muṣaddiq had lost so much of his support from the religious classes, many of the tribes and sections of the National Front as well as from landowners and the army.

Between 1953 and 1960 the Shah rebuilt his power. His political opponents, the Tūdah and the National Front, were crushed. The Tūdah Party had made extensive inroads in the army and it was claimed that the Tūdah military organisation had 500 members, mainly junior officers of lower middle class origin in support units. The army was thoroughly purged and enlarged from 120,000 in 1953 to over 200,000 in 1963. Muṣaddiq himself was tried and given three years imprisonment and subsequently confined to his country estate until his death in 1965. The Shah also began to build stronger security forces; in 1957 his secret police force, Savak, was founded.

The Shah established firmer control over the Majlis; in 1956 its numbers were increased from 136 to 400 deputies, a circumstance which made it more difficult for a tiny minority to control the assembly and sessions were extended from two years to four. Landowners still predominated in the membership of the Majlis although their proportion dropped from over 80 per cent in the pre-1952 assemblies to about 50 per cent in the post 1953 parliaments. The proposals for land reform put forward between 1950 and 1953 were set aside for some years. In 1957 an effort was made to create a two party system within the Majlis consisting of a government party and a loyal opposition. The system broke down, however, when it was attempted to conduct the 1960 elections on a two-party basis. The Shah also cultivated the religious classes and found an ally in the most prominent religious leader, Āyatallāh Muḥammad Ḥusayn Burūjirdī. The religious leaders were content to support a conservative monarchy and in return the Shah relaxed controls on religious schools and permitted a campaign against the Bahā'īs. By 1960, however, the disadvantages of relying on a conservative coalition of landowners and religious leaders were becoming increasingly apparent. The Shah wanted to move ahead with a programme of modernization.

Iran had recovered economically from the Muṣaddiq years. In 1954 agreement over oil was finally reached: oil nationalization endured and the Anglo–Iranian concession was transferred to a new international consortium which shared profits equally with Iran. The United States gave financial assistance to tide Iran over until oil revenues returned to the Iranian treasury and began to give large amounts of military aid. The growing demand for oil through the 1950s increased the revenues at Iran's disposal from 45 million dollars in 1950 to 285 million in 1960. In 1956 the second seven-year plan was inaugurated but its ambitious scope soon exhausted Iran's resources and led to heavy borrowing, printing money and inflation. By 1960 Iran was in a new economic crisis which demanded new measures.

NOTES

1. Quoted D.N. Wilbur, *Riza Shah Pahlavi*, Hicksville, NY 1975, 49.
2. Quoted Wilbur, *op.cit.*, 95.
3. Loraine to Curzon, No.551 of 4 September 1922, Public Records Office, FO 371/7830.

CHAPTER SEVEN

Arabia to the 1960s

GENERAL

The Arabian peninsula includes most of the Near East but in 1920 Arabia was the least modernized and most sparsely populated division of the region. The peninsula was largely desert; cultivation was confined to oases and a few highland regions, notably the Yemen and Oman, where sufficient rain fell to support agriculture. Industry consisted of handicrafts, fishing, pearling and servicing the pilgrim traffic. No-one knows how large the population was: at a guess it was seven million, although it may have been only half this total. Nor do we know how the population was distributed. The nomadic population is thought to have comprised between one-quarter and one-half of the whole, the urban population between 10 and 25 per cent, and settled cultivators to have made up the remainder. Nor do we know which was the largest town among Aden, Ṣanᶜā', Jidda and Mecca although none had more than 100,000 inhabitants. By 1950 little had changed, including our ignorance, but between 1950 and 1970 the region entered upon a greater transformation than any other region of the Near East.

Before 1914 two outside powers, the Ottomans and Britain, had exercised a preponderant influence over the coasts of Arabia and had divided the interior between them into spheres of influence, although these might better be described as spheres of marginal influence. As a result of the Ottoman collapse in the First World War the great political question of Arabia in 1920 was what was going to happen to the former Ottoman sphere. One possibility was that Britain would take it over by establishing a predominant influence over the local rulers. Britain did toy with variations on this possibility including the idea that local rulers might be grouped into some sort of confederation under the suzerainty of King Ḥusayn of the Ḥijāz who would thus be the principal agent of British control. But Britain abandoned this idea, partly because Ḥusayn was unco-operative but mainly because she thought the gains not worth the effort. As a consequence the question of who should succeed the Ottomans was left to local rulers to decide among themselves. The answer was ᶜAbd al-ᶜAzīz Āl Saᶜūd. Between 1921 and 1926 the ruler of Najd extended his control over all the former Ottoman territories with the exception of Yemen. Ḥā'il was annexed in 1921, the Ḥijāz in 1925, and ᶜAsīr in two bites in 1920 and 1926. Those successes left only Yemen which he defeated in 1934 and might have incorporated in his empire but for the intervention of Britain and Italy who preserved the independence of Yemen.

By 1926 the political structure of Arabia, as it was to exist until the end of the 1960s, was complete. The new structure was hardened by the creation of land frontiers. Before 1914 only the line between the British and Ottoman spheres had been traced; throughout Arabia authority was over men not land, and frontiers were as fluid as the tribes which moved through them. The establishment of European rule in the Fertile Crescent had the effect of completing the ringing of Arabia by a power which demanded the application of European notions of frontiers. This process of frontier making was begun in the 1920s when the frontiers with Kuwayt, Iraq and Transjordan were settled and the principle was ultimately extended to cover the whole of Arabia. The main sufferers were the nomadic tribes as frontiers were usually drawn through deserts. The main beneficiaries were states and historians, who can use the states as meaningful entities around which to write the history of Arabia. Before 1920 states in Arabia were little more than the assertions by oases of claims to tax their users, by religious dignitaries of claims to recognition, and military alliances among tribes.

SAUDI ARABIA TO 1964

The flavour of the state of Saudi Arabia in the form in which it existed in 1926 may be judged from the so-called constitution of that year which stated simply that "all administration is in the hands of His Majesty King ᶜAbd al-ᶜAzīz ibn Saᶜūd. His Majesty is bound by the laws of the Sharīᶜa."[1] The phrasing conveys exactly the orthodox Muslim concept of government: legislation was unnecessary because it was complete for all time in the Sharīᶜa and all that was required was a pious Muslim ruler to implement the law. ᶜAbd al-ᶜAzīz at that time was king only in the Ḥijāz, where he had in effect inherited the title assumed by the Hashimites in 1916; in his other great province of Najd he ruled as Sulṭan until the following year when he became king of Najd as well. Even so his father bore the older title of Imām until 1928. Only in 1932 did the Kingdom of Saudi Arabia come into existence, its name bearing witness to its origins as the dynastic possessions of the Saᶜūdī family. The founder of the state ruled until his death in 1953 when he was succeeded by his oldest son Saᶜūd, who had been designated heir in 1933 and who held the title until 1964, although not always the authority of ruler. The challenge by his brother Fayṣal to Saᶜūd's authority and the eventual resolution of the dispute between them mark a major change in the character of the Saᶜūdī state.

The government of Saudi Arabia was simple. The kingdom was divided into the two viceroyalties of Najd, ruled by Saᶜūd, and the Ḥijāz, ruled by Fayṣal. The viceroyalties were subdivided into provinces which were confided to other sons or relatives of ᶜAbd al-ᶜAzīz. Each governor had his own advisers and agents; in the more sophisticated Ḥijāz Fayṣal found in being the former Ottoman system of administration which he could adapt. The central government in Riyāḍ consisted of no more than the chosen advisers of the king. Until the 1940s there were only two ministries: foreign affairs which was given to Fayṣal whose territories included Jidda to which contact with the outside world was largely confined; and finance, which was held by a Najdī, ᶜAbdallāh Sulaymān, from 1932 until 1954. For the rest there were sundry trusted men, several of them from outside Arabia, including an Egyptian journalist, Shaykh Ḥāfiẓ Wahba, who subsequently wrote an almost unique account of the government of Saudi Arabia in this period. Ministers of defence and the interior were added in 1944 and 1952 respectively but only in 1953 did a full council of ten ministers emerge. That event marked the takeover of the central government of the kingdom by members of the Saᶜūdī family; eight of the ministers were Saᶜūdīs, including seven sons of ᶜAbd al-ᶜAzīz. Justice, however, was placed under a member of the Āl Shaykh family, the religious half of the alliance which had formed the Wahhābī state in the eighteenth century. Law remained the province of the orthodox ulema whose support was still vital to the Saᶜūdī dynasty.

Government was minimal until the 1950s, partly through Muslim tradition, partly because of opposition to any extension of government, but especially because the government could afford no more than the minimum. The revenues of Saudi Arabia were tiny. The

British subsidy ended in 1924 and thereafter the state depended upon collection of *zakāt* (the religious donation which effectively became a tax paid to the ruler), a share of the plunder won on raids, and customs duties. The total income of the state in 1932 was around $2.5 million. Much depended upon the pilgrimage and when pilgrims did not come, as in the early 1930s and during the Second World War, Saudi Arabia was in great financial difficulty. During the war ᶜAbd al-ᶜAzīz was again given a British subsidy but the fortunes of Saudi Arabian governments were not much improved until the end of the 1940s when oil revenues began to come in abundance, rising from 13 million in 1946 to 172 million in 1952. Oil revenues financed the expansion of government during the 1950s.

With so small a revenue before 1950 Saudi Arabia could afford only a tiny army. The original military forces were composed of Najdī townsmen, bedouin and Ikhwān. The last were the tribesmen settled in the new religious–agricultural settlements established by ᶜAbd al-ᶜAzīz from 1912. The Ikhwān formed the major element in the Saudi forces during the period of expansion from 1921 to 1926. After the last date ᶜAbd al-ᶜAzīz became concerned by their uncontrolled violence and sought to diminish their role and advance that of other forces. By the 1950s the Saudi forces had changed substantially and consisted of three main elements: tribal levies, a regular army based mainly on Ḥijāzī forces with ex-Ottoman officers and regarded as potentially disloyal, and the Royal Guard, a force of some 2,700 Najdīs wholly loyal to the king and thought to be the most effective fighting force in Saudi Arabia. Because of the small size of the army and its unreliability ᶜAbd al-ᶜAzīz had to rely on political skill and bargaining more than on coercion to hold his new state together.

The major problem of the state before 1950 was that of integrating the various parts into a single political unit, a problem never fully solved or even seriously attempted because of the continuing resentment on the part of many Ḥijāzīs towards Najdī rule, and the anarchy of the tribes. Before 1914 ᶜAbd al-ᶜAzīz had attempted to harness the tribes to the state by Islamic propaganda and settlement, devices which had produced the Ikhwān. By the late 1920s the Ikhwān were an embarrassment which threatened both internal security and foreign intervention because of the animosity aroused in neighbouring states by their raids. ᶜAbd al-ᶜAzīz succeeded in dividing the Ikhwān and forming a coalition of townsmen, cultivators and tribesmen against them. In 1929–30 he crushed them and thereafter the military threat of the tribes was much reduced. From that time on the state's dealings with the tribes were characterized by the gradual establishment of state authority and law through persuasion, coercion and subsidies to tribal leaders and by the encouragement of settlement. The problem of the tribes was ultimately solved by oil, which was the primary factor in bringing about the abandonment of nomadism and facilitating the process of settlement.

Before 1950 there was little economic change in Saudi Arabia. Agriculture and industry, other than oil, remained unaltered. Oil exploration began in 1931, a concession was given to Standard Oil of California in 1933 and production commenced in 1938. Because of the Second World War there was no substantial oil export until 1944, the year in which the great oil company, Aramco, was established to operate the concession. The oil operations in Saudi Arabia were tiny and remote; their effect on the economy was indirect through the funds made available for investment. In the 1950s the effects of these revenues began to be felt especially in the improvement of communications: roads, a railway from Riyāḍ to the Gulf coast, telegraph, telephone, radio and air traffic. Oil development also assisted the growth of towns, which had remained substantially unaltered since 1920, lacking even electricity. By 1955 Riyāḍ and Jidda had each grown to between 100,000 and 150,000, largely through the immigration of workers from outside Saudi Arabia. There was some investment in schools and a university was established at Riyāḍ in 1952.

The political effects of oil-induced change were experienced in the conflict which followed the death of ᶜAbd al-ᶜAzīz. This conflict was successfully contained within the Saᶜūdī family but it was a real dispute about the future development of Saudi Arabia. It was personalized in the opposition of Saᶜūd and Fayṣal. In simple terms Saᶜūd supposed that Saudi Arabia might go on much as before, that is as a grand tribal confederation, except that there would now be no shortage of money for its élite. Fayṣal stood for the view that Saudi Arabia must develop more elaborate state structures and invest in social and economic development if it was to cope with the influx of oil money. Both sought allies within the Saᶜūdī family, the household and state institutions and among the tribes and each sought to introduce his own close relatives and supporters into positions of power. The contest swayed this way and that; in 1958 Fayṣal prevailed and as prime minister exercised real power; in 1960 Saᶜūd recovered power and brought in his own supporters; in 1962 Fayṣal returned as prime minister; and in 1964 was finally victorious when Saᶜūd first abandoned all power to him and then abdicated in Fayṣal's favour on November 1964. In the decisive round in March 1964 Fayṣal had the support of his full brothers of the Sudayrī clan, the ulema, some tribal leaders and the National Guard; Saᶜūd rested on his sons and the Royal Guard but lost control of the latter. Fayṣal's victory was ultimately due to the circumstance that other members of the élite thought him better able to handle the two major problems of Saudi Arabia: bringing the state finances into some order and dealing with the menace of radical Arab nationalism, brought to the borders of Saudi Arabia by the 1962 revolution in the Yemen and the Egyptian intervention. It was literally a palace revolution but no less a revolution for that.

NORTH YEMEN TO 1962

North Yemen may be divided into three distinct geographical regions: the coastal plain known as the Tihāma, the mountainous interior and the eastern desert. In 1920 the latter region was the home of a few bedouin and played little or no part in events. The Tihāma was inhabited by Sunnī Arabs of the Shāfiᶜī school, many of part-African descent, who worked as sharecroppers on big landed estates. The mountainous region was the most fertile; in the northern area rainfall was sufficient to support a peasant subsistence agriculture. The peasants were Shīᶜī tribesmen of the Zaydī sect. In the south rainfall was less and as in the Tihāma cultivation depended mainly on irrigation. Large estates were again the norm and the inhabitants also Shāfiᶜīs. The great majority of the population were subsistence cultivators, although coffee and the narcotic *qāt* were produced for sale. Nomads were not more than 5 per cent and town dwellers about 10 per cent. The principal towns were the capital Ṣanᶜā' in the northern highlands, Taᶜizz in the southern uplands and the port of Ḥudayda on the Tihāma coast. The townspeople were non-tribal, mainly Shāfiᶜī, and included an aristocracy of *sayyids* (descendants of the Prophet) and *qāḍīs* (judges) as well as a lower class of artisans and shopkeepers. The towns were especially the stronghold of Islam; in the country areas customary tribal law mitigated by arbitration prevailed. North Yemen was inhabited almost entirely by Arabic-speaking Muslims although there was an influential Jewish population of some 50,000. The total population in 1920 was in the region of 3 or 4 million.

Most Yemenis, certainly those who lived in the mountainous areas, belonged to tribes and acknowledged the authority of tribal leaders at various levels and the supremacy of tribal law. The tribes were grouped in confederations, with most tribes belonging to one or other of four major confederations. Of these the great Zaydī confederations of the Ḥāshid and Bakīl were the most important and the paramount chiefs of these confederations were men to be reckoned with. The Madḥaj confederation included both Zaydī and Shāfiʿī tribes and the ʿAkk confederation was Shāfiʿī. The tribes controlled the countryside and government in those areas existed only by their permission.

In 1920 the mountainous region acknowledged in some degree the authority of the Zaydī Imām who was Imām Yaḥyā of the Ḥamīd al-Dīn family of *sayyids*. Yaḥyā had secured recognition from the Ottomans of a degree of autonomy under the treaty of Da'an in 1911 and with the collapse of Ottoman authority in 1918 hoped to become fully independent, inherit their position in the Tihāma and extend his authority over the Idrīsī territory of ʿAsīr to the north and over the Aden protectorates to the south. He failed to achieve all these ends. In 1919 he declined the offer of a deal with Britain which would have put him in possession of the southern Tihāma and still left him the possibility that at some future date he might extend his influence into the protectorate. As a result the British allowed the Idrīsī ruler of ʿAsīr to take over the Ottoman position in the Tihāma, including Ḥudayda, and Yaḥyā did not acquire the southern Tihāma until 1926. His ambitions in ʿAsīr were ended by his defeat at the hands of the Saʿūdīs in 1934 and in the same year he gave up his claims on the Aden protectorate from which his forces had been expelled in 1928. By 1934, therefore, although the eastern boundary of the state remained undemarcated and although the Imām still harboured expansionist ambitions, the state of North Yemen had been largely defined in territorial terms. In itself this was a revolutionary event for there had never been such a state in the past; the authority of the Imām had previously been a limited authority over men who accepted his law based on and constrained by religion.

The government established by the Imām was a minimalist government which performed limited functions mainly in the towns; his government in the countryside was the rule of the shaykhs although the Imām contrived progressively to introduce into their counsels some of his own officials. The Imām's administration consisted of his own family and household officers supplemented by members of the *sayyid* families, notably that of Āl Wazīr, *qāḍīs* and ex-Ottoman officials. In 1918 several former Ottoman officials threw in their lot with the Imām and in the Tihāma he inherited the Ottoman administrative system. Tribal leaders were excluded from the central government. The army, however, still consisted of tribal contingents; some attempt was made to build a regular army but this project made little progress before 1934. Ex-Ottoman officers of Syrian origin were used in the regular forces but during the 1930s the Imām sent military cadets to other Arab states for training, in particular to Iraq. Some idea of the minuscule nature of the government may be gauged from the circumstance that in 1931 only one ministry existed, the ministry of foreign affairs, which had six people in it, two of them typists. The meagre activities of government were supported by *zakāt*, the religious payment formerly collected by the shaykhs but which the Imām endeavoured to direct into his own treasury, and customs duties. It was however, the consistent object of the Imāms to increase their own control over government, to enlarge its functions and to extend its scope.

From the 1930s it is possible to discern two factors making for change in Yemen. One was the attempt, referred to above, by the Imāms to extend their power and which produced a reaction from those (tribesmen and *sayyids*) who felt their own position threatened. The second was the growth of a small number of modernist intellectuals who became aware of changes elsewhere in the Near East, often through study in other countries or employment in Aden, and who came to demand both modernization (especially of education) and liberalization in Yemen. The intellectuals formed the Free Yemeni Movement in the 1930s which developed into the Free Yemen Party founded in Cairo in 1944 and heavily influenced by the ideas of the Muslim Brothers. The leaders came from *sayyid*, *qāḍī* and some shaykhly families and included Aḥmad Muḥammad Nuᶜmān and Muḥammad Maḥmūd al-Zubayrī.

The first major outward sign of opposition in Yemen was the attempted coup of 1948 when the Imām Yaḥyā was assassinated, a new Imām from the Āl Wazīr family proclaimed and a constitution published. In this action the intellectuals played only a minor role; primarily it was a movement of discontented *sayyids* who resented their loss of traditional power. The rebels were defeated and crushed a month later by Yaḥyā's son and heir, Aḥmad, who called on tribal support. Imām Aḥmad reduced still further the power of the *sayyid* families. The Free Yemenis fled but revived in Cairo after 1952 with support from the new Free Officers' regime and their movement then took on a more radical tinge. From this time onwards radical and nationalist opinions disseminated from Cairo became a factor in stimulating opposition to the government of the Imām.

The army had played no part in the 1948 attempt but an army officer did try to overthrow the Imām in 1955. He was joined by a similar combination of discontented *sayyids* and radicals but once more the conspirators were defeated by tribal forces. The support of the tribes for the Imām was put in question, however, by the consequences of a different type of uprising in 1959–60. This latter rising was a conventional tribal disturbance among northern Zaydī tribes. It was, however, severely repressed by the Imām's forces and several tribal shaykhs were executed. As a consequence the Imām added a number of tribes to the groups of malcontents who disliked the sensation of subjection to stronger government.

By 1962 the Imām's government had lost the support of many of the ulema, of the modernist intellectuals and most townsmen, of some tribes, especially from the Ḥāshid confederacy, and of some army officers. It had never had significant support from the Shāfiʿī population. In 1961 a Free Officers' organization was founded and on 26 September 1962, a few days after the death of the Imām Aḥmad, a military coup took place. The leaders proclaimed the end of the Imamate and the establishment of a republic, with a senior officer, ʿAbdallāh al-Sallāl, as president of the revolutionary council.

SOUTH YEMEN TO 1967

In 1920 South Yemen was composed of three distinct elements: Aden Colony, the West Aden Protectorate and the East Aden Protectorate or Ḥaḍramawt. Aden Colony consisted of the settlements grouped around the port of Aden which had been under the rule of the British government of India since 1839. The main business of the port was concerned with regional trade and shipping services and had little to do with the local affairs of the protectorates. The port population reflected this emphasis; of its 50,000 inhabitants only a minority came from South Yemen and the greatest number were from North Yemen, Somalia, India and Europe. The protectorates consisted of a number of independent chiefly states whose rulers received small British stipends and allowed Britain to control their foreign relations. Their inhabitants, who numbered perhaps half a million, were mainly peasant cultivators with a few artisans in larger villages and the small towns. There was also an élite composed of tribal shaykhs, *sayyids* who performed important functions as educators, arbitrators and administrators outside the tribal structure, and merchants.

During the First World War Britain had provided very little protection for the protectorates, the greater part of which had been occupied by Ottoman troops or those of the Imām of the Yemen. In the aftermath of the war Britain reconsidered what to do with the protectorates. One proposal was to give them (except Lahej (Laḥj), the leading state of the west Aden protectorate) to the Imām of the Yemen. Another was to go back to a new version of the old system – persuade the Imām to recognize the frontier agreed with the Ottomans in 1905, and leave the chiefly states alone as far as possible, dealing with those in the west largely through the Sultan of Lahej, and using the Sultan of Mukallā in the same way in the east. The third option was to try to exercise greater direct influence over the states through Aden. The policy adopted was a mixture of the last two possibilities with the second predominating during the 1920s and the third coming to the fore in the 1930s and afterwards.

Throughout the 1920s the protectorates were subject to incursions from North Yemen as the Imām tried to assert his claims. Only in 1934 did the Imām reluctantly accept the 1905 boundaries. An important factor in his defeat was the use of air power. The RAF's search for a role and Britain's need for a cheap means of colonial policing were neatly married in Aden, enabling Britain to withdraw the large garrison of British and Indian soldiers between 1928 and 1930. Part of the garrison's duties were taken over by the reorganized police and levies which were progressively Arabized. The new levies were more effective than British and Indian forces in operations in the interior and during the 1930s were available to support the new policy of increased British influence.

Closer control in the protectorates included forming new treaties allowing for British advice via political agents in the internal affairs of the states. Grants were made to the rulers to enable them to maintain small military forces, known as tribal guards, to enforce greater security on the roads. There were also developments in health care, education and agriculture. From 1943 new irrigation projects were launched, notably the cotton development at Abyan. This new interventionist policy had much success in the eastern protectorate where internal security had completely broken down in some areas as a consequence of the struggle for power between the old *sayyid* élite and new men who had made money in the East Indies. Ḥaḍramawt had long exported men to India and Indonesia and was heavily dependent upon remittances from them; in 1930 this contribution to the economy amounted to 2.4 million dollars. With the money came disputes which soon produced tribal feuds and anarchy in the interior. The policy of relying on the Sultan of Mukallā alone would not answer and during the late 1930s Britain negotiated separate treaties with hundreds of local rulers to establish what was called Ingram's Peace after the political agent responsible for the new arrangements. Peace, of course, was relative; tribal disturbances continued and in 1943 there was a major uprising in the Kathīrī region of the eastern protectorate, linked to the drought and famine of that year. The 1943 experience, however, only acted as a spur to further British intervention to promote development. Finally, Britain also had some success in pacification in the bedouin region through the new Ḥaḍramī Bedouin Legion.

The interventionist policy brought greater prosperity to several regions. The principal beneficiaries were the notables – sultans, shaykhs, *sayyids* and merchants – whose wealth and power was enhanced by the changes. In Mukallā, for example, a new regular army replaced the old unreliable mercenaries; the finances and administration of the sultanate were placed on a better footing; schools and roads were built; and the Sultan's authority began to displace that of former claimants in remote areas. The Faḍlī and Yāfiʿī rulers benefited from the Abyan revenues. But new employment opportunities also opened up for lesser figures as bureaucrats in the new chiefly administrations, soldiers in the tribal guards or as teachers. Peasants also gained from the agricultural developments. Several notables, new and old, sent their children to Aden for secondary education to qualify them for the new jobs. One effect of the new policy was to strengthen the previously tenuous links between the Colony and the protectorates.

By the 1950s the social, economic and political changes in the protectorate states were beginning to have political repercussions at a higher level. In 1952 the South Arabian League was formed which was largely a grouping of rural notables under the leadership of the Sultan of Lahej to demand greater independence. Outside factors were also influential, notably the new ideas of radical Arab nationalism coming especially from Egypt after 1952 and events in Aden Colony itself.

Aden Colony experienced a major economic boom after the Second World War as a consequence of the increase in oil tanker traffic and the demand for refuelling facilities, which Aden was better able to supply after the construction of its own refinery in 1952. By 1958 Aden was by far the busiest port in the Near East. Its prosperity was demonstrated by hectic construction activity and an expansion of services. Two groups of Adenis began to demand a share of political power. One was composed of the prosperous Aden Arab merchant families who formed the Aden Association in 1950 to agitate for a gradual development of self-government. The second was a group of new young clerks mainly from middling families who found a role as organizers of the industrial labour force in Aden and formed the Aden

Trades Union Congress in 1956. Like the workers they represented, many came from North Yemen and coupled with their demands for independence were calls for the unity of the two Yemens.

During the 1950s Britain responded in two ways to these pressures. In Aden Britain sought agreement with the merchant notables and began a slow progress which led by 1959 to the election of a legislative council dominated by the notables. In the protectorates Britain opposed the South Arabian League and supported the demands put forward by opponents of Lahej for a federation. In 1954 Britain envisaged two federations covering the western and eastern protectorates with separate development for the colony. In 1959 a federation of western protectorate states was established. In essence it was a coalition of rulers but federal institutions were created, in particular the Federal Guards were formed from the old tribal guards to which were added in 1963 the Aden Levies. The rulers of the more prosperous eastern Aden states refused to join and the Aden politicians also objected to subjection to what were described, misleadingly, as the 'feudal' rulers of the protectorate and to subsidizing the interior. But in 1962 Aden Colony was persuaded to join what became the Federation of South Arabia.

Opposition grew rapidly after 1962, which was also the year of the Yemeni revolution. The Aden notables soon faded from the political scene which became dominated by two main groupings. One was composed of the young union organizers in Aden who were represented politically by first the People's Socialist Party (1962), then the Organisation for the Liberation of the Occupied South (1965) which included former supporters of the South Arabian League, and finally the Federation for the Liberation of South Yemen (FLOSY) (1966), which in its origin was a coalition of the Aden trade unionists with their main political rivals, the National Liberation Front (NLF).

The NLF was the second main opposition group of the 1960s. It was founded in 1963 following the North Yemeni revolution and was originally an amalgam of urban and tribal groups. Its programme, set out in its National Charter in 1965, was a characteristic product of 1960s radical Arab politics: it was anti-imperialist, anti-feudal and anti-capitalist. The NLF was less clear about positive measures because of the deep divisions within the party. The NLF was the product of at least two inspirations: one was the anti-*sayyid* movement which had begun in the Ḥaḍramawt and the other was the radical Arab doctrines of the Arab Nationalist Movement, a party founded by students in Beirut. The very different visions proclaimed by these two elements, compounded with tribal and personality differences and conflicts between northern and southern Yemenis, led to persistent animosities within the NLF.

The NLF was given an opportunity to grow by the Raḍfān uprising of 1963. The disturbances in Raḍfān were tribal in origin taking the form of objections by one tribe to the growth of the power of the local ruler. They coincided with a novel British capability to act against those who disturbed the status quo. The long search for a base east of Suez had ended at Aden which in 1960 became the main British military base in the region, collecting all the forces removed from east Africa. The temptation to use this force in Raḍfān was too great, the more so as it was thought necessary to make a stand against Egyptian and Yemeni republican radicalism. In turn the NLF came to dominate the resistance to British power and spread their influence from Raḍfān to surrounding areas, taking advantage of similar local disputes. Between 1963 and 1965 the NLF established a rural power base from which they launched their bid for power in 1967.

In February 1966 Britain announced her intention to leave Aden completely by the end of 1968. In 1964 she had promised independence to the Federation by 1968; now she proposed to abandon the base as well. The effect of the successive British announcements was to intensify the political struggle in South Yemen and to change its character; it now became a question of who and what would succeed British authority. Britain hoped it would be the moderates of the Federation; Cairo hoped it would be a radical coalition dominated by the Aden trade unionists led by ᶜAbdallāh al-Asnaj and therefore promoted the FLOSY enterprise; the radicals of the NLF intended that it should be them.

The NLF were the victors during the violent struggle of the years 1966 and 1967. At the end of 1966 the NLF withdrew from FLOSY and launched their own independent struggle. During the late summer of 1967 the NLF took over most of the states of the Federation while the tribal guards and the federal army stood by. On 29 August the chief minister of the Federation resigned announcing "this is a people's revolution; we cannot resist it".[2] The NLF also took over the sultanates of the east. Finally, the NLF fought and defeated the Adeni unionists of FLOSY. On 6 November Britain recognized the NLF victory and negotiated with that party for the transfer of power. On 29 November Britain withdrew and the following day the People's Republic of Southern Yemen was established with the NLF leader, Qaḥṭān al-Shaᶜbī, as first president.

The outcome in South Yemen was unique in the Near East; the only close parallel was in Algeria. In other areas élites of notables inherited power from the colonial ruler and lost it only later to new urban and military radical groups. In South Yemen the notables crumbled at the same time as colonial rule before a revolt of ragged tribesmen led by young radicals. Contemplating these events historians must fasten on the rapid collapse of the federal institutions and particularly of the army and the police. These forces were not the destroyers of the Federation but they did little or nothing to save it. Why they behaved as they did we do not know. We know that the core of the army was recruited from tribesmen from the ᶜAwdhalī and, especially, the ᶜAwlaqī federations, which inhabited an area remote from Aden and near the Yemeni frontier, and that these tribes supplied the bulk of senior officers. There was plainly discontent between the officers and the rank and file and among the officers themselves and it is evident that radical propaganda had made headway among officers and men. But how to turn this information into an explanation of the army's behaviour eludes me.

THE PERSIAN GULF STATES TO 1971

It will be convenient to treat the history of the city states of the Persian Gulf – Kuwayt, Baḥrayn, Qaṭar and Trucial Oman (now the United Arab Emirates) – together. Their traditional forms and their transformations during the period follow the same pattern.

In 1917 the population of the region was approximately 250,000, of whom perhaps 30,000 were nomadic. It is difficult to estimate the nomadic population because many of the bedouin tribes were not permanent residents; they moved into the territory of the city states during the winter and returned to Saᶜūdī territory or to Iraq during the summer. The settled population lived in towns or villages. The largest town was Kuwayt with 35,000; Manāma and Muḥarraq on Baḥrayn each had between 20,000 and 25,000; and there were several towns in the 10,000 to 15,000 range. Most towns were situated on the sea and the principal occupation was pearling which was the mainstay of the economies of all the states in 1920. Otherwise the inhabitants engaged in fishing, boat building and repair, a few domestic crafts, date cultivation in the oases, and maritime trade. Pearling was big business; in 1920 Kuwayt had 800 boats and 15,000 men engaged in the work and made one million dollars a year from it. Baḥrayn's commitment was similar. The collapse of pearling after 1929 due to the world depression and the competition of Japanese cultured pearls destroyed the traditional economy of the Gulf states and posed the question of what could replace pearling. The answer was ultimately oil and the transition from pearls to oil and its consequences is the theme of this section.

The people of the region were predominantly Arab and Muslim. The non-Arabs included some Persians and Indians settled in the towns for the purposes of trade; some of the Indians also formed the non-Muslim Hindu population. The Muslim Arabs were mainly Sunnī but a small majority of the population of Baḥrayn was Shīʿī and there was tension between that group and the Sunnī ruling élite on the islands. The social structure of the Arab population was tribal and the ruling families were themselves of tribal origin; branches of the ʿUtūb ruled in Kuwayt (Āl Ṣabāḥ), Baḥrayn (Āl Khalīfa) and Qaṭar (Āl Thānī); and Trucial Oman was divided between the Qawāsim and the Banū Ya's.

Government was a family affair. Shaykhs ruled as heads of family corporations; other members of the family were given fiefdoms or governorates. In 1920 there were no organized administrations or any real distinction between the income of the state and that of the ruler. Government was financed by levies on pearling and date plantations and customs duties. There were no regular armies and government necessarily involved bargaining and consent between the ruler and the notables, mainly tribal leaders and merchants.

A dominant factor in the situation was Britain. The Gulf states were in practice, although not in name, British protectorates as a consequence of treaties made with the rulers from the late nineteenth century onwards. Britain had seen these treaties as a way of excluding other major powers from the area and had no wish to become involved in the internal affairs of the Gulf states or in their disputes on land. Nevertheless, she was drawn into their internal affairs in the course of protecting Indian traders and to prevent disorders which might provide other powers with an entry into the region. The Gulf rulers did not want British interference in their internal affairs but they did want British assistance in dealing with tribes or other states which threatened them. The outcome of these differing views of the British role was friction and occasional British interventions to procure the replacement of a ruler and to facilitate reforms in the administration.

An example of British intervention was in Baḥrayn. In 1923 Britain deposed Shaykh ʿĪsā and through his successor introduced administrative reforms affecting the customs, law courts, shaykhly finances and established new departments. A British financial adviser was recruited to control the finances of the state. As a consequence of this partial modernization of the government Baḥrayn was better placed to use the oil revenues which began to flow in the 1930s. Attempts at reforms elsewhere had little success. In Kuwayt there was some modernization of government under Shaykh Aḥmad (1921–50) which led to dispute with wealthy merchants who sought a share in government. In Dubayy a similar reform movement in 1938–9 led to the setting up of a council with power over finances. The council, controlled by notables, clashed with the ruling family and was suppressed.

Baḥrayn, where oil was discovered in 1932 and exported from 1934 and which acquired a refinery in 1937, was unique among the Gulf states. Elsewhere the pattern was for concessions in the 1920s and 1930s, exploration in the 1930s and after, but no production for export until after the war. Production began in Kuwayt in 1946, Qaṭar in 1949, Abū Dhabī in 1962 and Dubayy in 1969. As a consequence the real revolution in the Gulf did not begin until the 1950s. In 1950 the Gulf was little changed in its main features from the situation in 1920. The population was not much greater and the social and political structures the same. Some small foundations of modern education had been laid but the Gulf was waiting for oil to replace pearls and it was often a painful wait with little employment and small revenues.

Social and economic modernization began in the 1950s. It would be superfluous in a book like this to rehearse statistics of barrels of oil and millions of dollars; what has to be borne in mind is that the populations of the Gulf city states were tiny and that oil wealth gave them the highest per capita income in the world. Further, oil revenues were paid to states which thereby controlled vast patronage. The states put a large amount of this money into education, health and housing and became the greatest welfare states in the world. In most of the states there was more than enough money for all citizens; the main problem was to protect it from outsiders whether they were other states, foreign workers or ideological revolutionaries. Disputes about the control of government were therefore muted. Power remained in the hands of the ruling families; the elaboration of government through the creation of departments, ministries and agencies and the creation of councils of ministers became a way in which power was further concentrated in the ruling families which dominated the ministries.

Kuwayt was the first state to enjoy the new wealth. Kuwaytī production and export were given a major boost by the Iranian oil dispute which shut down Iranian production in 1951. The state grew rapidly; by the end of our period 70 per cent of Kuwaytīs worked for the state. The question was: could Kuwayt keep its wealth? In 1961

Kuwayt became independent and was immediately claimed by Iraq. But Kuwayt was protected by an agreement which provided for British military assistance; British troops were sent to the scene and Iraq backed down and recognized Kuwayt in 1963. Kuwayt then set about safeguarding her position by winning or buying friends throughout the Arab world. She also introduced a constitution in 1962 providing for a national assembly (elected in 1963) and a council of ministers, although tension soon developed between the assembly and the council.

Baḥrayn did not find new oil wealth; her oil reserves were limited and wealth less abundant. Tensions continued between Shīʿīs and Sunnīs and between the ruling family and notables. There were also demands from a new working class which had developed around the oil industry. In Baḥrayn in 1954 the first embryonic political party in the Gulf was founded and there were strikes and demands for reforms. The opposition movement was suppressed in 1956 but there were further disturbances in 1965 during a major strike. Baḥrayn, however, had been claimed by Iran since the seventeenth century and this claim was resurrected in 1968 at the prospect of Baḥrayni independence. Iran, however, agreed to refer her claim to the United Nations which decided against Iran. In 1970 Baḥrayn established a council of ministers and in 1971 achieved full independence.

Oil production commenced in Qaṭar in 1949 and grew steadily thereafter. Development began after 1950. An educational programme was instituted in 1956 but the pace of change did not increase rapidly until after 1960 when Aḥmad ibn ʿAlī succeeded his father as ruler and Khalīfa ibn Ḥamad became prime minister and took control of the modernization programme. There followed the customary elaboration of government departments (a significant measure in Qaṭar because of the thousands of members of the Āl Thānī family to be found jobs) and legal reforms. The 1960s also saw the beginning of a surge in the population as a result of an influx of foreign workers. In 1970, in preparation for independence, Qaṭar introduced a provisional constitution which provided for an advisory assembly and a council of ministers. She became fully independent in 1971.

In Trucial Oman oil revenues did not begin to flow until the 1960s and major change was therefore late. However, some development did take place during the 1950s, partly through British assistance, partly through the help of other Arab states whose oil wealth had come earlier, notably Kuwayt, and partly through the enterprise of certain rulers, in particular Shaykh Rāshid of Dubayy, who became ruler in 1958, and instituted harbour works and tariff changes designed to make Dubayy a commercial entrepôt. There were also developments in education, notably in Shārja. It was Abū Dhabī under Shaykh Zayd which took the lead during the 1960s, however, as a result of the substantial oil revenues acquired by that state. Her new wealth gave Abū Dhabī the leadership of the states of Trucial Oman. Abū Dhabī then acquired the paraphernalia of a modern government including a substantial army which by 1971 numbered 10,000.

The future political structure of Trucial Oman was an open question in 1968 when the British decision to withdraw from the Gulf by 1971 was announced. Britain had contributed to the political evolution of the area in several ways but two features of her policy in relation to states call for comment here. One was the creation of states by recognition of their rulers as autonomous or independent and not as the representatives of some other ruler inside or outside the Gulf. Thus it was a British decision to treat the rulers of Kuwayt as more than Ottoman governors, the rulers of Baḥrayn as not Iranian dependents, the rulers of Qaṭar as independent of both the Ottomans and the prospective successor of the Ottomans, Ibn Saᶜūd. Similarly, it was Britain which identified as rulers various of the petty shaykhs of Trucial Oman. In its last form, completed as late as 1952, there were seven states: Abū Dhabī, Dubayy, Shārja, Ra's al-Khayma, ᶜAjmān, Umm al-Quwayn and Fujayra. The second feature of British policy was the territorial definition of the states by the demarcation of land boundaries. In relation to the Trucial States this process took place as late as the 1950s, partly as the result of the need for definition in relation to oil concessions. The demarcation of frontiers, however, caused rather than ended disputes about them.

When Britain decided to abandon political influence in the Gulf she had to decide whether she should undo the state system she had created. Kuwayt, of course, was already independent but Britain conceived the notion that the other states could not stand alone and therefore it would be sensible to encourage Baḥrayn, Qaṭar and the Trucial States to form a federation. This notion was pursued by the rulers from 1968 to 1970 but the scheme collapsed in 1970 principally because the states had acquired identities which they were unwilling to jeopardize. Baḥrayn and Qaṭar withdrew leaving the question of what would happen to the Trucial States: whether they would federate, each go it alone, or whether they would join with Oman in a new federation. A basis for a Trucial federation existed in institutions created by Britain in the 1950s, notably a military force (the Trucial Scouts, 1951), a consultative council (1952), chaired since 1965 by a a development office (1965). The decisive factors in the choice of a federated future, however, were an agreement to this end between the two leading states, Abū Dhabī and Dubayy, and the willingness of Shaykh Zayd to share the wealth of Abū Dhabī with the less fortunate states. So in 1971 Trucial Oman emerged as the independent state of the United Arab Emirates.

OMAN TO 1970

The population of Oman in 1920 was about 500,000. The most populous area, containing more than one-fifth of the population was the narrow coastal belt, densely packed with date groves. Another major area of settlement was the Jabal al-Akhḍar, a ridge of mountains which formed the backbone of Oman and which contained the small towns which were the heartland of the old Ibāḍī Imamate, the nucleus of the state which had existed before the nineteenth century rulers shifted their capital to the coast at Muscat. The third region was the large southern province of Dhufār, acquired in the nineteenth century more or less as a colonial possession to replace the lost Zanzibar. Leaving aside a number of Indian traders in the coastal towns and some of the inhabitants of Dhufār the population was Arab, Muslim (of the Ibāḍī sect), and tribal. A few tribesmen were still nomadic but most were settled cultivators who, nevertheless, still retained their tribal identities. Traditionally, the tribes grouped themselves into one or other of two political confederations, the Ghāfirī and the Hināwī, and the paramount chiefs of these confederacies possessed an authority additional to that which they derived from their own tribal leadership.

The government of Oman was in the hands of the Āl Bū Saʿīd dynasty represented during this period by Sultan Taymūr ibn Fayṣal (1913–32) and Sultan Saʿīd (1932–70). Taymūr became exasperated with British and other importunities and bored with the job of ruler and eventually abdicated and departed to a life of riotous living. Saʿīd, who began with reforming intent, took a different way out of the same problems and in 1958 moved permanently to the isolation of Dhufār. Both the functions and mechanisms of government were simple. Local government was consigned to various members of the Āl Bū Saʿīd family in the form of apanages. For central government there was a small number of departments (expanded after 1932) and a council of ministers from 1920–32. There were also British advisers and Britain effectively controlled the customs which were the main source of revenue. From 1921 a small military force existed, the Muscat Levy Corps recruited from Baluchi mercenaries. In 1955 this was converted into the Muscat and Oman Field Force and enlarged to 400 men.

Tension had long existed between the sultans of the Āl Bū Saᶜīd dynasty with their coastal and maritime preoccupations and the tribes of the interior with their loyalties to their tribal leaders and to the Imamate which was re-established in 1913. A succession of tribal risings led to the treaty of Sib in 1920 by which the Sultan agreed not to interfere in the internal affairs of the tribes. The sultans were never content with this situation and endeavoured to recover power over the interior. The tribes resisted their pressure and endeavoured to keep control over the Imamate, procuring the election of a new Imām in 1954. The episode coincided with a dispute over possession of the Buraymī oasis between Oman, Abū Dhabī and Saudi Arabia and in 1955 the Trucial Oman Scouts occupied Buraymī. The Sultan used the occasion to settle affairs with the rebellious tribes whom he defeated in October 1955. But the rebels subsequently secured Saᶜūdī help and returned to the Jabal in 1957. This time Saᶜīd was unable to suppress the rising with his own forces and obtained British military help for a successful campaign in 1959. Subsequently, the Sultan consolidated his authority over the Jabal.

The sultan was confronted with another challenge to his authority in the 1960s in Dhufār. The Dhufār rebellion began in 1963 as a conventional tribal uprising but subsequently acquired an ideological character, especially after the revolution in South Yemen. In 1968 the Dhufār Liberation Front became the Popular Front for the Liberation of the Occupied Arab Gulf (PFLOAG) and with South Yemeni support the rebellion became a much more serious affair. By 1969 the rebels controlled substantial areas of the province. From 1971 until 1975 the government mounted a major campaign with Iranian help until finally the rebellion was crushed and the authority of the government of Oman became greater than it had ever been in history. The state had been defined and its power established.

The ability of the Omani government to vindicate its authority in Dhufār owed much to the greater resources at its disposal from oil revenues. Oil exports began in 1967 and made possible a programme of modernization. In fact there was little change in the character of government because of the unwillingness of Saᶜīd to introduce any substantial reform. The impatience of reformers in Oman found an echo in British minds and Britain certainly did not discourage the coup on 23 July 1970 by which Saᶜīd was removed and replaced by his son, Qābūs. Saᶜīd went off to end his days in the comfort of the Dorchester Hotel in London as his father had ended his in Green's Hotel in Bombay. Under Qābūs Oman embarked on a belated transformation.

NOTES

1. Text of constitutions in Helen M. Davis, *Constitution, Electoral Laws and Treaties of the States in the Near and Middle East,* 2nd Edn, Durham, NC, 248–58.
2. Quoted Joseph Kostiner, *The Struggle for South Yemen,* 1984, 166.

SECTION II

THE YEARS OF REVOLUTION

CHAPTER EIGHT

Egypt since 1952

The Egyptian revolution of 1952 was the first radical revolution in the Arabic-speaking countries of the Near East. It had two main features. The first was the replacement of the old landed urban notables who had dominated the political system of Egypt since the nineteenth century by a new ruling élite, composed initially of military officers and subsequently of a mixed military–civilian class of state functionaries. The second was a major shift of political, economic and social power to the state.

The revolution was planned and carried through by a group of army and air force officers, organized in the Free Officers Society. The term "Free Officers" was first used in 1950 but the organization had been formed a year earlier. After the coup the officers formed a revolutionary command council (RCC) of 17 members. The chairman of the council was a senior officer, General Muḥammad Najīb (Neguib), who was chosen by the plotters at a late stage in the planning of the coup. The heart of the conspiracy was a group of some 13 officers led by Lieutenant Colonel Jamāl ᶜAbd al-Nāṣir (Nasser). The members of the core group had much in common: they were all between 28 and 35 years old with an average age of 33; no less than eight had graduated from military academy in 1938; all held the rank of major or lieutenant colonel; and nearly all were the sons of small landowners or minor government employees. Many had previously engaged in political activity as members or sympathizers of one of the extra-parliamentary parties, notably the Muslim Brothers and the Young Egypt Party. They were quite unlike the notables who had preponderated in the parliamentary parties.

The Free Officers dominated Egyptian politics for the next 20 years. To the original core group were added others including some younger officers who graduated in 1948 and after but the total number in this military–political élite was never more than a few hundreds. In 1952 there were some 4,000 officers in the army. Of these about 500 were purged, 2,300 remained in the army and 1,200 entered state service in administrative or economic capacities. They filled the great majority of posts of provincial governors and about one-third of all Cabinet posts, including the key posts. All presidents, prime ministers, defence ministers and all but one minister of the interior (and the exception was a policeman) had a military background. Only after 1973 did the dominance of the officers give way to civilian ministers, commonly with an engineering or legal background; the all powerful presidents continued to be from the military.

Until his death in September 1970 the leader of the Free Officers was Jamāl ᶜAbd al-Nāṣir. ᶜAbd al-Nāṣir was born in Alexandria in 1918, the son of a postal clerk who had moved to Alexandria from near Asyūṭ in upper Egypt. He had an unsettled childhood – his mother died young and his education was constantly interrupted as he moved back and forth between Alexandria and Cairo. In the mid-1930s he joined the Young Egypt Party and began to study law but in 1937 entered the military academy, graduating the following year. In 1948–9 he served in Palestine where he was wounded and in 1949 he helped to found the Free Officers movement of which he soon became leader. Determined, secretive and at once both cautious and bold he was an ideal leader of a conspiracy but he was too junior in July 1952 to assume the public direction of affairs. So the chairmanship of the RCC was given to Najīb, the leadership of the government to an old palace politician, ᶜAlī Māhir, and the headship of state to a regency council acting on behalf of Aḥmad Fu'ād, son of King Fārūq. Within two years, however, all these had gone and ᶜAbd al-Nāṣir was supreme.

The old politicians were soon eliminated. ᶜAlī Māhir resigned in September 1952 and the Wafdist demand for the restoration of the suspended constitution was met by the complete abolition of the constitution on 10 December 1952. The political parties did not long survive the loss of their arena; in January 1953 all political parties were banned. Their place was taken by the RCC which in the same month assumed power for three years. The monarchy was next to go. It was abolished on 18 June 1953 and Egypt was declared a republic with Najīb as president and prime minister. ᶜAbd al-Nāṣir became deputy prime minister and minister of the interior, and other officers began to move into government. Najīb's turn came in the early months of 1954. Two months of political struggle ended on 17 April 1954 with ᶜAbd al-Nāṣir as prime minister of a government which included eight other Free Officers. Najīb, reduced to no more than a figurehead, was dismissed from the presidency in November 1954 and placed under house arrest.

In popular esteem Najīb had greatly outranked ᶜAbd al-Nāṣir but the latter won the greatest support among the Free Officers and in the army. "My parliament is the army," ᶜAbd al-Nāṣir told General Sir Brian Robertson, with whom he was negotiating for a British evacuation of Egypt, and the army remained the base of his power until 1967.[1] In September 1952 almost all senior officers had been dismissed and thereafter the army had witnessed a contest for power among various revolutionary factions including the Muslim Brothers, the extreme left and the conservative nationalists. In the struggle between ᶜAbd al-Nāṣir and Najīb in 1954 the left had supported Najīb and the conservatives ᶜAbd al-Nāṣir. Already, however, in June 1953, ᶜAbd al-Nāṣir had placed his closest associate, ᶜAbd al-Ḥakīm ᶜĀmir, in the post of commander in chief and with the help of ᶜĀmir the Nasirites triumphed. From 1953 until 1967 ᶜĀmir controlled the army on behalf of ᶜAbd al-Nāṣir; he was effectively the second man in the regime and his own challenge to ᶜAbd al-Nāṣir in 1967 was the most serious threat to his power which the latter ever encountered. ᶜĀmir kept the army out of politics; in return military expenditures were steadily increased, in all seven times during the period 1950–65 from about 4 per cent of GNP to 12 per cent, and better pay and additional privileges were given to officers. As time went on the power of the army was both controlled and reinforced by an elaborate system of security services, built up within the army, the ministry of the interior, the party and the office of the president. The security services searched for dissidents and carefully watched each other. Those who controlled the services were among the most powerful figures in the regime, for example Zakariyyā Muḥyī al-Dīn, who served as minister of the interior for ten years.

The last major threat to the regime was also suppressed in 1954. This was the Muslim Brotherhood, the most powerful of all the street movements. In January 1954 the Brotherhood staged student demonstrations but the leaders were quickly arrested and the Brotherhood proscribed. Further clashes took place during the course of the year and in November a plot by Brothers in the army was discovered. There were then more arrests and trials and little was heard of the Brotherhood for ten years. The movement continued to exist underground, however, and in 1965–6 a further purge of Brotherhood supporters took place and their leading intellectual, Sayyid Quṭb, was executed. Also in 1954 potential sources of lesser opposition were purged, including the provincial and municipal councils, the press and in January 1955 the Bar Association. The left was repeatedly the subject of repression, notably in 1952 and in 1954–5. Trials of opponents of the regime were conducted by a special revolutionary tribunal consisting of three Free Officers. By 1955 there remained no serious rivals to the Free Officers.

In place of the institutions which it had destroyed the new regime began to create its own political institutions. The form of these changed over the years but until 1976 they consisted of three elements: a presidential system of government, a parliament and a mass political party. The institutions first emerged in a clear form in the constitution of 16 January 1956 which formally replaced the authority of the RCC with a civilian presidential government. Military officers who became ministers now had to resign from the army. The most striking element of the constitution was the power of the presidency. The president had extensive executive and legislative powers, determined the broad lines of policy and could appoint and dismiss ministers. The exceptional powers of the presidency (to which ᶜAbd al-Nāṣir was elected in June 1956) remained the leading feature of all subsequent constitutional documents including that of the United Arab Republic in 1958, the National Charter of 1962 and the new constitution of 1964. The 1956 constitution also provided for a single chamber parliament for which elections were held in 1957 but neither the assembly nor its successors proved to possess any real power.

The third element in the system was the mass party. The regime made three attempt to create a new political party. The first was the Liberation Rally, founded in February 1953 with ᶜAbd al-Nāṣir as Secretary General. It was not, he said, a political party, but a device to organize the people and rebuild society. The principal function of the Rally proved to be to muster street support for the policies of the regime. In 1956 it was replaced by a new organization, the National Union, the primary role of which was to choose candidates for elections to the new parliament. In 1962 came the most ambitious of all, the attempt to create a mass party, the Arab Socialist Union (ASU). Like that of its predecessors the purpose of the ASU was to mobilize the energies of the people and to select candidates for the new National Assembly. In appearance it was a party organized from the bottom upwards. Some 7,000 basic units were located in villages, urban quarters, schools and factories. The basic units produced district organizations and eventually a general national congress which was intended to have a central committee. In fact the affairs of the ASU were run by its supreme executive committee and its general secretariat. The secretariat was divided into branches each headed by a prominent leader of the regime who possessed ministerial status. In effect these branches became fiefdoms for the various leaders in which they established their clients and followers. In the rural basic units minor notables held sway and it has been suggested that the main purpose of the mass parties was to mobilize the support of rural notables against the threat of urban opposition. The ASU was, however, less a political party than a ramshackle collection of power bases. It had a further feature of significance. In 1962 the idea of creating a smaller, tightly organized, ideological party, something like the communist parties, had been contemplated. Although the notion was rejected in favour of another mass party an attempt was made subsequently to create within the ASU a small political vanguard giving the possibility of creating a new base of power which might rival the army. Under the secretary generalship of ᶜAlī Ṣabrī (1965–7, 1968–9) the ASU did become a base from which the party leader could challenge for the succession to ᶜAbd al-Nāṣir.

The regime also built wider support among bureaucrats, industrial workers and peasants. The period after 1952 saw a massive expansion of the state bureaucracy from 350,000 in 1952 to 1.2 million in 1970 and 1.9 million in 1978. If employees of state-owned companies are included the latter figure would be increased to 3.2 million. During the period 1959 to 1967 growth in expenditure on civil administration was second only to spending on the army. Although much of this increase was the consequence of the increase in state functions, part was fuelled by the desire to find jobs for friends of the regime. From 1962 all graduates were guaranteed a job in the public service (although they might have to wait some time for it) and by the 1970s about 100,000 graduates were produced every year. Industrial workers were another favoured group. During the period 1952–1967 real wages rose by 44 per cent not counting other benefits in the form of food subsidies, shorter hours, insurance and social security.

A bid for peasant support was made through land reform. The land reform law of 1952 was the most important measure of the early period of the Free Officer regime. It set a ceiling on land holding of 200 feddans (about 80 hectares) with an extra 100 feddans for dependants. (Subsequent amendments reduced the ceiling by 1969 to 50 feddans and a maximum of 100 for a family.) In fact the first stage of land reform seriously affected only a very small group of people. In 1952 70 per cent of the cultivable land of Egypt was owned by 4,000 families representing 1 per cent of the population. One-tenth of this number owned 20 per cent of the cultivable land of Egypt in holdings of more than 200 feddans. Most of these 400 landowning families were still in a category which most people would think of as modest since they held between 200 and 300 feddans and this group was little affected by the reform. However, the category also included the tiny number of great urban landed notables who had dominated the political scene before 1952. Land reform was a death blow to the economic basis of their political power; no single act did more to transform the political face of Egypt. Land over the ceiling was to be transferred to landless peasants or those with very small holdings, together with land that was confiscated from the royal family and others and some *waqf* land. In all about one million feddans or 15 per cent of the cultivable land of Egypt was redistributed in small packages. A second feature of the land reform was the promotion of co-operatives. All those who accepted redistributed land were obliged to join an agricultural co-operative and others were also encouraged to follow suit. Benefits were offered to co-operative members in the form of cheap credit, seeds and fertiliser. The hope was not only to increase the efficiency of farmers but also to tie them into the state system while avoiding nationalization of the land. Farmers were also favoured by taxation policy. For political reasons the regime kept taxation on agricultural incomes well below 10 per cent, preferring to rely on indirect taxes as its main source of domestic revenue.

A third feature of land reform was an ambitious attempt to increase the cultivated area by 50 per cent, notably by spectacular projects such as the Liberation Province and the New Valley. In fact the results achieved were much slighter than those claimed; most of the successes were on the fringes of the Nile Delta and the big projects were relative failures; land was brought under cultivation at a very high cost. Most notable of all was the construction of the new Aswan High Dam, completed in 1970, which created a vast new water storage capacity in Lake Nasser. The High Dam considerably increased the quantity of water available for the cultivation of summer crops but its principal significance was in the generation of electrical power for industrialization.

The land policy of the Free Officers had some successes in increasing production but its most striking achievement was political through its effect on the old wealthy landowners. It had much less success in attracting peasant support. Although many small peasants benefited from land reform more than half of the rural population remained landless and the chief gainers appear to have been the rural notables, owners of plots of 20–50 feddans, whose number remained almost unchanged. The increase of population soon swallowed up the small gain and the ratio of land to rural inhabitants fell from 1.3 hectares per family of five in 1947 to 0.8 in 1971. To help to understand what land reform meant on the ground one may consider the case of the village of Kamshish. Before 1952 the village had been dominated by the Fiqqī family which contrived to evade the land reform restrictions until 1961. Their ancient rivals, the Muqāllīd family, were quick to identify themselves with the new regime and exploit the new revolutionary institutions and became dominant as the Fiqqīs were eclipsed. But the rivalry continued and in 1966 the leader of the Muqāllīd family was killed by the Fiqqīs. The incident led to an inquiry and complaints about the survival of "feudalism" in the countryside. It may, however, indicate the failure of the regime to mobilize peasants on a new class basis; instead the revolution became only a new ingredient in a traditional mix.

One of the most important features of revolutionary Egypt was the growth of state economic power. This was not a development which had been planned in 1952. At that time the officers had little that could be called a programme; rather they had sentiments of romantic nationalism and social justice and experiences that had led to cynicism about the existing political and economic structure. In the six principles of 1952 it was stated vaguely that among the objectives of the regime were the destruction of imperialism, the eradication of feudalism and the ending of monopoly. In so far as the officers had an economic policy it was to continue with a basically private enterprise system moderated by nationalism and justice. The role of the state in the economy was envisaged as continuing to be the management of certain functions, including irrigation and railways, and the exercise of a general supervision. "We are not socialists," declared Jamāl Salīm, one of the most prominent of the Free Officers in the early years of the revolution. "I think our economy can only prosper under free enterprise."[2]

A major change in the regime's policy began in 1956 and the role of the state was transformed between 1959 and 1961. The first step, the nationalization of the Suez Canal Company in July 1956 followed by the nationalization of British and French banks in November of the same year, was largely prompted by nationalist assertion and a strong hostility to foreigners and especially the West. These moves were followed in January 1957 by the nationalization of all banks, insurance companies, commercial houses and agencies. Between 1959 and 1961 a series of measures involved the nationalization of Egyptian firms, state control of all imports and most exports, state control of labour through trade unions and co-operatives, the introduction of a system of steep progressive taxation and the sequestration of the property of many wealthy people. All this was linked to a policy of rapid industrialization under state ownership and control of investment. Between 1952 and 1972 the public sector grew from 15 per cent to 48 per cent of GDP.

A variety of explanations have been put forward to account for this dramatic alteration in the regime's policy. The regime itself emphasized economic factors; agriculture could not support Egypt's growing population; it was necessary to industrialize; private enterprise had failed to make sufficient investment in the right areas and so the state must step in to do the job. A second argument was political; just as the economic base of the landed urban notables had been eliminated by land reform so it was necessary to reduce the economic power of big business, both foreign and Egyptian. Moreover, the transfer of management to the state would find employment for bureaucrats whose loyalties were to the state. A third argument was ideological; the regime became convinced that Egypt should and must go down the path of socialism, the more so since it had shifted its foreign allegiance from the West to the USSR since 1955. In the National Charter of 1962 the ideological basis of the policy was spelled out. The issue of the National Charter followed one of the great reverses suffered by the regime, namely the breakdown of the United Arab Republic in 1961. At the time the loss of Syria was attributed to the strength of the reaction against socialism and the conclusion was drawn that the struggle against reaction and for socialism must be redoubled. The National Charter was essentially an elaboration of this message, an argument that the revolution was for freedom, socialism and Arab unity, that the key to success lay in economic development and that these objectives could be secured only through socialism and state ownership or control of the main part of the economy. The evidence does not permit any firm verdict as to which of these motives predominated and all no doubt played a part. The political and ideological arguments, however, may partake more of the nature of later rationalizations of a decision taken on pragmatic, economic grounds; that the economic arguments may not have been very good does not affect the issue. ᶜAzīz Ṣidqī, who as minister of industry from 1956 until 1966 was the driving force behind nationalization, belonged to the pragmatic school.

In fact Egypt underwent considerable economic changes during the period 1952 to 1970. In 1952 the Egyptian economy was mainly agricultural. Agriculture produced about 40 per cent of GDP, employed 65 per cent of the labour force and provided 90 per cent of exports, which were dominated by cotton. Industry, primarily construction, food processing and textiles, produced only 15 per cent of GDP and employed only 10 per cent of the labour force. Over the 18 year period agriculture grew at a rate of about 3 per cent a year and industry at 5.7 per cent, a rate considerably below that achieved between 1938 and 1951 although the effects were much more marked. By 1970 the share of industry in GDP had increased to 23 per cent and that of agriculture had been reduced to a similar size. The overall growth rate was around 4 per cent a year although per capita income rose by less than 2 per cent mainly because of the increase of population. The population of Egypt rose from around 20 million in 1952 to 30 million in 1966, 37 million in 1976 and 50 million in 1986.

Egypt also experienced noteworthy changes in social life. Most striking was the movement to the cities, in particular to Cairo and Alexandria. The population of Greater Cairo increased from 2.2 million in 1950 to 6.8 million at the census of 1976 and in 1986 reached 14 million; Alexandria grew from 1 million to 2.3 million between 1950 and 1976. Rent control protected those who were housed but did not encourage the provision of new housing with the consequence that there was a growth of shanty towns and in Cairo squatters filled the old Mamlūk tombs on the Muqaṭṭam Hills. A second feature of urbanization was the decline of the foreign population. In 1917 19 per cent of the population of Alexandria was foreign born, by 1960 the figure had fallen to 3 per cent.

Another aspect of social change was the expansion of education; between 1952 and 1970 the number of students at all levels grew by 8 per cent a year. By 1986 the number of children in primary school was approaching 8 million and over 1.5 million were in secondary schools. The regime gave a high priority to education. In 1953 it attempted a comprehensive reorganization of the system, in 1956 all education in public schools was made free and so in 1962 was higher education. All secondary school graduates were assured a place at university and a big effort made to achieve universal primary education. Foreign schools were Egyptianized and greater control was established over private schools; technical education was encouraged and a drive made against illiteracy. It is, however, easy to describe policies and to list statistics; more difficult and controversial is to make a qualitative assessment of the results. It is evident, however, that they fell some way short of both aspirations and claims. It is doubtful whether more than two-thirds of the age group attended primary school and, although it was claimed that illiteracy was reduced from 75 per cent in 1950 to 53 per cent in 1982 critics argued that in reality three-quarters of the population were still illiterate. The huge expansion of higher education, which by 1980 had produced 500,000 students in 13 universities, took place especially in the fields of arts, commerce and law, where staff/student ratios attained fearful levels; at Asyūṭ University in 1978 it was reported that the ratio was 1:1,500.

The position of Islam was also changed. Egypt under the Free Officers was in essence a secular state. It was not hostile to Islam which formed one of the three circles within which ᶜAbd al-Nāṣir claimed that Egypt operated; Islamic principles constituted one of the bases of the 1962 National Charter, Islam was stated to be the religion of the state in the 1964 constitution and Islamic links were used in foreign policy. Nevertheless, the government sought to bring Muslim institutions under state control. Accordingly, in 1952 family *waqfs* were abolished and in 1957 public *waqfs* were nationalized. (For similar attempts to control waqfs by Muḥammad ᶜAlī see *MMNE*, 149.) The Sharīᶜa courts were closed in 1956. The Ṣūfī brotherhoods were placed under close supervision and officially abolished in 1961, although they continued to flourish; in 1964 there were still more than 60 Ṣūfī orders. In 1961 reform was imposed upon the famous university of al-Azhar. In general the orthodox ulema made no objection to this increase of state control but co-operated with the regime; those who questioned the actions of the state, such as the Muslim Brotherhood, were firmly, even brutally, suppressed.

By the mid-1960s the Free Officers had accomplished a substantial transformation of Egyptian politics, society and economy. They had also contrived to reorientate the foreign policy of Egypt. This change also had not been foreseen in 1952 when the principles of foreign policy had been no more than Egyptian nationalism and a generalized dislike of Western influence. The first task was to regularize relations with Britain. In February 1953 the vexed question of the Sudan was disposed of by an arrangement that the Sudan should be given its independence in 1956 when it would be free to choose whether or not to unite with Egypt. In October 1954 a second agreement provided for the British evacuation of the Canal Zone and the last British forces left in June 1955. The agreements did not, however, lead to Anglo–Egyptian harmony because of Egyptian fears and resentments of British policy elsewhere in the region, notably the links between Britain and Iraq and their evolution in the Baghdad pact of 1955. A further disturbing factor was the worsening condition of Egyptian relations with Israel, in particular the serious Israeli raid on Gaza in March 1955.

In September 1955 Egypt made two important innovations in her foreign policy: at the Bandung conference ʿAbd al-Nāṣir appeared as a leader of the new non-aligned movement and an agreement was made to purchase Soviet arms via Czechoslovakia. In turn these innovations led to a deterioration of Egyptian relations with the United States culminating in the US decision in July 1956 to refuse funding for the Aswan Dam project, an act which led directly to the Egyptian nationalization of the Suez Canal Company in July 1956 and to the subsequent Suez War with Britain, France and Israel in the autumn of the same year (see pp. 402–10).

The events of 1955 and 1956 transformed ʿAbd al-Nāṣir from an Egyptian into an Arab leader and ushered in a period of more than ten years when Egypt played a dominant role in Arab affairs as the leader of opposition to Israel, a perpetual challenge to traditional regimes and the central element in all schemes of Arab unity. From 1958 until 1961 Egypt was joined with Syria in the United Arab Republic; from 1962 until 1967 she fought a long war in the Yemen in support of the republican government; she gave support to revolutionaries in North Africa and Arabia; she established and dominated the Palestine Liberation Organisation; and she demanded to be consulted in all the affairs of the region. In his book, *The Philosophy of the Revolution*, ʿAbd al-Nāṣir had described three circles within which Egypt moved: the Islamic, African and Arab. Although he gave support to African liberation movements and intervened in the Congo in 1964 it was the Arab circle which dominated Egyptian foreign policy during these years.

Egypt's Arab policy ended in tears. The schemes of unity all foundered; the radicals she had supported proved ungrateful; her promotion of Arab socialism incurred the hostility of traditional regimes and of their international supporters; and the cost to Egypt of her support for the Yemeni republicans and the Palestinians was heavy indeed. Egypt entered the Yemen war without sufficient knowledge of the situation in Yemen or evaluation of the costs of involvement. By others the Egyptian intervention was seen as evidence of a desire to extend Egyptian control over Arabia and in turn they gave assistance to the royalists. Attempts to find a negotiated settlement failed and the Yemen swallowed up a third of the Egyptian army and £E4 billion. "We never thought it could lead to what it did," ʿAbd al-Nāṣir confessed.[3] The results of Egypt's Palestinian policy were even worse: in 1967 war with Israel led to a comprehensive defeat for the Egyptian army, the loss of Sinai with its oil fields and the presence of an Israeli army on the Suez Canal which was closed. The hero of Arab nationalism in 1956 had become its victim in 1967.

The 1967 defeat contributed to a change of course by Egypt. Defeat called into question Egypt's Arab policy, the efficiency of her army, the suitability of Arab socialism and the competence of ᶜAbd al-Nāṣir. The question of ᶜAbd al-Nāṣir's competence was soon settled: on 9 June he accepted responsibility for the defeat and announced his intention of resigning the presidency. Massive popular demonstrations induced him to rescind his decision. ᶜAbd al-Nāṣir then blamed the army for the defeat and removed his old ally ᶜĀmir and 50 other commanders. Army and security chiefs responded with an attempt to overthrow ᶜAbd al-Nāṣir but the leaders of the conspiracy were arrested and ᶜĀmir himself committed suicide on 15 September 1967. ᶜAbd al-Nāṣir then began to rebuild Egypt's military strength with the help of substantial Soviet aid and greatly increased defence expenditure which amounted by 1970 to over 25 per cent of Egypt's national income.

Egypt also changed her Arab policy. Egyptian forces were withdrawn from the Yemen and better relations established with the conservative Arab states, led by Saudi Arabia. Arab unity was re-established and Arab aid began to make up some of the losses of revenues Egypt had suffered. ᶜAbd al-Nāṣir would not abandon his support for the Palestinians or enter into direct negotiations with Israel: Egypt's policy, it was stated, was no war and no negotiations. In fact the war went on in the form of the so-called war of attrition from March 1969 and ᶜAbd al-Nāṣir was prepared for indirect negotiations; in July 1969 he accepted the Rogers peace plan (see p.420).

It remained to be determined what changes should be made in the regime and its policies. The purges of 1967 had accelerated a change in the personnel of the regime which had already been taking place. Over the years there had been a steady attrition of the original Free Officers as they incurred ᶜAbd al-Nāṣir's displeasure. By March 1964 only seven of the original RCC members were still active in politics. In 1967 and 1968 other old stalwarts were dropped, including Zakariyyā Muḥyī al-Dīn, together with some of the younger officers who had come to prominence in the 1960s. Of the original members of the RCC only Ḥusayn al-Shāfiᶜī remained in the new government of March 1968 with ᶜAbd al-Nāṣir. Anwar al-Sādāt was speaker of the parliament. ᶜAbd al-Nāṣir himself was obliged to assume more and more direct authority as president, prime minister, commander in chief and head of the ASU. At the same time his health was rapidly declining: he was in constant pain and suffered heart attacks from 1965. At the head of affairs ᶜAbd al-Nāṣir remained in full control but in increasing isolation; it was as though he had convinced both himself and the Egyptian people that he was indispensable.

The new policy of Egypt was set out by ᶜAbd al-Nāṣir in the 30 March 1968 programme. Subsequently, it was claimed that the programme charted a new course for Egypt but at the time it appeared more ambiguous. On the one hand it reaffirmed the commitment to socialism and on the other promised more freedom and more modern, efficient government. Its principal emphasis was on the reconstruction of the ASU to make it more democratic and the vehicle of substantial change. In practice the changes made little difference to the organization. More interesting were the economic changes which went unnoticed. Again they were ambiguous: on the one hand was a tightening up of land reform and on the other a relaxation of controls on private economic activity – between 1966 and 1969 private sector imports increased five times. Egypt had to encourage private economic initiative both to facilitate Arab aid and to meet the demands of consumers, vividly demonstrated in the riots which took place in 1968. In fact, despite the continuation of hostilities some economic recovery did take place after 1967 aided by the development of oil production from the Morgan fields south of Suez and by higher cotton prices.

ᶜAbd al-Nāṣir died on 28 September 1970 before any clear lines for the future development of Egypt had been established and with no decision on the choice of a pathway out of her foreign policy dilemmas. He was succeeded by the vice-president (since December 1969), Anwar al-Sādāt. Sādāt was chosen primarily because he was the legal successor but also because he was one of only two of the original Free Officers surviving in high office and because he was considered by others who aspired to succeed ᶜAbd al-Nāṣir as a suitable temporary figurehead. In fact Sādāt proved to be more durable than his rivals and a real innovator in domestic and foreign policy.

Sādāt was born in 1918 in a village in the Delta, although he moved to Cairo when he was six. His father was a clerk in a military hospital. In 1936 he entered the military academy, became active in politics, joined the Free Officers and in 1953 became a member of the RCC. Subsequently he was employed in a variety of jobs in the party and parliamentary systems but he was never a leading figure in government under ᶜAbd al-Nāṣir. His reputation was as an active, even impulsive, but not a profound politician. It was commonly thought that he would be outmanoeuvred and replaced by ᶜAlī Ṣabrī, who had strong support in the ASU and in the security services and who also had the support of the left.

Sādāt defeated his rivals in what was called "the corrective revolution" of 14 May 1971. Ṣabrī challenged Sādāt's policy over a projected federation with Syria and Libya, defeated Sādāt in the executive committee of the ASU and was himself defeated in the parliament. Sādāt sealed his victory by the arrest of his opponents who included, in addition to Ṣabrī, the ministers of defence, the interior and information. Sādāt owed his victory partly to the cultivation of his rivals' deputies and to backing from parliament but principally to the powers of the presidency and the support of the army which resented the influence of the ASU. In the places of the conspirators Sādāt brought his own supporters into positions of power.

The immediate problem for Sādāt was still the confrontation with Israel. To defeat Israel was beyond the strength of Egypt but a small victory could give Sādāt a position from which to negotiate. While he prepared his victory he was obliged still to depend on Soviet military support – the Soviet–Egyptian Treaty of Friendship and Co-operation was signed 27 May 1971 – and to endure hostile demonstrations from leftist critics who called for more active prosecution of the war. Sādāt declared that 1971 would be the year of decision and when it passed without result criticism was redoubled. In 1972 there were riots and further demonstrations and pressure from anti-Soviet army officers and rightist Free Officers for a reduction of dependence on the Soviet Union and for action against the left. Sādāt removed both the complaining minister of war and the Soviet military advisers (and announced that Egypt would resume control of Soviet bases in Egypt) and took action against the left.

The October war of 1973 did for Sādāt what Suez did for ᶜAbd al-Nāṣir. Egyptian forces crossed the canal and inflicted defeat on the Israeli troops. Subsequently, things went wrong: Israeli forces themselves crossed the canal and cut off an Egyptian army. What would have been the military outcome is uncertain but a ceasefire brought the conflict to an end and Sādāt was able to claim that he had achieved his victory, restored the prestige of the Egyptian army and vindicated Arab honour. His own standing was greatly enhanced permitting him liberty to effect more substantial changes in domestic and foreign policy.

Sādāt introduced a number of political changes. Of the institutions established after 1952 the presidency remained very powerful; Sādāt's personal style of government made it yet more dominant. The army's political role was diminished, continuing the evolution begun in 1967. The number of men with a military background in government was reduced as they were replaced by civilians with backgrounds in engineering, business or the law. The military's monopoly of provincial governorships was also broken: under Sādāt only about one-third came from the army. And the dominance of the military in the party was ended.

The role of the ASU was completely changed under Sādāt. In 1974 Sādāt began to encourage a freer debate in the press and elsewhere and raised the possibility of the introduction of a multi-party system. In 1976 he found a compromise between those who wanted a single party and those who wanted a multiplicity of parties: this was the emergence of three "platforms" representing left, right and centre within the ASU. The three platforms were allowed to contest the parliamentary elections of 1976 and immediately afterwards converted into parties. In February 1978 a fourth party, the New Wafd, was added although it was disbanded the same year. Of the three parties which survived the centre party was completely dominant: at the elections of 1976 it won 280 seats. The centre party, named the Arab Socialist Party of Egypt and later the National Democratic Party, was indeed the government party: from 1978 until 1980 it was led by Sādāt himself and then by his trusted vice-president, Ḥusnī Mubārak. The other parties functioned as glorified pressure groups free to criticize within prescribed limits. Nevertheless, the monolithic mass party no longer existed (the ASU was finally dissolved in 1980) and the creation of the parties changed the character of parliament.

Under Sādāt the single chamber assembly had little real power but it became a more active centre of criticism and debate and was able to obstruct and modify legislation. It also began to serve as a channel through which politicians moved into the governing élite, partially replacing the army in this respect. The elections of 1972 and 1976 were relatively free although those of 1979 were under stricter control following the emergence of stronger opposition to the government from 1977 onwards. Taking into account the greater freedom enjoyed by the press and increased freedom of movement there was much more political freedom under Sādāt than under ᶜAbd al-Nāṣir.

Real power remained in the hands of Sādāt and his new entourage. His former colleagues were all gone: the last of the other Free Officers in power, Ḥusayn al-Shāfiᶜī stepped down in 1975. One study of the changing élite shows that of some 50 officers who held key posts under ᶜAbd al-Nāṣir 26 were still in high office when he died. Only eight still figured in Sādāt's élite. In their place were a group of businessmen, bureaucrats and technocrats and a few officers. Some of the most influential owed their position partly to their family links with Sādāt. Thus the powerful millionaire businessman, ᶜUthmān

Aḥmad ᶜUthmān, who made a fortune as a contractor on the Aswan Dam, was the father-in law of one of Sādāt's daughters. So was Sayyid Marᶜī, who was from an old landowning family of notables. A third member of the inner circle under Sādāt was Ḥusnī Mubārak, a former air force commander, who was clearly designated as second to Sādāt in the hierarchy. Another durable member of the élite was Mamdūḥ Salīm who served first as minister of the interior and then as prime minister. Other ministers came and went; most were chosen for their particular expertise, especially the economists like ᶜAbd al-Munᶜim Qaysūnī and ᶜAbd al-ᶜAzīz Ḥijāzī, the principal architect of the *infitāḥ* (see below). Relatively more men served as ministers than under ᶜAbd al-Nāṣir. Whereas in 18 years Nāṣir had had 18 cabinets with 131 individuals Sādāt had 11 cabinets with 127 individuals in seven years. Like ᶜAbd al-Nāṣir Sādāt relied heavily on the security apparatus, divided into three services under the president, the ministry of war and the ministry of the interior. Mamdūḥ Salīm and later Nabawī Ismāᶜīl were men who owed their importance to their control of security at the interior. In the army there was a constant turnover of men as Sādāt carefully balanced rivals and sought to avoid the emergence of any competitor from that quarter.

Sādāt made a considerable change in economic policy. The change (known as the opening – *infitāḥ*) took the form of freeing foreign trade and investment. Law 43 of 1974 offered several advantages to foreign investors, including tax exemptions and freedom from many legislative restrictions. Just as with the swing to state socialism under ᶜAbd al-Nāṣir there is dispute concerning the reasons for this move. On the one hand are those who stress the impetus given by the change in foreign policy and the forging of links with the conservative Arab states and with the United States. On the other hand are those who emphasize economic factors. According to the latter view socialism had failed to provide sufficient investment from domestic sources and among foreign sources Arab oil wealth promised to be the most considerable source of new funds. Arab capital married to Western technology, it was thought, could transform Egyptian industry, generating growth which would provide new opportunities for private Egyptian businessmen. Another factor was the earnings of Egyptian workers abroad. By 1980 an estimated 1.4 million Egyptians were employed abroad, half a million each in Saudi Arabia and Libya and the rest in the smaller Gulf countries. To facilitate their sorely-needed remittances a freer foreign exchange and trade system was required.

The economic opening had a marked effect on investment in Egypt. In 1975–7 about 26 per cent of GDP was invested compared to an average of around 17 per cent in the period 1960–7. On the other hand the proportion raised from domestic sources fell from about 75 per cent to only 14 per cent in 1979. Economic growth accelerated rapidly to an average of around 7 per cent per annum during the period 1973 to 1980. There were considerable costs, however: inflation at 30 per cent, a huge trade deficit and a vast increase in foreign debt. Moreover, the investment did not go into manufacturing industry but into services, particularly tourism, oil and construction. An undue share of the benefits was perceived to go to a small group of speculators whose lavish style of life stood in sharp contrast to the visible austerity of the ᶜAbd al-Nāṣir period and to the falling real wages of industrial workers and minor bureaucrats. The resulting discontent was a potent factor in the riots which took place in 1977.

Opposition to the Sādāt regime took a new form in January 1977 with the worst worker riots since 1952. The immediate cause of the riots was the government decision to reduce food subsidies which had risen ten times since 1972. The riots were suppressed but the government rescinded its decision to reduce the subsidies. Sādāt blamed the left but it is clear that the rioters embraced a much broader spectrum of opposition, including Islamic fundamentalists. In 1977 fundamentalists swept the student union elections, a traditional sign of the political times and in the summer of 1977 members of an Islamic group, *al-takfīr wa'l-hijra* (founded 1971), kidnapped and murdered the minister of waqfs.

The resurgence of Islam in Egypt after 1967 was part of a widespread phenomenon in the Muslim world but in Egypt it was sharpened by the 1967 defeat which appeared to show the barrenness of secular nationalism, by the rapid urbanization which brought into the big towns many traditionally-minded villagers, and by hostility to the *infitāḥ* and its manifestations. Islam in Egypt had many faces. The orthodox ulema supported the state, although they urged the restoration of Islamic law and more vigorous opposition to Israel. More vocal were the popular mosque preachers who wielded considerable influence. The Muslim Brotherhood also reappeared expressing hostility to several features of western influence but were excluded from direct involvement in politics and concentrated on their social work. The Brotherhood's avoidance of political action opened the way for a number of small, activist Muslim groups some of which preached armed uprising against what they described as the illegitimate government of Sādāt. Sādāt had had generally good relations with the Islamic groups before 1977. His policy was to maintain the divorce of religion from politics but to reduce controls on Islam. The Islamic groups demanded that public life should be regulated by Islamic law. Sādāt made concessions: in 1971 the constitution was amended to admit the Sharīʿa as a main source of law and again in 1980 to make the Sharīʿa the main source of legislation. The Islamic groups were unsatisfied and they also became more and more hostile towards Sādāt's foreign policy.

The 1973 war had opened the way for Sādāt, with United States' help, to negotiate a partial Israeli withdrawal from Sinai, recover the lost oil fields and reopen the Canal, so acquiring additional foreign exchange. By 1975 the so-called step-by-step approach seemed to have run its course and Sādāt then turned back towards the idea of a comprehensive settlement negotiated through the device of an international conference at Geneva. This programme enabled him to restore his relations with most other Arab states. He continued to look primarily to the United States for assistance; in March 1976 he abrogated the treaty with the USSR and the following month cancelled Soviet rights to use Egyptian ports. In October 1977 with the US/USSR joint declaration in support of a Geneva conference it seemed as if his new policy was on the verge of success. However, in November 1977 Sādāt made an astonishing visit to Jerusalem which set Egypt on a new course of direct negotiations with Israel culminating in the Camp David agreements of September 1978 and the 1979 Egyptian–Israeli peace treaty which provided for the completion of the Israeli evacuation of Egyptian territory, isolated Egypt within the Arab world and called down on Sādāt's head the full force of Muslim condemnation (see pp.423–4).

Several explanations have been put forward to account for Sādāt's remarkable change of policy. It has been suggested that he decided that the Geneva process would be too slow to procure the quick peace Egypt needed, that he was disappointed at the level of Arab aid to Egypt and less concerned about a breach with the rest of the Arab states, and that he believed that US attitudes would be decisive and a direct approach to Israel most likely to win US support. Other views stress his domestic difficulties and suggest that he needed a quick international success to quiet his Egyptian critics although, as it happened, his Israel initiative only fuelled the wrath of his Islamic and leftist critics. A third view is that Sādāt was an opportunist, that his offer to go to Jerusalem was a rhetorical flourish and his decision to accept Israel's invitation was made on the spur of the moment. This last view is contradicted by Sādāt's own claim that he had planned his move two months beforehand but there is no evidence to confirm Sādāt's claim and it is clear that all his associates were taken by surprise. A final point is that neither Sādāt nor anyone else appears to have perceived until later that the new initiative was an alternative and not a supplement to a comprehensive agreement.

The 1979 Egyptian–Israel treaty marked the culmination of the move away from Arabism in Egyptian policy which had begun in 1967 and had accelerated under Sādāt. The breach with all other Arab states was complete; Egypt was expelled from the Arab League which she had dominated since its foundation. Egypt was isolated in the Arab world and her remaining links with the USSR were also severely damaged. She could look only to the US for aid. Indeed Egypt became second only to Israel as a recipient of US assistance. Nevertheless, the change in Egyptian policy which gave a higher priority to Egyptian interests against Arab interests was only a shift back towards her pre-1956 position. Egypt continued to assert her Arab identity: the 1980 white paper reaffirmed Egypt's central role in the (ungrateful) Arab world but claimed that Egypt's new task was to lead that world towards peace. And within ten years Egypt had rebuilt her relations with Arab states.

In domestic as well as foreign policy Sādāt's rule marked a modification, but not a fundamental alteration of the basis of the system created by the Free Officers after 1952. The composition of the political élite had changed but it was still essentially a civil–military bureaucratic élite dependent upon a powerful, centralized state, loosely linked to a class of rural notables. Although the private sector had grown in importance, in particular that part which was linked to foreign trade, it had not regained its former significance in the Egyptian economy. The massive public sector of the economy remained intact and the power of the state continued to increase during the Sādāt period. Tax revenues increased from about 15 per cent of GDP under ᶜAbd al-Nāṣir to almost 25 per cent in the mid-1970s (although less later) and government revenue as a proportion of GDP grew from about one third in the early 1960s to about one half in 1980–1.

Sādāt was assassinated on 6 October 1981. His death (at the hands of an Islamic group in the army) was no more evidence of widespread discontent than ᶜAbd al-Nāṣir's narrow escape from assassination at the hands of an Islamic group on 26 October 1954 was evidence of the fundamental strength of his regime. It was chance which determined that one attempt succeeded and the other failed. In fact the system established by ᶜAbd al-Nāṣir and modified by Sādāt remained stable. Sādāt was succeeded by his vice-president, Ḥusnī Mubārak, and the army remained loyal under ᶜAbd al-Ḥalīm Abū Ghazāla. The coercive and attractive powers of the Egyptian state were not to be easily overturned.

The quiet style of the new president was wholly different from the dramatic periods of ᶜAbd al-Nāṣir or the flamboyance of Sādāt. Mubārak was a career air force officer until 1975. He was as anonymous as were his personal advisers led by Dr Usāma al-Bāz. Mubārak's right hand man was Field Marshal ᶜAbd al-Ḥalīm Abū Ghazāla who served as minister of defence from 1981 to 1989 and kept the army as loyal to Mubārak as ᶜĀmir had done for ᶜAbd al-Nāṣir. No other minister had his durability: the rest, including prime ministers and ministers of the interior, were frequently changed. The Mubārak period saw the final disappearance of the ᶜAbd al-Nāṣir men; Abū Ghazāla was almost the last in high office.

Mubārak developed the Sādāt policy of increasing political freedom and enlarging the role of parliament and parties. The elections of 1984 and 1987 were freer than those of the 1970s and although the government party (the NDP) won overwhelming victories at both elections a more substantial opposition also appeared. The leading element in this opposition was the Muslim Brotherhood. In 1984 the MB worked behind the Neo-Wafd Party which emerged as the second party with 58 seats; in 1987 the MB formed an alliance with the labour and liberal groups which won 56 seats. The MB also maintained its links with the Neo-Wafd which held 36 seats and several of the 48 independents elected were also Brothers. Altogether the Muslims could muster the support of more than a quarter of the parliament in a vote on an Islamic issue.

Islam represented the chief source of opposition to the regime. Apart from the parliamentary activities of the MB the militant Islamic groups continued to grow in number and influence down to 1987 and veils, beards, prayers and sermons became more common features of Egyptian life than they had been earlier. Concerned by the progress of militant Islam, in 1987 Mubārak appointed a new interior minister, Zakī Bādr, who began a policy of repression. By 1989 there were signs that the Islamic tide might be turning: at the 1989 student elections the Islamic candidates were defeated by representatives of the secular left.

Mubārak also maintained the liberal economic policies of Sādāt. Between 1952 and 1989 the Egyptian economy was transformed. In 1952 agriculture had dominated the economy with more than one third of GNP; cotton alone had provided 80 per cent of Egyptian exports. By 1989 the contribution of agriculture had declined to less than one fifth of GNP, cotton ranked a poor fifth in Egyptian exports and Egypt imported half of its food. Oil was Egypt's leading export; the next largest source of foreign exchange was remittances from Egyptian workers abroad, followed by tourism and the Suez Canal. Each of these four items was largely a creation of the 1970s. Also, aid from the USSR, which had amounted to 4 billion dollars during the period 1955 to 1973, had been replaced by aid from the USA to the tune of 10 billion dollars between 1975 and 1985. The years 1978 to 1984 were golden years for Egypt but Egypt had become as dependent upon oil in one form or another as she had previously depended on cotton. The collapse of oil prices in the late 1980s affected her entire economy. Egypt's debt grew from 21 billion dollars in 1981 to more than double that figure in 1989. The greatest change in the Egyptian economy, however, had been the switch from agriculture into services; without oil, industry's contribution was still modest.

NOTES

1. Quoted P.J. Vatikiotis, *Nasser and his Generation*, 1978, 164.
2. Quoted Patrick O'Brien, *The Revolution in Egypt's Economic System*, 1966, 68.
3. Quoted Robert Stephens, *Nasser*, 1971, 391.

CHAPTER NINE

Iraq since 1958

The revolution of July 1958 opened a period of far-reaching change in Iraq. The changes were most conspicuous in politics where they took the form of the replacement of the monarchy by a republic and of a landowning political élite by a state-orientated civil and military bureaucracy. They were also evident in matters related to social and economic organization but in these areas the changes incorporated developments which were already in progress under the monarchy and were closely linked to more fundamental processes such as the increase of population and the progress of urbanization. In the quarter of a century from 1958 to 1983 the population of Iraq more than doubled from less than 7 million to about 14 million and the proportion living in towns also doubled from 37 per cent to 75 per cent. By 1983 nearly half the urban population lived in Baghdad, the population of which increased from less than 1 million to nearly 4 million. Mosul and Basra had each become home to between 1 and 2 million people. Such fundamental transformations of the social and economic landscape constituted a revolution to which the political system was obliged to respond but which it did not create. At the end of the period came another cataclysmic event in the form of the Iran–Iraq war, which created its own imperatives. In considering the revolutionary changes in Iraq we are, as elsewhere, obliged to look at two revolutions: the one that was proclaimed and the one that happened. In Iraq the connections are more tenuous even than in other areas and in following the rough melodies of political fortune it is necessary to listen hard for the deeper rhythms of change. An historian must be as aware of what did not happen as he is of what did. And he must also be familiar with other events. Revolutionaries are peculiarly the victims of fashion; paradoxically they believe that a revolution should be like other revolutions. In Iraq men always looked over their shoulders at Egypt or spoke the language of the Baᶜth. But nature is more powerful than art and what they contrived was something different from the revolutions of Egypt and Syria.

The July 1958 revolution was planned and executed by a handful of men. In all there were about two hundred Free Officers of whom 14 were on the central council. The central council was fairly representative of Iraqi army officers: 12 were Sunnīs and 2 Shīᶜīs, 9 were from Baghdad and 9 also held the rank of colonel. Most were from middling families; the two leaders, ᶜAbd al-Karīm Qāsim and ᶜAbd al-Salām ᶜĀrif, were unusual in that they came from poor families. Qāsim, a brigadier, was the only general officer among them and, like Najīb in Egypt, may have been chosen as leader for that reason. Also, as in Egypt, the Free Officers held various political views and were in touch with a number of political groupings some of which, like their fellows in Egypt, cherished the hope that they might be the beneficiaries of the action of the officers. Indeed, the vague programme of the revolutionaries called for the establishment of a parliamentary democracy after a transitional period and the withdrawal of the army officers from politics. But the resemblances with Egypt began to break down immediately after the coup. No revolutionary command council was established but, to the annoyance of their colleagues, Qāsim and ᶜĀrif treated the revolution as their personal property.

One of the most distinctive features of the Iraqi revolution, especially during its first ten years, was the failure to create strong new institutions with the consequence that everything remained personal and factional. Under Qāsim there was a republic but no president. For form's sake a three-man sovereignty council was created consisting of one Sunnī, one Shīᶜī and one Kurd but it never had any authority. The government had little power itself. The first cabinet consisted of four army officers, including Qāsim as prime minister, minister of defence and commander in chief, and ᶜĀrif as deputy prime minister, minister of the interior and deputy commander in chief. The other members of the cabinet were chosen principally from older opposition politicians, notably from the moderate left party led by Kāmil al-Chādirchī representing the old Ahālī group. Rashīd ᶜĀlī al-Gaylānī returned to Baghdad hoping by choice or plot to come to power but he and his fellow conspirators were arrested in December 1958. Many of the civilian politicians resigned in disappointment at their exclusion from power in February 1959 and by May 1961 they had all gone, their places being taken by army officers and technocrats.

Qāsim dominated the regime. If ᶜĀrif had hoped to play ᶜAbd

al-Nāṣir to Qāsim's Najīb he was quickly disappointed. The occasion of the split between Qāsim and ᶜĀrif was a disagreement about the pace with which they should move towards union with Egypt and Syria; ᶜĀrif wanted immediate Arab union and Qāsim wanted to go more slowly. There was no disagreement about the principle of Arab unity; on that all were agreed. Essentially it was a personal dispute which ᶜĀrif lost. In September 1958 he was sent into diplomatic exile and in November he was arrested. Qāsim was now supreme but he was alone; he had enemies and rivals and he needed allies, if not friends. He might have chosen to create political parties or other institutions which would have provided a basis of stability; instead he relied on a few individuals such as Brigadier Aḥmad Ṣāliḥ al-ᶜAbdī, army chief of staff and military governor of Baghdad, and on uneasy compacts with various groups, in particular the Iraq Communist Party (ICP).

In 1958 the ICP was, with about 3,000 members, the largest, best organized and most active of the extra-parliamentary groups in Iraq. Since its origins in the 1920s and 1930s the ICP had experienced advances and reverses but under Ḥusayn al-Raḍī, secretary general from 1955 to 1963, its fortunes had improved. Communists were released from prison after the revolution together with other political prisoners and the party rapidly expanded its activities, began to recruit a following in the army and sought to organize a popular militia; the establishment of the Popular Resistance Force provided a ready-made organization which it endeavoured to control. It is said that at its peak the ICP had 20,000 members. The ICP was an urban party of students and intellectuals with only a small working class following but it aspired to be a party of the masses, in particular of the peasants. It was not, although it is sometimes said otherwise, a Shīᶜī party; in its early days it had been particularly attractive to minorities and at one point it had been dominated by Kurds but during the Qāsim period its leadership was Sunnī Arab with a strong element of representation from the Euphrates town of ᶜĀna. Down to 1963 it was Qāsim's most faithful ally but he never reciprocated its loyalty by offering the party any share of power. Communists were excluded from provincial governorships, given no important army posts in southern Iraq and held only one cabinet post. Nor were they allowed to arm the Popular Resistance Force.

Political parties were licensed in January 1960 but the ICP was not admitted to the privileged group. Instead Qāsim employed the same manoeuvre as had Atatürk in dealing with the Turkish communist party, that is he granted a licence to a loyal, but phantom, communist party and refused it to the real one. The ICP accepted the snub and continued, like the Soviet Union, to support Qāsim. In the eyes of the ICP Qāsim had two merits: he was anti-imperialist and he was lukewarm about Arab nationalism. The ICP was a party which put Iraq first and most of the alternatives to Qāsim took their stand on Arab unity.

The opposition to Qāsim is usually described as Arab nationalist, Pan-Arab, Nasirite or Baʿthist. With the exception of the last (and that only with qualifications) these labels did not represent parties. There was a movement rather than a party based in Lebanon and led by the Palestinian George Ḥabash called the Arab Nationalist Movement and this movement had some influence on individuals but the opposition to Qāsim had no stronger party base than had the "sole leader" himself. The attempted coups between the years 1958 to 1963 were mainly the work of factions and coalitions of factions of army officers. Of such a character was the revolt in Mosul in March 1959 where a local commander allied with local notables under the banner of Arab nationalism. The revolt was subdued with great violence with ICP help. Such credit as the ICP had gained in March at Mosul was dissipated in July at Kirkuk when communists were blamed for what was essentially a bloody confrontation between the local Turkoman élite and Kurdish immigrants. Popular hostility to the communists after Kirkuk may have made them lean more heavily on Qāsim's protection. A third challenge to Qāsim in 1959 came from the Baʿth which attempted to assassinate him in October but succeeded only in wounding him and paid the penalty for its failure. The opposition was further cowed by one of the few new institutions created by Qāsim and that a very familiar one, the revolutionary court. Presided over by his cousin, Faḍl ʿAbbās al-Mahdawī, the court was used to eliminate enemies of the regime. There were no further major challenges until February 1963.

Qāsim did build support among poorer urban groups by an extended social welfare programme. This programme included increased spending on health, education and house building and was accompanied by price and rent controls. Under Qāsim social welfare spending as a proportion of the budget doubled and spending continued at a high level down to 1974. This development indicates two of the significant changes brought about by the revolution: a switch from investment to consumption and a redistribution of wealth in favour of the towns against the countryside. Like all revolutions in the Near East the Iraqi revolution was an urban revolution.

The most dramatic feature of the revolution was land reform. It has previously been observed that the monarchical regime was a regime of big landholders. In 1958 2 per cent of landholders owned 68 per cent of cultivated land. The large estates were especially concentrated in the south where they belonged to tribal shaykhs who had turned themselves into landlords and their tribesmen into sharecroppers on new pump-irrigated land. In the north smaller holdings predominated although large estates existed, often in the hands of urban merchants who had taken advantage of the indebtedness of peasants. The land situation was much more like that of Syria than of Egypt because there was no absolute shortage of land; the average holding was 50 hectares even though three-quarters of farmers held less than 12.5 hectares. But the details mattered little to the new regime; it was sufficient that the old regime had been a landlord one. The object of land reform was to destroy big landlords and the Egyptian model would achieve this. In any case peasants in the provinces where the largest estates existed, Kūt and ᶜAmāra, were already taking matters into their own hands and seizing land.

The 1958 land reform imposed a ceiling of 250 hectares on wet (irrigated) land and 500 on dry (rainfed) land. Land over these limits was to be expropriated with compensation and distributed to cultivators in packages of around 12 hectares wet and 23 dry. Uncultivated *tapu* and *lazma* land was to revert to being state land. As in Egypt peasants who received land were obliged to become members of co-operatives. In fact the machinery was lacking to implement the new law; expropriation proceeded quickly and over 1 million hectares had been taken from landlords by the end of 1963 but distribution was much slower and the co-operatives were not formed. Succeeding regimes amended the law and made changes in implementation; the principal change came in 1969–70 when the ceilings were reduced and compensation was ended. During the 1970s redistribution was accelerated and land reform extended to the north which had been largely ignored during the 1960s. A further change was a switch from an emphasis on co-operatives, which by then embraced about half of the peasantry, to a preference for collective and state farms which increased in number rapidly during the 1970s. However, the collectives were not successful in increasing production and during the 1980s the regime reverted to encouraging private farming; in 1987 it was decided to sell off the state farms.

Land reform accomplished its main political aim of ending big landlordism. In its place it installed, not wholly by design, an agriculture dominated by middling landholders. Of the agricultural population of nearly 4 million in 1971 95 per cent owned land as compared with only 15 per cent of the 1958 farm population. This was not a result which all had wanted. The ICP had hoped for expropriation but not redistribution and the creation of a massive state agriculture which could be harnessed to the revolution. The Baᶜth too, in its radical phase, toyed with similar ideas. But instead the revolutionaries had contrived to create a conservative rural society. The secondary aim of land reform of increasing agricultural production had not been achieved. In 1958 Iraq was a food exporting country; by 1982 food constituted 15 per cent of all imports. During the first two decades of the revolution agricultural investment was low; only in 1976 was the decision made to give agriculture a higher priority. Agriculture's share of GNP fell from 17 per cent in 1960 to 8 per cent in 1980 and its share of employment from more than half to less than a third. The largest change which took place in the countryside was the massive movement from the land to the towns.

Under Qāsim and his successors down to 1976 the main priority was industrial development. In 1958 the principal industries in Iraq apart from oil were construction, food processing and textiles and they were still the principal industries in 1980. There had been some development of heavy industry – iron, steel, aluminium and petrochemicals – but the development had not transformed the Iraqi economy. If one excludes oil industrial production remained virtually constant at 15 per cent of GDP. The big growth areas of the Iraqi economy were services, especially government services, and oil.

Qāsim initiated a new policy towards the oil industry in Iraq. In an attempt to win greater state control of Iraqi oil production he entered into negotiations with the Iraq Petroleum Company. After three years he tired of bargaining and confiscated 99.5 per cent of the concession, leaving Kirkuk to the IPC but taking possession of the Rumayla field which he complained the company had failed to develop. In this way Qāsim launched Iraq into a protracted, damaging struggle with the oil companies, one which was carried on by his successors and ended in 1972 with the nationalization of the oil industry in Iraq. The continuance of the dispute meant that the growth of Iraqi production was held back and Iraq lost revenue. Only after 1972, during the great oil boom, did Iraqi oil production flourish. By 1979 Iraq was the second largest Gulf producer and had become in essence an oil state. Oil contributed 98 per cent of foreign exchange and 90 per cent of Iraq's revenues. By then the revolution floated on oil. But after 1980 the Iran–Iraq war forced Iraq to cut oil production severely and revenues from oil were halved.

Qāsim was overthrown and executed in February 1963. The support he had won from the poorer urban groups did not compensate for lack of support from private businessmen and from religious figures who were alienated by his policy of legal secularization marked by limitations on polygamy, the forbidding of child marriage and the introduction of equal rights in inheritance for women. In December 1962 there were student riots. Above all there was continuing hostility from army factions and it was a coalition of such factions with some civilians which carried out the bloody revolution of 8–9 February 1963.

Two groups were involved in the coup. One was a number of factions and discontented officers grouped under the generic term "Arab nationalist". The other was the Baʿth Party which had recovered from its setback in 1959. Its secretary, ʿAlī Ṣāliḥ al-Saʿdī, was the principal organizer of the coup and he made the necessary contacts with other groups. Saʿdī represented the radical wing of the Baʿth which was strongest among the civilian members and in the national guard, the Baʿthist militia which was recruited especially from the Baʿth stronghold of the Aʿẓamiyya quarter of Baghdad. Opposed to the radicals was another more moderate Baʿthist faction which was strongest in the army and included a number of men who had only recently joined the Baʿth together with some who were no more than lukewarm sympathizers with the aims of the party. The conspirators had been planning their coup since late 1961 when a committee composed of Baʿthists and various malcontents had been formed.

The new regime had at its head ʿAbd al-Salām ʿĀrif who was president of the National Council of the Revolutionary Command (NCRC) a body composed mainly of men drawn from the pre-coup committee but dominated by the Baʿthists who occupied 16 of the 18 seats. The Baʿth also formed the leading element in the government where they held 12 of 21 seats in the cabinet, including the posts of prime minister, and ministers of the interior and defence. The prime minister was Aḥmad Ḥasan al-Bakr, who had briefly served in the first Qāsim government before he had been dismissed from government and army alike. At the interior was Saʿdī and at defence Colonel Ṣāliḥ Mahdī al-ʿAmmāsh.

The imposing appearance which the Iraqi Baʿth made in the new regime grossly over-represented its true strength. In truth the party was small, divided and weak where it mattered – in the army. It is estimated that it had no more than 8,000 members. The Baʿth attempted to remedy its lack of command of a coercive force by rapidly building up the national guard to 34,000 by August 1963 but it experienced the same problem as the earlier communist militia; while such a force could accomplish something in street rioting it was no substitute for a disciplined force. However, the fall of the Baᶜth was due mainly to their own divisions. Quarrelling between factions led to a split in the autumn of 1963 and to the ejection of the radicals by the moderates. As a consequence the Baᶜth founder and head of the national command, Michel ᶜAflaq, was summoned to settle the problems of the Iraqi regional organization and did so by exiling the leading moderates as well. A few days later the Baᶜth lost power altogether when President ᶜĀrif carried out his own coup on 18 November.

The regime established by ᶜĀrif in November 1963 endured until 1968. Like the regimes of the preceding five years what was most distinctive about the ᶜĀrif regime was the flimsiness of its institutions. There was no permanent constitution, no parliament and no political parties of substance. The regime was a business of personalities, loose army factions and bureaucrats. There was a temporary constitution but it had little to offer Iraq as it was modelled on the constitution of Egypt in order to facilitate an eventual, distant union. A national revolutionary council (NRC) was established, composed of Baᶜthist and Arab nationalist officers and relatives and cronies of ᶜĀrif. The Baᶜthists, including Aḥmad Ḥasan al-Bakr, were quickly dropped in 1964, the Arab nationalists in the summer of 1965 and ᶜĀrif's men, many from his home district of al-Ramādī, were left in charge. But the NRC never had much power and was itself dissolved. There was also a political party, the Arab Socialist Union, formed on paper in July 1964 when ᶜĀrif announced that all political parties would be merged in a single new mass party modelled, of course, on the Egyptian party. But the party was of no consequence and the dominant institution was the presidency.

ᶜAbd al-Salām ᶜĀrif was president and commander in chief until he was killed in an aeroplane crash on 13 April 1966. His personality was the opposite of that of Qāsim, his former co-conspirator and rival. Whereas Qāsim was cautious and secretive like ᶜAbd al-Nāṣir, ᶜĀrif was dashing and extrovert like Anwar al-Sādāt. That two such different men should have run such similar regimes may suggest that the time was not ripe for more permanent institutions in Iraq. ᶜĀrif's brother and successor, ᶜAbd al-Raḥmān ᶜĀrif, who was president from April 1966 until his overthrow in July 1968, was a man of a greyer stripe. ᶜAbd al-Raḥmān's succession represented a temporary victory for the civilian and Arab nationalist elements in the regime over the military and particularist groups; his rival, a Mosuli officer named ᶜUqaylī, was presented as an Iraqi nationalist.

The increasing influence of civilian politicians in government had been visible since 1964. Like the NRC the first ᶜĀrif government had been composed largely of Baᶜthist and Arab nationalist officers. The first prime minister was a recent convert to Baᶜthism, Ṭāhir Yaḥyā, and the minister of defence was Ḥardān al-Takrītī. Both men were from Takrīt, a small town on the Tigris north of Baghdad, which was also the home of Aḥmad Ḥasan al-Bakr, who had served as prime minister in 1963. The emergence of the Takrītīs as the dominant regional faction within the Baᶜth Party, following the purges of radicals and moderates in 1963, was a significant development but it was one for the future as both ministers were dismissed in 1964. The Arab nationalist officers lasted longer but were finally ousted in September 1965 after their most prominent figure, the new prime minister, ᶜĀrif ᶜAbd al-Razzāq, former commander of the air force, failed in a coup attempt. The cabinet of September 1965 had only three army men and the new prime minister was ᶜAbd al-Raḥmān al-Bazzāz, a lawyer, diplomat and politician with a history of involvement in nationalist politics since the 1930s. He was also a man of considerable ability and his conduct of the government of Iraq during the following year helped to stabilize the situation.

The relationship of military and civilian in Iraq resembled that of nomad and settled in an earlier period. If they were not held firmly in check the military could not resist the temptation to encroach on the pastures of government. Such was the case in June 1966 when another attempted army coup weakened the position of Bazzāz who was replaced by an army officer in August 1966. In March 1967 ᶜAbd al-Raḥmān ᶜĀrif himself became prime minister for a time before handing over to Ṭāhir Yaḥyā again. His regime lasted until July 1968 when two coups in rapid succession installed a different sort of regime.

By 1968 ᶜĀrif had few supporters outside his own faction and the security services. The 1967 Israel war had helped to discredit the Iraqi regime as it had all other Arab governments and the continuing problems of Kurdistan formed a further question mark against ᶜĀrif's competence. Conservatives were irritated by the drift towards socialism after the fall of Bazzāz and nationalists by the failure to improve relations with other Arab states. Beyond these factors were the ambitions of individual army officers and factions and the rekindled enthusiasm of the Baᶜth. It was a coalition of military malcontents, led by men from ᶜĀrif's own home territory of al-Ramādī, and Baᶜthist officers which carried out the coup of 17 July which removed ᶜĀrif. In the second coup of 30 July the Baᶜthist officers expelled their army rivals and took power alone.

July 1968 saw the inauguration of the long-lasting Baᶜthist regime in Iraq. In 1968 the Baᶜth was a very different organization from that which had existed in 1963. The old leadership had gone; in 1966 a new faction had taken control of the Iraqi regional organization and in 1968 confirmed its victory and the division with the Syrian Baᶜth by establishing a new national command with ᶜAflaq as secretary general. Secondly, the organization of the Baᶜth Party was much improved in 1967–8; in particular a military intelligence apparatus was developed. Although the party was still only 5,000 strong in 1968 it was a more tightly knit and purposive organization than its predecessor.

It was the Baᶜth Party which dominated the new regime. The Iraqi Baᶜth after 1968 was a new type of institution in the Arab Near East. The ASU in Egypt was no more than an adjunct of the regime and the Syrian Baᶜth was a bonus awarded to the victorious army faction. Only the Yemen Socialist Party is comparable to the Iraqi Baᶜth, which was an élite party like the Communist Party of the Soviet Union. Its numbers were never large: in 1978 the membership was estimated to be 50,000 and purges reduced the size of the party in the subsequent years. An elaborate organization of cells, sections, divisions, branches and areas were developed, extending Baᶜth influence into the localities. The Baᶜth's position was guaranteed in the new interim constitution of 1970 which stated that Iraq was a People's Democratic Republic committed to Arab socialism and Islam. Under the constitution the principal authority in the state was the revolutionary command council whose members had also to be members of the Iraqi regional command of the Baᶜth. The Iraqi Baᶜth also dominated the government. Its secretary general, Aḥmad Ḥasan al-Bakr, became, in 1968, president, prime minister and commander in chief. In the early years of the regime the Baᶜth gave a substantial share of government posts to non-party men but after 1973 the party always retained about two-thirds of ministerial posts including all key portfolios. The party created its own militia, said to number 50,000 in 1978 but subsequently greatly increased in response to the war with Iran.

Around the party were created other institutions. In 1974 the National Progressive Front, an umbrella organization of political parties dominated by the Baᶜth, was formed. The ICP was included in the front but its uneasy alliance with the Baᶜth broke down in 1979 and the ICP withdrew to contest elections on its own. Another feature of the new Iraqi system was the creation of a number of associations of professional and industrial workers and peasants, which operated, like similar organizations in socialist countries, as links between party and people and were under Baᶜth control. Locally-elected councils were set up in the name of the democratization of government but also controlled by the party. Again the pattern of organization was one made familiar by the experience of socialist countries. Finally, in 1980 two parliamentary assemblies were established, one for the Kurdish territories and a national assembly elected by universal suffrage. At the 1980 elections the Baᶜth obtained an overwhelming majority.

The influence of the military was steadily reduced. In the government of 1968 two prominent Baᶜthist officers held key posts: Ḥardān al-Takrītī was minister of defence and Colonel Ṣāliḥ Mahdī al-ᶜAmmāsh minister of the interior. By 1971 both had gone and by 1974 Aḥmad Ḥasan al-Bakr was the only former officer in a key post. Opponents and dubious supporters of the dominant faction were systematically purged from the army and civil service during the years 1968–73. Conservatives, Arab nationalists and communists alike suffered from the repression, in particular the last group which was suppressed in 1970 and especially in 1978.

The dominant figures in the new regime were Aḥmad Ḥasan al-Bakr and Ṣaddām Ḥusayn al-Takrītī. Aḥmad Ḥasan al-Bakr was born in 1914, the son of a small landowner in Takrīt. He had entered the military academy in 1938, graduating in 1942, thus avoiding the great purge of officers which followed the fall of the Golden Square. He had joined the Free Officers in 1958 but under Qāsim he was forced out of the army and took up the study of law. From then on he was essentially a party man rather than an army officer and it was as a party organizer that he came back to the fore in 1966 as leader of the faction which took over the Iraqi Baᶜth. His principal supporter in that party coup was Ṣaddām Ḥusayn who became assistant secretary general of the Iraqi Baᶜth and was chiefly responsible for the reorganization of the party which took place in the following years. Ṣaddām Ḥusayn was a much younger man, being born in Takrīt in 1937, and came from a poor peasant background. He was reared by his uncle, a former officer purged in 1941. Ṣaddām Ḥusayn had no other connection with the army; the uniform he habitually wore was that of the Baᶜth militia. Ṣaddām was a party man who joined the Baᶜth in 1957 and quickly made a reputation as an activist. It is interesting that he especially admired Stalin. In 1959 he was wounded in the assassination attempt against Qāsim. A cautious, suspicious, courageous and ruthless conspirator Ṣaddām Ḥusayn resembled Qāsim, ᶜAbd al-Nāṣir and Asad. In the politics of Arab revolution his type of personality was that which was most successful. Aḥmad Ḥasan al-Bakr remained leader until 1979 when he stepped down, nominally, through ill-health, and was succeeded by Ṣaddām Ḥusayn whose powers had steadily increased during the preceding years as his rivals had been eliminated from contention. Nevertheless, Ṣaddām's succession was not easy. Following a reported coup attempt a very extensive purge took place which involved the execution of five members of the RCC. Ṣaddām Ḥusayn survived further coup attempts in 1982 and 1983.

Within the Baᶜth regime an important part was played by regional and kinship links. Regional factions were not new in Iraqi revolutionary politics but the Takrītī group was the most conspicuous and enduring of such factions. In 1987 one-third of the RCC and the Baᶜth regional command came from Takrīt. (Nearly all the others came from Mosul, Baghdad and ᶜĀna.) It is not easy to account for the importance of Takrīt, a small town which was once a centre of that curious and ancient Iraqi industry which involved the manufacture of inflatable skins for simple rafts to transport goods on the rivers. There were few career opportunities in Takrīt and many young men had gone into the army helped by the patronage of a Sharifian officer, Mawlūd Mukhliṣ. But Takrīt was no different in this respect from other towns, for example ᶜĀna, a similar town on the Euphrates, also once a centre of the skin raft industry and also the basis of an army faction. The success of the Takrītīs must be attributed partly to the circumstance that their rivals, notably the Mosulis in 1966 and the Ramādīs in 1968, were eliminated. Nor should one exaggerate the unity of regional factions. The Ramādīs fell out with one another and the Takrītīs also had their divisions, notably in the elimination of Ḥardān al-Takrītī, the dominant figure among the military Baᶜthists, who was removed from office in 1970 and assassinated a year later in Kuwayt. Regional factions were temporary coalitions of men who understood and occasionally trusted each other and who shared enemies. Kinship links were also important as they had been under the ᶜĀrifs. Ṣaddām Ḥusayn's al-Ṭalfāḥ clan held several leading posts. But, once again, it would be a mistake to suppose that kinship links were the sole or even the principal foundation of the regime. Ties of blood were a basis for trust and co-operation but were not wholly reliable; after the attempted coup of 1983 (in which they may have been involved) three of Ṣaddām's half brothers were removed from their posts, including Bārzān al-Takrītī, the head of intelligence.

The policy of the regime was set out in a number of documents including the constitution of 1970, the national charter of 1980 and the programme of the Baᶜth Party. It may be summarized as Arab socialism and rapid social and economic development in internal affairs, and non-alignment and Arab solidarity in foreign policy. It will now be appropriate to examine these different areas of activity before making an assessment of the changes wrought by the revolution.

Iraq turned to socialism, or at least to state capitalism, in July 1964 when banks, insurance companies and some industries including cement, tobacco manufacture and some sections of the flour and textile industries were nationalized, strict controls placed on foreign trade and increased taxes imposed on the rich. The motives behind this sudden shift from a private enterprise system appear to have been threefold. First was a desire to emulate Egypt and to make the Iraqi economic organization conform to that of Egypt with a view to eventual union. Second, there was the belief of some young technocrats, many trained abroad, that state industrial planning was a more efficient and speedy way of obtaining the rapid development which they sought. And third was the pressure for jobs in a state sector which was too small to accommodate all the revolutionary aspirants. In fact under ʿAbd al-Salām ʿĀrif socialism, like his political party, was more decorative than real. ʿĀrif was a political revolutionary but a social and economic conservative. Many of the changes remained on paper and controls were relaxed under Bazzāz in 1965-6 and the private sector was encouraged. After 1966 the move towards socialism grew stronger and more powerful still after the Baʿth took power in 1968. The share of the public sector in GDP grew from 31 per cent in 1968 to 80 per cent in 1977. Of course, much of this statistical change was due to the factor of oil. In 1972 Iraq nationalized the Iraq Petroleum Company and the following year took the remainder of the oil industry into state ownership. The oil boom and the great expansion of oil production which followed had the effect of boosting the share of the state sector. It also made available for state use additional oil revenues for investment. In turn these revenues were used to develop heavy industry – iron, steel and petrochemicals – as well as to finance a major development of communications (ports, roads, railways and airports). Even more, oil money went into services: by 1978 one-third of all those in work were in service industries. The main effect of the oil boom in Iraq was to finance the growth of employment in administration and defence; between 1960 and 1976 government employment grew at the rate of 6 per cent a year and the civil service increased from 27,000 in 1957 to 261,000 in 1973. By 1978 more than 20 per cent of the work force was employed by the state. Socialism in Iraq had created a network of interests around the state which gave substantial strength to the regime.

The main emphasis in social and economic development was on health, housing and especially education. Between 1958 and 1983 the number of elementary school pupils increased from 500,000 to 2.6 million, of secondary from 74,000 to 1 million, and higher education students increased from 8,500 to over 120,000. In 1958 only about 60 per cent of children in the relevant age group attended elementary school and less than 20 per cent secondary school. By 1980 virtually 100 per cent of Iraqi children went to elementary school and 60 per cent to secondary school. Illiteracy was down from 85 per cent in 1958 to just over half the population in 1977 when a new drive against illiteracy was launched. The education of women was especially advanced under the revolution.

The revolution was a secular revolution in the Near Eastern tradition of modernization from above. This is not to say that many of its leaders were not sincere Muslims but rather that they thought religion had little or no part in public life; in particular they considered that social reforms should be based upon what were regarded as universal principles of human development. In the comprehensive 1974 Baᶜth political report, which surveyed developments since 1968 and looked forward to 1979, for example, there was virtually no mention of Islam. Between 1958 and the end of the 1960s there was no significant religious opposition to the regime but from 1969 the Baᶜth found itself increasingly in confrontation with movements based on Islam, especially Shīᶜī movements. In 1969 a religious party was established to be closely followed by *al-daᶜwa al-islāmiyya*, a Shīᶜī movement with religious leaders. In 1977 and 1979 there were riots in Najaf and Karbalā.

The 1979 Islamic revolution in Iran and the Iran–Iraq war gave an impetus to Shīᶜī opposition to the Baᶜthist regime in Iraq. Shīᶜī organizations, notably *al-daᶜwa*, carried out armed attacks within Iraq, and in Tehran in 1982 organized the Supreme Assembly of the Islamic Revolution in Iraq under the leadership of a prominent Iraqi *mujtahid*, Sayyid Muḥammad Bāqir al-Ḥākim. The Iraqi regime replied with repression and religiosity. Shīᶜī *mujtahids* in Najaf were kept under strict surveillance. Many members of the Ḥākim family were arrested and several executed, and close controls were established over religious education. At the same time the regime abandoned its earlier secular stance, promoted Islamic conferences and enforced observation of Ramaḍān. Ṣaddām Ḥusayn prayed frequently and conspicuously in mosques.

The 1958 coup was followed by an increase in military expenditure from 7 per cent of GNP to 13 per cent in 1966 and during the same period Iraq's armed forces grew from under 50,000 in 1958 to 80,000.

Between 1967 and 1975 the Israel and Kurdish wars contributed to a further increase which raised the percentage of GNP spent on the military to 19 in 1974 by which year the army numbered 200,000. Iraq acquired sophisticated military equipment from the USSR and France. Between 1975 and 1980 the burden of military spending was reduced, although the size of the army continued to grow, but from the outbreak of the Iran–Iraq war there were large increases in military spending and by the end of the war in 1988 Iraq had a regular army of 950,000 and a popular army of 250,000.

The major internal security problem was that of the Kurds; in 1974 four-fifths of the army was occupied by this war. It will be useful to trace the development of this problem. After 1958 Muṣṭafā al-Bārzānī returned from exile and became president of the Kurdish Democratic Party (KDP), an organization of Kurdish intellectuals and workers in Baghdad. The Kurdish organizations brought forward several demands concerned with investment, jobs and cultural autonomy. Qāsim failed to satisfy these demands and in 1961 attempted repression. The KDP was closed down and the tribal group in the Kurdish opposition, under Muṣṭafā al-Bārzānī, organized for resistance in Kurdistan and proclaimed an independent Kurdish state. Qāsim tried to control the tribal opposition by playing off one Kurdish tribal group against another but this attempt failed (although tribal opposition to Bārzānī continued) and clashes took place between the army and the Bārzānī group. Some Kurdish officers deserted to the resistance. Eventually, in September 1961, Qāsim launched a military campaign against the Kurds. No quick result was obtained; the Kurdish rebels, who built up a force of 15,000, extended their control over much of the countryside and by February 1963 two-thirds of the Iraqi army was committed to the struggle in Kurdistan.

Between 1964 and 1966 negotiation and military force were tried and failed in attempts to solve the Kurdish problem. In 1964 ᶜAbd al-Salām ᶜĀrif tried a new strategy to divide the Kurds. A ceasefire arranged with Bārzānī divided him from the former leaders of the KDP, who had thrown in their lot with Bārzānī after the closure of their party and who wanted autonomy. Ibrāhīm Aḥmad and Jalāl al-Tālabānī, the leaders of a Kurdish intellectual group which later became known as the Patriotic Union of Kurdistan (PUK) separated their forces from the tribal group. But Bārzānī's forces remained the most powerful and Bārzānī employed the ceasefire to establish his own government in Kurdistan and to import arms from Iran. In 1965–6 war was renewed. In June 1966 a new agreement was made between the Kurds and the government of Bazzāz. The new arrangement was a compromise: it allowed for a decentralized administration although not autonomy in the Kurdish areas but permitted the use of the Kurdish language, representation for the Kurds in an eventual parliament and economic aid to the region. The agreement was not implemented and the war continued.

In 1970 another agreement was made between government and Kurds. The concessions to the Kurds were greater than in 1966: former promises concerning parliamentary representation and economic aid were repeated but now Kurdish autonomy was conceded, the Kurdish language was to become an official language with Arabic and there was to be a Kurdish vice-president. The Kurdish armed forces were to be integrated into the Iraqi army. The agreement broke down and in 1974 war was resumed. It is a question whether either side intended to implement the agreement which concealed some important differences of view concerning the extent of autonomy, the area in which it would be applied and the situation of the Kurdish forces within the Iraqi army. The Kurds wanted the inclusion of Kirkuk and its oil within the Kurdish autonomous area and they wanted to retain control of their military force, the Peshmerga.

Kurdish resistance collapsed in 1975 after the withdrawal of Iranian support following the Algiers agreement between Iran and Iraq. Bārzānī fled to the United States where he died in 1979 and his sons, Idrīs and Masᶜūd took control of the remnants of the KDP. The government implemented the 1970 agreement within a restricted area which included Sulaymāniyya but excluded Kirkuk and the western part of the Mosul region. Kurdistan was now opened to revolutionary transformation; land reform, which had been one of the causes of Kurdish tribal hostility in the early 1960s, was introduced in full measure, many schools were opened and economic investments made. The tribal isolation of much of Kurdistan, which had been preserved by the war, began to break down and there was a rapid move into the towns. But in isolated areas the resistance continued and after the outbreak of the Iran–Iraq war in 1980 it gathered strength again with Iranian support. Between 1980 and 1988 relations between government and Kurds consisted of a mixture of war and negotiation. The Bārzānī group (whose strength was mainly in the north) was irreconcilable and fought on with Iranian help; the PUK, led by Jalāl al-Tālabānī (with its principal base in Sulaymāniyya), was willing for a negotiated settlement providing that Kirkuk was included in the autonomous region. Neither resistance nor negotiation served the Kurds well and with the end of the Iran war Iraq turned on the

Kurdish rebels: a campaign in the north smashed the KDP and a major resettlement project removed Kurds from frontier areas.

The foreign policy of revolutionary Iraq was dominated by its relations with its fellow Arab states, with Iran and with the USSR. The revolutionaries were committed to Arab union but they faced the problem that Arab unity was unacceptable to the Kurds and to Shīʿī Iraqis by whom it was perceived as a device for strengthening Sunnī Arab control of the state. Accordingly, Iraq maintained rhetorical support for the principle of Arab unity and supported Arab causes, notably that of the Palestinians, but negotiations for the achievement of unity repeatedly failed. In 1958 Qāsim declined to pursue negotiations for union with Egypt and Syria and in 1963 only an empty agreement with the two states was made. Efforts to achieve union with Syria also failed and relations between the two Baʿthist regimes were almost invariably bad. After 1980 Syria aided Iran in the war between Iraq and Iran. And Iraqi relations with the Gulf states were always uneasy after Qāsim laid claim to Kuwayt in 1961. Iraq was commonly perceived by her Arab neighbours as an uncertain and violent state; only after 1975 did Iraq begin to win a reputation for greater moderation and develop better relations with Jordan and other states. Iraqi relations with Iran, like those with Syria, were dominated by regional rivalry between the two states. Disputes were sharp after 1969, were temporarily resolved in 1975 by the Algiers agreement and burst into flame in 1980 in the Gulf war. Relations with Iran are discussed in detail in Chapter 16.

In her relations with the great powers revolutionary Iraq made a clear break with the tradition of monarchical Iraq. The defence links with the west were immediately broken: Iraq's membership of the Baghdad pact was formally terminated in 1959. The difficult relations of Iraq with the Iraq Petroleum Company also had an adverse effect upon Iraq's relations with the west. Instead Iraq began to build close relations with the USSR which became a major trading partner of Iraq and a principal arms supplier. In 1972 a 15 year treaty of friendship was signed between Iraq and the USSR. Only after 1975 did Iraq begin to rebuild relations with the western powers.

As remarked at the opening of this chapter, it is difficult if not impossible, to disentangle the changes which were the consequence of revolution from the changes which Iraq experienced as a result of deeper processes which owed nothing to the revolution. One could say that it does not matter, that what is significant is what happened, but this is not a satisfactory answer. To the historian it is also important to know why something happened and especially interesting to contemplate the gulfs which separate men's motives for action from their expectations of the consequences of actions and divide their expectations from the future which came into being. In this light it may be said that in 1958 no-one intended the actual revolution which took place.

One object of the revolutionaries was to sweep away the monarchical regime and the élite which controlled Iraq and this was achieved. In 1958 it was not intended to change the economic structure of Iraq; the growth of a state-controlled economy was the result of a series of decisions taken for a variety of motives during the 1960s but the development transformed the Iraqi political system by creating a solid block of support for a strong state. A further unintended consequence of the revolution was a major transfer of resources from the rural to the urban sector. The Iraqi revolution was an urban revolution conducted in the interests of town dwellers who reaped the principal benefits in employment, rewards and services. It was especially the middle and lower urban classes who gained although some of their gains were lost to inflation and the greatest rewards went to entrepreneurs, contractors and higher bureaucrats including the managers of state enterprises. Government and state service replaced land as the main determinant of social status. This is not to say that there were not gainers in the countryside; in many areas peasants benefited, especially the middling landholders. It was also a generational revolution; the ageing élite of the Hashimite monarchy was replaced by new groups who became steadily younger until 1968. But youth is a wasting asset and the relative stability of the regime after 1968 meant an older élite. Nevertheless, the expansion of education tended to reduce the age of the élite as new groups of better trained technocrats claimed their share of power. It was also in some measure a sex revolution; one of the leading features of the changes was the improved position of women as the extended family declined, polygamy was reduced, and women gained greater access to education and jobs. There was also an element of a regional revolution: central Iraq including the Baghdad area gained most from the changes; the Shīʿī south and the Kurdish north enjoyed fewer advantages and suffered most from war.

The revolution was not a Shīʿī revolution: in 1958 it was supposed that Qāsim and the communists to some extent represented a Shīʿī reaction to Sunnī dominance but Sunnī Arabs dominated the Qāsim regime and even more those which succeeded it down to 1979. In that sense there was no change from the Hashimite situation and given the dominance of Sunnī army officers down to the early 1970s, the preponderance of Sunnīs in the Ba^{c}th Party and the circumstance that Shī^{c}ī landlords were the greatest sufferers under land reform it is unsurprising that this should have been so. But Shī^{c}īs did make gains from the revolution: Shī^{c}īs participated in the urban advantages; Shī^{c}ī immigration made Baghdad, like Basra, a majority Shī^{c}ī city and the great new suburb of Ṣaddām Ḥusayn City was a Shī^{c}ī stronghold. Shī^{c}īs, although they scarcely improved their position in the army before 1980, did much better in the bureaucracy and in business and as the regime became for a time more civilianized in the late 1970s Shī^{c}īs improved their relative standing. After 1980, as a consequence of the war with Iran, the Shī^{c}īs advanced more rapidly in the army and government.

The war of 1980–8 had a significant effect on the course of Iraq's development. From 1958 to 1968 the revolution developed no strong institutions: between 1968 and 1978 the Ba^{c}th Party emerged as the major new institution, dominating the army factions which had hitherto held sway. After 1980 the regime became a more personal adventure under the stress of war. Ṣaddām Ḥusayn made the party, like the army, obedient to his will, and the security services became the main institutional prop of his regime. The war also brought about economic changes: for the first time since 1958 the tide of state economic control was checked and partly reversed. Lastly, the war promoted the assertion of a new Iraqi national identity, a sense of patriotic feeling which could unite Sunnīs and Shī^{c}īs, Arabs and Kurds. The end of the war saw a more determined effort to end the long lasting Kurdish problem, to enforce the authority of the state and to crush traditional tribal resistance.

There was certainly an Iraqi revolution. It was not the revolution of its own rhetoric but it was real none the less. Arab unity, democracy and even social justice did not figure prominently in the development of Iraq after 1958 and the revolutionary regimes were at least as dependent upon their security forces as the monarchy had been, but changes there were. In part the changes were intended; in part they were the unintended consequence of human decisions; and in part they were the result of the growth of population, urbanization and the demand for oil.

CHAPTER TEN

Syria and Lebanon since 1958

SYRIA

In the years after 1958 Syria underwent a radical revolution similar to that experienced by Egypt after 1952 and Iraq after 1958. The principal changes in Syria were like those in Egypt and Iraq, namely the extinction of the political and economic power of the old landed urban notables who had dominated the Syrian scene before 1958 and the emergence of a new military and civilian élite dependent upon the greatly enhanced economic and political eminence of the state. The Syrian revolution was compressed into the years 1963 to 1970; the preceding period may be regarded as preparatory and the subsequent years as a time of consolidation. As in Egypt and Iraq the main agency of change was the army but the army officers who gained power came from more rural backgrounds than those in Egypt and Iraq; in fact, especially from a religious minority, the ʿAlawīs. Two other features distinguished the Syrian experience from that of Egypt. First, in Syria there was less of a tradition of state interventionism than in Egypt and therefore the change was more revolutionary and dramatic. And second, as in Iraq, the transition in Syria was punctuated by a series of often violent coups.

During the years 1958 – 1961 Syria was joined with Egypt in the United Arab Republic. The initiative for the union had come from Syria and had derived from a generalized sentiment in favour of Arab unity and from fears on the part of certain Syrian political groups of domination by the left. President ʿAbd al-Nāṣir had not sought the union for which he believed Syrians to be unprepared. In agreeing he had imposed three conditions: there should be a strong central government, the Syrian army should be kept out of politics, and all political parties should be dissolved. In forming a government ʿAbd al-Nāṣir had relied heavily on Egyptian personnel; Egyptians dominated the bureaucracy and his closest ally, ᶜAbd al-Ḥakīm ᶜĀmīr, presided over Syrian affairs. As his Syrian instrument ᶜAbd al-Nāṣir employed ᶜAbd al-Ḥamīd Sarrāj, who served as chairman of the Syrian provincial council until he was summoned to Cairo in 1961. These were the years when Egypt moved towards state control and ownership of economic activities and Syria shared in this experience; a measure of land reform was introduced and in July 1961 industries, banks, insurance companies, etc., were nationalized.

The union of Egypt and Syria was ended by a Syrian army coup on 28 September 1961. Partly the UAR broke down because of resentment of Egyptian dominance by Syrian army officers, bureaucrats and others. Wealthy Syrian landowners and merchants disliked land reform and nationalization, Syrian politicians of various colours were indignant at their exclusion from power and Syrian army officers were disgusted by the reduction of their pay to Egyptian levels. The leaders of the Baᶜth, who had hoped for much from the union were especially disappointed. Their candidates did badly at the elections of July 1959, in August the party split between Ḥawrānī, ᶜAflaq and other faction leaders and the Baᶜthist ministers resigned in December of the same year. Disillusionment was completed by the long drought which ravaged Syrian agriculture from 1959 to 1961 and contrasted vividly with the boom of the earlier 1950s. Agricultural output was reduced to half and rural incomes to 60 per cent of the 1957 figures. Finally, the Egyptians underestimated the strength of opposition to the union; in particular the removal of Sarrāj, who had kept close control over the Syrian army, proved to be a serious mistake.

It is difficult to estimate the significance of the episode of the UAR for Syria. One view is that it was an inconsequential interlude; the Egyptians went home, the old Syrian politicians returned to power and land reform and nationalization were promptly undone. Another view sees the union with Egypt as having consequences as far reaching as those of the Egyptian occupation of 1830 – 41. The mould of Syrian politics, already showing signs of cracking before 1958, was irretrievably shattered and could not be restored; Egyptian government had been more extensive and more radical than anything Syria had experienced before and within a few years UAR policies were back in force in Syria.

The immediate result of the coup was apparently to put the clock back to 1954. The coup had put the army in control but the army was unprepared to assume responsibility. The leader of the coup, a conservative Sunnī officer from Damascus, Lt. Col ᶜAbd al-Karīm al-

Naḥlawī, decided to restore a civilian government. A provisional constitution was published in November 1961 which provided for the election of a constituent assembly. The elections of 1961 saw the return of the old politicians, and the new government, like those before 1958, was dominated by landed urban notables. The new president was from the Qudsī family of Aleppo. The representation of the radical parties was much diminished. Ten seats were won by Muslim Brothers but the divided Baᶜth did badly; only the wing led by Akram al-Ḥawrānī, which won 15 seats, was successful. In other ways Syrian government from 1961 to 1963 resembled that of the period before 1958; there was a succession of weak governments dominated by factional rivalries and there were threats of army intervention. In March/April 1962 there were two attempted army coups, the first by Naḥlawī and the second by a group of officers from Homs and Aleppo who were opposed to the ambitions of the Damascus officers. The stalemate led to a new agreement again to restore power to the civilian politicians and the army leaders of both factions went into diplomatic exile. The new civilian government was more radical than its predecessors and its policies leaned towards those of the UAR; land reform was reintroduced and some renationalization took place.

Radical revolution in Syria was announced by the coup of 8 March 1963. The immediate cause was yet another crisis of weak government in Syria when ministers from the Muslim Brotherhood and the Ḥawrānī faction resigned over the question of the dismissal of 30 teachers. An important factor was the Baᶜthist coup which took place in Iraq on 8 February 1963 and which provided an inspiration and led to renewed talk of union with Iraq. A further element was the desire of some officers to revive the union with Egypt; indeed this was a proclaimed aim of the coup.

The new regime in Syria was dominated by Baᶜthists. The planning and execution of the coup was carried out by independent army officers of various opinions and the leading figure was Major Ziyād al-Ḥarīrī, a brother-in-law of Akram al-Ḥawrānī. Baᶜthist officers played a prominent but not a dominant part in the conspiracy. Moreover, the Baᶜthist officers constituted an organization separate from that of the Baᶜth Party. During the period of the UAR, when the civilian party had disintegrated, a secret military organization of Baᶜthist officers, known as the Military Committee, was formed. However, the Baᶜthists predominated in the institutions of the new regime. These were first, as the supreme authority, a 20 member national revolutionary council composed of equal numbers of army officers and civilians in which the Baᶜthists constituted the largest single group. The Baᶜthists confirmed their dominance by evicting the Nasirites at the end of April 1963. Second was the government in which half the members were from the Baᶜth and which was presided over by Ṣalāḥ al-Dīn al-Bīṭār, one of the two founders of the Baᶜth. The Baᶜth success led to a very rapid growth of party membership from only 400 civilian members in March 1963. As the new members came predominantly from rural areas the dominance of the old urban-based leadership of ᶜAflaq and Bīṭār was weakened and the party became more radical and more military in character. The party enlarged its support still further in 1964 – 5 when it organized workers in a trade union movement and peasants in a peasants' union.

No attempt will be made to relate in detail the confused story of the faction fighting of the following seven years of Syrian history. Instead the main features of the story will be indicated and the principal changes in the structure of Syria examined. During the period the real struggle for power took place within the ranks of the military Baᶜthists and especially within the military committee; civilian politicians, largely Baᶜthists, continued to occupy most posts in government and party, but played a subsidiary role in the power struggle. The struggle was essentially one of personalities and factions but it took on two other aspects concerned with disputes about policy and with communal or sectarian divisions. The policy disputes concerned both domestic and foreign policy, namely the pace of the extension of state control and Syria's attitude to her neighbours and especially to Israel. These policy matters will be considered in due course but it will be appropriate here to examine the sectarian aspect.

During the years 1963 to 1970 there was a shift of power from the Sunnī Syrian majority to the non-Sunnī minorities, the ᶜAlawīs, the Druzes and the Ismāᶜīlīs, and within the minorities to the ᶜAlawīs who had established their dominance over Syrian public life before the end of the period. This is not to say that these groups fought for power as sectarian parties; all factions embraced individuals from several sects and the most savage conflicts were often those between members of the same sect. Rather it is to point out first, that this shift of power did take place; and second, to suggest that it was linked to the struggle for power in that men looked first to their own communities for trusted supporters. First to go were the Sunnīs who had held the leading positions in the army before 1963 and had led every military coup down to that year. From 1963 to 1966 the leading figure in Syrian politics was a Sunnī Baᶜthist officer, Major General Amīn al-Ḥāfiẓ, who became president of the revolutionary command council following the bloody suppression of an attempted coup by Nasirite officers in July 1963, and later prime minister. The Sunnīs were weakened by their own rivalries, by their frequent inclinations towards ᶜAbd al-Nāṣir and by the purges of 1962, 1963 and 1966. The Druzes made their bid for power and lost in September 1966 and they and the Ismāilīs suffered in the purges of 1966 and 1968. After September 1966 the dominant figures in the contest for power were ᶜAlawīs.

The ᶜAlawīs, who constituted about 11 per cent of the population of Syria, were concentrated in the region of Latakia where they formed a majority of the population. In the course of time they spread out from their homeland and also settled on land in the plain of Homs and Hama. They were predominantly rural; down to 1945 ᶜAlawīs were only a minority in the population of the city of Latakia although subsequent immigration made them into a majority. The ᶜAlawīs were very divided among themselves and may be allocated to three main groups: a largely tribal population in the mountainous areas who lived as peasants or as sharecroppers on the lands of ᶜAlawī landlords: a partly detribalized population in the plains who lived as sharecroppers on the lands of Sunnī and Greek Orthodox landlords; and some ᶜAlawī immigrants who had left Hatay after its annexation to Turkey. This last group included some peasants but on the whole tended to be better educated and more urban than the older ᶜAlawī population. There were four tribal confederations each of which was divided into tribes and clans. These confederations were the Khayyāṭīn, Ḥaddādīn, Matāwira and Kalbiyya. There were also several religious sects, notably the Shamsiyya, the Qamariyya and the Murshidiyya. Although these tribal and religious groupings were loose, lacked any clear system for selecting leaders and were declining in importance because of the effects of modernization they remained significant linkage systems which could and did form the bases of alliances. Among the more prominent ᶜAlawī contenders were the three who constituted the military committee in 1963: Muḥammad ᶜUmrān from the Khayyāṭīn, Ṣalāḥ Jadīd from the Ḥaddādīn and Ḥāfiẓ al-Asad from the Numaylātiyya clan of the Matāwira, from the village of Qardaha, a centre of the Qamariyya sect. It was ᶜUmrān who first pursued a sectarian policy, bringing ᶜAlawī officers into key positions, Jadīd who inherited his supporters and developed the faction into a system of ᶜAlawī domination in 1966 – 8, and Asad who inherited the ᶜAlawī ascendancy.

The rise of the ᶜAlawīs within the French Troupes Spéciales has been described (see p. 99). A further factor of change was the policies pursued by the independent Syrian republic which set out to eradicate the separate identity which the ᶜAlawīs (and other minorities) had enjoyed under French domination. Communal representation in parliament was ended and the ᶜAlawīs lost their personal law and were subjected to the common law of Syria. ᶜAlawī opposition was crushed by force. Education and other aspects of modernization also tended to break down the isolation of the ᶜAlawīs. It is unsurprising that many ᶜAlawīs, once the option of autonomy was denied them, should have espoused a secular Syrian nationalism which would diminish the disadvantages of their sectarian identity in a predominantly Sunnī state. The choice was between the SSNP and the Baᶜth and most chose the latter. ᶜAlawī students in Damascus brought the Baᶜthist message back to Latakia and the Latakia branch soon became one of the strongest. When other Baᶜthist organizations declined under Egyptian domination the Latakia section, dominated by ᶜAlawīs, held firm. More important than the regional organization, however, was the rise of the ᶜAlawī Baᶜthists in the army.

A decisive event in the victory of the military Baᶜthist ᶜAlawīs was the coup of 23 February 1966 which ended months of struggle betwen Ḥāfiẓ, Bīṭār and the civilian Baᶜth ensconced in the national command of the Ba'th on the one hand, and Jadīd, Asad and the military ᶜAlawīs who dominated the regional command on the other. In December 1965 it had seemed that Ḥāfiẓ and Bīṭār had won when Bīṭār again became prime minister, dissolved the regional command and made an effort to remove the army from politics. But Jadīd retained his power in the army and in February gained the mastery. The victory of Jadīd marked the end of the ascendancy of the middle class urban groups which had once vied with the urban notables for power and the rise of the rural and small town radicals. The new regime had a Sunnī president and a Sunnī prime minister but power lay with Jadīd and Asad and their followers in the party and the army. It remained to determine whether Jadīd or Asad would triumph. Their rivalry was essentially personal and factional although it was expressed in terms of policy choices; in domestic policy Jadīd stood for radicalism and Asad for moderation; in foreign policy Jadīd advocated a popular war of liberation for Palestine whereas Asad favoured first building a coalition of Arab states. Institutionally. their rivalry was expressed in a contest between the Baᶜth Party, to which Jadīd devoted himself, and the army, in which Asad, as minister of defence, built up his own support. The final clash between the two, in November 1970, was won by Asad.

Attempts have been made to measure the extent of the change which took place in the political élite of Syria. These studies show that whereas before 1963 the élite was dominated by urban Sunnī notables mainly from Damascus and Aleppo, after 1966 the political élite was composed especially of men from the provinces, from rural areas and small towns, and contained a high proportion of members of minority groups. The change was pronounced in the Syrian regional command of the Baᶜth Party but it was also visible in government where the number of ministers from Damascus and Aleppo sank from two thirds before 1958 to less than one third between 1966 and 1976. In the key posts ministers from Latakia predominated. Another change was generational. Excluding the period of the UAR the median age of Syrian ministers before 1963 was 50. Between 1963 and 1966 it dropped to 40 before it began to climb again. These ages are almost identical with those of the Free Officers when they came to power in Egypt. As in Egypt the members of the new Syrian élite were all about the same age; most were born between 1928 and 1932. The Syrian revolution was a revolution of young, non-Sunnī provincials from the army.

In the destruction of the power of the old landed notables an important part was played by land reform. The land problem in Syria differed from that in Egypt in two respects: first, land was relatively abundant in Syria, especially in the east; and second, Syrian agriculture was much less dependent upon irrigation. Syria had big landlords and sharecropping peasants but it also had many prosperous middling land holders who in Egypt would have been accounted wealthy. Further, many of the sharecroppers were able to secure a relatively high proportion of the crop, depending upon what they contributed to production in addition to their labour. Regional variations were considerable. Attempts at land reform began with Shishaklī but the first major programme was that introduced under the UAR when ceilings of 80 hectares of irrigated and 300 hectares of rainfed land were set. It was estimated that 1.37 million hectares would become available for redistribution to peasants in packages of 8 hectares of irrigated and 30 hectares of rainfed land. The plan suffered from several weaknesses, chiefly that it was based upon the Egyptian reform and failed to distinguish between different types of irrigated land in Syria and that there was inadequate bureaucratic machinery to implement it. It also encountered strong opposition from landholders and became yet more unpopular when it coincided with the great drought. By the end of the UAR less than half of the 1.37 million hectares had been expropriated and only a small part redistributed. The new government promptly amended the land reform, raising the ceilings considerably and making other concessions to the landlords.

Subsequently, however, the Egyptian ceilings were restored and after the 1963 coup more drastic measures were introduced. Ceilings were lowered to a range of 15 – 50 hectares of irrigated land and 80 – 200 hectares of rainfed land. Implementation was accelerated. By 1972 it was claimed that the original 1.37 million hectares had been expropriated and 85 per cent of it distributed benefiting one-quarter of all peasants. The average holding was 9.7 hectares.

In considering the effects of land reform it is necessary first to note that the reliability of the statistics in the previous paragraph has been questioned. In particular it has been argued that redistribution did not keep pace with expropriation and that more land than is indicated remained in the possession of the state and was leased to peasants. Secondly, many peasants leased or rented back their land to landlords. Thirdly, an important element in land reform was the formation of peasant co-operatives for which considerable success was claimed after 1970 but other evidence suggests that co-operatives were unpopular and that the movement largely failed. One conclusion is that while the power of the absentee urban notable landlords was greatly reduced it was not eliminated and that land reform did not benefit the poorest peasants but led to the enhancement of the position of middling proprietors. Indeed, it has been argued that the regime itself was recruited from middling peasants and that the aim of land reform was to benefit this group. If this conclusion is correct it points to similarities in their results between the Egyptian, Syrian and Iraqi land reforms and suggests comparisons with the agrarian consequences of the French Revolution.

Under the revolution agriculture became less important in Syrian economic life. During the 1950s the Syrian boom had been sustained by an astonishing agricultural performance in which the key element was an alleged increase in the cultivated area from 1.75 million hectares in 1953 to an estimated 3.9 million in 1955 and the development of cotton cultivation. (One should not put too much faith in these statistics and it should be remembered that not all cultivated land was cultivated every year.) The rate of increase slowed after 1957 and between 1969 and 1982 the cultivated area increased by only 5 per cent to 6.2 million. The slower increase was primarily due to the circumstance that uncultivated rainfed land had become scarce and investment in irrigation was required to bring in new land. But the slower extension of cultivation was only partially compensated by the doubling of the irrigated area as a result of the construction of the Euphrates Dam (1968 to 1974). The annual growth rate of agricultural production fell to 3.5 per cent in the early 1960s and to only 0.25 per cent in the later 1960s. This decline may also be attributed to five years of drought (although harvests in the early 1960s were very favourable), reduced supplies of foreign machinery following the nationalization of foreign trade in 1965, and the dislocation caused by land reform itself. As a result of the poor performance of agriculture and the rise of industry the relative contribution of agriculture to GNP fell considerably. As late as 1970 agriculture still employed 60 per cent of the labour force but by 1984 this had reduced to 25 per cent and the share of agriculture in GDP had fallen from 35 per cent in the 1950s to under 20 per cent. In 1974 cotton lost its position as Syria's largest export item to oil. By the end of the 1970s agriculture had ceased to be the mainstay of the Syrian economy.

The economic policies of the revolutionaries down to 1980 were founded on the expansion of state owned industry. In May 1963 banks, insurance companies and big trading companies were nationalized; in January 1965 almost all of Syrian industry went the same way; and shortly afterwards foreign trade and most wholesale trade was taken into the public sector. Much of the transformation took place under the radical government of Amīn al-Ḥāfiẓ. As in the case of Egypt the motives for the change were economic and political; to direct investment into the industrial opportunities favoured by the revolutionaries and to reduce the economic power of the big urban business class. In Egypt the relative weight to be ascribed to these motives is fairly evenly balanced but in Syria it is plain that the political motive predominated; nationalization was the counterpart of land reform and its purpose was to reduce a second pillar of the old élite and transfer economic power (and patronage) to the institution controlled by the new élite. In planning priority was given to industrialization, electrification and to the development of communications; between 1968 and 1980 Syria doubled its road mileage, more than doubled the size of its railway network and its new and largest port was opened at Ṭarṭūs in 1970. Regionally, much investment was directed towards Latakia. An economic bonus was the development of the oil industry, also under state management; exports began in 1968 and Bāniyās, the terminal of the oil pipeline from Iraq, was developed as the major oil port. Industry remained dominated by food processing and textiles but during the 1970s there was a considerable expansion of chemicals, iron and steel (at Hama), engineering and cement. 1n 1971 the contribution of industry to GDP surpassed that of agriculture.

The change in emphasis from agriculture to industry was accompanied by an acceleration of urbanization. Until 1960 the rate of urbanization in Syria had been slower than that of other countries in the region because of the better opportunities in agriculture. After 1960 the movement to the cities increased in speed. Definitions of 'urban' differ but according to one measure the percentage of town dwellers increased from 37 in 1960 to 50 in 1980, more than half of whom lived in Aleppo and Damascus. The 1981 census ascribed populations in the region of 1 million to each of these cities.

The mainspring of economic change in Syria was not radical revolution but the growth of population. The population grew from 3 million at independence to 6 million in 1970, 9 million in 1980 and 10.6 million in 1986. During the 1970s the rate of growth reached nearly 3.5 per cent per annum. Agricultural growth could not accommodate this increase; the shift to an urban and industrial system was inevitable. All economic ventures, whether by the state or private initiative were no more than attempts to channel, manage or merely ride the flood. In fact Syria managed to keep ahead of the game. During the revolutionary decade of the 1960s growth fell behind the rate of the 1950s but just managed to keep ahead of the rate of population growth. During the 1970s, helped by the boom in oil prices and aid from wealthy Arab countries, Syria did much better but after 1980 growth declined to almost nil. Over the whole period from 1965 to 1985, it has been estimated, Syrian growth averaged 4.0 per cent per annum. A large part of the additional resources, however, was represented by the increase in defence spending.

Under Ḥāfiẓ al-Asad the revolution began a period of consolidation. Asad was born in 1930, obtained his secondary education in Latakia where he became involved in student politics and in 1947 joined the Ba^{c}th. In 1952 he entered the Homs military academy and subsequently trained as a jet pilot. Between 1958 and 1961 he was in Egypt where he helped to form the military committee of the Ba^{c}th. Asad took part in the coup of 1963 and within a year was in charge of the air force with the rank of major general. Over the following period he steered a skilful course, choosing the winning side in each conflict and in 1971 he became president of Syria. In many ways Asad resembled one of his own heroes, Jamāl ^{c}Abd al-Nāṣir. (Asad also shared his other hero, Saladin, with ^{c}Abd al-Nāṣir.) Both were cool, ruthless and thoughtful men driven by strong personal ambitions and national ideals. Both enjoyed a quiet, austere and private family life. Each had entered the army as a path to a political career and they took the same time (about 15 years) to progress from graduation to leaders of their country. It is curious that Asad should have come to power just when ᶜAbd al-Nāṣir died but no accident that he saw himself as ᶜAbd al-Nāṣir's successor as a leader of the Arab world.

The most important institution of the new Syria was the presidency. Under the 1973 constitution (which replaced the various provisional constitutions under which Syria had been governed since 1961) the president determined the general lines of state policy, appointed and dismissed prime ministers and cabinets, controlled other major appointments, chose the senior members of the judiciary and could veto legislation. The president was elected for seven years. Asad, who became president in February 1971 was re-elected in 1978 and 1985, each time by a vote of over 99 per cent of the electorate. He was surrounded by his presidential advisers and by a small group of influential individuals chosen for their personal qualities rather than the offices they held, although most were influential in the army or security services. They became known as the Company or The Ten Great Ones. In 1983, following a serious illness which had seemed likely to produce a succession crisis, Asad appointed three vice-presidents with specific areas of responsibility: his brother Rifᶜat al-Asad who was put in charge of military and national security matters, ᶜAbd al-Ḥalīm Khaddam, who was given responsibility for political affairs, and Zuhayr Mashāriqa, who was given control of party business. In fact none of these leading claimants to the succession was given supreme control of the sector concerned and by dividing powers Asad reinforced his own control.

Other institutions of government were much less important than the presidency. Ministries merely executed policy and were composed of a mixture of party men and technocrats; prime ministers tended to be long lasting servants of the president and between 1971 and 1988 only four men held this post. Parliament consisted of the single chamber people's council which was dominated by a Baᶜthist majority although other parties were allowed to function and several candidates were elected as independents.

In the 1973 constitution the Baᶜth Party was described as "the leading party of the society and state." It preserved its national and regional structures although the events of 1966 had made the distinction unreal. Also the party built around itself numerous social organizations through which the population could be mobilized. As a power base the party had proved inferior to the army in 1970 and it had become a prize which went to the victor; Asad became secretary general of both structures in 1970. As a party the Syrian Baᶜth was uneasily poised between an instrument of mass mobilization and an élite cadre; under Asad it inclined to the former. In 1987 it was claimed that the Baᶜth had 800,000 members but other estimates suggested that a true figure was less than half of that claimed. The party's two functions resembled those of the ASU in Egypt: to draw in support which was found among peasants, workers, bureaucrats, soldiers and youth; and to select candidates for the people's council. It thus served as a ladder by which individuals could move into positions of power. In 1972 a national progressive front was formed to bring together five left wing parties and to present a bloc of candidates for parliament. The front served both to permit a degree of multi-party activity and to ensure overall control by the Baᶜth; in this respect it resembled Sādāt's experiments in Egypt. The leader of the front was Asad. One of the constituents of the front was the Syrian Communist Party, still under the leadership of the durable Khālid Bakdāsh. In 1986 the communists ran independently and won nine seats.

The ultimate reservoir of power was the army and the security forces. Under the constitution the president was supreme army commander but Asad took care to secure that officers were especially privileged and senior appointments were held by men whom he trusted. Close allies were Muṣṭafā Ṭalās who served as minister of defence and Ḥikmat al-Shihābī, the chief of staff. Both of these men were Sunnī Muslims but in the officer corps as a whole Sunnīs (who came, like Muṣṭafā Ṭalās, mainly from humble backgrounds) were little more than a quarter compared to ᶜAlawīs who numbered more than half. Under Asad the regular military forces underwent a tremendous expansion from 60,500 in 1968 to 500,000 in 1986 equipped with 4,000 tanks and 600 aeroplanes.

The regular army was both supported and counterbalanced by a number of special forces employed mainly in internal security duties. By 1986 there were some 12 of these special forces, composed principally of ᶜAlawīs. They included the Special Elite Units, a force of 20,000 commanded by General ᶜAlī Ḥaydar, a Sunnī fellow villager of Asad, the Defence Detachments (18,000) commanded by Rifᶜat al-Asad, the Fighting Squadrons under another brother, ᶜAdnān al-Asad and the 2,000 strong presidential guard. There was also a peasant militia said to number 500,000 in 1986.

The purposes of these vast forces were to safeguard the security of the regime from domestic enemies and to further the aims of Syrian foreign policy. Under Asad the turbulent struggle for power within the regime which had characterized the 1960s was ended and challenges to the regime came from outside its ranks. These challenges came from various opposition groups, including Nasirites and pro-Iraqi Baᶜthists, but principally from Muslim organizations. During the early 1970s, which internally was a time of consolidation, economic development and the relaxation of some of the controls of the 1960s, opposition was subdued but it became strident and more violent after 1976.

The early growth of the Muslim Brotherhood in Syria has already been described. It was a mainly urban movement, drawing strength from the traditional bazaar and middle class professionals. Its programme was radical: to create an Islamic state which was defined as one with a powerful central government, a policy of industrialization and modernization but one which rejected western influence and several attributes of western or secular society. Dr Muṣṭafā al-Sibā^{c}ī, its leader until 1957, described the Brotherhood as "neither a [social welfare] society nor a [political] party but a spirit that permeates the very being of the Muslim community: it is a new revolution".[1] In 1963 the Brotherhood was banned and broke into factions. One group, based in Damascus, wished to confine itself to social activities: others, mainly in northern Syria, determined to oppose the secularist Ba^{c}th regime with violence. After an uprising in Hama in 1964 the regime violently suppressed the Brotherhood but armed resistance and repression continued. In 1973 Asad made some attempt to conciliate Muslims by conceding their demand that the president should be a Muslim but this did not satisfy the activists and in 1976 the northerners launched a *jihād* against the regime. A number of murders of supporters of the regime took place; in 1979 more than 60 ^{c}Alawī military cadets were killed in Aleppo. In 1980 the Muslim opposition formed the Islamic Front, a broad based coalition of Muslim groups which included the Muslim Brotherhood. Its programme closely followed that of the Brotherhood. The period from 1980 to 1982 was exceptionally violent with riots in Aleppo, Homs and Hama, culminating in an episode in February 1982 when the Islamic Front took over Hama for three weeks and the security forces almost destroyed the town and killed thousands of its inhabitants in retaking it. The defeat at Hama weakened the Islamic Front which subsequently entered an alliance (the National Alliance for the Liberation of Syria) with other opposition groups which in no way supported its programme. As a consequence the Islamic Front split and its activities were further reduced.

The emergence of radical Muslim groups in the 1970s and 1980s as the principal source of opposition to the Ba^{c}thist regime in Syria has obvious similarities to developments in Egypt. In both the Muslim Brotherhood played a part but it began to resemble a coalition of factions and its programme was adopted by other groups more inclined towards violence. The Muslim movement was essentially urban and owed some of its strength to new immigrants to the towns. But in Syria, where many of the immigrants were members of minority groups, the Islamic movement often took the form of an urban reaction against the rural intrusion and drew support from a broader group of urban groups including the ulema, merchants and notables. Ostensibly the Islamic Front was not opposed to ᶜAlawī domination: its accusation against the regime was not that it was ᶜAlawī but that it pursued secular policies; Asad was accused of being an agent of Israel and the West.

The foreign policy of Syria after 1958 was dominated by its relations with its Arab neighbours and with Israel. The search for Arab unity did not cease after the failure of the UAR; it remained the official raison d'être of the Baᶜth enshrined in its organization into national and regional commands. In 1963 the new regime immediately entered talks with Egypt and Iraq about unity but only paper agreement was reached and the union never materialized. The ambition persisted, however, and in the succeeding years Syria took part in various unsuccessful attempts to create some united Arab entity. In December 1970 the Tripoli Charter proposed a federation of Syria, Egypt, Libya and the Sudan; in 1971 a very loose federation with Egypt and Libya was formed; in 1978 it was announced that Syria and Iraq had united; and 1980 saw a proposed merger with Libya. The failure of the larger schemes involving Egypt and Iraq and the frequently poor relations of Syria with those countries turned Asad's attention more and more to Jordan, the Lebanon and Palestine and to the possibility of drawing these regions together into a federation of Greater Syria which might become a basis for a larger Arab unity when the time was ripe.

During the years after 1973 the problems of Greater Syria often seemed to dominate Syrian foreign policy. In 1973 Asad managed to improve relations with Jordan, broken off in 1970, and thereafter sought to draw that country into a closer alliance although Jordan remained suspicious of the military and economic power of her neighbour and Syria worried about Jordan's attitudes towards Palestine and Iraq. In 1976 Syrian troops were sent into Lebanon to end the civil war and to prevent the radical Palestinian coalition from gaining a complete victory over the Maronites. In 1977 Asad was within sight of his goal. He had support from the USA and (reluctantly) from the USSR and consent to the Syrian presence in Lebanon from other Arab states. Arrangements were made for formal defence, economic and cultural links between Syria, Jordan, Lebanon and the PLO. The project broke down because of the renewal of conflict in the Lebanon and difficulties with other Arab states. Nevertheless, Syria's influence in Lebanon persisted and after the failure of Israel to establish her influence in Lebanon in 1982–3 Syria became the dominant power in that country.

Syria's relations with her great Fertile Crescent neighbour and fellow Baᶜthist state, Iraq, remained a continued problem. Periods of occasional good relations were separated by long periods of bad relations. The reasons for this hostility are unclear. In part they were ideological, deriving from the great split in the Baᶜth in 1966 which resulted in the old leaders being driven from power in Syria and seeking refuge in Iraq. In part they were economic involving disputes about the transit of Iraqi oil through Syria and the use of the Euphrates waters. In part they were disputes about foreign policy, in particular about policies towards Israel, Lebanon and the PLO. But beneath these surface causes of tension was a deeper concern about interference in each other's affairs and ultimately about the leadership of the Fertile Crescent. In this last aspect the tension between revolutionary Syria and revolutionary Iraq reenacted the fears of the period before 1958. Between 1980 and 1988 the hostile relations between Iraq and Syria were exemplified by the support of Syria, almost alone among Arab states, for Iran in the war between Iraq and Iran.

LEBANON

The political system of Lebanon which developed between 1943 and 1958 depended upon three principles: first an agreement to share political power between the religious communities, second the restriction of the scope of state power and third, a tacit contract to set on one side the unresolved conflict about the nature of Lebanon – how much was it Arab and how much distinctively Lebanese. During the years 1958 to 1975 all of these principles were called into question and the consequence was the virtual destruction of the state.

As president from 1958 to 1964 Fu'ād Shihāb attempted to resolve the problems of Lebanon primarily by modifying the second principle. He preserved the political power sharing system of the National Pact and in foreign affairs he moved away from the emphasis placed by his predecessor, Kamīl Shamᶜūn, upon an independent Lebanon and its links with the west towards a more neutralist position. Shihāb improved relations with Egypt and the Arab world without impairing Lebanon's independence. He endeavoured to share benefits within Lebanon more evenly by increasing the role of the state in the economy and using state institutions to redistribute wealth. A central bank and a central planning organization were created and government investment was increased. Investment went especially into road-building and social activities, including schools, hospitals and social insurance. Help was directed to poorer areas of the country (the south, ᶜAkkār and the northern Biqāᶜ) and to poorer communities such as the Shīᶜīs, the Druzes and the Sunnī urban poor. In fact, the gap between rich and poor was not reduced. Increased state activity also meant more bureaucratic posts and Shihāb sought both to ensure a better share for the Shīᶜīs and other disadvantaged comunities and to make the administration more efficient and less confessional by setting up new organizations including a civil service council. These aims were contradictory and the end was that Sunnīs and Maronites continued to dominate the bureaucracy.

There was a more fundamental contradiction in the policies of Fu'ād Shihāb. It was to be expected that merchants and big business would resent the extension of state power but economic modernization also tended to turn acquiescent rural populations into discontented urban dwellers. The more prominent the role of the state the more importance was attached to the manner in which power was distributed within it. Far from deflecting criticism of the confessional system Shihāb's reforms tended to increase complaints about it. Subsequent events led several writers to view the Shihāb period as a golden age and to bemoan what were seen as the failures of his successors to maintain his system and policy. Yet it could be argued that Shihāb's policies contained within them the seeds of their own failure.

Under Shihāb the Lebanese political system, based on kin and confession and dominated by notables, remained more or less intact. Shihāb professed hostility to the old notables but was compelled to rely on them in government. The notables continued to dominate parliament and government; between 1947 and 1972 26 families held over one-third of all parliamentary seats and one-quarter of those elected in 1960 inherited their seats. Ministerial posts were filled by the familiar leaders. After first working with Ṣā'ib Salām, one of the victors of 1958, Shihāb established a good relationship with Rashīd al-Karāmī who was his longest serving prime minister. Power, however, tended to move from parliament to the presidency during the rule of Shihāb, who relied increasingly on the presidential office under Ilyās Sarkīs and on the army intelligence department, the Deuxième Bureau, which was used to influence elections and to maintain close surveillance of hostile groups. The army remained substantially unchanged in character and size under Shihāb; although it increased its share of resources it still consumed only 3.3 per cent of GNP in 1965. In 1952 and 1958, as commander in chief, Shihāb had kept the army out of politics and, with the exception of the Deuxième Bureau, he continued to do so as president. Although Shihāb created a more active state and a stronger presidency he failed to build either a strong army or a strong political party to support the system. Shihāb had no taste for political organization and relied on others to assemble a parliamentary majority. The task was left to Rashīd al-Karāmī who led the Shihābist Democratic Socialist Front which, with allies among the followings of other notables, supplied the parliamentary support for Shihāb's policies.

The weaknesses of the Shihāb system were experienced under his successor as president, Charles Ḥilū (1964–70). Shihāb had hoped that Sarkīs would succeed him and Ḥilū was a compromise candidate who lacked any substantial following of his own and, of course, inherited no presidential party. Ḥilū was obliged, therefore, to rely on the Deuxième Bureau and on parliamentary coalitions brought together under Rashīd al-Karāmī and ᶜAbdallāh al-Yāfī. Commonly Ḥilū played one group against another. One result of this policy was the increasing discontent with Ḥilū manifested by two of Shihāb's major supporters, Pierre Jumayyil, the leader of the Phalanges, and Kamāl Jānbulāṭ (Jumblatt), the leader of the Druzes. But Ḥilū's principal problems were caused by the link between foreign affairs and domestic discontent provided through the Palestine problem.

As a result of the 1948 war in Palestine Lebanon had become host to some 150,000 Palestinians many of whom lived in refugee camps which surrounded Beirut. There was no serious effort to integrate the Palestinians partly because to have given citizenship to more than a few would have tipped the population balance on which confessional power sharing was based further towards the Muslims. After the creation of the PLO in 1964 the camps became the scene of military training and from 1968 the Palestinians began to use bases in south Lebanon for operations against Israel resulting in retaliatory raids by Israel into Lebanese territory. Lebanese were divided about what to do; by and large most Christians, particularly Maronites, wished to restrain the Palestinians and most Muslims, particularly Sunnīs, wanted to support their activities. No Sunnī prime minister could be found to take action against the Palestinians and Ḥilū could do little except to hope that a political settlement of the Palestinian dispute would solve Lebanon's problems. In the meantime he employed the Deuxième Bureau. Ḥilū's attitude cost him the support of Kamāl Jānbulāṭ who threw himself on the side of the Palestinians after 1967 and in 1969 became leader of a radical alliance known as the Lebanese National Movement (LNM); and of Jumayyil, who in 1968 allied with other Maronite leaders, Shamᶜūn and Raymond Eddé (Raimūn Iddī), to press for a more active policy to control Palestinian activities. In 1969 the security forces clashed with the radicals and the Palestinians and finding a solution became urgent. A compromise was worked out at Cairo in November 1969 according to which the Palestinians were left free to operate from Lebanon but undertook not to interfere in internal Lebanese affairs.

The 1970 presidential election brought together the growing discontent with Shihabist policies as conducted under Ḥilū and the Palestinian question. Like previous elections, however, it was dominated by the ambitions of the traditional notables. The Shihabists had wanted Shihāb himself to stand again; not all were willing to switch their support to his replacement, Sarkīs. The three main Maronite leaders were also divided and eventually all three resigned their claims in favour of Sulaymān Faranjiyya, a notable from Zāghurtā in the north, who, it was thought, would be more acceptable to Muslims than any of the three Maronite alliance leaders. Faranjiyya defeated Sarkīs by a single vote largely because Kamāl Jānbulāṭ, at the last moment, threw his support to Faranjiyya against his old Shihabist allies.

The 1970 election marked the end of the Shihabist system. The army and administration were purged of Shihabists; the Deuxième Bureau lost all its top officers and was replaced by a much less efficient intelligence department. Faranjiyya put nothing new in its place, however. His purpose was to dismantle Shihabism and reward his followers and he had no plan for social and economic reforms which might reduce radical pressure. Faranjiyya was left with even fewer resources than his predecessor with which to deal with the polarizing problem of the activities of the Palestinians and he lacked the political skill to bring together a coalition of leaders. His position was in any case more difficult than that of Ḥilū because of two new factors. First, the expulsion of the Palestinian commandos from Jordan at the end of 1970 made Lebanon the only base for operations against Israel; the number of armed Palestinians in the south considerably increased as did their military activities and Israeli retaliation. Indeed, illegal immigration helped to swell the total number of Palestinians in Lebanon to an estimated 300,000. Second, the turmoil in the south increased the movement of Shīᶜīs into Beirut where many joined the radical groups.

To use the army against the Palestinians, as Faranjiyya was urged to do by other Maronites, was a course open to many objections. First, it was difficult to find any Sunnī leader of stature who would agree to such a policy; to employ a minor figure (as Faranjiyya did in 1973) would unite Sunnīs against the president. Second, Syria might not permit such an action. In 1973 a project to use the army to take control of Palestinian bases was abandoned when Syria threatened intervention. Third, the army itself might split if action against the Palestinians also involved action against the radical groups. The officer corps was dominated by Christians but the rank and file were largely Muslim. But if the army was not deployed against the Palestinians then the Maronites would employ their own militias. If the Maronite militias were employed then the radical militias which had been arming with Palestinian aid would also enter the conflict. Indeed this is what happened in 1975 when the Lebanese civil war began.

Historians dispute whether the Lebanese civil war was the result of internal causes, namely the challenge to Maronite dominance by other groups within the Lebanese system, or whether it was caused by an external factor, that is the presence on Lebanese soil of the Palestinians. It is clear that it was both: there were disputes but the factor which made them so difficult to resolve peacefully was the presence of the Palestinians. On the other hand the Palestinian problem could have been solved without overmuch difficulty if the Lebanese polity had been united. The civil war was not the product of a revolution but it was the cause of a fundamental change in the Lebanese system.

The civil war began in April 1975 when armed clashes took place between the Phalanges and Palestinians and the Lebanese National Movement threw in its lot with the Palestinians. The government fell and general fighting broke out. Soon the conflict became one mainly between Christians and Muslims. A decisive point was reached in January 1976 when the Maronites attacked the Palestinian camps in eastern and northern Beirut. The Palestinians then became formal parties to the conflict and they were strengthened by the arrival from Syria of additional Palestinian forces. Together the Palestinians and the LNM were too strong for the Maronites who were driven back to east Beirut and the northern part of Mount Lebanon. In February President Asad of Syria attempted to mediate a settlement based on a modification of the National Pact.

The February 1976 proposal involved equal Christian–Muslim representation in parliament (replacing the 6:5 ratio which had hitherto prevailed), the election of the prime minister by parliament, the naturalization of some Muslim residents in Lebanon, and the abolition of the confessional distribution of bureaucratic jobs with the exception of the highest posts. The question of the Palestinians was dealt with by confirmation of the 1969 Cairo agreement. The proposal was accepted by President Faranjiyya but rejected by Kamāl Jānbulāṭ, the Druze leader of the LNM. Jānbulāṭ stated that his object was not the modification of the confessional system but its complete abolition; Asad thought his purpose was simply to humiliate the Maronites.

The continuation of the civil war brought about the collapse of the Lebanese army. In January 1976 a Sunnī officer had refused orders and organized the Arab Army of Lebanon from Muslim recruits. In March the entire army of 19,000 dissolved: half went home and the other half joined rival groups in the battle. The Lebanese state now had no coercive force of its own; the Palestinians and the militias were supreme and it began to seem that the Palestinian–radical alliance might achieve a complete victory.

The first civil war was brought to an end by Syrian intervention. In January President Asad had assisted the Palestinians; in February he had sought a compromise settlement; in April he began to aid the Maronites; and at the end of May he sent Syrian regular troops into Lebanon. The Palestinian–radical alliance resisted the Syrian advance and fighting continued throughout the summer of 1976 before a ceasefire was arranged in October. Neither side had gained a complete victory; temporary peace came because Syrians and Palestinians alike were unwilling to fight any longer for their Lebanese allies. But the Syrians had saved the Lebanese state. The parliament still functioned and the new president, Ilyās Sarkīs, elected in May, succeeded Faranjiyya in September 1976. Few other institutions of the state functioned.

It is uncertain what motives predominated in Syrian calculations during 1976. There was concern about the prospect of the complete breakdown of the Lebanese state and the spread of disorder to Syria. There was worry about the likelihood that the Palestinians, predominant in Lebanon, might escape Syrian influence and bring about a conflict in the region which would expose Syria to Israeli attack. And there is the possibility that President Asad saw an opportunity to establish a predominant influence in Lebanon (by making Syria the arbiter of the balance of power) which might further his aims of Greater Syrian or Arab unity. In the circumstances he was able to obtain the consent of other Arab states to his intervention; an Arab deterrent force of 30,000 was formed to which Syria first contributed 22,000 troops and subsequently supplied the entire complement. It is also likely that having once staked his prestige by the February intervention Asad found it difficult to acquiesce in an outcome which involved the rejection of the settlement he had supported.

The results of the first round of civil war were far-reaching. The war had killed between 30,000 and 40,000 people; a substantial part of the Lebanese population had been made refugees (Asad claimed that over a million had entered Syria); and there had been extensive destruction of property (including most of Lebanese manufacturing industry). The population had been partly regrouped on confessional lines. The Christian population, except for surviving pockets in the south, had become concentrated in eastern Beirut and the northern part of the mountain. Apart from the Greek Orthodox nearly all Christian groups had rallied to the Phalanges and in September 1976 the Maronite factions had come together to form a military force, the Lebanese Forces, which was itself a powerful new factor on the scene. The Druzes had extended their control over the southern part of the mountain by the expulsion of Christians from the Shūf. West Beirut, firmly Muslim, was dominated by the radical groups but the LNM itself broke up after its defeat and the murder of Kamāl Jānbulāṭ on 16 March 1977. His son and succesor, Walīd Jānbulāṭ, functioned as a Druze leader rather than in the radical secularist style adopted by his father. The Palestinians had suffered a reverse but they remained a powerful factor in Lebanon; by 1980 they were the dominant force throughout western Lebanon from Beirut to the Līṭānī river. And Syria was firmly established in Lebanon; although in 1980 Syria made a partial withdrawal she retained her base in the eastern Biqā^c. Finally, the Lebanese state had suffered a tremendous blow; the system remained in place only because there was no agreement on what should replace it. Some of the forms of the state remained: the president resided in his palace; and parliament, in the impossibility of holding elections after 1972, had its life indefinitely prolonged. But real power had passed from the state.

After 1976 the history of Lebanon is a history of the separate development of various regions. Within the territories controlled by the different communities there was often something approaching normal life but on the borderlands and especially in west Beirut and in the south there was conflict, violence and even anarchy. In the period 1977 to 1982 the leading political feature was a bid for mastery by Bashīr Jumayyil, younger son of Pierre, who had found a power base in the Lebanese Forces and who strove to make himself the undisputed head of the Christian community, which he might use as a platform from which to take control of Lebanon. In 1978 he asserted supremacy over the Faranjiyyas and in 1980 over Sham^{c}ūn's militia. He then sought to extend his power over the town of Zaḥla threatening the

Syrian position in the Biqāᶜ, a challenge which precipitated a clash with Syria and drove Bashīr into alliance with Israel.

Israel's concern in Lebanon was primarily with the Palestinians. The purpose of her retaliatory raids before 1975 was to force the Lebanese government to take action to control the Palestinians. The effect of the raids, however, was to help destroy the Lebanese state. Israel, therefore, sought to control the Palestinians in the south by other means. It was made clear that Syrian forces would not be allowed to operate in the south and a limit was set to the Syrian advance 25 miles north of the Israeli frontier. In 1978 Israel launched an extended raid into Lebanon as far north as the Līṭānī river and when she withdrew handed over to a UN force (UNIFIL) and to a Lebanese militia commanded by a Lebanese Greek Catholic, Major Saᶜd Ḥaddād. Israel was still dissatisfied with the border security provided by this arrangement and decided to take advantage both of the situation in Lebanon and the freedom of manoeuvre obtained by the peace treaty with Egypt to try to rid herself of the Palestinian threat for ever. In 1982 she launched a new campaign in Lebanon known as "Peace for Galilee". Its stated objective was to stop raids into northern Israel; its concealed purpose was to defeat the Palestinians completely and establish a powerful Christian government in Lebanon under Bashīr Jumayyil which could prevent the recrudescence of the Palestinian attacks on Israel. This latter aim could be accomplished only by an advance to Beirut and the expulsion of the Syrians.

In the short term matters fell out much as Israel had hoped. The Palestinian forces in southern Lebanon were easily defeated and the Syrians withdrew from Beirut, although they remained in the Biqāᶜ. At Beirut from June to August the Israeli forces were checked by determined resistance from the Palestinians and radicals but it was eventually agreed that the Palestinian fighting men should be withdrawn from Beirut and replaced by a multinational force. On 23 August Bashīr Jumayyil was elected to succeed Sarkīs as president. It remained only to negotiate an agreement between Israel and Lebanon. This was accomplished on 17 May 1983: the state of war between Israel and Lebanon, which had endured since 1948, was brought to an end, a security zone was established in southern Lebanon and provision made for a joint Israel–Lebanon liaison committee to co-ordinate defensive arrangements. But this treaty was stillborn; indeed long before it was signed the Lebanese situation had changed dramatically.

On 14 September 1982, one week before he was due to take up his new office, Bashīr Jumayyil was killed in a bomb explosion. In his place his elder brother, Amīn Jumayyil, was elected president but he lacked the ability, energy and following of Bashīr. In apparent revenge for Bashīr's death Christian Lebanese forces entered the defenceless Palestinian camps of Sabra and Shatila with Israeli consent and massacred many of the inhabitants on 16 September. The resultant outcry helped to discredit the new government and made it more difficult for Israel to prosecute her aims in Lebanon. In the subsequent negotiations she was obliged to reduce her demands on Lebanon and the May agreement fell some way short of what Israel had wanted as the price of her withdrawal. Israel made her withdrawal conditional upon a Syrian withdrawal from the Biqāᶜ, a stipulation refused by Syria.

The May agreement was abrogated by Lebanon on 5 March 1984. Opposition to the agreement came from Sunnīs, Shīᶜīs, Druzes and some Maronites as well as from Syria. The Lebanese opposition pressed for abrogation and constitutional reforms. In factional fighting the opposition proved superior to the newly reconstituted Lebanese army and the Christian militias: the Druzes won in the Shūf, the Lebanese army began to disintegrate again and the multinational force withdrew. With neither competent armies nor allies Amīn Jumayyil was obliged to turn back to Syria at the end of February 1984 and accept the price of Syrian help, namely the abrogation of the agreement with Israel.

Israel's withdrawal from Lebanon was completed in 1985. In September 1983 Israeli forces had retired from the neighbourhood of Beirut to an area south of the Awwalī river. There they found themselves under attack from local resistance forces. Attempts to reach agreement with the Lebanese government on what troops should replace Israeli forces in the south having failed, Israel decided on a unilateral withdrawal which was carried out in three stages between February and June 1985. Israel left behind the South Lebanese Army, a new version of Ḥaddād's militia commanded by Major Antoine Lahad, to protect the frontier with Israeli support. A major factor in Israel's withdrawal was the determined resistance to Israeli occupation of southern Lebanon carried on chiefly by the local Shīᶜī population.

Between 1983 and 1989 prominent features of Lebanese history include the political rise of the Shīᶜī community, the decline of the old notables, the complete breakdown of the Lebanese political system and the imposition of Syrian hegemony over most of the country.

The Shīᶜīs of Lebanon inhabited three areas. The largest number lived in southern Lebanon as peasants and sharecroppers on the land of large landholders like the Asᶜads, who dominated the political life of the community. A second group lived in the Biqāᶜ, mainly as small peasants but also including substantial notable families, such as the Ḥamādas, who were active in politics. A third group was composed of recent immigrants to Beirut. A significant part of the community also worked abroad especially as traders in Africa. Until 1975 the Shīʿīs acquiesced in their modest position within the political system. However, changes were already taking place in their situation as a consequence of urbanization, changes in the population balance, religious revival and the rise of a new leadership.

The economic changes in Lebanon during the 1950s and 1960s helped to end the isolation of rural areas and stimulate emigration to Beirut and abroad; Shīʿīs moved into Beirut in considerable numbers, spurred by the disturbances in the south after 1970. It has been estimated that by 1975 about 40 per cent of the Shīʿīs of the south and 25 per cent of those in the Biqāʿ had left their native regions. The fertility of the Shīʿī community was higher than that of other communities and they replaced the Maronites as the largest single community with about 30 per cent of the total population of Lebanon. This new Shīʿī eminence led to demands for a revision of the National Pact in their favour. Educationally, the Shīʿīs were the least advanced of the Lebanese sects and they had benefited especially from the school building programme launched by the Shihāb government. The growth of state educational, health and other services made the Shīʿīs less dependent upon their traditional leaders. The religious revival was particularly associated with the work of Imām Mūsā al-Ṣadr, an Iranian Shīʿī teacher who settled in Lebanon in 1960 and with the encouragement of the Shihāb government began a campaign for social reform in the south, challenging the authority of the Asʿads and other notables. In 1969 the Imām found an organizational base in the newly-established Supreme Shīʿī Council and in 1974 he launched the Movement of the Deprived.

The civil war accelerated the development of the self-consciousness of the Shīʿīs and of a new radical view of society and politics. At first Shīʿīs fought only in the ranks of other militias but in 1975 a Shīʿī militia, known as Amal, was organized. ("Amal", meaning "hope" was also the acronym of the Arabic for Lebanese Resistance Detachments.) After 1978 Amal expanded rapidly in its role as protector of the Shīʿī villages of the south against the demands of the Palestinians. Like the Christian Lebanese Forces Amal was more than a militia. It was a movement rather than a party and composed of small groups with competing leaders. Its programme included the revival of Shīʿism but not a Shīʿī state, although this last question was the subject of a dispute within Amal which became more acute after the success of the 1979 Islamic revolution in Iran. Other elements in the Amal programme were the notion of an independent Arab Lebanon closely linked to Syria, the establishment of social justice through the social and economic initiatives of a more powerful state, and the end of the confessional system. It was recognized, however, that this last demand was incapable of realization in the near future so Amal also asked for a modification of the National Pact. From 1980 the leader of Amal was Nabīh Birrī, a Shīʿī lawyer born in West Africa of a family of low status and modest means. Mūsā al-Ṣadr had disappeared in 1978 while on a visit to Libya. Within Amal Birrī was challenged by Shīʿī clerics but a more serious challenge came from the growth of revivalist groups within the Shīʿī community after 1982. The radical Shīʿī groups found a base under Syrian protection in the Biqāʿ where they were supported from 1982 by a detachment of Iranian revolutionary guards and Iranian money. The most prominent group was the Ḥizballāh (the Party of God) which was founded in 1978 but came to prominence in 1982 with its headquarters in the Biqāʿ and branches in Beirut. Like Amal Ḥizballāh was a coalition of factions rather than a highly organized party. Associated with the Ḥizballāh in Beirut was a prominent Shīʿī cleric, al-Sayyid Ḥusayn Faḍlallāh. The radical Shīʿī groups were dominated by young religious teachers and adopted a campaign of violence and kidnapping. They demanded an Islamic state on the Iranian model and expressed extreme hostility to western influence.

From the latter part of 1983 onwards the Shīʿīs, through Amal, through the religious radicals and through other parties, became leading actors in the Lebanese drama. It was Shīʿī resistance led by Amal which drove Israel from southern Lebanon and the Shīʿī militias, in alliance with the Druzes, took control of west Beirut in April 1985, although they were unable to complete their victory over the Palestinians. In May 1984 Nabīh Birrī joined the new Lebanese government of national unity. The Shīʿīs were unable to convert their eminence into domination, however. In the first place they were divided into factions and Amal lost ground to Ḥizballāh. Second, they were confronted by the opposition of other groups, including the Druzes and secular radicals who were concerned about the growth of Shīʿī power. Third, Syria remained an important factor on the scene; in 1986 Syrian troops returned to Beirut, established control over the western section and began to challenge for control of the Shīʿī south of the city.

The continuing civil war in Lebanon accelerated the decline of the traditional notable leaders, the *zaʿīms*. Several of the older leaders passed from the scene after 1975. Of the three Maronite alliance leaders of 1968, Raymond Eddé went into exile in France in 1976, Pierre Jumayyil died in 1984 and Kamīl Sham^{c}ūn in 1987. Kamāl Jānbulāṭ was assassinated in 1977 and Rashīd al-Karāmī in 1987. The older *za^{c}īms* were partly successful in their attempt to pass their authority to their sons: the Jumayyil sons, of course, outshone their father and the Druze, Walīd Jānbulāṭ, succeeded to his father's full power. Others were challenged by new men. New leaders were most conspicuous among the Shī^{c}īs but also appeared among the Sunnīs and Maronites. In particular, the Lebanese Forces (LF) threw up a new leadership; in March 1985 Samīr Ja^{c}ja^{c} staged a revolt against an attempt to bring the militia under state control and although in February 1989 apparently he submitted to the similar demand of the Maronite prime minister, Michel ^{c}Awn, he retained his position in the LF. In government the dominance of the old notables also receded after 1976. With the exception of the brief and unsuccessful government of Taqī al-Dīn al-Ṣulḥ in 1980 and Rashīd al-Karāmī's so-called national unity government of 1984 (which rarely met), cabinets were led, until 1988, by two minor Sunnī figures, Salīm al-Ḥuṣṣ and Shafīq al-Wazzān, and composed largely of technocrats. Furthermore, the state institutions which the old notables had dominated no longer functioned effectively.

Economic factors also played a part in the waning of the traditional Lebanese notables. Most of them had had a rural base but rural Lebanon declined after 1960. Between 1960 and 1980 the proportion of the labour force employed in agriculture fell from 38 per cent to 11 per cent. By 1980 four-fifths of the population of Lebanon was urban, nearly half living in Beirut. To organize an urban party required different skills, although several *za^{c}īms* showed that they could develop them: the Phalanges was an early example of a party of middling Maronite city dwellers and its rise to prominence during the 1960s and 1970s reflected the new salience of the urban groups. Sunnī leaders, like Ṣā'ib Salām, had long practiced the art of mobilizing urban populations. But in Tripoli the old Karāmī influence was undermined by the fundamentalist Tawḥīd movement which came to dominate the life of the northern town until it was cut down by Syria in 1986.

In reducing the power of the traditional notables the Lebanese wars helped to accomplish a change similar to that which had taken place in other states of the Near East. Elsewhere, however, the decline of the old notables had been accompanied by the rise of a new élite dependent upon powerful state institutions; in Lebanon the decline of the notables was associated with the decline of the state itself and the rise of new institutions independent of the state.

From 1976 to 1989 Lebanese politicians sought and failed to find a permanent solution to Lebanon's problems through confessional constitutional reform. At the heart of the problem was the change in the confessional balance. By 1975, of a total resident population of about 3 million, 60 per cent were Muslim and 40 per cent Christian. The largest community was then the Shīʿīs with about 30 per cent, followed by the Maronites with 25, the Sunnīs 20 and the Druzes well under 10 per cent. The choice before Lebanon appeared to be either to revise the National Pact to take account of the population change, to adopt a non-confessional system or to break up the Lebanese state. In 1983–4 the all-party Geneva conference acknowledged the need for increased Muslim representation but failed to agree on the reduction of the powers of the Maronite president. In September 1984 the national unity cabinet agreed that the number of parliamentary deputies should be increased from 99 to 122 and Muslim and Christian representation should be equal but failed to agree on how the representatives should be divided among the sects; the Maronites demanded that they should continue to have the largest single sectarian representation. In December 1985 the Damascus Accord, signed by the leaders of the Druze, Shīʿī and Christian militias, looked to the abolition of the confessional system after a transitional period of three years and in the meantime provided for a new parliament with equal Muslim and Christian representation, reduced presidential and increased prime ministerial powers. The accord also proposed close integration with Syria. The Damascus Accord had no strong supporters except for Amal and was rejected by President Jumayyil.

By 1987 there was broad agreement that a reconstruction of the Lebanese political system would involve equal parliamentary representation of Muslims and Christians, a reduction of the powers of the Maronite president and an increase of those of the Sunnī prime minister, a larger share of higher posts for Muslims and a national army in which neither Muslims nor Christians would dominate. There was also agreement that the power of the Palestinians must be curtailed; in May 1987 the national assembly voted to terminate the Cairo agreement of 1969. One problem in the way of agreement was that reform on these lines would mean abandoning the sectarian enclaves built up since 1976, their administrations, revenues and other vested interests and in particular the militias which protected them. To this step there was considerable opposition from the Maronites in particular. As early as 1975 Maronites had contemplated partition as preferable to the loss of their traditional pre-eminence in Lebanon. After 1976 the Maronites had constructed their own institutions and ran their own economy in the consolidated Christian territory of east Beirut and the northern mountain which became a refuge for other Christian groups including those from the south expelled in 1985. Until 1982 the hope had remained that under Bashīr Jumayyil the Maronite ascendancy might be restored in all of Lebanon but from 1983 many Maronites took the view that their interests would be better served by holding what they had. This view was strongly represented among the new leaders emerging through the Lebanese Forces.

In September 1988 the Lebanese political system broke down completely when parliament failed to elect a successor to President Amīn Jumayyil. Jumayyil then departed from tradition by appointing a Maronite prime minister, Michel ᶜAwn, the army commander appointed to reconstruct the Lebanese army after the force rebuilt with US help had collapsed in 1984. ᶜAwn formed a three-man military cabinet. But the Muslim prime minister, Salīm al-Ḥuṣṣ, who was supported by Syria, refused to give way with the result that Lebanon had no president, two prime ministers and no parliament. Parliament, which had been elected in 1972, did not meet from September 1988 until November 1989.

The new Maronite prime minister resolved to make a further attempt to re-establish the authority of government, expel Syrian forces and restore the old Lebanese system. He persuaded the Lebanese Forces to accept his authority and in March 1989, helped by supplies of arms received from Iraq since the summer of 1988, tried to impose his authority over the ports under Muslim control. There followed a violent conflict in Beirut fought between the ᶜAwn government and the Syrians and the Muslim and Druze militias. The conflict accelerated the depopulation of Beirut which had begun in 1987. By August 1989 the population had sunk to an estimated 150,000. International efforts were made to arrange a ceasefire and talks.

In October 1989 a meeting of 62 Lebanese parliamentary deputies was called by the Arab league in Ṭā'if in Saudi Arabia. The resulting Ṭā'if agreement followed the lines of earlier proposals to modify the National Pact; presidential decisions were to be subject to cabinet veto. On 5 November 58 deputies met as the Lebanese parliament in north Lebanon to accept the Ṭā'if agreement and elected a speaker and a new president, René Muᶜawwaḍ, who appointed Salīm al-Ḥuṣṣ as prime minister. ᶜAwn, like the Shīᶜī fundamentalists, refused to recognize the legitimacy of the parliament or the authority of Muᶜawwaḍ who was assassinated on 22 November. Thereupon the deputies met again on 24 November and elected Ilyās Harāwī as president.

NOTE

1. Quoted Dr Umar F. Abd-Allah, *The Islamic Struggle in Syria*, Berkeley, Calif., 1983, 93.

CHAPTER ELEVEN

Israel, Jordan and the Palestinians since 1950

ISRAEL

By the time of the ceasefire at the end of 1948 the state of Israel, which was established on about 80 per cent of the territory of the former mandatory state, had a population of 800,000 of whom 80 per cent were Jewish and the remainder Arabs. By the census of 1983 Israel (including East Jerusalem, annexed from Jordan in 1967, and the Golan, effectively annexed from Syria in 1981) had a population of 4 million, of whom 83 per cent were Jewish. The growth of the Arab population was almost wholly the result of natural increase but more than half the increase of the Jewish population was attributable to immigration.

Jewish immigrants came in uneven bursts. The largest addition (nearly 700,000) took place during the first three years of the state. Many of the new immigrants came from Eastern Europe, the traditional source of Jewish immigrants, but half of them were from the Middle East. Another surge of immigrants took place after 1954 and among these newcomers were many from North Africa, in particular Morocco. By the mid-1960s most of the Jews of the Middle East and North Africa were in Israel and the flow of immigrants began to slacken. From 1967 to 1973 there was a further burst of immigration and another change in composition. Of the new immigrants half were from the USSR and one-eighth from the USA, the two non-Jewish states with the largest Jewish populations. After 1973 the pace of immigration dropped again and by the 1980s was down to an average of 15,000 a year. Although Jews continued to leave the USSR only one-quarter of emigrants chose to come to Israel, a majority preferring to settle in North America, just as a majority of Algerian Jews had preferred to go to France. Further, there was an increase in Jewish emigration from Israel: between 1948 and 1973 for every six Jews who came into Israel one left; after 1973 the corresponding ratio was 3:1. By 1989 it was estimated that up to 500,000 Israelis were living abroad, most of them in the United States and Western Europe.

The state of Israel had been founded as a Jewish state in fulfilment of the Zionist purpose which was to bring to the land of Israel the Jews of the Diaspora. Jewish immigrants were also needed to ensure the development and security of the new state. There could be no question of excluding would-be immigrants and by the 1950 Law of Return all Jews were guaranteed the right to live in Israel as citizens of the state. But the task of absorbing some 1.75 million immigrants between 1948 and 1989 was a very considerable one, especially during the early years of the state; indeed the pressures imposed by the flood of immigrants during the first three years induced the government to impose temporary restrictions on numbers during the following two years. The problems were in the first instance those of finding housing and employment for the immigrants and during the early years many were directed into agricultural settlements on lands abandoned by fleeing Palestinian Arabs.

A second set of problems was cultural and these were magnified by the high proportion of Jews from Asia and Africa among the new immigrants. These so-called Oriental or Sephardic Jews were much less well educated than the Ashkenazis, the earlier Jewish immigrants from Eastern Europe, and much poorer, and these disadvantages persisted after their arrival; over the period 1960 to 1973 the average per capita income of Oriental Jews stayed below half that of Jews of European origin. The Oriental Jews also had much larger families and by 1965 their numbers were equal to those of the Europeans. The Oriental Jews tended to move into cities where they took poorly paid jobs and were prone to unemployment; in 1959 there were riots against their conditions of life by Moroccan Jews in Haifa. It was only slowly that these inequalities began to diminish.

The principal factors in the absorption of the immigrants and the gradual creation of a sense of common Israeli citizenship over and beyond the cultural differences which remained were the language, modern Hebrew, and the institutions developed by the Jewish community and elaborated by the Israeli state, in particular the educational system, the army, Histadrut and the political institutions of the country. Most important of all was the extraordinary performance of the economy after 1948. It was her economic success which enabled Israel to meet the costs of settlement and to provide a rapidly increasing standard of living for all.

Between 1948 and 1970 Israel's gross national product grew at the rate of about 10 per cent a year and per capita income at about 5 per cent a year, figures which made Israel the most successful state in the Near East and one of the most successful states in the world in economic terms. This result was achieved through the annual investment of about 25 per cent of national income. Almost none of this investment came from within Israel; virtually all was provided by foreign aid. The major source of income for most of the period was from the Diaspora which contributed about $200 million a year before 1967 and $700 million a year during the following six years. Another important source during the early years of the state was German reparations which amounted to $125 million a year before 1966, when they came to an end. Nevertheless, West German aid continued at a higher level than before. And after 1967 the United States became a major provider of aid to Israel. Before 1967 US government help had been comparatively small at $50 million a year but after 1967 this contribution rose to reach a level of $3 billion ($1,200 million economic and $1,800 million military) by 1986. Israel had become the highest per capita recipient of US aid in the world and US government aid was five times as great as the contributions of the Diaspora. It should be noted, however, that 90 per cent of US government assistance was in the form of loans, whereas the bulk of other contributions had been made as outright grants; in consequence after 1967 a growing part of Israel's foreign income was paid out again in the form of interest, although postponements diminished the burden.

The flow of foreign aid financed a continuing deficit in Israel's balance of trade. Before 1973 exports were increasing more rapidly than imports and therefore, although the total deficit increased year by year, Israel was on the way to closing the gap. But after 1973 this tendency was reversed as imports rose more rapidly than exports. By 1989 Israel was more dependent on a continuing and increasing flow of foreign aid in order to finance her standard of living than ever before. On the other hand the fall in the number of immigrants meant that her requirements were smaller.

Israel's economic success was also due to other factors. One was the constant dynamic provided by the flow of immigrants who supplied a pool of cheap labour and whose wants supported a high level of economic activity. As the numbers of new immigrants fell off after 1973 use was made of Arab labour from the occupied territories; by 1975 about one-quarter of the labour force of the West Bank and Gaza was employed in Israel, especially in construction. A second factor was the high level of education and skills in the Israeli labour force which enabled Israel to achieve considerable increases in productivity in traditional industries and to establish new high technology industries. One example of her skills was the diamond cutting and polishing industry which was established by Jewish immigrants from the Netherlands in the 1930s and which became statistically Israel's most significant export industry, although its true contribution to foreign earnings was only about one-fifth of its nominal contribution. An example of the development of advanced technological industry is provided by the defence industry; in 1948 Israel imported rifles and by 1989 she was exporting advanced aircraft and missiles.

After 1970 Israel found it impossible to sustain her earlier rate of economic growth. The general reduction in world economic activity, the fall in net immigration, the burden of debt repayments, the high level of state expenditure, especially military spending after 1967 and more particularly after 1973, and persistent inflation brought about a change. Between 1970 and 1980 per capita income still grew at the comforting rate of about 2 per cent a year but in 1982–3 growth fell to almost zero and in 1983 a deflationary policy was introduced, public expenditure diminished and food subsidies were reduced. The result was an improvement in Israel's international economic position and a reduction in inflation, but also a substantial fall in workers' incomes and a plethora of strikes.

During the period 1948 to 1980 there were interesting and familiar changes in the shape of Israel's economic activity. Services were always the leading sector of the economy but over the period as a whole tended to loom still larger as a result of the enhanced role of the state. In 1948 about 20 per cent of the work force was engaged in agriculture and this proportion did not diminish during the early years of the state when an agricultural boom took place based on the resettlement of Arab lands. But from 1960 the relative importance of agriculture began to decline and by 1980 it employed only about 6 per cent of Israelis. A quarter of the population was then employed in industry (a proportion of the Jewish population which had remained fairly constant since the 1930s although the statistic conceals the important switch from small scale to large scale industry). Services had mopped up the decline in agricultural employment: in 1980 over half the working population was employed in services, the balance being made up by so-called "social overheads". The economic changes were reflected in changes in the distribution of the population: in 1948 one quarter of the Jewish population and two-thirds of the Arab population had lived in the countryside; by 1983 only one-tenth of the population were classified as rural. In its economic structure and in its standard of living Israel resembled a West European state.

Between 1948 and 1989 Israel created the most powerful state system in the Near East. In 1982 50 per cent of the GNP went to the government in taxes and because most of the money available for investment passed through government hands the state had a dominant position in the economy. Through the National Land Authority to which all of the Jewish National Fund land was transferred in 1959 92 per cent of land belonged to the state. In 1981 30% of the labour force was employed by the state. The Israeli state also controlled the most effective armed forces in the region and its security services were renowned for their capabilities. Its educational provision (including seven universities) and its social services were more extensive than those of any other state. How had this situation come to be and how was it controlled?

The institutions of the Israeli republic were based on those of the Yishuv of the mandatory period; only the weak presidency was new. No written constitution was adopted by the 1949 constituent assembly which made do with a few basic laws. In effect, via the constituent assembly, the old National Council became the Knesset, the single chamber Israeli parliament. The Israeli parliament was all-powerful; within the Near East only the Turkish Grand National Assembly, as it existed until 1960, compared to it. The 120 seat Knesset was elected by a system of proportional representation by which the whole country was treated as a single constituency and seats were allocated to political parties in accordance with their share of the vote. Any party which secured 1 per cent of the vote was represented in the Knesset. Party leaders chose Knesset members. This system of election was taken over from the National Council and also avoided the necessity of defining the territorial boundaries of Israel. But principally it reflected the dominant position which political parties had obtained within the Jewish community under the mandate. The effect of the system of proportional representation was to give great weight to the smaller political parties since no political party was ever able to obtain a majority of the votes and therefore of Knesset seats. All Israeli governments were coalitions.

The Israeli system fostered the growth of a large number of political parties, whose existence was in any case enjoined by the variety of the origins and interests of the population. More than 20 parties usually contested Israeli elections and about 15 were commonly represented in the Knesset. For convenience the political parties may be divided into four groups: the left dominated by Mapai and transformed in 1968 into the Israel Labour Party and subsequently into the Labour Alignment; the right represented by two main groups, Herut (founded 1948) which was in effect the old Revisionist party, and the liberal general Zionists, who allied with Herut in 1964 to form Gahal, the forerunner of Likud (1973); the religious parties; and others, such as the communists, whose opinions effectively ruled them out of government.

From 1949, when the interim government came to an end, until 1977 Israeli governments were formed by coalitions led by Mapai. Until his retirement in 1963 the dominant political figure was David Ben Gurion, who served as prime minister for the whole of the period, except in 1954–5 when Moshe Sharrett substituted for him. Only five individuals held the post of prime minister before 1977, indicating a remarkable degree of stability in the leadership. This ministerial stability was reflected in other important posts, notably finance, foreign affairs, and defence, all of which were occupied by five or fewer individuals. Cabinets were dominated by Ashkenazi immigrants, mainly from Russia and Poland: 80 per cent of cabinet ministers were in this category; 10 per cent, including one prime minister, Yitzhak Rabin, were sabras, that is born in Israel; and only 10 per cent were Orientals, despite the circumstance that Orientals constituted a majority of the population after the mid-1960s.

No dominant personality replaced Ben Gurion. The left was divided between the old guard, being contemporaries and former subordinates of Ben Gurion, and the young guard, being those whom Ben Gurion had advanced in his later years. From the first group came Ben Gurion's two successors as prime minister, Levi Eshkol (1963–9) and Golda Meir (1969–74) and from the second group came their challengers, among whom the most notable were Moshe Dayan and Shimon Peres together with Yigal Allon. The old guard had built their careers under the mandate and were essentially civilian politicians; the young guard were the product of the post-independence period and they had close connections with the military.

The 1967 war greatly enhanced the reputations of the young guard and particularly of Dayan who took the post of minister of defence in June 1967 and received a large share of the credit for the stunning victory of the Israeli forces. Dayan might have become prime minister in 1969 but for the challenge of Allon, the military leader of the 1948 war; instead Golda Meir emerged as a compromise candidate. However, Meir lacked the control exercised by Ben Gurion and her government became a system of apanages in which individual ministers exercised more or less independent authority within their spheres of responsibility; Dayan dominated defence including the arrangements for the occupied territories. Allon's health failed and Dayan would probably have succeeded Meir in 1974 but war, which had established his reputation in 1967, destroyed it in 1973 and the leadership fell to Yitzhak Rabin, who had been chief of staff in 1967. Rabin's government was dominated by the younger generation and marks the point at which political leadership passed from the old pre-independence politicians.

Labour's domination of government between 1948 and 1977 was reflected in its predominance in two other major Israeli institutions each of which had its origins in the mandatory period. These were Histadrut and the army. After independence Histadrut retained its position as the principal economic institution of Israel being at once trade union, employer, friendly society and provider of social services. By 1983 it had 1.6 million members (representing 60 per cent of the population after allowing for dependents), employed more than a quarter of a million people, and ran the largest industrial enterprise, Koor Industries. Its only major economic rival was the state itself. Histadrut was a voluntary oganization independent of any political party and all political parties shared in its management. But in its origins it had been closely linked with Labour and that association continued and was of key importance in providing a link between government and the powerful economic organization.

The Israel Defence Forces (IDF) were formed in 1948 from the Mapai-dominated Hagana. The IDF was a conscript force based on two years military service for men and one year for women. In 1975 service was increased to three years and two respectively. Active service was followed by a long period of reserve service. There was a small regular component of officers and NCOs serving on short term contracts. The system relied on rapid mobilization to produce a force which numbered 300,000 in 1967 and 500,000 in 1982, of which 174,000 (including 120,000 conscripts) represented the active element. The IDF was designed to fight short sharp campaigns and in 1967 had the highest proportion of combatants to noncombatants (50 per cent) of any force in the world. The largest part of the IDF was the army but there was also a well-equipped navy and air force. A secondary function of the army was to serve as a means of educating and integrating new immigrants. Israel also created efficient intelligence serices: external (Mossad), internal (Shin Bet) and military (Aman).

The military forces of the other political parties were dissolved or amalgamated with the new force. It was Ben Gurion's intention to terminate the system by which military forces had been party militias and to create a unified national army which, unlike almost all other Israeli institutions, would be outside politics. In practice Ben Gurion chose senior officers from among the Hagana veterans he trusted, although most senior commanders in 1948 were from Mapam, the left wing Marxist group which broke away from Mapai in 1944. A high proportion of IDF officers (30 per cent of airforce pilots and 22 per cent of army officers in 1967) came from the 5 per cent of Israelis who lived in the *kibbutzim* which were a particular stronghold of Labour. As with Histadrut the sympathy between government and army was an important factor in the development of the state. After 1967 this harmony began to break down with first the increasing tendency of military officers to enter politics on retiring from service and, secondly, more marked political divisions within the army following on the army's assumption of a political role in the occupied territories and more especially after Likud assumed the conduct of government in 1977.

Increasingly the main business of the state became the maintenance of the IDF. Between 1948 and 1978 the military budget increased at an average rate of 21 per cent a year, a figure which conceals a much more rapid increase of spending after 1967. From 1973 to 1982 nearly 50 per cent of the budget went on the IDF. From 6 per cent of GNP in the early 1950s military outlays rose to a peak of 47 per cent in 1976. Although a substantial part of the cost was met from US military aid the burden shaped all political decisions on Israel's development after 1967.

Until 1969 the left parties regularly secured about half the votes and seats, the right about a quarter and the remainder was divided fairly equally between the religious parties and the others. From the election of 1969 a decline was visible in the size of the vote for the left and an increase in that of the right until in the election of 1977 Likud emerged as victors and formed a government. Partly the success of the right was due to short term factors which made the Rabin government unpopular, notably financial scandals, economic difficulties, personality divisions and a loss of reputation which went back to the 1973 war, when the Israeli forces had been taken unprepared and had suffered more than 6,000 casualties. In fact the left's lost support in 1977 went not to the right but to a new short-lived protest centre party, the Democratic Movement for Change. But, as became apparent in subsequent elections, the rise of the right partly reflected the change in the composition of the Israeli population; Likud was more successful than Labour in attracting the support of the Orientals. The vote for the other two groups during the 1970s and 1980s remained much the same but these groups also underwent changes. Among the religious voters there was a switch of support towards the more orthodox religious parties and away from the relatively tolerant National Religious Party (founded 1956). And among the other parties there was a change in 1988 which illustrated the greater consciousness of Arab voters.

Until 1977 most Arab voters had voted for Zionist parties and mainly for Mapai; of the remainder the greatest number voted communist. One reason for this practice was the difficulty for any purely Arab party of devising a programme which would not be deemed to challenge the raison d'être of the state and hence make the party ineligible to take part in the elections. Another reason was the dominance within the Arab community of the conservative leadership of traditional village notables. In 1977, however, a number of Arab voters switched from Labour to the communists, in 1984 a majority voted for non-Zionist parties, and in 1988 many Arabs voted for a purely Arab party. This change in behaviour may be attributed to the decline of the older Arab leadership and the rise of a new, younger, more radical and professional leadership and to the increase of political consciousness arising from the Palestinian agitation outside Israel.

From 1977 until 1984 Israel was governed by coalitions led by Likud in which the dominant personality was the Herut prime minister (1977–83), Menachem Begin, former Revisionist and one time leader of Irgun Zvai Leumi. In 1948 the Revisionists had challenged the authority of the state by claiming the right to maintain their own armed forces but they had been defeated by Ben Gurion in a clash which took place over the Revisionist attempt to bring in a shipment of their own arms. Thereafter the Revisionists, through Herut, had entered the political system but their continued demand for the extension of the Israeli state to include all of mandatory Palestine and Transjordan had made them impossible allies in government until 1967; Ben Gurion regarded them with the greatest antipathy. In 1967 the Revisionists joined the national unity government which fought the war of that year and extended Israeli control over all Palestine. The Revisionists and their demands now appeared more respectable and in alliance with the old liberals they emerged as a real alternative to Labour. Despite its greater appeal to Oriental Jews Likud remained, like Labour, essentially an Ashkenazi party whose leaders were mainly from Eastern Europe.

In 1984 the Likud government lost the election. Doubts about the Lebanese war and concerns about increasing economic problems led to a shift of support to the extreme right parties rather than to Labour. As a result there came into being another coalition government, this time of Labour and Likud. The two parties shared power and the prime ministership was held first by the Labour leader, Shimon Peres, and next by the Likud leader, Yitzhak Shamir, a former member of the Stern Gang. The 1988 election also resulted in a stalemate although the balance shifted slightly towards Likud and in the new coalition Shamir continued as prime minister. For both Labour and Likud a problem existed in that the small parties who were alternative coalition partners had become more radical and more demanding in the price of their support. This phenomenon was especially a consequence of the growth of Jewish fundamentalism.

In its conception Israel was an ideological state and it faced continual problems of definition concerned with its Jewish character, its relations with Jews outside Israel and its relation to the land of Israel. The concepts of Judaism, the Jewish people and Eretz Israel all long predated the state and many people saw it as the job of the state to accommodate itself to these rather than the other way about. Ultra-orthodox Jews had opposed as blasphemous the creation of a Jewish state in Palestine and only grudgingly accepted its existence. In 1947 a concordat was reached between state and religion by which the state undertook to support dietary restrictions and Sabbath observance and leave personal law to the religious courts under the rabbinate. Further concessions were granted subsequently by the state; in 1952 orthodox women were exempted from military service and in 1953 state support was given to religious schools. A ministry of religion was created and was always held by a member of one of the religious parties. Until 1973 the arrangement worked reasonably well although there were clashes between secular and religious Israelis over education, law and the operation of state enterprises subjected to religious restrictions. From 1973 the demands of the religious and their ability through the balance of the political system to extract concessions increased. Whereas previously the religious had concentrated on preserving areas of Israeli life as zones of religion the tendency of the new, more aggressive religious leadership was to demand that the state should be governed by Jewish law. In particular they demanded acceptance of their definition of a Jew with its implications for Israeli citizenship, and annexation of the occupied territories as part of the land of Israel. Orthodox Jews, notably through the Gush Emunim movement (founded 1974), began to establish settlements on the West Bank. In 1977 as the price of their support for Likud the religious obtained two additional ministries, interior and education, and they made further gains in the years before 1988. Total support for the religious parties changed little, remaining at about 15 per cent of the electorate, but

Oriental voters increasingly gave their support to the more fundamentalist ultra-orthodox parties which rose at the expense of the National Religious Party.

Israel's relationship with Jews outside the state was ambivalent. On the one hand was a strong Zionist feeling that all Jews should come to the Jewish state and contempt for those who did not. Israel demanded an exclusive right to speak for Jews everywhere. On the other hand was the circumstance that Israel required the support of a prosperous Diaspora to sustain its existence. The Jewish Agency, dominated by Israelis and Zionists but supported by the contributions of Jews throughout the world, was the principal instrument for the settlement of emigrants in Israel. Diaspora financial contributions were required to support the state and Diaspora political pressure was needed to induce other states to lend their assistance to Israel. In fact most Jews in the Diaspora were content to accept a subsidiary role and to allow Israel to occupy the central position it claimed. Partly this was because of pride in the achievements of the Jewish state, notably its success in the 1967 war which led to a powerful demonstration of Diaspora support even from Jewish communities, such as those of France and South America, which had not previously been strongly Zionist. Partly it was the consequence of a view of Israel as an insurance policy for Jews everywhere, a view strengthened by the stress placed on what came to be known as the Holocaust, the murder of the greater part of European Jewry by Nazi Germany during the Second World War. Long show trials of war criminals such as those of Adolf Eichmann (1961) and John Demjanjuk ("Ivan the Terrible") (1988) served to keep remembrance vivid.

Most important of all was the relationship between the state of Israel and the land of Israel. The land of Israel was never precisely defined but may be taken to include Palestine and Transjordan. The decision of the Zionist leaders in 1947 to accept partition and a state in only part of this area was regarded by many, notably the Revisionists, as a betrayal. A number of Zionists regarded the acceptance as marking only a stage on the way to the acquisition of the whole and looked to the chapter of accidents to enable them to expand further. In fact the war of 1948 left Israel in possession of four-fifths of mandatory Palestine and the 1967 war put her in possession of the remainder. After 1948 Israel refused to surrender any of the additional territory she had secured during the war nor did she return any of the Palestinian territory gained in 1967.

Likud and the other right wing parties together with the religious parties opposed surrendering any of the territory. A minority of

Israelis, perhaps 10 per cent, would, according to their votes, have favoured surrendering all the territory acquired in 1967 in return for peace and to be rid of the problem of ruling so many Arabs. The Labour Alignment's original policy (the Allon Plan) was that it would return some of the territory under certain conditions (which excluded establishing a Palestinian state) and would retain an undefined amount for security and other purposes. Later, in 1970–1, a policy was adopted by Dayan of functional or creeping annexation. The occupied territories were also seen as a valuable market and a source of cheap labour. Labour began a policy of forming Jewish settlements on the West Bank (referred to as Judaea and Samaria) for security purposes and the policy of settlement was accelerated under the Likud government from 1977 to 1984. Land in the occupied territories was acquired through leasing, requisition and purchase so that by 1983 Israel had acquired direct control of a third of all the occupied land. An independent settlement policy was organized by religious and secular Zionist groups from 1968. East Jerusalem, annexed for essentially ideological reasons in 1967, was treated as a separate matter.

JORDAN

No country in the Near East endured greater territorial convulsions during the period following the Second World War than did Jordan; nor did any country, except Israel, enjoy greater political stability, economic growth and educational expansion. To explain this curious paradox is not easy and the difficulties are enhanced by the circumstance that Jordan (except for its foreign policy) is one of the least studied states of the Near East. Similar in size to Lebanon and Israel it has attracted only a fraction of the attention.

In terms of population Jordan was trebled in size in 1948-9 by the addition of the West Bank. In the following years the population grew rapidly but its balance changed. By 1961 of the 1.7 million Jordanians more than half lived on the East Bank compared to one-third in 1949. During this period there had been a major movement of people from the West to the growing towns of the East Bank, especially Amman which more than doubled its size to 433,000. Another change was the settlement and urbanization of the bedouin whose numbers fell from an estimated 200,000 in 1949 to 56,000 in 1961 with perhaps as many again classified as semi-nomad. By 1967 it was thought that more than half the population was urban. The 1967 war, which resulted in the

Israeli occupation of the West Bank, brought about a further, dramatic change in the population. An estimated 350,000 people fled to the East Bank and the movement continued in subsequent years; between 1967 and 1989 about 65,000 residents in the occupied territories moved to the east. The 1979 census showed 2.1 million residents on the East Bank, a figure roughly equal to the total population of both banks in 1967, and by 1989 this figure had risen to some 3 million, of whom about two-thirds lived in towns, nearly 1 million in Amman alone.

One may summarize the changes in Jordan as follows. Jordan's population grew from 400,000 to 3 million, changed its character from being basically pastoral and agricultural to urban, and changed its composition from being mainly east Jordanian tribes to 50 per cent or more of Palestinian origin. The challenge of domestic politics was to manage this change, to provide the resources necessary to satisfy the aspirations of the people and to integrate the different elements of the population.

A high rate of economic growth was essential in order to provide for so rapidly growing a population. This was achieved. Between 1951 and 1967 Jordan experienced an almost continuous boom, based on the development of agriculture (notably by irrigation of the Jordan valley), tourism, light manufacturing industry and the exploitation of minerals, especially potash and phosphates. In the seven years before the 1967 war growth averaged over 9 per cent per annum. The 1967 war completely disrupted Jordan's economic development; the West Bank had contributed about 40 per cent of GNP, including most of Jordan's agricultural production, as well as being a considerable asset to tourism through the existence of Jerusalem and the Holy Places. However, growth resumed in the 1970s and between 1974 and 1982 averaged nearly 10 per cent per annum, falling thereafter to around 3 per cent.

This economic success was achieved principally through private enterprise: Jordan introduced a succession of plans from 1962 but remained a country of small peasant landholders and businessmen. Jordan was greatly assisted by foreign aid. Until 1956 outside aid came chiefly from Britain, principally in the form of payments for the Arab Legion; thereafter the United States provided assistance and between 1958 and 1965 Jordan was the largest recipient of US aid in per capita terms. After 1967 Jordan also received payments from Arab countries. UNRWA spending on the Palestinian refugees provided a continuing stimulus to the Jordan economy and during the 1970s and 1980s remittances from Jordanians employed abroad, mainly in other Near Eastern countries, was an important source of foreign exchange.

Jordan also benefited from the Lebanese civil war, which resulted in the transfer of banking and other services to Jordan, and from the Iran–Iraq war when Jordan's port of ᶜAqaba became a conduit for Iraqi imports. After 1982 the inability of Iraq to pay for imports and the decline in the oil revenues of Arab states adversely affected Jordan and led to a fall in the rate of growth. Jordan then began to experience serious economic difficulties; she could no longer afford the abundant imports of consumer goods or the large apparatus of food subsidies which she had developed during the easy years. But when she began to take measures to redress the balance popular discontent manifested itself in riots. Jordan found herself in much the same plight as Egypt and several other Near Eastern states in the 1980s.

The economic boom helped to pay for the provision of social services, in particular education; already by 1960 Jordan had more children per head in government schools than any other Arab country and Jordan continued to invest heavily in education. The University of Jordan in Amman was opened in 1962 and was followed by other universities and colleges. By 1985 Jordan had 50,000 students in higher education at home and a further 60,000 abroad. Nevertheless, a third of Jordanians remained illiterate.

The political system of Jordan was dominated by the monarchy and by the personality of King Ḥusayn ibn Ṭalāl, the grandson of ᶜAbdallāh ibn Ḥusayn. After ᶜAbdallāh's assassination on 20 July 1951, his eldest son, Ṭalāl, came to the throne. Ṭalāl was, however, already mentally sick and suffered a complete breakdown a year later when he was deposed in favour of his young son, Ḥusayn, who was preferred to Ṭalāl's half brother, Nāyif, who was held to be of inferior birth. Ḥusayn came of age in May 1953 and began a reign which exceeded in length that of all other Arab leaders. The Hashimites possessed certain advantages in terms of their descent from the Prophet, their tribal links and their Arab nationalist credentials but during the era of radical Arab nationalism these merits were seemingly outweighed by antipathy to the notion of monarchy in general and to the Hashimites in particular because of their pro-Western inclinations and because of ᶜAbdallāh's ambiguous role in Palestine in 1948–9. Hashimite rule was resented by many Palestinians who found themselves citizens of Jordan. In these circumstances singular political skills were required from the ruler and these Ḥusayn supplied in full measure. The king made foreign policy and dominated domestic politics. In 1965 he settled the problem of the succession by choosing his brother, Ḥasan, as Crown Prince, bypassing his own children, whose mother was English. Ḥasan became increasingly associated with the making of policy.

Ḥusayn was assisted by a royal council recruited from tribal and other notables, which provided a link with bedouin elements, a source of political advice and a training ground for future ministers.

The political system of Jordan was based on the constitution of 1952, subsequently amended. The 1952 constitution, introduced by Ṭalāl, made the cabinet responsible to parliament and not, as formerly, to the king, limited the king's legislative powers and gave parliament some financial powers. Parliament was composed of two chambers: an elected chamber of deputies which from 1950 to 1963 consisted of 40 members, including 20 from each bank of the Jordan, and a senate appointed by the king and consisting of notables including senior politicians and military figures. In 1963 the number of deputies was increased to 60, parity between the two banks being preserved. Political activity was strictly controlled; few political parties were legalized and all were banned completely from time to time. Nevertheless, political groupings which resembled parties existed and took part in elections. Elections were closely supervised until 1956 when Jordan had something approaching free elections which, for the first time, produced a majority of deputies opposed to the regime. Thereafter controls were again introduced at subsequent elections down to 1967. From 1974 until 1984 parliament was suspended, being replaced from 1978 to 1984 by an appointed national consultative council. Another representative device was a tribal council established in 1971 to deal with the affairs of tribal areas. When parliament was reconvened in 1984 the seats of members who had died were filled by means of by-elections. In 1989 in the first general election since 1967 a new 80 member lower house was elected from the East Bank alone. Political parties were permitted and the elections were more or less free from government interference. The fluctuating fortunes of parliament were related both to internal considerations and to the progress of inter-Arab affairs, in particular to developments in relation to Palestine.

Except briefly between 1971 and 1974, when the king established the Jordanian National Union as the single official party, there was no real government party if one excludes the Constitutional Bloc of the 1950s; most members sat as independents and supported the regime. The opposition parties reflected currents of opinion outside Jordan. During the 1950s and 1960s most of the opposition groupings belonged to the radical Arab spectrum, Nasirist, Communist and Baʿthist, although there was always some support for the Muslim Brotherhood. By the 1980s the balance had switched and in the 1984 by-elections and the 1989 general election the Muslim fundamentalist candidates made the strongest showing. In 1989 they captured 34 of the 80 seats. A moderate leftist grouping, the Democratic Bloc, came second.

The king appointed the chief minister. Governments were short-lived; between 1951 and 1989 the average life of governments was well under one year. Nevertheless, there was much ministerial continuity. The most important ministers were drawn from a group of east bank notables and, especially during the early years, from old advisers of ᶜAbdallāh. In this respect the year 1958 marks something of a turning point. From the 1930s until that year four men dominated governments: Ibrāhīm Hāshim, Samīr al-Rifāᶜī, Tawfīq Abu'l Hudā and Saᶜīd al-Muftī. The first three were of Palestinian origin, had entered the service of ᶜAbdallāh during the 1920s and subsequently identified themselves completely with the fortunes of Jordan. Among them Tawfīq Abu'l Hudā, who served a total of 12 years as chief minister, was an outstanding statesman and was chiefly responsible for steering Jordan safely through the difficult period between the death of ᶜAbdallāh and the accession of Ḥusayn. The fourth member of the group, Saᶜīd al-Muftī, was a Circassian, a member of the small but highly influential community which provided a quite disproportionate number of ministers; between 1947 and 1965 there was at least one Circassian in 27 out of 36 cabinets. But the predominance of the old ᶜAbdallāh men ended in 1958: Tawfīq Abu'l Hudā killed himself in 1956 and Ibrāhīm Hāshim died in the Iraqi revolution of 1958. Only Samīr al-Rifāᶜī served as chief minister after 1959 and for less than a month.

The passing of the old guard coincided with a major crisis in the history of Jordan, which had two points of origin. The first was internal and was related to the demands of Palestinians and some discontented east Jordanians, particularly from the East Bank towns, for a greater share of power. The second was external and was connected to the struggle for dominance in the Arab world between Egypt and Iraq and the problem of Western influence. The internal and external conflicts came together at the end of 1955 when an attempt was made to draw Jordan into the Baghdad pact, an attempt opposed by Egypt and by the internal opposition, led by Sulaymān al-Nābulsī. Nābulsī had formed a series of political groupings culminating in the National Socialists who won 11 seats and emerged as the largest single grouping at the elections of 1956. The king had endeavoured to postpone the elections but riots in January 1956 forced him to try to placate the opposition first by disavowing any intention of joining the Baghdad pact and then, on 1 March 1956, by dismissing General John Glubb, the British commander of the Arab Legion.

Ḥusayn's efforts failed, however, and the opposition won the elections of October 1956 which were fought largely on the issue of the Anglo–Jordanian treaty. The new government, led by Nābulsī, signed a military agreement with Egypt and on 12 February 1957 the Anglo–Jordanian treaty was ended by agreement. In the aftermath of the Suez campaign the treaty could hardly have been saved. But the opposition was not content with its success and began to challenge the king in other areas; in particular the king's authority over the army was threatened by the new CGS, General ᶜAlī Abū Nawwār. The crisis came to a head in April 1957 when Ḥusayn dismissed Nābulsī and Abū Nawwār. A new government under Ibrāhīm Hāshim suspended the constitution, dissolved parliament, abolished political parties and trade unions and imposed martial law. Opposition leaders were arrested and tried before military courts.

Throughout the crisis Egypt had supported the opposition and the affair had demonstrated the difficulties of Jordan in standing alone in the turbulent world of inter-Arab rivalries. It was, indeed, a commonplace of political discussion at the time that Jordan was politically and economically unviable and must form some association with another Arab state. Egypt, Syria and Iraq were the partners most frequently mentioned but the radical fervours of the first two made them unattractive to Ḥusayn and most speculation, supported by Britain, leaned towards a link between Jordan and Iraq. Neither state, however, pursued the possibility with any real enthusiasm until Egypt and Syria came together in the United Arab Republic in 1958. At that time a Jordanian–Iraqi link seemed a matter of survival and was accomplished through the creation of the Arab Federation on 14 February 1958. The Iraqi revolution of July 1958 brought the Hashimite federation to a rapid end, however, and Jordan now had no real alternative to subordination to Egypt but to stand alone with the support of the West. The period from 1958 to 1963, when the last major attempt at Arab political union collapsed, was a difficult and isolated time for Jordan.

The prolonged political crisis of 1955–8 changed the face of Jordanian politics. It ended the long relation with Britain and substituted a new link with the United States; it ended the attempt to solve the problems of Jordan by domestic conciliation of radical Arabism; it ended the hopes of solving Jordan's problems by federation; and it marked the point at which Ḥusayn took full control of his country's affairs. From 1958 onwards chief ministers were much more executors of the king's will than they had been before that date. This is not to say that they were not able men; in particular, Waṣfī al-Tall, the former radical who was prime minister on a number of occasions between 1962 and 1971, was a skilful politician who also brought into government a new generation of ministers, including many Palestinians. Similarly, Zayd al-Rifāʿī, the eldest son of Samīr al-Rifāʿī and a childhood friend of Ḥusayn, demonstrated considerable abilities as prime minister from 1973–6 and 1985–9. But essentially they and other ministers did what Ḥusayn wanted and were appointed and dismissed in accordance with the initiatives which the king wished to make in domestic and foreign affairs.

The crisis also demonstrated the ultimate reliance of the regime on the security services. As a result of the war of 1948–9 the Arab Legion had been expanded from 6,000 to 12,000 and it continued to grow in subsequent years and reached 25,000 in 1956. At that time it was merged with the 30,000 strong National Guard, composed of Palestinians and established in 1951 to perform border duties. By 1967 the reformed army numbered 55,000. In 1967 the army was heavily defeated and temporarily reduced to 30,000, its air force and most of its armoured equipment gone. But the army was quickly rebuilt and by 1970 was 65,000 strong.

Tensions existed within the army between the bedouin and Palestinian elements in the officer corps and these became more marked after the departure in 1956 of the 40 British officers who had served with the Legion. In 1956 the king almost lost control of the army and there were attempted coups in 1960, 1961 and 1963. Between 1968 and 1970 there was a major crisis within the army because of the Palestinian guerrilla problem; there were further problems in 1974; and in 1976 disturbances in the army forced the resignation of the prime minister. On each occasion the king kept ultimate control of the army because of the continued loyalty of the bedouin element which still amounted to about one-third in 1967 and was dominant in the armoured units. Even as the number of bedouin declined the bedouin ethos remained powerful in the army where bedouin played a role similar to that of the kibbutzniks in the Israeli army. The king maintained the personal links between the monarchy and the army by control of all senior appointments and by appointing close relatives to command: his uncle Sharīf Nāṣir ibn Jamīl and his cousin Sharīf Zayd ibn Shākir served as commanders in chief for many years. And officers were given special privileges in housing, health and education. The monarchy also developed other security services, a police force and the general intelligence department which kept strict watch on domestic opposition.

The army saved the regime again during the second great crisis of the state in 1967–70. In 1967 Jordan was defeated and the West Bank was lost. The defeat of the Arab states opened the way to the development of the Palestinian guerrilla forces which operated from Jordan and which began to create within Jordan their own state within a state, centred on the fortified refugee camps within which the guerrillas established their own services and from which they flouted the laws of Jordan. At first the guerrillas co-operated with the army but clashes between the two groups began in November 1968. For a long while Ḥusayn was unable to take effective action against the guerrillas: apart from their own strength of some 15,000 armed men, there were on Jordanian soil 12,000 Iraqi and 6,000 Syrian troops who might be expected to come to the aid of the guerrillas. The key to the resolution of the problem was the attitude of Egypt. In the summer of 1970 the PLO parted company with Egypt over the Rogers peace plan and radical factions within the PLO attempted to wreck the plan by hijacking Western aircraft. It was Ḥusayn's opportunity and he turned his bedouin troops against the guerrillas in September 1970, completing the destruction of their power in Jordan by July 1971. The Iraqi troops withdrew from the field: the Syrians attempted to intervene in support of the guerrillas but were defeated and also left the scene.

The action of September 1970 was one episode in the most enduring problem of Jordan during the years after 1948, namely the integration of Palestinians and East Jordanians within a single state. There was considerable opposition among Palestinians to the unification of the West Bank with old Transjordan in April 1950. Palestinians were more numerous and better educated and considered themselves to be more sophisticated than the Transjordanians. More than twice as many West Bank children were in school and the West Bankers had more doctors, newspapers, trade unions and political institutions. Former supporters of the Ḥusaynī party (of mandatory Palestine) resented the extinction of Arab Palestine. Palestinian refugees wished to prosecute their struggle against Israel in order to recover their lands and rightly believed that the monarchy was more concerned with reaching a settlement with Israel. As a result many supported radical Arab nationalism which promised the continuation of the struggle.

During the 1950s the monarchy sought to obliterate the sense of Palestinian identity: the use of the word "Palestine" in official documents was forbidden, Palestinian political parties and other institutions were closed, there were strict controls on the press and the legal systems and currency were unified. At first the West Bank was ruled as a single entity from Jerusalem but later it was divided into provinces and ruled from Amman. Tight security was maintained over the region, especially after the 1958 crisis. The monarchy dealt for choice with old notable families which would co-operate with it, including the Nashāshībīs and the Tawqāns; indeed between 1950 and 1967 the West Bank was one of the last bastions of traditional notable politics in the Near East. Palestinians, mainly notables, were brought into the Jordanian central government. It was supposed that Palestinians might comprise half of each cabinet but they usually fell below that proportion and were commonly found in less sensitive posts. Of the 20 Jordanian prime ministers between 1950 and 1989 only four were Palestinians and none held their posts for long. Palestinians complained of the preference given to East Bankers in employment, contracts and licences and of their exclusion from combat commands in the army.

Jordanian policy worked fairly successfully until 1956 but the great political crisis of the late 1950s produced a partial change of emphasis and more efforts to conciliate Palestinians with jobs and with pardons for former opponents of the regime. The declining attractiveness of Pan-Arabism to Palestinians after the collapse of the UAR in 1961 led to greater Jordanian integration. But this process was upset by the revival of the notion of Palestinian identity following the creation of the PLO in 1964. Thereafter the monarchy was involved in a prolonged contest with the PLO for the loyalties of Jordanian Palestinians. Until 1967 the monarchy had the advantage of direct authority over the West Bank but subsequently the problem assumed a different aspect.

After 1967 the monarchy was engaged in a double struggle, first for the loyalties of citizens of the East Bank of whom about one-half were of Palestinian origin and second for the loyalty of the West Bankers. The defeat of the Palestinian guerrillas in 1970–1 ended the greatest challenge to the monarchy's authority on the East Bank but the contest for the West Bank continued and was interfused with the problem of ending the Israeli occupation. After 1967 Jordan maintained her claim to the West Bank and with Arab assistance continued to pay the salaries of West Bank civil servants and to subsidize schools, hospitals and local government. At first this policy seemed successful; Jordanian supporters won an overwhelming victory at the 1972 West Bank municipal elections and Ḥusayn put forward a plan for a federation of the two regions, sharing only a common defence and foreign policy. But afterwards the contest moved against the monarchy. In 1974 the Arab states recognized the PLO as the sole legitimate representative of the Palestinian people with the right to establish a national entity on the West Bank and in Gaza. Arab money was now funnelled to the West Bank through the PLO, new younger PLO supporters displaced the older notables in the political leadership of the West Bank and Jordanian influence declined. Still Ḥusayn kept alive the federation scheme and endeavoured to reach agreement with the PLO on the distribution of funds to the West Bank and on a basis for negotiation with Israel. These efforts were ultimately unsuccessful. In February 1986 Ḥusayn broke off his attempt to reach agreement with the PLO. At the end of 1987 came a further demonstration of the decline of support for Jordanian pretensions on the West Bank with the *intifāḍa*, a movement which owed nothing to Jordan and made no acknowledgement of Jordanian authority. On 31 July 1988 Ḥusayn gave up the struggle and surrendered Jordan's claims to the West Bank.

Ḥusayn's abandonment of his claims to the West Bank marks a period in the history of Jordan. But if it was partly a recognition that he had lost the contest with the PLO in the West it was also a recognition of the comparative insignificance of the West Bank in the context of Jordan. By 1988 there were nearly 3 million people on the East Bank and less than a million on the West. The progress of assimilation on the East Bank had continued. Although there were still some 750,000 refugees in the East only 200,000 were in camps. The majority of Palestinians were integrated into Jordanian society or were among the 350,000 Jordanians working abroad. It was UNRWA's money which fostered identification as refugees and was a potent factor in promoting the notion of a Palestinian identity within Jordan. But by 1989 Jordan was nearer to being a unified state than it had ever been.

THE PALESTINIANS

It may reasonably be asked why a history of a people should appear in a book which is otherwise concerned with the histories of states. If the Palestinians why not the Kurds or the Baluchis or any other group which has no state of its own? The answer lies in two circumstances: first that the Palestinians have achieved a degree of international recognition as possessing some of the attributes of a state, and second because whereas the history of other peoples may be contained within the states to which they belong that is not true of the Palestinians; leaving aside the question of the status of refugees in general, in Gaza since 1948 and on the West Bank since 1988 Palestinians have not been members of any state.

The decision to write about the Palestinians, however, raises a major problem which is not presented by the history of states, namely, who is a Palestinian? There can be no objective answer to such a question but if one takes the subjective response – a Palestinian is one who thinks he is a Palestinian – one is at once faced with the circumstance that impressions of identity change over time; he who thought he was a Palestinian yesterday may think he is Jordanian today and a Palestinian again tomorrow. Or he may adopt both identities today for different purposes.

In 1947 there were about 1.3 million Palestinian Arabs. About one-third lived in towns, two-thirds in 800 or so villages and there were also some 70,000 bedouin. About half the Arab land of Palestine was owned by small peasant cultivators and the other half by mainly absentee landlords. Palestinian agriculture was fairly prosperous: grain was the principal crop but a substantial area of land (75,000 hectares) grew fruit for export. In other ways villages were economically and socially self-sufficient and largely indifferent to urban politics which were the affairs of notables.

The conflict of 1947–9 destroyed this society throughout much of Palestine. Of the 1.3 million Palestinians about 700,000 were displaced. 150,000 still lived in territories under Israeli rule, while 400,000 remained in their homes on the West Bank and 50,000 in the Gaza strip. Of the 700,000 refugees about 400,000 were in Jordan, mainly on the West Bank, 150,000 in Gaza and 150,000 divided between Syria and Lebanon. (These figures are contested and estimates of the total number of refugees have varied between 500,000 and 900,000.)

After the war the refugees wished to return to their homes but Israel refused to admit more than a small number, took over the property of the refugees and declined to pay compensation. Israel expected the refugees to be absorbed by Arab states. In fact only Jordan gave the Palestinians, refugees and non-refugees, full citizenship: in Gaza the Palestinians lived under Egyptian military administration, and neither Lebanon nor Syria would grant citizenship to more than a small number of Palestinians. Nor could the Arab countries easily afford the burden of caring for the refugees, a duty which in 1950 was assumed by the United Nations Relief and Works Agency (UNRWA) and financed by Western powers, especially the United States.

The existence and activities of UNRWA were key factors in preserving the Palestinian identity. At first UNRWA was concerned with administering short term relief, including the distribution of food rations, but as time went on it became more concerned with other activities, notably with health and education. This shift in emphasis was temporarily upset by the new refugee disturbances caused by the 1967 war and again by the Lebanese troubles but the trend continued and by 1986 only 11 per cent of UNRWA's budget went on relief against 22 per cent on health and the remainder on education. Thus UNRWA's existence was an inducement to people to identify themselves as Palestinians and the health and educational institutions which it set up became effectively Palestinian institutions.

In 1950 UNRWA registered 960,000 Palestinian refugees. By May 1967 the total number of registered refugees had risen by natural increase to 1.34 million. The June 1967 war produced a further displacement of Palestinians: 150,000 existing refugees moved on and an estimated 300,000 became refugees for the first time. By 1968 the number of registered refugees had risen to 1.56 million. In 1987 there were 2.19 million registered refugees of whom about one-third lived in camps and the remainder in villages and towns. Of the 2.19 million there were 840,000 in East Jordan, 370,000 on the West Bank, 440,000 in Gaza, 280,000 in Lebanon and 260,000 in Syria.

The total number of Palestinians, meaning those non-Jews who lived in Palestine in 1947 together with their progeny, was between 4.5 and 5.0 million in 1987. Because of differences in the ways different states collect statistics apportionment of non-refugees is difficult but roughly 650,000 lived in Israel, 500,000 on the West Bank, 300,000 in Kuwayt and the remainder in Jordan, Gaza and other countries. Many of those living outside the boundaries of mandatory Palestine had Jordanian nationality. The greatest uncertainty attends the number of non-refugees of Palestinian origin living on the East Bank, but it may be estimated that these numbered about 500,000 in 1987. What is most arguable of all is the extent to which these different groups regarded themselves as Palestinian. As a general proposition it may be suggested that the strongest sense of identity was felt by those who lived in refugee camps and those who lived within the bounds of mandatory Palestine.

Between 1949 and 1964 the Palestinians were seen primarily as a refugee problem. Neither Israel nor Jordan recognized the existence of a Palestinian problem; to the Israelis they were Arabs and to the Jordanians they were Jordanian. Other Arab states and the world at large recognized the Palestinians as such but saw their problem as being that of refugees to be returned or resettled. International action focused on temporary relief and plans for resettlement through co-operative action to irrigate land. Palestinians had no political institutions of their own; the Ḥusaynī government of Arab Palestine based in

Gaza was dissolved at the end of 1948 and al-Ḥājj Amīn taken to Cairo. Nevertheless, the old Arab Higher Committee continued to claim leadership down to 1964. Palestinian political thinking was divided during this period: some looked to assimilation within the states in which they now dwelled; some to a continuation of the lonely struggle for an Arab Palestine; and some to the support of a united Arab world. Among this last group were those who believed that the liberation of Palestine must be preceded by revolutions within each Arab country so as to bring to power radical pan-Arab regimes.

In 1964 the establishment of the Palestine Liberation Organisation (PLO) gave Palestinians a new political focus. Proposals to establish a Palestine entity had been advanced by Egypt and Iraq in 1959 but had come to nothing. The failure of attempts to agree on the division of Jordan waters and the Israeli decision to proceed unilaterally with a scheme to use Jordan water to irrigate the Negev caused the Arab leaders to turn back to the notion of the creation of a Palestine entity as part of their response. The lead was taken by Egypt who wished to keep firm control of the organization.

At the founding conference of the PLO in East Jerusalem in May 1964 a statement of aims (the Palestine National Charter or Covenant) and a constitution were adopted. The Charter asserted that the Palestinian identity was an inherent characteristic and that Palestinians were an integral part of the Arab nation and proposed the establishment of a united Palestinian state with the same boundaries as mandatory Palestine. It denied any national identity to Jews, condemned Zionism and accepted as Palestinians only those Jews who were present in Palestine before the beginning of "the Zionist invasion". The constitution established a Palestine national council as the supreme representative body for Palestinians and an executive committee as an embryonic cabinet. Eventually the members of the executive committee became virtually ministers in charge of departments. The first chairman of the executive committee was Aḥmad Shuqayrī, a diplomat from a Palestinian notable family. A further Palestinian institution which was established was the Palestine Liberation Army, formed from Palestinian units in the Iraqi army.

In its early years the PLO commanded little respect or attention. Its claims to represent them were dismissed by many Palestinians, Shuqayrī was widely regarded as a noisy Egyptian puppet, and Jordan was strongly opposed to the pretensions of the PLO to authority over Jordanian Palestinians. The PLO and its army performed dismally during the 1967 war and Shuqayrī resigned in December 1967. Control of the PLO then passed to another group of Palestinians, namely the guerrillas led by the organization, al-Fataḥ. The guerrillas took over the national council in July 1968, amending the Charter to give prominence to a programme of armed struggle, and took over the executive committee in February 1969. Yāsir ᶜArafāt, the leader of al-Fataḥ, became chairman.

Sporadic guerrilla attacks by Palestinians against Israel had occurred ever since 1949 but, with the exception of the months which preceded the Suez campaign when guerrillas had struck at Israel from Gaza they had not been organized. The radical Palestinian groups thought guerrilla activity premature and wasteful and preached the doctrine that the first task was to secure Arab unity. In the aftermath of Suez, however, there grew up the notion that Palestinians should not wait for Arab unity but should wage their own campaign with Arab support for the liberation of Palestine. This view was espoused by a number of Palestinians in Kuwayt and they became the nucleus of al-Fataḥ. It is difficult to establish a precise date for the conversion of al-Fataḥ from a movement into an organization; it was a gradual process which took place between 1958 and 1962. Al-Fataḥ took part doubtfully in the foundation of the PLO and turned to Egypt's rival, Syria, for support in launching its own guerrilla campaign in 1965.

It was the Arab defeat in the 1967 war which gave al-Fataḥ and the other guerrilla organizations their opportunity. The Israeli occupation of the West Bank seemingly provided a scene for guerrilla operations. In fact their efforts to mount an offensive from inside the West Bank were defeated by popular indifference and Israeli repression. In 1968 the guerrillas moved their bases to the east bank of the Jordan whence they conducted operations in Israel. On 21 March 1968 the guerrillas, with Jordanian army assistance, fought against an Israeli retaliatory raid at Karameh. Karameh was not a victory for the guerrillas – Israel achieved its objective of forcing the guerrillas to move their bases into the interior – but it was a great propaganda success. At a time when many Arabs had come to believe that Israel was invincible the guerrillas had helped to show that armed resistance was feasible. Their popularity was assured, thousands of volunteers flocked to join them and money flowed into their war chest.

Armed struggle required a base and since no base could be maintained in Israeli occupied territory the base had to be on the territory of Israel's neighbours, in effect Syria, Jordan or Lebanon. Of these Jordan, which had the longest frontier with Israel and the largest Palestinian population, was the obvious choice. But Jordan resented the PLO's claims on the loyalty of its Palestinian citizens, the disregard of its laws and its exposure to Israeli retaliation. At one time the guerrillas took over a Jordanian town, Irbid. Attempts to reach agreement on the conditions under which the guerrillas could operate from Jordan failed and in the end Jordan crushed the guerrillas and expelled them in 1970–1.

In 1971 the guerrillas moved their main base to Lebanon and disposed their forces along Israel's northern border in what became known as Fatahland. The cycle of raids and retaliatory raids brought about a situation in Lebanon similar to that which had existed in Jordan. Again attempts to reach agreement about guerrilla activities were unsuccessful. But the Lebanese government was more divided than that of Jordan, its army was weaker and its communities deeply separated on other issues. In Lebanon the outcome was civil war into which the Palestinians were drawn in 1975. There followed a prolonged struggle in which both Syria and Israel took a hand. In 1976 the Palestinians were defeated by Syrian forces but were allowed to continue their operations against Israel from their southern bases. In 1982 Israel made a determined effort to crush the Palestinians in Lebanon, defeated their forces in the south but was unable to complete a victory in Beirut. In August 1982, however, the guerrillas agreed to withdraw from Beirut with the honours of war and a US guarantee for the safety of civilians. In fact their withdrawal was followed by Maronite massacres of Palestinians in the Beirut refugee camps of Sabra and Shatila. Following the Israeli withdrawal from Lebanon in 1983 the Palestinians resumed their operations in south Lebanon on a much reduced scale. The Palestinians also suffered a set back in the north of Lebanon when Syria, determined to bring the PLO under control, sponsored a break away movement within al-Fataḥ and expelled ᶜArafāt and other leaders from Lebanon in December 1983. By that date it could be said that the guerrilla attempt to convert Lebanon into the main base for operations against Israel had failed. Some guerrillas remained but their operations were severely curtailed. The PLO headquarters was moved to Tunis.

Another feature of the guerrillas' armed struggle against Israel was operations conducted mainly outside the Near East against Israeli or related targets. These operations took various forms and included attacks on Israeli officials or organizations but the most dramatic were the hijackings of civilian aircraft. Hijacks began in July 1968 and reached a peak in September 1970 when four aircraft were hijacked and destroyed. Other spectacular operations included the killing of Israeli athletes at the Munich Olympics (September 1972), an attack on the Saᶜūdī embassy at Khartoum (February 1973), the hijacking of an Italian cruiseliner, the *Achille Lauro* (September 1985) and terrorist attacks at Rome and Vienna airports (December 1985). Sometimes operations were carried out by other groups acting on behalf of the guerrillas, for example the Lod airport massacre of 1972 executed by a Japanese terrorist group. Israel retaliated by attacks on Palestinian targets in Arab countries and on guerrilla leaders. Operations included commando attacks on Beirut in 1968, which resulted in the destruction of 13 Arab aircraft, and in 1973, in which three PLO leaders were killed. A notable success was the assassination of the Fataḥ military leader, Khalīl al-Wazīr (Abū Jihād), in Tunis in April 1988.

Most of the Palestinian operations described in the previous paragraph were the work of the radical groups which joined the PLO in 1969 and not of al-Fataḥ. Most of these groups were established during the period 1967–9 although some were descended from earlier organizations. One of the most prominent was the Popular Front for the Liberation of Palestine (PFLP) led by George Ḥabash, which was responsible for most of the hijackings during the period 1968–70. The PFLP was itself a descendant of the Palestinian branch of the Arab Nationalist Movement (ANM), the radical Pan-Arab movement founded by students in Beirut in 1950. Other groups were formed by splinter movements within the PFLP. These included the Popular Democratic Front for the Liberation of Palestine (PDFLP) founded by Nāyif Hawatma, like Ḥabash a Christian Arab, and the Wādī Ḥaddād group which persisted with hijacks after the PFLP abandoned that tactic in 1972. Other groups were sponsored by different Arab countries. Among them were the PFLP-General Command, founded by Aḥmad Jibrīl in 1968, and al-Ṣāʿiqa, led by Zuhayr Muḥsīn until his death in 1979, both of which were supported by Syria; and the Arab Liberation Front, founded in 1969 and supported by Iraq. Another group, backed first by Iraq and then by Syria, was led by Ṣabrī al-Bannā (Abū Niḍāl), who broke away from al-Fataḥ in 1973. Abū Niḍāl's group became notorious for assassinations, especially of moderates within the PLO. There were many more small guerrilla groups often formed as a result of divisions within the radical groups.

The divisions between and sometimes within the guerrilla groups made it difficult for the PLO to agree on any new policy direction. In particular the radical groups endeavoured to obstruct any project which would compromise the goal of establishing a united, democratic, secular Palestine. In 1970 the radicals' hijackings were intended to disrupt the Rogers peace plan; between 1974 and 1978 a number of radical groups formed the Rejection Front to oppose plans to work for a Palestinian state on the West Bank and in Gaza: and in 1984–5 dissident guerrillas endeavoured to prevent PLO–Jordanian agreement on a basis for negotiation with Israel.

The PLO also pursued its goals through diplomatic action. Its first aim was to obtain recognition by other Arab states as the sole legitimate representative of the Palestinian people. This end was accomplished first at the Algiers summit in 1973 and confirmed at the Rabat meeting in 1974. It also tried to obtain wider international recognition and assistance. In 1974 ᶜArafāt addressed the General Assembly of the UNO, which gave the PLO observer status and similar recognition was obtained from the Non-Aligned Movement and from the Islamic Conference, which subsequently admitted the PLO to full membership. Help and a degree of recognition were obtained from China, the USSR and the countries of Western Europe. In accordance with an undertaking to Israel in 1975 the USA long refused to accord any recognition to the PLO but in 1988 agreed to talk to PLO representatives.

To convert diplomatic successes into success in Palestine required that the PLO should modify its goal of a united Palestine, accept the existence of Israel and aim for a smaller Palestinian state. In particular it was demanded that the PLO should accept UN resolution 242 (see p.420) as a basis for negotiation. Because of the divisions within its own ranks and because of opposition on the part of some Arab states the PLO found this acceptance very difficult; the PLO would accept a mini-state, if at all, only as a step towards its original goal. As a result the PLO was shut out of the peace initiatives of the 1970s and early 1980s. Only in 1988 did the PLO finally accept 242. At the same time Jordan's decision to abandon its claims to the West Bank left the way clear for the PLO which on 15 November 1988 proclaimed the state of Palestine, which achieved widespread international recognition. In April 1989 ᶜArafāt was appointed first president.

The scene for direct action by Palestinians had shifted to Palestine itself. Gaza had always been a centre of violent hostility to Israeli occupation and in 1971 Israel had vigorously repressed the resistance there. The West Bank was for long more docile but evidence of deep-rooted antipathy to Israeli control and to Jewish settlements was manifested during the later 1970s and 1980s. This phenomenon coincided with the decline of Jordanian influence which was replaced by that of the PLO. In the municipal elections of 1976 PLO supporters, drawn mainly from the younger professional classes, defeated Jordanian sympathizers who belonged to older notable families. In 1978 the West Bank mayors organized themselves into an informal National Guidance Committee to oppose the Camp David plans for the area.

Opposition to the intensification of Jewish settlement, which took place after the Likud victory in the 1977 Israeli elections, grew and in 1980 there were widespread demonstrations on the West Bank. In 1981 Israel declared the National Guidance Committee illegal, established a so-called civil administration and endeavoured to create its own political structure on the West Bank by appealing to the rural population through new village leagues. This policy failed and PLO influence remained dominant. In 1982 there were much more serious riots on the West Bank against Israeli efforts to control the mayors. In the following years there was further violence involving both Palestinians and Jewish settlers.

Within occupied Palestine a new departure occurred at the end of 1987 with the beginning of the so-called *intifāḍa*, a campaign of demonstrations against Israeli rule. What distinguished the *intifāḍa* from previous movements were its widespread character, its long duration and the circumstance that it was the work of new, local groups, including Muslim radicals, communists and secular nationalists as well as organizations linked to the PLO. In an attempt to control the *intifāḍa* Israel was obliged to commit large numbers of troops to peace-keeping duties on the West Bank and in Gaza. The harsh treatment of protesters caused an outcry against Israeli rule and the persistence of the demonstrations provided evidence of the strength of Palestinian feeling. The *intifāḍa* was a serious blow to Israel's attempt to argue that Palestinian opposition was merely the result of PLO terrorism against those who accepted Israeli rule, although those who co-operated with Israel were also attacked.

CHAPTER TWELVE

Turkey since 1950

Between 1950 and 1989 Turkey experienced rapid social, economic and political change. The driving force behind these changes was a rate of economic growth which averaged around 6 per cent a year. Allowing for population growth at nearly 3 per cent a year economic growth represented an increase in per capita income of at least 3 per cent a year. A starting point for any inquiry into Turkey's fortunes during these years are the questions: from where did the growth come and where did the benefits go?

Agriculture made the smallest contribution to Turkey's economic growth: its share of GNP fell from 37 per cent in 1950 to 20 per cent in 1986. The share of industry rose from 16.5 per cent to 28 per cent during the same period. Services (including construction) represented 42 per cent of GNP in 1950 and 46 per cent in 1986 after having reached 51 per cent in the late 1970s. The changed contributions were reflected in employment. In 1950 four out of five Turks worked in agriculture; in 1986 only one in two. Leaving aside those who were working abroad (mainly in industry) the rest had gone into industry and services. Because of the increase in population the number employed in agriculture remained about the same and one can say, therefore, that nearly all the increase in the working population (apart from those who went abroad to work) was absorbed in industry and services. The dynamic sector of the economy was industry which was the major contributor to Turkey's economic growth; indeed it would not be too much to say that during these years Turkey underwent an industrial revolution.

Before considering the distribution of the benefits of economic growth one must first examine the demographic changes which took place in Turkey during these years. Turkey's population increased from 21 million in 1950 to 52 million in 1986. Part of this increase was accounted for by the continuing influx of Turkish immigrants from Balkan countries although this addition to the population was partly counterbalanced by the half a million or so Turks who went to work in Western Europe and who are not included in the 52 million. By far the largest part of the increase was the consequence of natural increase at an average of nearly 3 per cent a year. One effect of so rapid a rate of natural increase was that the average age of the population fell year by year and the ratio of young dependents to workers increased. A substantial part of the benefits of economic growth therefore went on bringing up young Turks, in particular on health care and education although expenditure on education in Turkey at 2–3 per cent a year was below the average for the Near East. Nevertheless, by the 1970s primary education was almost universal and the effects of this may be illustrated by the statistics for literacy; in 1950 just under one-third of Turks were literate; by 1970 one Turk in every two could read and write and by 1989 two out of every three. By and large this change had been accomplished by educating the new generation rather than by an increase of literacy among adults.

Turkey's population also underwent a substantial redistribution. In 1950 25 per cent of Turks lived in urban areas, by 1986 the percentage had risen to 46. Much of this increased urban population was concentrated in a few large cities. Istanbul's population rose from 1 million in 1950 to 5.5 million in 1985; Ankara from 290,000 to 2.2 million; and Izmir from 230,000 to 1.5 million. The connection between industrial development and urban growth may be witnessed by the case of Istanbul which in 1972 had 45 per cent of Turkey's private manufacturing plants and 54 per cent of all workers in the private industrial sector. Ankara owed its rise especially to the expansion of government services and Izmir retained its position as the major export port, although Mersin, which served the Cilician plain and the rapidly expanding city of Adana (population 0.8 million in 1985) and became a major port for exports of grain and oil, was of increasing importance. Another part of the proceeds of economic growth had been spent on providing housing and other urban services for a greatly increased urban population. Furthermore, urban populations were much greater consumers of services such as health care and education than were people who lived in the countryside.

Part of the increase in Turkey's wealth went to the state and to people who worked for the state. In 1950 the number of state employees, including central and local government bureaucrats and employees of the state economic enterprises but excluding military personnel, was around 200,000. By 1960 the figure had doubled and during the 1970s the number employed in the state economic enterprises increased dramatically from 362,000 in 1970 to 650,000 in 1978. By 1986 there were five times as many people on the government payroll as in 1950. It is also clear that productivity in the state industrial sector was much lower than in the private sector and during the 1970s the public sector incurred very large deficits, the financing of which represented a subsidy to the state sector. The growth and persistence of the large public industrial sector took place despite the circumstance that for much of the period governments were formed by political parties which were ideologically hostile to a large state economic sector. In fact debate revolved more around the efficiency of the state sector than its size but not until after 1980 was there any major effort to achieve greater efficiency. Unlike other countries in the Near East, however, Turkey began the period with a large state sector and its rate of increase was much less than that of other countries; taxation in 1963 amounted to only 17.5 per cent of GNP. Indeed, whereas in many other countries the growth of the state sector was the principal economic dynamo, in Turkey it was the private sector which performed this role.

Before 1950 it had been assumed that the state had the major role to play in industrialization: in fact by 1975 62 per cent of the output of manufacturing industry came from the private sector. Within the private sector there was a tendency for large firms to grow much faster than small firms. Thus in 1963 firms with less than ten workers employed 52.5 per cent of the work force and in 1975 only 43 per cent. Workers in private industry were major beneficiaries of Turkey's economic growth as also were a group of big businessmen who came to figure increasingly prominently in political life during the period.

Turkey's industrial growth was achieved mainly by exploiting the expanding home market. By a variety of duties, taxes, levies and quotas Turkish industry was securely protected from foreign competition. A survey in 1972 showed that the average level of protection was 42 per cent, although it varied greatly from product to product. Turkish industry was therefore built on import substitution and in international terms much of it was uncompetitive. In effect the Turkish consumer subsidized industrial growth by paying higher prices for the industrial goods purchased. This situation implied an additional transfer of resources from the farmer to those who participated in industry although this transfer was partly offset by the lower taxes paid by farmers. Until the 1970s Turkish industrial growth was financed mainly from internal sources but during the 1970s, and especially after the great increase in the price of oil, it was financed more by foreign loans. By 1980 the size of the foreign debt and the need to improve the competitiveness of Turkish industry, if Turkey was to have any prospect of fulfilling her ambition to join the European Economic Community, made it clear that the path of economic development which Turkey had followed with such success since 1950 could not be followed in the next decade. New initiatives were required if Turkey's economic momentum was to be sustained just as it appeared that new political arrangements were needed to replace those which had come under increasing strain during the 1970s.

In 1950 Turkey began a new era in her political affairs when the Democrat Party (DP) took office and the Republican People's Party (RPP), the ruling party since the establishment of the Republic and for most of the time the only party, formed the opposition. For both parties it was a novel experience; neither was sure how to behave in the new situation. Celâl Bayar became president but the leading personality in the Democrat government was the prime minister, Adnan Menderes who dominated Turkish politics for the next ten years. A gifted communicator, to his devoted followers Menderes seemed like a man who could work miracles, an impression reinforced when he escaped from an aeroplane crash in 1959. To his opponents Menderes seemed more sinister, a demagogue who threatened to become a dictator.

The Democrats had won the election with a programme of economic and political liberalization. In fact they made little impression on the state sector but they did preside over an economic boom. In this they were helped by two factors, a succession of good harvests and the spur to world economic activity provided by the Korean War. The early 1950s were a period of unprecedented prosperity for Turkey. Cereal production in 1953 was 85 per cent higher than in 1950 and output of cotton and tobacco also increased substantially. Receiving prices for their produce higher than world prices (as they had done since 1932) the peasants of western Anatolia, whose support had been a major factor in putting the Democrats into power, were much better off and able (with help from United States aid) to invest in mechanization. The number of tractors in use increased from 14,000 in 1950 to 44,000 six years later and there was considerable expansion in the cultivated area. Other beneficiaries were members of the commercial and industrial middle class. The liberalization of trade, which ultimately contributed to a large trade deficit, produced immediate results in goods in the shops. There was some growth of private industry, notably of textiles. The Democrats also inaugurated a major programme of road construction. Before 1950 Turkey had emphasized rail transport and in 1950 Turkey had only 1,600 kilometres of hard surfaced roads compared with around 8,000 kilometres of railway lines. By 1960 the Democrats had endowed Turkey with a network of 7,000 kilometres of hard roads. The number of motor vehicles increased by over 150 per cent. The Democrats had laid the basis of a reshaping of Turkish transport and as a consequence the integration of many small towns and country areas into the national economy.

The Democrats reaped their political reward in 1954 when they achieved a landslide victory in the election to the Grand National Assembly. But subsequently things began to go wrong. The economic boom slowed down and inflation increased from 9 per cent in 1954 to 15 per cent in 1958. The trade gap widened and in 1958 Turkey was obliged to ask for assistance from the IMF and to accept, in return for new credits, some measures of restriction. Nevertheless, the overall economic situation remained satisfactory. The more serious problems were political.

The Democrats failed to carry through their promise of greater political liberalization. They remained suspicious of the RPP and determined to reduce its continuing power and influence. At the heart of the problem was the circumstance that the RPP had been for so long the party of government that its institutions had become intermixed with those of the state and its supporters were strongly entrenched in the state apparatus, the judiciary, the bureaucracy, the army, the schools and the state economic institutions. The Democrats began to try to separate the RPP from the state. In 1951 they closed the People's Houses, nominally agencies of state mobilization but in practice instruments of RPP propaganda. In 1953 they confiscated all property of the RPP which was not necessary for party activities; the party newspaper, *Ulus*, was taken over by the state. In 1954 the Democrat government turned its attention to bureaucrats and judges; laws were passed putting them under closer control and some were retired. Restrictions were placed on the press and on public meetings. To their critics it seemed that the Democrats had moved into the realms of more general repression and were intent upon silencing the opposition with a view to retaining power. The opponents of the Democrats were encouraged by the results of the 1957 election. Although the Democrats won a comfortable majority of the Assembly seats their total vote fell below 50 per cent. At the same time the resentment of the critics was increased by the electoral law which forbade coalitions and so helped to ensure a Democrat majority.

One major complaint against the Democrats was that they had departed from the secular principles of the Republic by making concessions to the Muslim leaders who had supported them. In fact the relaxation of the laws against Islamic teaching had begun in 1949 and the Democrats' additional concessions to religion were modest. In 1950 the ban on religious broadcasting was lifted and prayers in Arabic were permitted; in 1952 special secondary schools with some religious teaching were established and in 1956 religious teaching was allowed in middle schools. In 1957 religious schools were given official recognition. It was clear that there was much popular support for these government measures and they were paralleled by an increase in religious activity, notably mosque attendance, pilgrimage and the observation of the fast, and in religious publishing. Pilgrimages to Mecca, however, were stopped in 1956 as a means of economizing on foreign exchange, an indication of the small importance which the Democrat government attached to support of Islam. The Democrats also suppressed in 1952 the Tijānī order the rapid rise of which recalled the dangerous association of Ṣūfī orders and violent opposition which had been a feature of the Kurdish rising of 1925. Political parties based on religion remained illegal but the Nation Party, founded in 1954 under the leadership of Fevzi Çakmak and successively reincarnated as the Republican Nation Party and the Republican Peasants Nation Party, clearly hoped to appeal to the Muslim vote. It made little impact on the political scene. In hindsight it is evident that the Democrats' Islamic policy was no more than a minor gesture by a secular government towards a powerful sentiment; to those at the time who lived nearer to the shattering conflicts of the Atatürk period, the Democrats seemed like men playing with fire in a powder magazine. Readers in the last years of the twentieth century may have some sympathy with their fears.

The growing tension between the Democrats and their opponents came to a head in 1960. The Democrats' attempts to control the activities of the RPP, including the employment of the army in an endeavour to obstruct a speaking tour by the RPP leader, İsmet İnönü, and the threat of an investigation into the RPP's affairs, led to demonstrations by university students, a most unusual event in Turkey at that time. The army was called in to quell the disturbances. To the army its use in support of a civil power which it mistrusted, coming on top of a long period in which it had felt neglected by government and starved of the resources it required, was too much. On 3 May the CGS, General Cemâl Gürsel, demanded political reforms including the resignation of the President and when these demands were refused he resigned. On 27 May he led a virtually bloodless military coup claiming that the Democrats had flouted the constitution, used public power for private profit, involved the army in politics, repressed the people and divided the nation.

The 1960 coup was a surprising and, it may seem, unnecessary affair. Central to the business were the suspicions of the Democrats' intentions. It was feared that Menderes intended to call an election with the opposition paralysed and ensure a further period of office. In fact Menderes had no need to call an election for he had an ample majority and he had decided against doing so. Subsequent evidence of support for the Democrats suggests that it was unnecessary for them to manipulate the voting and that they would have won in a fair election. The RPP feared that Menderes intended to use the proposed investigation as a means of closing the party down and the army feared that Menderes intended a purge of officers sympathetic to the RPP. On top of all was the vague charge that the Democrats were undermining the foundations of Atatürkism. The evidence suggests that these fears were insubstantial and that they resulted in a coup indicates that the opponents of the Democrats had a short fuse. Indeed both the army and the RPP still retained in some degree the notion that they were the especial guardians of the Republic, the leading institutions and the rightful rulers; to them the Democrats still looked like upstarts but upstarts who seemed to be becoming fixtures.

The military leaders of the coup had no clear idea of what they might substitute for the Democrat government or what policy they might pursue. A National Unity Committee (NUC) was established which was dominated by junior officers and had an average age of only 42, and a cabinet of military officers and non-party experts was formed. Among the junior officers were men who wanted to retain power indefinitely and to push through radical reforms. A conflict developed between them and the senior officers which was won by the latter. On 13 November 1960 14 of the 37 members of the NUC were dismissed, most of them being sent into diplomatic exile. An Armed Forces Union of senior officers now possessed real power in Turkey and the generals were determined to move quickly back towards constitutional government and to withdraw the army from the corruptions of politics, allowing it to resume what they conceived to be its position as the ultimate guardian of republican principle.

The Turkish army's decision to return to barracks was a momentous one for it established a clear distinction between Turkey and most of the Arab states. In the Arab states the pattern was for power to pass to relatively junior officers who clung to power and established what were in practice if not in name military regimes. That in Turkey it was the senior officers who led the coup and who retained control of it and that they decided to withdraw from politics may be attributed to the circumstances that the Turkish army had developed from the Ottoman reforming tradition, that it possessed a structure, discipline and habit of obedience which other Middle Eastern armies did not possess and that it saw itself as both the predecessor and the creator of the republic. Further, the existence of the RPP provided the possibility of an alternative government in which the army might have confidence. In his small town or middling rural background the average Turkish officer was not very different from his Arab counterpart although his father was more likely to have been a public servant.

Before handing power back to the politicians the army and its supporters carried through some important measures. First was the demolition of the Democrat party. The party was abolished, its leaders imprisoned and brought to face a long drawn out state trial which was intended to serve as a lesson in political behaviour and republican principle. Two of the leading Democrats, including Menderes, were hanged, others were given long sentences and all were banned from political life. Second was a series of purges of institutions including the army and the universities. Third came a new constitution approved by a constituent assembly on 26 May 1961.

The new constitution was intended to safeguard against a recurrence of the phenomenon of the Democrat ascendancy by introducing a number of checks and balances. Atatürk had developed the Grand National Assembly as the single expression of the nation's will and, under the control of the party he commanded, it had proved a singularly efficient way of achieving rapid decision. The experience of the Democrats had shown, however, that any party in control of the GNA could do what it liked. The new checks and balances consisted of a detailed statement of individual rights, a constitutional court, a second chamber and guarantees of independence to the universities and the judiciary. The first parliament elected under the new constitution met on 25 October 1961. The NUC ceased to exist and its 22 surviving members became members of the Senate from which point they could maintain observation of the political process which they had set in motion. They also endeavoured to insure themselves against reprisals for their actions by a clause inserted in the constitution.

The results of the elections for the 1961 parliament were a disappointment to the army. The 1960 coup had been the work of yesterday's élite but its leaders had hoped that their accomplishment would receive popular endorsement through a vote for the Republican People's Party. The RPP did secure the largest number of seats in the Assembly but it did not achieve a majority and a new party, the Justice

Party (JP), ran it close and obtained a larger number of seats in the Senate. The balance was held by two small parties. It was plain that the Justice Party was in many ways the reincarnation of the banned Democrat party with a similar programme and enjoying support from the same areas. So ominous was the success of the JP that several senior officers wanted to set aside the elections but others, supported by İsmet İnönü, argued that the elections should stand and their views prevailed. Gürsel was elected president for seven years and a government formed consisting of a grand coalition between the RPP and a reluctant JP. The RPP dominated the new government.

The story of the years 1961 to 1965 is of the victory of democracy and of the consequent gradual transfer of power to the JP, the successor to the Democrats in popular favour. The result was achieved through the restraint exercised by army and JP and especially through the political skill of İsmet İnönü, the leader of the RPP. The prestige of the aged İnönü as one of the heroes of the nationalist resistance in 1919–22 and the prime minister and chosen successor of Atatürk was employed to persuade the army to permit the gradual transition, in particular to grant the JP's demand for the release of the imprisoned DP leaders in 1964. In 1969 their political rights were also restored. İnönü subordinated other goals to the task of rebuilding a consensus which would enable the politicians to work the new political system; his successive governments between 1961 and 1965 introduced no significant reforms. The coalition with the JP quickly broke down; from June 1962 until December 1963 the RPP governed in coalition with the two minor parties; and from December 1963 until February 1965 the RPP formed virtually a minority government. In February 1965 the transition was made to a JP dominated coalition from which the RPP was excluded. At the elections of October 1965 the JP obtained a majority of the vote and of the seats; the RPP trailed with only 29 per cent of the vote. The JP formed a single party government with its leader, Süleyman Demirel as Prime Minister.

Like that of the DP, the programme of the JP was economic and political liberalization. Although the military government had established in 1960 a state planning organization and revived the concept of centralized economic planning the JP shared the DP's hostility to the notion and preferred to rely on foreign investment in manufacturing as the principal element in economic development. The results were impressive and it was in this period that industry began to overtake agriculture (favoured by the DP) as the main contributor to GNP. In October 1969 the JP again obtained a majority of the seats although its share of the vote slipped to 47 per cent. The RPP, however, slipped even further to 27 per cent and the smaller parties took a larger share of the votes although a new electoral system ensured that they were less favourably treated in terms of seats than they had been in 1965.

The JP's economic successes were not matched by its political stability. The JP was a coalition of different groups. Part of its support came from the prosperous peasantry of western Anatolia and part from commercial and industrial interests. It was this latter group, in particular, that Süleyman Demirel, an engineer elected leader of the party in 1964 at the age of 40, represented. Demirel never achieved within his party the ascendancy which Menderes had exercised over the factions which made up the DP. There was growing discontent from the agricultural interests and from some small businessmen with a policy which they saw as favouring big business. Further, there were personal rivalries within the party. In February 1970 the party split and Demirel was left at the head of a weak, minority government which was unable to confront the growing political violence in Turkey.

The 1960s had seen the rise of new actors on the Turkish political stage, namely an extreme left and a radical nationalist and religious right. Neither wing represented new sentiments, of course; both had been present in various forms since the earliest days of the nationalist resistance. What was new was the organized and violent manner in which they pursued their ends. In their new forms they were a product of the economic development of the period since 1960, of the process of urbanization, of the expansion of education, in particular of the considerable growth of universities during the 1960s, and of the growth of anti-Western sentiment, especially after the failure of the United States to support Turkey over Cyprus in 1964.

One factor in the growth of the left was the development of the trade union movement. Although there had been some relaxation of the strict controls over trade union activity after the Second World War and trade unions were legalized in 1947, trade unions had remained under strict government control and were kept out of politics. In 1963 trade unions were given the right to strike. Thereafter, there was a rapid development of trade unionism among industrial workers; by 1989 about half of non-agricultural workers were members of a trade union. The conservative trade union confederation, Türk Iş (established 1952), which carefully avoided becoming involved in politics and refused to establish links with the RPP, remained the largest organization but other more radical labour organizations, notably DISK (founded 1967), began to adopt a more political stance. The 1960s also saw the emergence of a political party claiming to represent the interests of workers. This was the Turkish Workers Party (TWP), founded in 1961 and led from 1962 by a Marxist lawyer, Mehmet Ali Aybar. Its support was narrow, however, mainly from a minority of industrial workers in the big cities, a few intellectuals and some Kurds. The TWP obtained 3 per cent of the vote in 1965 and 1969. The TWP and a number of even smaller leftist parties attracted some support from university students.

The development of the new nationalist right may be traced back to the radical officers of the 1960 coup. In 1962 and 1963 one officer, Colonel Talât Aydemir, formerly the commander of the Ankara War Academy but a man who had missed the 1960 coup, launched unsuccessful attempts at coups of his own and was hanged in 1964. Another officer, a former member of the NUC, Alparslan Türkeş, left the armed forces and entered politics by taking over the old Republican Peasants Nation Party, which was renamed the National Action Party (NAP) in 1963. The programme of the new party was a mixture of Islam and Turkish nationalism and was set out in the so-called nine lights, a collection of isms which recalled the arrows of Kemalism. Emphasis was placed upon modernization and above all on education. The organization of the party stressed the role of the leader, Türkeş, and a prominent feature was the development of a paramilitary section known as the Grey Wolves. In many ways the party was reminiscent of the fascist style parties of the Arab world of the 1930s. The party attracted a strong urban and student following and obtained 3 per cent of the vote in 1969.

The new parties of the left and right were at the centre of the urban violence which became a feature of Turkish life from the late 1960s and which disrupted universities. The weak JP government seemed unable to take effective action to quell the unrest and on 27 March 1970 the military leaders represented on the National Security Council (established 1962) delivered a warning. The unrest worsened in 1970 and 1971 and there were attacks on the armed forces themselves. An alarming feature was the appearance of armed revolt in Kurdistan. The senior officers began to fear that the divisions within Turkish society would spread to the army itself as they had threatened to do in 1960.

On 12 March 1971 the army, led by the CGS, General Memduh Tağmaç, took action, forced the Demirel government to resign and installed a new government composed of conservative politicians and technocrats with instructions to restore law and order. For the next two years Turkey was ruled by governments of this character during which time martial law was established in some provinces, the TWP was closed, the constitution amended to limit freedoms and the security forces encouraged to hunt down those who disturbed the peace. There was no sweeping political reorganization such as had occurred in 1960–1, however; the constitution, parliament and the main political parties remained in being.

The second period of military-dominated government in Turkey came to an end in 1973. The occasion was a trial of strength between the army and the politicians over the election of a new president. Gürsel had died in 1966 and been succeeded as CGS by General Cevdet Sunay, whose position as president had been an important factor in facilitating the execution of the army's will in 1971. When Sunay's term expired the army wanted him to be succeeded by the existing CGS but the assembly chose instead a retired admiral, Fahri Korutürk. A new government which included the JP was formed to prepare for elections. The army, led by the new CGS, General Semih Sancar, who was opposed to army involvement in politics, withdrew to barracks once more. Its intervention proved to have done little more than provide a breathing space; although order had been to some extent restored there was no fundamental alteration in the political situation which had produced the military intervention of 1971. The army had been too quick to act and too quick to go.

Between 1973 and 1980 the politicians and the army wrestled with the consequences of their failure to deal with the problems of 1970–1. During these years there were a succession of weak governments, the consequence of the factionalization of the main parties and their dependence upon minor parties which were unwilling to permit effective action against urban violence. The violence of left and right steadily increased and in the eastern provinces Kurdish separatists launched a guerrilla movement. The toll of deaths from political violence rose year by year from 34 in 1975 to 1250 in the first seven months of 1980.

A novel feature of the 1970s was the emergence of a religious party. Although the constitution banned either class or religious parties the National Salvation Party (NSP) was as Islamic as the TWP had been Marxist. Islam had come into greater prominence during the more open political atmosphere of the 1960s. The Nurist movement, founded by Saidi Nursi (1873–1960), which had developed during the 1950s among the small town dwellers of western Anatolia, demonstrated the extent of support for the restoration of Islamic values in social and political life and of opposition to the secularist style of Turkish politics. The NAP had appealed to Islamic sentiment. The Islamic movement cut into the support for the JP which was obliged to make concessions to appease its Islamic faction. In 1970, however, the Islamists led by Necmettin Erbakan, a former university teacher, organized the National Order Party. The party was closed down in 1971 but quickly re-emerged as the NSP. The effect of the growth of the NAP and the NSP, combined with factional disputes, was to break up the JP coalition and to divide the right wing vote (a majority at every election) among several parties and thereby prevent the emergence of a strong, single party government which could deal with the economic and political problems which confronted Turkey during the 1970s.

The fragmentation of the conservative vote allowed the RPP to emerge as the strongest party at the 1973 election although it did not command a majority in the Assembly. The RPP secured 33 per cent of the vote and the JP 30 per cent. The NSP came third with 12 per cent of the vote, an unprecedented score for a minor party. In all the minor parties obtained more than a quarter of the seats in the Assembly.

The RPP was itself a different party with a new leader. The old RPP was a coalition of conservative landowners from eastern Anatolia and urban intellectuals, with a strong following in the public services and among urban workers and a radical programme. The tensions between the two wings of the party had first become apparent during the minority governments led by Inönü in 1961–5 and the radicals had criticized Inönü for his failure to carry through reforms. Bülent Ecevit, who, as minister of labour in 1963 had given unions the right to strike, had emerged as leader of the radical faction and was elected secretary general in 1966. Inönü resisted the demands for more radical policies and tried to hold a balance between the conservative and radical wings of his party. But he was unable to prevent a drift to the left, a breakaway of conservatives to form the Reliance Party and the alienation of eastern Anatolian landowners by the adoption of a land reform programme. The dispute finally came to a head in 1972 when Ecevit defeated Inönü (who died the following year) and assumed the leadership of the party. Ecevit, a journalist by profession, was 47 when he replaced the 90 year old Inönü. The change in the RPP was generational as well as ideological and completed a process which had produced as leaders of the four principal political parties men all born in the mid-1920s. The new RPP programme was social democratic although it eschewed appeals to class loyalties.

In January 1974 an RPP/NSP coalition government was formed. In domestic affairs its most notable accomplishment was the passage of a land reform act. There had been attempts at land reform between 1945 and 1960 as a result of which about 1.7 million hectares of arable land

and 1.5 million hectares of pasture were redistributed, but there were continued complaints of unequal distribution and exploitation particularly from the Kurdish areas in the east. It was calculated that in 1960 15 per cent of landowners owned half the land and the biggest estates were in the east. The RPP included in its ranks a number of radicals who were Kurds. Under a plan of land reform introduced by the last of the non-party governments in 1973 it was proposed to redistribute 3.2 million hectares (three-quarters state land and the remainder taken from private landlords) to 500,000 peasants over a period of 15 years. In 1974 the Ecevit government proposed to establish new ceilings on land holding, reducing the former ceilings of 500 hectares of irrigated land and 1,000 hectares of dry land to 100 and 200 hectares respectively. In the event implementation was very slow and in 1977 the law was annulled by the constitutional court. It could be argued that little was lost by the failure of land reform. In the region of prosperous western Anatolia and the Black Sea coast, where commercial agriculture prevailed, a land reform designed to create small peasant proprietors was an irrelevency. In eastern Anatolia the situation resembled that of Ireland in the nineteenth century where land reform failed to check what was essentially a political movement. Land reform was unlikely to satisfy the demands of Kurdish nationalists.

The principal matter with which the RPP-dominated government had to deal was in foreign affairs, namely the Cyprus question and Ecevit's successful invasion of Cyprus brought him great popularity. Hoping to exploit his popularity he resigned in September 1974 expecting to precipitate a general election at which the RPP might improve its position. Ecevit had miscalculated: there was no general election, instead there followed a non-party government which in 1975 was succeeded by a quarrelsome right wing coalition led by Demirel. When the elections finally took place in June 1977 the RPP increased its share of the vote to 41 per cent against the 37 per cent of the JP. The rest of the right wing vote went to the NSP which obtained 9 per cent and the NAP which received 6 per cent. Although the RPP held the largest number of seats it did not command an absolute majority and Ecevit could not form a government against the combined opposition of the right wing parties. It was Demirel who eventually formed a right wing coalition government in July 1977.

From 1977 until 1980 there was a succession of weak governments. Demirel's government was replaced by an Ecevit-led coalition in January 1978 which in turn gave way to a minority JP government in October 1979. None proved capable of dealing with the increasing violence of left and right, Kurd and Turk and Sunnī and Shīʿī. Ecevit took measures against the right but when he attempted to deal with terrorism of the left by re-introducing special courts there were defections from his party. The rightists were willing to support action against the left and the Kurds but refused to tolerate effective action against the right. In the same period the economic problems of Turkey became more difficult. Turkey was badly hit by the oil price rise of the 1970s both because of the increased price she was obliged to pay for her oil and because of the fall in remittances from Turkish workers abroad consequent upon the slowdown of economic activity in Europe. The persistent gap in Turkey's trade account widened and she was compelled to seek additional foreign credits to balance her payments. The IMF eventually demanded some domestic economic restraint as the price of assistance but no Turkish government felt strong enough to face the consequences of checking the sustained Turkish economic boom. Meanwhile, inflation increased to 50 per cent in 1978. A coalition of JP and RPP might have had the strength to tackle the security problem and the growing economic difficulties but Demirel and Ecevit could not agree on such a move. It is a curious circumstance that four out of five Turks voted fairly consistently for two moderate parties of the centre left and the centre right but were unable to secure a stable government. Rather it was the remaining fifth which called the tune.

Once more it was the senior command of the armed forces which intervened under the leadership of the CGS, General Kenan Evren. On 12 September 1980 the leading politicians were arrested and on 18 September a five-man National Security Council took control. Martial law was established throughout Turkey, parliament was dissolved and a new civilian government under Bülent Ulusu installed. The military intervention had been caused primarily by the evident inability of the politicians or of the heavily politicized police force to deal with political violence in Turkey and in particular by the upsurge of guerrilla activity in Kurdistan and by the threat of Islam. The Iranian revolution of 1979 had further encouraged the Islamists in Turkey and in August 1980 the NSP had called for the restoration of Sharīʿa law in Turkey, a fundamental challenge to a basic principle of the secular republic. Once again the army had felt obliged to act to safeguard Kemalism as well as the integrity of the republic.

The first priority of the new government was to restore law and order and the following months saw a major security operation designed to eradicate terrorism. It was accompanied by armed clashes, arrests, imprisonment, torture and executions. During 1981 the level of political violence through most of Turkey was greatly reduced although disturbances continued in the Kurdish regions. A second aim was to restore economic stability and a programme of austerity was introduced which led to an actual fall in GNP; this programme, however, was not sustained. The third objective was to restore parliamentary government but before this was done the army decided to introduce a new constitution in another attempt to improve the political situation by changing the rules. In the meantime Turkey was governed under a provisional constitution (October 1980) which left unlimited power to the military commanders. In 1981 all the old politicians were banned from political activity and all political parties were disbanded. The soldiers were determined to start with a clean slate.

The new constitution was approved by referendum on 7 November 1982. Its central feature was a strong president who appointed the prime minister and the senior judges and could dismiss parliament and declare a state of emergency. The CGS, Kenan Evren, became president for seven years. Behind him was a presidential council of senior generals. The 1960 experiment with a second chamber was abandoned and Turkey reverted to a single chamber system. There were also close controls over trade unions, the press, and political parties. To prevent small parties dominating the political scene it was decreed that no party should obtain representation with less than 10 per cent of the vote.

The first election held under the new constitution in November 1983 was as disappointing to the military as that of 1961 had been. The army had hoped that two semi-official parties would harvest the greatest number of votes. The old parties (and most of the old politicians) had been banned and attempts to resurrect them under new names were foiled by the government. Victory, however, went to a quite new party, the Motherland Party (MP), a heterogeneous coalition of liberal and Islamic groups led by Turgut Özal, which obtained 211 seats out of the 400 at stake and formed a government in December 1983. The victory of the MP may be attributed partly to the reputation of its leader as an economic wizard, partly to the MP's appeal to diverse groups and partly to the persistent hostility of Turks to military efforts to prescribe what was good for them. The legacy of Atatürk was a difficult one.

The MP and Özal dominated Turkish political life for the next six years, winning a second election in November 1987 with 36 per cent of the vote and 292 out of 450 seats. Economically its policy represented a sharp change from that of previous governments: it mounted an attack on the powerful state sector, cut taxes and encouraged private industry and tourism. The government also exploited the economic opportunities created by the Gulf War, considerably increasing its trade with Iran and Iraq. The policy produced favourable results: austerity was relaxed, trade boomed and growth was resumed. But the older problems persisted, a large trade gap and inflation which reached 75 per cent a year in 1989. Politically, the new government continued the repression of political violence while seeking to restore greater political freedom. In the campaign against urban violence it was relatively successful. Strong security measures, including arrests, trials, imprisonment and alleged torture, crushed opposition but attracted widespread obloquy from liberal critics outside Turkey. The government also continued the struggle against armed guerrillas in Kurdistan where the task of restoring order was made more difficult by the effects of the Gulf War.

The lifting of the ban on the old politicians in 1987 allowed Demirel, Ecevit, Erbakan and Türkeş to resume their activities. Their parties also reappeared under new names. The Social Democratic Populist Party (SDPP), led by Erdal İnönü, son of İsmet, was substantially the old RPP; and the True Path Party (TPP), led by Demirel, was the former JP. These two parties became the principal opposition groups within the Assembly. The Welfare Party of Erbakan was the old NSP, and in all but name – the 1982 constitution retained the former ban on religious and class parties – was Islamic and sought the creation of an Islamic state. The National Work Party of Türkeş was the former NAP. In 1987 the SDPP took 25 per cent of the vote and the TPP 19 per cent; the other parties failed to cross the 10 per cent threshhold. The revival of these older parties began to squeeze the MP which was the scene of a constant struggle for mastery betwen its liberal secular and religious wings; in 1988 the religious group seemed to have triumphed and in 1989 the secularists. Özal's personality still dominated the party but he came under increasing criticism for his reliance upon his family and friends. At the 1989 local elections the MP suffered a crushing defeat when both the SDPP and the TPP won more votes; Özal changed most of his cabinet, sacrificing his brother and nephew, and some Islamist ministers. On 31 October 1989 he was elected president in succession to Evren. By 1989 it seemed that the pattern of Turkish political life which had prevailed from 1950 to 1980 was beginning to reassert itself.

In conclusion it will be appropriate to review, elaborate and evaluate some of the changes in Turkish social, economic and political life which were partly adumbrated in the introduction to this section. Socially, Turks were more urban, more educated, more mobile and more aware in 1989 than in 1950. Urbanization was linked to the decline of the extended family. In broad terms twice the proportion of Turks were in educational establishments in 1989 compared with 1960, although only about 50 per cent completed primary education. The growth of women's education was especially remarkable: in 1950 about one in five women was literate; in 1980 more than half were in that category. Turks travelled regularly between village and city and from 1962 an increasing number went abroad to work; by the 1970s around 500,000 were abroad, mainly in West Germany. Turks also read more – after 1945 publication expanded rapidly and by 1975 more than 7,000 titles were published each year. They listened to radio, went to the cinema (where half preferred foreign films) and from 1972 watched television. It may be easiest to indicate the extent of social change by considering a single village, Susurluk, situated in north west Anatolia. In the 1930s Susurluk was a typical Turkish peasant community, recruited in large part from Balkan immigrants. Its population of 4,000 lived by subsistence agriculture, less than one in five of the men was literate and virtually no women, and its contacts with the outside world were minimal. Susurluk was a beneficiary of the Democrat reforms of the 1950s when a new road gave it access to Istanbul and Izmir and a sugar refinery provided industrial employment. A study conducted in 1969 showed that over 90 per cent of the inhabitants had visited Istanbul and three-quarters had been to Ankara, that 80 per cent of the males were literate and nearly all of them read a daily newspaper, that many had gone away to work and most were dissatisfied with their lives and anxious to better themselves. Nearly half of the family budget still went on food but the proportion was steadily dropping.

The study of Susurluk also revealed the persistence of Islamic values and of Muslim observance. A feature of Turkish development was the apparent revival of Islam after 1950. Examples of this process have been given; one might add that from the 1960s there was a growth of trade and artisan associations with a religious character and after 1975 a remarkable expansion of religious schools. What seems clear is that this phenomenon was the consequence of the drawing of villages like Susurluk and their inhabitants into the national life through modernization and the greater freedom given them to express their demands; it was not that they had become more Muslim but that they demanded that their religious beliefs should be accommodated. In Susurluk they were content with the accommodation they received through the DP and the JP; elsewhere religious sentiment was expressed through a religious party. Islam was never identified with a single party; different sects variously supported the NSP, MP and DP/JP/TPP. The main support of the NSP was drawn from eastern and central Anatolia, that is to say from the least advanced regions of the country, and from the big cities, presumably from recent migrants from the poorer regions, although the most notable centre of NSP activities was the ancient city of Konya with its powerful religious traditions. It may be that the impact of modernization in these areas was sharper because of the absence of the longer acclimatization which western Anatolia experienced from the nineteenth century or it may be that the secular RPP found it more difficult to accommodate Muslim sentiment than did the DP, JP and MP.

It has been remarked earlier that Turkey became economically more prosperous and more industrial. Yet, rapid as it was, economic growth failed to keep up with the growth of the population; unemployment increased steadily throughout the period after 1950. It reached 1 million in 1962, 1.6 million in 1972 and 3.2 million in 1977. In 1989 more than 15 per cent of the work force was unemployed. Although these figures are effectively inflated by the growth of the urban population they indicate the extent of the pressure on the Turkish economic system (and on the political system) to provide jobs for the growing population and the constraints on economic and political action imposed by demography. In 1963 Turkey conceived the ambition to join the EEC and by various subsequent agreements promised to adapt her economic structure to that of the Community. Throughout the subsequent years she maintained her ambition and in 1987 submitted a formal application to join but was unable to make the necessary adaptations for to do so would have meant to relinquish the imperative of economic growth.

Politically, Turkey maintained the ideal and for the most part the practice of parliamentary democracy throughout the period from 1950 to 1989. She did so within limits designed to repress the extreme left, religious radicalism, ethnic parties and any who were thought to intend to abolish choice. In particular limits were placed on political violence. Turkey's success owed much to three institutions which traced their history to the Ottoman period: the bureaucracy, the army and parliament. Before 1950 the Turkish bureaucracy had been dominated by the Ottoman tradition, either through men who had been brought up in it or through their sons. As late as 1964 half of senior officials were the sons of bureaucratic and military families. The subsequent expansion of the bureaucracy and the retirement of the older officials meant that the Turkish bureaucracy became one produced by the Turkish republic but it maintained an expertise which enabled government to be carried on when the political system was in abeyance or working inefficiently. During the 1970s sections of the bureaucracy became politicized but these were purged in the 1980s and the administrative system survived as a professional apparatus; red tape helped to carry it through.

The army intervened thrice during the period and threatened to do so on other occasions. It has been remarked that unlike military interventions in most other regions of the Near East the Turkish military interventions were conducted by the military leaders and were intended to protect the principles of the republic which included the sovereignty of parliament. They were also intended to protect the army itself: in 1960 and at other times there were divisions within the army between radicals who believed the army should participate in the government of Turkey and those who saw its role as that of ultimate guardian of the state. In 1960 these divisions separated a number of junior officers from the army leaders but in the 1970s some leaders also held the radical view. The army was itself in danger of becoming politicized and the timing and scale of its interventions may be seen as compromises between radicals and conservatives. As Evren remarked in 1980: "we had to implement this operation within a chain of command and orders to save the army from politics and to cleanse it from political dirt". [1] Pressure on the army was increased by the politicization of other security institutions, notably the police, in the 1970s and one object of intervention was to create a stronger civilian security system which would lessen the need for army interventions. In particular, a secret police force was created.

The third institution was parliament. It has been noted that 1950 marked the beginning of a new era in the composition of parliament; the number of deputies with an official or military background fell and the proportion of those with a professional or business background rose to account for three-quarters of all deputies by 1977. It is interesting to observe that the parliaments of the 1980s, although they contained many new faces, were in social composition, age, education, etc., very similar to other parliaments since 1950. A second feature was the end of single party domination. During the decade of the 1950s the Democrats promised to replace the RPP as the single governing party but this prospect, if it ever existed, was ended by the 1960 military intevention. In the following years Turkey developed a system in which up to 80 per cent of the vote went to a centre left and a centre right party, leaving the remainder to be divided among a number of nationalist and religious parties with a much smaller number going to the extreme left. One problem which the Turkish political system failed to solve was whether this radical vote could be absorbed by the main parties or whether it should be repressed. It was clear, however, that the Ottoman character of the parliaments and parties of the early Turkish republic had gone.

The three outstanding features of Turkish political history in the period after 1950 were the establishment and maintenance of a system of limited parliamentary democracy, the de-Ottomanization of the three main institutions of parliament, the army and the bureaucracy, and the sustained effort to cope with the social and economic consequences of the increase of population and its redistribution. Turkish political history from 1950 is the story of the attempts of the political system to accommodate the great numbers of the newly politicized. Its successes seem much more remarkable than its failures.

NOTE

1. *12 September in Turkey: Before and After*, Ankara 1982, 302.

CHAPTER THIRTEEN

Iran since 1960

Between 1960 and 1979 Iran was transformed. The growth of population accelerated. Between 1920 and 1960 the population doubled to 23 million; by 1979 a further cohort equivalent to the entire population of 1920 had been added. Most of the increase in population went into towns and into industry or services. It has been calculated that 3.7 million people left villages for towns between 1956 and 1976 compared to virtually none before 1934 and under three-quarters of a million between 1934 and 1956. In 1960 about one-third of the population lived in towns; in 1979 very nearly half were urban. The number of inhabitants of Tehran grew most rapidly of all from nearly 2 million in 1960 to 4.5 million in 1976, a number which represented 30 per cent of the urban population and 13 per cent of the total population of Iran, compared with only 2 per cent in 1920. No other town had more than 700,000 people in 1976. Tehran was the centre of government, higher education and industry; it contained two-thirds of all university students, nearly one-third of high school students and nearly one-third of all literates; about half of all factories were in or around Tehran.

By 1979 25 per cent of the male working population was in manufacturing industry (up from 15 per cent in 1960) and the proportion of those in agriculture had fallen from a half to one-third. During the period industry surpassed agriculture in its contribution to GNP; in 1960 the share of agriculture was three times as large as that of industry; in 1976 it supplied only 9 per cent of GNP compared with 16 per cent for industry. Between 1965 and 1975 coal and cement output each trebled and the production of iron ore rose from 2,000 tons to 900,000 tons. It was in this period that a new iron and steel complex was constructed at Isfahan. Communications also developed – ports, railways and especially roads, of which more than 20,000 kilometres were constructed.

Social life underwent major changes. The numbers in school more than doubled between 1963 and 1977 and with the establishment of 12 new institutions the number in higher education rose from 25,000 to 154,000 with about 80,000 studying abroad. Literacy also doubled from less than 20 per cent in 1960 to around 40 per cent in 1979. Health care improved, especially in the towns: the number of hospital beds doubled, the number of doctors trebled and infant mortality was halved. Entertainment also expanded: during the period the number of radios doubled and that of televisions increased to 1.7 million.

No country in the Near East, outside Arabia, was changed more in these years than was Iran; over the whole period the average rate of economic growth was of the order of 12 per cent per annum. It is true that at the end of the period Iran was behind Israel, Turkey, Egypt and other countries in several indicators, notably the numbers in higher education, but Iran had started from a much lower baseline and compressed her growth into a much shorter period.

The money to pay for the economic growth and the additional services came from oil. In 1960 Iran received 285 million dollars from oil, itself a sum nearly equal in size if not in value to the total revenues from oil before 1950. By 1970 Iran was receiving 1 billion dollars a year and in 1976 as a consequence of the great rise in oil prices which took place during the early 1970s oil revenues reached 20 billion dollars. In 1977–8 38 per cent of Iran's GNP, 77 per cent of national revenue and 87 per cent of her foreign exchange came from oil. As a result, under successive seven year plans, the state took the lead in investment. About half of total investment came from the state, channelled through state banks, the remainder coming from other domestic sources and from foreign loans. The state loomed large in the economy. Apart from security forces of some 400,000 (including 200,000 army, 100,000 airforce and 60,000 gendarmerie) and some 800,000 civil servants (including teachers) the state employed many people in state economic enterprises so that it is calculated that in 1977 about 10 per cent of all workers were in the state sector.

The state's role in this process of transformation was given the name "White Revolution" by Muḥammad Riżā Shāh. In its content and many of its effects the White Revolution was almost identical with the other great secular revolutions of the Near East which took place between 1950 and 1970 and which mark a watershed in the history of the modern Near East. It involved the transfer of the centre of gravity of Iran from agriculture to industry, from countryside to town, and from landowning notables to the state.

The White Revolution took shape between 1960 and 1963. By 1960 it seemed that the Pahlavī state was securely established on the basis of a working arrangement with conservative landowners who dominated the Majlis and conservative religious dignitaries who controlled the bazaar. The Shah, however, was dissatisfied with this situation; he wanted radical change, partly because of outside pressures, partly because of internal discontent and partly out of a desire to carry forward the process begun by his father of making Iran a powerful, independent state and thereby achieving his own special place in history.

In 1961, annoyed with the failure of his attempt to make a loyal two party system work and with the unwillingness of the Majlis to support reform, the Shah dismissed parliament and governed without it for two years. It was in this period that he also began the transformation of government. Previously, governments had been formed by notable politicians who were subservient to the Shah but who required the support of the Majlis. For nearly four years Manūchihr Iqbāl had been such a faithful prime minister. The Shah began to replace these semi-independent ministers with men who were no more than advisers. The last prime minister of the old school was Dr ᶜAlī Amīnī, a wealthy landowner with a reputation as a reformer. ᶜAlī Amīnī was too independent, however, and he was dismissed in 1962.

The Shah eventually found a suitable prime minister in Ḥasan ᶜAlī Manṣūr. Manṣūr was the son of a politician who had risen under Riżā Shāh and he brought with him into government a group of young, western-educated men who became the chief agents of the White Revolution. After the assassination of Manṣūr in January 1965 one of them, Amīr ᶜAbbās Huvaydā, a member of an old bureaucratic family and the brother-in-law of Manṣūr, became prime minister, retaining the post until 1976. Huvaydā was a man of great ability and charm but he never asserted himself against the Shah and was content to be the instrument of his civil policies. Another principal adviser of the Shah during these years was his boyhood friend, the former prime minister, Asadallāh ᶜAlam, who served as minister of court (in effect head of the Shah's personal staff); the Empress Faraḥ and the Shah's twin sister, Ashraf, also possessed considerable influence.

The Shah intervened personally in all matters of government, notably economic planning, approved all major appointments and kept direct control of defence and foreign affairs, by-passing his ministers and dealing directly with ambassadors and generals. Until his death in

1975 the Shah's brother-in-law, General Muḥammad Khātamī, the commander of the airforce, was a powerful instrument of the Shah's control of the armed services. The Shah took great care with the army: army officers were given considerable privileges but they were kept under close observation; no general could visit Tehran without the permission of the Shah and he dismissed them often without giving any reason. Internal security matters were also under the eye of the Shah. Separate security organizations were maintained partly in order to watch each other and the Shah ensured that men personally loyal to himself were in control: for example another boyhood friend, General Ḥusayn Fardūst, was in charge of the Imperial Inspectorate founded in 1958, and from 1965 until 1978 the secret police, Savak, was under another old friend, General Niᶜmatallāh Nāṣirī, the officer once chosen to present to Muṣaddiq his letter of dismissal. The Shah was protected by the Imperial Guard, an élite unit of 2,000.

No traditional organization of government had real power. The cabinet had little collective existence; ministers and the heads of agencies were more or less individually responsible to the Shah. The Majlis, when it resumed its career, had no control over government; the often extravagant debates which had been a feature of the 1950s were no more. The two party system functioned until 1975 when it was replaced by a single party, the Resurgence Party, which acted as a mass rally, rather like the Arab Socialist Union in Egypt. Huvaydā was secretary general of the new party and great pressure was put on men to join it; non-membership was an implied rejection of the White Revolution. By the end of 1976 the membership was claimed to be five million. The party had two wings, intended to promote debate within a liberal consensus.

By his changes in government the Shah had transformed an inefficient autocracy into an efficient dictatorship. There was no official censorship but there was strict control over the press and other publications; in 1975 the government closed down all publications with a circulation of less than 3,000 which meant that the great majority ceased to exist. Trade unions were under close supervision, usually exercised through Savak, and were confined to dealing with workers' affairs narrowly defined. The judiciary was under complete government dominion and increasing use was made of military and special administrative tribunals. Most feared of all the institutions of the new state was Savak which was virtually outside the law and interfered in many areas of life. Savak made secret arrests, tortured suspects and carried out executions and assassinations.

In all these features the Pahlavī regime was similar to other secular dictatorships in the Near East; in fact it was one of the milder and more benevolent of them and that is one reason why we know more about its workings than we do about others. The Pahlavī regime relied on coercion because it was an élite regime pushing a reluctant people in a direction in which the people did not wish to move but which the regime believed was necessary and desirable for the nation, namely towards what the Shah called the great civilization. The situation was precisely that described earlier by the famous Iranian poet, writer and liberal, Malik al-Shuaᶜrāᶜ Bahār. The government was liberal, he remarked, but the people were not. The Shah and his supporters were confident they knew best and believed that the opposition to their policies was dangerous and extremist and for an indefinite period must be kept under strict control.

The centrepiece of the White Revolution was land reform. Rather more than half the land surface of Iran is unusable mountain and desert. Of the remainder about 10 per cent is woodland, and 10 per cent arable of which more than half was left fallow each year principally for want of water. Of the less than 5 per cent of Iran's land cultivated in any year 40 per cent was irrigated. The cultivators lived in some 70,000 villages. Until the 1950s these villages were commonly protected by strong walls but with the decline of nomadism and greater security the walls were allowed to fall into disrepair. Houses were usually one room, mud brick structures built around a courtyard. Villages were surrounded by fields. Of the peasants about 5 per cent owned sufficient land to maintain themselves and the remainder were sharecroppers. Of the sharecroppers 60 per cent possessed cultivation rights (*nasaq*) and 40 per cent (mainly labourers) had no rights. The main crop was wheat.

The dominant figures in the countryside were the landowners. It is calculated that about half of Iran's cultivated land was held by big landowners, those who controlled one or more villages, a typical holding being between 20 and 40 villages. These landowners were absentees and included members of the royal family, military officers, tribal shaykhs, religious dignitaries and big merchants. Other categories of absentee landowners included small proprietors who owned part of a village and administrators of *waqf*. The absentee landlords employed agents or the village headman to look after their interests in the villages. The landowners shared the crop with the peasants according to who supplied the different inputs of land, water, seed, animals and labour.

Reformers had talked about land reform since the beginning of the twentieth century but nothing had been done; Riżā Shāh was uninterested and landowners were opposed. After his return to power in 1953 Muḥammad Rižā Shāh began to consider land reform seriously primarily as a means of reducing the social, economic and political power of the landowners whom he saw as a brake on progress and a threat to his power. He also began to hope that he could build a firmer base for his regime if he could win the support of a loyal class of peasant proprietors, a delusion which has inspired not only many revolutionaries but also British agrarian reformers in India and the Near East. But the Shah's early attempts at legislation were ineffectual; the modest 1960 land law, which finally struggled through the Majlis, depended for its implementation on a cadastral survey which had not been carried out and could not be accomplished for many years given the absence of machinery to do so. (The same lack of information means that most of the statistics and proportions cited in this section should be regarded as approximations only.)

A breakthrough came with the appointment of the Amīnī government in 1961 and the choice of Dr Ḥasan Arsānjānī, a proponent of land reform since the 1940s, as minister of agriculture. Arsānjānī adopted a simple solution to the problem of the absence of information: instead of providing for the customary ceilings on wet and dry landholding he worked on the basis of the village. The 1961 land law limited holdings to one village. Successive amendments to the law defined various procedures and limited its application in some respects but did not change the basic thrust of the measure and the process of land reform continued until 1971. Arsānjānī resigned in 1963 and the Shah thereafter took the leading role in the reform.

The effects of the Iranian land reform were dramatic. The big losers were the large landlords. Their power and influence in the countryside was extinguished; many took their compensation and invested in industry or services. Smaller absentee landlords survived and in 1971 they still owned half of all cultivated land. The benefits went to the *nasaq* peasants of whom there were about 2 million in 1960. By 1971 90 per cent of them had been transformed into peasant proprietors. Many of these, however, acquired holdings too small to support their families and were compelled to seek other employment to supplement their income. The agricultural labourers got nothing. A new class of commercial farmers appeared in the countryside especially as a consequence of the emphasis in the third stage of land reform in the late 1960s on what were called agri-businesses. The increase in production which had been expected did not materialize, however, and food production declined during the 1970s. This was a particularly disappointing result in view of the other inputs into agriculture: fertilizer production rose from 47,000 tons in 1963 to nearly 1 million in 1977, the number of tractors from 3,000 to 50,000, and irrigated lands grew by 240,000 hectares as a result of major projects (and declined by an unknown amount as the result of the decay of the traditional *qanāts* or underground channels).

The state was a major gainer from land reform because it replaced the big landlord as the dominant social, economic and political factor in the countryside. Peasants receiving land had been obliged to join co-operatives which became agencies of government control. The headman, who had formerly served both landlord and government was now exclusively a government agent; village councils and new rural courts were set up under government supervision. The nationalization of forests and pastures in 1963 also increased the presence of the state. Most important, however, was the invasion of the countryside by a host of new agencies set up under the White Revolution. But the regime failed in its object of securing the gratitude of the peasants; no mass of loyal peasants came to rescue the regime in 1978 and the countryside remained largely apolitical.

The creation of several new agencies was an integral part of the revolution; their purpose was to transform the countryside. Their functions were indicated by their titles: the literacy corps (1963), the health corps (1964), the reconstruction and development corps (1964) and the religious corps (1971). They were staffed by young graduates sent out from the cities to modernize rural areas. The religious corps consisted of graduates of secular universities, usually of faculties of theology, not of graduates of the *madrasas*, and they were termed 'mullās of modernization'. Both the literacy corps and the religious corps were seen as a direct challenge to the religious classes as they seemed to usurp the traditional functions of the ulema. In fact, before 1960 the penetration of formal Islam into the countryside was slight: only about 10 per cent of villages had *mullās* and these were often men of little learning. Itinerant religious figures had a reputation as tricksters. It was after land reform that the ulema made a greater effort to spread into the countryside and encountered competition from the propagandists of the secular revolution.

Other parts of the revolution were concerned with winning the support of the new class of industrial workers and of women. The original six principles of the White Revolution which were submitted to a referendum in 1963 included provision for the sale of state-owned factories and for profit-sharing in industry. In 1975 an ambitious plan for employee and public ownership through the transfer of shares to workers was announced. Votes for women was another of the original principles and women strengthened their legal position through the Family Protection Law of 1967 which increased their rights in divorce. A state-controlled women's organization was established. The remainder of the ultimate total of 17 principles of the White Revolution, as they were set out in stages between 1963 and 1975, were concerned with social reforms, governmental reform and urban development.

Opposition to the White Revolution and the Shah's regime proceeded from several sources. The most acute resistance was experienced in 1963 when landowners, tribal leaders and religious figures opposed the regime on several issues but most prominently on land reform. The National Front, crushed in the 1950s, revived in the early 1960s but was crushed again in 1963 and subsequently flourished mainly among exiles. Much the same applies to the Tūdah Party. Tribal opposition was experienced, especially among the Qashqā'īs who were the most inveterate tribal opponents of the Pahlavīs. Most serious was religious opposition because of the support the religious leaders enjoyed within the traditional bazaar. In the summer of 1963 there were major disturbances in Tehran which required heavy military interventions to subdue. Religious opposition was partly the consequence of the direct threat to the income of the ulema through land reform and its application to *waqf* lands but it had more complex origins which must now be considered.

Shīʿī Islam in Iran was a major institution. No accurate figures exist and estimates of its size vary, an indication of the decentralized character of Iranian Islam: a reasonable estimate is that in Iran during the 1960s there were about 100 *mujtahids*, 10,000 *mullās*, 80,000 other religious functionaries, 5,000 major mosques and perhaps another 15,000 minor ones, and 4 major seminaries, in all more than 100 *madrasas* with nearly 10,000 students. There were also innumerable shrines including the great shrine of the Imām Riżā at Mashhad which received 3.5 million pilgrims in 1976–7, representing a ten-fold increase over ten years. Apart from their income from *waqfs* and providing services the ulema received payments from the faithful in the form of the religious taxes known as *zakāt* and *khums*. It has been suggested that taxes paid to the ulema exceeded those paid to government. Just as in India it was the banyas who were most generous to the pious so it was in Iran that the traditional bazaar was the main source of the ulema's income. In return for these payments the ulema provided certain services, principally legal, educational, religious and what may be called articulatory – in effect expressing popular grievances to government. But by the 1960s many of their traditional legal and educational functions had gone as a consequence of the modernization of government under the Pahlavīs.

Modernization, its effect upon their role and its broader effects upon the society in which they lived, precipitated a major debate among the ulema of Iran. In particular it raised questions about their relationship with government which they perceived as the main agent of change and the principal challenger to their traditional role. Historically, in the attitude of the ulema to government there had been a gap between theory and practice. In theory government belonged to the Imāms, the last of whom had disappeared from view in the ninth century AD. Since then Shīʿī jurists had debated the question of who should exercise the powers of the Hidden Imām until he returned and a consensus had emerged that the *mujtahids* should take on most, if not all of his functions. A further debate had centred on the way in which the ulema should reach decisions, whether by reference only to the Qur'ān and the traditions of the Prophet and the Imāms or whether they could also use deductive reasoning. By the end of the eighteenth century those who upheld the use of deductive reasoning had triumphed and thereafter the true leaders of Shīʿī Islam were the great *mujtahids*. So much for the theory, which left little place for kings except as executors of the decisions of the *mujtahids*. In practice Shīʿī jurists recognized that kings held power and that anarchy was the likely consequence of their being deprived of it. Hence most Shīʿīs accepted secular authority providing the ruler made it possible for them to live according to the Sharīʿa. Most *mujtahids* tried to remain aloof from politics, some co-operated with government and only a few indulged in persistent opposition.

A *mujtahid* became a *mujtahid* by being recognized as one who was worthy in intelligence, learning, justice, faith and maturity to exercise *ijtihād* or interpretation. He underwent a long period of training, usually between 15 and 35 years, obtaining certificates from several *mujtahids*, before, as it were, inviting business and collecting his own followers. From this point in his career two attributes were especially important: family connections and good health. It is no accident that the great majority of *mujtahids* came from families of *mujtahids* and those families were in turn linked by marriage alliances. There was a powerful *mujtahid* aristocracy and it was difficult for an outsider to break in except through patronage often sealed by marriage. Good health was important because progress from graduation to the rank of Āyatallāh was partly a matter of survival. The emphasis on maturity ensured that the reputation of the oldest continued to rise and as their seniors and contemporaries died so they eventually reached the highest rank, often at more than 80 years of age. The standing of a *mujtahid* depended upon his reputation but during the nineteenth and twentieth centuries titles came into use, in particular those of Ḥujjat al-Islām (the proof of Islam) and Āyatallāh (the sign of God). One title, however, came to be reserved only for the most distinguished *mujtahids*: this was marjaᶜ al-taqlīd (the model for emulation).

The last *mujtahid* who won such distinction as to acquire the title of model for emulation was Āyatallāh Muḥammad Ḥusayn Burūjirdī, the leading Shīᶜī jurist at Qum from 1947 to 1961. As remarked earlier, Burūjirdī stayed on good terms with the regime, supporting its conduct in some matters and opposing it on others, notably on the question of land reform immediately prior to his death in 1961. At the time of Burūjirdī's death no other *mujtahid* was thought worthy to exercise the same authority although there were several prominent contenders. Āyatallāh Rūḥallāh Mūsavī Khumaynī (Khomeini) was not among these but it was he who asserted leadership of the anti-government movement in 1963 and acquired thereby a position of leadership among the radical ulema.

Khumaynī did not come from one of the great *mujtahid* families; his father was a trader but the son had formed marriage alliances including one with Burūjirdī himself. Nor was he renowned as a *mujtahid*; his speciality had been philosophy rather than *fiqh*, the usual choice of the jurist. But like Kāshānī ten years earlier he forced his way into prominence through politics. Whereas other *mujtahids* remained aloof from the anti-government campaign or kept to moderate opposition Khumaynī denounced the government for corruption, oppression, jeopardizing the independence of Iran, permitting the inroads of the West and sacrificing Islam. The troubles of Iran he depicted as part of a conspiracy against Islam by Jews, Bahā'īs and the USA. Khumaynī said little about the issues on which other religious critics fastened, namely land reform and women's rights, and focused on broader matters which attracted wider support in the bazaar. Certainly, the government saw Khumaynī as its principal religious opponent, imprisoned him and would probably have executed him but for the intervention of other *mujtahids*. In the end, after a further attack on the government for subservience to the USA, Khumaynī was exiled to Turkey in October 1964. In October 1965 Khumaynī moved to Najaf and it was in Iraq that he developed new political ideas, switching his emphasis from the conduct of government to its very nature, and elaborated his concept of Islamic government.

Khumaynī became a symbol around which several different elements in Shīᶜī radical thought rallied; some of them he incorporated in his own critique. One such was the emphasis on excessive westernization, or westoxication as it was called by the popularizer of the concept, Jalāl Āl-i Aḥmad. Another was the notion that Shīʿīs, and particularly the ulema, must involve themselves more directly in social and political action. This was especially the theme of Dr ʿAlī Sharīʿatī, who endeavoured to reconcile Shiʿism with Marxist sociology, and achieved a considerable reputation with a series of lectures delivered in Tehran. Sharīʿatī attacked the conservative ulema and recommended the model of activists and modernists like the nineteenth century reformer, Jamāl al-Dīn al-Afghānī. Sharīʿatī emphasized the duty to resist oppression and found a model in the conduct of the Imām Ḥusayn at Karbalā. Islam was the religion of protest and the oppressed, he argued.

In 1971 some young men began an armed revolt against the government. One group, the Mujāhidīn-i Khalq, which was established in 1966, drew primarily on the new modernist radical religious thinking and also on Marxism. Another group, the Fidā'iyān-i Khalq, was decidedly secular and was a breakaway movement from the Tūdah party formed in 1963. Together with some smaller factions the two groups conducted a campaign of assassinations and attacks on government property. Most of their members were university or *madrasa* students from poor backgrounds. They had small success and suffered heavily in the campaign against them conducted by the security services.

Influential as they were the radicals remained a minority and the success of Shīʿī protest depended on the support of a substantial group of the *mujtahids* for a stand against the government. The policies of the regime during the 1970s and especially during the period 1975 to 1977 helped to accomplish this end. Moderate religious leaders objected to the activities of the literacy and religious corps; to the claims of the new Resurgence party to be the mobilizer of popular opinion in support of the regime; to the government's increasing control over ulema incomes through the ministry of waqfs; to the substitution for the Islamic calendar of a new calendar which commenced from a date in the early history of pre-Islamic Iran and to the cult of monarchy; and to the arrest, exile, and even murder of ulema who spoke out against government policies. Above all, they complained of the corruption, luxury and injustice which appeared to characterize the regime. Further, the *mujtahids* were forced into opposition by the complaints of their principal clients, the traders of the bazaar who objected to the government's attack on profiteering and efforts at price control, actions which were perceived as an attempt to make the bazaar pay for the government's errors in pushing ahead with too rapid economic development after 1973.

In 1976 Iran's boom came to a sudden end. Carried away by the enchanting visions raised by the torrent of oil revenues which began in 1973 the government raised all its targets and embarked on a spending spree which ended in a flood of goods which neither the ports, roads nor the economy of Iran could handle. Three years of feverish activity concluded with an economy drive which brought growth to a halt and led to widespread unemployment. The consequent disappointment of those whose expectations had been raised and the bitterness of those who had paid the price of boom in inflation without adequate return were further important causes of the unrest which followed.

Protest began among middle class intellectuals in May 1977. The government did not immediately stifle criticism with the consequence that criticism and demands for greater freedom increased. The Shah made concessions; Huvaydā, who was worn out by his long spell in office, was replaced as prime minister. In November 1977 opposition took a new form – street demonstrations by university students. So far the religious classes had not been involved but in January 1988 there were riots at Qum following an attack on Khumaynī in a government-controlled newspaper. Thereafter a cycle of rioting developed: 40 days after each riot and its suppression, following the end of the period of mourning for those who were killed, new demonstrations or riots took place. The riots grew in intensity and spread to engulf more towns. The government's response was to mix conciliation and repression. In August a new prime minister was installed to conciliate the religious critics; the Islamic calendar was reinstated, gambling casinos and night clubs were closed and the hated Resurgence Party was abolished. On the other hand, on 7 September, following a massive demonstration in Tehran the government introduced martial law and troops killed a large number of demonstrators on the following day. In October 1978 the campaign took on a new dimension with a wave of strikes which brought much of industry, particularly oil production, to a halt. In November the Shah appointed a military government but abandoned the policy of suppression after the greatest demonstrations of all in Tehran in December 1978, coinciding with the month of Muḥarram in which the martyrdom of Ḥusayn at Karbalā is commemorated. Government now began to break down and there were mutinies in some army units. The Shah made a last desperate effort at conciliation, this time of his secular middle class critics, by appointing a member of the National Front, Shāpūr Bakhtiyār, as prime minister. Bakhtiyār demanded that the Shah should leave Iran which he did on 16 January 1979. But Bakhtiyār himself survived less than a month longer. On 1 February Khumaynī returned to Iran from Paris, whither he had gone when he was expelled from Iraq in October 1978 and whence he conducted a skilful campaign against the regime, and on 11 February Bakhtiyār fled.

The Islamic revolution of 1978–9 in Iran was unique among Near Eastern revolutions. A powerful regime was brought to its knees by street demonstrations. Before 1978 most observers assumed that the only real threat to the regime came from its own security forces but these remained loyal almost to the end. Bakhtiyār dissolved Savak in January 1979 but the army remained substantially intact, despite the mutinies which had taken place in some units, until after the return of Khumaynī. The size and the persistence of the demonstrations, however, made the regime unwilling to use the army systematically and ruthlessly against them. One must inquire who participated in these demonstrations and why they were so persistent?

Massive street demonstrations began in Tehran in September 1978. Before that time opposition had come mainly from the middle class, represented on the streets especially by students, from the religious classes and from the traditional bazaar, in fact much the same groups which had been defeated by repression in the bloody conflict of June 1963. But from September 1978 the largest element in the street demonstrations was the new urban poor, that is the new immigrants, living in squatter areas and slums in south Tehran. Traditionally, the urban poor was apolitical, primarily concerned with housing, jobs and education and loath to take part in political activity or demonstrations. On the whole the most recent arrivals, living in squatter settlements, took little part in the events of 1978–9 despite their grievances over recent demolition of their dwellings. But those who lived in the slums, mainly the semi-skilled workers who had some education and including second generation immigrants, did become mobilized during the revolution. They were disturbed by inflation, high rents, unemployment and they were open to religious appeals. Islam was the principal attribute which they carried over from the village to the city and their Muslim values were offended by the evidence of luxury and injustice. Their Muslim associations became instruments of mobilization.

The Islamic revolution was an urban phenomenon. Although the upheaval in Tehran was by far the largest and most significant of the disturbances, riots and demonstrations took place in every town in Iran. In the countryside, however, except in those villages from which workers travelled to their urban employment, very little happened before 1979. The peasantry remained sturdily apolitical. The urban character of the revolution reflects both the influence of Islam and of modernization.

A key role in the revolution was played by the network of mosques and Muslim associations. It was through these that information and calls to action were relayed, tapes of Khumaynī's speeches played and action planned. Foreign radio broadcasts also assisted in the progress of the revolution. But neither the existence of combustible urban material nor of a potentially revolutionary organization could have availed without the leadership of Āyatallāh Khumaynī. From first Iraq and then Paris he dominated the revolution in 1978–9. No other *mujtahid*, however inclined to compromise, could stand against the appeal of Khumaynī to the Iranian people. Nor could the middle class leadership of the National Front; its leader, Karīm Sinjābī, accepted Khumaynī's leadership and denounced Bakhtiyār's attempt to turn the revolution to the advantage of the liberals. Throughout the period Khumaynī was unrelenting in his demand for the end of the Pahlavīs and of oppression, and the establishment of an Islamic republic and the rule of justice.

Finally, one must consider the role of the Shah and his supporters. Leaving aside the distraction of a foreign war, the response of most regimes to threatened revolution is either repression or conciliation or a mixture of both. Throughout, the Shah chose the last course; in 1977 he allowed the middle class some freedom, in 1978 he sought to repress the liberals and conciliate the moderate ulema, and in 1979 he returned to an attempt to conciliate the liberals. Towards the disorders in the streets his policy was uncertain; sometimes he left them alone in the hope that peaceful demonstrations would burn themselves out and violence would alienate support; at other times he tried to clear the streets. His wavering policy has been criticized and writers have adduced his failing health and his fear of human rights critics abroad as reasons for his failure to take more determined repressive action, and his stubborn determination to hold on to power as the cause of his failure to pursue conciliation more systematically. Given the size and character of the movement against his regime it is not easy to see what tactics might have succeeded; the fateful decision was made in 1973 when he chose an accelerated programme of modernization. As for his regime the most interesting feature is the way in which the Pahlavī institutions stood up for so long; it was after his departure that they collapsed.

THE ISLAMIC REPUBLIC

The fall of the last Pahlavī government was followed by a confused period during which the revolutionaries took control. In localities power was assumed by committees, usually based upon the mosque, which gave orders to the local institutions of government and endeavoured to enforce their will with the help of local militias. In factories power was taken by committees of workers. In Tehran there was a revolutionary council, formed in January 1979, of which the membership was undisclosed but which consisted of a number of laymen and clerics selected by Khumaynī on the advice of his advisers in Paris. On 5 February Khumaynī also nominated a provisional government with Mahdī Bāzargān as prime minister. Bāzargān chose a government of moderate, middle class professionals with only one cleric. Tension quickly developed between the government and the revolutionary council which was remodelled after Bāzargān and others left to form the government and which in its new form was more clerical, more radical and more powerful. Revolutionary tribunals sprang into being and were employed against Pahlavī supporters, particularly members of the security forces. In this period there were a number of executions of former military and civilian leaders, most notably of Amīr ᶜAbbās Huvaydā.

At the end of March 1979 a referendum gave overwhelming approval to an Islamic republic as the future form of government for Iran. There was, however, little agreement about what an Islamic republic was and this question remained to be answered in a new constitution. Leaving aside the views of the left wing secular radicals of the Tūdah Party and the ambitions of ethnic autonomists there were two main views about the constitution. On the one hand was the view of the Bāzargān government that an Islamic republic was basically an ordinary state conducted on Islamic principles and therefore a modified version of the 1906 Iranian constitution in which a strong president was substituted for the monarchy would suffice. On the other hand were the religious radicals who wanted a very different constitution in which real power was wielded by the ulema through new revolutionary Islamic institutions such as the revolutionary council and the revolutionary guards. Khumaynī himself seems to have had no clear view in the early part of 1979; his own inclination was to argue that very little government was needed as its only purpose was to implement the Sharīᶜa as interpreted by the *mujtahids*; and there was no need for parliament or parties. The decision was left to a constituent assembly, known as the Assembly of Experts which was dominated by the radical ulema led by Āyatallāh Muḥammad Ḥusaynī Bihishtī. In November 1979 the assembly produced a constitution for an Islamic state.

Although the constitution provided for the usual republican apparatus of president, cabinet and parliament it was very different from conventional constitutions. The government should strive for the political, cultural and economic unity of the Islamic world, ran the preamble; and government and army had a duty to "extend the sovereignty of God's law throughout the world". [1] All laws and regulations must be based on Islamic criteria, it was stated. And the constitution provided for three distinctively Islamic institutions: the revolutionary guards, a council of 12 guardians to examine and if necessary veto all legislation, and a supreme guide, the *vālī faqīh*, on whom was conferred the "vicegerency and leadership of the nation" and who controlled all important civil, military, judicial and religious appointments. Khumaynī was named as *vālī faqīh* for life. Effectively, the constitution gave him supreme power if he chose to exercise it.

One dominant political party had already come into existence. This was the Islamic Republican Party (IRP) founded in 1978. Its leaders were radical ulema, most of them former students of Khumaynī at Qum or men who had followed him since the 1960s. One of these men, Bihishtī, was the major figure in the party during its first two years, and was most influential in shaping the Islamic republic. Other parties succumbed to the IRP. The National Front withered away. The National Democratic Party, a basically secular group of middle class professionals was closed down in the summer of 1979. The Islamic People's Republican Party, led by Āyatullāh Sayyid Kāẓim Sharīʿatmadārī, which could be said to represent the moderate ulema and which had a strong following in Azerbaijan, was banned in December 1979. The Tūdah Party, living on the hope that eventually Islamic government would collapse and it would inherit power, gave its support to the regime but was eventually shut down in February 1983. Thereafter, the only party of consequence which functioned legally was Bāzargān's Iran Freedom Movement and that was severely constrained in its activities by threats of violence. The IRP dominated the Majlis following its victories at the elections of 1980 and 1984 but in 1987 it was dissolved by Khumaynī, being held to have fulfilled its purpose.

New revolutionary institutions were created from 1979 onwards and especially after the beginning of the war with Iraq in September 1980. They were often called foundations (*bunyād*) or crusades (*jihād*) and included the Foundation for the Disinherited (*mustażʿafīn*), the

Martyrs' Foundation, the Foundation for War Refugees, the Crusade for Reconstruction, the Organisation for Economic Mobilization (*basīj*), and the Centre for Commanding Good and Avoiding Evil. These institutions were in some ways similar to the corps created by Muḥammad Riżā Shāh; they enlisted supporters in pursuit of specific aims and acted as instruments of mass mobilization. They also became centres of wealth and power in their own right. The Foundation for the Disinherited acquired considerable property through the confiscation of the assets of former supporters of the regime and the Crusade for Reconstruction virtually supplanted the ordinary departments of government in war-ravaged areas of western Iran. During the war with Iraq the *basīj* organization exercised great power as a recruiting agency for the revolutionary forces. Unlike the Pahlavī corps the Islamic organizations appeared as rivals to the state system and as power bases for aspiring candidates for power. Like all other institutions, however, they were subject to the over-riding authority of Khumaynī.

The most important of all the new revolutionary institutions was the Revolutionary Guards (*pāsdārān*), founded in May 1979. In its origins the Pāsdārān was a militia created to provide the radical ulema with a force with which they could challenge the well-armed groups of the left, notably the Mujāhidīn, the Fidā'iyān and the Tūdah. The collapse of the Pahlavī army in February 1979 had scattered large quantities of arms throughout the population and many weapons had fallen into the hands of the radicals of the left. At first Pāsdārān recruits were found through the local committees; subsequently the guards absorbed the personal bodyguards of religious leaders. The role of the Pāsdārān grew rapidly. Initially it was used to restore order in the cities, then against political opponents of the radicals, both leftists and ethnic autonomists. From the autumn of 1980 it was used extensively in the war against Iraq. The Pāsdārān grew in size to 50,000 in 1981 and by 1985 had reached 250,000. By that time it was no longer a revolutionary militia but had acquired the equipment and training of a modern army. It was recruited mainly from poorer urban groups but insisted on a high educational standard. In 1985 the decision was taken to establish Pāsdārān naval and air force units as well. By 1987 the whole force totalled 450,000. Although it was not the direct military wing of the IRP the Pāsdārān resembled in structure and ideological motivation the German Waffen SS and was a vital element in the power structure of the Islamic Republic. Many of its officers had close personal links to ulema leaders.

After the revolutionary regime became established and the radical ulema confirmed their control a process began of linking the older institutions of the state with the new revolutionary institutions which had originally grown up in competition with them. This was done partly by incorporating the new institutions into the state apparatus. Thus in 1982 a ministry of Pāsdārān was created and the Reconstruction Crusade also became a ministry. The revolutionary committees were placed under the ministry of the interior and the independence of the factory committees restricted. This process reflected the greater confidence which the ulema felt in their control of state institutions after they had purged them of Pahlavī supporters and other opponents.

The purge and reconstruction of the army was a slow process. In 1978 the Pahlavī armed forces had totalled 415,000 men, including 60,000 officers of whom 400 were of general officer rank. The first purges focused on the internal security forces – the police, gendarmerie and Savak – and the army, apart from the removal of many general officers, was left intact. At that time the moderate government of Bāzargān hoped and expected that the republic could change the leadership of Pahlavī institutions and then take them over. The discovery of plots against the regime among the military and the predominance of the radical ulema in the summer of 1979, however, led to a much more far-reaching purge which continued until the outbreak of the Iran – Iraq war. In this second stage committees were set up to investigate the reliability of officers and many thousands were removed. The war with Iraq brought an end to the drastic purges although minor purges continued during the following years. The main focus now was on the Islamization of the army and on rebuilding it as the principal instrument for the defence of Iran against outside enemies, although the Pāsdārān shared this duty. Islamization was accomplished through creating, in December 1980, a system of religious commissars whose job was to maintain the ideological purity of the army. In the training of new officers great attention was paid to Islamic indoctrination and good Islamic credentials became a qualification for command. Gradually a new group of senior officers emerged from the ranks of those who had held the rank of colonel before the revolution and who had passed the loyalty investigation. The army which had been reduced in numbers to 150,000 in 1980 was expanded during the war to attain a size of 350,000 by 1987.

Other state institutions underwent a process of Islamization. The bureaucracy was subjected to purges and civil servants to ideological tests. The educational system was also overhauled and checks made on Islamic credentials; nevertheless the structure of universities and the content of the science curriculum remained basically unchanged. In 1982 drastic changes were introduced in the legal system. All laws not in conformity with Islam were revoked, all courts abolished and all judges not conversant with Islamic law removed. It was found more difficult to replace them, however. Islamic penal, civil and commercial codes were drafted but only the penal code was introduced in 1983. Special courts were established to try military personnel, clerics and drug offenders and itinerant justices appointed to dispense swift, Islamic justice.

The first three years of the revolution formed a period of strife and turmoil. During 1979 disturbances took place in Gurgān in the north east, Ahwāz in the south west and in Kurdistan. These disturbances contained elements of ethnic opposition to Persian domination. The first two were suppressed but the rising in Kurdistan continued for several years.

The Bāzargān government fell in November 1979. Its position had been weakened by the radical ulema in the revolutionary council and the invasion of the United States Embassy by young radicals, who disregarded the government and made prisoners of the staff, was the last straw. Khumaynī refused to condemn the invaders who claimed to be following his line. Until the first elections under the new constitution were held in January 1980 the revolutionary council ruled Iran.

Iran's first president was Abu'l Ḥasan Banī-Ṣadr, an Islamic radical lay follower of Khumaynī who had been one of his closest advisers in Paris and who had served briefly in the government since November 1979. He won the January 1980 presidential election with a large majority principally because Khumaynī prevented the radical ulema from running a strong candidate. Before 1980 the most distinctive feature of Banī-Ṣadr's politics had been his hostility to authority but once in office he became a powerful advocate of a strong central government, the rapid reconstruction of the traditional institutions of the state and the reduction of the revolutionary institutions. His policies brought him into a conflict with the IRP which dominated Iranian politics for the next 18 months and which ended in the defeat and flight of Banī-Ṣadr.

At first Banī-Ṣadr appeared likely to establish his ascendancy; in February he became chairman of the revolutionary council and acting commander in chief. The IRP gained an important victory in the Majlis elections in the spring of 1980 and used its domination of parliament to force on Banī-Ṣadr a government which he did not want. The long dispute between Banī-Ṣadr and the prime minister,

Muḥammad ᶜAlī Rajā'ī, over the composition of the cabinet paralysed the government of Iran for months. In addition to their sway over parliament and government the radical ulema acquired control over the judiciary, the radio, the Pāsdārān and other revolutionary institutions as well as the mosques. The purging of the bureaucracy and army removed potential allies of the president. The Iraqi invasion of September 1980 offered Banī-Ṣadr the possibility of recovering his position by emerging as the single war leader but that chance was lost when the ulema secured control of the Supreme Defence Council and the Pāsdārān's size and reputation grew.

In 1981 the political battle was fought out increasingly on the streets between the radicals of the left, the Mujāhidīn and the Fidā'iyān, who now leaned towards the president, and the supporters of the ulema, the revolutionary guards and the roughs who were known as the party of God. The issue was decided, however, by Khumaynī, who came down against Banī-Ṣadr at the end of May. Within two weeks Banī-Ṣadr was in hiding and on 21 June the Majlis declared him to be incompetent.

The IRP under the leadership of Bihishtī was triumphant but the party was now plunged into a violent confrontation with the Mujāhidīn. On 28 June 1981 120 people were killed, among them Bihishtī, when the headquarters of the IRP was bombed and on 30 August the prime minister's office suffered the same fate. Among the victims of this second attack were Rajā'ī, who had succeeded Banī-Ṣadr as president, and the new prime minister, Muḥammad Javād Bāhunar. The radical ulema struck back in a ruthless campaign of repression which lasted for 18 months and which the ulema won. During the campaign they eliminated other enemies and cowed their critics into silence. The most prominent of the moderate religious leaders, Sharīᶜatmadārī, was placed under house arrest.

By the end of 1982 the most radical phase of the revolution seemed to have come to an end. The defeat of the radical left coincided with an improvement in the war situation. "We should no longer say we are in a revolutionary situation," said Khumaynī in December 1982 and he issued a declaration aimed at curbing the excesses of the revolutionary courts.[2] It was time to consolidate what had been won and complete the process of Islamization of Iran's institutions and to try to rebuild Iran's battered economy.

After 1982 political disputes revolved around two issues of policy. One concerned foreign affairs and whether Iran should seek an end to the Iraq war and concentrate on internal reconstruction or whether she should prosecute the war against Iraq to victory and aim at extending the Islamic revolution further, notably in Lebanon. The second dispute concerned domestic policy and divided those who favoured a conservative economic policy from those who wished to carry through a radical policy of nationalization and land reform. These two issues were cross-cutting, that is to say that not all who supported a radical foreign policy supported a radical domestic policy and so on. A third element in the political situation was the struggle for power. As long as Āyatallāh Khumaynī lived there was no question of who had supreme power but left open were the questions of who could win his support and who would succeed him. Political disputes and the struggle for power produced political factions within Iran and rapidly shifting alliances as the factions sought support within various institutions.

By the end of 1981 a new political leadership had emerged from within the IRP in Iran. The new president was Ḥujjat al-Islām ᶜAlī Khāmani'ī, the new prime minister Ḥusayn Mūsavī, and Ḥujjat al-Iṣlam ᶜAlī Akbar Hāshimī Rafsanjānī, as speaker of the Majlis, achieved increasing prominence. In addition Āyatallāh Ḥasan ᶜAlī Muntaẓirī was designated as prospective successor to Khumaynī in November 1985. In the political disputes which followed these men were principal actors. It would be too complicated to describe their shifting policy positions and alliances. Mūsavī became identified with a radical domestic policy and was in frequent conflict with a more conservative Majlis, responsive to pressures from the traditional bazaar, and an even more conservative Council of Guardians in which the more traditional ulema found an institution which enabled them to reassert themselves in some degree. Rafsānjanī, who, like Khāmani'ī, adopted an intermediate position in domestic affairs, became the principal supporter of a peace policy abroad. Muntaẓirī, who was a strong supporter of the conservative faction in domestic policy, held to a radical policy in foreign affairs.

On 4 June 1989 Khumaynī died. His death marked the end of an extraordinary decade which had witnessed the Islamic revolution and the most destructive war ever waged by Iran. So long as Khumaynī had lived his authority had been unassailable although in his last, sick years his son and mouthpiece, Aḥmad Khumaynī had come to exercise power in his father's name and had used it to place sympathetic, radical ulema in important posts. The matter of the succession, however, was quickly settled by the Assembly of Experts. In March 1989 Muntaẓirī had been compelled to resign his position as prospective successor to Khumaynī and the Assembly chose the president, ᶜAlī Khāmani'ī, to succeed Khumaynī as *vālī faqīh* and gave him the title of Āyatallāh. On 18 July Rafsanjānī was elected to succeed Khāmani'ī as president. At the same time important constitutional changes were approved by which the powers of the president were strengthened and the post of prime minister was abolished. Rafsanjānī gave primacy to economic reconstruction, mainly through the private sector, at home, and to rebuilding relations abroad. His opponents argued for state control of the economy and support of Islamic revolution outside Iran.

The economic performance of the Islamic republic was poor. The main cause was the fall in oil production and oil revenues in consequence of the war with Iraq which led to the destruction of the Ābādān refinery and restrictions on Iran's ability to produce and export oil, and of the fall in oil prices which meant that Iran received much less for the oil she did sell. Iran had far less money to invest and less foreign exchange with which to buy goods. The oil factor was the main reason why GNP fell under the republic as fast as it had risen during the Pahlavī boom. A subsidiary cause, however, was the regime's uncertainty about the policy which it wished to pursue and the disruption caused by its internal disputes.

The Islamic republic wanted a system of Islamic economics but no-one was sure what this could be. Banī-Ṣadr and others had written on the subject before 1979 but their analysis was more in terms of general principles than specific measures and more concerned with distribution than production. The leading concept behind Islamic economics was social justice, implying a more equal distribution of wealth. There was a fundamental difference between factions concerning the ownership of property: the radicals supported a policy of nationalization and the conservatives one of private ownership. Each claimed Sharīʿa support for their arguments. There was also a vague feeling against bigness and in favour of moderate economic growth, small scale industry and small farmers. This last feeling was partly influenced by a prejudice in favour of conservation of Iran's oil which, as in 1951–3, assumed a symbolic importance which outweighed its economic significance. Finally, it was intended to apply Sharīʿa law to certain economic transactions, notably banking where it was desired to abolish interest.

In the early days of the revolution the radicals had matters much their own way. The flight of many Pahlavī owners and managers provided a strong argument for nationalization. In June and July 1979 banks and most large manufacturing enterprises were nationalized. A national industries' organization was set up to administer them. The radicals also supported unofficial seizures of property by courts, committees, factory committees and the new foundations, notably the Foundation for the Disinherited which took over most of the property of the wealthy Pahlavī Foundation. In several areas, for example Gurgān, peasants seized the property of landlords although in others landlords tried to recover lands lost under the Pahlavī land reform. In April 1980 a radical land law to limit holdings to 20 hectares was introduced. From 1982, however, the pendulum swung back towards the conservatives, whose theoretical arguments were strengthened by the evidence of corrupt dealings during the radical phase. There was resistance in the Majlis to new radical legislation and the Council of Guardians rejected bills to nationalize foreign trade and for land reform; the 1980 law was suspended. In factories the government succeeded in imposing management structures in place of the worker councils. In many areas, however, government was unable to influence the outcome which was decided by local considerations.

In practice pragmatic considerations played a more important part than ideology and the economic performance of the Islamic republic contradicted most of the ideological assumptions. The republic favoured a greater emphasis on traditional agriculture both to increase food production and to keep peasants on the land. But its incentives to grow wheat failed to achieve their purpose, food production fell, Iran remained heavily dependent on imported food and the years after 1979 saw the greatest of all movements from countryside to town. The republic also theoretically favoured the traditional bazaar and small industry, where its strongest support resided, but in the event it gave more emphasis to big industry; steel and petrochemicals continued to be the most dynamic sector under the republic. However, in the black economy which sprang up during the Iraq war, the traditional bazaar merchants did well. But industrial production as a whole fell during the early years of the republic.

By 1989 Iran was a much poorer country than it had been in 1978. Population, aided by an influx of refugees from Afghanistan and Iraq, had grown even more quickly than under the Pahlavīs to reach 50 million in 1986. The redistribution of population had also taken place at a faster rate. By 1989 three-quarters of the population of Iran lived in urban areas; the population of Tehran in 1986 was 6 million. Partly this increase in urbanization was the result of the improved housing provided by the republic and the subsidies on food given to the urban poor. But the fall in GNP, added to the cost of the war with Iraq until 1988 meant a very considerable decline in per capita income.

NOTES

1. Quotations from the Iranian republican constitution are taken from *Constitution of the Islamic Republic of Iran* (trans. Hamid Algar), Berkeley, Calif., 1980.
2. Quoted Shaul Bakhash, *The Reign of the Ayatollahs*, 1985, 228.

CHAPTER FOURTEEN

Arabia since the 1960s

GENERAL

By 1971 European colonial authority in Arabia had passed away and the new state structure was complete. With minor exceptions the boundaries of states were defined and central governments had extended their power and elaborated their institutions. Significant changes in economic and social institutions had begun in some areas but only in Saudi Arabia, Kuwayt and Qaṭar had oil wealth been sufficient to generate substantial alterations by the 1960s. It was the extraordinary increase in oil revenues during the 1970s which made possible development programmes which resulted in much deeper social transformations in those and other states. It was during the 1970s and 1980s that the two Yemens also entered on periods of rapid political, economic and social change, partly as a by product of the oil wealth in neighbouring countries but also as a consequence of revolutionary political changes within those states. Finally, it was after 1971 that Oman began a programme of modernization.

Two broad points may be made about the results of change. The first concerns the relations between the peripheral, coastal regions and the interior. Here it may be useful to adapt the geopolitical theory of Halford Mackinder concerning the conflict between heartland and periphery or between powers based on the land and those based on the sea. Until the nineteenth century it was the heartland which dominated the affairs of Arabia but the advent of two peripheral powers, Britain and the Ottomans, which established their power on the coasts and thence exercised some influence on the interior, changed the balance in favour of the periphery. The eclipse, first of the Ottomans and then of the British, led to the resurgence of the interior through much of the peninsula. Thus in North Yemen it was Ṣanʿāʾ which triumphed over Ḥudayda, in South Yemen the Dathīna over Aden, and in Saudi Arabia Riyāḍ over Jidda. On the Gulf coast, however, the coastal powers hung on in Kuwayt, Baḥrayn, Qaṭar and the United Arab Emirates; and in Oman Muscat defeated Rastāq. In these areas oil and the balance of power operated to favour the periphery.

The second point relates to a theme which runs throughout this book, namely the fate of the notables. In much of the Near East it was the notables, primarily the large landowners, who were the immediate beneficiaries of the end of colonial power but they were unable to retain control in the face of a challenge from other groups which included both a new urban class and a class of middling rural landholders. This pattern was broken in Arabia. In Saudi Arabia and all along the Gulf coast the notables hung on to power, although the basis of their wealth became oil or offshoots from it. In North Yemen the *sayyid* class did lose power but the tribal notables managed to retain much of their power and to claim a share in government. Only in South Yemen was the old notable class swept away; their demise coincided with that of the colonial power which had fostered their rise. In trying to explain the Arabian outcome two factors are worth considering. The first is oil which placed in the hands of those who controlled the states vast amounts of wealth and patronage which helped them to retain power. The men of the old regimes survived in Arabian states which had oil. The second factor is that notables in Arabia differed from those elsewhere. In those areas of Arabia where there was substantial cultivation the pattern was not one of large landowning but of a smallholding peasantry. The wealth and power of traditional notables had derived less from land and more from tribal authority, religious status, and trade. In Arabia the great destructive force of land reform had little on which to work.

To say that notables retained power in most of Arabia, however, conceals a significant change. In former times Arabian rulers had been little more than first among equals; only those with some peculiar claim to eminence within Islam were especially distinguished from others and even then eminence was not confined to them and it conferred no considerable power. British and Ottoman recognition and subsidies began a process, continued and enlarged by oil revenues and the operation of the international system, which gradually marked off royal households from other groups and converted them into strong regimes which disposed of all the power and patronage of modernized, centralized states. The size of the royal households, running into many thousands, was as large as that of the élites which ran other states in the Near East. The new style royal households often found it worth their while to patronize the traditional notables but they themselves had moved up to occupy a position comparable in some respects to the British and Ottoman states. The other traditional notables were useful but rarely essential intermediaries and they also took on new functions.

SAUDI ARABIA SINCE 1964

A persistent problem for students of Saudi Arabia is that they have no accurate statistics of the population of the state. Censuses have been held but the results have either not been published or they have been made available in contradictory and puzzling forms. A further problem concerns the counting of foreign workers and their dependents. The number of these seemingly rose from perhaps half a million in 1964 to a peak of 3 million in 1984, subsequently falling by about a million during the following years. As these workers were almost wholly urban one effect of their presence was to complicate the statistics of urbanization. A reasonable guess at the population of Saᶜūdi Arabia at the end of the 1980s would be 8 million Saudis and 2 million foreign workers, of whom about half were from North Yemen and the rest from other Arab countries, Pakistan and Europe. About two-thirds of the population was urban, one-quarter villagers and the rest nomad. Of the urban population well over a million lived in Riyāḍ, rather less than a million in Jidda and about half a million in Medina. The urban population included a substantial new middle class, largely dependent on the state, composed of teachers, bureaucrats, army officers and professionals. The growth of the population, its composition and its redistribution are indications of the dramatic changes in Saudi Arabia.

At the end of the 1980s the people of Saudi Arabia were much healthier, better housed and much better educated than they had been in 1964. A large part of public expenditure had gone on public health, hospitals, housing and education. Between 1964 and 1986 the number studying at all levels increased by ten times to 2.2 million. By the latter date there were seven universities. These changes were paid for out of the revenues from oil which rose from under 1 billion dollars in 1964 to a peak of 102 billion dollars in 1981 although they fell substantially after that date to only 23 billion in 1985. These revenues financed major development projects, organized from 1970 as five-year plans. A very large sum went into defence but the money also financed a considerable programme of road, port and airport construction, large industrial projects centred principally around petrochemicals and including two industrial cities at Jubayl and Yanbuᶜ, and agricultural expansion through irrigation and mechanization which greatly increased wheat production.

During this period Saudi Arabia was transformed politically into a centralized state. The state controlled the oil revenues and to arrange their distribution was obliged to develop the ministries, departments, agencies and other institutions of a modern state. Saudi Arabia remained a monarchy but the nature of the monarchy changed under Fayṣal and his successors. The state became a corporate venture of the Saᶜūdī family. In the mid-1980s it was estimated that the total size of the family, including collateral branches, was around 20,000 of whom about 250 were direct male descendants of ᶜAbd al-ᶜAzīz. A central characteristic of Saᶜūdī politics was the competition for jobs among this group. Saᶜūdīs dominated central and provincial governments, government agencies, the armed forces and spilled over into private business. In search of jobs and the power and patronage which went with them they formed alliances among themselves and with outsiders, often cementing alliances with marriage ties.

In 1964 the Sudayrī clan (also known as the Āl Fahd) emerged as the leading group within the Saᶜūdī family. The Sudayrīs were the sons of ᶜAbd al-ᶜAzīz by a wife from the important Sudayrī tribal family. Fayṣal was the leading member of this group and under his rule his brothers, Fahd, Sulṭān and Nāyif rapidly advanced at the expense of the relatives of the former ruler, Saᶜūd. Saᶜūd's supporters were excluded from Fayṣal's 1962 cabinet in which the most important five posts were held by Saᶜūdīs, who included Fayṣal himself as prime minister, Fahd in charge of the interior and Sulṭān at defence. The remaining posts were held by notables and commoners. Although the size of cabinets grew this pattern was repeated throughout the following years. In 1975 Saᶜūdīs held 7 of 25 posts and in 1987 12 of 32 posts. Always the key posts, including those concerned with foreign affairs and security and the principal provincial governorships, remained in Saᶜūdī hands. Further, there was very striking ministerial continuity. Sulṭān retained control of defence in all cabinets and Fahd of interior until he surrendered it to his brother, Nāyif. Non-Saᶜūdī ministers also remained in the same posts for many years: for example, Aḥmad Zakī Yamānī, a Ḥijāzī lawyer appointed minister of petroleum in 1962, retained the portfolio until 1986. Ḥijāzīs formed the largest contingent of non-Saᶜūdī ministers. A further feature of the evolution of Saᶜūdī government was the introduction of a new generation of younger Saᶜūdī princes, mainly the sons of the Sudayrī brothers and usually educated abroad. The most notable member of this group was Saᶜūd ibn Fayṣal, who became foreign minister.

The succession, which was carefully managed, broadly followed the rule of seniority among the male sons of ᶜAbd al-ᶜAzīz. A pattern was established by which the successor and the second in line were designated in advance by appointment as first and second deputy prime ministers, the monarch holding the post of prime minister whether he performed the functions or not. Thus Khālid ibn ᶜAbd al-ᶜAzīz was appointed deputy to Fayṣal in 1964 and succeeded to the throne when Fayṣal was assassinated by his nephew in 1975. Fahd, who had been designated second deputy prime minister in 1967 became first deputy in 1975 and succeeded Khālid in 1982. ᶜAbdallāh ibn ᶜAbd al-ᶜAzīz, who had been made second deputy at Khālid's accession in 1975, then became first deputy and Sulṭān second deputy under Fahd. These decisions, endorsed by the senior members of the family and accepted by religious and tribal notables, regulated competition for the succession and effectively concentrated it on the post of second deputy prime minister.

Until his death Saudi government was dominated by Fayṣal but subsequently it assumed the characteristics of a company in which the directors both assumed collective responsibility for decisions under the leadership of the managing director (monarch) and also operated as divisional executives. Partly this evolution was due to the elaboration of a system of institutional apanages as princes developed the departmental fiefs they had secured during the 1960s; and partly it was due to the personality of Khālid, who was more inclined to act as a chairman than a chief executive. Under Khālid the mainspring of Saudi government was Fahd although his power was delimited by the apanages of his brothers. There were differences of personality and policy, represented by a debate between those who leaned more towards tradition, such as Khālid and ᶜAbdallāh, and those, like Fahd and his brothers, who wished to press on more quickly with modernization, but these disputes were all well contained. That the system worked with such little friction was due in no small measure to the circumstance that until 1981 new resources came forward year by year in such abundance as to enable the system to satisfy all claims upon it.

Outside the Saᶜūdī family three groups counted in the political scene: tribal leaders, religious dignitaries and the new professionals. Although nomadism had declined to insignificance tribal allegiances remained of primary importance in creating networks which linked to the political system. The leaders of the major tribes were conciliated with pensions, jobs for their followers and privileged treatment in legal matters; and it was through them that the tribally-based National Guard was recruited. The tribal leaders were also the recipients of royal hospitality. Khālid and ᶜAbdallāh in particular cultivated this constituency and all the Saudi provincial governors gave especial attention to their dealings with tribal leaders. The ulema were an important factor in the working of the system as they were called upon to endorse major changes in policy. For example the ulema played a role in 1964 both in supporting Fayṣal and in legitimizing the Saᶜūdī household decision to depose Saᶜūd. In return the ulema were left in charge of the law courts and the Sharīᶜa remained the only law of Saudi Arabia. The Āl Shaykh family regularly held two or three ministerial posts, particularly the ministry of justice established in 1970. Moreover, in Saudi Arabia there was no change in dress and visible styles of living such as had taken place in other parts of the Near East during the secular revolutions. The new professionals occupied a much greater area in state employment and in trade but had little political influence. As a group they were indispensable but as individuals they were used and discarded. Their hopes of greater influence lay in the constitutional developments discussed since the 1960s and the creation of some form of parliament, but although in 1980 a committee was established to consider the matter nothing emerged from it.

The system was ultimately underpinned by the security forces. There were two elements in the army: the regular army (including the air force) and the National Guard. The regular army had been kept small under Saᶜūd and numbered around 12,000 at the accession of Fayṣal. Under Fayṣal and his successors it was decided to strive for a small, highly trained and well equipped force and particular emphasis was placed upon the development of a system of air defence. By 1986 a force of 57,000 existed, including 40,000 in the army and 14,000 in the air force. Its equipment was second to none in the world and it was constantly upgraded. The second force was the tribally-based National Guard which was rebuilt after 1970 as a counterbalance to the regular army and for use in internal security. Its numbers rose to 35,000 but were subsequently reduced to 23,000 by 1982. In their evolution the roles of the regular and tribal forces had become reversed. Under ᶜAbd al-ᶜAzīz the tribal army had been for external defence but was unreliable against the principal internal enemy which was the tribes themselves. The regular army, therefore, was the primary support of civil government. By the end of the 1970s the regular army had become the main weapon against external enemies and the National Guard was used for internal security where the principal enemy was perceived to be the secular radicals. In fact during the 1980s it began to seem that the main internal enemy was partly tribal and partly religious fundamentalism against which the National Guard was seen to be unreliable. The tendency, therefore, was to rely more on a new internal security force created in 1980. Moreover, during the Gulf war of the 1980s the principal enemy was seen to be external. The effect of these developments was to reduce the importance attached to the National Guard and to enhance that given to the regular forces. This shifting emphasis was reflected in the outcome of the long argument about the introduction of conscription. Sulṭān, in charge of the defence ministry, supported conscription and ᶜAbdallāh, in charge of the National Guard, opposed the change. A decision in principle in favour of conscription was made in 1985.

Three important turning points may be detected in the history of Saudi Arabia during the period 1964 to 1989. The first was in 1967 when the result of the Arab–Israeli war forced Egypt to withdraw from North Yemen, drop its radical challenge to Saudi Arabia and establish good relations which endured until 1978. Saudi Arabia was thereby relieved of a major security threat. The second turning point was the 1973 oil price rise which provided the resources to fuel Saudi Arabia's domestic development and to support a major programme of outside aid as well as endowing Saudi Arabia with a new power in the form of the so-called oil weapon. The third turning point occurred in 1979–80 as a result of a combination of events: the Islamic revolution in Iran; the Israeli–Egyptian peace treaty; the seizure of the grand mosque at Mecca on 20 November 1979 by a group of ᶜUtayba tribesmen and religious fundamentalists and the prolonged siege which followed; the Soviet invasion of Afghanistan; and the outbreak of the Iran–Iraq war. These events were soon followed by the downturn of oil prices. The effect of these developments was to dent Saudi confidence: the Egyptian alliance was broken, the stability of the Gulf region destroyed, the security and prestige of the Saudi regime called into question at home and the resources to buy the country's way out of trouble diminished. There was no change in the main lines of Saudi policy but an even greater emphasis was placed on defence and a more conservative demeanour adopted in an effort to conciliate traditional forces. It was ironic that this development should have coincided with the accession of the liberal modernizer, Fahd.

NORTH YEMEN SINCE 1962

The military coup of 26 September 1962 which established the Yemen Arab Republic plunged North Yemen into civil war. The republican side consisted of army officers, townsmen, intellectuals, most of the Shāfiᶜī population, and some important Zaydī shaykhs. The royalist side consisted of the Ḥamīd al-Dīn family, led by the Imām Muḥammad al-Badr, most of the *sayyid* class, and most of the Zaydī tribes. Both sides secured outside help. The republicans turned to Egypt which sent troops to a peak number of 60,000 and the royalists secured financial aid from Saudi Arabia and military advisers from Jordan. The struggle lasted six years. Various attempts to establish peace by negotiation between the parties and by international efforts all failed until the withdrawal of Egyptian forces (partly as a consequence of the Israeli victory in 1967) and the ending of Saudi assistance to the royalists left the internal factions to fight it out. A royalist victory seemed inevitable but the Zaydī tribes failed to take Ṣanᶜā' during a protracted siege in 1968 and went home. Ṣanᶜā's survival was due to the resistance of the republican radicals (mainly Shāfiᶜīs), who organized a citizens' militia, but immediately after their victory the radicals were defeated by the moderate faction which went on to purge the army of radicals and to dissolve the citizens' militias. Moderate Zaydīs now controlled affairs on both sides and they found a compromise through national reconciliation in 1970.

The republic had survived but the result of the civil war was a victory for the Zaydī tribes who had enriched themselves from both sides during the conflict and who dictated the shape of the settlement. The tribes wanted a weak government, a share in government to ensure that it remained weak and control of its patronage. They dominated the consultative assembly elected under the new constitution in 1971 and took most important government jobs including six of the ten provincial governorships. They also dominated the republican army which was based on tribal contingents with their own leaders. Until 1973 the tribes had an independent source of income in the form of Saudi subsidies paid directly to them. The main losers were the *sayyids* whose former dominant position in the central government was taken by non-*sayyids*, mainly men from Zaydī *qāḍī* families.

The dominance of the great Zaydī tribal confederations continued throughout the presidency of Qāḍī ᶜAbd al-Raḥmān al-Iryānī. Iryānī's government had little money and little authority. Moreover, from 1967 to 1973 Yemen suffered a disastrous drought. The tribes did much as they liked, plunged North Yemen into a war with South Yemen in 1972, and overthrew Iryānī when they decided that he was too soft on the radicals. The instrument of Iryānī's dismissal on 13 June 1974 was Lt Col Ibrāhīm Muḥammad al-Ḥamdī, the deputy army commander, who came from a Zaydī *qāḍī* family. Ḥamdī suspended the 1971 constitution and made himself chairman of a command council which became the ruling body. Together with other army leaders Ḥamdī dominated the government but he did not govern in the interests of the tribes.

The political history of North Yemen since 1974 may be crudely represented as a struggle between tribal groups who wanted a weak central government and technocrats who wanted a strong modernizing government, a struggle in which the balance was held by the army and progressively tipped by it in favour of the technocrats. The term "technocrats" is used here to describe a group of civilians with higher educational qualifications who had returned from abroad after 1962 when the republic was anxious to find Yemenis of ability to fill the governmental jobs which it was creating. The technocrats had no power base in the traditional society and if they had ambitions to take power they had no means of realizing them; their power lay in their indispensability and their interest was in the expansion of their own arena of the state and its agencies. Indeed the bureaucracy did acquire an institutional framework after 1962 – a civil service commission and an institute for training public servants were created in 1963 – and was increased in size after 1974 to reach 35,000 in 1982. This petty figure may serve to highlight once more the great weakness of the baseline of traditional government in North Yemen from which the new system developed.

The technocrats came to the fore under Ḥamdī and were by far the largest group in all governments after 1974. ʿAbd al-ʿAzīz ʿAbd al-Ghānī, who served as chairman of the central bank founded in 1971, was prime minister from 1975 to 1980 and became prime minister for another long stint in 1983. Another man who served in many posts, including that of prime minister from 1980 to 1983, was ʿAbd al-Karīm al-Iryānī. Ḥasan Makkī, prime minister in 1974 and Muḥammad Saʿīd al-ʿAṭṭār were also prominent technocrats. The technocrats dominated the central planning organization founded in 1972 and similar agencies. Through their posts they were able to shape the main lines of economic development. They did not press for political liberalization, however; in North Yemen more democracy meant less development and less government. The technocrats wanted a government of the élite. Military rule suited them because it kept the tribes away.

From 1975 Ḥamdī began to reduce the power of the tribes. He played off one confederation against another, first picking off the Bakīl and then the Ḥāshid. In December 1975 the Ḥāshid leader, Shaykh al-Aḥmar, called for a tribal rebellion against Ḥamdī but Ḥamdī ignored the call and so did the tribes. Ḥamdī benefited from the ending of the direct Saudi subsidy to the tribal leaders which made them turn instead to the state and he profited also from the upturn in Yemen's economic fortunes through the great increase in the value of remittances from Yemeni workers abroad. A further limitation on the power of the tribes was Ḥamdī's strengthening of the army, although he was unable to break its tribal structure. Ḥamdī also began to sap the power of the religious groups. The *sayyids*' power had already been reduced but Ḥamdī now dropped some of the *qāḍī*s from government. Furthermore, he began to reduce the extent of their legal powers by inroads into the monopoly of the Sharīʿa; in 1975 he introduced a commercial code and in 1976 courts to implement it. By the time of his mysterious murder on 11 October 1977 Ḥamdī had gone some way towards reversing the decline of state power. He had also incurred the hatred of tribal and religious groups and his successor, the deputy army commander, Aḥmad Ḥusayn al-Ghashmī, tried to purge the Ḥamdī men and their radical supporters and to re-establish better relations with the tribes. But before he could accomplish anything of significance Ghashmī too was murdered in June 1978.

In 1978 the future shape of the Yemen Arab Republic seemed in considerable doubt. The new president, Lt Col ʿAlī ʿAbdallāh Ṣāliḥ, a protége of Ghashmī and, like him, an uneducated man from a minor Zaydī tribe, appeared unlikely to hold on to power. He had no apparent power base, was thought to be incompetent and was regarded as a Saudi puppet. The tribes were expected to recover the power lost to Ḥamdī. But the career of Ṣāliḥ was a classic case of the job making the man and the fact that the headship of the state (and army) could make the man was proof of how much these institutions had evolved. It was also evidence of the marriage between the modern institution and the traditional network because Ṣāliḥ was quick to introduce into the state apparatus members of his own family and fellow tribesmen from the Sanḥān section of the Ḥāshid confederacy.

Ṣāliḥ found an answer to one of the most persistent problems of North Yemen since 1968, namely the activities of the southern radicals who, with help from South Yemen, had persistently defied government. Attempts to subdue them brought the Ṣanʿā' government into conflict with Aden and leaving them alone brought trouble with the tribes and with Saudi Arabia. Yemen could not afford to quarrel with Saudi Arabia because it was Saudi aid which kept the state afloat. In February 1979 armed conflict with South Yemen began again. Between 1979 and 1982, however, Ṣāliḥ achieved first an agreement with Aden and then a military victory over the southern rebels. Ṣāliḥ combined his military campaign with political advances through a national dialogue committee which he established in 1980 to carry through a policy of national reconciliation which bore fruit in a national pact.

Ṣāliḥ also strengthened the army and began to develop other state institutions. In 1979 he introduced conscription, an act which began to weaken the tribal element in the army as well as increase the army's size. By 1986 he had 37,000 troops and in addition a national security force of 5,000 for use against internal enemies. These forces at the disposal of the state may be contrasted with the 20,000 tribal levies which existed. Ṣāliḥ continued the work, begun by Ghashmī, of restoring the constitution suspended by Ḥamdī. He established representative bodies including a general people's congress in 1982. The congress was a substitute for a political party. It was built on a grassroots movement of local development associations which in turn had grown out of the co-operatives (established after 1962) which had assumed responsibility for several local services. In 1973 Ḥamdī created a national organization of these associations and Ṣāliḥ used them both as agencies of local government and as building blocks for national organizations. They provided a means by which state authority could be inserted into rural areas in place of tribal authority or by which state authority could be integrated with tribal power. One must be careful, however, not to exaggerate the extent of this growth in state power; in 1980 government took only 8 per cent of GNP in the form of revenue and by this measure the state in the Yemen Arab Republic still ranked as one of the weakest in the world.

During the 1980s Yemen experienced considerable economic difficulties. The later 1970s had seen a boom founded on remittances and outside aid which had made possible new investment, especially in roads and education. The three main towns of Ṣanʿā', Taʿizz and Ḥudayda were linked by roads, and feeder roads struck off towards remoter places. The number of schools increased from 700 in 1970 to 5,000 in 1985 and the University of Ṣanʿā' was opened in 1971. Literacy grew from 2.5 per cent in 1962 to 13 per cent in 1985. But the end of the oil boom in Arabia cut employment in the oil states and remittances fell; also aid was harder to obtain. The cotton boom of the mid 1970s was long since exhausted. The state needed a new injection of resources and it found it in oil. Oil was discovered in eastern Yemen in 1984, a pipeline and a refinery were built and export began in 1988.

Between 1962 and 1988 North Yemen had a revolution but not one of the same character as those which took place elsewhere in the Near East during the second half of the twentieth century. Its domestic economy remained one of subsistence agriculture and not much more than one-tenth of its population of 9 million lived in towns. Although Ṣanʿāʾ grew rapidly during the 1970s and 1980s it was still below 500,000 at the end of the period. Socially, North Yemen remained tribal and largely illiterate. Despite the growth of its state institutions the state was a very modest force. The most important changes which took place in Yemen were the consequence of other peoples' revolutions, especially that of Saudi Arabia. By 1980 something like one-third of the labour force of North Yemen was working in Saudi Arabia; rural workers become temporary immigrants in Saudi towns. It was their earnings which were the major dynamo of change in North Yemen.

SOUTH YEMEN SINCE 1967

South Yemen began its independent life in considerable economic difficulties. It was naturally a poor country and its situation was made worse by the closure of the Suez Canal in 1967, which event reduced to insignificance the movement of ships through its port of Aden and thereby almost eliminated one of South Yemen's major sources of employment and income. The departure of the British garrison and of many of Aden's prosperous merchants were also blows to the new state and the long drought in the interior injured agriculture. During the following 20 years South Yemen continued to struggle economically: the reopening of the Suez Canal in 1975 did not result in the return of the old prosperity; in the face of the socialist policies of the new state the merchants did not come back; agriculture continued to perform poorly; and industry did not develop – even during the 1980s 80 per cent of industrial output came from the antiquated Aden refinery. The only bright spot on the South Yemeni economic horizon was the remittances of the 15 per cent of Yemeni workers who went abroad to take employment in the oil rich states of Arabia. It was their money together with some overseas aid which financed development projects and accounted for the economic growth of the late 1970s and early 1980s. In 1984 half of GNP came from remittances.

By 1986 the population of South Yemen had increased from just under 1.5 million at independence to 2.4 million. Because of the development of Aden with its population of 350,000 South Yemen was much more urbanized than its northern neighbour; some 38 per cent of the population lived in towns, 10 per cent was nomadic and just over half was rural, mainly small peasant cultivators. South Yemen's greater urbanization was reflected in its greater literacy, which increased from 20 per cent at independence to 40 per cent in 1980. South Yemen had spent heavily on education and pupils in schools increased from 65,000 at independence to 270,000 in 1980. The University of Aden was founded in 1975.

Another striking difference between the development of southern and northern Yemen concerned the role of the state. Even at the end of the period the northern state accounted for less than 10 per cent of GNP; in South Yemen the state's share rose from 25 per cent in 1973 to 56 per cent in 1980. To a considerable extent the difference is explained by the different policies of the two regimes but in this area as in others South Yemen was building on a much more substantial British base than the Imamate base from which the Yemen Arab Republic began.

The nature of the South Yemen state may account for an apparent difference in social development. In the north the tribal structure was fundamental to the history of the area and although there was some diminution in the role of tribes between 1975 and 1988 they remained of great significance. By contrast, in writing on South Yemen one encounters little concern with tribal loyalties; instead its history is explained in terms of ideology, party and personality. An unanswered question is whether the difference is real or whether it is one of perception, influenced by the persistent hostility of the South Yemeni regime to tribalism or to any mention of tribal affiliation. In 1968 the tribal reconciliation decree attempted to stop feuding, in 1969 a ban on wearing arms was imposed and provincial government boundaries were redrawn on a non-tribal basis, in 1970 tribal associations were declared illegal, and tribal designations have disappeared from personal names. In favour of the 'real' explanation is the greater urbanization and the absence of any tribal organization comparable to the Zaydī confederations of northern Yemen; tribal loyalties have been less pronounced among the northern Sunnīs who may be compared to the tribes of the south. In favour of the explanation linked to perception is the evidence that during several power struggles in the south alliances seem to have been based on regional or tribal links.

The political conflicts in South Yemen which took place after independence involved several factors: tribal, ideological, institutional (state versus party), international (involving relations with North Yemen and Saudi Arabia) and personal. They began immediately after the British departure and were expressed in terms of a difference between those who emphasized the necessity for stability and those who demanded a programme of revolutionary change, in particular nationalization and land reform. The radicals gained control of the National Liberation Front at the March 1968 party congress and dislodged Qaḥṭān al-Shaᶜbī the following year. Shaᶜbī failed to secure the support of the old federation army which was also a loser in the contest; ᶜAwlaqī officers, who had stood on the side lines in 1967, rebelled and were crushed. By 1969 the radicals were in charge of the institutions of the state as well as the party and implemented a socialist programme. The state was given a new name in 1970: the People's Democratic Republic of Yemen.

State institutions were remodelled. The most important institution of government became the presidential council composed of the president, the prime minister and the general secretary of the party. A highly centralized system of local government was introduced. The bureaucracy was virtually reconstructed because of the loss of senior civil servants at the time of independence. In the interests of economy salaries were cut severely in 1968 and 1972. As the programme of extending state control got underway the bureaucracy was expanded from 13,000 in 1970 to 32,000 in 1977. The army was also rebuilt after the purges of 1968. Conscription was introduced and the size of the army increased from 10,000 at independence to 27,500 in 1986. As a control on the army a militia was formed out of the military forces of the NLF. Formally constituted in 1973 it numbered 15,000. Internal security was the responsibility of a special 30,000 strong police force under the ministry of the interior and of a revolutionary security force created in 1974 and placed under the ministry of state security. For so small a state this was a formidable collection of coercive forces. The federation courts were also replaced by a system of people's courts which administered rough revolutionary justice from 1968 to 1979. As time went on the courts were given new legal codes with which to work including codes of family law (1974), personal law (1976) and civil law (1983). The legal reforms represented a far-reaching assault on tribal and Sharīᶜa law and a major increase of state intervention.

One striking innovation was the introduction of a new-style political party. The NLF, in its origins a coalition of groups, was transformed by stages into a party whose structures and style were those of an orthodox communist party, with central committee, secretariat and politburo. The organizational change was made in 1972: in 1978 the name Yemeni Socialist Party was adopted and the party became a vanguard party, that is a small (26,000) party of dedicated activists. As in socialist countries the party surrounded itself with a number of social organizations which it dominated. These included organizations of workers, women and, most importantly, of youth. What is difficult to say is whether the party played the same role which it did in socialist countries as the dominant political institution. While it is true that whoever controlled the party emerged as victor in every political conflict except that of 1980 it is also the case that the initiative often lay with other institutions. At all events the emergence of the Yemeni party was a unique phenomenon in Arabia and although the Baᶜth parties of Syria and especially Iraq had some similarities the role of the party in South Yemen was quite distinctive in the Near East.

There were also major social and economic changes. In 1970 a programme of land reform was introduced which established ceilings for individual holdings of 8.5 hectares for irrigated land and 17 hectares for dry land and double these limits for family holdings. In fact there had been few large landholdings before independence; what there were consisted principally of the lands of shaykhs and sultans. Many of these had fled but land reform completed the demolition of their fortunes and administered a severe blow to the traditional tribal structure. As elsewhere in the Near East the power of the notables was replaced by that of the state. Those who benefited from land reform were obliged to join co-operatives which were effectively at the mercy of the state which controlled all water supplies. In fact what the state had done was to take charge of a process which had begun with independent peasant action to seize lands, especially in Ḥaḍramawt. It is claimed that about half the cultivated land changed hands. All foreign-owned enterprises were nationalized in 1969 with the exception of the largest of all, the refinery, which remained in the hands of British Petroleum until 1977. The regime also took over the property of the many people who had fled.

The effect of the social and economic changes was to destroy the power of the traditional notables and the influence of foreign business. This was also the expressed intention but it could be argued that the economic and political changes of 1967 had already delivered a fatal blow to many of the old structures and the regime was obliged to pick up the pieces itself. It is also true that the radical programme helped to complete the disenchantment of the former dominant groups and to hasten their departure from the scene. Their withdrawal meant that the politics of South Yemen became the story of the conflicts among the radicals, men whose outstanding characteristic was their youth. At independence the average age of the NLF leaders was under 30 and this circumstance may help to explain the turbulence of the political history of the PDRY.

The structure of the revolutionary government implied the existence of major power centres in the state, the party and the army and to some extent in provincial governments. Rivals for power sought control of these power centres from which to bid for supreme power. In the years 1969 to 1986 four men in particular dominated the political scene. These were: Salīm Rubayᶜī ᶜAlī, who was president from 1970 to 1978; ᶜAlī Nāṣir Muḥammad, who was prime minister from 1971 until 1980 and president, prime minister and general secretary of the party from 1980 to 1986; ᶜAbd al-Fattāḥ Ismāᶜīl, who was general secretary throughout the 1970s and president from 1978 to 1980; and ᶜAlī Aḥmad Nāṣir ᶜAntar, who commanded the army. Rubayᶜī ᶜAlī and ᶜAlī Nāṣir were both from Dathīna, Ismāᶜīl from North Yemen and ᶜAntar from Ḍāliᶜ. From 1970 to 1978 the leading antagonists were Rubayᶜī ᶜAlī, who represented the rural radical element in the NLF, and Ismāᶜīl who looked for support to the Adeni workers and who was the principal architect of the development of a strong Soviet style party.

Rubayᶜī ᶜAlī was overthrown in a coup in 1978, immediately following the murder of Ghashmī in North Yemen, an event with which the coup was obscurely connected. Rubayᶜī ᶜAlī resisted with support from Abyan but this support was partly neutralized by the local influence of ᶜAlī Nāṣir Muḥammad and a decisive role was played by ᶜAlī ᶜAntar who brought the army against the president. Rubayᶜī ᶜAlī and his supporters were executed and Ismāᶜīl became president. There now began a contest for power between Ismāᶜīl, with his strength in the party and the internal security organization and a following among fellow North Yemenis, and ᶜAlī Nāṣir Muḥammad, who had a regional and tribal following in the Dathīna and won the support of ᶜAlī ᶜAntar and the army. In 1980 Ismāᶜīl was forced out and ᶜAlī Nāṣir Muḥammad took control of the main power centres as president, prime minister and general secretary of the party. He remodelled the central committee and politburo to guarantee his control. In 1981 he removed ᶜAlī Antar from control of defence and seemed to have no rival. ᶜAlī Nāṣir Muḥammad began to institute changes in policy, a more liberal economic regime at home and better relations with neighbouring states.

In January 1986 ᶜAlī Nāṣir Muḥammad was overthrown in a struggle so bloody that it amounted to a brief civil war. From 1984 ᶜAlī Nāṣir's power had been steadily undermined. We can trace the process but the causes are obscure; probably ᶜAlī Nāṣir had alienated too many influential men, most notably ᶜAlī ᶜAntar. In 1984 ᶜAlī Nāṣir lost control of the party in which Ismāᶜīl and his supporters recovered power and the following year he was obliged to give up the prime ministership. His strength now lay primarily in the internal security forces and in his following in Abyan. On 13 January 1986 ᶜAlī Nāṣir attempted to recover his position by murdering his leading opponents at a Politburo meeting. Four died including Ismāᶜīl and ᶜAntar but his opponents rallied under the leadership of the prime minister, Ḥaydar Abū Bakr al-ᶜAṭṭās. At first the army held aloof from the struggle but in the end threw its weight decisively against ᶜAlī Nāṣir who fled with many of his supporters. Al-ᶜAṭṭās took over as president and general secretary of the party. No new men appeared on the scene; there had been yet another reshuffle among the original small group of radicals. The episode showed how little we understand of the mainsprings of South Yemeni politics.

THE PERSIAN GULF STATES SINCE 1971

Between 1961 and 1971 the smaller Gulf states of Kuwayt, Baḥrayn, Qaṭar and the United Arab Emirates had achieved independence. The subsequent period may be divided into two periods. During the first, optimistic period which continued until 1980 the states obtained extended international recognition and acceptance of their independence and enjoyed a flood of prosperity from oil. During the second, darker period of the 1980s the political prospect clouded. The Iran–Iraq war posed problems for the Gulf states in preserving their independence. All wished to remain neutral; to demonstrate sympathy for the Arab cause represented by Iraq lest they should subsequently be abandoned by other Arab states; to show that their regimes were truly Islamic; and to come together for collective security. But collective security in the form of the 1981 Gulf Co-operation Council (GCC), ostensibly for economic but actually for defence co-ordination, also imposed a limitation on independence by forcing them into dependence on Saudi Arabia.

The economic situation also became more gloomy following the fall in oil revenues. The citizens of the Gulf states, with the exception of the people of Baḥrayn, were still among the wealthiest in the world but they became more conscious of the precariousness of their prosperity and their vulnerability, dependent as they were on one product and on imported labour. The states began to look at other options which would reduce their dependence. There were broadly three options: to conserve oil supplies and spread their consumption over a longer period; to invest the proceeds outside the Gulf and live off the income; or to diversify their economies. All these variations were employed and Kuwayt tried all three; indeed, by 1982 Kuwayt drew more from her overseas investments than she did from oil. Economic diversification involved agriculture, industry and services. In agriculture all states attempted to increase their output of vegetables, dairy products and chickens but all ran up against the shortage of water which imposed severe limits on agricultural development. Water consumption in Kuwayt, for example, increased from 255 million gallons in 1954 to 38.5 billion gallons (38,500 million) in 1986, much of it extracted from the sea at an extravagant cost. In industry all tried petrochemicals and some went on to iron and steel, aluminium and ship repair. The result was a proliferation of high cost industries and gross over-capacity. In services the Gulf states looked at banking, insurance and stock markets but all proved to have problems. Moreover, all diversification required more foreign workers and the citizens of the Gulf states (except Baḥrayn) were becoming more and more uneasily conscious of their situation as a minority in their own states.

Both the states and the regimes which ran them survived throughout the period and emerged at the end apparently stronger than they were at the beginning. State institutions, bureaucratic and military, were developed and the royal households extended their control over them. Problems of succession were managed within the households with little friction; only in Qaṭar did change take place with force and only in Shārja was there violence. And although there was criticism of the dominance of ruling families, notably in Kuwayt and Baḥrayn, the criticism was contained without great difficulties or major concessions.

In Kuwayt the Āl Ṣabāḥ family dominated the new institutions created after independence. The amirs ᶜAbdallāh (1950–65), Ṣabāḥ (1965–78) and Jābir (1978–) controlled the political system. The 1963 constitution provided for a national assembly and a council of ministers. Key posts were held by members of the Amir's family. Although the proportion of ministries held by the Āl Ṣabāḥ fell from three-quarters in 1962 to between one-quarter and one-half (except in 1971 when it dropped to 15 per cent) the principal posts of foreign affairs, interior, defence and information (that is to say intelligence) were always held by Āl Ṣabāḥs. A pattern was established by which the heir apparent was prime minister. In 1987 the Āl Ṣabāḥ held 7 of 22 ministries and 3 of the 4 provincial governorships. The national assembly was elected on a narrow suffrage consisting of those descended from Kuwaytī citizens before 1920, a group which comprised only 6.4 per cent of the population in 1981. The assembly, however, was critical of government policy. Political parties were illegal but groups of men representing non-conformist views were elected. In the 1960s and 1970s the most vocal opposition was composed of Arab Nationalist Movement supporters, who drew strength from the large, unenfranchized Palestinian element in the population of Kuwayt. They found support among Kuwaytīs critical of Āl Ṣabāḥ domination and their criticisms led to the dismissal of the assembly in 1976 and a revision of the constitution. A new national assembly was elected in 1981 in which the radical secularists had been replaced as the principal opposition by Muslim fundamentalists, who looked to the 30 per cent of Shīʿīs in the population for support. In 1986 the assembly was again dismissed because of its inability to work with the council of ministers.

There was a steady growth in the number of ministries and in the size of the civil service, which was reserved for Kuwaytī citizens. The security forces were also expanded. Conscription was introduced in 1979 and by 1986 the Kuwayt army numbered 12,000. In addition there was a national guard and a national security force under the ministry of the interior of some 18,000. These forces constituted a control on each other and on the police. Leaving aside the constant threat of being drawn into the Gulf war the main duty of the security forces was to combat isolated acts of terrorism which threatened Kuwayt. In this they were successful and the prosperity of Kuwayt increased. Its population grew from about 250,000 in 1961 to 1.7 million in 1985 (of whom 43 per cent were Kuwaytīs and perhaps 25 per cent Palestinians). Seventy per cent of the population was literate in 1985. Although the non-Kuwaytīs had no political rights they enjoyed many of the benefits of the welfare state.

Baḥrayn remained under the control of the Āl Khalīfa family. As in Kuwayt the ruler (Shaykh ʿĪsā) took the title of Amir at independence and the 1973 Baḥraynī constitution also provided for a council of ministers and a national assembly. The heir apparent (Shaykh Khalīfa) was prime minister and the key ministries were controlled by members of the royal family; in 1987 they held 7 of 16 ministries. The partly-elected national assembly encountered similar problems to those of its Kuwayt counterpart and was dissolved in 1975. The opposition in Baḥrayn was composed especially of members of the Shīʿī majority who were excluded from positions of power in the Sunnī-dominated state. After 1979 a continual concern was that the Shīʿīs would respond to appeals from Iran and that Iran would revive her claims to the islands. Baḥrayn also had a powerful, organized labour force which continued to agitate for better conditions. Baḥrayn was less able to buy off opposition with welfare benefits. Its oil was running out, its refinery out of date and its strenuous attempts at industrial diversification after 1966 brought in little new income although its banking activities grew rapidly after 1975. Baḥrayn imported few foreign workers and its population grew mainly by natural increase from 216,000 in 1971 to 416,000 in 1987 of whom about 75 per cent were literate. Its armed forces remained tiny; there was no conscription and in 1987 the regular forces totalled under 3,000. For internal security Baḥrayn relied principally on a public security force of similar size. In these circumstances Baḥrayn was obliged to look outside for support, to the GCC and notably to Saudi Arabia which financed a causeway to link Baḥrayn to the mainland. If Kuwayt was one model of a second generation Gulf state Baḥrayn was another.

The political evolution of Qaṭar was similar to that of Kuwayt and Baḥrayn. The vast Āl Thānī family imposed its control over the new institutions created after independence. The 1970 constitution called for a council of ministers and an advisory council. Āl Thānīs dominated the council of ministers; Shaykh Khalīfa, who replaced his cousin Aḥmad as Amir in 1972 by a bloodless palace coup, retained his post as prime minister, and gave the majority of other ministerial posts to members of the ruling family; in 1987 8 of the 15 ministers were Āl Thānīs. The advisory council was appointed; provision was made for elections but none was held. Opposition remained muted. Qaṭar was a small state; its population rose from about 100,000 at independence to an estimated 230,000 in 1988 and a majority of its people were foreign workers. Its armed forces numbered only 6,000 in 1987 and, like Baḥrayn, it looked outside for help to the GCC and by tradition to Saudi Arabia. Unlike Baḥrayn, however, its oil revenues remained abundant and provided a very high standard of living for its people.

The United Arab Emirates (UAE) had peculiar political problems. The federation had come reluctantly into existence in 1971 and consisted of a group of mutually suspicious states held together by the wealth of Abū Dhabī and fear of the outside. One, Ra's al-Khayma, did not join the others until 1972. It was the hope of Shaykh Zayd of Abū Dhabī to turn the UAE into a unified, centralized structure by developing powerful union institutions and it was the desire of the other rulers to circumvent this ambition or at least to slow down the process.

The 1971 UAE constitution established a president, council of ministers, consultative assembly and a supreme council of rulers. The last institution was dominant and within it the rulers of Abū Dhabī and Dubayy possessed vetoes. Abū Dhabī and Dubayy also shared the principal union posts: Shaykh Zayd became president, Shaykh Rāshid of Dubayy vice president and Rāshid's son prime minister. In 1979 Rāshid took over the office of prime minister as well. At first the council of ministers was composed of the nominees of rulers but in 1977 an attempt was made to make appointments dependent upon individual merit. Even so, ruling families continued to dominate the union government; in 1987 11 of 25 ministers came from the shaykhly houses. The consultative assembly had little importance. The other main union institutions were legal – a union system of courts was established in 1978 – and military. In 1976 a union defence force was established to integrate the separate armies of the shaykhdoms. By 1986 it numbered 43,000.

Throughout Shaykh Zayd sought to expand the role of the union institutions at the expense of those of the shaykhdoms. In 1973 Abū Dhabī dissolved its own government and merged wholly with the union. But Abū Dhabī was the largest, most populous and wealthiest state and to the other states it seemed that the union would become merely Abū Dhabī writ large. The other states endeavoured to preserve shaykhly independence and resisted attempts to co-ordinate economic policy. Resistance to the further extension of union authority was led by Dubayy, especially after the assumption of the prime ministership by Shaykh Rāshid. Nevertheless, union authority continued to advance: the development of roads linked the UAE more closely and the establishment of first a currency board (1973) and later a central bank (1980) marked the progress of ideas of greater economic co-ordination.

Despite these tensions the UAE was highly successful principally because of the abundance of oil revenues. Abū Dhabī continued to be the largest oil producer but Dubayy and Shārja joined the ranks of the elect. A large part of the revenues went on social services, especially health and education, on communications, agriculture and industrial diversification, although there was much duplication of industrial effort. The principal activity was construction which attracted large numbers of foreign workers, especially from the Indian subcontinent. The population of the UAE increased very rapidly from 320,000 in 1972 to 1.6 million at the census of 1985. Approximately one-third of this number was regarded as indigenous. As elsewhere in the Gulf the main question was how to safeguard the great wealth of the former poor tribesmen.

OMAN SINCE 1970

The coup of 1970 brought to power Sultan Qābūs, then aged 29, and he quickly established complete domination over the government of what was renamed the Sultanate of Oman. At first he brought back his uncle as prime minister but at the end of 1971 Qābūs took direct control of the government and of the ministries of foreign affairs, defence and finance. Āl Bū Saʿīds figured largely in other departments of government which greatly expanded to accommodate them and others. Of 24 ministers in 1987 nine, apart from the Sultan, were members of the ruling family, the remainder being drawn from old bureaucratic families and tribal leaders. A feature of the years after 1970 was the monopoly of posts by Omani Arabs at the expense of those of Zanzibari, Baluchi and Indian origin and of the foreign advisers who had previously played so large a role. As elsewhere in the Gulf one may see the new political élite in terms of concentric circles composed of ruler, household, notables and citizens, narrowly defined. One may also observe the same process of the elevation of the ruler and his household above other groups. In particular the role of tribal leaders declined after 1970, for example, Aḥmad ibn Muḥammad al-Ḥārithī, whose support had been vital to the success of the Sultan in his struggle with the tribal rebels of Oman in 1957 and who had played a major role in Omani politics thereafter, was arrested in 1970. Tribal forces were reduced in importance as the Sultan's forces grew in response to the security problems of Dhufār. By 1986 the armed forces (Omanized by the replacement of the previously dominant Baluchis after 1970) numbered 21,500 against 5,000 tribal militia.

The rapid development of Oman after 1970 was paid for by oil. By 1985 oil and gas accounted for 47 per cent of GDP and 90 per cent of foreign earnings. A large part of the proceeds went on defence but there was substantial investment in economic development, especially communications, and social services. In 1970 Oman had only 16 schools; in 1985 it had nearly 600 and a university was opened in 1986. Economic investment was concentrated on construction during the 1970s and early 1980s and foreign workers were imported mainly from India and Pakistan. The collapse of oil prices hurt Oman more than other countries, brought many projects to a stop and led to a switch back to agriculture in which Oman had greater potential than any other state of the region outside North Yemen. Oman remained the least developed country in eastern Arabia, however, despite its rapid growth. Most of the population remained in rural areas; of a population estimated at 1.2 million in 1985 only 50,000 lived in the largest town, Muscat.

SECTION III

THE NEAR EAST IN INTERNATIONAL RELATIONS

CHAPTER FIFTEEN

European Predominance and Its Decline, 1923–56

EUROPEAN SUPREMACY, 1923–39

The post First World War settlement had the effect of partially insulating the Near East from international affairs. In a great band running through most of the Arab world, from Morocco to Iraq, British and French influence predominated. North and south of that band were independent states but they had nowhere to go since no other great power either could or would challenge British and French influence: Germany was beaten, Italy was too weak, the Soviet Union was absorbed in revolutionary reconstruction and the United States had returned to isolation. Only if Britain and France had fallen out would there have been an opportunity for Near Eastern states to manoeuvre in the international field and this did not happen. Until Anglo–French supremacy was threatened in the late 1930s the international history of the Near East was quite different from the pre-Lausanne period of international contention, the age of the Eastern Question.

A contrary view has been expressed, namely that what distinguished the period 1923 to 1939 was the appearance of Near Eastern states in an active role of national self-assertion. It is quite true that some Near Eastern states (Iraq, Saudi Arabia and Egypt) secured their independence during this period and some took up their places in the League of Nations (Iran from its foundation, Turkey and Iraq in 1932, Afghanistan in 1934 and Egypt in 1936). There are several examples of regional diplomatic dealings between Near Eastern states, notably the Saadabad pact of 1937 and many cases where regional states successfully asserted themselves against the Great Powers. But this assertion was contained within narrowly confined limits; in no sense were the Near Eastern states free players on the international stage. They operated within a framework built and maintained primarily by Britain and France.

Britain's greatest interest in the Near East, as in other parts of the world, was in the preservation of peace. She had all she wanted and more, and was unsure if she could hold what she had if there were war. Bonar Law's anguished cry over Chanak in 1922 – "we cannot alone act as the policemen of the world" [1] is one that echoes through British foreign policy in this period. Doubtful of the adequacy of her own resources she turned to collective security through the League of Nations as the main guarantee of peace. For Britain the League was not a mere idealistic aspiration but a practical and necessary device for her own protection and the safeguarding of her interests, an attitude which may help to explain the extraordinary attention she paid to the League's opinions concerning Britain's discharge of her obligations under the Palestine mandate.

The Near East occupied a lowly place in Britain's scale of international priorities. First was the defence of the United Kingdom itself with its associated concerns with the Channel, the Low Countries and resistance to any power which sought to dominate Europe. Then came Britain's imperial defence obligations followed by the defence of the Far East. Only in fourth place came the Near East which was thought by naval strategists to be indefensible in time of war because of the probability that the Mediterranean would be closed to British shipping by Italian submarine and air attacks. The Near East could not be defended from India because Indian resources were almost entirely committed to India's own defence.

Until 1938 the Near East was starved of defence resources. Outside Egypt and the Sudan there were few troops except for those engaged in peacekeeping in Palestine since 1930 and most of the work of imperial policing was done by the Royal Air Force. The main base for the support of the Near East was vulnerable Malta; Haifa could not be used because of mandate restrictions, Alexandria's utility was reduced because of Britain's dubious position in Egypt and the Canal Zone base did not then exist, and Famagusta, briefly considered in the 1930s, was rejected when the 1938 Anglo–Italian agreement made Cyprus ineligible as a base. During the 1920s and early 1930s there was no substantial outside threat but the rise of Germany and Italy apparently altered the situation. Still there was no idea that the Near East should be defended by arms; it was to be defended by diplomacy which meant the conciliation of Italy. In 1935 the policy of conciliation clashed over the Italian invasion of Ethiopia with Britain's other great interest of upholding collective security through the League and plunged British diplomacy into desperate contortions as it attempted to reconcile the two policies.

Britain's lack of defence capability in the Near East also implied the conciliation of regional states; hence the desire to appease Turkey over Alexandretta in 1937–9 and the Arab states over Palestine after 1937. The commitment of 50,000 troops to suppress the Arab rising in Palestine in 1938 offended against all Britain's strategic principles in the Near East. Palestine was of minor consequence, the troops were required elsewhere and Arab friendship was needed. Once again Britain's problem was to reconcile Near Eastern strategy with her obligations to the League; the 1939 White Paper was an attempt to accomplish this trick. But at the same time Britain took another decision, namely to regrade the Near East above the Far East and to fight Italy for the Mediterranean if it became necessary. This crucial decision, however, was less the outcome of a new sense of the importance of British interests in the Near East than a conviction that Britain's position in the region, as in the world, ultimately depended on her prestige and her prestige depended on her being seen to be ready to fight for her interests. To do otherwise would be to hand over the region to Italy.

British interests in the Near East were those of communications and oil. The concern with the balance of power in Europe, which had dominated Near Eastern policy before the First World War, was no longer seen as directly affecting the region; indeed that concern had been related more to Ottoman territories in Europe and to the Straits than to the non-European territories of the region. The concept of communications had, however, widened to embrace communications by sea, air and land. Sea communications meant, above all, the Suez Canal, through which between 9 and 14 per cent of Britain's trade passed during this period and which was the principal conduit for warships and troop carrriers proceeding to the east. The Red Sea and Indian Ocean formed an extension of the Suez communication system. "It has always been, and it is today," declared the Foreign Secretary, Anthony Eden, in 1937, "a major British interest that no great Power should establish itself on the eastern shore of the Red Sea." [2] It is interesting to observe, however, first, that there was no question of excluding foreign powers from the western shore where Italy was securely located (and the French base of Djibouti was near at hand), and secondly that the prohibition was held to apply equally to Britain. Moreover, it should be noted that it was generally, and correctly assumed that the utility of the canal route would be greatly diminished in the event of war because of the insecurity of the

Mediterranean and that the main route of sea communications with the east would necessarily become the Cape of Good Hope route or (in the case of Australia and New Zealand) the route by way of Panama. These limitations on the use of the canal also applied to the use of the land route through Palestine to ᶜAqaba and thence by water via the Red Sea to the east, a route discussed as an alternative to the Egyptian route if conditions in Egypt denied use of the canal to Britain, but never developed.

Air communications were the great innovation of the interwar period. Due to the relatively short range of contemporary aircraft numerous landing fields and facilities were required along the routes. These routes and their impedimenta were planned and developed during the late 1920s and early 1930s. Their main use was for the transport of passengers and their potential strategic value was for the rapid movement of troops in the event of crisis, although it was always understood that large numbers of troops and their equipment could only be moved by sea and land. Imperial Airways air routes crisscrossed the Near East but the principal junction was in Egypt through which passed the routes to India, Australia and South Africa. A second route to the East traversed Palestine, Transjordan, Iraq and the Arab shore of the Persian Gulf, after Iran had made difficulties which led to the abandonment in 1932 of the original plan to use the Iranian shore. There was no particular reason why the protection of commercial operations should have been a matter of military strategy; Imperial Airways could have made commercial agreements with the governments concerned in the same way as other airlines or other commercial operations. Alternative routes through Turkey or French territories were available. It was the military uses which made the protection of airways of strategic importance although contemporary strategic argument commonly confused the two issues.

Land communications were of much less importance mainly because few of the various plans for roads and railways through the region reached fruition. Of the railways the Ḥijāz railway remained closed, the Baghdad railway ran mainly through non-British territory, the Cairo–Haifa line was little used because of the variations in gauges and the contemplated line from Haifa to Baghdad was never built. Nor was the road planned to link Palestine to Iraq built either and the main east–west land route was that which ran northwards through Palestine to Damascus and thence across the Syrian desert to Baghdad, outside British control.

Britain's second major interest was oil. In 1938 about 18 per cent of Britain's oil requirements was met by Iran, the site of the operations of the Anglo–Iranian Oil Company and of the refinery at Ābādān. Iran was second only to the Caribbean as a fount of oil for Britain and was more important still as a source of oil for naval, air force and military uses. Nevertheless, valuable as Iranian oil was to Britain it was not irreplaceable. Britain's second great oil interest in the Near East was much less important; only 4 per cent of Iraqi oil which came through the pipeline to Haifa was used by Britain. The oil of Iran and Iraq was, of course, a valuable commercial asset.

In any balance of British interests in the Near Eastern region Egypt, as the great junction of sea and air communications to Africa and the East, stood out as the most important country. From 1922 until 1936 Britain sought to make an agreement which would safeguard her interests there and finally achieved a settlement by the 1936 Anglo–Egyptian treaty which provided for the continuation of the British garrison and for the use of Egyptian facilities in time of war. Palestine was regarded as important as a protection for the flank of the Egyptian position (although Sinai and the Western Desert were thought adequate against a land threat, at least until the Italian build up in Libya, and discussions of Egyptian defence concentrated chiefly on the threat of attack from the sea) and as the centre of a secondary system of communications. Possession of Palestine also had a less tangible value: "the religious associations of the Holy Land [Christian, Muslim and Jewish] are of the first importance to Great Britain" ran a 1938 assessment.[3]

The second centre of British interests in the Near East was in the eastern part of the region. Before 1914 the creation of an insulated buffer zone against the prospect of the approach of Russia towards India had always been a British objective but from 1921 to 1940 there was no British alarm about a Russian advance. British interests in Iran were now primarily economic and centred on oil and her interests in Iraq were concerned with economics (wheat perhaps more than oil), communications and the fulfilment of her treaty obligations. The 1930 Anglo–Iraq treaty was similar to the later treaty with Egypt; Britain had the use of certain facilities in Iraq, namely the air bases near Baghdad and Basra, and more extensive rights in time of war. In return she undertook responsibilities for the defence of Iraq.

Britain's position in Arabia was strong. From Kuwayt to Aden she controlled all the Arabian shoreline with the exception of the Saudi possession of al-Ḥasā on the Gulf coast and could prevent any foreign power obtaining bases from which to threaten British sea or air communications. Inland her power and knowledge were slighter and she was taken by surprise by Ibn Saʿūd's conquest of the Ḥijāz in 1925.

During the 1920s Britain sought a negotiated settlement to the territorial disputes which threatened to disrupt Arabia. Such a settlement could only be obtained by drawing lines on maps and substituting territorial boundaries for claims over tribes and their pastures. In this way Britain contributed further to the process of state definition in the Near East. In 1925 by the agreements of Bahra and Hadda she sought to establish the frontiers between Saudi Arabia and Iraq and Transjordan respectively. The first agreement was largely successful but Ibn Saᶜūd's continuing unwillingness to accept the loss of ᶜAqaba meant that the Hadda frontier was only partially accepted until 1965. By the 1927 treaty of Jidda Britain recognized the complete independence of Ibn Saᶜūd in Najd and the Ḥijāz. Throughout, Britain sought to conciliate Ibn Saᶜūd, even to the extent of limiting her rights of protection over the smaller Gulf states, but could never overcome his distrust of her relations with the Hashimites of Iraq and Transjordan. However, Ibn Saᶜūd had no other realistic option until 1942 and British influence prevailed throughout the period. Finally, in 1934 Britain achieved an agreement with Yemen by which the Imām ceased his interference in the Aden protectorate. British interest in Arabia remained negative; she wished to keep other powers out but there was nothing she coveted for herself.

At the end of the First World War Britain was deeply involved in the construction of a new state system in the Near East and in the internal government of the region. Between 1919 and 1921 she had decided that the effort was beyond her resources and considerably reduced her commitments. Subsequently, her object was to strive for good relations with strong regional powers and to safeguard her limited interests by treaties. With the exception of Palestine she was broadly successful in this endeavour.

French interests in the Near East were slighter than those of Britain. France's main concern outside Europe was with the western Mediterranean and with the maintenance of her position in the three North African territories of Morocco, Algeria and Tunisia. Most of the great French bases were in the western Mediterranean at Toulon, in Corsica, at Bizerta and near Oran. By comparison France's position in the eastern Mediterranean was weak; mandate restrictions inhibited the development of Tripoli in Lebanon as a base. France's possessions in Indo-China, Somaliland and Madagascar, however, meant that she too was concerned with safe communications through the Near East although she was effectively dependent upon Britain in this respect. Nevertheless, the French mandated territories in Syria and Lebanon were used for air links to the east. More important to France, however, was the Suez Canal in which Frenchmen were also major shareholders.

France earnestly strove to make her Near Eastern territories pay through economic development. She sought for oil without success and became increasingly dependent on the flow of oil from Iraq through the pipeline to Tripoli. France was the principal buyer of Iraqi oil during the 1930s: she bought three-quarters of Iraqi output amounting to half of France's imports of oil in 1938. France also hoped to make Syria and Lebanon once more the main entrepôt for the trade of the interior: she planned a railway to supplement the Damascus-Baghdad desert road and during the 1930s cultivated good relations with the newly independent government of Iraq, at one time even floating the idea of a Hashimite ruler in Damascus.

France also had extensive cultural interests in the Near East. Since the nineteenth century France had proclaimed her civilizing mission in the Near East, a concept which embraced both the notion of France as the protector and promoter of Catholic interests in the region and a broader duty to extend the benefits of French civilization and values, particularly through French schools and the French language. Although there was a substantial development of French schools in Syria and Lebanon during the interwar period French cultural influence was not confined to the Levant. Through most of the Near East before 1914 France had been the leading European cultural influence and a model for educational and legal reforms. Most of the writers and politicians who emerged after the First World War had French as their first foreign language. It was France's endeavour to retain this cultural pre-eminence against the challenge of English and to lay the foundation for close French relations with Egypt, Turkey and Iran in the future.

Finally, like Britain, France was concerned by the repercussions of developments in the Near East on her situation elsewhere. In particular France was concerned that political developments in Syria and Lebanon might influence Muslims in North Africa. And in the late 1930s she became worried that challenges to her power in the Near East might inhibit her ability to resist German designs in Europe. It was this last concern that prompted her to surrender Alexandretta to Turkey in 1939. In this, as in other matters, France worked in concert with Britain. Rather more slowly than Britain France came to the same conclusion: the best and cheapest way to safeguard her interests in the region was to try to establish treaty relations with independent states. In 1936 she came near to achieving this by the treaties signed with Syria and Lebanon but by 1939 she had not succeeded in resolving all the problems which arose and the treaties remained unratified.

Italy emerged from the First World War with few gains in the Near East, only minor improvements to her frontiers in Libya and Somaliland and confirmation of her possession of the Dodecanese. Italy's interests were primarily in the Mediterranean, through which passed nearly all her trade, and the Adriatic. She developed naval bases on the Italian mainland, in Sicily, Sardinia and Pantelleria, on Leros and in Libya at Tripoli, which was linked by a new military road to Tobruk. But between 1923 and 1932 Italy was content to pursue a policy which did not challenge Britain or France. Rather she relied on economic and cultural penetration of the Near East, an enterprise which involved the development of shipping and banking and an attempt to assert a position as protector of Catholics. More ambitious schemes put forward by Italian governors and officials were not followed through: talk of the revival of Italian claims in Asia Minor in 1926 only alienated Turkey; the effect of the 1926 treaty with Yemen was cancelled by an agreement with Britain the following year to keep out of Arabia; and the proposal of the Italian ambassador in Egypt to attempt to take over the British position in that country was flatly rejected.

From 1932 Italy began to pursue a more ambitious policy in the Near East. The most dramatic examples of the new policy were the Italian conquest of Ethiopia in 1935, which raised the possibility of a new Italian initiative in Arabia, and the invasion of Albania in April 1939 which posed the threat, most alarming to Turkey, of further Italian penetration of the Balkans. Radio broadcasts in Arabic began in 1934, Italian communities in the Near East (estimated at 200,000 in 1938 of which 60,000 were in Egypt) were encouraged to organize and be more assertive, shipping and airline interests were pushed more aggressively, schools, scholarships and societies were founded, subsidies distributed, and arms sold. Italy posed as the protector of both Islam and the Jews. Benito Mussolini aspired to be all things to all men in the Near East; he wanted a Jewish state in Palestine but one which should be small enough as not to offend the Arabs.

In fact there was very little substance to the new Italian policy. Italian prestige rose in the Near East after her Ethiopian success, although her policies also gave rise to Egyptian and Turkish concern; Italian commercial penetration increased but still only 10 per cent of Italian trade was conducted with the Levant in the later 1930s; and she remained unwilling to alienate Britain. In 1938 Britain and Italy concluded a treaty intended to settle their differences; the two powers agreed to recognize the independence of Saudi Arabia and the Yemen, and Italy undertook to avoid areas where British influence predominated. It was only with the defeat of France in 1940 that Italian ambitions took on flesh.

The First World War set a term to the powerful German economic and cultural influence which had developed in the Near East before and during the war. During the 1920s Germany avoided any political involvement in the Near East and confined herself to modest economic and cultural ventures. By and large this policy continued under the Third Reich after 1933. Germany's main interest was in Eastern Europe, her main rival was the Soviet Union and she had no wish to quarrel with Britain and France. As in the years before 1914 her principal interest in the Near East was in the Northern Tier, that is in Turkey, Iran and Afghanistan. Partly this interest was an extension of her eastern ambitions, partly it was a way of developing political influence among the states on the southern frontier of the Soviet Union, an influence which might be useful in the event of a dispute with that country, and partly it was a commercial interest. German trade with this region grew rapidly in the later 1930s: in 1938–9 Germany had nearly half of the trade of Turkey and one-third of Iran's; and her trade with Afghanistan increased five times between 1937 and 1939. Germany supplied advisers and arms and German firms were active in construction. In 1938 the German air service to Iran, established since 1925, was extended to Afghanistan. Too much should not be read into this activity, however. Important as trade with Germany was to the states of the Northern Tier it was of little value to Germany. And Germany was still unwilling to be drawn into political commitments to the states of the region; their help might eventually be useful but she was not going to quarrel with the USSR and Britain for the sake of any of them.

German activity in the Arab world was very slight. Germany was uninterested in oil concessions because she feared to become dependent upon Near Eastern oil and could see no political advantage worth the price of annoying Britain, France and Italy. An alternative policy was advocated by some Germans from 1936 according to which Germany should bid for the support of Arab nationalism and make agreements with Iraq and Saudi Arabia. In fact an arms deal with Saudi Arabia was made in May 1939 but Saudi Arabia got very little from it. A sizeable trade was conducted with Egypt during the period 1925–30 but it collapsed during the depression and was never rebuilt. A pro-Arab policy implied an anti-Zionist policy over Palestine but Nazi ideology pointed in favour of support for the Jewish national home as a suitable receptacle for unwanted German Jews. In 1933

Germany concluded a profitable agreement with the Zionists by which Jews emigrating to Palestine could take property in the form of German exports. Only briefly in 1937 did Germany hesitate over Palestine when she feared that a Jewish state hostile to Germany might come into being under the provisions of the Peel plan.

The interests of the United States in the Near East during the period 1920 to 1939 were negligible. Such interests as existed were almost wholly private and included the educational activities of Protestant missionaries and others, a restrained interest by some Jews in the progress of the national home policy in Palestine and a strong dislike on the part of Americans of Greek and Armenian origin for the republic of Turkey, a modest interest in trade, construction and the provision of expertise, and the involvement of American oil interests in Iraq and Arabia. But the Near East remained near the bottom of the United States' scale of world priorities.

A clear distinction should be made in Soviet policy towards the Near East between policy towards the Northern Tier and policy in the Arab world. In Turkey, Iran and Afghanistan the USSR had a strong interest. Through the Straits of the Bosphorus and the Dardanelles passed much of Soviet seaborne trade and the Straits were also a gateway to the Black Sea for an enemy of the USSR. The three countries all bordered the southern regions of the Soviet Union, their Muslim inhabitants could appeal to Soviet Muslims across the frontier and their governments could give facilities to a powerful international enemy of the USSR. Much Soviet trade was conducted with the three countries. In February–March 1921 the young Soviet state abandoned the policy of fostering revolution in the region and concluded treaties with the existing governments of the three states. Further treaties were made in 1925–7 and again in 1933. The purpose of the treaties was to try to ensure that the states concerned would ally with no hostile power against the USSR and to provide a satisfactory basis for economic relations. The Soviet Union planned no expansion into the region but wanted weak, dependent states on her southern frontier. At the same time she wanted advantageous economic relations and the two aims came into conflict in her dealings with Iran when Soviet insistence on strict terms for economic transactions induced Iran to look elsewhere for help. Nor was the USSR able to exercise as much pressure as she wished on Turkey. The USSR hoped to achieve a more satisfactory arrangement for the Straits, one which would place their control in the hands of the Black Sea powers. But at Lausanne (1923) and Montreux (1936) the USSR was obliged to accept regimes which gave her little control over the Straits.

Soviet interest in the Arab world was very slight. Diplomatic relations were opened with the Ḥijāz (1924), Saudi Arabia (1926) and the Yemen (1928) but dealings amounted to little and the Soviet missions were closed in 1938. The Comintern, which dealt with local communist parties, was more interested in and more knowledgeable about the Arab world than was the USSR but it was no more effective; in fact the activities of minority-dominated local communist parties reacted unfavourably on the reputation of the Soviet Union. The old Orthodox link with Syria and Palestine was temporarily broken.

The regional powers were primarily concerned with domestic developments and anxious for peace. Turkey always identified the USSR as her main enemy and Italy as a possible threat. She endeavoured to protect herself against these threats in three ways. First, by conciliation of the USSR, second, by looking towards Britain as the strongest naval power in the Mediterranean and third, by regional alliances, notably the Balkans Entente (1934) with Greece, Yugoslavia and Rumania and the Saadabad Pact (1937) with Iran, Iraq and Afghanistan. Iran was also concerned with the threat of Russia but perceived Britain additionally as a threat to her independence by virtue of the British position in Iraq, the Gulf and British dominance of Iranian oil. Accordingly, Iran tried conciliation but also strove for regional alliances and for the help of a third power. Neither the United States nor Germany was willing to fill this last role. The international relations of Iraq and Egypt were dominated by their dealings with Britain; both, however, also had regional interests. In the period under discussion, however, these regional interests did not clash; Egyptian interest was focused on the Nile and Iraqi interest on the old Ottoman Arab provinces. Iraq also had border problems with her neighbours which required adjustment; the frontier with Turkey was settled in 1926 by the award of Mosul to Iraq and the frontier with Iran by the agreement of 1937 which left most of the Shaṭṭ al-ᶜArab in Iraq. Iraq did not abandon the hope of eventually acquiring Kuwayt.

THE NEAR EAST IN THE SECOND WORLD WAR

The Second World War had none of the importance of the war of 1914–18 for the Near East. The first war had led to the destruction of the Ottoman Empire, the political reconstruction of the Near East and the establishment of French, and more especially British dominion in the Arab region. By comparison the second war merely hastened the demise of French influence, momentarily revived and briefly prolonged British domination, and gave an additional impetus to the advance of the USA and the USSR in the region. The economic effects of the second war were similar to those of the first: in the early years hardship due to the disruption of traditional patterns of trade and in the later years prosperity due to the demands of Allied forces in the region. One final result might be mentioned: the second war changed the way people thought about the Near East. Political, military and economic planning fostered and redefined the notion of the Near East as a region and the formation of the Arab League promoted the notion of an Arab world. Indeed, it could be said that the Second World War marks the period when the old concept of a Near East with its core in the former Ottoman territories gives way to a new concept of a Middle East with its heartland in the Arab world.

The main reason why the Near East did not assume greater importance during the Second World War was that Germany was not very interested in the region. From September 1939 until June 1940 the Near East was little affected by the war. The fall of France in June 1940 did offer Germany the option of taking up the policy of attacking British influence in the region by exploiting the links already established with the Northern Tier and supporting the ambitions of Arab malcontents. Britons, who were much more conscious of the opportunities which beckoned to Germany, contemplated the possibility of a German bid to win over the countries of the Balkans and Turkey and then a drive down towards the canal and the Gulf timed to coincide with another thrust led by Italy from the west. From November 1940 to July 1941 British planners were obsessed by this strategy and were led by their obsession to attach far too much importance to the Near East.

Adolf Hitler was uninterested in a strategy focused on the Near East. He had no faith in Arabs as allies and no wish to break down the British empire in the Near East. Contrary to British speculations he was uninterested in the oil of the region which amounted to less than 5 per cent of world production in 1940. Germany preferred to concentrate first on the possibility of a direct attack on Britain and then on preparations for the attack on the USSR. The Vichy regime in Syria and Lebanon was left alone and Italy, which now entered the war, was given a free hand in the Near East. Italy rejected the Arab option and her main objective was to replace Britain as the leading European power in the region by taking over the British position. In fact Italy proved quite incapable of executing this ambition despite a large superiority in troops in the region. By the early months of 1941 she had been defeated in East Africa and in Libya and thereafter her importance was only as an auxiliary to Germany in the Near East. The British campaigns in Iraq, Syria and Lebanon in the spring and early summer of 1941 ended for a time the possibility of the accomplishment of the drive from the north.

The German invasion of the USSR in June 1941 changed the complexion of affairs in the Near East. Before that event British planners had seen the USSR, linked to Germany by the 1939 Nazi–Soviet pact, as a major threat in the Near East and in the winter of 1940 had even contemplated bombing Baku. In fact the USSR had had little interest in advancing towards the Gulf, despite the famous Hitler–Molotov conversations of November 1940 and the subsequent German–Soviet agreement when the interests of the USSR were defined as extending southwards from Batum and Baku in the general direction of the Persian Gulf. At issue between Germany and the USSR in 1940–1 was the advance of Germany in central and south-eastern Europe which the USSR wished to reverse and against which it hoped to guard by establishing a base in the vicinity of the Straits. Hitler was concerned to divert Soviet attention away from Europe and the Straits towards India in the hope of embroiling the USSR and Britain. The USSR was uninterested in this possibility and the agreement was a non-meeting of minds in which the much quoted definition of Soviet interests was a compromise between Hitler's effort to push the USSR in a direction in which she did not intend to move and the Soviet hope to obstruct German and Italian designs in the Near East.

The German invasion made Britain and the USSR allies and the effects were soon felt in the Northern Tier. Afghanistan was compelled to expel her German technicians and advisers; Iran was occupied; and Turkey came under pressure to abandon her neutrality and enter the war. The effects in the Arab world were much less although the new respectability of the USSR paved the way for her establishment of diplomatic relations with Arab states in 1943. The invasion also gave rise to visions of a new giant Axis pincer threat during 1942. The German successes against the USSR and the drive into the Caucasus awakened the possibility that the USSR would collapse and that a German advance into the Near East from the north would be combined with an invasion of Egypt by Rommel's Afrika Corps in the west. The whole Near East might then fall to Germany which could advance south-eastwards to link up with the Japanese in India. From such nightmarish speculations the Near East was preserved first by lack of interest in the scheme on the part of either Germany or Japan and second by the defeat of German forces at Stalingrad and Alamein (al-ᶜAlamayn) in the autumn of 1942, the landings in French North Africa and the subsequent expulsion of the Axis powers from the region. By the end of 1942 Germany was not a factor in the Near East and the only question which remained was what the Allies might do with the region.

The fears and tension of the years 1940–2 had left their mark on the Near East. Britain's concern was to support friendly regimes and to eliminate regimes thought to be unreliable. The regime of Rashīd ᶜĀlī in Iraq and its army supporters were destroyed by force in May 1941 and Hashimite authority was restored. In Syria and Lebanon the Vichy regime was also overthrown in June–July 1941 by arms and a Free French regime installed. But the Free French regime existed on sufferance and was obliged to pledge itself to the independence of Syria and Lebanon and to conduct itself in a way acceptable to the demands of nationalists with the result that its authority was eventually compromised and the independence of Syria and Lebanon secured. The Egyptian regime survived on a knife edge; in February 1942 Britain was ready to force King Fārūq to abdicate but he saved himself by consenting to deliver the government to the pro-British Wafd party. The Iranian regime did not survive: in September 1941 Riżā Shāh was obliged to abdicate although the monarchy continued. Turkey struggled desperately to remain neutral, resist Soviet demands and continue trading with the Axis and was successful. By contrast Transjordan and Saudi Arabia did well out of the war. Transjordan proved herself a faithful and useful ally and ended with a much expanded Arab Legion. Saudi Arabia, after a painful period of economic difficulty, found a friend in the USA and began to reap the benefits of her oil.

The early years of the war had produced great economic problems throughout the Near East. These problems were the result of, first, the diversion of European goods to home markets which had a serious impact on the modernization programmes of Near Eastern states and, second, the dislocation of commerce due to the restrictions on trade with belligerents and the shortage of shipping which was required for war purposes. This last problem was very grave for those countries which could not feed themselves as they could not import sufficient food, prices rose and in some areas there was famine. Britain eventually decided that it was necessary to plan distribution on a regional basis and set up in Cairo in 1941 the Middle East Supply Centre (MESC) which, mainly through a licensing policy aimed at reducing civilian imports by 80 per cent, maintained essential supplies to the different parts of the region. The MESC did not save the Near East and particularly Iran, Syria and Lebanon from heavy inflation between 1941 and 1945. From 1942 the United States took part in the system, branches were set up in different countries and the MESC eventually began to assume a much larger role in planning for economic development. The ideas pioneered by the MESC, notably in the matter of land reform, were to have a considerable influence on subsequent economic development. In particular the MESC's scope promoted the notion of regional economic planning. The notion of the Near and Middle East as a region was also stimulated by other military and political institutions, notably the existence of Middle East Command with its HQ in Cairo to conduct the war in the region, the creation of the Middle East War Council and the establishment of a British minister of state for the Middle East (1941). It is worthy of note that Turkey was excluded from the orbit of these institutions thereby underlining the growing separation of that state from the region of which it had once been the fulcrum.

The new centre of what was now referred to as the Middle East was Egypt, and Cairo, which was the focus of so much regional activity during the war, also became the centre of a new political initiative, the Arab League. Ideas of Arab unity had been floating around for more than half a century but between the two world wars they had received an impetus from the ambitions of Arab rulers, notably the Hashimites of Iraq and Transjordan and ʿAbd al-ʿAzīz ibn Saʿūd, the activities of radical parties in the Levant and Iraq, the writings of Arab intellectuals such as Sāṭiʿ al-Ḥusrī, and the popular enthusiasms generated by Arab issues, notably the Palestine dispute. Egypt had not been wholly detached from these developments but Egyptians had tended to stand on the side lines and to regard Arabism as only one, and not the most important of the activities with which they were concerned; the government of ʿAlī Māhir in 1939 was the first Egyptian government which gave a prominent place to Pan-Arabism. In Egypt, as elsewhere, it was not easy to distinguish between Muslim and Arab enthusiasms.

The war gave a fresh energy to Pan-Arab ideas through the experience of regional economic planning and because of the political questions raised by the future of Syria and Lebanon in particular. From 1941 various projects of Arab federations were put forward and the movement received British backing when the foreign secretary, Anthony Eden, spoke approvingly of such ambitions at the Mansion House on 29 May 1941. Britain now believed that the movement for Arab unity, which she had formerly regarded without enthusiasm, was sufficiently strong that she would be unwise to stand aside and perhaps surrender leadership to an enemy state. It was also thought that it would be easier to solve the Palestine problem within the context of an Arab federation. There still remained real British doubts whether a political federation would advance British interests and Britain tried to confine the movement to economic and cultural areas. The initiative then passed to Arab hands and especially to Egypt which now came forward as a main supporter of Arab unity. Egypt was unwilling to allow the Arab movement to become a Hashimite-dominated scheme of Fertile Crescent union and this attitude was shared by other states including Syria, Lebanon and Saudi Arabia. The Hashimites too were divided between Iraq and Transjordan. In these circumstances Egypt took the lead, a conference was called in Egypt and on 7 October 1944 the Alexandria Protocol set out a plan for an Arab League. The League came into being on 10 May 1945.

THE POST-WAR NEAR EAST, 1945–54

At the end of the Second World War the leading Great Powers in the Near East were the USSR and Britain. Germany and Italy were defeated; France had been unable to hold on to her position in Syria and Lebanon and was now limited to the western Mediterranean; and the United States had little more than a foothold in the region and was doubtful whether she wished to increase her involvement. During the immediate postwar period the USSR and Britain tried to consolidate their positions, the USSR in the northern area and Britain in the south. They failed to accomplish their ends but the manner of their failure had the effect of drawing the USA into playing a much greater role in the region.

Well before the end of the war the USSR began an attempt to gain greater control over Turkey. Soviet discontent with the Straits regime established at Montreux had been manifest since 1936. The Montreux regime had allowed the passage of foreign warships through the Straits under certain conditions and had given Turkey exclusive control over the waters. The USSR wanted the warships of non-Black Sea states excluded from the Straits while those of Black Sea states were allowed to pass freely into the Mediterranean. To ensure that Turkey kept to this arrangement the USSR sought an agreement which would give her a military base in the vicinity of the Straits. The Soviet Union had discussed the question of a revision of Montreux with Germany in 1940 and raised the question again at the Moscow conference in October 1944 and at Yalta in February 1945. "It was impossible," remarked Stalin at the latter conference, "to accept a situation in which Turkey had a hand on Russia's throat."[4] The USSR began to put pressure on Turkey to agree: on 19 March 1945 she denounced the 1925 Turko–Soviet neutrality treaty and in June lodged a claim to Kars and Ardahan, territories in eastern Turkey conquered from the Ottomans in 1878 and returned to Turkish rule in 1921. In addition an unofficial claim to a considerable stretch of Turkish Black Sea coast was put forward on behalf of Georgia.

The dispute over the Straits went on until October 1946. Turkey and Britain both appealed to the United States to persuade the USSR to desist. The United States was not anxious to intervene and was willing that the Montreux convention should be modified in favour of the USSR, although disinclined to concede any Soviet base at the Straits. Britain and the USA agreed that an international conference should discuss the matter. But the Soviet Union insisted that an international conference should only ratify a previous bilateral agreement between Turkey and the USSR and in 1946 continued to demand a joint Soviet–Turkish defence pact. Taken in conjunction with Soviet actions elsewhere, the Soviet demands appeared to President Truman in January 1946 to demonstrate an intention to invade Turkey and control the Straits. With British and US support Turkey stood firm. In October 1946 the USSR dropped the matter and did not press for a conference to discuss the revision of Montreux.

The second country in which the USSR tried to convert a wartime advantage into a permanent gain was Iran. Following the Anglo–Soviet invasion of Iran in 1941 the USSR had occupied the northern area from which she excluded Iranian authority. The Soviet Union endeavoured to use her strength in northern Iran to reduce Iran to a dependent position by the protection of autonomous movements in northern Iran, by promoting Tūdah party membership of the central government and by securing an oil concession for the five northern provinces of Iran. By the tripartite alliance of 29 January 1942 occupying forces were to leave Iran within six months of the end of hostilities. Fearing that the USSR would not do so Britain attempted at Yalta in January 1945 to set a date. In May 1945 the Iranian government also opened the question. But the USSR evaded the demand that she should bind herself to leave Iran by 2 March 1946.

The USA was slow to adopt a firm position over the Soviet occupation of northern Iran. Iran had sedulously endeavoured to involve the USA in Iran since 1942; US advisers had been employed and concessions offered. But the USA was reluctant to acknowledge that she had important interests in Iran and inclined to agree with the Soviet view that relations between Iran and the USSR were a matter for those countries alone. In January 1946, however, Iran insisted on involving the United Nations, but 2 March came and went and Soviet forces remained and were reinforced. The US concluded that this represented a Soviet military invasion of Iran but was still doubtful whether to take any firm action beyond supporting Iran at the UN.

The USSR failed to attain its objectives in Iran. By an agreement dated 4 April between the Soviet Union and Iran Soviet troops were evacuated in return for a Soviet oil concession. The Soviet troops were withdrawn but the USSR never got its oil concession having been outmanoeuvred by the Iranian prime minister, Aḥmad Qavām. What part the US played in the Soviet acceptance of the agreement is uncertain; some writers claim that a message from Truman to Stalin delivered on 4 April was decisive; others that it was Iranian diplomatic skill that won the day.

Soviet policy in the Northern Tier in 1945–6 had as its objective the creation on the southern borders of the USSR and at the Straits a system of dependent or buffer states similar to that which she was in process of creating in eastern Europe. The policy was defensive; there is no evidence to support contemporary speculations that the USSR aimed at the acquisition of a warm water port on the Indian Ocean and her policy at the Straits appears to have been intended to keep outsiders away from the Black Sea, not to open the Mediterranean to Soviet penetration. Soviet policy failed partly through the resistance of Turkey and Iran to the pressure put upon them, partly because of the opposition of the Western powers and partly due to a loss of will by the USSR itself. Had the USSR chosen to resort to force it must have succeeded for no power could or would have resisted Soviet force in that region. Britain, although she took a leading part in the opposition to Soviet moves, lacked the strength to resist; she contented herself with preventing a communist takeover of Greece. To neither Turkey nor Iran did the USA ever give unequivocal support against the USSR. The episodes marked stages in the advance of the USA in the Near East but were not decisive in the involvement of that country. The USA was still not wholly convinced that major American interests were at stake in the region.

The failure was most significant for the USSR. The Soviet Union was regarded by both Turkey and Iran as the major enemy but both were willing to adopt a conciliatory policy towards their northern neighbour as they had done in the pre-war period. The Soviet bid for domination drove them into alliance with the rivals of the USSR and destroyed Soviet influence in the Northern Tier. From 1947 to 1949 relations between the USSR, Turkey and Iran were at a low level as the USSR sought to undermine their governments by propaganda and subversion. Relations remained unhappy for years thereafter. Only in 1953 did the USSR return to the policy of seeking good relations with established regimes in the Northern Tier and by that time it was not easy to recover lost ground.

At the end of the war Britain had troops in almost every Near Eastern country, dominated some and had alliances with others. The task she faced was to convert this position into a lasting peace time preponderance. In charge of the negotiation was the new British foreign secretary, Ernest Bevin. Britain's effort was concentrated on the Arab world; in the Northern Tier she dared not face the USSR, could not afford the cost of financial support to the states concerned and wished to slough off responsibility to the United States. In February 1947 Britain informed the United States that she was ending economic aid to Turkey and Greece, a burden assumed by the USA under the Truman Doctrine (12 March 1947).

In the Arab Near East Bevin's policy called for a military confederacy under British leadership and a programme of economic development. The two were closely linked: the confederacy would provide protection (mainly against the Soviet threat) and the development would benefit the people of the area. Bevin was insistent that he was proposing a partnership of mutual benefit between Britain and the people, not the old élite of the Near East, whom he dismissed as pashas. His hope was to reach agreement with moderate nationalists, isolating extremists of all kinds. To Britain the benefits would be first, the protection of her interests in the Near East, most notably oil; and second, the provision of a Near Eastern shield for the protection of Africa, the continent whose economic development was to be to Britain in the future the source of wealth that India had been in the past. Thus it was that the importance of the Near East to Britain was held to be unaffected by her prospective departure from India.

The key to the success of Bevin's policy was agreement with Egypt. By virtue of the leading role Egypt had assumed in the Arab League she was now pre-eminent in the Arab world. More especially, Egypt had the Suez Canal and the Canal Zone base, 500 square miles of military installations (including ten airfields) valued at £300 million. Although British policy was conceived in regional terms, which derived from the regional institutions established during the war, Bevin was persuaded to try to bring his regional military and economic organizations into being through bilateral negotiations, beginning with Egypt. In 1945 Egypt called for the renegotiation of the 1936 Anglo–Egyptian treaty. In reply Britain offered only minor concessions; the chiefs of staff insisted that continued British occupation of the Canal Zone was essential to the defence of the Near East. Riots in Egypt, however, convinced the British negotiators that Britain must evacuate Egypt and on 6 May 1946 the cabinet agreed. Subsequently, negotiations focused on the problems of the maintenance of the canal base and the conditions under which British forces could return in case of war. Gradually the Egyptians whittled down the British demands until by the time agreement was reached between Bevin and the Egyptian prime minister, Ismāᶜīl Ṣidqī, in October 1946, the British position in Egypt was to rest on Egyptian goodwill alone. At this point, however, the negotiations collapsed, not over Egypt but over the question of Egyptian sovereignty over the Sudan.

The failure to reach agreement with Egypt was disastrous for the success of Bevin's plan for the Near East. In the course of the negotiations Britain had agreed to surrender the base which the military advised was essential to the defence of the region. Britain had made the concession because she believed that ultimately the base was useless if Egypt was hostile and therefore that the defence of the region must depend on agreement and Egyptian goodwill. But neither had been secured in 1946 and the effects of both the attempt and the failure had a powerful influence on negotiations in other parts of the region. Other states also demanded treaty revision and found it difficult to accept anything less than Egypt had been offered.

Britain attempted to reach agreement with Iraq on a new treaty in late 1947. The 1930 treaty had provided for British control of the two bases of Habbāniyya and Shayba and for British use of Iraqi facilities in time of war. There were those who argued that Britain could not hope to be allowed to keep the bases and should plan to evacuate them and move to Kuwayt and Transjordan, but Bevin decided to try to retain use of the bases. Under the Treaty of Portsmouth it was agreed that Britain should share the bases with Iraq under a similar arrangement to that proposed for Egypt. In January 1948 riots in Baghdad caused the Iraqi government to abandon the new treaty.

An important element in the proposed new Near Eastern system was a satisfactory settlement of the Palestine problem. The problem of Palestine was political rather than strategic. The chiefs of staff claimed Palestine was of considerable strategic value as a shield to Egypt and even, in 1946–7, as a partial substitute for it, and looked to a treaty with an eventual Palestinian government to safeguard British bases in

Palestine. But to the chiefs of staff every place was valuable and they certainly never thought that Palestine could be a full substitute for Egypt. Securing Britain's strategic position in Palestine was of less moment than finding a solution which would not unduly antagonize other Arab states and so make the execution of Bevin's Near Eastern plans more difficult, and which would also win US acquiescence. In 1945–6 Bevin tried to find a solution which the US would support and failed. He also failed to find a solution acceptable to Jews and Arabs. By September 1947 Palestine was seen to be an economic and strategic liability and Britain's problem one of damage limitation. Therefore Britain decided to give up the mandate and refused to implement the UN recommendation of partition. In this way she hoped that the Palestine denouement would not damage her relations with the Arab states and that she might save something from the wreckage if Jordan took over the territories assigned to the Arab state. It was quite late before she came to believe that other Arab states would fight in Palestine.

Britain's only success was with the tiny state of Transjordan. In March 1946, before the decision was taken to evacuate Egypt, Britain concluded a treaty with Transjordan which terminated the mandate and secured British military use of Transjordanian bases and facilities. It was a treaty very much on the 1930s model and it was quickly found unacceptable. In February 1948 it was replaced by a new treaty intended to give the appearance that Jordan had some control over the British bases at Amman and Mafraq; a joint military board similar to those proposed for Egypt and Iraq was established. Britain had secured from Jordan what she had failed to obtain from the other states.

At the time the dust had settled in Palestine in 1949 Britain's situation in the Near East still appeared to be strong. Her position in most of Palestine had gone but she still had treaties with Egypt, Iraq and Transjordan and British forces and bases in all those countries; and her positions in the Sudan, southwest Arabia and the Gulf were intact. Her two greatest assets, the Canal Zone base and the Ābādān refinery, were still under British control. Indeed, when Bevin reviewed British policy in the Near East in July 1949 he saw no reason to make any major changes: Britain should still strive to create a regional security system which might eventually include Turkey, Iran and Israel as well as the Arab states and which would use the Canal Zone as its main base, although he now believed that the United States should also be brought into the system. And Britain, with United States' help, should persevere with the plan of regional economic development even though her financial contribution would necessarily be meagre.

In fact Britain's position had been seriously weakened by the failure to achieve a revised treaty arrangement in 1946–8. The old treaties had been undermined by the proposal to revise them and in 1951 Egypt denounced the 1936 treaty. And the British position in all her bases had been weakened. Whatever was said in future years there was no real question of going back on the concessions made to Egypt in 1946; any future settlement would have to start from that point and the eventual agreement reached in 1954–5 for the evacuation of the Suez base did follow the 1946 lines. And in other bases the British position rested mainly on consent and the bases could hardly be held when consent was withdrawn or used if the purpose was unacceptable to the state concerned. In the 1930s Britain had successfully moved from a position where her influence was guaranteed by control to one where her interests were secured by treaty; in the late 1940s she tried to move to a situation in which her influence rested on Arab goodwill and she failed. In the 1950s she harvested the consequences of that failure.

The British position in the Near East received one further blow in the post-war period through the nationalization of the Anglo–Iranian Oil Company in 1951. Although the British Government held a majority of the shares of the company it did not normally interfere in its ordinary commercial transactions among which were included the arrangements between the company and the Iranian government for the division of profits. But when negotiations on that matter failed and the Majlis voted to nationalize the company in March 1951 the government could not be indifferent. Apart from its stake in the company with its refinery at Ābādān, the largest in the world, Britain needed Iranian oil. Also British prestige in the region was at stake. Britain was not hostile to nationalization in principle but demanded compensation and control over the operation of oil production. She also seriously considered military intervention in 1951, either the occupation of southern Iran or of Ābādān alone. In the end she rejected a military solution and adopted a legal and economic approach, hoping in this way to force Iran to accept a compromise. When this approach failed she conspired with the United States to help to overthrow the Iranian government in 1953. But the eventual compromise reached over oil in 1954, although financially satisfactory, did not restore the former British position in Iran.

The decline of British power and influence in the Near East may be explained in various ways: that it was faulty British conception or execution of policy; that it was the competition of the new superpowers; that it was Britain's inability to prevail against the forces of nationalism; that it was a loss of British will.

The conception of British policy was criticized on the grounds that the regional approach was fundamentally mistaken because of the differences between the regional powers, that the economic content was beyond British powers, that the purposes were too vague, in particular that the economic development of Africa was a mirage, and, as the prime minister, Clement Attlee, argued, that it should have been the UN and not Britain at the centre of the scheme. Attlee also argued that the whole strategic concept of bases was outdated by the atomic bomb. The execution of British policy was also criticized; the negotiators in Egypt were thought to have surrendered too much too quickly and the presentation of the Treaty of Portsmouth to have been badly handled. British policy in Palestine suffered from continual divisions between the different departments of government.

The USSR and the USA were also blamed but unreasonably; the problem with the USSR was that it did very little in the Arab world and so made it more difficult for Britain to obtain acceptance for her arguments that the USSR constituted a major threat to the region. The main criticism of the USA was that it declined to support British imperial ambitions and was a commercial competitor, that it favoured small nations and it did not underwrite the British solution in Palestine. But if the USA did little to support Britain it did little to undermine the British position either.

Nationalist opposition has been the preferred explanation for Britain's failure. In Egypt Ṣidqī was unable to obtain acceptance of his agreement with Bevin partly because of popular opposition and in Iraq the pro-British regime abandoned the Treaty of Portsmouth in the face of hostile demonstrations. In Palestine the conflicting claims of Arab and Jewish nationalism made a peaceful solution impossible. In each case it could be said that popular feeling was less powerful than appeared; that urban crowds were not representative of national sentiment and were manipulated by political factions motivated by narrower ambitions or that governments surrendered to terrorism. Many Britons argued that national feeling was weak and would melt away if resolutely confronted. But there were also many who believed that nationalism had come to stay and that it could not be overcome by any force that could be brought against it; further, that the world had moved beyond the stage of the forcible suppression of popular demands. When Britain decided against the use of force against Iran in 1951 she did so especially because she thought that its use would offend against the principles of the UN and world opinion, especially that of the USA. The same scruples prevented her acting more resolutely against Zionist terrorism in Palestine. The same arguments which had led Britain to support the League of Nations and collective security between the wars persuaded her to uphold the United Nations after the war; her adherence to the principles of the Atlantic Charter was not merely a pious obeisance.

These last remarks bring us to the question of the loss of will. The Second World War had cost Britain dear: £1.2 billion of overseas investments liquidated; £3 billion pounds of overseas debt acquired (£500 million in the Near East); the National Debt doubled; Britain's trade severely damaged with exports less than a third of what they had been in 1939; considerable damage to housing and industry; and so many men under arms that there was a shortage of manpower for industrial reconstruction. At the same time the new Labour government was elected on a programme which included a great extension of welfare services. At a critical period of post-war decision Britain experienced one of its worst winters of the century. In the early months of 1947 the country was blanketed in snow and ice and industrial production almost came to a stop. Something had to go and in February 1947 Britain decided to stop economic assistance to Greece and Turkey, refer Palestine to the UN and announce a date for India's independence. It is reasonable to argue that as nationalism increased the cost of maintaining the British position in the Near East so loss of will reduced the price Britain was willing to pay for it.

THE SUEZ WAR

The Suez War of 1956 marks a period in the influence of Europe in the Near East. It was the last occasion on which Britain and France attempted to impose their will on a major regional power by force and although both of them continued to play a significant role in parts of the region thereafter, theirs was a declining role. After Suez it was the United States and the USSR which became the principal international powers in the region. More important still Suez represented the new assertion of the regional powers.

The Suez War had two points of origin: regional and international. The regional aspect derives from the Arab–Israeli dispute. The conclusion of the 1948 Arab–Israeli war had not led to a settlement of the points at issue. The war was ended by armistice agreements signed at Rhodes in 1949 and it was intended that the armistice should be followed by a peace agreement negotiated under the auspices of the United Nations. But the UN Conciliation Commission failed to produce a solution and conferences at Lausanne (1949), Geneva (1950) and Paris (1951) achieved no success. The two main points in dispute were the frontiers of Israel; whether they should be those indicated by the UN in 1947, those established by the armistices in 1949 or some compromise between those lines: and the future of the Palestinian refugees; whether they should be allowed to return to their homes, compensated or resettled. To these points of difference were added others arising from continued friction along the armistice lines and the Egyptian refusal to allow Israel to use the Suez Canal. For the Arab states the problem of a settlement was complicated by the question of Arab Palestine, whether an Arab state should be established or whether the annexation of the West Bank to Jordan should be accepted.

Various approaches to a settlement by international action and regional contacts were tried and failed. Agreement between Jordan and Israel was near in 1950 but failed partly because of the reluctance of Israel to recognize Jordanian possession of the West Bank and partly because opposition within Jordan caused ᶜAbdallāh to abandon the project. From 1952 until 1956 there were discussions of a settlement which linked Egypt and Israel and which received British and US support. In 1954–5 an elaborate plan was concocted involving a compromise on frontiers, an Egyptian–Jordanian corridor in the Negev, a free port for Jordan at Haifa, a non-aggression pact, the return of some refugees and the resettlement of others. That plan also failed partly because Israel suspected that she would be called upon to surrender much of the Negev and partly because Egypt seemingly lost interest. Another approach towards agreement was the Johnston plan for the sharing of the Jordan waters. The plan began as a way of settling some 200,000 refugees on irrigated land in the Jordan valley but developed into a detailed scheme for a Jordan Valley Authority involving co-operation between Israel, Syria and Jordan. But in October 1955 the Arab League shelved the plan.

During the same years there was increasing tension along the borders of Israel. On the Syrian frontier there was friction arising from the Israeli efforts to develop Arab and waste land in the demilitarized zones north of lake Tiberias and Syrian hostility to these efforts. There was shelling and counter shelling and raids. On the Jordanian frontier there was trouble arising from the resentment felt by refugees at Israeli appropriation of their lands. Guerrillas crossed the frontier and attacked Israeli posts and settlements. Israel retaliated, notably with the raid on the village of Qibya in October 1953 which left 50 dead and the village destroyed. But from 1954 the worst troubles arose on the frontier with Egyptian-controlled Gaza. On the Jordan frontier guerrilla raids had not had official support, although they may have been conducted with the connivance of officials. On the Gaza frontier from 1954, however, they were directed by Egypt and threatened the development of the Negev. On 28 February 1955 Israel launched a massive reprisal raid on Gaza in which 32 Egyptian soldiers were killed and on 31 August 1955 a further raid on Khān Yūnus which killed 36 Egyptians. In general Israel gave more than she received. During the period 1954–6 Israel suffered rather more than 200 casualties a year from guerrilla activities while Arab casualties were more than twice as many.

Arab raids into Israel were motivated by Palestinian resentments or by a desire to prevent Israel from developing former Arab lands. If Israel were allowed to proceed in peace she would have little inducement to come to a compromise settlement. Israeli retaliation was partly the outcome of a new, militant philosophy which held that Israel would only be secure if she struck back hard at any who threatened her. Israel also feared that her successful development would be prevented if she tolerated Arab actions; in particular she resented the economic boycott organized by the Arab states and the closure of the Suez Canal for most of the period after 1947 to shipping bound to or from Israel. Still more serious for the future of Israel was the Egyptian blockade of the Strait of Tirān at the mouth of the Gulf of ᶜAqaba. The Tirān blockade, which became total in 1955, made the Israeli port of Eilat unusable and Israel meditated war against Egypt in order to force the opening of the strait. The friction also owed something to elements on both sides who feared that any settlement would involve a sacrifice for which they were unready and who saw the inflammation of disputes as a way of preventing such a settlement. Perhaps most of all, as time went on, prestige was at stake on both sides.

The international aspect of the Suez War may be traced back to Egyptian hostility to European influence in the Near East. In particular, Egypt opposed the British-backed scheme for a Middle East defence organization which remained at the heart of British plans for the Near East throughout the early 1950s. In October 1951 Egypt rejected a joint approach, involving the end of the Anglo–Egyptian treaty of 1936 and the internationalization of the canal base, from Britain, the United States, France and Turkey. But Britain renewed negotiations with the Free Officers' regime and in July 1954 reached agreement on the evacuation of the base with an understanding that she could reoccupy it in case of an attack from the USSR. But for the time being Britain abandoned the effort to bring Egypt into a full regional military alliance and with United States' encouragement turned her attention to the Northern Tier.

The formation of the Baghdad pact in 1954 was a major development in the international history of the Near East. The pact's origins go back to Western fears of Soviet aggression (inflamed by the Berlin Blockade and the takeover of Czechoslovakia in 1948) which led to the formation of the North Atlantic Treaty Organisation (NATO) in 1949. Following the experience of the Korean War the Eisenhower administration developed the concept of containment into a world wide scheme of collective defence against international communism, represented by the USSR and China. The South-East Asia Treaty Organisation (SEATO) was formed in 1954. The question arose of what should be done in the Near East. It was decided to form the states of the northern part of the region (those which seemed most conscious of a Soviet threat) into a Western alliance. Turkey was already, since 1951, a member of NATO. In April 1954 Turkey and Pakistan signed a treaty of friendship and co-operation and on 24 February 1955 Turkey and Iraq signed the Baghdad pact. Britain joined the pact in April (a separate agreement ended the 1930 treaty with Iraq and provided for Iraqi control of the two bases), Pakistan became a member in September and Iran in October. The United States, the inspiration of the scheme, did not join the pact, although she took part as an observer and had military assistance agreements with individual members.

The Baghdad pact had many curious features. Its ostensible purpose was collective military defence against the USSR but it had little military strength because its members' forces were either too weak or committed elsewhere. Most, if not all, of its members had joined to win favour with the United States and expected little from their fellow members. Turkey was content with NATO membership and Pakistan was primarily concerned with winning US support against India, not the USSR. But the oddest feature was the membership of Iraq which, like Pakistan, had no frontier with the USSR. The membership of Iraq clearly pointed to an intention to involve the Arab world, that is to resurrect the Middle East regional defence scheme under British leadership. Britain had turned the whole Northern Tier concept upside down; instead of being a shield against the USSR it now seemed to its critics to be a sword pointed into the Arab world.

Egypt stridently attacked Iraq's membership of the Baghdad pact as being a betrayal of schemes of purely Arab collective security under the Arab League and successfully used her influence to prevent any other Arab state from joining the pact; a British attempt to persuade Jordan to adhere to the pact in January 1956 failed and, on 1 March, King Ḥusayn dismissed his British commander in chief, General John Glubb. Iraq was now isolated in the Arab world. The possibility that Egypt might take such an attitude had been foreseen and Iraq had taken pains to ascertain that President ᶜAbd al-Nāṣir had no objection to Iraq's membership. Only after receiving assurances on this point had Iraq signed the pact. Egypt's violent attack on Iraq seemed, therefore, to be motivated less by a real fear of European influence in the Arab world than a desire to discredit Iraq in the struggle for Arab leadership.

The Egyptian attack on the pact and particularly the damage to British relations with Jordan were decisive in changing Britain's attitude to Egypt. Hitherto, Britain had striven for agreement and in pursuit of that end had evacuated the canal base. Now it seemed that leaving the canal base, far from being a prelude to friendship, was all that ᶜAbd al-Nāṣir had wanted before he destroyed Britain's remaining influence in the Arab world. The British prime minister, Sir Anthony Eden, felt like the victim of a confidence trick and was uncomfortably reminded of Chamberlain, Hitler and Munich.

In the same month that ᶜAbd al-Nāṣir alienated Britain he also contrived to alienate France. France was hostile to the Baghdad pact, partly because it was an Anglo–Saxon-dominated enterprise and partly because she believed that it was the wrong way to confront the USSR; economic development, not military alliances, would be more effective in the Near East, France thought. France was, therefore, a potential supporter of ᶜAbd al-Nāṣir in his opposition to the pact. But France had a more pressing problem in Algeria where the rebellion against French rule had begun on 1 November 1954. Of her imperial possessions France had lost Indo–China in 1954 and gave independence to Morocco and Tunis in March 1956. But Algeria, with its 1 million settlers, she was determined to keep. Already, however, she had committed a quarter of a million French troops to the suppression of the rising and she was anxious to find a cheaper way of dealing with the opposition. France believed that if the Egyptian president ended support for the revolt she could easily suppress it. In March 1956 she asked him to stop and he refused. From that time on France was convinced that an Algerian solution must be preceded by the departure of ᶜAbd al-Nāṣir.

ᶜAbd al-Nāṣir also contrived to alienate the United States. He angered the United States first by his neutralism; in April 1955 ᶜAbd al-Nāṣir emerged from the Bandung conference as one of the principal enthusiasts for non-alignment. Second, he bought arms from the USSR. By the Tripartite Declaration of 1950 Britain, France and the United States had effectively guaranteed the frontiers of Israel and its neighbours and agreed to regulate supplies of arms to the opposing sides so that no side should gain a marked advantage. Since that time the three powers had been the sole suppliers of arms to Israel and the Arabs. In August 1954 and February 1955, however, France had supplied arms to Israel which could be regarded as having upset the balance of advantage. But in May 1955 ᶜAbd al-Nāṣir went outside the Western powers and asked the USSR to sell him arms. It may be that his intention was to persuade the USA to sell him more arms but the USA did not respond and the Soviet deal, negotiated through Czechoslovakia, went ahead and was announced on 27 September 1955. ᶜAbd al-Nāṣir gave two reasons for his decision to buy Soviet weapons: the Baghdad Pact and the Gaza raid.

Although dismayed by Egypt's attitudes the United States did not immediately turn against ᶜAbd al-Nāṣir. Israel's requests for additional arms to match the Soviet deliveries to Egypt were refused and in December 1955 the United States agreed to give financial support to the central element in Egypt's development programme, the High Dam at Aswan. It was only gradually in the course of 1956 that the United States came to the conclusion that some rebuff should be administered to ᶜAbd al-Nāṣir. That rebuff came on 19 July 1956 when Egypt was told that the US offer to finance the dam was withdrawn. Various technical and economic reasons were given for the decision but it seems clear that the balance was tipped by the political arguments.

ᶜAbd al-Nāṣir responded to the rebuff on 26 July 1956 by nationalizing the Suez Canal Company. Egypt had had disputes with the canal company but these appeared to have been temporarily adjusted by new agreements in early 1956 and although the company was regarded as an unacceptable relic of colonialism in Egypt its concession would run out in any case in 1968. The nationalization was clearly linked with the US refusal to finance the Aswan Dam by ᶜAbd al-Nāṣir's statement that the revenues would be used to pay for the Aswan Dam.

Egyptian nationalization of the canal raised two sets of questions. One set was concerned with the ownership and operation of the canal. There could be no legal objection to Egyptian nationalization of an Egyptian company; compensation should be paid and ᶜAbd al-Nāṣir promised this although there remained a question whether Egypt could pay it. Also the canal was an international waterway protected by an international convention and its secure operation was a matter of great concern to several states; for example, nearly a quarter of British imports including most of her oil came through the canal and through it also ran her imperial communications with the Far East. Whether Egypt could or would operate the canal safely was, like the question of compensation, a matter susceptible of possible arrangement through international discussion. This was the course pressed by the United States and it was in keeping with what had come to be the British tradition of settling disputes through international agreement.

The second set of questions had to do with the position of Britain and France in the Near East. As the two governments saw the matter ᶜAbd al-Nāṣir had been steadily undermining their position for some time and the nationalization of so great a symbol of the Anglo–French presence in the region would be the last straw. If ᶜAbd al-Nāṣir were allowed to get away with it Britain and France would be finished in the region; no-one would believe that they would ever stand up for their supporters. In this view, if not revoked the nationalization of the canal was a challenge which could only be met by arms and the forcible deposition of ᶜAbd al-Nāṣir.

Had it been possible Britain and France would have launched a military expedition against Egypt immediately. The difficulty was that they had no base from which an expedition of the size which their military advisers informed them was necessary could be launched. An expedition would take several weeks to prepare. In the meantime they had little alternative but to negotiate under the leadership of the American Secretary of State, John Foster Dulles. The negotiations, however, did not promise a solution satisfactory to Britain and France; furthermore, their desire for a prestige victory over ᶜAbd al-Nāṣir could hardly be fulfilled by negotiations. But with negotiations in progress it became more difficult to contemplate the use of force, particularly as Egypt had not obviously offended against international law. A device was needed which would permit Britain and France to launch an expedition against Egypt seemingly unconnected with the canal dispute, an expedition of which the United States had no knowledge. It was at this point that the regional and the international factors came together. For her own reasons Israel also wanted to attack Egypt and unseat ᶜAbd al-Nāṣir. The stage was set for collusion.

It was France which brought the different parties secretly together. At Sèvres on 24 October it was decided that Israel would attack Egypt and Britain and France would call on the two sides to stop fighting and retire from either side of the canal. Israel would agree and Egypt, of course, would refuse, since agreement would involve retiring from Egyptian Sinai. Britain and France would then occupy the Canal Zone and ᶜAbd al-Nāṣir would be utterly discredited and would fall from power. Such was the plan in which little thought was given to what should replace ᶜAbd al-Nāṣir's government and what would be the effects of the international reaction and particularly that of the United States.

Israel attacked on 29 October. On 30 October Britain and France delivered the prearranged ultimatum. Israel accepted and Egypt rejected the demand. On 31 October Britain and France began air attacks on Egyptian airfields and ᶜAbd al-Nāṣir gave the order to retreat to the west bank and to block the canal. On 5 November British and French paratroops dropped at Port Said and on 6 November seaborne troops began to land from the main expedition which had loaded at Malta on 28 October. An advance on Suez began but was arrested at midnight on 6 November by British and French acceptance of the UN call for a ceasefire.

The decision to call off the Suez operation before it had achieved its objectives of the seizure of the Canal Zone and the fall of ᶜAbd al-Nāṣir was a British decision; the French government wanted to continue until the canal was in allied hands. One reason for the decision to stop was that the ostensible justification for the operation had ended when Israel and Egypt stopped fighting; having obtained her objectives Israel was anxious to accept the ceasefire call originally made by the UN on 30 October. Other reasons were a threat of Soviet intervention and political opposition within Britain. The main reason, however, was the threat to sterling. Already weak before the operation began sterling had been subject to heavy selling subsequently, the reserves were being drained and international support was not available because of the hostility of the USA to the British and French action.

The Eisenhower administration had strongly opposed the Anglo–French resort to arms. It seems to have been supposed that Eisenhower would have been too busy with the presidential election campaign to take much action but the president abandoned the campaign and gave all his attention to the crisis. It was the USA which led the UN demands for a ceasefire and, by refusing to support sterling or to supply oil to make up the deficiency caused in Europe by the closure of the canal, the US maintained pressure on Britain and France causing them first to accept the ceasefire and subsequently to withdraw ignominiously from Egypt without achieving any advantage from the operation. US policy was based on a view that it was wrong to go to through the UN. Britain miscalculated both the strength of the US reaction (wrongly supposing that Dulles did not speak for Eisenhower) and the effects which US hostility might have, particularly on the situation of sterling.

The Suez fiasco did not end European influence in the Near East; France did not leave Algeria until 1962 and Britain remained a force in south west Arabia until 1967 and in the Persian Gulf until 1971. But Suez confirmed in dramatic style two features which had been evident since 1945; that European influence could not prevail in the face of the hostility of the regional powers and of the United States. If Europe had the resources she certainly did not have the will. Suez hastened the process of the removal of European influence from the Near East and ensured that neither Britain nor France would again aspire to play a major role in the region; the notions of the Middle East military confederacy and of regional economic development under British leadership were dead.

NOTES

1. Letter from A. Bonar Law, *The Times*, 7 October 1922.
2. Anthony Eden, House of Commons, 19 July 1937. Quoted in The Earl of Avon, *The Eden memoirs: Facing the Dictators*, 1962, 450.
3. RIIA, *Political and Strategic Interests of the United Kingdom*, 1939, 143.
4. *Foreign Relations of the United States: Malta and Yalta Papers*, Washington DC, 1955, 903.

CHAPTER SIXTEEN

Superpowers and Regional Powers, 1956–89

THE SUPERPOWERS

To the USSR by far the most important region of the Near East was that part which bordered the southern areas of the Soviet Union, the region which is described in this book as the Northern Tier, namely Turkey, Iran and Afghanistan. The failure of the Soviet attempt to dominate the Northern Tier in 1945–7 and the consequential turning of Turkey and Iran towards the West left Soviet policy towards the Near East in disarray. It was six years before a new Soviet policy for the Northern Tier emerged; in the meantime relations between the Soviet Union and its southern neighbours were hostile. During the years 1947–9 the Soviet Union looked mainly to the overthrow of the Turkish and Iranian regimes by communist or minority groups; from 1949–53 it hoped broader opposition coalitions would effect a similar change. In the meantime the USSR tried economic and political pressure and maintained a continuous propaganda campaign. Although events in Iran under Muṣaddiq appeared to favour Soviet hopes the results of Soviet policy were ultimately disappointing and by the end of 1953 pro-Western regimes were strongly entrenched in Turkey and Iran.

The new Soviet policy launched in 1953 was similar to that which had been adopted in 1921, namely to establish good relations with established governments without being concerned about their social bases. In 1953 the Soviet Union withdrew the territorial demands made on Turkey in 1945 and dropped the request for a revision of the Straits regime. Border problems with Iran were settled in 1955 and a comprehensive treaty signed in 1957 when an agreement was made covering the use of the waters of the Aras and Atrek rivers which separated the two states. Trade agreements were signed, including, in

1957, a transit agreement of particular importance to Iran. But this new policy was very slow to produce any result; the two states clung firmly to their Western links and strengthened them. Turkey, which had joined NATO in 1952, became a member with Greece and Yugoslavia of the Balkan Pact in 1954 and of the Baghdad Pact with Iraq the same year. In 1957 Turkey allowed US Jupiter missiles to be located on her soil. Iran also joined the Baghdad Pact and, like Turkey, signed military assistance agreements with the USA. In 1959 Iran rejected a Soviet offer of a non-aggression treaty by which the USSR undertook to renounce the detested articles 5 and 6 (giving the USSR a right of intervention in Iran under certain circumstances) of the 1921 treaty. Iran thereupon unilaterally denounced the articles concerned.

The Soviet Union was disappointed with the results of the new policy of conciliation which had failed to shake Western predominance in the Northern Tier. In particular she was dismayed by the formation in 1954 of the Baghdad Pact. She persevered with the policy but from 1955 supplemented it with a new initiative in the southern region of the Near East. Hitherto, the USSR had paid little attention to the Arab world; indeed she had seen Israel as a more likely ally in the region and had supported the Jewish state during its early years. Soviet relations with Israel had cooled after 1950 and were severed in 1953, although for some Zionist groups the USSR remained the preferred ally until 1955. But the continuing dispute between Israel and her Arab neighbours provided an opportunity for the USSR to gain influence in Arab countries and Egyptian hostility to the Baghdad Pact gave further impetus to Soviet intervention. When approached by ᶜAbd al-Nāṣir in May 1955 the USSR agreed to supply arms to Egypt so breaking the Western monopoly.

The Soviet entry into the Arab world was not the consequence of the discovery of some new great interest in the region; the USSR had neither need nor desire for Middle Eastern oil, nor, at that time, any interest in naval facilities in the eastern Mediterranean or ambitions to maintain a fleet in the Indian Ocean. Soviet Arab policy began as a challenge to the Western position, in a region of importance to the West, as a counter to the Western challenge to the USSR in the Northern Tier. It was quickly developed; a friendship treaty with North Yemen was signed in 1955 and arms supplies to Syria were also commenced. In 1958 the Iraqi revolution provided another major opportunity for the extension of Soviet relations and soon the USSR was well established as the ally of radical Arab nationalism in what was depicted as a struggle against imperialism and its regional allies.

Soviet influence in the Arab world was at a peak during the heyday of Arab radicalism during the 1960s. The USSR did not seek military allies; it was content with Arab neutralism. And it did not ask for Marxist governments; it saw the adoption of socialist ideologies and statist policies by the revolutionary Arab states during the period as part of an irresistible movement towards socialism and kept almost silent about the suppression of communist parties in Egypt and elsewhere. It did not attempt to interfere in Arab internal affairs. The USSR became the principal supplier of weapons to the radical Arab states, an important trading partner for them and gave economic and technical assistance. In particular the USSR replaced the USA as the financier of the High Dam. This happy period was brought to an end by the 1967 Arab–Israeli war.

United States' interest in the Near East was slow to develop. The first major commitment was in the Northern Tier through the 1947 Truman Doctrine by which the USA agreed to replace Britain as the supplier of economic aid to Greece and Turkey. The USA did not hurry to enlarge its commitments despite the appeals of Turkey and Iran. Iran's request to be included in the Truman Doctrine was refused and the Shah's hopes of massive US military assistance were rebuffed in 1949. Turkey won greater favour as a result of her participation in the Korean War which helped her to gain admittance to NATO in 1952. It was only after 1952 that the USA showed greater interest with the extension to the Northern Tier of the concept of containment; thereafter, US influence grew rapidly and from 1954 the USA–Iran alliance was well established. The main US interest remained negative; the purpose of US policy was primarily to deny the USSR a foothold in the region rather than to gain any special advantage for the USA.

United States' commitments in the southern, Arab region were slower still to form. The oldest interest was oil. In 1919 fears of depletion of US reserves, combined with apprehension that the European powers would monopolize Near Eastern oil, prompted the USA to insist on an open door policy and a share for the United States. US oil interests became participants in Iraqi oil and during the 1930s acquired concessions in Arabia. The most important of these oil concessions was in Saudi Arabia, where it was worked by the company which became known in 1944 as ARAMCO. The US government was still very reluctant to concede that any national US interest was involved in Saudi Arabia, preferring to leave political affairs to Britain. But in 1943, in response to the urgings of various pressure groups which pointed to British and Russian threats, the great value of

Saudi oil and the importance of ᶜAbd al-ᶜAzīz ibn Saᶜūd in the Arab and Muslim worlds, President Roosevelt made the formal declaration that Saudi Arabia was of vital interest to the security of the United States which was necessary in order that Ibn Saᶜūd might qualify for assistance under the wartime system of aid known as Lend–Lease. Subsequently, the USA became the principal supporter of Saudi Arabia which itself became the centre of US interests in the Arab world. Roosevelt's declaration was a formula not a conviction; important as Saudi oil was to ARAMCO it was scarcely vital to the United States which in 1948 imported much less than 10 per cent of the oil it used and less than 1 per cent from Saudi Arabia. In 1951 the USA signed a defence agreement with Saudi Arabia but refused to make a treaty of alliance.

Despite the role played by the United States in the foundation of the state of Israel in 1948 and the popular and Congressional sympathy for the Jewish state which prevailed, the USA was not committed to the support of Israel. To the Departments of State and Defense, which valued Arab support more than Israeli, Israel was a strategic liability and remained so until the late 1950s. US arms supplies to Israel were negligible. The Israeli request to join NATO in 1954 was rejected and the USA declined an Israeli proposal for a mutual defence treaty. In 1956 US pressure on Britain and France to withdraw from Suez was applied equally to Israel although in the end Israel obtained an important concession over the Straits of Tirān.

US involvement in the Arab Near East increased after 1956. Until that date, despite a residual distaste for British colonialism, the US had been inclined to view the region as a British responsibility and accepted a subordinate role in the various British-designed regional defence schemes. The region was rated in 1948 as of critical rather than vital importance and the 1950 tripartite declaration on arms and frontiers was made without enthusiasm or any feeling of strong commitment. After 1956 it was plain that neither Britain nor France could discharge their former leading roles. At the same time the Egyptian arms deal seemed to presage a Soviet bid for influence in the region. Accordingly, the Eisenhower Doctrine was issued on 9 March 1957. The Doctrine stated that US military and economic assistance would be available to any state in the Middle East which requested it and was threatened by international communism. The Doctrine was an attempt to avoid involvement in regional entanglements and confine US assistance to defence against the USSR. It was founded on an assumption that the reverse suffered by Britain and France had left a political vacuum in the area, an assumption which ignored the rise of the regional powers.

The Eisenhower Doctrine became a device through which the USA was drawn into local disputes in the Near East. In 1957 the US encouraged King Ḥusayn of Jordan in his struggle against his domestic critics and became involved in an obscure plot to overthrow the regime in Syria with the aid of Turkey. In 1958 the Iraqi revolution led to fears that the whole Near East was in danger of succumbing to revolution and US troops were sent to Lebanon at the same time as British troops were sent to Jordan. Inevitably, radical Arab nationalism had become identified in US minds with international communism, an identification made more plausible by the links formed between the USSR and the radical Arab states and by the rhetorical denunciations of imperialism, capitalism, etc., in which the radicals indulged. Equally, regimes which felt threatened by the claims of the radicals found it convenient to depict themselves as defenders of the West against communism. Among this number was Israel which now began to rise in the scale of United States' favour. President Kennedy strove to resist the polarization of the region and the linking of the Cold War and regional disputes and sought to find a compromise with the radical Arab states but he failed. Egyptian involvement in Arabia following the 1962 Yemen revolution increased US apprehensions and under Kennedy's successor, Lyndon Johnson, the US tilt towards Israel became more pronounced. It was not until after the 1967 war, however, that the US–Israel alliance was firmly established.

THE ARAB–ISRAELI WAR OF 1967

The 1967 Arab–Israeli war changed the face of international relations in the Near East. It elevated the Arab–Israeli dispute from what was essentially a regional quarrel into one which involved the major powers. It also made the dispute much more difficult to compose.

The origins of the 1967 war may be found first in the continuation of the unsolved problems of frontiers and refugees which had existed since 1948. Indeed, the problem of the refugees had worsened as their number had risen through natural increase. Also the Palestinians could not be regarded as a purely refugee problem after the creation of the Palestine Liberation Organisation in 1964. The Palestinians were now a political, and to a limited extent, a military factor; from 1965 the Palestinian guerrilla organization, al-Fataḥ, commenced raids into

Israel from Syria and Jordan and the Palestinian Liberation Army was organized. Israel retaliated against Jordan, notably in a raid in November 1966 on the village of al-Samu.

The second point of origin was in the arms race in the Near East. In 1950 Israel and the principal Arab states had each spent between 4 and 6 per cent of GNP on arms. By 1966 all were spending about 12 per cent of their much larger GNPs. The Near East had become one of the most heavily armed regions of the world. The arms race was encouraged by a basic asymmetry; to Israel all Arab states were potential enemies and her level of spending was geared to meeting a threat from them all. But each Arab state had its own enemies against whom it armed as well as against Israel.

A third point of origin was a consequence of the Suez War. When Israel had withdrawn from Sinai she had retained troops in Gaza and at the Straits of Tirān and had surrendered these areas to the United Nations Emergency Force (UNEF) only upon certain assurances. Although Gaza had been transferred back to Egyptian military rule UNEF remained to police the frontier and to keep open the Strait of Tirān enabling Israel to develop the port of Eilat. This Israeli gain from the war remained a source of Egyptian resentment.

The most persistent problem, however, was the question of the Jordan waters which gave rise to an Arab military alliance. After the failure of the Johnston plan Israel determined to go ahead with her own schemes to abstract water for the Negev. In reply the Arab states announced in January 1964 their intention to divert the waters at a point nearer the sources and to create a united Arab command of Egypt, Jordan and Syria to defend the works and prevent Israel diverting the waters. Israel retaliated by bombarding the works but it was clear that Israel's irrigation plans were vulnerable so long as she did not control the sources of the rivers. Furthermore, the creation of an Arab military confederacy was a potential threat to Israeli security.

The united Arab command was not a serious threat to Israel. Since the ineffectual 1950 Arab League Collective Security Pact there had been several attempts to create Arab alliances including the Syrian–Jordan alliance of 1956, the short-lived Arab Solidarity Pact of 1957, the United Arab Republic and the Iraq–Jordan Union of 1958. All had failed because of the different objectives and mutual mistrust of the Arab states. The 1964 alliance was also impotent because Egyptian forces were fully engaged in the Yemen and ᶜAbd al-Nāṣir did not want to be drawn into a conflict with Israel before his troops were back; and because Jordan, the key state in any war with Israel, did not want Arab forces stationed on her territory (except in a real emergency) fearing that they would be used to subvert her monarchical regime. Egypt and Jordan existed in a state of mutual dislike; when Egypt, supported by Syria, criticized Jordan for failing to enter more enthusiastically into the struggle with Israel, Ḥusayn retaliated by accusing Egypt of hiding behind UNEF in Sinai and permitting Israeli ships to sail through the Tirān strait.

The chain of events which led to the war began with the deterioration of Israeli–Syrian relations, the consequence of renewed squabbles over the demilitarized zones and Syrian support for guerrilla attacks on Israel. In April 1967 Israeli aircraft shot down six Syrian jets and in May Israel warned Syria of further retaliation if trouble continued. On 12–13 May the USSR apparently informed Syria and Egypt that Israeli forces were preparing to attack Syria on 16–17 May with a view to overthrowing the Syrian government. This report was incorrect but ᶜAbd al-Nāṣir seemingly believed that a threat did exist and felt obliged to make some response in order to vindicate Egypt's claims to Arab leadership. But ᶜAbd al-Nāṣir could make no convincing demonstration while UNEF remained on his borders so he ordered Egyptian mobilization and UNEF was removed. UNEF also left its post at the Strait of Tirān which Egyptian forces occupied and closed to Israeli shipping on 22 May.

ᶜAbd al-Nāṣir had apparently won a bloodless victory. The threat to Syria, if it ever existed, had been dispelled. ᶜAbd al-Nāṣir had re-established Egypt's credentials as the leader of the Arab states and reformed the Arab alliance; Ḥusayn felt obliged by strong demonstrations in support of Egypt to hasten to Cairo to sign a mutual defence treaty on 30 May. And the last consequence of Suez was expunged by the closure of the Tirān strait. Despite his threats against Israel it is plain that beyond this point ᶜAbd al-Nāṣir did not intend to proceed in 1967. His object was to keep by diplomacy what he had won. It seemed likely that he might accomplish this end with Soviet assistance for, although the United States had made a declaration in favour of the free passage of Israeli ships through the strait, it became apparent that the USA and its allies wished to leave the matter to the United Nations and the ordinary processes of diplomacy, even though President Johnson did promise that something would be done to open the strait for Israel. It is still unclear whether ᶜAbd al-Nāṣir calculated that Israel would not fight or whether he believed that Israel would fight and that the Arabs could defeat her.

Israel decided to fight as soon as it became clear that no-one else would stand up firmly for Israeli freedom to use the strait and after the Arab military alliance was formed on 30 May. On 1 June a national government was formed and on 5 June Israel attacked. By 10 June it was all over; Egypt, Syria and Jordan had been routed and Israel was in occupation of the whole of mandatory Palestine together with Sinai (including the Strait of Tirān and the Egyptian oil fields) and the Golan heights. Israeli forces were at the Suez Canal which was blocked. The speed and comprehensiveness of the Israeli victory took everyone by surprise; it was achieved by the use of air power to destroy the Arab air forces on the first day and, subsequently, in combination with Israeli armour and other ground forces, to defeat the Arab armies. So devastating was the Arab defeat that ᶜAbd al-Nāṣir wrongly claimed that US and British aircraft had supported Israel.

The 1967 war made Israel the dominant power in the region: her prestige stood high, her ailing economy received a boost, and in flowed overseas aid and immigrants. The result was a devastating blow to Egypt's claims to leadership and in the longer term led to a reduction of her involvement and a refocus on domestic concerns; immediately, Egypt abandoned the Yemen. The war cost Jordan dear: a substantial part of her territory was under Israeli occupation. Syria had escaped more lightly but still had lost the Golan. The defeat of these states gave a greater role to other Arab states, in particular to Saudi Arabia which alone had the money to support the defeated states. It was in 1967 that the Arab states first employed the so-called oil weapon: on 6 June, following ᶜAbd al-Nāṣir's accusations against Britain and the US, ten Arab states stopped oil supplies to those countries. The embargo was lifted in August.

The result of the war also had consequences for the great powers. The prestige of the USSR was severely damaged. The Soviet Union was held partly responsible for the misinformation which had contributed to the outbreak of war and was blamed by the Arabs for failing to support them. The USSR had issued threats but done no more. In fact the USSR had urged caution throughout the crisis but could not escape a share of blame and to restore her influence was obliged to increase considerably her aid to Egypt and Syria to rebuild their forces. The USA had also urged caution and reliance on diplomacy but now basked in the reflected glory of the success of the state which was commonly regarded as her client. To the USA Israel began to seem a valuable tool which could prevent the spread of Soviet influence in the Near East by defeating Soviet clients. In Europe, however, matters looked different. The European powers were much more dependent on Near Eastern oil and on the Suez Canal. They observed that the war had damaged their interests and France, once the leading supporter of Israel, promptly cancelled an Israeli order for aircraft. The beginning of the slow drift of Europe towards support for the Arabs and a rift in the western alliance started in 1967. In the Near East support for the defeated Arab countries was almost universal; even Turkey took a pro-Arab line. In the long run the war contributed to the greater isolation of Israel.

THE ARAB–ISRAELI CONFRONTATION, 1967–79

As in 1949 and 1956 war was not followed by peace in 1967; instead a UN ceasefire was succeeded by informal hostilities and in 1973 by another major war. The Arab states refused to make peace: the Israelis could not decide what to offer for peace: and the outside powers lacked the will and the ability to enforce a peace.

All the Arab regimes survived their defeat; President ᶜAbd al-Nāṣir offered to resign but was recalled by popular acclaim and the blame for the defeat was born by others. Soviet military assistance enabled the Arab states to continue resistance and Arab money supported their crippled economies. At the Arab summit meeting at Khartoum in August 1967 it was agreed that Egypt and Syria would continue the struggle and that the oil-rich states would support them. Arab recognition of Israel, a peace treaty or direct negotiations were all rejected. The maintenance of prestige permitted no other posture although Egypt and Jordan were quietly ready for a peaceful settlement if one which did not sacrifice their pride could be found; they were ready to accept the 1949 borders and a compromise on the Palestinian refugees as a basis for peace. More radical states including Syria, Iraq, Algeria and the Sudan, were more obdurate and a new factor was the independent action against Israel undertaken by the Palestinian guerrillas.

Israel had three main possibilities: to return the conquered land as quickly as possible in return for a permanent settlement; to keep all, or nearly all the conquered territory; or to return some territory in return for peace, retaining control of certain areas for security purposes. Only a small minority, mainly from the left, advocated the first course; a substantial group, centred around the old Revisionists and religious groups, favoured the second option which would fulfil the original Zionist purposes; a majority of the ruling Labour group preferred the third course – in the so-called Allon plan this was defined as keeping security settlements in the Jordan valley, retaining the Golan from which Syrian artillery had bombarded Israeli settlements, making some strategic adjustments to frontiers, and returning the remaining territory to Egypt and Jordan. One conquest stood outside all these calculations, however; for ideological reasons East Jerusalem was effectively annexed on 27 June 1967. Between the various possibilities Israel could not decide, nor did she see any reason to hasten to make up her mind as her military position was apparently unassailable. The effect of delay was to strengthen the position of those who wished to keep everything.

The outside powers wanted peace in the region. A framework for a possible settlement was UN Security Council resolution 242 of 22 November 1967 which referred to the inadmissibility of the acquisition of territories by war and the need to work for a just and lasting peace based on the withdrawal of Israeli armed forces "from territories occupied in the recent conflict". The resolution also called for the end of all claims or states of belligerency and "respect for the acknowledgement of the sovereignty, territorial integrity and political independence of every State in the area and their right to live in peace within secure and recognized boundaries free from threats or acts of force". It further affirmed the necessity of free navigation in international waterways, finding a just solution of the refugee problem, and guaranteeing the territorial inviolability and political independence of every state in the area through measures which included the establishment of demilitarized zones.[1] Resolution 242 became the basis of all subsequent attempts to achieve an Arab–Israeli settlement.

Resolution 242 was accepted by Israel and by Egypt, Jordan and Lebanon but was rejected by Syria and some other Arab states and by the Palestinians who complained that there was no recognition of their rights other than as refugees. There were, however, different interpretations of what the resolution meant: Israel claimed that she was not required to withdraw from all territories and that her 1949 boundaries had not been secure; and there was no agreement as to what was a just solution to the refugee problem. Moreover, the resolution did not deal with procedure; Israel insisted on direct negotiations which were not acceptable to the Arabs. On this point and on Syria's refusal to participate the first efforts to negotiate a settlement on the basis of 242 (the Jarring Mission of 1967–8) failed. A second peace project, this time sponsored by the United States and known as the Rogers plan, was launched at the end of 1969. The Rogers plan attempted to resolve the territorial dispute by allowing only minor modifications in Israel's favour in the 1949 frontiers. It was supported by Egypt and Jordan but bitterly opposed by Israel, the radical Arab states and the Palestinians and it effectively collapsed in the latter part of 1970.

Egypt had become increasingly concerned at the lack of progress in the peace negotiations and perceived that the delays favoured those Israelis who hoped to keep what had been conquered. To break the deadlock Egypt launched in March 1969 what became known as the War of Attrition, a series of exchanges along the canal frontier intended to force Israel to maintain a high degree of mobilization at considerable cost and thereby to induce her to make peace. The strategy failed; Israel constructed a heavily fortified defensive line and her reprisal attacks on Egyptian industry around Cairo inflicted more injury on Egypt than was suffered by Israel. Egypt called off the war of attrition in August 1970. One of its principal effects was to bring into Egypt a supply of more advanced Soviet aeroplanes and missiles together with Russian "technicians" and pilots to operate them.

By the end of 1970 a change had taken place in the position of the USSR and the USA. In 1967 they had agreed to use their influence to restrain their respective "clients" in the Near East and induce them to make peace on the basis of 242. The failure to achieve peace and the continuing hostilities allowed the "clients" to draw their patrons more closely towards their sides. Both superpowers supplied increasing quantities of advanced weapons to their clients. Furthermore, they became more and more suspicious of each other. Thus the USA came to believe that the USSR was exploiting the situation for its own advantage and to the eventual detriment of western interests in the region. In September 1970 the USA decided that the USSR was supporting Syria in an attempt to take over Jordan and believed that only Israel stood in the way of her success. The 1971 Soviet–Egyptian treaty, which was followed in April 1972 by a similar treaty with Iraq, appeared to confirm this judgement. In fact the treaties represented no change in Soviet policy nor any increase in Soviet influence; they merely provided a legal basis for the flow of Soviet weapons and advisers into those countries. As subsequently became apparent, most obviously when Egypt dismissed its Soviet advisers in July 1972, the terms of the exchanges were controlled by the Arab states. But the US response was to give Israel greater importance as a bulwark against Soviet penetration of the region. It was not so much the Cold War as the myth of the Cold War which was imported into the Near East in this period.

The deadlock in the Near East was broken by Egypt and Syria when they went to war with Israel in 1973. President Sādāt, who had succeeded ᶜAbd al-Nāṣir in September 1970, soon became convinced of the necessity of a limited war to persuade Israel to make peace on terms acceptable to the Arabs and the world to support a settlement. He proposed an operation to seize the east bank of the canal supported by a Syrian offensive in the Golan. Jordan would not take part but Saudi Arabia agreed to support an oil embargo. Planning began in March 1973 and the attack was launched on 6 October. During the first three days the war went well for the Arabs; the east bank was seized and Syrian troops broke through in the Golan and threatened Israel proper. Thereafter Israel recovered: Syrian forces were repelled by 11 October and by 18 October Egyptian forces, which had unwisely advanced beyond their planned objectives on the east bank, were in danger of being cut off by an Israeli operation on the west bank of the canal. On 22 October Egypt and Israel, but not Syria, accepted a UN ceasefire call (resolution 338).

During the course of the 1973 war both superpowers had supported their clients with fresh supplies of arms and diplomatic action. But they had also agreed on concerted action through the UN to achieve a ceasefire. However, the ceasefire left the Egyptian Third Army on the east bank of the Canal in a very vulnerable position at the mercy of Israel, which seemed inclined to exploit the advantage. The USSR then threatened to send troops to the support of Egypt whereupon the USA announced a red alert (placing her forces on a war footing) on 24 October. It seemed that the Near Eastern situation had at last brought the two superpowers to the brink of war but this appearance is misleading. In fact the USSR had no intention of sending troops but wished only to put pressure on the USA to restrain Israel. On the part of the USA the red alert served to disguise the USA's compliance with this demand. On October 25 agreement was reached and on 27 October the resupply of the stranded Egyptian army began. Thus Israel was denied the possibility of a complete victory.

Another feature of the 1973 war was the renewed use of the oil weapon. In October the Arab oil states imposed cuts in production and a total ban on supplies to the USA. The embargo was maintained until March 1974 and it contributed to a considerable rise in the price of oil. The oil embargo of 1973 had much greater impact than that of 1967 because of changes which had taken place in the world oil position in the intervening period. In 1967 there had been plenty of cheap oil in the world, oil production was still controlled by a few great oil companies and the USA produced as much oil as the whole of the Middle East. Around 1970 a shortage of oil developed, US production began to decline rapidly, estimates of reserves ceased to increase more rapidly than production and there was a sudden consciousness that oil was finite and that well over half of the world's known reserves was in the Middle East. The bargaining position of the Middle Eastern oil states was greatly improved and they took advantage of the new situation to take control of production, either by outright nationalization or by taking a controlling share in the oil companies, and to raise prices. By 1973 the whole world was sensitive to their decisions; in particular the policies of most European countries, which had already been inclining towards support for the Arabs since 1967, more strongly favoured the Arab states in 1973. It was the oil factor rather than the international terror campaign waged by Palestinian guerrillas between 1968 and 1972 which brought about this change in European attitudes. A clear division between the USA and Europe on the question of the Near East now existed and the USA needed a settlement to consolidate the western alliance.

The United States's new peace initiative, conducted by the secretary of state, Henry Kissinger, took a new form. Although nominally aiming at a general peace at a full peace conference Kissinger concentrated on a series of small local disengagement agreements leading to a partial Israeli withdrawal in Sinai and the Golan. Agreements were made between Israel and Egypt on 18 January 1974 and 4 September 1975 and between Israel and Syria on 29 May 1974. To persuade Israel to agree to the withdrawals the USA gave Israel extensive assurances of support, including an undertaking not to deal with the PLO so long as it did not accept 242. The agreements did benefit Egypt, which recovered the Sinai oilfields and was able to reopen the Suez Canal, but when the step by step approach appeared to have reached the end of its possibilities Israel was still in occupation of most of Sinai and the Golan. To the new US president, Jimmy Carter, it seemed time to return to the idea of a general peace conference at Geneva. On 1 October 1977 the USA and the USSR agreed to summon a conference at Geneva.

The plan for a new Geneva conference was frustrated by a dramatic new development which opened the prospect of direct Israeli–Egyptian negotiations for peace. This was the visit of President Sādāt of Egypt to Jerusalem where he conferred with Israel's new prime minister, Menachem Begin, in November 1977. At first the move was seen as one intended to contribute to the Geneva initiative but its effect was the reverse for it alienated other Arab states and eventually led to a separate peace treaty between Israel and Egypt on 26 March 1979. That agreement was produced largely through the mediation of President Carter and was part of what were called the Camp David accords of September 1978. The accords were intended to provide an agreed framework for a general settlement and contemplated both separate peace treaties between Israel and the Arab states and a staged settlement of the problem of the West Bank and Gaza by which a self-governing, elected Palestinian authority should replace Israeli military government. Using 242 as a basis Egypt, Israel and Jordan were to negotiate an agreement concerning the powers of the authority and its boundaries. After the authority had been in place for not more than three years, new negotiations, involving Israel, Egypt, Jordan and elected Palestinian representatives, would determine the final status of the West Bank and Gaza and conclude a peace treaty between Israel and Jordan.

The Camp David accords failed to produce a general settlement. Whether the complicated plans for the West Bank and Gaza could have provided a basis for a settlement is unknown because they depended on the participation of Jordan and, like every other Arab state except Egypt, Jordan declined to have anything to do with the Camp David accords. The Israeli–Egyptian treaty was the only result. By that treaty the state of war which had existed since 1948 was terminated, the two countries agreed to establish normal relations and Israel withdrew her forces from Sinai by 25 April 1982. The treaty also provided for talks on Palestinian autonomy but these talks made no progress. The main results of the treaty were that Egypt was able to concentrate on domestic reconstruction at the price of isolation in the Arab world and expulsion from the Arab League; and Israel was relieved of fears of attack by her most formidable Arab neighbour. Pressure on Israel to reach a general settlement was now much less and she took advantage of her freedom to annex (de facto) the Golan heights on 14 December 1981, to attempt to deal with the Palestinians in Lebanon in 1982–3 and to try to impose her own settlement on the West Bank and Gaza.

THE NORTHERN TIER AND THE GULF

During the 1960s the conciliatory Soviet policy in the Northern Tier began to achieve better relations with Turkey and Iran. These improved relations were manifested primarily in the economic field; a trade agreement with Turkey was signed in 1965 and Soviet economic aid was given to that state; improved trade and transit agreements were made with Iran and in 1966 the USSR agreed to build a steel mill, a gas line and a machine tool factory (all completed 1970–3) and Iran undertook to supply natural gas to the USSR. Visits were exchanged and cultural and technical agreements made. Political successes came more slowly but were also achieved, particularly with Turkey.

Turkey's receptiveness to Soviet approaches was partly influenced by her disillusionment with the USA, especially over Cyprus. The Cyprus problem originated in the 1950s with the Greek Cypriot demand for union with Greece and the campaign of violence against British rule. When Britain decided to concede independence to Cyprus Turkey became concerned about the future of the Turkish community on the island. By the Zurich and London agreements of 1959 an independent republic of Cyprus was established with safeguards for the Turkish minority. Britain, Greece and Turkey became guarantors of the settlement. But difficulties arose between the Greek and Turkish communities and in December 1963 civil war broke out. Turkey contemplated intervention in the summer of 1964 but was warned by President Johnson that if she did intervene NATO might not come to her support in other matters. Turkey thereupon resolved to rely less on the United States in the future and to seek to improve her relations with the Middle East, the USSR and above all, Europe. She was confirmed in her new view by events in Cyprus in July 1974 when a Greek-sponsored coup overthrew the government of Archbishop Makarios and the rebel regime announced union with Greece. Unable to persuade Britain or the United States to take effective action Turkey invaded Cyprus. The United States disapproved of this action and imposed an arms embargo which lasted until 1978. Turkey became convinced that she could not rely on United States' support in any dispute involving Greece.

Turkey did not cease to look to the United States for military and other assistance but she increasingly diversified her options. In 1963 she signed an association agreement with the European Economic Community and in subsequent years worked towards eventual membership of that institution with which half her trade was conducted. With the Soviet Union her relations grew warmer; in 1977 the prime minister, Bülent Ecevit, declared that the USSR was no longer a threat to Turkey and in 1978 a document of friendship was signed by the two countries. Turkey was generous in permitting the USSR easy use of the Straits to support the Soviet Mediterranean squadron.

With Iran Soviet relations were less comfortable. The Shah continued to regard the USSR with suspicion, the more so because of the alliance between the USSR and Iraq and Soviet use of Iraqi facilities in the Gulf. To Iran the USSR was an ally of Arab radicalism and a potentially disturbing factor in the Gulf. For Iran the alliance with the United States remained the main plank of her foreign policy. Nevertheless, the Soviet Union was reasonably content with the improvement in her relations with Iran and could even find features to praise in the White revolution.

The principal Soviet success was the decline of the western-supported military confederacy of the Northern Tier. The Baghdad Pact had collapsed in 1959 when Iraq withdrew and had been replaced by the Central Treaty Organisation (CENTO) consisting of Turkey, Iran, Pakistan and Britain, but the members were little interested in its military purposes. The Northern Tier states also established a regional organization for economic and cultural co-operation, Regional Co-operation for Development (RCD), in 1964 but this organization also had little vigour. Nevertheless, it did represent a continuing concept of regional organization which went back to the Saadabad pact of 1937.

In terms of international relations the Near East in 1978 seemed more stable than it had done for some years. The confrontation between the USA and the USSR, first in the Northern Tier and then in the Arab world, which had begun in 1945 appeared to have stabilized. In the Northern Tier Turkey and Iran seemed to have found a way of working with the two superpowers while pursuing their own regional interests and in the southern region Camp David gave some hope of agreement although it had temporarily produced a polarization of the region in which the two superpowers found themselves on opposite sides. In Arabia the last embers of colonial power had been extinguished when Britain had left the region in 1971. Britain had remained an influential power in Arabia after 1956 but during the 1960s she had come to the conclusion that to sustain commitments east of Suez without the facilities of the Suez base and consistently with her European commitments was too great a burden. Between 1966 and 1968 Britain had decided to withdraw from Aden and the Gulf and she left the first at the end of 1967 and the Gulf at the end of 1971. The dire results anticipated from her departure had not materialized; the local powers had adjusted their differences and Iran had come forward to claim the role of policeman of the Gulf. The apparent menace of the growth of Soviet influence in south-west Arabia had receded with the ending of the rebellion in Oman.

The pleasing prospect described in the preceding paragraph was upset in 1979 by two events: the Islamic revolution in Iran and the Soviet invasion of Afghanistan. To the United States these two events represented, first, the replacement of her most trusted ally (excepting Israel) in the region by a dangerously unstable and unpredictable revolutionary power which seemed bent on a course opposed to the USA, and, second, the advance of the Soviet Union towards the

Persian Gulf. Together, the two events seemed to threaten the disruption of vital western interests in the Near East. The United States reacted in a variety of ways but especially by giving aid to states in the region and by creating a special force for rapid deployment in what was now described as the arc of crisis. A new situation had arisen which had two aspects: superpower and regional confrontation.

The United States had misinterpreted the Soviet role in events. The Soviet invasion of Afghanistan was a miscalculation based upon defensive and ideological considerations and was not part of a plan to gain a foothold on the Gulf or challenge Western interests in the region. The Soviet Union had had no hand in events in Iran and welcomed them little more than the USA did; it was pleasing that the USA had lost an ally but not at the price of so tinderous a power on the southern frontier of the USSR. Regional perceptions were clearer; those states which accepted US aid did so for their own purposes, often unconnected with the Soviet threat, and others were reluctant to become part of US designs. As time went on it became clearer that there was no real basis for superpower confrontation and that the heart of the matter was regional conflict, a civil war in Afghanistan and a struggle for mastery between Iran and Iraq.

THE IRAN–IRAQ WAR, 1980–88

The Iran–Iraq war, sometimes called the Gulf War (although the Gulf was neither the principal bone of contention nor the main theatre of operations) was a regional contest between the two principal states in the eastern Near East. Other powers viewed the struggle with uninterest or fear and were involved reluctantly. It was also the largest interstate conflict since the Second World War in terms of its duration, its cost and its casualties. The war lasted eight years, cost an estimated $200 billion directly and another $1,000 billion indirectly, and inflicted some 1 million casualties, perhaps 60 per cent sustained by Iran. By the end of the war each side had between 1.3 and 1.6 million men under arms, representing in the case of Iraq more than half of the total number of males of military age and in the case of Iran about one-sixth.

There were disputes about hegemony in the Gulf. After the Iraq revolution of 1958 Muḥammad Riżā Shāh had become increasingly worried about the progress of radical Arab nationalism, supported by Iraq and Egypt, in the Gulf region; and his concern had deepened after the announcement in 1968 of the British intention to leave the region. To Iran the security of the Gulf was important because it was a main artery of trade, especially for Iran's oil exports, and the site of oil production from offshore installations. Iran prepared to replace Britain as the principal guardian of regional security. She composed her disputes with Gulf states by agreements with Kuwayt (1965), Saudi Arabia (1968), Qaṭar (1969) and Baḥrayn (1970). In two areas there were more violent clashes: in 1971 Iran seized the Tūnb islands and Abū Mūsā at the mouth of the Gulf and a prolonged dispute with Iraq over the Shaṭṭ al-ᶜArab ended only in 1975 when Iraq conceded Iran's demand that the deep water channel should form the frontier between the two states and not, as hitherto under the 1937 treaty, the Iranian shore with the exception of a small area around Ābādān. Although Iran established her authority with care and the situation was generally accepted by the states of the region there were resentments, especially on the part of Iraq, which claimed leadership among the Arab states of the region and regarded herself as the principal upholder of the concept of the Arab Gulf, a notion which embraced the proposition, enunciated in 1964, that the Iranian south-western province of Khūzistān was Arab.

The desire to avenge the loss of prestige involved in conceding Iran's demands in 1975 was a principal reason for Iraq's attack on Iran on 22 September 1980. Other reasons are given, including the rivalry of Sunnī and Shīᶜī, Persian and Arab, secularist and Muslim, but none of these vague animosities was the direct cause of the war. And although President Ṣaddām Ḥusayn resented the appeals of the Islamic Republic of Iran to Muslims (and especially to Shīᶜīs in Iraq) to overthrow his government it was not necessary for him to go to war to deal with these matters. The motive for war was simply that Iran was thought to be too much weakened by revolutionary turmoil and army purges to resist a limited attack and would concede Iraq's demands relating to the Shaṭṭ al-ᶜArab, minor border disputes arising out of the 1975 agreement and perhaps also grant some alteration in the position of Khūzistān.

Iraq's calculations went astray: although Iraqi forces captured Khurramshahr and penetrated deep into south-west Iran, they achieved no decisive victory and Iranian resistance, by regular and irregular forces, held the Iraqi advance. For two years there was stalemate and then the war began to turn against Iraq. In 1982 Iranian offensives cleared Iraqi forces out of most of the Iranian territory which they had captured and the way was open for peace on the basis of the *status quo ante bellum*. But Iran decided to go on fighting and to carry the war into Iraq.

What her objectives were remained obscure. She had no territorial claims and her demand for the complete withdrawal of Iraqi forces from Iran was conceded. She demanded reparations and an admission of war guilt from Iraq. It was reported and sometimes denied that she demanded the removal of Ṣaddām Ḥusayn and it was also suggested that she wished to establish an Islamic government in Iran, although these alleged goals never became clear war aims. Most Iranians believed they were fighting for good against evil. Mainly, Iran was fighting for prestige.

Having decided to take the war to Iraq Iran had a choice of three main lines of attack. She could attack on the central front and drive directly on Baghdad but she lacked the air superiority and armour which would be required for success in such an enterprise. She could advance in the north, seeking to control Iraq's oilfields at Kirkuk and enlist the help of Kurdish opponents of Iraq's government. This strategy, however, would involve promises to Kurds which could have repercussions among Iran's Kurds. The third strategy was to assault Basra in the south, cutting Iraq off from the Gulf and raising the possibility that Iraq's Shīʿī population would join hands with the invader. Iran adopted the southern front as her main line of advance and made the others subsidiary to it. Between 1983 and 1986 she mounted a series of attacks which culminated in the capture of Fao in February 1986 but she failed to break the Iraqi defences in front of Basra. Nevertheless, by 1986 it seemed only a matter of time before superior Iranian manpower resources finally wore Iraqi defences down.

From 1982 Iraq was on the defensive. With her oil exports through the Gulf and through Syria blocked her revenues declined and she became more vulnerable in a long war. Her strategy was to raise the cost of the war to Iran by exploiting her superior airpower and to try to involve other states. She attacked Iranian cities, oil installations and tankers and succeeded in reducing Iran's oil exports. She appealed for Arab financial help which was freely given by the Gulf states, and she opened up channels for supplies through Kuwayt, Jordan and Turkey. And she strove to win the support of the superpowers. From 1982 onwards both the USSR and the USA inclined towards Iraq. The USSR became, with France, a principal supplier of arms to Iraq.

In 1987 Iraq achieved some success in drawing in the superpowers. In retaliation for Iraqi attacks on shipping using Iranian ports Iran began, in 1986, naval attacks on the vessels of states which sympathized with Iraq, in particular Kuwayti vessels. Kuwayt appealed for assistance which was given first by the USSR. To prevent the further extension of Soviet influence and to retain her own influence among the states of the Arab Gulf the USA agreed in May 1987 to place Kuwayti vessels under her own flag and escort them through the Gulf. This action brought US warships into action against Iranian craft and opened the possibility of wider hostilities in the Gulf.

In 1988 the war turned against Iran and she at last accepted a ceasefire. In April 1988 Iraqi forces recovered Fao and from May to July launched other successful offensives. In the face of Iraqi chemical weapons and aerial attacks Iranian morale appeared to have sunk low. On 20 July 1988 Iran accepted UN resolution 598 of 20 July 1987. "God knows," said Āyatallāh Khumaynī, "that were it not that all our honour and prestige should be sacrificed for Islam, I would never have consented.... I repeat that accepting this [resolution] was more deadly for me than taking poison."[2]

The war had ended in a draw, a result which might have been secured as early as 1982. The real question is why Iran, with her superior resources of wealth and manpower, failed to win a convincing victory. The answer appears to be that Iraq was more anxious not to lose than Iran was to win and that Iraq was prepared to make a greater effort and was better at winning friends. Iraq mobilized a far higher proportion of her manpower than did Iran and she maintained the equipment and training of her forces at a higher level. Iraq was willing to borrow heavily abroad to sustain the struggle but Iran sought no foreign loans and actually paid off debt during the war. Iraq was quite ruthless in her demands on other Arab countries for assistance and also attracted aid from other powers. Iran was more proficient in the gentle art of making enemies; she alienated Britain and France quite wantonly, made no effort to conciliate the USSR, and her dabblings with the USA in 1985–7 ended in disclosure and the so-called Irangate (Iran-Contra) affair, that is the scandal caused by the attempt of certain US officials to evade Congressional prohibitions on aid to the Nicaraguan rebels by supplying them with arms paid for out of the profits from arms sales to Iran.

All other states remained officially neutral but of the regional powers all the Arab states except Syria and Libya supported Iraq. Egypt's assistance to Iraq speeded her rehabilitation in Arab eyes after the so-called betrayal of the treaty with Israel. At the Amman summit of November 1987 most Arab states agreed to resume diplomatic relations with Egypt. Jordan greatly strengthened her position in the Arab world by becoming the strongest supporter of Iraq and allowing supplies to be channelled through ʿAqaba. Relations between the two countries became better than at any time since 1958. And Saudi Arabia also increased her influence among the Gulf states who found it convenient to come together with Saudi Arabia in the Gulf Cooperation Council. Of the other states in the region Israel gave covert help to Iran on the basis that she was the enemy of Iraq; and Turkey was the perfect neutral, profiting considerably from the closure of the Gulf routes and greatly increasing her trade with both belligerent states.

Of the great powers France supplied Iraq with key weapons from 1983 and won some consequential Arab goodwill. The Soviet Union inclined towards Iran during the first two years of the war, condemning Iraq for its breach of the peace and suspending arms supplies, but after Iran took the war into Iraqi territory the USSR leaned towards Iraq and resumed arms supplies. The USA long stood aloof, regarding both regimes with aversion and hardly knowing which she would prefer to see defeated. But under Arab pressure she eventually came to believe that an Iranian victory would be injurious to US interests because it might lead to the collapse of the pro-Western regimes in the Gulf. Her attempt to win influence with Iran through arms supplies ended in humiliation and in 1987 she agreed to assist Kuwayt. At that time the US did not intend to take sides in the war but the inevitable result was that she became pitted against Iran. But none of the great powers, with the possible exception of France and her supplies of Exocet missiles to Iraq, exercised a major influence on the course of the conflict. Nor did the divisions of the superpowers influence events materially; rather their similar views promoted co-operation between them at the United Nations which remained their principal arena of intervention.

The Iran–Iraq war was interesting for its effects on the international trade in oil. The war took place at the end of a decade which had seen the demand for oil from the Gulf greatly increase and the price rise several times. Indeed it was only the reserves accumulated through the sale of oil which enabled the two countries to fight as long and as hard as they did. Before the war the conventional wisdom had been that the world could scarcely afford the loss of one major producer, let alone of two, and it certainly could not tolerate a war in the Gulf through which passed so much of the world's oil. In fact, Iraqi and Iranian production was greatly reduced and the war raged in the Gulf for eight years with tankers and oil installations becoming prime targets and yet the world found more than enough oil for its wants and the price fell through most of the period. Oil did, however, find new routes by pipeline direct to the Red Sea and the Mediterranean and one effect of the war was to reduce the importance of the Persian Gulf to the world;

in 1978 nearly 20 million barrels a day (mbd) went out from the Gulf and by 1985 this was reduced to 6.4 mbd.

Despite its ramifications the war ended as it began, as a conflict primarily about prestige between two regional powers. Its long endurance had been especially the consequence of the dominance of the two main protaganists, Ṣaddām Ḥusayn of Iraq and Āyatallāh Khumaynī of Iran. Neither was prepared to give way and both retained sufficient power and influence to defeat attempts to replace them or to reduce their control of decision making. Indeed the most interesting result of the greatest interstate conflict of the second half of the twentieth century in the Near East was a negative one; it resulted in no alteration in the state system and no change of regime. The outcome was a demonstration of the strength of the state system which had emerged from the First World War and of the power of regimes to ensure their own survival.

THE SOUTHERN NEAR EAST, 1979–89

The Israeli–Arab peace treaty of 1979 isolated Egypt and united the other Arab states. The subsequent decade saw the rehabilitation of Egypt and a renewed division of the Arab states. The main factors in these changes were the Iran–Iraq war, events in Lebanon, and the question of an Arab–Israeli settlement.

The Iran–Iraq war had the effect of diminishing the influence of Iraq which had previously been numbered among those states least inclined to compromise with Israel; isolating Syria, which was alone, but for Libya, in her support of Iran; and enabling Egypt to reappear as an important pillar of the Arab cause.

The Lebanon situation was the consequence of the struggle for power among the different communities and factions in Lebanon and the involvement of several outside powers. Syria had intervened in 1976 and had won Arab approval for her role. Her presence did not, however, end the hostility between the different communities or lead to a cessation of Palestinian guerrilla attacks on Israel. In June 1982, taking advantage of the neutralization of Egypt, Israel invaded Lebanon in an attempt to crush the PLO and clear the way for a settlement of the West Bank on her own terms. The Israeli forces clashed with those of Syria, and Israel contrived to eliminate Syrian missile sites (established in 1981 and the subject of repeated Israeli complaints) and destroy a large number of Syrian aircraft. Syria decided to seek a truce and to withdraw from contact with the Israeli forces. Israel then had an opportunity to destroy the PLO forces and establish a congenial government in Lebanon but her plans went awry: the PLO fighters left Beirut in August 1982 undefeated, no stable government could be created, Israel's treaty with Lebanon of 17 May 1983 was never ratified and was cancelled in March 1984 by the Lebanese government and Israel gradually withdrew her forces between July 1983 and June 1985. By the latter date Israel had returned to the position she occupied in June 1982, that is with a security zone along her frontier held in the Israeli interest by a Lebanese militia. Syrian forces returned and recovered their predominant influence and the struggle between the Lebanese communities and factions was resumed although outside intervention had helped to change the balance between them.

Israel's Lebanese war had international repercussions. The United States, preoccupied by the notion of a Soviet threat, saw Syria as the agent of the USSR in the region and considered her occupation of Lebanon as a preliminary to the extension of Soviet influence. The USA was not unhappy, therefore, that Israel should have forced Syria to retire and was willing to assist in the negotiation of the Israel–Lebanese treaty and in establishing a strong government in Lebanon which would exclude outside powers. The United States also agreed to take part in a multinational peacekeeping operation following the departure of the Palestinians. The USA soon found, however, that she had involved herself in a complex local situation. In September 1983 she was persuaded to support the Lebanese army with force and the Sixth Fleet shelled Druze positions near Beirut. As a result US forces and those of France became the target of attacks by Shīʿī groups; on 23 October 1983 the headquarters of the US and French forces in Beirut were destroyed by car bombs and 241 US Marines and 58 French soldiers were killed. The USA blamed Iran, Syria and the USSR for instigating the attacks and drew still closer to Israel. The USA soldiered on in Lebanon for a few more months but it became plain that naval bombardments achieved little and that a massive deployment of US troops would be required to uphold the authority of the Lebanese government. In February 1984 the USA gave up and withdrew its troops in company with the other members of the multinational force.

The withdrawal of the multinational force led to the reassertion of the power of the community militias and of Syria. Syria then found herself sucked further and further into Lebanese politics. In 1983–5 she set herself to reduce the Palestinians and the Sunnī Lebanese militias to subjection; in February 1987 she was obliged to occupy West Beirut when her Amal allies were defeated by a coalition of other groups and to try to bring those rival groups to heel. In 1989 the Syrian occupation was challenged by the Maronite Lebanese government which was backed by Iraq. Like other states Syria was enmeshed in Lebanese conflicts and incurred by her actions the hostility of states which supported groups antagonistic to Syria. By 1989 almost all Arab states wished her out of Lebanon and her policies towards the PLO had alienated both Arabs and the USSR. Lebanon contributed to the isolation of Syria in the Arab world even while Syria was seen as an element of stability in Lebanon.

The years 1980–9 witnessed several initiatives intended to advance what was euphemistically known as the peace process involving Israel and the Arab states. In June 1980 came a European Community initiative, the Venice Declaration, which expressed support for the principles of resolution 242, endorsed the Palestinian right to self-determination, demanded the association of the PLO in negotiations and urged an Israeli withdrawal from the occupied territories and an end to the settlement policy. In August 1981 the Fahd plan was drawn up which offered recognition of Israel in return for a withdrawal to the 1949 frontiers, an independent Palestinian state on the West Bank and in Gaza and return or compensation for the refugees. The plan was rejected at the Arab summit in Fez in November 1981 but adopted in a remodelled form to acknowledge the leadership of the PLO at the September 1982 Fez summit. In September 1982 came the Reagan Plan which was a development of the Camp David framework and looked to an autonomous Palestinian entity confederated with Jordan. The entity's frontiers were to be negotiated with Israel, that is to say it was supposed that Israel would not return to the 1949 frontiers. In February 1985 a joint plan based on the Fez proposals but incorporating Palestinian self-determination within a confederation with Jordan was put forward by Jordan and by Yāsir ᶜArafāt for the PLO. ᶜArafāt could not carry his PLO colleagues with him, however, and the plan collapsed in 1986. It was evident that a major stumbling block was the PLO's refusal to relinquish armed struggle and to accept Resolution 242 and in 1988 ᶜArafāt was able to persuade the PLO to agree to these terms and thus allow a dialogue to begin with the USA. On 15 November 1988 the Palestine National Council proclaimed the establishment of an independent state in the West Bank and Gaza, accepted resolution 242 and the notion of an international conference under the UN and renounced terrorism. There remained, however, many major problems including acceptance of the Palestinian state, the definition of its frontiers and the position of the refugees, and beyond these questions the matter of whether Israel would accept any settlement which obliged her to withdraw from the occupied territories.

Israel attempted to find her own solution to the matter but without substantial success. One solution was piecemeal annexation including Jerusalem (1967), the Golan (1981) and the establishment of settlements in the occupied territories. Immediately after 1967 official policy was to encourage settlements in strategic locations but quickly an unofficial movement sprang up (the Land of Israel Movement) which promoted settlements in all areas with a view to future annexation. After 1977 this movement received official encouragement from the Likud government. Most settlements were located in areas adjacent to existing Israeli towns, notably Jerusalem. While the process of settlement went on some interim arrangement for the government of the West Bank and Gaza was sought. At first the Jordanian system and personnel were used but in 1976 these were displaced by PLO supporters and Israel sought to create a new class of collaborators through the village leagues (1981). When this failed Israel returned to the notion of trying to secure the election of suitable mayors but this hope also failed. Mayors opposed Israeli policy and a new autonomy plan in 1986 foundered for this reason. The failure of the 1986 plan led to increasing disturbances on the West Bank and in Gaza which in December 1987 produced the *intifāḍa*, an expression of general hostility to Israeli occupation and settlements.

Israel had tried to avoid international intervention in a settlement of the Arab–Israeli dispute and insisted that it was a matter for direct negotiation with the Arab states. Her only success with this policy was with Egypt in 1979 and that agreement did not solve the Palestinian question. Israel's refusal to recognize the PLO blocked any international conference at which the PLO was represented. In 1988 the change in policy of the PLO which produced USA–PLO talks compelled some Israeli rethinking which led in 1988 to Shimon Peres, the Labour leader in the coalition government accepting the principle of an international conference, a notion still resisted by the Likud element. In 1989 the Likud party became divided over a proposal put forward by the prime minister, Yitzhak Shamir, to build on the Camp David approach by holding free elections on the West Bank and Gaza after the *intifāḍa* had ceased. Likud, and perhaps a majority of Israelis, believed that the territories should never be surrendered, that there should be no Palestinian state, and that sometime, as a result of future contingencies, the land would become the permanent possession of Israel and most of the Arab population would leave.

CONCLUSION

The most noteworthy result of the international transactions of the states of the Near East after 1923 is that they left almost intact, with the exceptions of the Ḥijāz and Palestine, the structure of states and their frontiers which was created in the post First World War settlement. This result may be thought surprising bearing in mind that the structure was denounced at the time as one imposed from outside without reference to the wishes of the peoples concerned; criticized subsequently by groups which espoused philosophies justifying a reorganization of the state system on some new ethnic, historical, geographical or religious basis; and attacked by states which felt themselves to be placed at a disadvantage by the existing state structure. Did the persistence of the 1923 state structure owe more to factors external to the region or internal?

In the period 1923–56 Britain and, to a lesser extent, France were the dominant presence in the region. British influence was exerted to preserve the 1923 settlement. In central Arabia she allowed the rival contenders their struggle for power and contented herself with preventing encroachment on areas in which she was more intimately involved. Thereby Britain helped to impose frontiers on Arabia, extending the principles of the 1923 settlement thither. In Palestine she decided in 1947 that the task of upholding the 1923 settlement was beyond her powers and limited her involvement to trying to reduce disruption outside Palestine. Elsewhere she endeavoured to preserve the status quo and in the Gulf region continued to do so until 1971. Britain and France were able to play the role they did because their position in the area had a legal basis and was supported by armed forces operating from bases. Until 1939 they had no serious challenge from outside the region and the strategy pursued by Nazi Germany during the Second World War meant that the challenge during that period was much slighter than it might otherwise have been. British influence declined quite rapidly after the Second World War as a result of a regional challenge and a loss of will.

No outside power subsequently played a role in the Near East comparable to that which Britain had played. There are three reasons for this decline in the importance of outside intervention: the absence of sound legal grounds for intervention and of bases as opposed to facilities; a smaller interest by outside powers, except for the interest of the USSR in the Northern Tier; and the rise of the regional powers. Near Eastern oil was never vital to either superpower; both had their own sources or access to other supplies. Those powers which did depend on Near Eastern oil – Europe and Japan – had little or no power to control events; indeed it is a curious irony, with which proponents of theories of economic-based imperialism must wrestle, that the decline of European power exactly matched the rise of Europe's principal economic interest in the area. The influence of the superpowers depended more on indirect means: offers of economic and military aid, the supply of weapons and promises of diplomatic support. Often the superpowers preferred to operate through the United Nations. They were unwilling to commit troops to the region. There were occasions when superpowers employed force; the US used Marines in Lebanon in 1958 and 1983–4, naval power in the Gulf and the Mediterranean and air power against Libya in 1986; the USSR used its forces in Egypt in 1970 and in Afghanistan in 1979–89. In no case were forces used to alter the state structure, rather they were introduced in the hope of preventing a threatened alteration. What influence outside powers exerted was cast in favour of the established state system.

It is in general true to say that while the international system is neutral concerning changes of regimes it is hostile to changes in the state structure. The United Nations represents established states which wish the world of the states they know to continue. Economic and political dealings are with states and not, with very few exceptions, with groups. The weight of the international system is everywhere cast in favour of the international status quo and the survival of the state system of the Near East may be no more surprising than that of Africa. But the operation of the international system is not the only or the main reason for the survival of the state system of the Near East or perhaps that of other regions. In the end the international system will ratify changes in state structures agreed by the states concerned; in the Near East the states did not agree and the survival of the state system owed most to the states themselves.

In considering the role of the states of the Near East there are four points which should be borne in mind: the development of powerful security systems which supported regimes and states; the growth of groups whose members' interests were served by the existing states; the identification of national interests; and the formation of national identities conterminous with the states themselves. These factors all contributed to consolidating the state system of the region. Groups which sought to challenge the state system were defeated by the states themselves, alone or in alliance; such was the fate of the Kurds, and outside intervention in the Lebanon was intended, whatever its result, to maintain the state. Despite the widespread Arab commitment to

Arab political union and in spite of the circumstance that regimes dedicated to the proposition that their own states were unnatural held power, leaving aside the UAE, no proposed merger succeeded and every failure seemed to confirm the desire of states to preserve their identity. Their regional pacts served to maintain the identity of the states which formed them; thus the Arab League, the Gulf Co-operation Council and others served to preserve the existence of the states which composed them.

New states and new regimes begin with an international tabula rasa; quickly they define interests and pursue them. Contemplating the international history of the Near East one is struck by the persistence with which states pursued the goals they identified although regimes came and went. Thus Turkey steadily pursued her European ambitions in various forms after 1923, Israel her ambitions to rule all Palestine, Iraq developed a consistent aim to become the predominant Arab power in the eastern region, Syria sought persistently to dominate the Arab lands of the eastern Mediterranean, and Egypt endeavoured to avoid an exclusive commitment to any of the fields within which her position required her to operate.

In considering the relations between international and regional powers one may conclude that the dominant feature was the manipulation of the international powers by regional powers. The Cold War was not exported to the Near East but imported by the states of the region to serve their own purposes. From 1945 Turkey and Iran presented their traditional disputes with Russia as part of a world-wide conflict and secured US and other aid in reward. In 1955 Egypt won Soviet support by presenting her regional ambitions as part of a struggle against imperialism. Syria and Iraq later followed suit. In 1958 Kamīl Shamʿūn placed his personal ambitions in Lebanon in the frame of a fight between radical Arabism and Western values, an argument cultivated by Maronites at other times. From 1970 Israel successfully presented her local problems as being linked to the super-power conflict and improbably persuaded the United States that she was a strategic asset in that arena. And from 1982 to 1988 Iraq displayed her quarrel with Iran as part of a greater clash between revolutionary Islamic fundamentalism and secularism. This is not to say that the international powers were always unaware of the manipulation and that it did not sometimes suit their purposes to fall in with regional ambitions. Nor is it to contend that international intervention always worked to the advantage of the regional powers which were as capable of miscalculation as were others. But it is to say that on balance the regional pipers called the tune.

The state system of the Near East survived partly because it was supported by the international system but principally because it was not in the interests of the regional powers to overthrow it. Tempting as it was to individual states and regimes to meditate projects of Greater Syrian, Fertile Crescent, Arabian, Yemeni, Arab or Muslim unity and inviting as were the prospects of statehood to discontented groups within and across state boundaries the projects and prospects were all found to contain more debits than credits, more opponents than supporters; and the status quo usually seemed more attractive.

There are two exceptions to this generalization. One is Lebanon where regional ambition and factional contention combined to threaten the integrity of the state. But Lebanon's state structure was the weakest in the whole region (outside Arabia) and its plight perhaps reinforces the contention concerning the dominance of modern states. The other is Israel, which other states and a discontented, stateless group apparently sought to obliterate. Israel's establishment and continued existence owed more to international intervention than any other state in the region and yet that intervention was not the decisive factor. The United Nations' decision to partition Palestine in 1947 was no more than the recognition of the circumstance that no-one was prepared to coerce a group which already possessed many of the attributes of a state and the survival of Israel owed more to the abilities of Israelis to mobilize their own resources and tap those of others than to direct intervention in Israel's support. And the history of the Arab–Israeli dispute suggests that it persisted as much because of the ambitions of Israel as because of the rhetorical Arab ambition to destroy the Jewish state.

What one observes, in fact, is the emergence of a regional balance of power in the Near East, created by the finer apprehension of state interest and by a balance of force. Alliances were formed to prevent any one state from upsetting that balance as Egypt threatened to do in the 1960s and Iran in the 1980s. The interest of outside powers, the delicacy of the balance of power, and the wealth available to sustain the struggle, ensured that the balance of force was struck at a very high level. From the 1960s onwards the Near East spent a higher proportion of its wealth on defence than any other region of the world. Regional hegemony or dominance by one international power might have come much cheaper.

NOTES

1. UN Document Security Council Resolution 242 (22 November 1967).
2. Quoted Dilip Hiro, *The Longest War*, 1989, 243.

Epilogue

The typescript of this book was completed in the late summer of 1989 and it is a history of the Near and Middle East from the First World War peace settlement until that date. There is an artistic untidiness about contemporary history which by definition has no end. It is therefore worth emphasising the point made in the preface that this is a work of history which does not attempt to predict the future. To put the matter in an extreme and highly unlikely form the state system of the Near East could collapse tomorrow and the Europeans and the notables could return and yet the truth of the observation that the stability of the first and the departure of the second were prominent features of the history of the Near East between 1923 and 1989 would be unaltered.

It is, nevertheless, interesting to contemplate some events which have occurred in the year since the work was completed. The most noteworthy events have taken place in Arabia (with Turkey one of the two areas of the Near East which have diverged significantly from the patterns of change which characterized the rest of the region). One significant development attracted little attention: this was the announcement on 15 May 1990 of the unification of the two Yemens. If it endures the merger will constitute a major alteration in the state system of Arabia. The second episode dominates the headlines as I write this epilogue: it is the Iraqi invasion of Kuwayt on 2 August 1990, its annexation a week later and the accompanying Gulf crisis. If the disappearance of the Kuwayt state proves to be permanent a second significant change in the Arabian state system will have been accomplished. In addition the conjunction of a united Yemen (in population easily the largest state in Arabia) and an expansionist Iraq would threaten the position of Saudi Arabia, the small Gulf states and Oman and usher in the possibility of the greatest political revolution in Arabia since the 1920s. On the other hand if Kuwayt is restored to life we shall debate (as in the case of the 1961 affair) whether regional or international factors proved decisive in that outcome.

Although history does not predict it fills the present with resonances. To the historian the events of August 1990 recall enduring patterns of Iraqi history: the long-standing commitment to Arab unity which began with the Hashimite legacy and was carried on by the followers of Fayṣal I; the vision of Iraq as the Prussia of Arab nationalism which is associated with Sāmī Shawkat; the belief of Ṣalāḥ al-Dīn al-Ṣabbāgh and the Golden Square in the central role of the Iraqi army in the achievement of Arab unity; and the perennial detestation of the Baᶜth for the notables. But whether we come to see the Kuwayt adventure as just another blind alley or as the Schleswig-Holstein question of Arab unity is not yet a matter for history.

M.E. Yapp. August 1990.

Bibliographical Guide

NOTE

The following guide can be no more than an illustration of the immense range of source material available for the study of the Near East in the twentieth century and an indication of the more important books among the great number which have been written on the subject. The amount of source material available for the twentieth century and the quantity of the secondary literature dwarf the totals for all earlier periods of Near Eastern history. In listing books, subtitles, publishers' names and the place of publication, if it is London, have normally been omitted. The list is confined to works in English, apart from a few in French and German, and primarily to books. Readers are advised below which are the more important journals. Other evidence used by historians, including sound recordings and film material, is excluded.

PRIMARY SOURCES

One would have expected that the principal source used by historians writing on the modern history of the Near East would have been the archives of the Near Eastern states. In fact this is not so mainly because archives have not been open to scholars or if open have been usable only with great difficulty. Of the states of the Near East the only ones which make available their unpublished records are Turkey, Egypt and Israel and then not later than the middle of the century. (It is true that occasionally archival material from other states appears for fortuitous reasons as when Jordanian intelligence archives fell into Israeli hands at the capture of Jerusalem in 1967). The Egyptian national archives (*Dār al-wathā'iq al-qawmiyya*) are poorly catalogued and cramped and much material is unavailable. In fact, because of problems of storage, many documents from the old *Dār al-mahfūzāt* are rotting in the open air. There is in theory a rule by which material more than 50 years old is made available to scholars but it has not been observed in practice. In contrast to the well-furnished Central Zionist Archives the Israel State Archives are also cramped and inadequate. Only the materials for the mandate period (which are largely duplicated in London) are normally open for inspection. Turkish archives for the period of the Republic, in contrast to those for the Ottoman period, were not available for scholarly research until very recently but in May 1989 a fifty year rule was introduced. It remains to be seen how it is applied. One cannot see the government archives of Iran or of Arab states other than Egypt. Lack of money, fear of disclosure, and a habit of regarding government archives as the working documents of bureaucracy rather than as the basic materials of historical research have combined to produce this sad situation which may now be on the verge of improvement.

It should not be supposed, however, that government documents are not available. All Near Eastern governments publish large quantities of documents containing information about their economic, social, political and diplomatic transactions. For example, the Egyptian government presently produces about 120 official publications, mainly in Arabic, together with a host of special publications. Important speeches are published by the ministry of information, usually in English translation. Other Near Eastern governments have similar publication programmes; in 1973 the Turkish foreign ministry began publishing an 11 volume collection of documents on foreign policy covering the years since 1923. The Israeli government has recently begun publishing diplomatic documents covering the late 1940s. Those Near Eastern governments which have parliaments publish records of their debates. A great deal more material is available than many people suppose; the problem is often to identify and locate the material; sometimes the national or parliament libraries of the states concerned are the only places where a student can be reasonably sure of finding them. Certainly, no centre in the West has anything like a full collection of Near Eastern government publications; for the most recent period of history the US Library of Congress is considered to be the best but, even so, it has extensive gaps in its collections. Near Eastern national libraries are also the main sources for comprehensive collections of newspapers and periodicals covering the whole of the twentieth century. The amount of newspaper material available may be gauged by the estimate that Egypt alone currently publishes about 400 titles, and although more newspapers are published today than in the past the volume of twentieth century newspaper material is very great. National libraries also contain some of the collections of private papers of Near Eastern politicians, although many more of these are in private hands. In short, the amount of source material available is enormous; the problem for scholars is that of other students of modern history, namely to read and digest the material that exists; not, as in the past, to try and fill the gaps in the material.

The archives of European states and of the United States are also an important source for historians of the modern Near East. Britain and France were directly responsible for the governments of Iraq (to 1930), Palestine (to 1948), Syria and Lebanon (to 1945) and Aden (to 1968). In addition, Britain had responsibilities in Egypt to 1936 and in Arabia to 1971 which entailed keeping detailed records of the internal affairs of these countries. Lastly, like those of other states, the foreign ministries of European states and of the United States kept (and keep) elaborate records relating to the states of the Near East. Because of these circumstances and because the European states and the United States are much more willing and able to make available their archives to scholars, European and American archives have become the principal sources used by serious historians writing about the history of the period of Near Eastern history before about 1960. (Because of the opportunities offered to researchers under the Freedom of Information Act US materials for later periods are also available.) Briefly, the principal repositories are: in Britain, the Public Records Office and the India Office Library in London; in France, the Archive du Ministère des Affaires Etrangères in Paris, the Archives d'Outre Mer in Aix-en-Provence and the recently deposited records of Syria and Lebanon in Nantes; in Italy, the Archivio Storico del Ministero degli Affari Esteri in Rome; in Germany, the Archiv des Auswărtigen Amts in Bonn and the Nazi Party archives in Koblenz; and in the United States, the National Archives in Washington, DC. Soviet archives for this period are not at present available for use. Those who wish to use these archives should consult the guides published by the archival administrations but a simple start is to use one of the relevant research handbooks published in Wilmington, Delaware, namely S. Asher, *British Foreign Policy, 1918–1945*, R.J. Young, *French Foreign Policy 1918–1945*, C.M. Kimnich, *German Foreign Policy, 1918–1945*, and Alan Cassels, *Italian Foreign Policy, 1918–1945.* League of Nations records in Geneva are also important, as are those of the United

Nations and a helpful guide to these is G. W. Baer, *International Organisations, 1918–1945*.

Considerable quantities of materials from the European and US archives have been published either in microfilm or in book form. Microfilm publications from the US archives by University Publications of America have been particularly extensive and include, for example, the US diplomatic post records for the Middle East, 1925–1954. The same firm has also published the British series of confidential prints covering the Middle East down to 1939. Research Collections (New Haven) have published a large collection of League of Nations Documents on microfilm including all the records of the Permanent Mandates Commission. Every government has also instigated its own publication of diplomatic correspondence in book form. The principal series are, for Britain, the *Documents on British Foreign Policy*, (65 volumes in three series covering the period 1919–39); for France, the *Documents Diplomatiques Françaises* (32 volumes in two series covering the period 1932–1939); for Germany, the *Akten Zür Deutschen Auswärtigen Politik* (54 volumes in five series to date covering the years 1918–45; an English language version of the third and fourth series covering the years 1933–1941 has been published in 19 volumes); for Italy, *I Documenti Diplomatici Italiani* (21 volumes in four series to date covering the years 1918–1943); for the USSR, *Dokumenty Vneshnej Politiki SSSR* (21 volumes covering the period 1918–1938); and for the United States, the *Foreign Relations of the United States*, a very large collection of documents which has reached the year 1963. The above collections are those of diplomatic correspondence generated by foreign ministries. As mentioned above, Britain and France also had direct governmental responsibilities which involved other departments of government and documents relating to these responsibilities were published extensively, notably administration reports, reports of commissions of inquiry and a variety of material relating to social, economic and political affairs. Some material in this category is still being published or reprinted, for example the 25-volume collection of British documents on *Arabian Boundaries, 1853–1957*, (ed. R. Schofield and G. Blake), Archive Editions, 1988.

Another major category of source material is memoirs. Because of the absence of archival material from 1960 onwards memoirs (with government publications and newspapers) are the principal source for the historian of the contemporary Near East. Memoir material is abundant especially in European languages but also in Hebrew, Arabic, Turkish and Persian. Some memoirs are mentioned below but the list is very far from exhaustive and is limited to material available in

English. A large quantity of memoir material is untranslated and sometimes difficult to obtain; for example, for political reasons some of the Arabic material was published in newspapers and periodicals, notably in Beirut.

The most convenient source of statistical material is often the publications of the United Nations and its agencies, together with those of the World Bank and the International Monetary Fund. Usually, UN material is based on the publications of Near Eastern governments and while it may not be accurate – indeed it is dispiriting to observe that among Near Eastern states only Israeli population figures are rated "reliable" in the regular UN statistical publication (the *Monthly Bulletin of Statistics*) – there is no obviously better source than the states themselves. With all their inaccuracies and other disadvantages, the statistics available for contemporary Near Eastern history are infinitely better than any statistics (or, more commonly, impressionistic estimates) for earlier periods of the history of the region. The existence of series of statistics which at least approximate to accuracy enables the historian to express conclusions in terms of quantities, a mode of writing which facilitates comparisons and is especially suited to a broad survey such as the present book. I have availed myself freely of the facility provided and am in no way deterred by the circumstance that the quantities I have offered are subject to a large margin of error. To a Western trained economist such uncertainty may inspire trepidation but to an historian arriving at the second half of the twentieth century from the eighteenth and nineteenth centuries the ground seems exceptionally firm. Such an historian may revel in the opportunities presented, regarding the occasional tumble as a price well worth paying for his new freedom.

Finally, oral evidence should be mentioned. It is a peculiarity of contemporary history that participants in events can be questioned about those events and their testimonies are used by many writers, usually in the form of formal interviews which are commonly tape-recorded, although occasionally reference is made to private conversations. Another type of oral evidence relates to social history; the observations made by an anthropologist in a study of a Near Eastern village, for example, constitute a form of recorded oral testimony. The use of oral evidence gives rise to certain philosophical problems in the discipline of history which is the study of the past based upon written documents. This is not the place to discuss those problems; it is sufficient to note that historians use oral evidence either directly by setting out to collect evidence from participants or indirectly through reliance on the books of the social and political scientists who habitually employ such materials, often placing their chief reliance on them.

As remarked above, the quantity of source material for the history of the Near East in the twentieth century exceeds that for all previous periods of its history. One would also say that the quality of the material is superior. Many historians dismiss this second proposition, pointing to the absence of much archival material, the inaccuracies of newspapers and the self-serving deceptions of many memoirs. But once one makes the comparison with earlier periods one sees how fortunate is the historian of the contemporary Near East. At least he has some archival material, and what would the historian of earlier periods not give for newspapers describing, however badly, the events of the time? How much would that other historian like to have a collection of memoirs of the time of Harūn al-Rashīd as large as that available to the historian of, for example, Hashimite Iraq? And for all the scepticism which has been expressed about the use of oral evidence how much the historian of the origins of Islam would welcome the chance to interrogate the companions of the Prophet.

SECONDARY SOURCES

General

Jere L. Bacharach, *A Middle East Studies Handbook*, 1985, offers general information useful to students of the modern Middle East and contains an historical atlas. A more elaborate atlas is Gerald Blake, John Dewdney and Jonathan Mitchell, *The Cambridge Atlas of the Middle East and North Africa*, Cambridge 1988. The Middle East Libraries Committee has produced a bibliography compiled by D. Grimwood Jones, *Middle East and Islam*, 1979. A supplement covering the years 1977 to 1983 has been edited by P. Auchterlonie, 1986. George N. Atiyah, *The Contemporary Middle East, 1948–1973,* Boston 1975, is also a useful annotated bibliography. An annual survey which supplies basic political and economic information on each country of the region and up to date accounts of historical events is *The Middle East and North Africa*, (Europa Publications). Another annual with excellent articles on each state and on particular problems is *The Middle East Contemporary Survey*, a successor to the *Middle East Record*. *The Survey*, which is written mainly by members of the Shiloah Institute and Dayan Center in Tel Aviv, appears about two or three years after the events it describes. More recent information must be sought in the

London-based *Middle East Economic Digest* (which in 1979 absorbed the *Arab Report and Record*, which ran from 1967 to 1979) and similar journals specializing in the region, notably the Beirut *Arab World File* and the *Middle East Economic Survey* (Cyprus), which carries useful information on oil affairs. The Economist Intelligence Unit *Quarterly Economic Reviews* are also invaluable for economic affairs and *Middle East International* (London) is good for political developments. Biographical information may be obtained from *Who's Who in the Arab World* (Mansell), currently in its ninth edition. The work also includes country studies and historical articles. Details of cabinets during the early period may be obtained from R. Bidwell, *Bidwell's Guide to Government Ministers, vol 2: The Arab World*, 1973. For statistical information down to 1975 see B.R. Mitchell, *International Historical Statistics: Africa and Asia*, 1982. There are several academic journals which publish articles on the modern history of the Near East but the leading journals are *Middle Eastern Studies* (London), the *International Journal of Middle East Studies* (Cambridge), the *Middle East Journal* (Washington DC), *Asian and African Studies* (Haifa) and the *Journal of Palestine Studies* (Washington DC). *International Affairs and Foreign Affairs* (Washington DC) also often carry important articles on the Near East.

On social life Ira M. Lapidus, *A History of Islamic Societies*, Cambridge 1988, provides a sound background and C.A.O. Van Niewenhuijze, *Sociology of the Middle East*, 1971 and M. Zeltzner, *Aspects of Near East Society*, New York 1962, are broad surveys. Gabriel Baer, *Population and Society in the Arab East*, 1964 is a good account of the social structure of the Arab world in the 1950s, including sections on the family and social stratification. A thoughtful book, strong on Turkey, is D. Lerner, *The Passing of Traditional Society*, Glencoe, Ill., 1958. On village life see R.Lawless (ed.), *The Middle Eastern Village*, 1987, and on urban life there are some useful collections of papers including A.H. Hourani and S.M. Stern (eds.), *The Islamic City*, Oxford 1970, I.M. Lapidus (ed.), *Middle East Cities*, Berkeley, Calif. 1969, L.C. Brown (ed.), *From Madina to Metropolis*, Princeton 1973, and G.H. Blake and R.I. Lawless (eds), *The Changing Middle Eastern City*, 1980. A comprehensive review is still needed: V. Costello, *Urbanization in the Middle East*, Cambridge 1977, is not quite full enough. The most detailed survey of educational development is Joseph S. Syzliowicz, *Education and Modernization in the Middle East*, Ithaca NY, 1973. A.L. Tibawi, *Islamic Education*, 1972, considers traditional and modern Arab systems. An excellent survey is Fahim H. Qubain, *Education and Science in the Arab World*, Baltimore 1966.

There has been a reluctance to undertake a general account of population change in the modern Near East: J.I. Clarke and W.B. Fisher (eds), *Populations of the Middle East and North Africa*, 1972, was a pioneering work but it lacks historical depth and is now rather old. Ali Banuazizi, *Social Stratification in the Middle East and North Africa*, 1984, is a useful bibliography of social change.

We also need a general economic history of the modern Near East. Most studies lack an historic dimension and are geared towards prophecy. Z.Y. Herschlag, *Introduction to the Modern Economic History of the Middle East*, 2nd edn., Leiden 1980, is the nearest to what is sought. C.A. Cooper and S. Alexander (eds), *Economic Development and Population Growth in the Middle East*, New York 1972, is a useful review of the economic history of various countries. Y.A. Sayigh, *The Economies of the Arab World*, 1978 is a survey covering the period since 1945; and Rodney Wilson, *The Economics of the Middle East*, 1979, is comprehensive and contains much serviceable information. Jean Ducruet, *Les Capitaux Européens au Proche Orient*, Paris 1964, is good on aspects of European intervention. On agrarian history two pioneering classics are Doreen Warriner, *Land Reform and Development in the Middle East*, 1957, and *Land and Poverty in the Near East*, 1968, although both may best be regarded as characterizations of a bygone age. More recent is Tarif Khalidi, *Land Tenure and Social Transformation in the Middle East*, Beirut 1984.

The starting point for study of the history of the Middle East oil industry is S.H. Longrigg, *Oil in the Middle East*, 3rd edn, 1968. See also G.W. Stocking, *Middle Eastern Oil*, Nashville 1970. Other good accounts of the early history of the industry are B. Shwadran, *The Middle East, Oil and the Great Powers*, 1955 and G. Lenczowski, *Oil and State in the Middle East*, Ithaca, NY 1960. J.E. Hartshorn, *Oil Companies and Governments*, 1962, is only partly concerned with the Near East. A recent historical account of the development of OPEC is Ian Skeet, *OPEC*, Cambridge 1988, which takes the story down to 1985. Mary Anne Tetresault, *The Organisation of Arab Petroleum Exporting Countries*, 1981, is only partly historical. Returns on oil operations are analysed in Zuhayr Mikdashi, *A Financial Analysis of Middle Eastern Oil Concessions, 1901–65*, New York 1966. For recent developments see B. Shwadran, *Middle East Oil Crises since 1973*, Boulder 1986.

Turning to political history there are several regional studies of value. Ann T. Schulz, *International and Regional Politics in the Middle East and North Africa*, Detroit 1977, is a useful bibliography and guide to information sources. On the nature and development of the state Michael Hudson, *Arab Politics: The Search for Legitimacy*, Cambridge,

Mass. 1977, is both a textbook and an argument about the character of Arab regimes. It may be read with Gabriel Ben-Dor, *State and Conflict in the Middle East*, New York 1983, and Giacomo Luciani (ed.), *The Arab State*, 1989, a collection of essays which follows the publication of a four-volume work edited by Luciani entitled *Nation, State and Integration in the Arab World*, 1987. Sylvia Haim's anthology of nationalist writings, *Arab Nationalism*, Berkeley, Calif. 1962, is still a very convenient collection on this topic and has an excellent introduction. An elegantly written account of the intellectual evolution of nationalist movements down to 1939 is in A.H. Hourani, *Arabic Thought in the Liberal Age*, Oxford, 1962. A more recent study of ideas which is weighted towards Shīʿī thought is Hamid Enayat, *Modern Islamic Political Thought*, 1982, and a study of one influential thinker, Shakīb Arslān, is contained in William Cleveland, *Islam against the West*, Austin, Texas 1985. The relation between Islam and the state at a broader level is the concern of a short, stimulating book by P.J. Vatikiotis, *Islam and the Nation State*, 1987. Radical movements are dealt with in Adeed Dawisha, *The Arab Radicals*, 1986, and Sami A. Hanna and G.H. Gardner (eds), *Arab Socialism*, Salt Lake City, 1969, is a compilation of documents on the topic. Hisham Sharabi, *Nationalism and Revolution in the Arab World*, New York 1966, is useful for its treatment of the political vocabulary of Arab radicals, a subject dealt with in greater detail in B. Lewis, *The Political Language of Islam*, 1988. Two books on Pan-Arabism may be mentioned: Yehoshua Porath, *In Search of Arab Unity*, 1986, which traces the various initiatives from 1930 to 1945, and Ahmad M. Gomaa, *The Foundation of the League of Arab States*, 1977 , which describes the establishment of the principal institutional success of the movement. Both draw heavily on British documents.

Political élites have been a fashionable subject of concern and two collections of papers dealing with the subject are George Lenczowski (ed.), *Political Elites in the Middle East*, Washington, 1975 and Frank Tachau (ed.), *Political Elites and Political Development in the Middle East*, New York 1975. One major source of élite recruitment has been lawyers, the subject of Donald M. Reid, *Lawyers and Politics in the Arab World, 1880–1960*, Minneapolis 1981. Another has been the military and on the role of armies in politics see Sidney Fisher (ed.), *The Military in the Middle East*, Columbus, Ohio 1963, J.C. Hurewitz, *Middle East Politics: the Military Dimension*, New York 1969, and E. Be'eri, *Arab Army Officers in Arab Politics and Society*, New York 1970, which looks at the social origins of officers. Turkey and Iran are dealt with in G.M. Haddad, *Revolutions and Military Rule in the Middle East*, New York 1965.

Although old, Walter Laqueur's, *Communism and Nationalism in the Middle East*, 1956, is still useful for its treatment of the early communist parties. See also M.S. Agwani, *Communism in the Arab East*, 1969. Students of Middle East minorities should start with A.H. Hourani, *Minorities in the Arab World*, 1947, but a more recent work is R.D. McLaurin (ed.), *The Political Role of Minority Groups in the Middle East*, New York 1979. The often sad fortunes of minorities have always been among the many interests of Elie Kedourie and this is a convenient place in which to mention three collections of his essays: *The Chatham House Version*, 1970, *Arabic Political Memoirs*, 1974, and *Islam in the Modern World*, 1980. Modern Near Eastern history has been fortunate in that it has been graced by three writers of unusual intellectual distinction and literary merit, Elie Kedourie, Albert Hourani and Bernard Lewis, and anything written by these men is worth reading. A relevant collection of essays by Albert Hourani is *Europe and the Middle East*, 1980. Bernard Lewis, *The Middle East and the West*, 1964, is still useful.

Since the 1979 Islamic revolution in Iran there has been a great upsurge of interest in Islamic fundamentalism or revivalism and its political role. A good starting point is E. Mortimer, *Faith and Power*, 1982. Other general studies include J.O. Voll, *Islam*, Boulder 1982, D. Piper, *In the Path of God*, New York 1983, J.L. Esposito, *Islam and Politics*, Syracuse, NY, 1984, H. Munson, *Islam and Revolution in the Middle East*, 1988, which has an anthropological approach; and H. Dekmejian, *Islam in Revolution*, Syracuse, NY, 1985, which deals with the Arab states. Other recent works are W. Montgomery Watt, *Islamic Fundamentalism and Modernity*, 1988, and D. Hiro, *Islamic Fundamentalism*, 1988. Sami Zubaida, *Islam, the People and the State*, 1989, argues that fundamentalism is essentially a response to modernity. There are several good collections of papers on the role of Islam, including Alexander S. Cudsi and Ali E. Hillal (eds), *Islam and Power*, London 1981; Michael Curtis (ed.), *Religion and Politics in the Middle East*, Boulder 1981; Muhammad Ayoob (ed.), *The Politics of Islamic Reassertion*, London 1981; J.P. Piscatori (ed.), *Islam in the Political Process*, Cambridge 1983; and S.A. Arjomand, *From Nationalism to Revolutionary Islam*, 1984. A useful collection of source material is John L. Donahue and John L. Esposito, (eds), *Islam in Transition*, 1982, although it would have been more helpful if greater editorial guidance had been given, in particular the dating of the source extracts. Among more specialized works the following are worthy of study: Emmanuel

Sivan, *Radical Islam*, 1985, which contains abundant information about fundamentalism in Egypt and Syria; and Gilles Kepel, *The Prophet and Pharaoh*, 1985, which deals with recent movements in Egypt and may be read as a continuation of Richard Mitchell, *The Society of the Muslim Brothers*, 1969, which is still the best study of the first major fundamentalist group in the region. Some of the more important writings of two prominent Brothers are in C. Wendell, *Five Tracts of Hasan al-Banna*, Los Angeles 1978, and Sayed Kotb, *Social Justice in Islam*, New York 1970. By far the best descriptive account of Shiᶜism is Moojan Momen, *An Introduction to Shiᶜi Islam*, 1985, and a serviceable collection of essays is Martin Kramer (ed.), *Shi-ism, Resistance and Revolution*, Boulder 1987. Some source material has been translated by Hamid Algar, namely Ali Shariati, *On the Sociology of Islam*, Berkeley, Calif. 1979, and Ruhullah Khumayni, *Islam and Revolution*, Berkeley Calif. 1981. Khumayni's *Islamic Government*, 1979, has also been translated, although the translation is accompanied by a diatribe against the Islamic Republic,

On international relations the usual (substantial) starting point is G. Lenczowski, *The Middle East in World Affairs*, 4th edn, Ithaca, NY 1980, which includes studies of the foreign policies of various countries and accounts of particular problems. Two books describe the approach of Muslims towards international relations. These are J.H. Proctor (ed.), *Islam and International Relations*, New York 1965, and Majid Khadduri, *The Islamic Law of Nations*, Baltimore 1966. See also A. Dawisha (ed), *Islam in Foreign Policy*, New York 1983. L. Carl Brown, *International Relations and the Middle East*, Princeton 1984, argues that international relations in the modern Middle East have many of the characteristics of the old Eastern Question. His book also contains a useful critical bibliography of international relations in the region. Domestic influences on foreign policy-making are the subject of R.D. McLaurin *et al*, *Foreign Policy Making in the Middle East*, New York 1977. A convenient collection of source material for the years to 1945 is in J.C. Hurewitz (ed.), *The Middle East and North Africa in World Politics*, vol. 2, 1914–45, New Haven 1979. For documentary selections relating to the subsequent period see M. Khalili, *The Arab States and the Arab League*, vol. 2, Beirut 1962, and *Arab Political Documents*, Beirut 1963–5. A small, but helpful collection concentrating on Arab and Israeli affairs is T.G. Fraser, *The Middle East, 1914–1979*, 1980.

Egypt

There are several good general histories of modern Egypt. J. Marlowe,

Anglo–Egyptian Relations, 1800–1956, 1965, T. Little, *Modern Egypt,* 1967, and J.C.B. Richmond, *Egypt, 1798–1952,* are all clear, sympathetic and readable. D. Hopwood, *Egypt, 1945–1981,* 1982, is short and well balanced and includes some information about cultural developments. A. Goldstein, *Modern Egypt,* Boulder 1988 is the most recent and has an excellent bibliographical essay, but P.J. Vatikiotis, *The Modern History of Egypt,* 1980, is the best. Jacques Berque, *Egypt: Imperialism and Revolution,* 1972, is full of ideas but needs to be approached with caution. For the period before 1952 we have some good studies based on archives. These include two works on the Wafd: Marius Deeb, *Party Politics in Egypt. 1919–39,* 1979, and Janice J. Terry, *The Wafd, 1919–1952,* 1982. Afaf Lutfi al-Sayyid-Marsot has written a study focused on the Liberal Constitutional party, *Egypt's Liberal Experiment, 1922–1936,* 1977. Aḥmad Ḥusayn's Young Egypt party is the subject of J.P. Jankowski, *Egypt's Young Rebels,* Stanford 1975. The communist parties are dealt with in S. Botman, *The Rise of Egyptian Communism, 1939–1970,* Syracuse, NY, 1988, which has much material on earlier periods and not a great deal after 1952. Communism had not had much to do with the labour movement which is described in J. Beinin and Z. Lockman, *Workers on the Nile,* Princeton 1988, and E. Goldberg, *Tinker, Tailor and Textile Worker,* Berkeley, Calif. 1986. B.L. Carter, *The Copts in Egyptian Politics,* 1986, is concerned with the period 1919–52. In addition to the book by Richard Mitchell, C.P. Harris, *Nationalism and Revolution in Egypt,* Stanford 1964, is valuable for the Muslim Brotherhood. On relations with Britain there is still a lot to be gleaned from the work of Lord Lloyd, *Egypt Since Cromer,* 2 vols, 1933–4, and from the Chatham House study, *Great Britain and Egypt, 1914–1951,* 1952. Thomas Mayer, *Egypt and the Palestine Question, 1936–1945,* Berlin 1983, describes the involvement of Egypt in a regional problem. We are well provided with studies of intellectual changes in Egypt during this period. J.M. Ahmed, *The Intellectual Origins of Egyptian Nationalism,* 1960, Nadav Safran, *Egypt in Search of Political Community,* Cambridge, Mass 1961, Charles Wendell, *The Evolution of the Egyptian National Image,* Berkeley, Calif. 1973, and I. Gershoni and J.P. Jankowski, *Egypt, Islam and the Arabs,* 1986, all repay reading. Gershoni has also produced a study of the development of Pan-Arab ideas in Egypt, *The Emergence of Pan-Arabism in Egypt,* Tel Aviv 1981. One of the most significant intellectual figures of the period, Muḥammad Ḥusayn Haykal, is the subject of C.D. Smith, *Islam and the Search for Social Order in Modern Egypt,* Albany, NY 1983. On economic changes two books by Charles Issawi, *Egypt: an Economic and Social Analysis,*

1947, and *Egypt in Mid-Century,* 1954, are recommended. Two recent studies describe the efforts of private industrialists in Egypt: Eric Davis, *Challenging Colonialism,* Princeton 1983, a study of the Bank Misr group, and R. Tignor, *State, Private Enterprise and Economic Change in Egypt, 1918–1952,* Princeton 1984.

On the revolution of 1952 J. and S. Lacouture, *Egypt in Transition,* 1958, is still useful but we now have a number of studies of ᶜAbd al-Nāṣir and his times. Foremost among them is P.J. Vatikiotis, *Nasser and His Generation,* 1978, but there are two worthy biographies of ᶜAbd al-Nāṣir: Robert Stephens, *Nasser,* 1971, and J. Lacouture, *Nasser,* New York 1973. R.H. Dekmejian, *Egypt Under Nasir,* Albany 1971, is especially valuable for the pioneering analysis of the political élite of the period. L. Binder, *In a Moment of Enthusiasm,* Chicago 1978, is an absorbing study of a second élite, the rural notables. It may be read with I. Harik, *The Political Mobilization of Peasants,* Bloomington 1974, and James B. Mayfield, *Rural Politics in Nasser's Egypt,* 1971. On the land reform see G.S. Saab, *The Egyptian Agrarian Reform, 1952–1962,* 1967, and S. Radwan, *Agrarian Reform and Rural Poverty,* 1952–1975, Geneva 1977. An interesting imaginative study is R. Critchfield, *Shahat, an Egyptian,* Syracuse, NY 1978, a study of an Egyptian village. The best general account of the economic history of Egypt under ᶜAbd al-Nāṣir is Robert Mabro, *The Egyptian Economy, 1952–1972,* 1974, with which may be read the joint work produced by Mabro and Radwan, *The Industrialisation of Egypt, 1939–73,* Oxford 1976. P. O'Brien, *The Revolution in Egypt's Economic System,* 1967, is a good study of the movement towards socialism and centralized planning during the late 1950s and early 1960s. One should not forget the accounts by participants: Gamal Abdul Nasser, *The Philosophy of the Revolution,* 1954; Anwar Sadat, *Revolt on the Nile,* 1957 and *In Search of Identity,* 1977, and Mohammad Neguib, *Egypt's Destiny,* 1955.

The period of Sādāt and Mubārak is less well covered. R.W. Baker, *Egypt's Uncertain Revolution under Nasser and Sadat,* Cambridge, Mass 1978, is an attempt to discern the pattern of change between the periods before and after 1970. John Waterbury, *The Egypt of Nasser and Sadat,* Princeton 1983, covers the same topic in rather greater depth. R.A. Hinnebusch, *Egyptian Politics under Sadat,* Cambridge 1985 (new edition 1988), indicates the extent of political change under Sadat and considers the changing pattern of the élite. Anthony McDermott, *Egypt from Nasser to Mubarak,* 1988, is a rather sketchy account. C. Tripp and R. Owen (eds), *Egypt Under Mubarak,* 1989, is a wide-ranging collection of essays on contemporary Egyptian problems. Of biographies of Sadat, D. Hirst and I. Beeson, *Sadat,* 1981, is informative but hostile, and Raphael Israeli, *Man of Defiance,* 1985, is more sympathetic. An understanding of the working of family politics may be gained from a study of Sayyid Marᶜi by Robert Springborg, *Family Power and Politics in Egypt,* Philadelphia, 1982.

On the role of Islam in the period since 1952 see, in addition to the works listed in the general section, Morroe Berger, *Islam in Egypt Today,* 1970, and M. Gilsenan, *Saint and Sufi in Modern Egypt,* Oxford 1973. Berger has also written on the bureaucracy, *Bureaucracy and Society in Modern Egypt,* Princeton 1957. Another more recent study of the same important subject is Nazih N.M. Ayyubi, *Bureaucracy and Politics in Contemporary Egypt,* London 1980. We have no recent study of the role of the other great Egyptian institution, the army. P. J. Vatikiotis, *The Egyptian Army in Politics,* Bloomington 1961, although valuable for the 1930s change in the character of the force, is rather old and does not consider the army's evolution and functions under ᶜAbd al-Nāṣir and Sādāt. Higher education is the subject of two recent works: Haggai Erlich, *Students and University in Twentieth Century Egyptian Politics,* 1989, and Ahmad Abdalla, *The Student Movement and National Politics in Egypt,* 1985, which is especially valuable for the student movements against Sādāt, in which events the author was a participant. The feminist movement has produced a rash of studies of women in Egypt including Soha.A. Kader, *Egyptian Women in a Changing Society, 1899–1987,* 1988, which summarizes changes in politics, education, law, and other aspects of social life.

Iraq

General information about Iraq may be found in the Naval Intelligence manual, *Iraq and the Persian Gulf,* 1944, and in R.F. Nyrop, (ed.), *Iraq: A Country Study,* Washington 1979. Of general histories of Iraq, S.H. Longrigg, *Iraq 1900 to 1950,* 1953, is old but still contains abundant information on the details of administration during the mandatory period. It should be supplemented by P. Sluglett, *Britain in Iraq, 1914–32,* 1976. P. Ireland, *Iraq,* 1938, is a remarkable study of the early years of the states which makes one wonder how the author came to be so well informed. Two recent studies of the early period are M.A. Tarbush, *The Role of the Military in Politics,* 1982, which stops in 1941 and Reeva S. Simon, *Iraq Between the Two Wars,* New York 1986, which focuses on the role of education and the army in forming nationalist ideology. H. Mejcher, *The Imperial Quest for Oil,* 1976, is an informative study of the role of oil in British policy towards Iraq between 1910 and 1928 which contrives, nevertheless, to exaggerate the importance of that factor. Another work on the subject of Iraqi oil is W. Stivers, *Supremacy and Oil,* Ithaca NY 1982. A recent study of British relations with Iraq from the granting of independence until the 1941 intervention is Daniel Silverfarb, *Britain's Informal Empire in the Middle East,* 1986. Like other scholarly studies of this period it is based on British documents and is informative on strategic questions. We are short of published biographies of Iraqi politicians of this period; we have no good life of Fayṣal, and Lord Birdwood, *Nuri al-Said,* 1959, though sympathetic, fails to locate him in his Iraqi political background. This is an appropriate place in which to mention the three studies of Iraqi history by Majid Khadduri: *Independent Iraq,* 1960, which covers the period down to 1958, *Republican Iraq,* 1969, which takes the story on to 1968, and *Socialist Iraq,* 1978, which deals with the Baᶜthist revolution. But overshadowing all other books in English on Iraq is the massive, discursive, shapeless, yet highly analytical work of Hanna Batatu, *The Old Social Classes and the Revolutionary Movements of Iraq,* Princeton 1978. A work which no future writer on the politics of the period can ignore with safety is ᶜAbd al-Razzāq al-Ḥasanī, *Ta'rikh al-wizārāt al-ᶜirāqiyya,* 10 vols Sidon 1953–67, an enormous study of the composition and workings of Iraqi governments.

Uriel Dann, *Iraq Under Qassem,* 1969, is a detailed account of the first five years of revolutionary Iraq and his *Foundations of the Ba'th Regime in Iraq, 1968–73,* Tel Aviv 1974, forms a sort of sequel. They may be read with the works of Khadduri and Batatu cited above. M. and P. Sluglett, *Iraq since 1958,* 1987, is a very informative study, although the authors do not disguise their distaste for the regime. E. and E.F. Penrose, *Iraq, International Relations and National Development,* Boulder 1978, on the other hand, is more sympathetic. Christine Moss Helms, *Iraq,* Washington 1984, is a short but serviceable work. But for the student approaching the history of modern Iraq probably the most useful account is Phoebe Marr, *The Modern History of Iraq,* 1985, a well informed, straightforward history of the sort we wish we had for every state in the region. Once more we are short of biographies although Amir Iskandar, *Saddam Husain,* Hachette 1980, contains a lot of information about the man. Two collections of essays should also be mentioned: Abbas Kelidar (ed.), *The Integration of Modern Iraq,* 1979, and T. Niblock, (ed.), *Iraq: The Contemporary State,* 1982. On economic development readers should consult, in addition to the Penrose book, Ferhang Jalal, *The Role of Government in the Industrialization of Iraq 1950–1965,* 1968, and Khair al-Din Haseeb, *The National Income of Iraq, 1953–1961,* 1964. We lack a good study of the land reform: R. Gabbay, *Communism and Agrarian Reform in Iraq,* 1978, is really the story of the land reform which did not take place, namely that envisaged by the communists.

Syria

General information about Syria may be obtained from R.F. Nyrop (ed.), *Syria: A Country Study,* Washington 1979, and John Devlin, *Syria: A Country Profile,* Boulder 1987. Two general histories of modern Syria can also be mentioned: A.L. Tibawi, *A Modern History of Syria including Lebanon and Palestine,* 1969 which takes in the nineteenth and twentieth centuries and Tabitha Petran, *Syria,* 1972. The outstanding study of the mandatory period is P. Khoury, *Syria and the French Mandate,* Princeton 1987, a substantial work securely based on French and British archival sources and on Arabic materials. It has largely replaced the reliable but pedestrian work of S.H. Longrigg, *Syria and Lebanon under the French Mandate,* 1958, but it should not be allowed to overshadow Albert Hourani's old but fascinating sketch, *Syria and Lebanon,* 1946, and the important and neglected book of Safiuddin Joarder, *Syria under the French Mandate,* Dacca 1977, which deals with the period down to 1927.

Derek Hopwood's short, *Syrian Politics and Society, 1945–1986,* 1988, is a good introduction to the period since independence. It may be followed by P. Seale, *The Struggle for Syria,* 1965, which is still valuable for its details of Syrian political struggles before 1958 and G.H. Torrey, *Syrian Politics and the Military,* Columbus, 1964, which covered similar ground and reached similar conclusions. There is still no detailed study of the years of the United Arab Republic but N. Van Dam, *The Struggle for Power in Syria,* 2nd edn, 1980, is a short but highly analytical account of the years 1961–1978. The turbulent years of the Baʿth's rise to power may be followed in I. Rabinovich, *Syria under the Baath, 1963–6,* Jerusalem 1972 and we have good histories of the Baʿth party itself by John F. Devlin, *The Baʿth Party,* Stanford 1976, which takes the story up to 1966, and Robert W. Olson, *The Ba'th and Syria, 1947–1982,* Princeton 1982. The Baʿth's rival for the affections of nationalists, the SSNP, is the subject of L.Z. Yamak, *The Syrian Social Nationalist Party,* Cambridge, Mass 1966, The Islamic opposition is described by Dr Umar F. Abd-Allah, *The Islamic Struggle in Syria,* Berkeley, Calif. 1983. The author makes no bones about his strong sympathies for the Muslim opposition, but he provides much new information. We now have two biographies of Ḥāfiẓ al-Asad: P. Seale, *Asad of Syria,* 1988, and M.Ma'oz, *Asad: The Sphinx of Damascus,* 1988. The first provides more information about the man and his internal policies but both lean heavily towards foreign affairs. Ma'oz has also edited (with A. Yaniv), *Syria Under Asad,* 1986, a collection of essays. For Syrian economic development see E. Kanovsky, *The Economic Development of Syria,* Tel Aviv 1977. Finally, two important articles should be mentioned: R. Bayly Winder, "Syrian Deputies and Cabinet Ministers, 1919–1959" in *MEJ*, 16 (1962) and 17 (1963) and A. Drysdale, "The Syrian Political Elite, 1966–1976" in *MES,* 17 (1981).

Lebanon

Kamal S. Salibi, *The Modern History of Lebanon,* is the best general history but has to be supplemented for the period after 1958 by his *Crossroads to Civil War,* 1976, which covers the period from 1958 to 1976. Readers who are interested in the historical myths which sustain the parties to the Lebanese conflict may also like to read his *A House of Many Mansions,* 1988. Helena Cobban, *The Making of Modern Lebanon,* 1985, is a more recent history. For the early history of the state, Meir Zamir, *The Formation of Modern Lebanon,* 1985, is the best guide and is based upon archival sources. Some archival material is available in W.L. Browne (ed.) *The Political History of Lebanon 1920–1950,* Salisbury, NC 1976, a collection of US State Department records. L. Binder (ed.), *Politics in Lebanon,* New York 1966, is a valuable collection of essays which successfully displays the working of the Lebanese system before its time of severe trial. So does M.C. Hudson, *The Precarious Republic,* New York 1968. Interesting on the personalities and functions of the *za*^{c}*īms* of Lebanon is Wade R. Goria, *Sovereignty and Leadership in Lebanon, 1943–1976,* 1985. Of the political parties we have a good study of the Phalanges by J. Entelis, *Pluralism and Party Transformation in Lebanon,* Leiden 1974, and a useful and informative, but occasionally ill-arranged history of the parties by Michael W. Suleiman, *Political Parties in Lebanon,* Ithaca, NY 1967. Not surprisingly, the civil war in Lebanon has attracted the greatest attention and only a small selection of the books written on this topic can be mentioned. Salibi's *Crossroads to Civil War* is a good starting point and is as notable for the author's detachment as for his knowledge of the subject. Some other books on the origins of the conflict, although knowledgeable, have more obvious sympathies, including John Bulloch, *Death of a Country,* 1977 and W. Khalidi, *Conflict and Violence in Lebanon,* Cambridge, Mass 1979. Other works on the civil war include I. Harik, *Lebanon, Anatomy of a Conflict,* Hanover 1981, and Ilana Kass, *The Lebanese Civil War, 1975–77,* Jerusalem 1979. Perhaps the most comprehensive and detailed history of the struggle (if not the most readable), however, is Itamar Rabinovich, *The War for Lebanon, 1970–1985,* rev. edn, 1985. Turning to special aspects of the Lebanese conflict A.R. Norton, *Amal and the Shiʿa,* Austin, Texas, 1987, considers the development of Shīʿī consciousness. Yair Evron, *War and Intervention in the Lebanon,* 1987, is a substantial study of Syrian and Israeli involvement in Lebanon between 1975 and 1985. Syrian policies are also studied by A. Dawisha, *Syria and the Lebanese Crisis,* 1980. A. Yaniv, *Dilemmas of Security,* Oxford 1987, is a detailed study of Israeli planning of the 1982 expedition into Lebanon, and B. Hamizrachi, *The Emergence of the South Lebanon Security Belt,* 1988, deals with the role of Major Ḥaddād between 1975 and 1978. The unfortunate UN force established in south Lebanon is the subject of B. Skogmo, *UNIFIL,* 1989, which covers the period from 1978 to 1988.

Jordan

R.F. Nyrop (ed.), *Jordan: A Country Study*, Washington, 1980, provides basic information and two other general books are P. Gubser, *Jordan,* 1983, and Anne Sinai and A. Pollock (ed), *The Hashemite Kingdom of Jordan and the West Bank,* New York 1977. We badly need a good general history of Jordan. In its absence it is necessary to patch together various studies, some of them rather old, of different topics in the history of that interesting country. A starting point is N.H. Aruri, *Jordan,* The Hague 1972, which covers the period from 1921 to 1965. It can be supplemented for the reign of ʿAbdallāh by a new study by Mary C. Wilson, *King Abdullah, Britain and the Making of Jordan,* Cambridge 1988, and by a collection of essays by U. Dann, *Studies in the History of Transjordan, 1920–1949,* Boulder 1984. Nevertheless, we still have no full account of political activities during the 1920s and 1930s. Anne Deardon, *Jordan,* 1958, Benjamin Shwadran, *Jordan: A State of Tension,* New York 1959, and R. Patai, *The Kingdom of Jordan,* Princeton 1958,(an old Human Relations Area File volume, the precursors of the Nyrop studies) are still useful, especially for the political clashes of the 1950s, a subject also covered by H.H. Abidi, *Jordan: A Political Study 1948–57,* 1965. The most recent and best investigation of this topic, however, is U. Dann, *King Hussein and the Challenge of Arab Radicalism,* Oxford 1989, an examination of the period from 1955 until 1967. The relations between Jordan and the Palestinians and the problems of integration have been the subject of several studies among which may be mentioned Clinton Bailey, *Jordan's Palestinian Challenge, 1948–1983,* Boulder 1984.Two studies of the Jordanian army exist: S.A. El-Edroos, *The Hashemite Arab Army, 1908–1979,* Amman 1980, is a comprehensive military history and P.J. Vatikiotis, *Politics and the Military in Jordan,* 1967, has a rather wider scope.

Little has been written on the last 20 years of Jordan's history which can be confidently recommended. S.A. Mutawi, *Jordan in the 1967 War,* Cambridge 1967, is good as far as it goes and includes some useful comments on Jordanian decision making in addition to the military history of the war. But on the internal political reconstruction of Jordan in the following years we have no substantial work. P. Mazur, *Economic Growth and Development in Jordan,* Boulder 1979, B. Khader and A. Badran, *The Economic Development of Jordan,* 1987, and O. Aresvik, *The Agricultural Development of Jordan,* New York 1976, are helpful on the economic side. Jane M. Hacker, *Modern Amman,* Durham 1960, is an interesting study of social change. Nor do we have any major work on Jordanian foreign policy since 1967. M.I. Faddah, *The Middle East in Transition,* 1974, stops in 1967. King Ḥusayn's own memoirs, *Uneasy Lies the Head,* 1962, and *My War with Israel,* 1969, also deal with the years to 1967, although Crown Prince Ḥasan's book, *Search for Peace,* New York 1984, does take the story down to more recent times.

Palestine, 1920–48

Two basic sources of information on the mandate period are the *Survey of Palestine,* 2 vols, 1946, produced by the British Palestine administration for the Anglo–American Committee of Enquiry, and the ESCO Foundation's *Palestine,* 2 vols, Cambridge, Mass 1947. Anyone wishing to undertake research in the period should consult Philip Jones, *Britain in Palestine, 1914–1948,* 1979, a list of archival sources. Three of the general histories can be recommended: J. Marlowe, *The Seat of Pilate,* 1959, C. Sykes, *Crossroads to Israel,* 1965, and A.W. Kayyali, *Palestine: A Modern History,* 1978. J.C. Hurewitz, *The Struggle for Palestine,* New York 1950, and Nicholas Bethell, *The Palestine Triangle,* 1979, cover the period 1935 to 1948. On the first years of British rule Bernard Wasserstein, *The British in Palestine,* 1978, is excellent. The book may be supplemented by three other studies based on work in the archives: J. McTague, *British Policy in Palestine, 1917–22,* Lanham, 1983, D.E. Knox, *The Making of a Near Eastern Question,* Washington 1981 and Muhammad Y. Muslih, *The Origins of Palestinian Nationalism,* New York 1988. The years 1925–1936 are less well studied; the best work on the Passfield White Paper is the article by G. Sheffer, "Intentions and Results of British Policy in

Palestine: Passfield's White Paper", *MES,* 9 (1974). For the period from 1936 we are better served by Michael Cohen, *Palestine: Retreat from the Mandate,* 1978, and *Palestine and the Great Powers,* 1982, R.W. Zweig, *Britain and Palestine during the Second World War,* 1986, which describes attempts to operate the 1939 White Paper policy, and M. Jones, *Failure in Palestine,* 1986, the best account of Anglo–US attempts to agree on policy in 1945–7 and of the British decision to go to the UN. The most recent account is Ritchie Ovendale, *Britain, the United States and the End of the Palestine Mandate, 1942–1948,* 1989. We have the luxury of two specialized studies of the Anglo–American Committee of Inquiry: A. Nachmani, *Great Power Discord in Palestine,* 1987, and A.H. Podet, *The Success and Failure of the Anglo-American Committee of Inquiry, 1945–1946,* New York 1986. A. Shlaim, *Collusion Across the Jordan,* Oxford 1988, is a very full, well-written account of the role of King ʿAbdallāh and his links with the Zionists.

For the development of Palestinian nationalism the two books by Y. Porath, *The Emergence of the Palestinian-Arab Nationalist Movement,1918–1929,* 1972 and *The Palestinian Arab National Movement, 1929–1939,* 1977, are outstanding, and Ann M. Lesch, *Arab Politics in Palestine, 1917–1939,* 1979, is very good. One should also look at J. Migdal (ed.), *Palestinian Society and Politics,* Princeton 1980, and Ylana M. Miller, *Government and Society in Rural Palestine, 1920–1948,* Austin 1984, which exposes the dilemma of Arab district officials of the British administration. There are so many books on the development of the Yishuv that it is difficult to know which to single out but W. Laqueur, *A History of Zionism,* 1972, is reliable, and B. Halpern, *The Idea of the Jewish State,* Cambridge, Mass 1969, stimulating. See also D. Horowitz and M. Lissak, *The Origins of the Israeli Polity,* Chicago 1978. Y. Bauer, *From Diplomacy to Resistance,* Philadelphia 1970, examines the development of armed resistance after 1934. Yosef Gorny, *Zionism and the Arabs, 1882–1948,* Oxford 1987, is a recent study of attitudes towards the Palestinian Arabs, and K. Stein, *The Land Question in Palestine, 1917–1939,* Chapel Hill, NC 1984, a good examination of the problems of land purchase. The growth of the Jewish labour force is studied in A. Ben-Porat, *Between Class and Nation,* 1986. For the end of the mandate see, on the military side, D.A. Charters, T*he British Army and Jewish Insurgency in Palestine, 1945*–7, 1989, and Natanel Lorch, *The Edge of the Sword,* New York 1961; on the diplomatic side, A. Ilan, *Bernadotte in Palestine, 1948,* Oxford 1989; and for a re-examination of all aspects, the collection of essays edited by W.R. Louis and R.W. Stookey, *The End of the Palestine Mandate,* 1984.

Israel

Noah Lucas, *The Modern History of Israel,* 1975, is a sound history; Howard M. Sachar, *A History of Israel,* 2 vols, 1976–1987, is much more detailed. Uri Davis, *Israel Incorporated,* 1977, is a bright and controversial read; W. Frankel, *Israel Observed,* 1980, a balanced examination; and N. Safran, *Israel, The Embattled Ally,* Cambridge, Mass 1981, although concerned with foreign policy also contains a good deal about recent Israeli history. S.N. Eisenstadt has written two substantial studies of social organization and change, *Israeli Society,* 1967, and *The Transformation of Israeli Society,* 1985. On political change see M. Bernstein, *The Politics of Israel,* Princeton 1957, O. Kraines, *Government and Politics in Israel,* 1961, D. Peretz, *The Government and Politics of Israel,* Boulder 1983, and R.J. Isaac, *Party and Politics in Israel,* New York 1982. On the religious parties see Gary S. Schiff, *Tradition and Politics,* Detroit 1977. Y. Peri, *Between Battles and Ballots,* Cambridge 1983, is both a study of the development of the Israeli army and of its political influence. I wish I had been able to find a good straightforward economic history of Israel but was obliged to flounder among specialized studies. Readers may try a combination of D. Patinkin, *The Israeli Economy,* Jerusalem 1967, N. Halev and R. Klinov-Malul, *The Economic Development of Israel,* New York 1968, and Y. Ben-Porath (ed.), *The Israeli Economy,* Cambridge, Mass 1986. There is no shortage of memoirs: almost every notable Israeli politician has left some sort of autobiography and some, like Ben Gurion, Meir, Eban and Dayan, have had more than one try. Israeli foreign policy is dealt with elsewhere but some books should be considered here, in particular the works of Michael Brecher for they cast much light on the internal workings of Israeli cabinets. They are *The Foreign Policy System of Israel,* 1972, *Decisions in Israel's Foreign Policy,* 1974, and *Decisions in Crisis,* Berkeley, Calif. 1980. I. Peleg, *Begin's Foreign Policy 1977–1983,* 1987, is a helpful analysis of the role of the right in foreign policy-making.

The Palestinians

Benny Morris, *The Birth of the Palestinian Refugee Problem, 1947–1949,* Cambridge 1987, is an outstanding examination of the circumstances which led to the Palestinian exodus and demolishes the view of J.B. Schechtman, *The Arab Refugee Problem,* New York 1952. Rosemary Sayigh, *The Palestinians,* 1979, is a Palestinian account of their history. A collection of essays edited by G. Ben-Dor, *The Palestinians and the*

Middle East Conflict, Ramat Gan, 1978, is wide-ranging. On the fortunes of Palestinians on the West Bank see Ammon Cohen, *Political Parties in the West Bank under the Jordanian Regime, 1949–1967,* Ithaca, New York 1982, which is based on captured Jordanian intelligence reports, and S. Mishal, *West Bank/East Bank,* New Haven 1978. R. Khalisi and C. Mansour (eds), *Palestine and the Gulf,* Beirut 1982, contains helpful information on émigré Palestinians and their activities. The best account of the PLO is H. Cobban, *The Palestinian Liberation Organisation,* Cambridge 1984. See also Moshe Ma'oz (ed.), *Palestine Arab Politics,* Jerusalem 1975, and W.B. Quandt *et al., The Politics of Palestinian Nationalism,* Berkeley, 1973. Aspects of PLO activities may be studied in R. Israel, *The PLO in Lebanon,* New York 1983, Galia Golan, *The Soviet Union and the Palestine Liberation Organisation,* New York 1980, and Muhammad Shadid, *The United States and the Palestinians,* New York 1981. For more recent events see Moshe Ma'oz and M. Nisan, *Palestinian Leadership in the West Bank,* 1984, and G. Aronson, *Israel, Palestinians and the Intifada,* 1989.

The Kurds

D. McDowell, *The Kurds,* 1985, is a useful booklet issued by the Minority Rights Group and makes a convenient starting point. D. Kinnard, *The Kurds in Kurdistan,* Oxford 1964, is also a useful general account and S.C. Pelletiere, *The Kurds,* Boulder 1984, brings the story nearer to the present. G. Chaliand, (ed.), *People Without a Country,* 1980, contains essays on the Kurds in various states; that by Kendal is one of the few accounts of the Kurds in Turkey and that by the late A.R. Ghassemlou on Iran is also valuable. Ghassemlou also wrote a major book on *Kurdistan and the Kurds,* Prague, 1965. Another broad survey which contains a great deal of information is Christiane More, *Les kurdes aujourd'hui,* Paris 1984. M. Van Brunuissen, *Agha, Shaikh and State,* Utrecht 1978, provides the best analytical background as well as a good account of the Shaykh Saᶜid uprising. Another anthropological perspective is that of F. Barth, *Principles of Social Organisation in South Kurdistan,* Oslo 1953. We have most information about the Kurds of Iraq. C.J. Edmunds, *Kurds, Turks and Arabs,* 1957, is a good starting point and may be followed by E. Ghareeb, *The Kurdish Question in Iraq,* Syracuse, New York 1981, and S. Jawad, *Iraq and the Kurdish Question, 1958–1970,* 1981. For the Kurdish problem at the end of the Second World War see W. Eagleton, *The Kurdish Republic of 1946,* 1963.

Turkey

The Admiralty handbook, *Turkey,* 2 vols, 1942, contains abundant information which provides a background for the study of Turkey before intensive economic modernization began. D.A. Rustow, *Turkey: America's Forgotten Ally,* 1987, is a very useful and up to date short sketch of Turkey. For the period down to 1950 the most readable history is B. Lewis, *The Emergence of Modern Turkey,* 1961. Another general history with a full bibliography is that by Stanford J. Shaw, *History of the Ottoman Empire and Turkey,* vol 2, Cambridge 1977, and all aspects of development during the period since 1923 are also covered in W.F. Weiker, *The Modernization of Turkey,* New York 1981. W. Hale, *The Political and Economic Development of Modern Turkey,* 1981, has more on economics than politics but is clearly written and well balanced. The best biography of *Atatürk is that by Lord Kinross, Ataturk,* 1964. More recent studies of Kemalism include, Jacob M. Landau (ed.), *Ataturk: the Modernization of Turkey,* Boulder 1984 and A. Kazancigil and E. Ožbudun (eds), *Ataturk,* 1981. The legitimate opposition to Atatürk from the Liberal Party in the 1930s is the subject of W.F. Weiker, *Political Tutelage and Democracy in Turkey,* Leiden 1973. R.D. Robinson, *The First Turkish Republic,* Cambridge, Mass 1963, covers the period down to 1960 and is more concerned with development than with history. I. Giritli, *Fifty Years of Turkish Political Development, 1919–1969,* Istanbul 1969, is also broad in scope. An important book which describes fundamental changes in Turkish political development during the period is F.W. Frey, *The Turkish Political Elite,* Cambridge, Mass 1965. The best narrative history of Turkey covering the period after 1950 is Feroz Ahmad, *The Turkish Experiment in Democracy, 1950–1975,* 1977. It may be read with K.H. Karpat, *Turkey's Politics,* Princeton 1964, and two books by C.H. Dodd, *Politics and Government in Turkey,* Manchester 1969, and *Democracy and Development in Turkey,* Walkington, 1979. The army's role in 1960 is explored in E. Ŏzbudun, *The Role of the Military in Recent Turkish Politics,* Cambridge, Mass 1966, and the role of Islam in politics since 1950 is the subject of M.Y. Geyikdagi, *Political Parties in Turkey,* New York 1984. For the 1980 coup see M.A. Birand, *The Generals' Coup in Turkey,* 1987, which is based on interviews with military participants. Lucille W. Pevsner, *Turkey's Political Crisis,* New York 1984, is a short account of the same events. and F. Tachau, *Turkey,* New York 1984, is also useful. A recent collection of papers on the changes in Turkey since 1980 and the re-establishment of the parliamentary system is M. Heper and A. Evin (ed.), *State, Democracy and the Military,* Boston 1988. Heper has also produced a thoughtful book on *The State Tradition in Turkey,* Walkington 1985. See also the essays edited by E.D. Akarli and G. Ben-Dor, *Political Participation in Turkey,* Istanbul 1975. Another pioneering contribution to political history is R. Bianchi, *Interest Groups and Political Development in Turkey,* Princeton 1984 and Jacob M. Landau, *Pan-Turkism in Turkey,* 1981, contains much information on ideological groups.

The most useful general introduction to Turkish economic history is Z.Y. Herschlag, *Turkey: The Challenge of Growth,* Leiden 1968, which traces developments from the Ottoman period. Although written from the prevalent and occasionally irritating perspective of the world economy, C. Keydar, *The Definition of a Peripheral Economy,* Cambridge, 1981, is still a useful guide to economic change in the 1920s. Morris Singer, *The Economic Advance of Turkey, 1938–1960,* Ankara 1977, describes the effects of the Second World War and liberalization; and the period from 1950 to 1971 is well covered by Anne O. Krueger, *Turkey,* New York 1974. The latest period of liberalization since 1980 is described in T.F. Nas and M. Odekon (ed.), *Liberalization and the Turkish Economy,* 1988. For agrarian changes see O. Aresvik, *The Agricultural Development of Turkey,* New York 1975. The social effects of modernization in the countryside may be observed in the study by Paul Stirling, *Turkish Village,* 1965. Another anthropological study shows changes in a small town (Susurluk) – P.J.Magnarella, *Tradition and Change in a Turkish Town,* Cambridge, Mass 1974. Immigration to large towns is the subject of Kemal H. Karpat, *The Gecekondu,* Cambridge 1976, and information on emigrant Turkish workers may be obtained from N. Abadan-Unat (ed.), *Turkish Workers in Europe, 1960–1975,* Leiden 1976. Kemal H. Karpat *et al., Social Change and Politics in Turkey,* 1973, picks up a number of developments.

Turkish foreign policy is a thing apart from the preoccupations of many of the other countries in the Near East. Ference A. Vali, *Bridge Across the Bosporus,* Baltimore 1971,is an attempt by a former Turkish foreign minister to set out the strategic imperatives of Turkish diplomacy in the context of an account of its development. Inevitably, the Straits question figures largely in his discussion. Relations with Britain loomed large in the life of the young republic and may be studied in S.F. Evans, *The Slow Rapprochement,* Walkington 1982. Several good studies of Turkish policy during the Second World War exist, among them Edward Weisband, *Turkish Foreign Policy, 1943–1945,* Princeton 1973, Selim Deringil, *Turkish Foreign Policy During the Second World War,* 1989, Frank G. Weber, *The Evasive Neutral,* Columbia, Missouri, 1979, and J. Robertson, *Turkey and Allied Strategy, 1941–1945,* 1985. On the conflict over the Straits in 1945–6 see H.N. Howard, *Turkey, The Straits and U.S.Policy,* Baltimore 1974. Relations with the United States are outlined in G.S. Harris, *Troubled Alliance,* Washington 1972 but the best account of the changes in Turkish foreign policy is that by Kemal H. Karpat, *Turkey's Foreign Policy in Transition, 1950–1974,* Leiden 1975.

Iran

There are several general accounts of Iranian history before the Islamic revolution. Peter Avery, *Modern Iran,* 1965, is reliable if unexciting. Hossein Amirsadeghi (ed.), *Twentieth Century Iran,* 1977, and George Lenczowski (ed.), *Iran Under the Pahlevis,* Stanford 1978, are collections of essays each of which aims at presenting a more or less comprehensive picture of Iranian development. M. Reza Ghods, *Iran in the Twentieth Century,* 1989, is a Persian view which emphasizes Persian culture as a determining factor in developments. Although patchy in its coverage, Ervand Abrahamian, *Iran Between Two Revolutions,* Princeton 1982, is perhaps the most stimulating work and it is especially valuable for the period of Iranian history embracing the Second World War and its aftermath and for the growth of the left. Another challenging work is L. Binder, *Iran,* Berkeley 1962. For changes under Riżā Shāh, Amin Banani, *The Modernization of Iran,* Stanford 1961, is clear and succinct. A biography of Riżā Shāh has been written by D. Wilber, *Riza Shah Pahlevi,* New York 1975, a rather starry eyed work with some obvious errors but more information than anyone else has contrived to collect about this little known man. For the early years of Riżā's reign R.W. Cottam, *Nationalism in Iran,* Pittsburgh 1979, is valuable. Economic developments are well described in the lucid monograph by J. Bharier, *Economic Development in Iran, 1900–1970,* 1971. Two major foreign institutions are also the subject of imposing studies: R.W. Ferrier, *The History of the British Petroleum Company,* Vol. 1, Cambridge 1982, which takes the story down to the early 1930s, and G. Jones, *Banking and Empire in Iran,* Cambridge 1986, the history of the Imperial Bank of Persia down to its withdrawal from Iran in 1952. On Iranian oil see also F. Fesharaki, *The Development of the Iranian Oil Industry,* New York 1976.

Internal developments during the early part of the reign of Muḥammad Riżā Shah are less well covered, apart from Abrahamian's book and Fakhreddin Azemi, *Iran: The Crisis of Democracy,* 1989. Three books on the Muṣaddiq crisis are worth mentioning: J.A. Bill and

W.R. Louis (eds), *Musaddiq, Iranian Nationalism and Oil,* 1988, *Musaddiq's Memoirs* (ed. Homa Katouzian), 1988, and S. Zabih, *The Mossadegh Era,* Chicago 1982. For the period after 1960 we are better served. H. Bashiriyeh, *The State and Revolution in Iran, 1962–1982,* 1983, covers the period of the White Revolution. Marvin Zonis, *The Political Elite of Iran,* Princeton 1971, is an important study of the composition and attitudes of the Iranian ruling class mainly in the 1960s. On the later years of the Pahlavi regime, Robert Graham, *Iran: The Illusion of Power,* 1978, is short but very much to the point and Fred Halliday, *Iran: Dictatorship and Development,* 1980, contains much information and careful analysis. There are several books on the Iranian land reform. Ann K.S. Lambton, *The Persian Land Reform, 1962–66,* Oxford 1969, is written from the closest observation and should be read in conjunction with her masterly survey, *Landlord and Peasant in Persia,* Oxford 1953. Eric J. Hooglund, *Land and Revolution in Iran, 1960–1980,* Austin 1982, a more recent study, includes a discussion of the later stages of land reform and the experiments with agri-businesses. Finally, K.S. McLachlan, *The Neglected Garden,* 1989, is the product of many years of research and reflection on the political and environmental problems of Iranian agriculture.

The role of Islam in Iran has attracted much attention since the revolution but some good work was produced before that event, notably M.M.J. Fischer, *Iran: From Religious Dispute to Revolution,* Cambridge, Mass 1980, based on research in Qum during the 1970s, and S. Akhavi, *Religion and Politics in Contemporary Iran,* Albany 1980. The atmosphere of change in Shīᶜī Islam may be felt in Roy Mottahedeh's imaginative *The Mantle of the Prophet,* 1986. Nikki R. Keddie also has long been interested in the role of Islam and her works, written and edited, including *Roots of Revolution,* 1984, *Religion and Politics in Iran,* 1983, and *Shi'ism and Social Protest,* (edited with J.R.I. Cole), 1986, are worth studying for the background to the revolution. The most interesting study of the new immigrants to towns is Farhad Kazemi, *Poverty and Revolution in Iran,* New York 1980. For the revolution itself we have very ample material in the memoirs of several participants including the Shah (*Answer to History,* 1980), Chapour (Shapur) Bakhtiar (*Ma Fidélité,* Paris 1982) General Robert F.Huyser (*Mission to Tehran,* 1986) the US Ambassador William Sullivan, (*Mission to Iran,* 1981), and the British Ambassador Anthony Parsons (*The Pride and the Fall,* 1984). General ᶜAbbās Qarābāghī's account is as yet untranslated, like the memoirs of Mahdī Bāzargān. Students of Iran since the revolution should begin with Shaul Bakhash, *The Reign of the Ayatollahs,* 1985, a scholarly account by a distinguished Iranian academic. Said Amir Arjomand tore himself away from his studies of Shīʿī theology to produce *The Turban for the Crown*, 1988. Also useful are several books by the prolific Sepehr Zabih, including *Iran since the Revolution*, 1982, *The Left in Contemporary Iran*, Stanford 1986, and *The Iranian Military in Revolution and War*, 1988. Ervand Abrahamian has written an account of the Iranian *mujahidin*, *Radical Islam*, 1989. Two collections of articles are B.M. Rosen (ed.), *Iran since the Revolution*, New York 1985, and H. Amirahmadi and M. Parvin (eds), *Post Revolutionary Iran*, 1988.

The doyen of studies of Iranian foreign policy is Rouhollah K. Ramazani and three of his books, *The Foreign Policy of Iran 1500–1941*, Charlottesville 1966, *Iran's Foreign Policy, 1941–1973*, Charlottesville 1975, and *Revolutionary Iran*, Baltimore 1986 (which deals with the foreign policy of the Islamic republic) will give a comprehensive picture. G. Lenczowski's old study of *Russia and the West in Iran, 1918–48*, Ithaca, NY 1949, is still useful for the early period. A recent, rather idiosyncratic account of Soviet–Iranian relations duing the years 1925–41 is M. Rezun, *The Soviet Union and Iran*, Geneva 1981 and D.B. Nissman, *The Soviet Union and Iranian Azerbaijan*, 1987, is a short analysis of relations between the two Azerbaijans after 1945. For the period 1941 to 1953 we have a number of studies focused on US involvement. They include M.H. Lytle, *The Origins of the Iranian–American Alliance, 1941–1953*, New York 1987, which belongs to the revisionist school and Kuross A. Samii, *Involvement by Invitation*, 1987. A recent denunciation of US policy in Iran is J.A. Bill, *The Eagle and the Lion*, 1988. Other books are included under international relations.

Arabia

J.B. Kelly, *Arabia, the Gulf and the West*, 1980, is a powerful, wide-ranging mixture of scholarship and polemics, which covers all the century but concentrates especially on the period 1970 to 1980. Readers should also consult Kelly's study of boundary-making in Arabia, *Eastern Arabian Frontiers*, 1964. Fred Halliday, *Arabia Without Sultans*, 1975, approaches the peninsula from a very different viewpoint. See also D. Hopwood, *The Arabian Peninsula*, 1972. The two Admiralty handbooks, *Iraq and the Persian Gulf*, 1944 and *Western Arabia and the Red Sea*, 1946 are still useful.

R.F. Nyrop (ed.), *Area Handbook for Saudi Arabia*, Washington 1977, provides basic information on the state. On the formation of the state of Saudi Arabia, Christine M. Helms, *The Cohesion of Saudi*

Arabia, 1981, is valuable. J.S. Habib, *Ibn Sa'ud's Warriors of Islam*, 1978 describes the conflict with the Ikhwān. The early years of the state are described in several books by H.St.J. Philby, of which *Saudi Arabia*, 1955, is perhaps the most useful. Two pictures of Ibn Saᶜūd's state from the inside are Hafiz Wahba, *Arabian Days*, 1964, and Muhammad Almana, *Arabia Unified*, 1980. A good account of relations with Britain during the early years is Clive Leatherdale, *Britain and Saudi Arabia, 1925–1939*, 1983. With it readers can examine Sir Gilbert Clayton, *An Arabian Diary*, Berkeley, Calif. 1969. D. Holden and R. Johns, *The House of Saud*, 1981, is good. The two best known books on the state are R. Lacey, *The Kingdom*, 1981, and N. Safran, *Saudi Arabia*, Cambridge, Mass 1985, where it is argued that the main dynamic in the state is external, namely the search for security. These books may be supplemented by three collections of essays: N. Anderson (ed.), *The Kingdom of Saudi Arabia*, 1977, W. Beling (ed.), *King Faisal and the Modernization of Saudi Arabia*, 1980, and T. Niblock (ed.), *State, Society and Economy in Saudi Arabia*, 1982.

A number of books treat the two Yemens together, notably B.R. Pridham (ed.) *Contemporary Yemen*, 1983, and *Economy, Society and Culture in Contemporary Yemen*, 1985, works which contain some helpful essays; and R. Bidwell, *The Two Yemens*, Boulder 1983. Turning to North Yemen, Manfred W. Wenner, *Modern Yemen, 1918–1966*, Baltimore 1968, is a useful account of the Imām's precarious government but for the period of the republic has been superseded by R.W. Stookey, *Yemen*, Boulder 1978, and J.E. Peterson, *Yemen: The Search for a Modern State*, 1982. Probably the best account of the period since the end of the civil war, however, is R. Burrows, *The Yemen Arab Republic*, 1987. The development of opposition to the Imām is described in the late J. Leigh Douglas, *The Free Yemeni Movement, 1935–1962*, Syracuse, NY 1988. An interesting, if discursive examination of the tribal background is Paul Dresch, *Tribes, Government and History in Yemen*, 1989. For the history of South Yemen before independence the two books of greatest use are R.J. Gavin, *Aden under British Rule, 1839–1967*, 1975, which considers matters from the British viewpoint, and J. Kostiner, *The Struggle for South Yemen*, 1984, which examines the growth of the opposition movements. On the independent state there are two useful and informative accounts by Helen Lackner, *P.D.R. Yemen*, 1985 and Tareq Y. Ismael and Jacqueline S. Ismael, *The People's Democratic Republic of Yemen*, 1986. Both are sympathetic towards the aspirations, if not always the performance of the regime, Lackner especially so. Fred Halliday, *Revolution and Foreign Policy*, Cambridge 1989, is a study of the foreign policy of the republic of South Yemen and is especially useful for relations with the USSR.

The best starting point for the study of the Gulf is A.L. Cottrell (ed.), *The Persian Gulf States*, Baltimore 1980. Often with the patronage of the states themselves several scholarly studies have been produced in recent years and the picture for students is much brighter than it was. M.M. Abdullah, *The United Arab Emirates*, 1978, and Rosemarie Said Zahlan, *The Origins of the United Arab Emirates*, 1978 are both sound histories using British documents. They have largely replaced the older works of K.G. Fenelon, *The United Arab Emirates*, 1973, D. Hawley, *The Trucial States*, 1970 and J.D. Anthony, *Arab States of the Lower Gulf*, Washington 1975. For social change F. Heard-Bey, *From Trucial States to United Arab Emirates*, 1982, may also be recommended. A.O. Taryam, *The Establishment of the United Arab Emirates*, 1987, is an account of the first 15 years of the new state. For Qaṭar also we have a fair history in Rosemarie Said Zahlan, *The Creation of Qatar*, 1979. Baḥraynī history may be studied in two books: Mahdi Abdalla al-Tajir, *Bahrain 1920–1945*, 1987, and M.G. Rumaihi, *Bahrein: Social and Political Change since the First World War*, 1976. Unfortunately we have nothing of value on the most recent period of Baḥraynī history and little scholarly work on the modern history of Kuwayt. Husayn al-Baharna, *The Legal Status of the Arabian Gulf States*, Manchester 1968, provides useful background to disputes both at the time and subsequently.

R.G. Landen, *Oman since 1856*, Princeton, 1967, covers the early period of the history of Oman and may be supplemented by J.E. Peterson, *Oman in the Twentieth Century*, 1978, which is well informed but ill-arranged. Other books are J. Townsend, *Oman: the Making of the Modern State*, 1977, F. Clements, *Oman*, 1980, and C.H. Allen, *Oman*, 1987, an account of the process of modernization.

International Relations

There is no general study of international relations in the Near East over the period since 1923; writers have concentrated on shorter periods, smaller areas and particular topics. Some periods, areas and topics have attracted little attention, a circumstance which may strengthen the view that the region was less important to the great powers than is sometimes supposed. This observation seems especially applicable to the period 1923 to 1939. There is no full account, based on archival sources, of British strategic and political interests in the region as a whole, as opposed to her interests in particular states.

The closest approximation is E. Monroe, *Britain's Moment in the Middle East, 1914 to 1956*, 1963, a beautifully written elegy based mainly on published sources. One should also read her *Mediterranean in Politics*, 1938. R. Bullard, *Britain and the Middle East*, 1951, is only a short introduction to the subject. The growth of the interest in air communications may be traced in R. Higham, *Britain's Imperial Air Routes, 1918 to 1939*, 1961. A useful examination of British interests is the Chatham House survey, *Political and Strategic Interests of the United Kingdom*, 1939, and indeed the annual RIIA survey volumes are extremely helpful. The first volume of the war history of *Grand Strategy*, by N.H. Gibbs, 1976, and the first volume of I.S.O. Playfair, *The Mediterranean and the Middle East*, 1954, are also valuable.

The situation with regard to French interests is still worse; no-one has undertaken a dissection of French interests in the Near East in this period. To put French Near Eastern interests in perspective it is best to use a general history of foreign relations such as P. Renouvin, *Histoire des relations internationales: Le crise du xxe siècle*, 2 vols, Paris, 1958, and a general account of colonial policy, for example, H. Deschamps, *Méthodes et doctrines coloniales de la France du XVIe siècle à nos jours*, Paris 1953. On French interests at the end of the period see I. Lipschits, *La politique de la France au Levant, 1939–41*, Paris 1941. In English there is H.I. Priestley, *France Overseas*, 1938. Oddly enough the lesser interests of the Axis powers have received more careful examination: for Italy, D. Mack Smith, *Mussolini's Roman Empire*, 1977, is a good starting point and may be followed by C.J. Lowe and E. Marzari, *Italian Foreign Policy, 1870–1940*, 1975 and J.L. Miège, *L'impérialisme colonial italien de 1870 a` nos jours*, Paris 1968. For German interests in the Near East see J.L. Wallach (ed.), *Germany and the Middle East, 1835–1939*, Tel Aviv 1975, F. Hirszowicz, *The Third Reich and the Arab East*, 1966 which deals mainly with the period 1930–42, and F.R. Nicosia, *The Third Reich and the Palestine Question*, 1985, which examines the years 1933–9. Books on Soviet policy are discussed below.

For the Second World War we are better furnished with books. German interests are described in H. Tillman, *Deutschland's Araberpolitik im zweiten Weltkrieges*, East Berlin 1965, and B.P. Schroder, *Deutschland und der Mittlere Osten im zweiten Weltkrieges*, Frankfurt 1975. British activities are the subject of the official war history volumes on *Grand Strategy* (1957–1976) and *The Mediterranean and the Middle East* (5 vols, 1954–73). G. Warner, *Iraq and Syria, 1941*, 1974, sets those two campaigns against the background of British strategic thinking. A recent study of inter-Allied difficulties in the Levant is A.B. Gaunson, *The Anglo–French Clash in Lebanon and Syria, 1940–45*, 1987. An important institution is described in M.W. Wilmington, *The Middle East Supply Center*, Albany, 1971. The best general account is still the RIIA volume by G. Kirk, *The Middle East in the War*, 1953, and Kirk's second volume, *The Middle East, 1945–1950*, 1954, is still useful for post-war British policy although it has been largely displaced by the excellent and comprehensive examination of archival evidence by W.R. Louis, *The British Empire in the Middle East, 1945–1951*, Oxford 1984. See also I. Pappé, *Britain and the Arab–Israeli Conflict, 1948–51*, Oxford 1988. Books on the war and its aftermath often form part of the study of the origins of the Cold War and such is the case with Barry Rubin, *The Great Powers in the Middle East, 1941–1947*, 1980, and B.R. Kuniholm, *The Origins of the Cold War in the Near East*, 1980, which is a study of mainly US policy towards Iran, Turkey and Greece, projected against a background of British policy-making. We now move into the field of the European withdrawal from the Near East of which process there is a general account by Howard M. Sachar, *Europe Leaves the Middle East, 1936–1954*, 1972. A recent account of British decline, emphasizing domestic weakness, is J. Abadi, *Britain's Withdrawal from the Middle East*, 1947–1971. Princeton 1982. See also, M.A. Fitzsimons, *Empire by Treaty*, 1965. The role of the United Nations in partially plugging the gap is described in Rosalyn Higgins, *United Nations Peace Keeping*, 1946–67, vol. 1, 1969. J.C. Campbell, *Defense of the Middle East*, New York 1960, is still a very useful guide to the defence projects of the early 1950s. P. Darby, *British Defence Policy East of Suez, 1947–68*, 1973, shows how remaining British Middle Eastern interests were rationalized into an Indian ocean strategy. From a very large literature on the Suez affair five books may be mentioned: D.A. Farnie, *East and West of Suez*, Oxford 1969, is a general history of the operation of the canal which provides a background to Hugh Thomas, *The Suez Affair*, 1967, which is short and well informed on British policy; K. Love, *Suez, the Twice Fought War*, 1969, which is detailed and fuller on the Arab–Israeli dimension; W.R. Louis and R. Owen (eds), *Suez 1956*, 1989, a retrospective collection of essays which benefit from the newly opened archival material; and D. Carlton, *Britain and the Suez Crisis*, 1988, a short survey of Britain's role in the light of the new material.

We are now quite well provided with serious studies of US policy in the Near East. General works include T.A. Bryson, *American Diplomatic Relations in the Middle East, 1782–1925*, Metuchen, 1977, and J.A. De Novo, *American Interests and Policies in the Middle East, 1900–1939*, Minneapolis 1963. Philip J. Baram, *The Department of State in the Middle East, 1919–1945*, Philadelphia 1978, is a valuable work which should be read with the Kuniholm book cited above. Early US relations with Turkey, such as they were, are studied in R.R. Trask, *The United States Response to Turkish Nationalism and Reform, 1914–1939*, Minneapolis 1971. Most writing, however, has centred on US oil interests in Saudi Arabia and on Palestine. On oil interests see the general conspectus by E.W. Chester, *United States Oil Policy and Diplomacy*, 1983, A.D. Miller, *Search for Security*, Chapel Hill, NC 1980, a study of policy towards Saudi Arabia from 1939 to 1949; M.B. Stoff, *Oil, War and American Security*, New Haven 1980, which considers oil policy between 1941 and 1947, I.H. Anderson, *Aramco, the United States and Saudi Arabia*, Princeton 1981, which covers the same period, and N. Kokxhoorn, *Oil and Politics*, Frankfurt 1977, which is concerned with the relationship between US perception of domestic oil supplies and her interests in the Near East. D.S. Painter, *Private Power and Public Policy*, 1986, contains a detailed examination of US oil policy in the Near East during the 1940s and 1950s. For Palestine we have J.B. Schechtman, *The United States and the Jewish State Movement, 1939–1949*, New York 1966, Z. Ganin, *Truman, American Jewry and Israel, 1945–1948*, New York 1979, Evan Wilson, *Decision on Palestine*, Stanford 1979, P. Grose, *Israel in the Mind of America*, New York 1983, and J. Snetsinger, *Truman, The Jewish Vote and the Creation of Israel*, Stanford 1974. Two books by Bernard Reich, *Quest for Peace*, 1980, and *The United States and Israel*, New York 1984, trace the continuing involvement of the United States and Israel. A good introduction to the later period is T.G. Fraser, *The USA and the Middle East since World War 2*, Oxford 1989. On later developments see also S.L.Spiegel, *The Other Arab–Israeli Conflict*, Chicago 1985, an account of US policy in the Near East from 1945 to the 1980s and A. Dowty, *Middle East Crisis*, Berkeley, Calif. 1984, a study of US decision-making in 1958, 1970 and 1973. We also have, of course, the many memoirs of US presidents and secretaries of state which it is unnecessary to list here.

The archival foundations which underpin most of the above studies are, of course, not present in studies of Soviet policy. Two works by W. Laqueur, *The Soviet Union and the Middle East*, 1959 and *The Struggle for the Middle East*, 1969, which takes the story on from 1958 to 1968, make a good starting point. Both include consideration of the Northern Tier as well as of the Arab world and the second has a good documentary selection. Documents relating to Soviet policy in the 1920s are assembled in X.J. Eudin and R.C. North, *Soviet Russia and the East, 1920–1927*, Stanford 1957. Another documentary survey, covering the period 1945–1973, is Yaacov Ro'i, *From Encroachment to Involvement*, New York 1974. Most studies of more recent Soviet policy concentrate on the Arab world. A. Yodfat and M. Abir, *In the Direction of the Persian Gulf*, 1977, analyses Soviet policy towards the Gulf and oil and provides an historical background. Ro'i has also produced a study of Soviet policy towards the young state of Israel, *Soviet Decision Making*, New Brunswick, NJ 1980, and *The Limits to Power*, 1979, a collection of essays on different aspects of Soviet policy in the Middle East, mainly the Arab–Israeli question. Yet another assemblage of useful papers is M. Confino and S. Shamir, (eds), *The USSR and the Middle East*, New York 1973. Oleg Smolensky, *The Soviet Union and the Arab East under Khrushchev*, Lewisburg, Pennsylvania 1974, Charles B. McClane, *Soviet–Middle Eastern Relations*, 1973, and Hélène Carrère d'Encausse, *La politique soviétique au Moyen-orient, 1955–1975*, Paris 1975 are useful accounts of Soviet policy in the Arab world; the last work argues that ideology declined in importance after 1968. The close connections of the USSR and Egypt attracted much attention: see A.Z. Rubinstein, *Red Star on the Nile*, Princeton 1977, K. Dawisha, *Soviet Foreign Policy towards Egypt*, 1979 and R.O. Freedman, *Soviet Policy towards the Middle East since 1970*, New York 1975. Soviet policy in Arabia is the subject of M.N. Katz, *Russia and Arabia*, Baltimore 1986. The 1970s are also described by Galia Golan, *Yom Kippur and After*, Cambridge 1979. Noteworthy for its use of Egyptian naval archives is M.M. El Husseini, *Soviet–Egyptian Relations, 1945–85,* 1987. Finally, for the period since 1979 see C.R. Salvetz, *The Soviet Union and the Gulf in the 1980s*, Boulder 1989.

Some books relevant to the Arab–Israeli conflict have already been mentioned. There is a bibliography edited by J. Sherman, *The Arab–Israeli Conflict, 1945–1971*, New York 1978. Serious students should examine the collection of documents and readings edited by J.N. Moore, The *Arab–Israeli Conflict*, 3 vols, Princeton 1974. T. Dupuy, *Elusive Victory*, New York 1978, provides a guide to the wars from 1947–74. Earl Berger, *The Covenant and the Sword*, 1965, is a convenient account of Arab–Israeli relations between 1948 and 1956. It may be followed by N. Safran, *From War to War*, New York 1969. W. Laqueur, *The Road to War*, 1968, and D. Kimche and D. Bawley, *The Sandstorm*, 1968, are also useful on the 1967 war. Israeli memoirs which relate to this episode include those of Dayan, Eban and Rabin. For the period 1967–73 see W. Laqueur, *Confrontation*, 1974, and on the 1973 war see also Zeev Schiff, *October Earthquake*, 1974. On the Egyptian side see the memoirs of Mahmud Riad, *The Struggle for Peace in the Middle East*, 1981, and Sādāt's own account. About the Camp David agreement W.B. Quandt, *Camp David*, Washington 1986, is very well informed. Y. Lukacs and A. Battah, *The Arab–Israeli Con-*

flict, Washington 1988 is a substantial collection of essays examining regional, superpower and diplomatic initiatives over the period 1967 to 1987.

For military and strategic problems in the Gulf war see A.H. Cordesman, *The Gulf and the Search for Strategic Security*, Boulder 1984, and *The Iran–Iraq War and Western Security, 1984–1987*, 1987. Dilip Hiro, *The Longest War*, 1989, is a straightforward blow-by-blow history of the war. Majid Khadduri's *The Gulf War*, Oxford 1988, was written before the end of the war but is still a serviceable examination. Ephraim Karsh (ed.), *The Iran–Iraq War*, 1987, is a collection of essays of above average quality, but the best analysis of the impact of the war is S. Chubin and C. Tripp, *Iran and Iraq at War*, 1988. A recent retrospective is H. Maull and O. Pick, *The Gulf War*, 1989.

Glossary

Ahl(Āl). Family or clan.
ᶜ*Alawī*. Member of a Shīᶜī sect also known as Nuṣayrī and inhabiting northern Syria.
Amīr. Military commander, governor, minor ruler, prince. Title used by ruler of Transjordan until 1946 and by some rulers in the Gulf since 1961.
Āyatallāh. Literally "the sign of God". Title used increasingly by eminent ulema in Iran since the nineteenth century. *Āyatallāh al-ᶜuzmā* = the greatest sign of God, usually rendered as Grand Āyatallāh
Bahā'ī. Follower of the teachings of Bahā'allāh, leader of a branch of the Bābī sect in Iran. The branch became a universalist, syncretist religion with its headquarters in Haifa.
Basīj. Prepared for an enterprise, hence mobilization. Term applied to the youth brigades mobilized as reserves for Iran's war with Iraq.
Caliph. (Arabic *khalīfa*). Deputy or successor (sc. of the Prophet). After the abolition of the Ottoman Caliphate several Muslim rulers sought to obtain wide acceptance of their claims to the title. Some Muslim jurists held that any Muslim ruler was entitled to call himself Caliph.
Capitulations. Grants or treaties establishing a system of extraterritorial jurisdiction and tariff limitation in the Ottoman empire. Similar restrictions were placed on Iran. The capitulatory regime declined rapidly from 1923 and was swept away by the Montreux agreement of 1937.
Bunyād. Foundation.
Dawla. The state.
Diaspora. Word of Greek origin meaning "dispersion" and used to describe Jewish communities living outside the land of Israel.
Dūnum. A measure of land area originally corresponding to 919 square

metres (2,500 in Iraq) and now standardized as 1,000 square metres.

Efendi (*effendi*). Ottoman title of Greek origin used to describe civilian bureaucrats and literate townsmen generally.

Faqīh. One who is learned in *fiqh*. An expert in Sharīʿa law.

Feddan (*faddan*). A measure of land area corresponding to 4.201 square metres in Egypt. Used also in Syria with a wide range of meanings.

Fidā'iyān (plural of *fidā'ī*. One who gives up his life for another). Term used generally by devotees of various causes in Iran and particularly by groups engaged in violent or terrorist activities.

Fidā'iyān-i khalq. Literally, "devotees of the people", a left wing terrorist group in Iran which originated as an offshoot of the Tūdah party in 1963.

Fidā'iyān-i Islām. Literally "devotees of Islam", a politico–religious terrorist group in Iran active from 1943 to 1955 which committed political assassinations. The group was revived during the 1970s.

Fiqh. Islamic jurisprudence, the usual course of study by ulema, eg. *muftīs* and *mujtahids*.

Ḥājj. Arabic title indicating one who has performed the pilgrimage to Mecca.

Hashimite. A descendant of Hāshim, the great-grandfather of the Prophet, in particular King Ḥusayn of the Ḥijāz and his descendants in Iraq, Syria and Jordan. Also sometimes termed Sharifians.

Hijra. The flight of Muḥammad from Mecca to Medina in AD 622, the year from which the Muslim calendar commences.

Ḥujjat al-Islām. Literally "the proof of God", a title below that of Āyatallāh adopted by Iranian ulema from the nineteenth century.

Ijtihād. The practice of reasoning in order to interpret the Sharīʿa.

Ikhwān. Brethren. *al-Ikhwān al-Muslimūn* = the Muslim Brotherhood.

Imām. Originally a prayer leader but also extended to denote the leader of the Muslim community or of sections of it. In Shīʿī usage one of the divinely guided descendants of Muḥammad.

Infitāḥ. Literally "a cleft or opening". Term applied to the policy of economic liberalization introduced in Egypt during the 1970s.

Intifāḍa. From a word meaning to destroy or annihilate. Name given to demonstrations and especially to the Palestinian protest movement which began in 1987 and was directed against Israeli occupation of the West Bank and Gaza.

Istiṣlāḥ. Mode of Islamic reasoning which emphasizes the principle of expediency or concern for human welfare.

Jihād. The struggle against evil or unbelief, in particular the holy war against unbelievers.

Khedive. Title of Persian origin held by the Muḥammad ᶜAlī dynasty in Egypt from 1867 to 1914.
Khums. Tax equal to one-fifth of income to be paid to the descendants of the Prophet. In Iran one-half of the tax (i.e. one-tenth of income) was claimed by the ulema as "the share of the Imām".
khuṭba. Friday sermon in the mosque when by tradition the name of the sovereign was mentioned.
Kibbutz. Hebrew word used for Jewish communal agricultural settlement.
Lazma. Category of land in Iraq from a word signifying necessity, scrupulousness, careful judgement.
Madrasa. College of higher Islamic education.
Majlis. Council, parliament.
Maktab. Muslim primary school.
Mamlūk. Slave imported into Muslim territories normally for military service. Name applied to dynasties in Egypt and Iraq of such origin.
Marjaᶜ al-taqlīd. Literally, "a model for emulation or imitation". In Iran a title given to the most renowned *mujtahids*.
Milk. Form of land tenure approximating to freehold.
Millet. Officially recognized religious community in the Ottoman Empire. The term later acquired a broader meaning nearer to that of "nation".
Mīrī. Appertaining to the state, state land.
Muftī. Muslim jurist qualified to give opinions on matters of legal interpretation and to issue a ruling (*fatwā*).
Muḥarram. The first month of the Muslim year of which the tenth day is the anniversary of the battle of Karbalā', an event of the greatest significance in Shiᶜism.
Mujtahid. Jurists qualified to give authentic legal rulings, especially among the Shīᶜa.
Mülkiye. Appertaining to civil government, Ottoman civil service college in Istanbul.
Mullā. Lesser member of the religious classes, cf. Persian *ākhūnd*.
Mustaḍᶜafīn (*mustażᶜafīn*). Term which occurs five times in the Qur'ān where it signifies orphans or the disinherited and perhaps the weak and oppressed generally. In radical Shīᶜī political theology came to be used in a sociological sense to denote the oppressed classes.
Nā'ib. Deputy.
Naqīb. Chief or leader.
Nasaq. Literally, order, method, arrangement; something fixed or established. In Iran used to describe a form of land tenure which gave significant rights to the holder.

Pāsdārān. Guards. *sipāh-i pāsdārān-i inqilāb-i islāmī* = Islamic revolutionary guard.
Pasha. Ottoman official title, usually borne by those with rank of minister, governor or equivalent and continued in some post-Ottoman states as a title of respect.
Qabīla. Tribe.
Qāḍī. Muslim judge appointed by the state with administrative as well as judicial duties.
Qanāt. Underground channel used to convey water for drinking or irrigation.
Qāt. Supposedly narcotic shrub grown in Yemen.
Qur'ān. The definitive written collection of the divine revelations of Muḥammad.
Ramaḍān. Ninth month of the Muslim calendar during which Muslims fast from dawn to dusk.
Sanjak (*sanjaq*). Ottoman administrative division, corresponding to a district of a province and by origin military.
Sayyid. Originally a title of respect which came to signify a descendant of the Prophet, normally in the line of Ḥusayn, although often used with a broader meaning, sometimes corresponding to Mr.
Shāh. Persian word meaning king. The correct title of the Pahlavī rulers of Iran was *Shāhinshāh*, or "king of kings", usually rendered as emperor. *Padishāh* was used in some other Muslim states with a similar meaning.
Sharīʿa. Islamic law.
Sharīf (plural *ashrāf*). Literally "noble". A descendant of the Prophet (normally in the line of Ḥasan), especially the *sharīf* of Mecca. c.f. *naqīb al-ashrāf* = leader of the *sharīfs*.
Shaykh. Literally "old man". Term used to denote heads of tribes, Ṣūfī orders, guilds and petty states.
Shaykh al-Islām. Religious title, in particular the chief religious officer (*muftī*) of the Ottoman Empire.
Shīʿī. Follower of an Islamic religious sect which originated in a political dispute over the succession to the leadership of the Muslim community. The Shīʿīs espoused the claims of ʿAlī and his descendants, whom they came to regard as divinely guided. The Shīʿīs are divided into numerous sects of which the largest is the Imāmī or Twelver Shīʿī sect in Iran.
Sirf. Form of land tenure from a word signifying change.
Ṣūfī. Religious mystic, member of a religious order or *tarīqa*
Sulṭān. Title of a Muslim ruler from a word meaning power or rule.
Sunnī. One who follows the Sunna or traditions of the Prophet, a

member of the largest Muslim group, that which is commonly termed orthodox. Sunnī Muslims follow one of four main schools of law: Ḥanafī, Ḥanbalī, Mālikī and Shāfiʿī.
Tapu. Register. Land registered in accordance with the 1858 Ottoman land law.
Ulema. Anglicized version of *ʿulamā'*, the plural of *ʿālim*, those with religious knowledge, commonly those who have completed a course at a *madrasa*.
Vilāyet. Ottoman province, governed by a *vālī*.
Wafd. Arabic word meaning delegation adopted as the name of a political party in Egypt.
Wahhābī. Name of puritanical Muslim sect deriving its teachings from Ibn Ḥanbal, established in Arabia in the eighteenth century and now the dominant sect in Saudi Arabia and some Gulf states.
Wālī (vālī) faqīh. The leader of the jurists, post established in the Islamic Republic of Iran and held first by Āyatallāh Khumaynī.
Waqf. Charitable endowment, usually of land.
Wazīr. Official in Muslim regimes, now often minister.
Yishuv. Hebrew word meaning settlement, used to describe the Jewish community in Palestine and Israel.
Zakāt. Muslim tax prescribed in the Qur'ān.
Zaydī. Shīʿī sect, principally in North Yemen.
Zaʿīm. Leader, term used especially to describe notables in Lebanon.

Lists of Rulers

Note. The following lists are those of rulers, that is to say of the dominant personalities (a sometimes elusive concept) in governments or regimes at any time. In most cases such personalities were also the heads of states; in any case the title or post is indicated. Where there was no dominant personality the name of the head of state is listed. The dates given are the years in which individuals took up their office.

EGYPT

1917 Sulṭān Aḥmad Fu'ād (King Fu'ād I, 1922)
1936 King Fārūq (regency to 1937)
1952 King Aḥmad Fu'ād II (regency)
1953 Muḥammad Najīb (president)
1954 Jamāl ᶜAbd al-Nāṣir (chairman RCC, president 1956)
1970 Anwar al-Sādāt (president)
1981 Muḥammad Ḥusnī Mubārak (president)

IRAQ

1921 King Fayṣal I
1933 King Ghāzī I
1939 King Fayṣal II (regency [ᶜAbd al-Ilāh] to 1953)
1958 ᶜAbd al-Karīm Qāsim (prime minister)
1963 ᶜAbd al-Salām ᶜĀrif (president)
1966 ᶜAbd al-Raḥmān ᶜĀrif (president)

1968 Aḥmad Ḥasan al-Bakr (president)
1979 Ṣaddām Ḥusayn (president)

SYRIA

1919 General Henri Gouraud (high commissioner = HC)
1923 General Maxime Weygand (HC)
1925 General Maurice Sarrail (HC)
1925 Henri de Jouvenal (HC)
1926 Henri Ponsot (HC)
1933 Charles Damien de Martel (HC)
1938 Gabriel Puaux (HC)
1940 General Henri-Fernand Dentz (HC)
1941 General Georges Catroux (delegate general = DG)
1943 Jean Helleu (DG)
1944 General Paul Emile Beynet (DG)
1945 Shukrī al-Quwwatlī (president)
1949 Ḥusnī al-Zaᶜīm (chief of staff, president)
1949 Sāmī al-Ḥinnāwī (chief of staff)
1949 Adīb al-Shishaklī (chief of staff, president 1953)
1954 Hāshim al-Atāsī (president)
1955 Shukrī al-Quwwatlī (president)
1958 Jamāl ᶜAbd al-Nāṣir (president UAR)
1961 Naẓīm al-Qudsī (president)
1963 Amīn al-Ḥāfiẓ (prime minister)
1966 Ṣalāḥ Jadīd (assistant secretary Baᶜth Regional Command)
1970 Ḥāfiẓ al-Asad (prime minister, president 1971)

LEBANON (presidents)

1926 Charles Dabbās
1934 Ḥabīb al-Saᶜd
1936 Emile Eddé
1941 Alfred Naqqāsh
1943 ᶜAyyūb Thābit
1943 Petro Ṭrād
1943 Bishāra al-Khūrī
1952 Kamīl Shamᶜūn

1958 Fu'ād Shihāb
1964 Charles Ḥilū
1970 Sulaymān Faranjiyya
1976 Ilyās Sarkīs
1982 Amīn al-Jumayyil
1989 René Muᶜawwaḍ
1989 Ilyās Harāwī

PALESTINE (high commissioners)

1920 Sir Herbert Samuel
1925 Herbert, Lord Plumer
1928 Sir John Chancellor
1931 Sir Arthur Wauchope
1937 Sir Harold MacMichael
1944 John, Viscount Gort
1945 Sir Alan Cunningham

JORDAN

1921 ᶜAbdallāh (amīr, king 1946)
1951 King Ṭalāl
1952 King Ḥusayn

ISRAEL (prime ministers)

1949 David Ben-Gurion
1953 Moshe Sharrett
1955 David Ben-Gurion
1963 Levi Eshkol
1969 Golda Meir
1974 Yitzhak Rabin
1977 Menachem Begin
1983 Yitzhak Shamir
1984 Shimon Peres
1986 Yitzhak Shamir

TURKEY (presidents)

1923 Mustafa Kemal Atatürk
1938 İsmet İnönü
1950 Celâl Bayar
1961 Cemal Gürsel
1966 Cevdet Sunay
1973 Fahri Korutürk
1980 Kenan Evren
1989 Turgut Özal

IRAN

1909 Aḥmad Shāh Qājār (regency to 1914 and 1923–5))
1925 Riżā Shāh Pahlavī
1941 Muḥammad Riżā Shāh Pahlavī
1979 Āyatallāh Rūḥallāh Mūsavī Khumayni (vālī faqīh)
1989 Āyatallāh ᶜAlī Khāmani'ī (vālī faqīh)
Ḥujjat al-Islām ᶜAlī Akbar Hāshimī Rafsanjānī (president)

ḤIJĀZ (kings)

1916 Ḥusayn ibn ᶜAlī
1924 ᶜAli ibn Ḥusayn
1926 ᶜAbd al-ᶜAzīz Āl Saᶜūd

SAUDI ARABIA (kings)

1902 ᶜAbd al-ᶜAzīz Āl Saᶜud (amīr, king 1926)
1953 Saᶜūd ibn ᶜAbd al-ᶜAzīz
1964 Fayṣal ibn ᶜAbd al-ᶜAzīz
1975 Khālid ibn ᶜAbd al-ᶜAzīz
1982 Fahd ibn ᶜAbd al-ᶜAzīz

NORTH YEMEN

1904	Imām Yaḥyā Āl Ḥamīd al-Dīn
1948	Imām Aḥmad
1962	Imām Muḥammad al-Badr
1962	^{c}Abdallāh al-Sallāl (president)
1967	^{c}Abd al-Rahmān al-Iryānī (chairman of presidential council)
1974	Ibrāhīm Muḥammad al-Ḥamdī (chairman of the command council)
1977	Aḥmad Ḥusayn al-Ghashmī (chairman of the command council, president 1978)
1978	^{c}Alī ^{c}Abdallāh Ṣāliḥ (president)

SOUTH YEMEN

1920	Major-General T.E.Scott (political resident = PR, Aden)
1925	Major-General J.H.K.Stewart (PR)
1928	Lt Col Sir G.S.Symes (PR)
1930	Lt Col B.R.Reilly (PR, chief commissioner 1932, governor of Aden 1937)
1940	Sir John Hathorn Hall (governor)
1944	Sir Reginald Champion (governor)
1951	Sir Tom Hickinbotham (governor)
1956	Sir William Luce (governor)
1960	Sir Charles Johnstone (governor)
1963	Sir Kennedy Trevaskis (HC)
1965	Sir Richard Turnbull (HC)
1967	Sir Humphrey Trevelyan (HC)
1967	Qaḥṭān al-Sha^{c}bī (president)
1969	Salīm Rubay^{c}ī ^{c}Alī (president)
1978	^{c}Abd al-Fattāḥ Ismā^{c}īl (president)
1980	^{c}Alī Nāṣir Muḥammad (president)
1986	Ḥaydar Abū Bakr al-^{c}Aṭṭās (president)

KUWAYT

1921 Aḥmad ibn Jābir Āl Ṣabāḥ (shaykh)
1950 ^{c}Abdallāh ibn Sālim (shaykh, amīr 1961)
1965 Ṣabāḥ ibn Sālim (amīr)
1977 Jābir ibn Aḥmad (amīr)

BAḤRAYN

1922 Ḥamad ibn ^{c}Īsā Āl Khalīfa (shaykh)
1942 Salmān ibn Ḥamad (shaykh)
1961 ^{c}Īsā ibn Salmān (shaykh, amīr 1971)

QAṬAR

1913 ^{c}Abdallāh ibn Qāsim Āl Thānī (shaykh)
1948 ^{c}Ali ibn ^{c}Abdallāh (shaykh)
1960 Aḥmad ibn ^{c}Alī (shaykh, amīr 1971)
1972 Khalīfa ibn Ḥamad (amīr)

ABŪ DHABĪ (shaykhs)

1922 Sulṭān ibn Zayd Āl Bū Falāḥ (Āl Nihayyān)
1927 Saqr ibn Zayd
1928 Shaykh Shakhbūṭ ibn Sulṭān
1966 Shaykh Zayd ibn Sulṭān (president United Arab Emirates 1971)

^{c}AJMĀN (shaykhs)

1908 Ḥumayd ibn ^{c}Abd al-^{c}Aziz Āl Bū Khuraybān (Āl Nu^{c}aym)
1928 Rāshid ibn Ḥumayd
1981 Ḥumayd ibn Rāshid

DUBAYY (shaykhs)

1912 Saᶜīd ibn Maktūm Āl Maktūm
1958 Rāshid ibn Saᶜīd

FUJAYRA (shaykhs)

1932 Muḥammad ibn Ḥamad Āl Sharqī
1974 Ḥamad ibn Muḥammad

RA'S AL-KHAYMA (shaykhs)

1919 Sulṭān ibn Sālim Āl Qawāsim
1948 Saqr ibn Muḥammad

SHĀRJA (shaykhs)

1913 Khālid ibn Aḥmad Āl Qawāsim
1924 Sulṭān ibn Saqr
1951 Saqr ibn Sulṭān
1965 Khālid ibn Muḥammad
1972 Sulṭān ibn Muḥammad

UMM AL-QUWAYN (shaykhs)

1922 ᶜAbdallāh ibn Rāshid Āl Muᶜallā
1923 Aḥmad ibn Ibrāhīm
1929 Aḥmad ibn Rāshid
1981 Rāshid ibn Aḥmad

OMAN (sulṭāns)

1913 Taymūr ibn Fayṣal
1932 Saᶜīd ibn Taymūr
1970 Qābūs ibn Saᶜīd

Maps

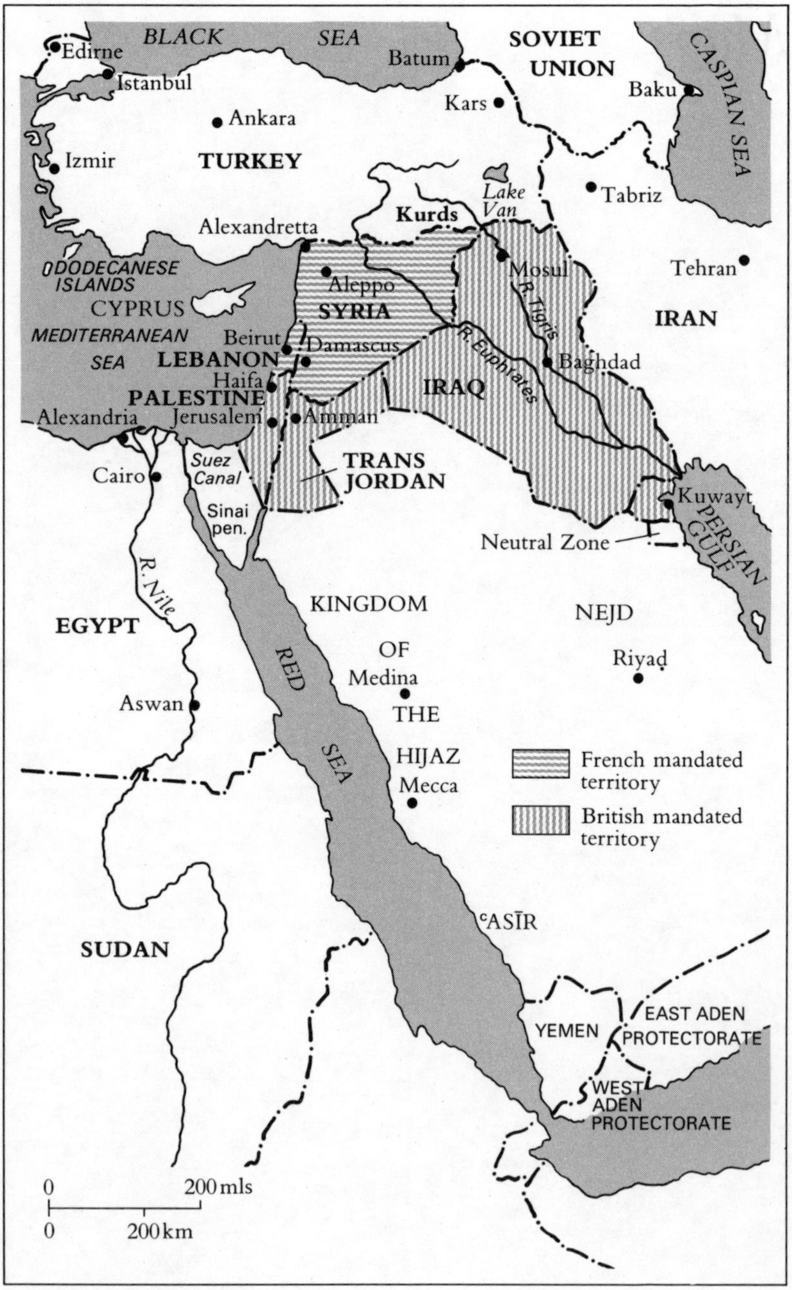

1. The Near East in 1923

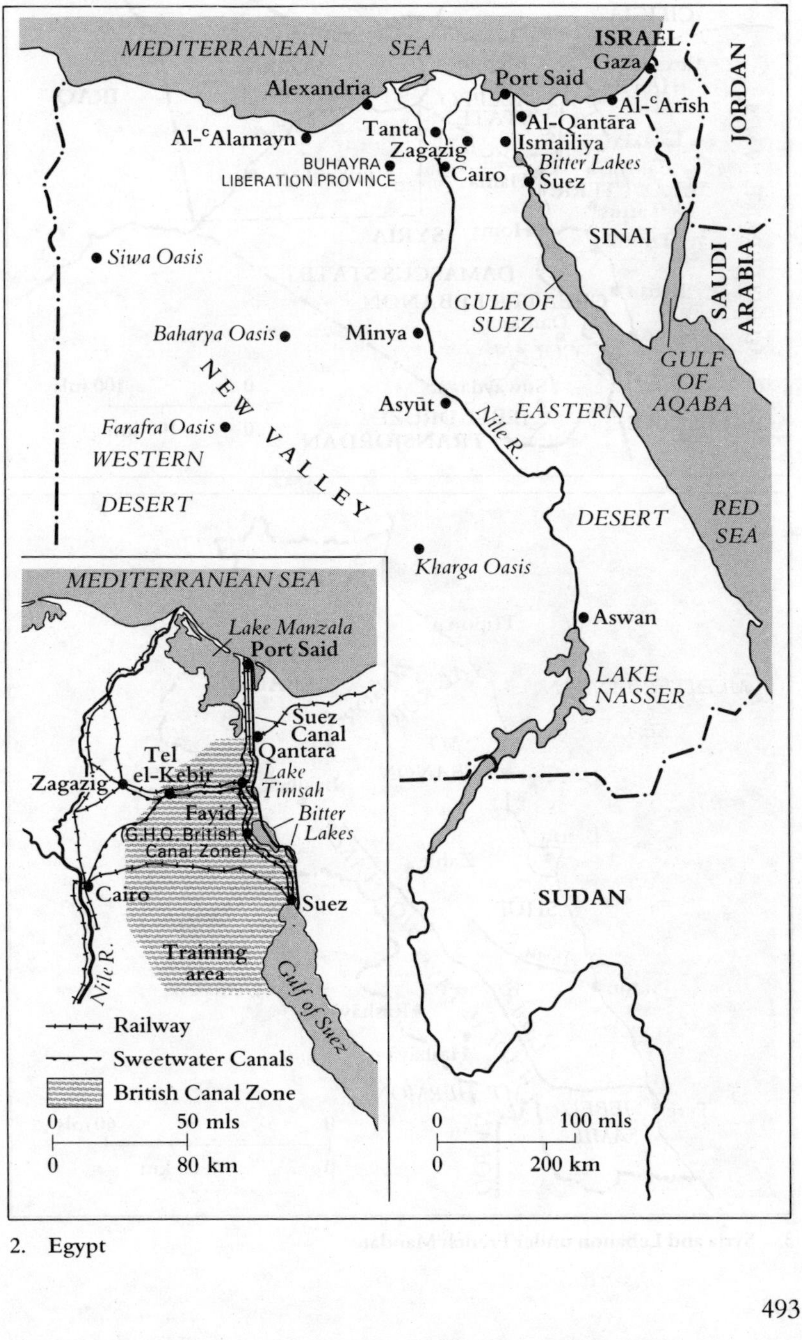
MEDITERRANEAN SEA
ISRAEL
Gaza
JORDAN
Alexandria
Port Said
Al-cArish
Tanta
Al-Qantāra
Al-cAlamayn
Zagazig
Ismailiya
BUHAYRA
LIBERATION PROVINCE
Cairo
Bitter Lakes
Suez
SINAI
Siwa Oasis
SAUDI ARABIA
GULF OF SUEZ
Baharya Oasis
Minya
NEW VALLEY
GULF OF AQABA
Asyūt
Nile R.
EASTERN
Farafra Oasis
WESTERN
DESERT
DESERT
RED SEA
Kharga Oasis
Aswan
LAKE NASSER
SUDAN
0
100 mls
0
200 km
MEDITERRANEAN SEA
Lake Manzala
Port Said
Suez Canal
Qantara
Tel el-Kebir
Lake Timsah
Zagazig
Fayid
(G.H.Q. British Canal Zone)
Bitter Lakes
Cairo
Suez
Training area
Nile R.
Gulf of Suez
Railway
Sweetwater Canals
British Canal Zone
0
50 mls
0
80 km

2. Egypt

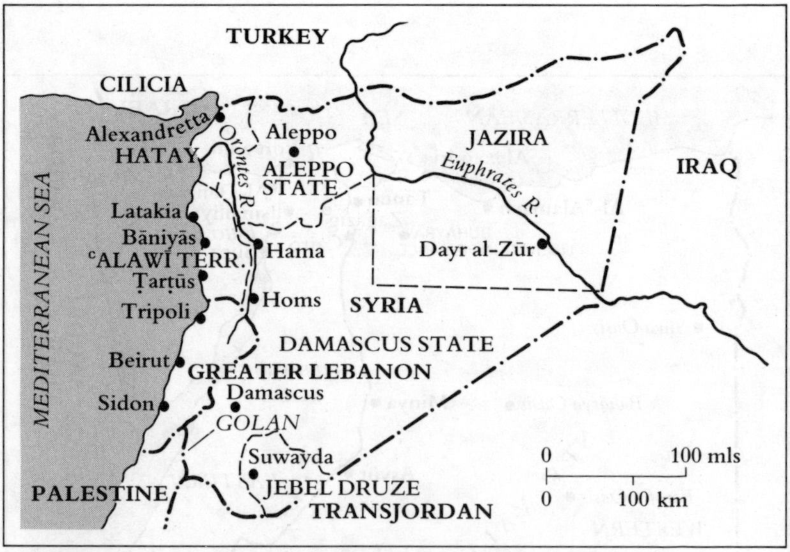

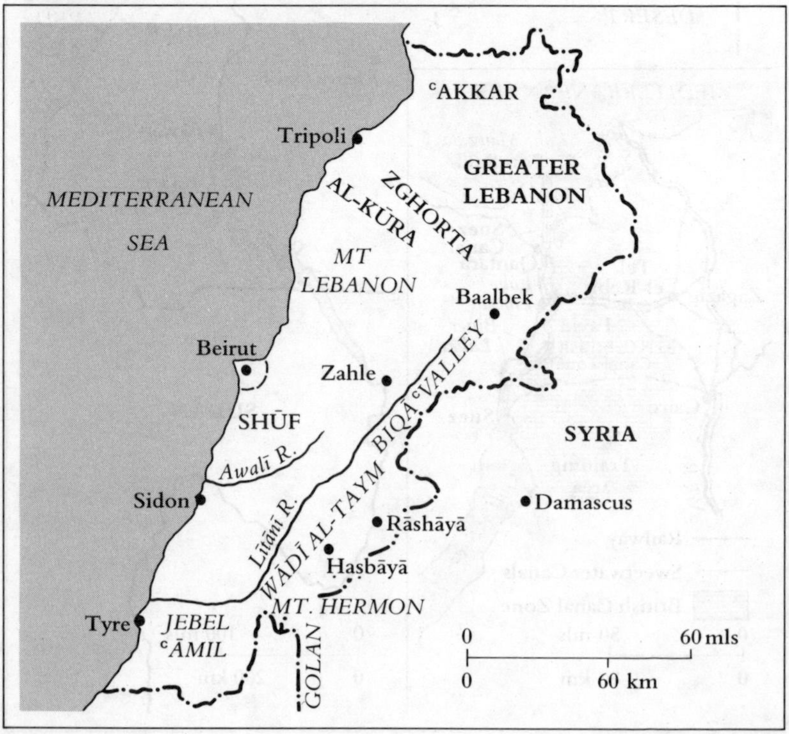

3. Syria and Lebanon under French Mandate

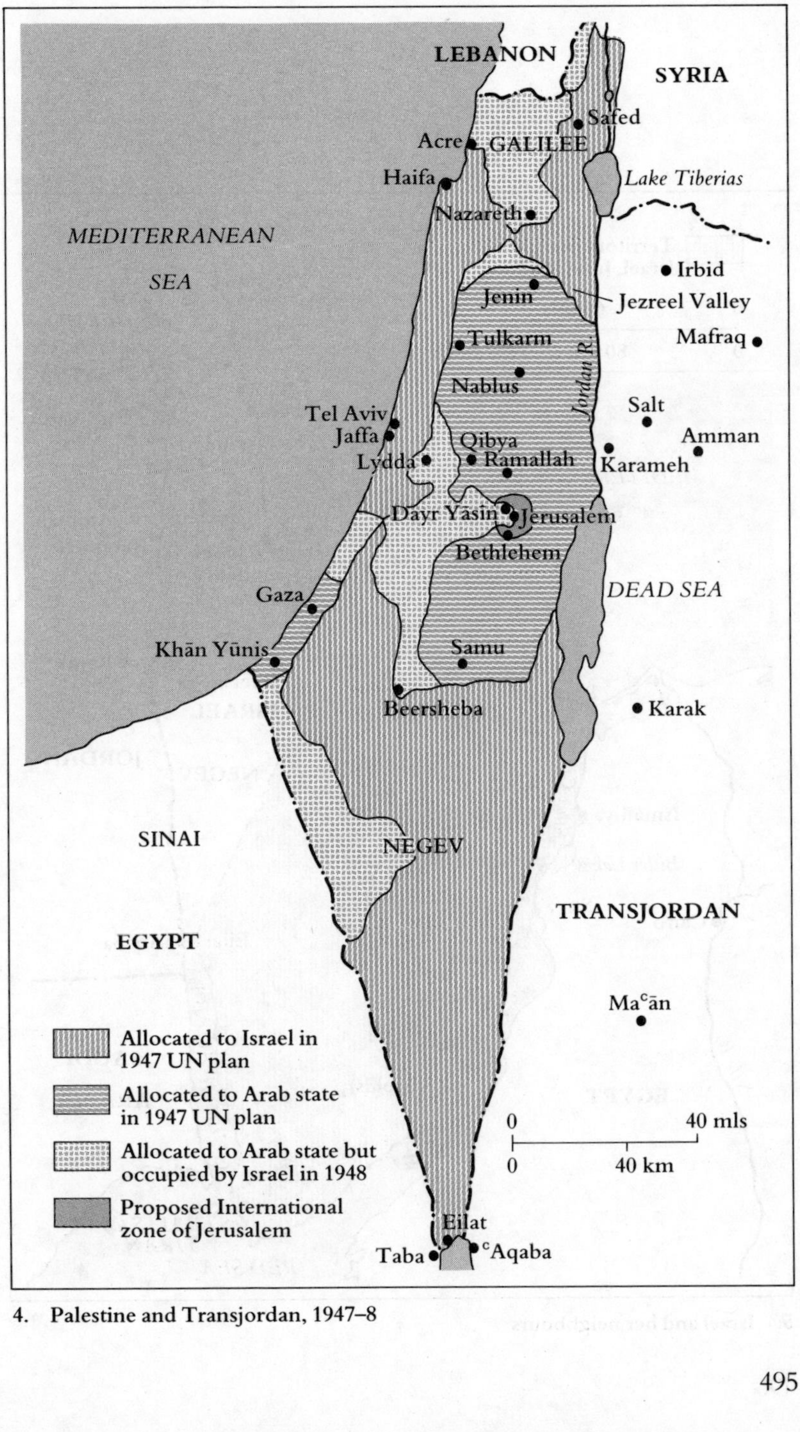
LEBANON
SYRIA
Safed
Acre
GALILEE
Haifa
Lake Tiberias
Nazareth
MEDITERRANEAN
SEA
Irbid
Jenin
Jezreel Valley
Tulkarm
Mafraq
Jordan R.
Nablus
Tel Aviv
Salt
Jaffa
Amman
Qibya
Lydda
Ramallah
Karameh
Dayr Yāsīn
Jerusalem
Bethlehem
DEAD SEA
Gaza
Samu
Khān Yūnis
Beersheba
Karak
SINAI
NEGEV
TRANSJORDAN
EGYPT
Ma^c^ān
Allocated to Israel in 1947 UN plan
Allocated to Arab state in 1947 UN plan
Allocated to Arab state but occupied by Israel in 1948
Proposed International zone of Jerusalem
0
40 mls
0
40 km
Eilat
Taba
^c^Aqaba

4. Palestine and Transjordan, 1947–8

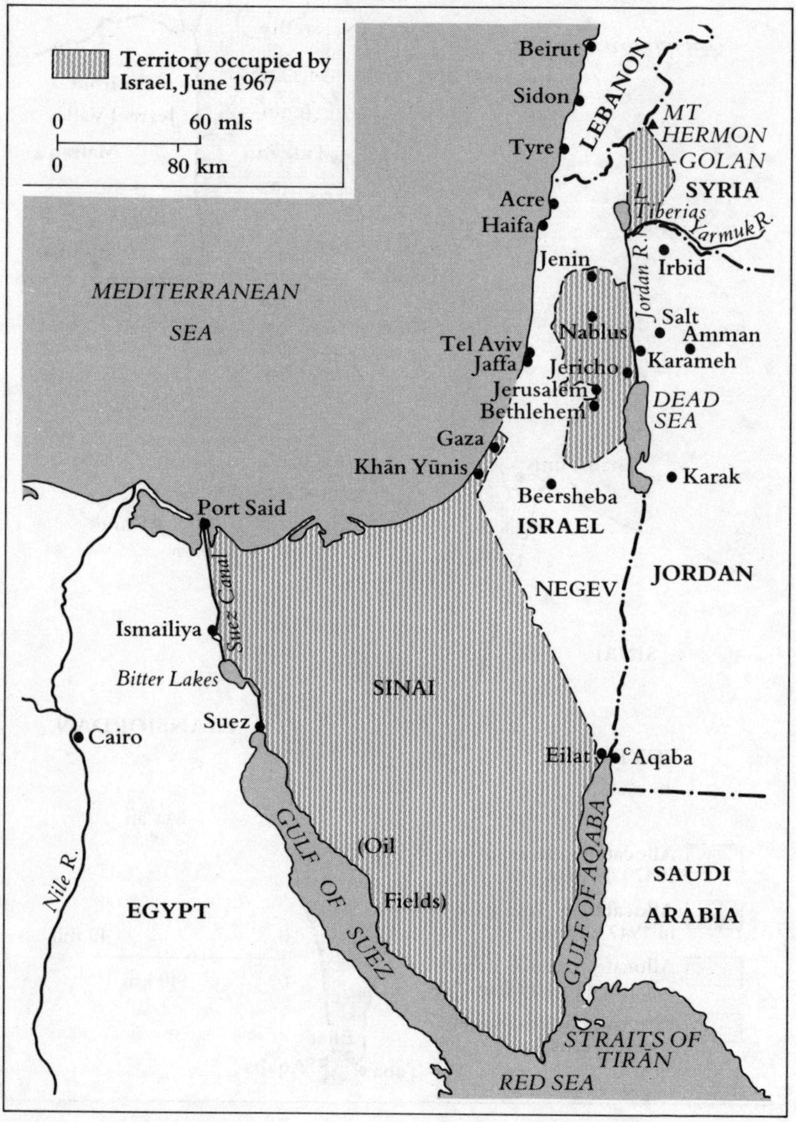
Territory occupied by Israel, June 1967
0
60 mls
0
80 km
Beirut
Sidon
Tyre
LEBANON
MT HERMON
GOLAN
SYRIA
Acre
Haifa
L Tiberias
Yarmuk R.
Jenin
Irbid
Jordan R.
MEDITERRANEAN SEA
Nablus
Salt
Amman
Tel Aviv
Jaffa
Jericho
Karameh
Jerusalem
Bethlehem
DEAD SEA
Gaza
Khān Yūnis
Karak
Beersheba
Port Said
ISRAEL
JORDAN
NEGEV
Suez Canal
Ismailiya
Bitter Lakes
SINAI
Suez
Cairo
Eilat
ᶜAqaba
GULF OF SUEZ
(Oil Fields)
GULF OF AQABA
SAUDI ARABIA
Nile R.
EGYPT
STRAITS OF TIRĀN
RED SEA

5. Israel and her neighbours

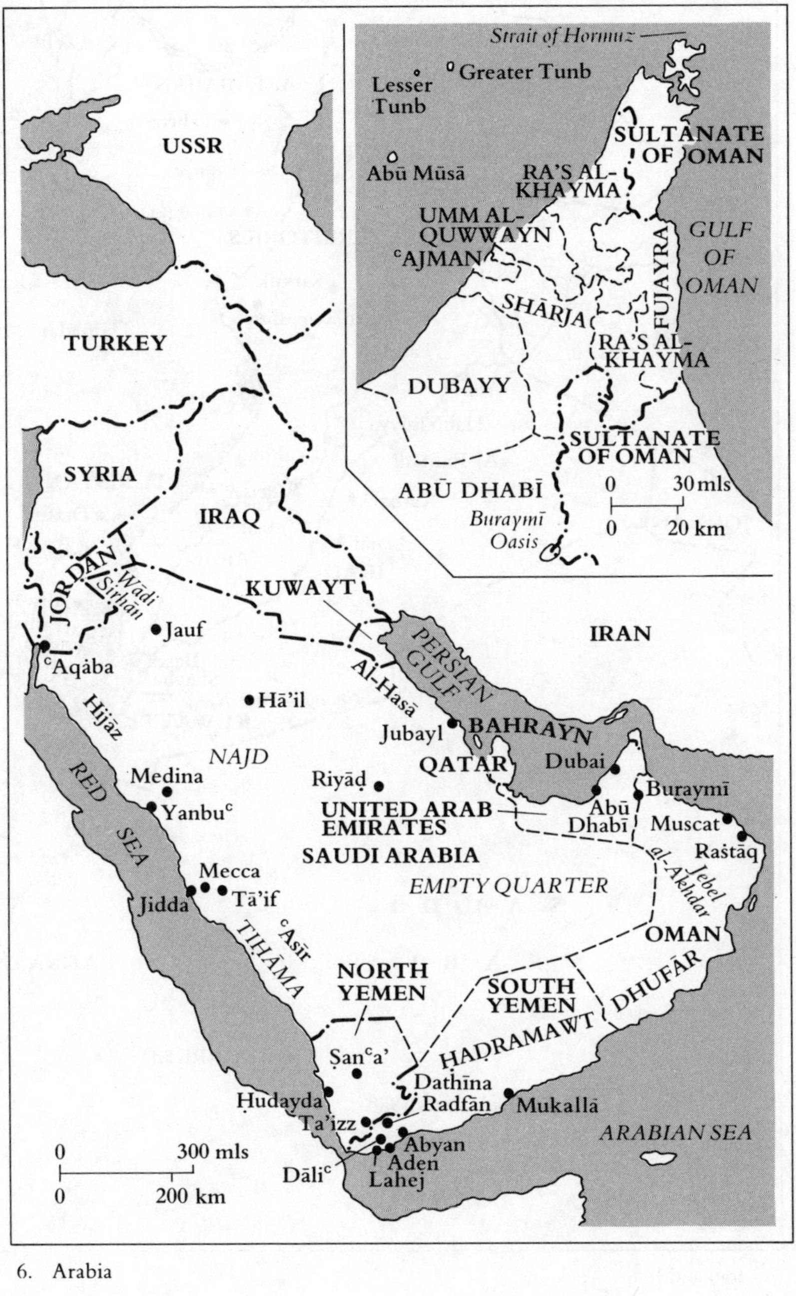
Strait of Hormuz
Greater Tunb
Lesser Tunb
Abū Mūsā
SULTANATE OF OMAN
RA'S AL-KHAYMA
UMM AL-QUWWAYN
ᶜAJMAN
GULF OF OMAN
FUJAYRA
SHĀRJA
RA'S AL-KHAYMA
DUBAYY
SULTANATE OF OMAN
ABŪ DHABĪ
Buraymī Oasis
0 30 mls
0 20 km
USSR
TURKEY
SYRIA
IRAQ
JORDAN
Wādi Sirḥān
KUWAYT
IRAN
Jauf
ᶜAqāba
PERSIAN GULF
Al-Hasā
Hā'il
Hijāz
Jubayl
BAHRAYN
NAJD
RED SEA
QATAR
Dubai
Medina
Riyāḍ
Buraymī
Yanbuᶜ
UNITED ARAB EMIRATES
Abū Dhabī
Muscat
Rasṭāq
SAUDI ARABIA
Mecca
Jebel al-Akhdar
EMPTY QUARTER
Jidda
Tā'if
ᶜAsīr
TIHĀMA
OMAN
NORTH YEMEN
SOUTH YEMEN
DHUFĀR
HADRAMAWT
Ṣanᶜa'
Dathīna
Ḥudayda
Radfān
Mukallā
Ta'izz
ARABIAN SEA
Abyan
Aden
Lahej
Dāliᶜ
0 300 mls
0 200 km

6. Arabia

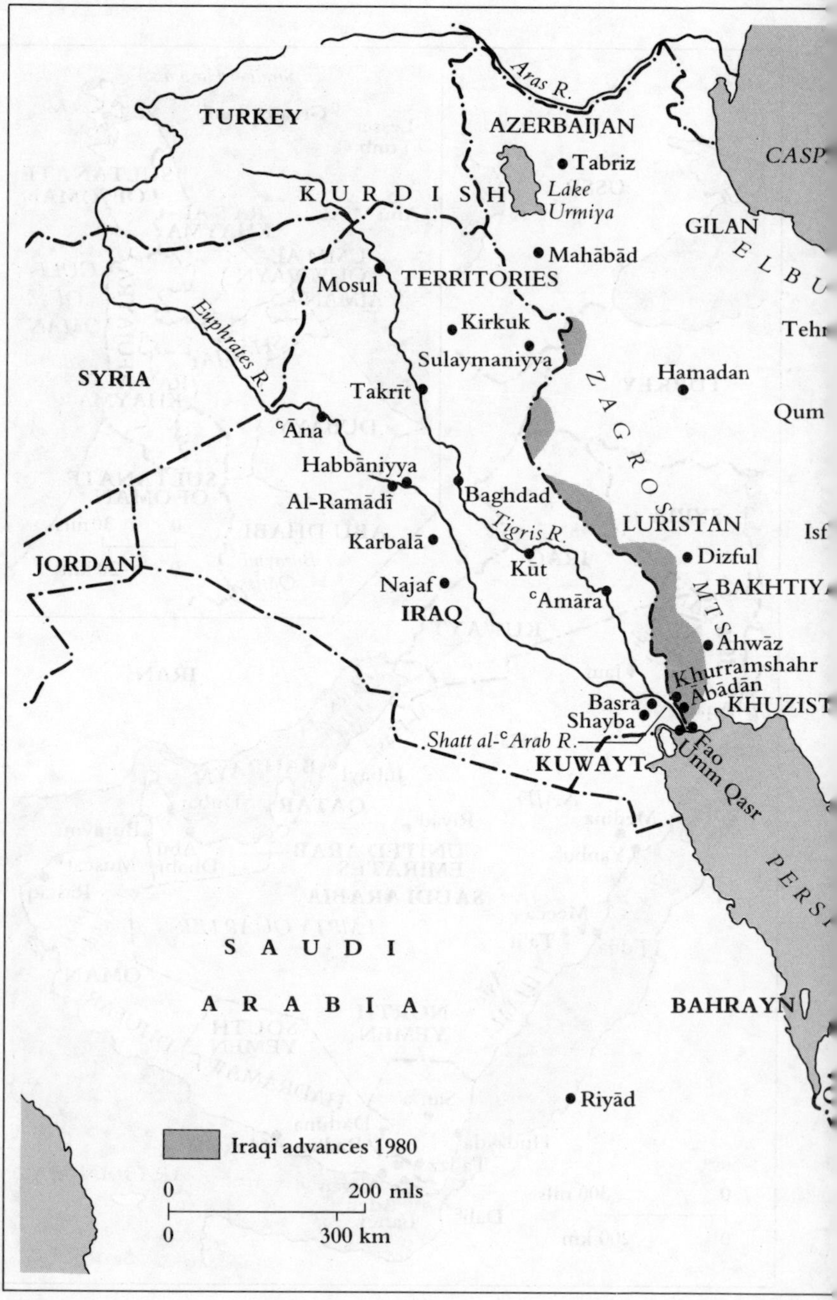

7. Iran and Iraq

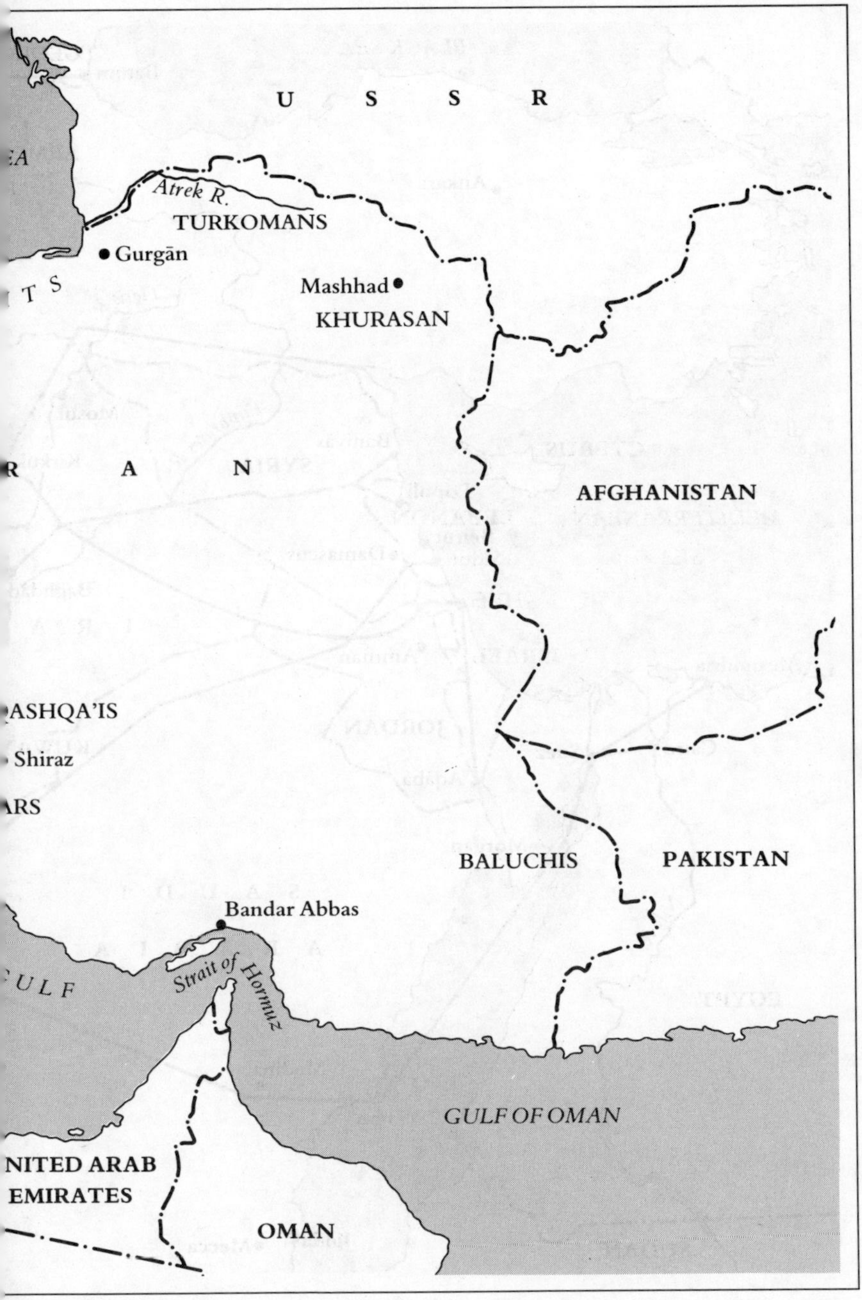
U S S R
EA
Atrek R.
TURKOMANS
Gurgān
T S
Mashhad
KHURASAN
R A N
AFGHANISTAN
ASHQA'IS
Shiraz
ARS
BALUCHIS
PAKISTAN
Bandar Abbas
ULF
Strait of Hormuz
GULF OF OMAN
NITED ARAB
EMIRATES
OMAN

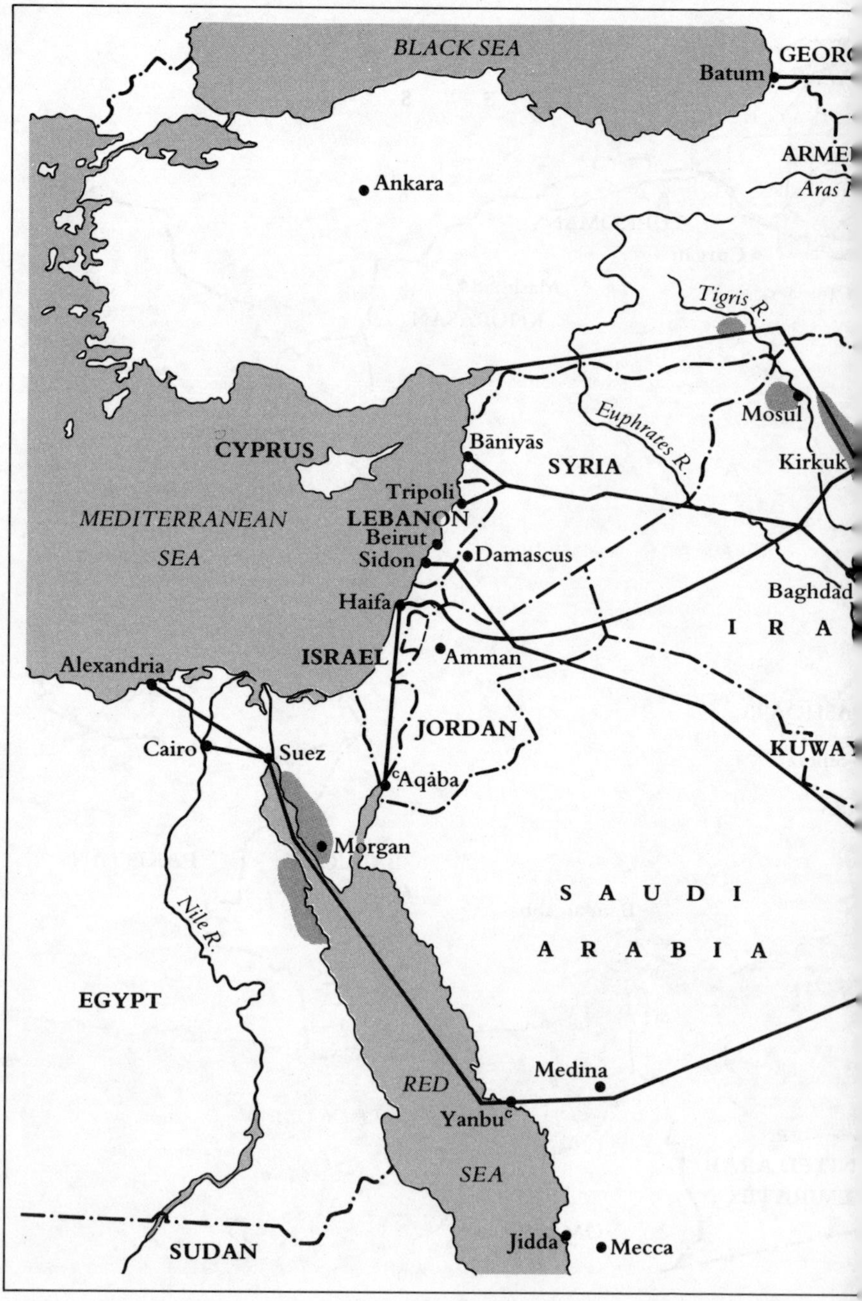

8. Major oilfields and pipelines in the Near East

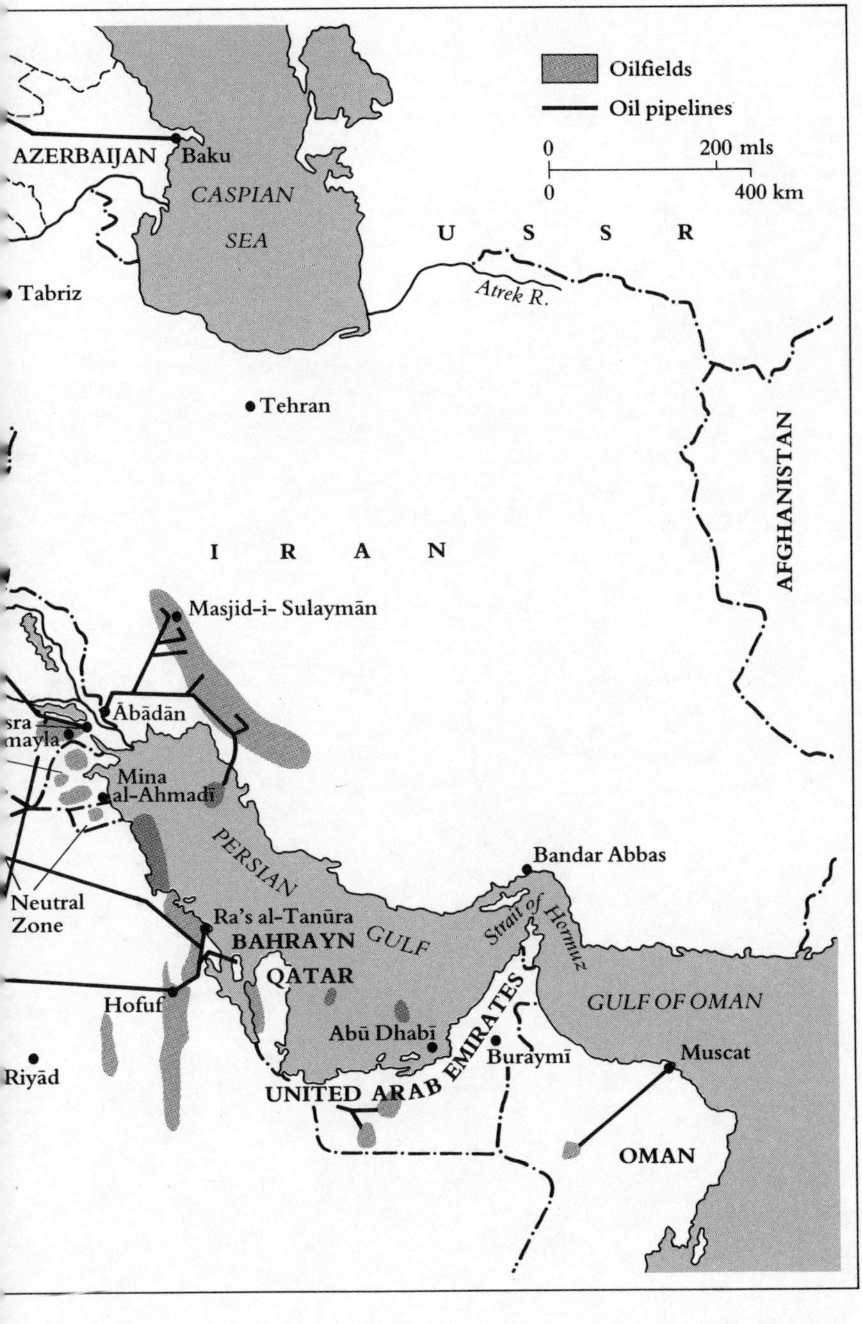

Oilfields
Oil pipelines
0
200 mls
0
400 km
AZERBAIJAN
Baku
CASPIAN
SEA
U S S R
Atrek R.
Tabriz
Tehran
AFGHANISTAN
I R A N
Masjid-i- Sulaymān
Ābādān
sra
mayla
Mina
al-Ahmadī
PERSIAN
GULF
Bandar Abbas
Strait of Hormuz
Neutral
Zone
Ra's al-Tanūra
BAHRAYN
QATAR
Hofuf
GULF OF OMAN
Abū Dhabī
Buraymī
Muscat
Riyād
UNITED ARAB EMIRATES
OMAN

Index